THE LAW OF
FUND-RAISING

NONPROFIT LAW, FINANCE, AND MANAGEMENT SERIES

The Law of Fund-Raising by Bruce R. Hopkins

The Law of Tax-Exempt Organizations, Fifth Edition by Bruce R. Hopkins

The Nonprofit Counsel by Bruce R. Hopkins

Starting and Managing a Nonprofit Organization: A Legal Guide by Bruce R. Hopkins

Tax and Financial Planning for Tax-Exempt Organizations: Forms, Checklists, Procedures by Jody Blazek

THE LAW OF FUND-RAISING

Bruce R. Hopkins

JOHN WILEY & SONS

New York • Chichester • Brisbane • Toronto • Singapore

Library of Congress Cataloging in Publication Data:

Hopkins, Bruce R.
  The law of fund-raising / Bruce R. Hopkins.
     p.   cm. —(Nonprofit law, finance, and management series)
  Includes bibliographical references and index.
  ISBN 0-471-50870-5 (cloth)
  1. Fund-raising—Law and legislation—United States.
2. Charitable uses, trusts, and foundations—United States.
I. Title. II. Series.
KF1389.5.H66   1991
344.73′03170681—dc20
[347.3043170681]   90-42408

This book is dedicated to Carolyn, with appreciation

Preface

While it does not seem that long ago, it was on January 20, 1973, that I received a telephone call in my office from a client nonprofit organization inquiring about a hearing that was to be held in a few days before a House of Representatives subcommittee chaired by Congressman Lionel Van Deerlin. This impending hearing was to concern legislation that would introduce a law to regulate, by the federal government, fund-raising by charitable organizations. Knowing nothing of the legislation or the upcoming hearing (or, for that matter, fund-raising regulation), I promised the caller that I would explore the matter and report back. Although it was a Saturday, I telephoned Representative Van Deerlin's office, hoping to find some knowledgeable staff person in his office and was surprised to have the call answered by the congressman himself. We discussed the matter, and the "hearing" turned out to be an informal briefing on the bill in the congressman's office for interested (and concerned) persons. I attended that briefing, spoke out, found myself appointed to an ad hoc group deputed to redraft the legislation, and was thereby led into the realm of fund-raising for charity and its regulation (present and prospective) by government. From that one call unfolded a progression of bills, hearings, acquaintances, research, court opinions, new organizations, and a swirl of other developments that today comprise a substantial body of regulatory law directed at charities. And the regulation is snowballing.

Regulation of fund-raising by or on behalf of charitable organizations has been part of the law of several states and localities for many years. Yet, until recently, enforcement of these statutes and ordinances has been, at best, casual.

Occasional abuses in the past attracted brief public notice and little punitive action. In today's consumer-oriented climate, however, a few well-publicized fund-raising misdeeds have resulted in a regulatory drive that threatens to engulf all charitable institutions. With society's institutions distrusted and under attack, and with the pressure for additional tax revenue, the public climate appears supportive of this intense regulation.

These developments have combined to heighten awareness of and sophistication about the methods and results of charitable giving on the part of federal and state regulators, voluntary standards agencies, the media and, in rare instances, donors themselves.

Significantly, this onslaught of regulation and expansion of enforcement has not attracted nearly the general attention and concern that is warranted, largely because of the insidious nature of recent regulatory developments. State law enforcement in this field is on the brink of becoming a major regulatory force, and federal regulation on a massive scale is on the immediate horizon—yet few seem to understand or even care.

The reason for this impassivity is that the philanthropic community has become conditioned to receive its jolts of new regulation by means of enactment of federal legislation, usually in the tax field. However, fund-raising regulation has not come upon the voluntary sector by means of a single law, but is, instead, an amalgam of slowly building and encompassing local, state, and federal administrative regulation. Unfortunately, the charitable world is now wholly exposed to creeping regulation by federal, state, and local agencies. This regulation has intensified in recent years.

Ten years ago I wrote a book entitled *Charity Under Siege: Government Regulation of Fund Raising.* This book described the fund-raising regulatory picture at that time. (Some portions of that book have found their way into this one.) I thought the volume of fund-raising regulation was striking then; but over the intervening decade the extent of the explosion of regulation in this field is mind-numbing. (My surmise is that the annual supplements to this book will reflect continuation of this trend.) One sometimes wonders (1) how the philanthropic world manages to do what it does while laboring under the burden of these laws, and (2) whether all of this regulation is really worth the effort.

The range of problems caused by the state charitable solicitation acts is considerable. The worst situation is faced by the organization that raises its funds by direct mail in every state of the union. Such an organization is confronted with a bewildering array of differing requirements, forms, due dates, exemptions, and accounting principles. All too frequently the organization "solves" this problem by registering in only a few states—or, perhaps, in none at all.

Direct mail users are not the only types of charitable organizations facing regulation. These laws affect organizations that acquire funds by means of capital campaigns, planned giving programs, special events, annual giving solicitations, bequest programs, or whatever. The regulatory requirements apply (with exceptions) to churches and other religious organizations; schools, colleges, and universities; hospitals and other health care institutions; assorted related "foundations"; publicly supported charities; civic and patriotic groups; those seeking foundation and government grants and corporate gifts; and more.

This body of law directly affects both new and old groups, unpopular or controversial as well as established organizations, those with an existing constituency and those searching for support.

These laws also impose registration and reporting requirements on professional fund-raising consultants and professional solicitors. In a majority of cases, it appears that, like the charities they serve, these individuals and companies are not in full compliance with all of these laws.

Most managers of charitable organizations and their consultants—fund-raisers, lawyers, accountants, and the like—are not aware of the many difficulties, including the immense cost of compliance, posed by the existing and burgeoning number of laws regulating fund-raising. They require background information and a general understanding about the charitable solicitation acts and their applicability to various types of philanthropic institutions. A purpose of this book is to sketch out for them the regulatory picture and the many dilemmas it poses.

Many organizations and their fund-raisers are willing to make a reasonable effort to come into compliance with these laws but do not know where to begin. Thus, another purpose of this book is to describe means by which the organizations and their fund-raisers can rationally approach these laws and develop a procedure for effective compliance with them.

Finally, some organizations—and their numbers are growing—are in basic compliance with some of the applicable laws but need guidance about what to do when their registration is being reevaluated and perhaps threatened. A purpose of the book is to describe the process and the available rationales for keeping an organization in—or bringing one back into—compliance with these laws.

A number of legal problems are inherent in the administration and enforcement of these laws. These legal aspects are discussed in the book, to provide both a basis for further research and a guide to fund-raising organizations and their advisers about the reach of various statutory and constitutional law principles.

In addition to coverage of the state law and regulatory scene, the book analyzes the scope of existing federal regulation of charitable fund-raising and surveys the issues that must be faced in designing a federal statute in this area. Additionally, examination is made of the ways in which the Internal Revenue Service is at present establishing itself by administrative action as a monitor of charitable fund-raising. Also, legislation has been introduced in the U.S. Congress to provide comprehensive regulatory schemes, and the book offers an evaluation of these proposals.

Thus, as state regulation in the field of charitable fund-raising explodes and federal regulation looms, coupled with the effects of local ordinances and the growing role of the voluntary standards agencies, it is clear that guidance for the regulated is necessary. Consequently, the book is designed to be a guide for fund-raising charitable organizations and their advisers—to help them come into compliance with the regulatory requirements and to stay that way.

My thanks go to Jim Greenfield, David Ormstedt, Del Staecker, and Bill Warshauer for their very interesting and useful contributions to Chapter 2 of the book. Also, my gratitude goes to my friends at John Wiley & Sons, particularly Jeffrey Brown, Marla Bobowick, and Mary Daniello, for their efforts in seeing the book to completion.

BRUCE R. HOPKINS

Washington, D.C.
November 1990

Contents

4   The State Charitable Solicitation Acts: A Comparative Analysis   252

5   State Regulation of Fund-Raising: Legal Issues   294

Appendices

1

Government Regulation of Fund-Raising for Charity: Origins and the Future

Charitable organizations are an integral part of U.S. society, and most of them must engage in the solicitation of contributions to continue their work, which benefits that society. Yet both these organizations and their fund-raising efforts are under intense criticism and immense regulation. Some of this regulation comes from the many state "charitable solicitation acts"—statutes that are designed to regulate the process of raising funds for charitable purposes. Other aspects of this regulation are found in the federal tax law, particularly in its application by the Internal Revenue Service[1] and the courts.

One of the pressing questions facing philanthropy in the United States is whether this form of regulation is on the verge of stifling or even smothering the nation's independent and voluntary sector. A conflicting attitude is that charity, and fund-raising for it, has become "big business," and warrants regulation to minimize abuse, protect prospective and actual donors from fraud and other forms of misrepresentation, and reduce waste of the charitable dollar.

Before examining the extent of this regulation, and the accompanying contemporary issues and trends, one should place the role of charitable organizations in its historical and public policy context.

§ 1.1 The Independent Sector and American Political Philosophy

Because modern U.S. charity evolved out of the common law of charitable trusts and has been accorded exemption from income and property

[1] Throughout this book, the Internal Revenue Service is referred to as the IRS.

1

taxation since the beginnings of state and federal tax policy, the contemporary treatment of charitable organizations is best reflected in the federal tax laws.

The public policy rationale for exempting organizations from tax is illustrated by the category of organizations that are charitable, educational, religious, scientific, literary and similar entities[2] and, to a lesser extent, social welfare organizations.[3] The federal tax exemption for charitable and other organizations may be traced to the origins of the income tax,[4] although most of the committee reports accompanying the 1913 act and subsequent revenue acts are silent on the reasons for initiating and continuing the exemption.

One may nevertheless safely venture that the exemption for charitable organizations in the federal tax statutes is largely an extension of comparable practice throughout the whole of history. Presumably, Congress simply believed that these organizations should not be taxed, and found the proposition sufficiently obvious as not to warrant extensive explanation. Some clues may be found in the definition of "charitable" activities in the income tax regulations,[5] wherein are included such purposes as relief of the poor, advancement of education or science, erection or maintenance of public buildings, and lessening of the burdens of government. Clearly the exemption for charitable organizations is a derivative of the concept that they perform functions which, in the organizations' absence, government would have to perform; therefore, government is willing to

---

[2] These are the organizations described in section (hereinafter §) 501(c)(3) of the Internal Revenue Code of 1986, Title 26, United States Code. Throughout this book, the Internal Revenue Code is referred to as the IRC.

[3] IRC § 501(c)(4).

[4] 38 Stat. 166. The income tax charitable contribution deduction originated in the 1894 statute (28 Stat. 556, § 32), which was declared unconstitutional in *Pollock* v. *Farmers' Loan and Trust Co.*, 157 U.S. 429 (1895). In general, see McGovern, "The Exemption Provisions of Subchapter F," 29 *Tax Lawyer* 523 (1976), and Bittker & Rahdert, "The Exemption of Nonprofit Organizations from Federal Income Taxation," 85 *Yale L. J.* 299 (1976).

A companion book by the author describes the federal tax law as it applies to nonprofit organizations. Chapter 1 of the book, *The Law of Tax-Exempt Organizations*, 5th ed. (New York: John Wiley & Sons, Inc., 1987), contains a fuller analysis of this aspect of public policy and of the independent sector. Throughout this book, the volume on tax-exempt organizations is referred to as *Law of Tax-Exempt Organizations*.

[5] Income Tax Regulations (hereinafter Reg.) § 1.501(c)(3)-1 (d)(2).

forego the tax revenues it would otherwise receive in return for the public services rendered.

Since the founding of the United States, and earlier in the colonial period, tax exemption—particularly with respect to religious organizations—was common.[6] The churches were openly and uniformly spared taxation.[7] This practice has been sustained throughout the nation's history—not only at the federal but at the state and local levels, most significantly with property taxation.[8] The U.S. Supreme Court, in upholding the constitutionality of the religious tax exemption, observed that "[t]he State has an affirmative policy that considers these groups as beneficial and stabilizing influences in community life and finds this classification [exemption] useful, desirable, and in the public interest."[9]

The Supreme Court early concluded that the foregoing rationalization was the basis for the federal tax exemption for charitable entities. In one case, the Court noted that "[e]vidently the exemption is made in recognition of the benefit which the public derives from corporate activities of the class named, and is intended to aid them when not conducted for private gain."[10]

The U.S. Court of Appeals for the Eighth Circuit has observed, as respects the exemption for charitable organizations, that "[o]ne stated reason for a deduction or exemption of this kind is that the favored entity performs a public service and benefits the public or relieves it of a burden which otherwise belongs to it."[11] One of the rare congressional pronouncements on this subject is further evidence of the public policy rationale. In its committee report accompanying the Revenue Act of 1938, the House Ways and Means Committee stated:

> The exemption from taxation of money or property devoted to charitable and other purposes is based upon the theory that the government is compensated for the loss of revenue by its relief from financial burden which would otherwise have to be met by appropriations from public

---

[6] Cobb, *The Rise of Religious Liberty in America* 482–528 (1902); Lecky, *History of European Morals* (1868).

[7] Torpey, *Judicial Doctrines of Religious Rights in America* 171 (1948).

[8] *Trustees of the First Methodist Episcopal Church* v. *City of Atlanta*, 76 Ga. 181 (1886); *Trinity Church* v. *City of Boston*, 118 Mass. 164 (1875).

[9] *Walz* v. *Tax Commissioner*, 397 U.S. 664, 673 (1970).

[10] *Trinidad* v. *Sagrada Orden de Predicadores*, 263 U.S. 578, 581 (1924).

[11] *St. Louis Union Trust Company* v. *United States*, 374 F.2d 427, 432 (8th Cir. 1967). Also *Duffy* v. *Birmingham*, 190 F.2d 738, 740 (8th Cir. 1951).

funds, and by the benefits resulting from the promotion of the general welfare.[12]

One federal court observed that the reason for the charitable contribution deduction has "historically been that by doing so, the Government relieves itself of the burden of meeting public needs which in the absence of charitable activity would fall on the shoulders of the Government."[13]

Other aspects of the public policy rationale are reflected in case law and the literature. Charitable organizations are regarded as fostering voluntarism and pluralism in the American social order.[14] That is, society is regarded as benefiting not only from the application of private wealth to specific purposes in the public interest but also from the variety of choices made by individual philanthropists as to which activities to further.[15] This decentralized choicemaking is arguably more efficient and responsive to public needs than the cumbersome and less flexible allocation process of government administration.[16]

The principle of pluralism was stated by John Stuart Mill, in *On Liberty* (1859), as follows:

> In many cases, though individuals may not do the particular thing so well, on the average, as the officers of government, it is nevertheless desirable that it should be done by them, rather than by the government, as a means to their own mental education—a mode of strengthening their active faculties, exercising their judgment, and giving them a familiar knowledge of the subjects with which they are thus left to deal. This is a principal, though not the sole, recommendation of jury trial (in cases not political); of free and popular local and municipal institutions; of the conduct of industrial and philanthropic enterprises by voluntary associations. These are not questions of liberty, and are connected with that subject only by remote tendencies; but they are questions of development. . . . The management of purely local businesses by the localities, and of the great enterprises of industry by the union of those who voluntarily supply the pecuniary means, is further recommended by all the advantages which have been set forth in this Essay as belonging to individuality of devel-

---

[12] H. R. Rep. No. 1860, 75th Cong., 3d Sess. (1939), at 19.

[13] *McGlotten* v. *Connally*, 338 F. Supp. 448, 456 (D.D.C. 1972).

[14] *Green* v. *Connally*, 330 F. Supp. 1150, 1162 (D.D.C. 1971), aff'd sub nom, *Coit* v. *Green*, 404 U.S. 997 (1971).

[15] Rabin, "Charitable Trusts and Charitable Deductions," 41 *N.Y.U.L. Rev.* 912, 920–925 (1966).

[16] Saks, "The Role of Philanthropy: An Institutional View," 46 *Va. L. Rev.* 516 (1960).

opment, and diversity of modes of action. Government operations tend to be everywhere alike. With individuals and voluntary associations, on the contrary, there are varied experiments, and endless diversity of experience. What the State can usefully do is to make itself a central depository, and active circulator and diffuser, of the experience resulting from many trials. Its business is to enable each experimentalist to benefit by the experiments of others; instead of tolerating no experiments but its own.

This same theme was echoed by then-Secretary of the Treasury George P. Shultz, in testimony before the House Committee on Ways and Means in 1973, when he observed:

These organizations ["voluntary charities, which depend heavily on gifts and bequests"] are an important influence for diversity and a bulwark against over-reliance on big government. The tax privileges extended to these institutions were purged of abuse in 1969 and we believe the existing deductions for charitable gifts and bequests are an appropriate way to encourage those institutions. We believe the public accepts them as fair.[17]

The principle of voluntarism in the United States was expressed by another commentator as follows:

Voluntarism has been responsible for the creation and maintenance of churches, schools, colleges, universities, laboratories, hospitals, libraries, museums, and the performing arts; voluntarism has given rise to the private and public health and welfare systems and many other functions and services that are now an integral part of the American civilization. In no other country has private philanthropy become so vital a part of the national culture or so effective an instrument in prodding government to closer attention to social needs.[18]

Charitable organizations, maintained by tax exemption and nurtured by the ability to attract deductible contributions, are reflective of the American philosophy that all policymaking should not be reposed in the governmental sector. "Philanthropy," wrote one jurist,

is the very possibility of doing something different than government can do, of creating an institution free to make choices government cannot—even seemingly arbitrary ones—without having to provide a justification

[17] "Proposals for Tax Change," Department of the Treasury, Apr. 30, 1973, at 72.
[18] Fink, "Taxation and Philanthropy—A 1976 Perspective," 3 *J. C. & U. L.* 1, 6–7 (1975).

that will be examined in a court of law, which stimulates much private giving and interest.[19]

The public policy rationale for tax exemption (particularly for charitable organizations) was reexamined and reaffirmed by the Commission on Private Philanthropy and Public Needs in its findings and recommendations in 1975.[20] The Commission observed:

> Few aspects of American society are more characteristically, more famously American than the nation's array of voluntary organizations, and the support in both time and money that is given to them by its citizens. Our country has been decisively different in this regard, historian Daniel Boorstin observes, "from the beginning." As the country was settled, "communities existed before governments were there to care for public needs." The result, Boorstin says, was that "voluntary collaborative activities" were set up to provide basic social services. Government followed later.

> The practice of attending to community needs outside of government has profoundly shaped American society and its institutional framework. While in most other countries, major social institutions such as universities, hospitals, schools, libraries, museums and social welfare agencies are state-run and state-funded, in the United States many of the same organizations are privately controlled and voluntarily supported. The institutional landscape of America is, in fact, teeming with nongovernmental, noncommercial organizations, all the way from some of the world's leading educational and cultural institutions to local garden clubs, from politically powerful national associations to block associations—literally millions of groups in all. This vast and varied array is, and has long been widely recognized as, part of the very fabric of American life. It reflects a national belief in the philosophy of pluralism and in the profound importance to society of individual initiative.

> Underpinning the virtual omnipresence of voluntary organizations, and a form of individual initiative in its own right, is the practice—in the case of many Americans, the deeply ingrained habit—of philanthropy, of private giving, which provides the resource base for voluntary organizations. Between money gifts and the contributions of time and labor in the form of volunteer work, giving is valued at more than $50 billion a year, according to Commission estimates.

> These two interrelated elements, then, are sizable forces in American society, far larger than in any other country. And they have contributed

---

[19] Friendly, "The Dartmouth College Case and the Public-Private Penumbra," 12 *Tex. Q.* (2d Supp.) 141, 171 (1969).

[20] *Giving in America—Toward a Stronger Voluntary Sector* (1975). All quotations herein from the Commission's report are by permission.

immeasurably to this country's social and scientific progress. On the ledger of recent contributions are such diverse advances as the creation of non-commercial "public" television, the development of environmental, con-sumerist and demographic consciousness, community-oriented museum programs, the protecting of land and landmarks from the often heedless rush of "progress." The list is endless and still growing; both the number and deeds of voluntary organizations are increasing. "Americans are forever forming associations," wrote de Tocqueville. They still are: tens of thousands of environmental organizations have sprung up in the last few years alone. Private giving is growing, too, at least in current dollar amounts.[21]

Exemption from taxation for certain types of nonprofit organizations is a principle that is larger than the Internal Revenue Code. Citizens combating problems and reaching solutions on a collective basis—in "association"—are inherent in the very nature of American societal structure. Nonprofit associations are traditional in the United States and their role and responsibility are not diminished in modern society. Rather, some contend that the need for the efforts of nonprofit organizations is greater today than previously, in view of the growing complexity and inefficiency of government. To tax these entities would be to flatly repudiate and contravene this doctrine which is so much a part of the nation's heritage.

This view of nonprofit associations operating in the United States has been most eloquently stated by Alexis de Tocqueville. He, too, espoused the principle of pluralism, as expressed in his *Democracy in America*:

Feelings and opinions are required, the heart is enlarged, and the human mind is developed only by the reciprocal influence of men upon one another. I have shown that these influences are almost null in democratic countries; they must therefore be artificially created, and this can only be accomplished by associations. . . . A government can no more be competent to keep alive and to renew the circulation of opinions and feelings among a great people than to manage all the speculations of productive industry. No sooner does a government attempt to go beyond its political sphere and to enter upon this new track than it exercises, even unintentionally, an insupportable tyranny; for a government can only dictate strict rules, the opinions which it favors are rigidly enforced, and it is never easy to discriminate between its advice and its commands. Worse still will be the case if the government really believes itself interested in preventing all circulation of ideas: it will then stand motionless and oppressed by the heaviness of voluntary torpor. Governments, therefore, should not be the only active powers; associations ought, in democratic

---

[21] *Id.* at 9–10.

nations, to stand in lieu of those powerful private individuals whom the equality of conditions has swept away.

But de Tocqueville's classic formulation on this subject came in his portrayal of the use by Americans of "public associations" in civil life:

> Americans of all ages, all conditions, and all dispositions constantly form associations. They have not only commercial and manufacturing companies, in which all take part, but associations of a thousand other kinds, religious, moral, serious, futile, general or restricted, enormous or diminutive. The Americans make associations to give entertainments, to found seminaries, to build inns, to construct churches, to diffuse books, to send missionaries to the antipodes; in this manner they found hospitals, prisons, and schools. It is proposed to inculcate some truth or to foster some feeling by the encouragement of a great example, they form a society. Wherever at the head of some new undertaking you see the government in France, or a man of rank in England, in the United States you will be sure to find an association.

One distinguished philanthropist believes that if the leadership of the government and business sectors of U.S. society were to assume the responsibility for support of the private sector, "[w]e would surprise ourselves and the world, because American democracy, which all too many observers believe is on a downward slide, would come alive with unimagined creativity and energy."[22]

Contemporary writing is replete with examples of these fundamental principles. Those who have addressed the subject include:

> . . . the associative impulse is strong in American life; no other civilization can show as many secret fraternal orders, businessmen's "service clubs," trade and occupational associations, social clubs, garden clubs, women's clubs, church clubs, theater groups, political and reform associations, veterans' groups, ethnic societies, and other clusterings of trivial or substantial importance. —Max Lerner

> . . . in America, even in modern times, communities existed before governments were here to care for public needs. —Daniel J. Boorstin

> . . . voluntary association with others in common causes has been thought to be strikingly characteristic of American life. —Merle Curti

---

[22] Rockefeller 3d, "America's Threatened Third Sector," *The Reader's Digest* Apr. 1978, at 105, 108.

We have been unique because another sector, clearly distinct from the other two [business and government], has, in the past, borne a heavy load of public responsibility. —Richard C. Cornuelle

The third sector is . . . the seedbed for organized efforts to deal with social problems. —John D. Rockefeller

. . . the ultimate contribution of the Third Sector to our national life— namely, what it does to ensure the continuing responsiveness, creativity and self-renewal of our democratic society. . . . —Waldemar A. Neilsen

. . . an array of its [the independent sector's] virtues that is by now fairly familiar: its contributions to pluralism and diversity, its tendency to enable individuals to participate in civil life in ways that make sense to them and help to combat that corrosive feeling of powerlessness that is among the dread social diseases of our era, its encouragement of innovation and its capacity to act as a check on the inadequacies of government. —Richard W. Lyman

The problems of contemporary society are more complex, the solutions more involved and the satisfactions more obscure, but the basic ingredients are still the caring and the resolve to make things better. —Brian O'Connell[23]

Tax exemption for charities and the charitable contribution deduction, therefore, are not anachronisms, nor are they loopholes. Rather, they are a bulwark against overdomination by government and a hallmark of a free society. These elements of tax law help nourish the voluntary sector of this nation, preserve individual initiative, and reflect the pluralistic philosophy that has been the guiding spirit of democratic America. The charitable deduction has been proven to be fair and efficient, and without it the philanthropic sector of U.S. society would be rendered unrecognizable by present standards.

In sum, there needs to be a realization that the charitable deduction and exemption are predicated on principles that are more fundamental than tax doctrines and are larger than technical considerations of the

---

[23] These quotations in fuller form, and others, are collected in O'Connell, *America's Voluntary Spirit* (New York: The Foundation Center, 1983).

A companion book by the author addresses this point in additional detail, and traces the origins and development of a hypothetical charitable organization to illustrate applicability of the various laws, including fund-raising regulation requirements. The book, *Starting and Managing a Nonprofit Organization: A Legal Guide* (New York: John Wiley & Sons, Inc., 1989), is referred to in this book as *Starting and Managing a Nonprofit Organization*.

federal tax law. The federal tax provisions that enhance charity exist as a reflection of the affirmative national policy of not inhibiting by taxation the beneficial activities of qualified organizations striving to advance the quality of the American social order.

Likewise, in the zeal to regulate charitable solicitations, government must take care not to destroy the very institutions that compose the essence of the American societal fabric.

§ 1.2 The Independent Sector Today

During the course of 1989, total giving to charity in the United States was $114.7 billion, an increase of 10.43 percent in relation to the revised estimate for 1988 of $103.89 billion.[24] Living individuals provided $96.43 billion of this giving, with bequests yielding $6.57 billion; private foundations, $6.7 billion; and corporations, $5 billion.

This $114.7 billion was allocated as follows: $54.32 billion for religion, $11.39 billion for human services, $10.69 billion for education, $10.04 billion for health, $7.49 billion for the arts and humanities, $3.62 billion for civic and public causes, and $17.15 billion for other purposes.

The most recent attempt to comprehensively profile the contemporary independent sector of the United States principally utilizes data for 1984.[25] This analysis, in estimating the dimensions of the sector within the context of the entire U.S. economy, concluded that, of total national income ($3.144 trillion), the independent sector's share was 5.6 percent, as contrasted with the for-profit sector's share of 79.3 percent and the government's share of 14.5 percent. Of the earnings from work ($2.169 trillion) generated by Americans in 1984, the independent sector accounted for 7.2 percent, while the for-profit sector accounted for 75.3 percent and the governmental sector, 16.8 percent. Of the total number of entities in the United States in 1984 (19.4 million), the independent sector accounted for 4.2 percent, the business sector, about 94 percent; and the governmental sector, less than 1 percent. Current operating expenditures for all nonprofit organizations (not just those comprising

---

[24] *Giving USA* (1990), published by the AAFRC [American Association of Fund Raising Counsel] Trust for Philanthropy.

[25] Hodgkinson and Weitzman, *Dimensions of the Independent Sector* (2d ed. 1986). For purposes of this analysis, the term "independent sector" was defined to constitute only IRC § 501(c)(3) organizations (352,884 IRS-recognized organizations plus 338,244 churches and the like) and IRC § 501(c)(4) organizations (130,344 organizations).

the independent sector) in 1984 were $209.8 billion. Although the independent sector grew faster than other sectors of the U.S. economy throughout the 1970s, by 1984 the independent sector was declining in comparison with the other two sectors on most national indicators.

According to this analysis, the total sources of funds for the independent sector in 1984 were dues, fees, and other charges (37.8 percent), contributions (26.9 percent), government (26.9 percent), and other receipts (including investment income) (8.4 percent). During this year, about 80 percent of the funds were used for current operations, with 5.7 percent expended for construction and capital improvements. Of the total expenditures for current operations ($201.5 billion), 52 percent was for health, 24 percent for education and research, nearly 10 percent for social services, 8.5 percent for religion, and 3 percent for civic and social purposes. In 1984, the total full-time employment equivalent of volunteers (5 million in the independent sector) had an assigned value of $80 billion, representing 24 percent of total sources of support. The proportion of total employment represented by the independent sector was 7.1 percent in 1984; 67.3 percent of these employees were female and nearly 14 percent were black.

Private charitable contributions in 1984 totaled $73.3 billion, representing 32.7 percent of operating expenditures (as contrasted with 70.6 percent in 1955) and 2.4 percent of national income. Most of these gifts came from living persons (82.8 percent), with the balance from bequests (6.7 percent), private foundations (5.3 percent), and business corporations (5.2 percent). In 1984, 89 percent of Americans made charitable contributions, with an average gift of $640; 39 percent of the donors gave at least 2 percent of their incomes, and 70 percent of the gifts went to religious organizations. Persons with household incomes of $50,000 or more, while accounting for 13 percent of the nation's households, made 37 percent of total individual contributions in 1984. In 1983, private foundations granted $4.5 billion for charitable ends, while corporate contributions totaled $3.8 billion in 1984.

This analysis also profiles the independent sector in terms of trends in funding and expenditures, by subsector, namely, health services; education and research; religious organizations; civic, social, and fraternal organizations; arts and culture; foundations; and legal services. Of the total annual funds received by the independent sector in 1984 ($253.5 billion), health services (primarily hospitals) accounted for one-half; education and research, 23 percent; religion, nearly 12 percent; social services, 8 percent; civic, social, and fraternal organizations, nearly 3 percent; and arts and culture, and foundations (including international activities), about 2.5 percent each. For this purpose, support includes private contributions; dues, fees, and like charges; government funds; and endowment funds. The health services subsector received 48 percent of its 1984 support from the private sector, 35 percent from government, and 8 percent from contributions. The comparable percentages for education and research were 53, 17, and 14.5 percent; social services, 12.6, 44, and 37 percent; civic, social, and fraternal, 13, 50, and 30 percent; and arts and culture, 10, 13, and 66.7 percent. The percentage of funds used by the subsectors for current operating expenditures in 1984 was: health services, over 80 percent; education and research, also over 80 percent; religious organizations, 59 percent; social service organizations, 93 percent; civic, social, and fraternal organizations, 95 percent; legal services, 100 percent; and arts and culture, 49 percent.

Of the 94.5 million nonagricultural employees in the United States in 1984, 7.2 million were employees of nonprofit organizations; of these, 6.7 were employed in the independent sector. Wages and salaries in the independent sector in 1984 totaled $90.6 billion. The health services subsector was responsible for 46.7 percent of this employment; education and research, 22 percent; religion, 9.7 percent; civic, social, and fraternal, 5 percent; and arts and culture, 1.5 percent.

Other 1984 data on the health services subsector show that it represents 52 percent of the independent sector's total current operating expenditures; of these expenditures, 88 percent were by hospitals (3,539 institutions); 5.3 percent of these expenditures were by nursing and personal care facilities; 6.5 percent of these expenditures were by the outpatient care and allied services component of the subsector; and the estimated value of volunteer time for the subsector was $8 billion. The education and research subsector included 27,694 private elementary, secondary, and special schools, 1,803 private colleges (1983 data), 1,338 libraries and information centers, and 1,946 educational and scientific research organizations (1982 data); independent colleges and universities accounted for nearly 52 percent of this subsector's total operating expenditures; and the estimated value of volunteer time for this subsector was $6.1 billion. There were 52,571 social service organizations in 1982; individual and family services consumed 26 percent of this subsector's operating expenditures; job training and related services represented 10 percent of this subsector's operating expenditures; and the estimated value of volunteer time for this subsector was $17 billion. In 1984, there were approximtely 4,200 entities such as public radio and television broadcasting organizations, nonprofit theaters, symphony orchestras, operas and dance companies, museums, and botanical and zoological gardens, that attracted volunteer time with an estimated value of about $2.5 billion. Otherwise, in 1982, there were 24,261 private foundations; 35,457 civic, social, and fraternal organizations; and 1,302 legal services organizations; there were an estimated 338,000 religious organizations in 1983.

Total revenue for charitable organizations (other than private foundations) was $196.3 billion in 1982. Contributions and program revenue combined provided 84 percent of this amount.

The philanthropic scene means more than just dollars; it means people. It is believed that one of every four American citizens is engaged in some form of service in the conduct of philanthropic programs and causes. There may be as many as 20 million voluntary workers and leaders working to further the programs of the agencies supported by the United Way alone. A survey of 20 national charitable agencies indicates that they attract the service of 20.8 million volunteers plus 15.7 million fund-raising volunteers.

With nonprofit institutions and organizations now numbering in excess of 800,000, the independent sector of American society is truly a major "enterprise."[26]

§ 1.3   Evolution of Government Regulation: The Focus on Fund-Raising Costs

"'Helping' Children" ran the front-page headline in *The Washington Post*, which continued: "Va. Charity Raised Nearly $1 Million, but 93 Percent Went for Expenses."[27] That headline encapsulates one of the prime issues facing America's philanthropic community today: the reasonableness of fund-raising costs, as perceived by federal and state legislators and regulators and the general public—as well as those who manage or are generally responsible for the charities involved. Government regulation of fund-raising for charity, while encompassing other matters, is fixed on the single issue of fund-raising expenses: their measurement, reporting, and "proper" amount.[28] In fact, the origin of government

---

[26] In general, Cutlip, *Fund Raising in the United States* 157 (1965).

[27] *The Washington Post*, Feb. 7, 1980, at A1. Also see "Correction," *The Washington Post*, May 11, 1980, at 2.

[28] One commentator observed that many states "are beginning to reexamine laws regulating charitable solicitations in the wake of recent disclosures revealing the actual expenditure patterns of many organizations" and concluded: "Of primary concern have been the revelations that in many instances only a small percentage of the money given to further a charitable cause is expended on that cause." Quandt, "The Regulation of Charitable Fundraising and Spending Activities," 1975 *Wis. L. Rev.* 1158, 1159 (1975).

regulation of fund-raising is traceable to the fund-raising cost issue; the history of this field of regulation reflects reaction to a pageant of alleged abuses by charities soliciting gifts, each of which featured an ostensibly "high" percentage of fund-raising costs.

The Washington Post article detailed the direct mail fund-raising activities of an organization headquartered in Alexandria, Virginia, by the name of Children's Aid International. According to the account, the organization raised nearly $1 million over a two-year period—"money it promised to spend on packages of high-protein food for malnourished children around the world"—yet expended less than 7 cents out of each dollar raised on "food for children." The breakdown on CAI's expenditures: 25 percent for management fees, 17 percent for other administrative costs, 51 percent for fund-raising, and the balance—7 percent—for "starving children."

The clear implication gained from the article is that a 93 percent fund-raising cost experienced by a charity is "improper," may be close to "fraudulent," certainly "wrong." The closest the article came to express criticism was to observe that CAI's fund-raising costs are "high in comparison with that of many established charities," followed by the observation that the fund-raising costs of the local United Way agency are less than 7 percent. The organization's defense—unavoidably high start-up costs—went unanalyzed and was buried deep in the story. It may be safely assumed that the article helped fuel public suspicion about charitable institutions generally.

Some months beforehand, another headline in The Washington Post announced: "Pallottines Say Nearly 75% Spent for Fund-Raising."[29] This story featured the celebrated case of the Pallottine Fathers, a Catholic order based in Baltimore, Maryland, that conducted a massive direct mail fund-raising effort and allegedly devoted, in one 18-month period, 2½ cents out of every dollar received for missionary work. Apparently, in 1976, the order raised $7.6 million and spent $5.6 million to do so. This undertaking eventuated in a grand jury investigation, which developed evidence of extensive real estate dealings by the order and a loan to the then governor of the state to help finance his divorce. Little of the proceeds of the order's solicitations went to support Pallottine missions in underdeveloped countries as claimed. The publicity became so intense that the Vatican rector general of the order commanded that Pallottine

---

[29] The Washington Post, Nov. 3, 1977, at C1.

fund-raising activities cease and formed a special investigating commission; the father who headed the order's fund-raising operations was banished from the state by the archbishop of Baltimore.

Again, the public was exposed to a fund-raising abuse that was framed in terms of high expenses in relation to contributions received.

These episodes are, unfortunately, only two in a series of like exposés that have haunted legitimate charities for years and helped taint the term "fund-raising."[30] These events also fueled the machinery that has been built by and for government to regulate fund-raising by charitable organizations. Many an aspiring or practicing politican has parlayed a probe of a charity "scandal" into high office. Thus *Time Magazine*, for example, was moved to characterize the Pallottine order scandal as indicative of widespread wrongdoing: "The Pallottine mess provides Americans with one more excuse not to give money to church agencies, even those that make full public accountings"[31] and "[t]he Pallottines were not the only agency that used 80% or more of their gifts to cover the exorbitant costs of direct mail."[32]

Other episodes—isolated instances having major impact on public and regulatory attitudes—include the solicitation activities of Father Flanagan's Boys Town, the Sister Kenny Foundation, the Police Hall of Fame,[33] the Freedom for All Forever Foundation, the Korean Cultural

---

[30] Also "Solicitors Cash In on Budget Pinch Felt by Nonprofit Groups," *The Washington Post*, Oct. 18, 1982 (Washington Business), at 19; "Many Charity Shows Benefit Mostly The Fundraiser," *The Charlotte Observer*, Mar. 22, 1981, at 1.

[31] "Radix Malorum Est Cupiditas?" *Time Magazine*, Jan. 23, 1978, at 75.

[32] "Wrist Tap," *Time Magazine*, May 22, 1978, at 64.

[33] In this matter, the Circuit Court of Cook County, Illinois, ordered fund-raisers to pay $528,231.52 (including $150,000 in punitive damages) into a trust fund for widows and children of slain law enforcement officers, as the result of a fund-raising effort that generated $785,731, of which the fund-raisers received $622,000 for costs and compensation. One contract allowed up to 75 percent of total contributions to be consumed in fund-raising expenses; the court characterized this and other contracts as authorizing "illegitimate commissions and expenses and were outrageous, unconscionable and an assault upon the public conscience in violation of public policy and Illinois law relating to charitable solicitations." *People of the State of Illinois v. Police Hall of Fame, Inc.*, No. 74 CH 5015 (order dated October 19, 1976).

and Freedom Foundation,[34] and the Children's Relief Fund.[35] Thus the public media remain alive with one report after another of the alleged misdeeds of charities. Invariably, the scandals involve solicitations of charitable contributions from the general public, by or for organizations that derive their principal support from public giving,[36] with an ostensibly excessive amount of funds devoted to direct mail campaigns, questionable investments, or administration.[37]

Thirty years ago, federal regulation of fund-raising for charity did not exist (other than by means of the charitable contribution deduction), and state regulation in the field was just beginning to flower. Prior to that time, fund-raising regulation (such as it was) was a combination of occasional IRS audits and state attorneys general inquiries, the latter predicated on their historical role of enforcing the requirements imposed on the administration of charitable trusts.[38] These efforts were based on one premise, and today's vast and growing governmental apparatuses overseeing charitable fund-raising continue to be guided by that premise: "The greatest possible portion of the wealth donated to private charity must be conserved and used to further the charitable, public purpose; waste must be minimized and diversion of funds for private gain is intolerable."[39] Out of the inadequacies of common law principles and tax enforcement efforts has grown—and is still growing—a comprehensive

---

[34] In one instance, the Attorney General of the State of New York charged the Foundation with raising $1,508,256 and expending only $95,674 (6.3 percent) for charitable purposes, and characterized the Foundation as "perpetrating a fraud upon the contributing public." News release dated February 16, 1977.

[35] For a litany of fund-raising "abuses," see *Hearing on Children's Charities Before the Subcommittee on Children and Youth of the Senate Committee on Labor and Public Welfare*, 93d Cong., 2d Sess. (1974), chaired by then-Senator Walter F. Mondale. Also *Hearings on Fund Raising By or In Behalf of Veterans Before the House Committee on Veterans' Affairs*, 85th Cong., 2d Sess. (1958); *Hearings on Federal Agencies and Philanthropies Before a Subcommittee of the House Committee on Government Operations*, 85th Cong., 2d Sess. (1958).

[36] E.g., Baldwin, "Ideology By Mail," *The New Republic*, July 7 and 14, 1979, at 19.

[37] These developments have spawned articles in the popular media such as Smith, "New Guidelines for Giving" (subtitled "Our 10 commandments help you separate top charities from wastrels"), *Money*, Dec. 1989, at 141.

[38] Bogert, "Proposed Legislation Regarding State Supervision of Charities," 52 *Mich. L. Rev.* 633 (1954).

[39] Karst, "The Efficiency of the Charitable Dollar: An Unfulfilled State Responsibility," 73 *Harv. L. Rev.* 433–434 (1960).

supervisory and regulatory program governing the fund-raising efforts by charitable organizations at the federal, state, and local levels.

Statutory regulation of fund-raising for charity began with codification of the supervisory and investigatory authority of states' attorneys general. Thereafter, there came into being provisions seeking to prevent fraud in charitable solicitations or to promote disclosure of information about such solicitations, or both. Municipal ordinances earlier introduced the concepts of licensing and periodic reporting of charities' fund collection activities, and this approach was adopted by the states as their charitable solicitation acts were written. As the years passed, the statutes became more extensive and stringent, the staffs of the regulatory agencies increased, and regulations, rules, and forms unfolded. In general, the call of one observer, who declaimed that "the evils of inefficient or unscrupulous charitable organizations must be attacked head on by strong government regulation,"[40] was heard.

However, the process is by no means wholly an instance of government regulation increasing merely for the sake of increase. The nature of organized philanthropy, and the perception of it by the public, lawmakers, and regulators, have altered dramatically over the past two decades.

§ 1.4   The Contemporary Regulatory Climate

The number of nonprofit organizations remains steadily on the rise. Most of these are exempt from federal and state income and property taxation, many are eligible to attract tax-deductible contributions, and many utilize preferred postal rates. The involvement of these groups in the day-to-day management and change of American life has never been greater.

Concurrent with the rise in state regulation of fund-raising for charity has been a significant upsurge in regulatory activity at the federal level by means of administration of the nation's tax laws. The process got under way in 1950, when Congress enacted laws taxing the unrelated business income of otherwise tax-exempt organizations. In 1969, the Internal Revenue Code was sizably thickened by a battery of rules defining, regulating, and taxing private foundations, seeking to prevent self-dealing and large stockholdings and to increase grant making and public involvement in the affairs of foundations. In 1974, Congress authorized the formation, within the IRS, of an Office of Employee Plans and Exempt Organizations, which has stepped up federal oversight and

[40] Quandt, *supra* note 28, at 1187.

audit of the nation's nonprofit, including charitable, organizations. Congress, in 1987, enacted disclosure laws for noncharitable tax-exempt organizations engaged in fund-raising and, in 1989, the IRS launched a renewed effort to require disclosures in the course of fund-raising for charitable organizations.

Still, notwithstanding this rise in government regulation, all is not well. The malady was evidenced several years ago by a blast from a normally rather staid publication, hurling the following charges against some nonprofit organizations—they:

1. Pay their executives fat salaries and allow them generous fringe benefits.

2. Award contracts to their trustees and board members.

3. Serve as fronts for commercial enterprises with which they have "sweetheart" deals.

4. Enjoy special mailing privileges and property-tax breaks that give them a competitive edge against tax-paying establishments.

5. Engage in wasteful and sometimes fraudulent fund-raising with little accountability to the public.[41]

The last allegation is the most immediate concern herein, but this inventory of wrongdoings is indicative of the state of the nonprofit sector as perceived by some. Public regard is essential to the successful functioning of charitable groups; this regard—which has remained high throughout the country's existence—may be eroding in the face of well-publicized abuses and other pressures.

This, then, is the dilemma of the charities: abuses appear to be on the increase, triggering greater governmental regulation, which makes operations more difficult for authentic charitable undertakings and the public climate more critical of these undertakings. The inroads being made by a few unscrupulous and fraduent operators in tapping the resources of philanthropy are threatening to undermine the seriously needed solicitation programs conducted by legitimate charitable organizations.

Coincidentally, the public is demanding greater accountability from nonprofit, principally charitable, organizations. The consumerism movement is causing individual and corporate donors to be more concerned

[41] "For Many, There Are Big Profits in 'Nonprofits,'" *U.S. News & World Report*, Nov. 6, 1978, at 45.

and sophisticated about the uses of their gift dollars. The emphasis now is on disclosure; donors—prospective and actual—are demonstrating greater proclivity to inquire of federal, state, and local agencies, lawmakers, and the independent "watchdog" agencies, and the philanthropic community about the fund-raising and fund-expenditure practices of charitable organizations.

In this age where the tax bills being levied are rising annually, taxpayers often lack sympathy for and even resent organizations that do not pay tax. Greater understanding of the principle that taxes forgone by one must be made up by others may be fostering a public attitude toward nonprofits that is somewhat less lofty than that captured by concepts of voluntarism and pluralism. Likewise, the lure of the standard deduction (now used by a substantial majority of taxpayers) is pulling people away from deductible charitable giving, thereby severing still another traditional nexus between Americans and their charities.

Therefore, in the face of seemingly inadequate disclosure of meaningful information to the public, excessive administrative and fund-raising costs, and insufficient portions of the proceeds of charitable gifts passing for charitable purposes, government regulation of fund-raising for charity is thriving. Some states that currently lack a charitable solicitation act are busily engaged in the process of trying to enact one. Many states with such a law are contemplating toughening it, either by amending the act or by increasing reporting and like regulatory burdens. And, although the drive for a federal charitable solicitations law has temporarily slowed, the IRS, expanding its administrative capabilities, is quietly but assuredly embarking on a program of substantial regulation in this field.

Despite all this activity, the pressure for still more regulation seems to continue, ultimately to be manifested in some form of a federal charitable solicitations statute. The drive for such a law, now dormant, may be awaiting only the spark of a well-publicized charity scandal to trigger action by Congress. Part of the interest in federal law in this field derives from dissatisfaction with the present state-by-state regulatory scheme. Such critics voice a variety of complaints about the federal law, including these:

1. There is no requirement (as there is for private foundations) that public charities annually distribute a portion of their funds for charitable purposes.

2. There is no requirement that charities disclose to potential contributors the portion of their funds actually devoted to charitable purposes.

3. There are no common requirements regarding registration, licensing, periodic reporting, disclosure of financial information, and limitations on compensation of fund-raisers.

4. There are no uniform accounting standards for public charities imposed by law.

5. Some charitable and other nonprofit organizations are escaping taxation of unrelated activities, in part by portraying those activities as "fund-raising."

However, there are certain nonlegislative developments (all as discussed in subsequent chapters) that may serve to mute some of this criticism, such as development of a new federal annual information return and several proposed innovative ways to regulate charities' fund-raising costs. Also, efforts going forward under the auspices of the National Association of State Charity Officials may result in significant progress toward uniformity of administration and enforcement in this area.

There are parallel developments that may also introduce federal law governing charitable solicitations. These concern the fact that, in the wake of two decades of experience in strenuously regulating the operations and activities of private foundations, many in the IRS and the Department of the Treasury and some in Congress are seriously contemplating comparable regulation of the affairs of one or more categories of public charities.

Unlike the torrents of alleged scandals that preceded the revolution in the federal tax laws pertaining to private foundations, which culminated in a major portion of the Tax Reform Act of 1969, there has been no parade of ostensible abuses warranting strict supervision of public charities. Rather, it appears that this is a last frontier for reformers in the field of charitable organizations and that most of the reforms are being advocated because the statutory basis for the rules is already in place;[42] furthermore, the imposition of these rules on public charities strikes many as the thing to do as a logical extension of existing regulation. Hence the not-too-far-distant future may well see extension of many of the private foundation restrictions to some or all public charities: most likely, the prohibitions (perhaps in some modified form) on self-dealing, excess business holdings, and jeopardizing investments, and the rules mandating payout of funds and restricting the uses of such funds. It is in this context that the recent attention to the matter of government supervision or regulation of solicitations for charitable contributions may bring some

[42] IRC ch. 42.

new federally enforced rules to govern the fund-raising activities of public charities, that is, as part of a comprehensive effort to regulate public charities to the same degree as is at present the case for private foundations.[43]

Whatever happens, one aspect of the matter is clear: both state and federal regulation are on the rise. The former is not likely to be preempted by the latter. Students of this regulatory scene astutely observed that, "[a]s legislators continue efforts to devise schemes which comply with the [Supreme Court] decision [finding a state charitable solicitation act unconstitutional as violating free speech rights], they will certainly not renounce long-standing views on the important role of state regulation of charitable solicitation."[44]

Probably the most difficult issue to cope with is what all of this regulation is and will be doing to the philanthropic sector. Will fund-raising regulation improve the solicitation picture for legitimate charitable groups or will it smother the entirety of the sector? Is there actually sufficient abuse taking place in this area to warrant the massive costs of compliance? Is the overall panoply of nonprofit organizations, tax exemption, and charitable giving becoming an anachronism, in the process of evolutionary departure in the face of the growth of the state? Is fund-raising for charity the wave of the past, because charity itself is becoming obsolete?[45]

Although no one knows the answers to these questions, the march of government regulation of fund-raising for charity continues inexorably. This new form of regulation, arising from humble origins only a few years ago, is now one of philanthropy's major concerns. How and whether these new governmental policies and philanthropy can coexist will say much about the nature of the charitable sector in the coming years.[46]

[43] In early 1989, a task force at the IRS recommended that many of the federal tax rules that are presently applicable only to private foundations be extended to apply to some or all public charities (Report of the IRS Commissioner's Executive Task Force on Civil Penalties). A summary of and commentary on these recommendations appears in VI *The Nonprofit Counsel* (No. 5) 1 (1989).
[44] Harris, Holley, & McCaffrey, *Fundraising Into the 1990's: State Regulation of Charitable Solicitation After* Riley 90 (1989).
[45] See Cook, "Is charity obsolete?" *Forbes*, Feb. 5, 1979, at 45. Also Mayer, "End of an era," *The Progressive*, Oct. 1979, at 32; Morganthau, "The Charity Battle," *Newsweek*, May 7, 1979, at 33; and Delloff, "Private Philanthropy and the Public Interest," *The Christian Century*, Feb. 21, 1979, at 188.
[46] See Hopkins, "Coming: New Law, More Regulation," 20 *Fund Raising Management* (No. 11) 28 (1990); Hopkins, "Fund-Raisers and The Tax Law: 20 Years' Experience," 20 *Fund Raising Management* (No. 2) 32 (1989).

2

The Anatomy of Charitable Fund-Raising

Certain basic factual aspects of fund-raising for charity warrant summary prior to any analysis of federal and state governmental regulation of this type of fund-raising.[1] These aspects include the types of organizations encompassed by the various laws, the many fund-raising techniques, and the roles of those individuals (other than the regulators) who are, along with the charitable organizations themselves, enmeshed in this regulatory process: the fund-raising professionals, the lawyers, and the accountants.

§ 2.1 Scope of the Term "Charitable" Organization

The many laws governing the process of soliciting gifts for charitable purposes principally apply, of course, to charitable organizations and those who raise funds for them. Thus, it is necessary to understand the scope of the term "charitable" organization as it is employed in these laws.

The term "charitable" organization as used in the state charitable solicitation acts has a meaning considerably broader than that traditionally employed under state law and under the federal tax law.[2] Therefore, the soliciting organizations encompassed by the federal definition of what is "charitable" must comply with the requirements of the federal regulation of fund-raising for charity as well as that of the various states (unless specifically exempted). However, there are organizations that are tax-

---

[1] There are, of course, other forms of fund-raising, such as fund-raising for political parties and candidates; the governmental regulation of these forms of fund-raising is outside the scope of this book.
[2] See Ch. 4 § 4.1.

exempt under federal law for reasons other than advancement of charitable purposes that are obligated to comply with the panoply of state and local charitable solicitation laws.

The federal tax law definition of the term "charitable" is based upon the English common law and charitable trust law precepts. The federal income tax regulations recognize this fact by stating that the term is used in its "generally accepted legal sense."[3] At the same time, court decisions continue to expand the concept of "charity" by introducing additional applications of the term.[4] As one court observed, evolutions in the definition of the word "charitable" are "wrought by changes in moral and ethical precepts generally held, or by changes in relative values assigned to different and sometimes competing and even conflicting interests of society."[5]

For the most part, the institutions and other organizations that are subject to these laws are those that have their federal tax status based on their classification as "charitable" organizations. These are the entities categorized as "charitable," "religious," "educational," "scientific," or "literary," or certain organizations that are engaged in the fostering of "national or international amateur sports competition."[6] Each one of these terms is defined in the federal tax law.

The term "charitable" in the federal income tax setting embraces a variety of purposes and activities. These include the relief of the poor and distressed or of the underprivileged,[7] the advancement of religion,[8] the advancement of education or science,[9] lessening of the burdens of

---

[3] Reg. § 1.501(c)(3)–1(d)(2).

[4] See *Law of Tax-Exempt Organizations* at 55–79.

[5] *Green* v. *Connally*, 330 F. Supp. 1150, 1159 (D.D.C. 1971), aff'd sub nom., *Coit* v. *Green*, 404 U.S. 997 (1971).

[6] IRC §§ 501(c)(3) & 170(c)(2). The first of these provisions is the basis for federal tax-exempt status; the second is the basis for eligibility for donee status for purposes of the federal charitable contribution deduction. (Most organizations that engage in fund-raising are able to offer their donors assurances that their gifts are deductible for federal and state income tax purposes because these organizations are described in IRC § 170(c)(2).) Organizations that are engaged in "testing for public safety" are referenced in IRC § 501(c)(3) but not IRC § 170(c)(2).

The charitable giving rules are summarized in Ch. 6 § 6.11.

[7] Reg. § 1.501(c)(3)-1(d)(2). See *Law of Tax-Exempt Organizations* at 92–96.

[8] Reg. § 1.501(c)(3)-1(d)(2). See *Law of Tax-Exempt Organizations* at 96–98.

[9] Reg. § 1.501(c)(3)-1(d)(2). See *Law of Tax-Exempt Organizations* at 98–101.

government,[10] community beautification and maintenance,[11] promotion of health,[12] promotion of social welfare,[13] promotion of environmental conservancy,[14] advancement of patriotism,[15] care of orphans,[16] maintenance of public confidence in the legal system,[17] facilitating student and cultural exchanges,[18] and the promotion and advancement of amateur sports.[19]

The federal tax law also encompasses organizations defined as "charitable" in the broadest sense;[20] these include entities considered "educational," "religious," and "scientific." Nonetheless, the term "charitable" as used in the federal tax context—including "education,"[21] "religion,"[22] and "science"[23]—is not as broad as the concept of tax exemption. Certainly the term is not as far-ranging as the concept of nonprofit organizations. Stated another way, nonprofit organizations are not necessarily tax exempt, and tax-exempt organizations are not always charitable.

To be tax-exempt under federal law, a nonprofit organization must satisfy the rules pertaining to at least one of the categories of tax-exempt

---

[10] Reg. § 1.501(c)(3)-1(d)(2). See *Law of Tax-Exempt Organizations* at 101–3.

[11] Rev. Rul. 78-85, 1978-1 C.B. 150. See *Law of Tax-Exempt Organizations* at 103–4.

[12] Rev. Rul. 69-545, 1969-2 C.B. 117. See *Law of Tax-Exempt Organizations* at 104–13.

[13] Reg. § 1.501(c)(3)-1(d)(2). See *Law of Tax-Exempt Organizations* at 113–17.

[14] Rev. Rul. 76-204, 1976-1 C.B. 152. See *Law of Tax-Exempt Organizations* at 117–18.

[15] Rev. Rul. 78-84, 1978-1 C.B. 150. See *Law of Tax-Exempt Organizations* at 118.

[16] Rev. Rul. 80-200, 1980-2 C.B. 173. See *Law of Tax-Exempt Organizations* at 118.

[17] *Kentucky Bar Foundation, Inc.* v. *Commissioner*, 78 T.C. 921 (1982). See *Law of Tax-Exempt Organizations* at 118.

[18] Rev. Rul. 80-286, 1980-2 C.B. 179. See *Law of Tax-Exempt Organizations* at 118.

[19] *Hutchinson Baseball Enterprises, Inc.* v. *Commissioner*, 73 T.C. 144 (1979), aff'd, 696 F.2d 757 (10th Cir. 1982). See *Law of Tax-Exempt Organizations* at 118. Also IRC § 501(j). See *Law of Tax-Exempt Organizations* at 223–24.

[20] The U.S. Supreme Court has held that all organizations encompassed by IRC § 501(c)(3), including those that are "educational" and "religious," are "charitable" in nature for federal tax law purposes (*Bob Jones University* v. *United States*, 461 U.S. 574 (1983)).

[21] See *Law of Tax-Exempt Organizations* at 160–80.

[22] See *Law of Tax-Exempt Organizations* at 181–209.

[23] See *Law of Tax-Exempt Organizations* at 210–16.

organizations set forth in the Internal Revenue Code.[24] In addition to those organizations that are recognized as charitable entities,[25] the realm of tax-exempt organizations under federal law embraces social welfare (including advocacy) organizations,[26] labor organizations,[27] trade and professional associations,[28] social clubs,[29] fraternal organizations,[30] veterans' organizations,[31] and political organizations.[32] Generally, with the exception of veterans' organizations,[33] contributions to these organizations are not deductible as charitable gifts.[34]

In general, the sweep of the states' charitable solicitation acts is not so broad as to encompass all nonprofit organizations, nor is it so broad as to encompass all tax-exempt organizations. For example, these laws do not normally embrace trade and professional associations[35] that are financially supported largely by dues (payments for services), rather than by contributions. Likewise, they do not normally cover private foundations,[36] which, while charitable in nature, do not normally solicit

---

[24] The Internal Revenue Code provides for tax-exempt status under IRC § 501(a) for those nonprofit organizations that are listed in IRC § 501(c). Other categories of tax-exempt organizations are described in IRC §§ 521, 527, & 528. See *Law of Tax-Exempt Organizations* at 396–411. Governmental entities are also tax-exempt. See *Law of Tax-Exempt Organizations* at 154–59, 417–22.

[25] That is, organizations described in IRC § 501(c)(3).

[26] Organizations described in IRC § 501(c)(4). See *Law of Tax-Exempt Organizations* at 297–339. Social welfare organizations are the type of noncharitable organizations that are most likely to be subject to the state charitable solicitation acts.

[27] Organizations described in IRC § 501(c)(5). See *Law of Tax-Exempt Organizations* at 356–60.

[28] IRC § 501(c)(6). See *Law of Tax-Exempt Organizations* at 316–39.

[29] IRC § 501(c)(7). See *Law of Tax-Exempt Organizations* at 340–55.

[30] Organizations described in IRC § 501(c)(8) & (10). See *Law of Tax-Exempt Organizations* at 370–74, 377–79.

[31] IRC § 501(c)(4) or § 501(c)(19). See *Law of Tax-Exempt Organizations* at 393–96.

[32] IRC § 527. See *Law of Tax-Exempt Organizations* at 404–9.

[33] Contributions to veterans' organizations are deductible by reason of IRC § 170(c)(3).

[34] Only organizations described in IRC § 170(c) are eligible charitable donees. See *supra* note 6.

[35] See *supra* note 28.

[36] See *Law of Tax-Exempt Organizations* at 436–90.

contributions. By contrast, these laws are likely to be attributable to organizations (other than purely charitable ones) that are tax-exempt but cannot attract deductible contributions,[37] or are eligible to receive deductible contributions but are not usually regarded as charitable organizations, such as veterans' groups.[38]

Generally, the organizations that need to be concerned with the state charitable solicitation laws are the following:

1. Churches and other membership and nonmembership religious organizations.[39]

2. Educational institutions, including schools, colleges, and universities.[40]

3. Hospitals and other forms of health care providers.[41]

4. Publicly supported charitable organizations.[42]

5. Social welfare organizations.[43]

Consequently, an organization recognized as a "charitable" entity under federal tax law, that engages in fund-raising, is (unless specifically exempted)[44] assuredly subject to the state charitable solicitation laws. However, these laws may also encompass other types of tax-exempt organizations that solicit contributions.[45]

§ 2.2 Methods of Fund-Raising

Critical to an understanding of government regulation of charitable fund-raising is an understanding of "fund-raising" itself.[46]

---

[37] E.g., organizations described in IRC § 501(c)(4). See *supra* notes 26 & 34.

[38] IRC § 501(c)(19). See *supra* note 31.

[39] IRC § 170(b)(1)(A)(i). See *Law of Tax-Exempt Organizations* at 198–206, 438.

[40] IRC § 170(b)(1)(A)(ii). See *Law of Tax-Exempt Organizations* at 436–39.

[41] IRC § 170(b)(1)(A)(iii). See *Law of Tax-Exempt Organizations* at 439–41.

[42] IRC §§ 170(b)(1)(A)(vi) (IRC § 509(a)(1) & 509(a)(2)). See *Law of Tax-Exempt Organizations* at 442–58.

[43] See *supra* notes 26 & 34.

[44] See Ch. 4 § 4.4.

[45] See Chs. 3 & 4.

[46] This analysis, and the one in § 3 of this chapter, was prepared by James M. Greenfield, FNAHD, CFRE, author of *Fund-Raising: Evaluating and Managing the Development Process* (New York: John Wiley & Sons, in press). His contribution is gratefully acknowledged by the author.

Every "charitable" organization is entitled to receive and, indeed, welcomes support in the form of contributions. Contributed funds can be used only to support the goals and objectives of the organization consistent with its stated mission, usually to provide a benefit to others. When goals, mission, and public benefits are communicated as institutional needs to the public, they can stimulate gift support. Replies are acts of philanthropy that are motivated by numerous factors, including a sincere concern and a willingness to help others, to improve quality of service, or to advance knowledge. Such voluntary responses, whether of time, talent, or treasure, uplift the human spirit because they are directed to a charitable organization.

Requests for contributions are conducted by one or more fund-raising methods. Fund-raising is, in itself, a unique form of communication that "promotes" and "sells" the product (cause) and "asks for the order" at the same time. There is a common perception that there is a single type of activity called fund-raising and that all gifts are made in cash. Most regulatory approaches seem founded on this perception, as are public attitudes—both positive and negative—toward charitable solicitations. In fact, charitable organizations employ several methods and techniques to solicit contributions. Gifts can be in several forms (such as cash, securities, real property, and real estate), all of which are embraced within the term "fund-raising." The one feature shared equally is the objective—to ask for a gift that benefits someone else.

Asking is simple. There are only three ways: by mail, by telephone, or in person. Mail solicitation is 16 times less effective than in-person contact, but most fund-raising uses this most impersonal of approaches. Organizing institutions and agencies to perform fund-raising is much more complex and requires the careful, and sometimes simultaneous, application of many individual methods of solicitation by volunteers and employees working together. Each individual method of fund-raising has its own characteristics regarding suitability for use, public acceptance, potential or capacity for success (gift revenue), and cost-effectiveness. Likewise, the reporting and enforcement aspects of regulatory systems—to be fair—should distinguish between the varieties of fundraising technique and their performance.

The methods of asking are best understood by dividing them into three program areas: annual giving, special purpose, and estate planning. The "pyramid of giving" (see page 38) illustrates how each area functions to perform its individual task and to aid the progression of donor interest and involvement leading to increased gift results with each chosen charitable organization. A total of 15 methods of fund-raising are included within the three program areas.

Annual Giving Programs

The basic concept of annual giving programs is to recruit new donors and renew prior donors whose gifts provide for annual operating needs. Some programs require only a staff professional to manage, but most require both staff and a volume of volunteer leaders and workers. Charities frequently conduct two or more forms of annual solicitation within a 12-month period, the net effect of which is to contact the same audience with multiple requests within the year. Churches make appeals weekly through the collection plate; United Way uses payroll deductions to assure frequent payments. Such gift support is basic to the financial success of the organization; their needs are urgent, and the funds are consumed immediately upon receipt.

The design behind the choice of any one of these several methods offered during any one year is always the same—to recruit new donors and to renew (and upgrade) the gifts of the prior year's donors. Some donors prefer one method of giving over all others because it is their favorite or they are most comfortable with that style. For example, benefit events are popular because they include attendance at social activities. Multiple-gift requests to present donors will increase net revenues faster than efforts to acquire new donors because present donors are the best prospects for added gifts. Obviously no one organization will be able to use every fund-raising method (chiefly because of donor resistance or saturation), so rational selections are required.

A brief explanation of each method and its special value to the annual giving process is presented below, arranged in the order of least productive to most efficient.

1. *Direct Mail: Donor Acquisition.*   Direct mail/donor acquisition fund-raising uses direct mail response advertising (usually third class, bulk rate) in the form of letters to individuals who are not present donors, inviting them to participate at modest levels. One of the best methods to find and recruit new contributors, this program is perhaps best known to the public because it receives so many mail requests. Usually a charity can expect only a 1 to 2 percent rate of return on "bulk mail requests," but this is considered satisfactory. Successful "customer development" may require an investment of from $1.25 to $1.50 to raise $1.00, a formula well accepted in for-profit business circles but often criticized within charitable organizations. The value of new donors is not their first gift, however, but their potential for repeat gifts. Such first-time

donors, with care and attention, can become future leaders, volunteer workers, and even benefactors.

The mail process includes: (1) selecting audiences likely to reply to this organization; (2) buying, renting, or leasing up-to-date mailing lists of audiences selected; (3) preparing a package containing a letter signed by someone whose name is recognized by most people, a response form with gift amounts suggested, a reply envelope, and a brochure or other information about the charity or the program offered for gift support; (4) scheduling the "mail drop" during the most productive times in the year for mail solicitation (October through December, March through June); and (5) preparing for replies, including gift processing, setting up donor records, and sending "thank you" messages.

2. *Direct Mail: Donor Renewal.* Direct mail/donor renewal fund-raising is used to ask previous donors, who are the best prospects for annual giving, to give again. If some contact has occurred since the first gift, such as a report on the use of their gifts to render services to others, it is likely that 50 percent of prior donors will give again—at a minimum cost to the organization of a renewal letter. A feature called "upgrading," a request to consider a gift slightly above the last amount, works 15 percent of the time, with the added value of preserving the current gift level. Prior donor support is predictable income for organizations who can estimate their ability to meet current needs because of committed levels of donor support.

3. *Telephone and Television.* Telephone calls to prospects and donors permit dialogue and are more successful than direct mail. Public response is not high (around 5 to 8 percent), perhaps because of the intrusive nature of phone calls and their frequent use by for-profit organizations. Television solicitation is more distant but is the best visual medium to convey the message (televangelists have perfected this technique). Both methods are expensive to initiate and require the instant response of donors (only 80 percent of pledge collections may be realized).

4. *Special and Benefit Events.* Special and benefit events are social occasions that use ticket sales and underwriting to generate revenue but incur direct costs for production support. While popular, especially with volunteers, such events are typically the most expensive and least profitable method of fund-raising in practice today. Events include everything from a bake sale and car wash to golf tournaments and formal balls. If well managed, they should produce a 50 percent net profit. While most fund-raising staff deplore the energy and hours required to support

events, their greater value is in public relations visibility, both for the charity and its volunteers.

5. *Support Group Organizations.* Support groups are used to organize donors in a quasi-independent association around the charitable organization. Membership dues and sponsorship of events are used as revenue sources as well as "friend-raising" opportunities. Support groups are like civic organizations, with a board of directors and active committees, except that their purposes are committed to one charity (for example, an alumni association). Valuable for their ability to develop committed annual donors, to organize and train volunteers, and to promote the charity in the community, support groups also require professional staff management. Smaller charities should consider support groups to secure annual gifts as well as the volunteers needed to produce benefit events and to aid the organization in other ways when needed.

6. *Donor Clubs and Associations.* Donor clubs and associations are donor-relations vehicles, similar to support groups, that are designed to enhance the link between donor and charity that will help preserve annual gift support. Most organizations use higher gift levels (say, $1,000 and up) and prestigious names (for example, President's Club) to separate these donors from all others. Their selectivity and privileges help justify the higher gift required, which is rewarded by access to top officials and other benefits. Donor club members also represent a concentration of major gift prospects, whom charitable organizations treat as benefactors, and whose cultivation will pay dividends in the future.

7. *Annual Giving Campaign Committees.* Campaign committees are volunteer committees of peers using in-person solicitation methods to recruit the largest and most important annual gifts. Whether committee members solicit 10 prospects or 100, the performance of such a committee will be the most lucrative of all the above-mentioned annual giving methods. The committee is structured as a true campaign, with a general chairman and division leaders for individual, business, and corporate prospects. Each volunteer may be assigned from three to five prospects to visit and to discuss their annual gift decision. Donors are receptive because someone they respect has taken the time to call upon them on behalf of an organization that the volunteer regards highly and has supported with a personal contribution first.

8. *Other Annual Giving Methods.* Several other methods remain that also can develop annual gift support.

(a) *Commemorative Giving.* A commemorative gift to a charity has the dual effect of honoring the recipient and aiding the donor's favorite charity at the same time. Most often such gifts are memorials following the death of a family member, friend, or business colleague, and are directed by the family to their favorite organization. Commemorative gifts can also be given to mark a birthday, anniversary, promotion, graduation, or other important occasion.

(b) *Gifts in Kind.* Instead of cash, donors can make gifts of items from attics, basements, and warehouses that can be used by the recipient organizations (such as Goodwill Industries, Salvation Army, St. Vincent Society) in their program activities. Businesses often donate products or excess merchandise, either for direct use (food or equipment) or for use as a benefit door prize or auction or raffle item.

(c) *Advertisements in Newspapers/Magazines.* Advertising, while the least likely solicitation method to stimulate a response, can promote an organization, a special campaign, a form of giving, or other purpose. Usually, direct mail or telephone follow-up is required to maximize the gift response from such "multi-media" techniques.

(d) *Door-to-Door and On-Street Solicitation.* While on-street solicitation is less common today because of limited volunteer time, some organizations benefit from "cold calls" during neighborhood drives because the public recognizes the organization's name (for example, the American Cancer Society's "Women's Walk"), or has come to trust the organization's purposes (for example, the Salvation Army's "kettle" collections at Christmastime). The difficulty in recent years has been abuse of public trust by a few other organizations or individuals who "hustle" the public too hard or who run afoul of local regulations restricting solicitation, such as in airports and other public areas.

(e) *Sweepstakes and Lotteries.* Where legal, charities can benefit from such forms of public solicitation as sweepstakes and lotteries. However, most charities prefer to avoid areas of questionable practice, which too often are viewed by the public as forms of gambling. Bingo remains the exception, but it too is carefully regulated and supervised.

(f) *Las Vegas and Monte Carlo Nights.* Again, where legal, Las Vegas and Monte Carlo nights can develop gift revenues for a charity. State and local regulations for conduct of such events are strict, and may include a 5 to 10 percent fee taken from net proceeds. Like other special and benefit events, "casino" nights are hard to manage profitably because of high direct costs and overhead expenses.

(g) *Mailings of Unsolicited Merchandise.* The theory behind the practice of mailing unsolicited merchandise is to engender guilt in the recipient—presumably recipients would feel guilty keeping something of value sent to them and thus would be more likely to respond with gift support. Such a method is less popular today because of rising postage and material costs, and potential adverse tax consequences, along with public resistance (lack of response).

(h) *In-Plant Solicitations.* Public solicitation in the workplace is usually controlled by the employer. Where in-plant solicitations are permitted, some employees resist being "cornered" and "pressured" to give. Usually, only United Way or other federated campaigns have been allowed into the workplace for such solicitation.

(i) *Federated Campaigns.* Federated campaigns are community-wide solicitations organized to support a large number of civic, social, and welfare organizations in the community with a single, once-a-year fund drive. Public acceptance is high, management and fund-raising costs are low (under 20 percent), and a "campaign period" is observed. Federated campaigns, such as United Way, are usually directed at local corporations for annual gifts and to their employees, who are encouraged to allow payroll deduction. Such campaigns require cooperation from those charitable organizations being supported, who must refrain from their own solicitations during the campaign period.

Special Purpose Programs

A successful base of annual giving support permits the charitable organization to conduct more selective programs of fund-raising that will secure major gifts, grants, and capital campaigns toward larger and more significant projects. Requests for large gifts differ from annual gift solicitation because the request is for a "one-time" gift, allows a multi-year pledge, and is directed toward one specific project or urgent need. Likely donors are skillful "investors" who will respond to a major gift request only after researching the organization and determining if the project justifies their commitment. If the request fails their examination, it is not likely to receive any but token support.

Following is a brief explanation of how the three forms of special purpose fund-raising are employed.

9. *Major Gifts from Individuals.*   First of all, it takes courage to ask someone for $1 million. Before the request is made, careful research should ascertain the candidate's capability and enthusiasm for the organization, preparedness to accept this special project, and likely response to the "team" assembled to make the call. Also important is an early resolution of the donor recognition to be offered (election to the board, name on the building, or both). The project must be a "big idea," worthy of the level of investment required, perceived as absolutely essential, and a unique opportunity offered only once. In short, major gift solicitations should be performed as though they were a request for the largest and most significant gift decisions from these donors at this point in their lives.

10. *Grants from Government Agencies, Foundations, and Corporations.*   Separate skills and tools are required to succeed at grantsmanship. Grants are institutional decisions to provide support based upon published policy and guidelines that demand careful observance of application procedures and deadlines, the decision is made by a group of people and, because of limited dollars, only one grant may be given for every 25 to 50 requests received. Usually, for a grant proposal to be accepted, the organization and its project must match perfectly the goals of the grantor.

11. *Capital Campaigns.*   Clearly, the capital campaign is the most successful, cost-effective, and enjoyable method of fund-raising yet invented. Why? Because everyone is working together for the same goal, the objective is significant to the future of the organization, major gifts are required (all through personal solicitation), start and end dates are followed, activities and excitement exists, and more. A capital campaign is the culmination of years of effort, both in design and consensus surrounding the master project and in development of the fund-raising team, along with experienced volunteers and enthusiastic donors. When everything comes together in a capital campaign, the result is success.

Planned Giving Programs

An increasingly active area of fund-raising involves gifts made by the donor now to be realized by the charitable organization in the future. The term "gift planning" best describes this concept. Such gifts either transfer assets to the charity now in exchange for the donor's retaining an income for life, or transfer the assets at the donor's death. Such planning allows the donors to remember their favorite charities in their estate and to plan gifts of their assets, now or at death. Such gift decisions are usually made by donors who have some history of involvement and participation with the charities named in their estate, and speak loudly of the donors' trust and confidence in the organization and its future.

The four broad areas of "planned giving" are guided by income tax, gift tax, and estate tax law plus layers of changing regulations. Estate planning is perhaps the single area of fund-raising in which the tax consequences of giving are most prominent.

12.   *Wills and Bequests*.   The easiest way for donors to leave a gift is to specify in their will or living trust that "ten percent (10%) of the residue of my estate is to go to XYZ Hospital." Organizations should provide suitable but simple bequest language to donors to encourage them to include the organization in the will. These gifts may be outright transfers from the estate or may involve funding by means of a charitable trust created by will.

13.   *Pooled Income Funds*.   A "starter gift" to show donors how gift planning works can be made by means of a pooled income fund. Individuals may join a "pool" of other donors whose funds are commingled and interest earnings paid out according to a pro rata shares distribution based on the annual value of the invested funds. Similar to mutual funds, pooled income funds require donors to execute a simple trust agreement and transfer cash or securities to the charity, which adds their gift to the pooled income fund. Upon a donor's death, the value of his or her shares is removed from the fund and transferred to the charity for its use.

14.   *Charitable Remainder Gifts*.   Major gifts of property with appreciated value make excellent assets to transfer to a charitable organization in exchange for a retained life income based on the value of the gift at the time of transfer. Such gifts are especially valuable to donors planning their retirement income and distribution of their assets. The structure of the trust agreement may be as a unitrust, annuity trust, or gift annuity. While the legal structure of the three agreements is slightly different, the charity in each case assumes responsibility to manage the asset or its cash value and to pay the donor an income at least annually.

15.   *Life Insurance/Wealth Replacement Trust*.   Any individual may name his or her favorite charity as a beneficiary, in whole or in part, to a life insurance policy. This decision qualifies the value as a charitable contribution deduction. Some charitable organizations offer their own life insurance product, and premiums paid to the charity represent

annual gifts for tax-deduction purposes. The charity uses the funds to pay premiums on a policy it owns and which names the charity as the sole beneficiary. The value to the donor is that the charity recognizes the death benefit value as the amount "credited" as a gift by the donor. The wealth replacement trust concept is linked to a charitable remainder trust; here the donor uses the annual income to purchase a life insurance policy, usually for the value of the asset placed in trust, and names his or her heirs as beneficiaries, thus transferring the same value upon the donor's death.

Reasonable Costs of Fund-Raising

Few charitable organizations will make use of all of the foregoing fund-raising techniques. Usually only mature fund development programs in established charities have the necessary numbers of volunteers, donors, and prospective donors as well as an adequate professional and support staff, budgets, and operating systems to coordinate such a massive effort with efficiency.

Most organizations begin with the need to define the audiences who will support their mission and to seek their first gifts. Thereafter, attention is focused on securing annual operating revenues to stay in business, which requires constant attention to the annual giving solicitation methods. The choice of method(s) depends on several factors, including the scope of the organization's mission and the cost of fund-raising. If the cause is national, the broadest solicitation outreach will be needed through direct mail, which is most expensive. If the purpose is local, concentration can expand audience selection to everyone in the area, again expensive. In time, major gifts, grant requests, capital campaigns, and estate planning may be included to balance overall program productivity and cost-effectiveness.

By contrast, several types of organizations have the ability to engage in multiple fund-raising methods simultaneously and with high profitability. Colleges pursue alumni constantly (annual gift, class gift, reunion gift, capital campaign, estate planning, plus requests for time and talent in leadership roles and as volunteers and workers). While private colleges do not approach the general public, they often expand their solicitations to "anyone who walked across the campus one day." Other organizations must appeal to the general public because their cause, as well as their needs, requires them to reach out. Thus advocacy groups combine fund-raising with a call to action; churches, with the offer of a way to salvation;

hospitals, with wellness education and provision of direct care; and the like.

Whatever the organization, its choice of fund-raising method carries with it a differing cost-effectiveness performance. "Charities are not the same in how they perform fund-raising nor does fund-raising perform the same for every charity. Equally, efficient fund-raising is not the measure of the importance or value of the cause."[47]

Choice of method requires attention to cost-effectiveness measurement. It costs money to raise money, but what are the reasonable cost levels? Studies by the American Association of Fund-Raising Counsel, the National Society of Fund Raising Executives, and National Association for Hospital Development reveal that, on average, it costs 20 cents to raise one dollar after a solicitation program has been in operation for a minimum of three years. Reasonable cost levels for various methods of fund-raising are given below.

Direct Mail Acquisition.   To make the first sale, whether in for-profit sales or nonprofit fund-raising, is expensive. Direct response advertising is a popular and effective form of direct mail acquisition used by both private and nonprofit enterprises. Reasonable cost levels for a nonprofit organization should not exceed $1.50 per dollar raised, with a corresponding 1 percent or higher level of participation (rate of return).

Direct Mail Renewal.   Once a donor is acquired, the effort to renew this gift, either in a few months or next year, will be more cost-effective. Renewal costs should be within 20 cents per dollar raised, with a 50 percent renewal rate among prior donors.

Special Events and Benefits.   While highly popular with volunteers, benefits are expensive to conduct and usually are valuable for reasons other than raising money. A net goal of 50 cents per dollar raised against direct costs is the recommended guideline.

Corporations and Foundations.   Solicitation of corporate and foundation support is a highly selective and competitive method of fund-raising. Expenses should not exceed 20 cents per dollar raised.

Planned Giving.   Planned gifts, being complex and individually designed, require time to prepare and plenty of patience to mature. An average of 25 cents per dollar raised is the recommended guideline.[48]

---

[47] Greenfield, "Fund-Raising Costs and Credibility: What the Public Needs to Know," *NSFRE J.*, Autumn 1988, at 49.

[48] N. Fink & H. Metzler, *The Costs and Benefits of Deferred Giving* (1982).

Capital Campaigns. The most profitable, cost-effective, and productive fund-raising method available is the capital campaign. Why? Because these campaigns focus on big ideas and solicit big gifts, require personal leadership and solicitation by volunteers, have professional staff direction, and the like. Capital campaign costs should not exceed from 5 to 10 cents per dollar raised.

Regulations that focus on costs compared with gift revenues treat unfairly the above realities of fund-raising performances by charitable organizations, whether old or new. Simple bottom-line analysis is inadequate, can be misleading, and seriously fails to understand the nature of individual organizations, their unique environment, and their separate capacity for raising charitable contributions.

New, start-up efforts (even for established charities) to begin a fund-raising program are not likely to meet these "reasonable cost" guidelines for at least three years. Charities representing new causes or previously unknown or unpopular needs will be even less successful. The critical factors inherent in success—environment and capacity—also must reflect the realities surrounding the organization. A realistic analysis of local conditions will help set reasonable expectations based on factors such as availability of prospects, access to wealth, competition, local regulations, geography, style, public image, access to volunteers (including leadership), fund-raising history, prior fiscal performance, volume and variety of fund-raising methods offered, use of professional staff or consultants, existing donors for renewal and upgrading, established fund development office procedures, and more.

§ 2.3 Role of the Fund-Raising Professional

Fund-raising executives refer to the development process as their guide. This process includes (1) acquiring donors, (2) renewing and upgrading donors, and (3) maximizing donors. Each phase represents an increased capacity to support charitable organizations, but the process starts at the bottom of the pyramid of giving [Exhibit 2.1]. Identification of prospects from those publics available to each charity is accomplished through the several annual giving methods. Each individual donor's progression up the pyramid requires time for information and interests to develop as well as a level of personal involvement with the organization (the "friend-raising" phase). Major gift opportunities, while less frequent, are usually centered in capital campaigns, and represent a continuing investment in response to a rising commitment and enthusiasm for the

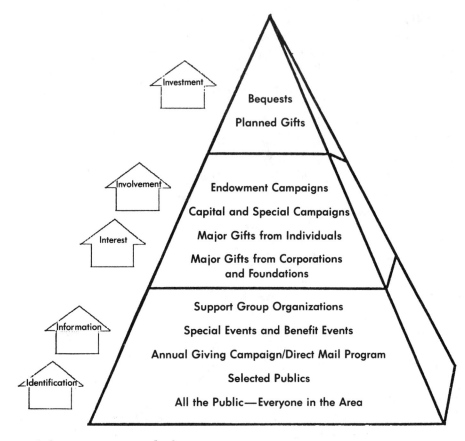

Exhibit 2.1.   Pyramid of giving.

programs and services of the organization. The ultimate investment decision usually is made last, is frequently the largest gift, and may even come as part of the donor's estate.

Fund-raising professionals are like symphony orchestra conductors. They need a number of competent musicians, all the right instruments, the correct sheet music for each player, a concert hall, rehearsals, and an audience before fine music can be produced. Any one of the 15 fund-raising methods can more easily be accomplished alone; to activate many methods simultaneously takes skill in managing the process of moving everyone forward together, in the same direction, toward the same objective, and all at the same time.

The desired net effect is to stimulate multiple forms of asking for multiple gift decisions from donors and prospects each year, while at the same time selectively soliciting larger gifts from a few who have demonstrated greater potential from previous gift performance.

Types of Professional Fund-Raisers

Three types of professional fund-raising executives work for and with charitable organizations to direct and manage fund-raising programs. Legislation and regulation provide guidelines for the relationship between organizations and those who perform fund-raising in their behalf and distinguish between the three types.

1. *Fund Development Officer.* A fund development officer is a full-time salaried employee of the organization and receives the same standard employment benefits as all other employees. Most regulations are silent about employees who perform fund-raising, choosing rather to regulate the organization itself. The fund development officer designs the fund-raising program in keeping with the organization's priority needs; selects the fund-raising methods required to produce the income needed; and supervises operations on a daily basis. To make the development process work, the development officer must also set and meet goals and objectives; identify committees; assign functions and manage them successfully; recruit and train leaders and volunteers; hire and train staff; write policies and procedures, have them approved, and see that they are followed; prepare budgets and supervise expenses; perform and report results and analysis; keep confidential records accurately and discreetly; design and implement a donor recognition system; and more.

2. *Fund-Raising Consultant.* A fund-raising consultant is an individual or firm who is hired for a fee to provide services of advice and counsel to charitable organizations on the design, conduct, and evaluation of their fund-raising enterprises. Most regulations require consultants to register with state authorities, file a copy of contracts for service, and be bonded when the handling of gift dollars will occur. Consultants are available to guide staff and volunteers on specific fund-raising methods (direct mail, telephone, planned giving, capital campaigns, and the like), to perform objective studies and analysis of the design and conduct of comprehensive fund-raising programs, as well as provide executive search, marketing, public relations, and other services. While consultants do not usually conduct solicitations directly, nor do they handle gift money, they can and do assist these efforts. Consulting staff can be retained to

perform all of the duties of the fund development officer, usually for a specified period until fund-time employees can be hired and trained.

3. *Professional Solicitor.* A professional solicitor is an individual or firm who is hired, for a fee or on a commission or percentage basis, to perform a fund-raising program or special event directly in the name of the organization, to solicit and receive all gifts, to deposit funds and pay expenses, and to deliver net proceeds to the charity. Legislation and regulations of professional solicitors are the most intense because of past conduct by those whose fees and expenses are high and who deliver net proceeds in the area of only 20 percent or less of gross revenues. Such firms are more likely to attract smaller and newer organizations (or "noncharities" for whom the gift deduction is no longer allowed) who believe they lack the ability to mount their own fund-raising programs and thus are easy prey to the sales pitch that promises gift income with no effort on the organization's part.

In making a choice of fund-raising professional, charitable organizations should compare their cost-effectiveness. Fund development officers and professional consultants perform similarly and produce net returns of from 75 to 80 percent of net income, while professional solicitors return 20 percent or less of net income.

Several other features that relate to the separate role of fund-raising professionals are discussed below.

Growth Toward a Profession

Fund-raisers may call themselves professionals and engage in professional practices, but their field has not yet achieved accepted professional status. To do so requires a commonly accepted body of knowledge, common standard of conduct (ethics), published literature, theoretical base from established methods of research, and an accreditation process. Progress continues on all fronts but remains incomplete at present.

Professional Associations and Societies

National and local organizations have expanded to meet the needs of fund-raisers, one of the fastest-growing new service areas of employment available in the United States. At the close of 1989, membership in the National Society of Fund Raising Executives (NSFRE), which was founded in 1962, exceeded 12,000 men and women (in nearly equal numbers) in over 110 chapters across the country. The Council for the Advancement and Support of Education (CASE) and the National Association for Hospital Development (NAHD) provide similar trade association services to their members. The American Association of Fund-Raising Counsel (AAFRC) represents many of the larger, national firms who practice as consultants. Hundreds of others who practice fund-raising as staff or consultants are not members of any society. New professional associations, such as the National Planned Giving Council, have emerged to meet the needs of specialists, while the Direct Mail Marketing Association includes members who service both for-profit and not-for-profit clients.

The primary purpose of these trade associations is to serve the members, usually by providing training in the profession through conferences, seminars, monthly meetings, workshops, journals, and newsletters. Serious efforts have begun to define a common curriculum of information organized along knowledge and experience levels to provide career development opportunities. College curricula and degrees have been slow to develop, perhaps because of a lack of literature and research base. Professional training, when linked to certification, can yield verification to members of their comprehension of basic principles plus a validation to employers of a level of competency.

Accreditation and Certification

Licensure of fund-raising professionals is not yet a serious consideration and could be unwieldy to implement, considering the more than 850,000 tax-exempt charitable organizations doing business in the United States. Fund-raising staff and consultants do benefit from participation in accreditation programs because they reflect a level of personal commitment to the craft and demonstrate levels of competency attained. Presently, the accepted certification programs are offered by NSFRE and NAHD.

Standards of Conduct and Professional Practice

As with any emerging profession, common standards require time for development. Within fund-raising, these standards originated as codes of ethics but have since matured into standards of conduct and professional practice. While AAFRC, CASE, NAHD, and NSFRE each have their written texts in this area, they have not yet achieved a common standard to govern what is, in essence, the same form of activity.

§ 2.4   Role of the Accountant

The accountant serving a charitable organization that engages in fund-raising also has a variety of responsibilities, as discussed in an analysis prepared by Price Waterhouse, which follows.[49]

Accounting for fund-raising costs is one of the most sensitive areas of financial accounting, reporting, and management for organizations that solicit funds from the public. The level of fund-raising expenses with respect to contributions is generally perceived as an index of management performance. Amounts reported as fund-raising expenses, accordingly, are carefully examined by organization constituents and directors, contributors, and regulatory agencies.

An accountant in an organization that solicits funds from the public has several important responsibilities, including accounting for fund-raising costs in a manner (1) consistent with "generally accepted accounting principles"; (2) consistent with the financial reporting requirements of state and other regulatory agencies; and (3) facilitating sound financial management of the organization.

Generally Accepted Accounting Principles

Professional accounting literature applicable to nonprofit organizations requires that organizations soliciting funds from the public report fund-raising expenses *separately* from other supporting expenses and program expenses.

Fund-raising expenses generally include all costs involved in inducing others to contribute resources without receipt of economic benefits in return. Fund-raising costs usually consist of the direct costs of solicitation (such as the cost of personnel, printing, postage, occupancy, etc.) and a fair allocation of overhead.

One aspect of accounting for fund-raising costs is subject to considerable judgment—accounting for the joint cost of multiple-purpose materials, such as educational literature that also includes a request for funds. Formerly, accounting literature (and industry practice) was inconsistent on this issue. Some organizations allocated joint costs between respective functions. Other organizations did not allocate joint costs, and reported joint fund-raising and educational costs exclusively as fund-raising expenses.

---

[49] This analysis was prepared by William Warshauer, Jr., chairman of Nonprofit Industry Services, Price Waterhouse, for use as part of this chapter. His contribution is gratefully acknowledged by the author.

Functional allocation of multiple-purpose expenses is now required by the accounting profession in its most recent pronouncement on the subject if certain criteria are met. Recommended bases of allocation include use made of materials and costs associated with different functions.

Financial Reporting Requirements

Nonprofit organizations that solicit funds in several states are confronted with a web of financial reporting requirements. Regulation of charities in different states is the responsibility of different agencies with different reporting requirements and different filing deadlines. In addition, charities are often subject to the registration and reporting requirements of local units of government.

Fund-raising expenses frequently are a focus of state and local regulators. Different jurisdictions require different detail in reporting fund-raising costs. Some states and municipalities have attempted to restrict the right of solicitation to organizations whose fund-raising costs do not exceed a fixed percentage of contributions, but the Federal courts have ruled this to be unconstitutional.

State and local regulation of charities is fluid and subject to unanticipated changes. Accountants, therefore, must closely monitor the reporting requirements of all jurisdictions in which their organization solicits funds from the public.

Accountants must also be alert to guidelines established by private "watchdog" agencies. These agencies, notably the Philanthropic Advisory Service of the Council of Better Business Bureaus and the National Charities Information Bureau, establish "standards" for nonprofit organizations. Deviation from these standards may result in public censure, and sanctions in the form of reduced or withheld contributions from corporations and other grant-making organizations.

Financial Management

In addition to conforming with generally accepted accounting principles and with reporting requirements of various regulatory bodies, accounting for fund-raising expenses should provide information that facilitates sound financial management.

Creation of information of this type usually requires a system of cost identification and cost allocation. Effective analysis of fund-raising costs requires an accurate identification of fund-raising cost components and an objective allocation of joint costs and overhead.

By relating the cost of various fund-raising activities with the amount of contributions received—that is, identifying the cost of each dollar raised—fund-raising policy may be enhanced and fund-raising activities may be improved.

§ 2.5 Role of the Lawyer

The legal counsel who represents or otherwise works for a charitable organization that is ensnarled in regulation of its fund-raising likewise has a multitude of responsibilities. In addition to all other tasks that must be undertaken in serving the organization, he or she should:

1. Review the law of each jurisdiction in which the organization solicits contributions and advise it of its compliance responsibilities.

2. See to it that all applications, forms, reports, and the like, are properly prepared and timely filed.

3. Assist the organization where it is having difficulties with enforcement authorities, such as by helping prepare a statement in explanation of its fund-raising costs or by arguing its case before administrative staff(s), state commission(s) or court(s).

4. Review and advise as to agreements between the organization and professional fund-raisers and/or professional solicitors.

5. Assist the organization in the preparation of annual reports and like materials by which it presents its programs, sources of support, and expenses to the general public.

6. Keep abreast of recent developments bearing on regulation of fund-raising by charitable organizations.

As is so often the case in general, the lawyer's role in relation to fund-raising regulation should not be performed in isolation but should be carefully coordinated, not only with the charitable organization's staff, officers, and governing board, but with other consultants, principally the accountant and the professional fund-raiser.

§ 2.6 Viewpoint of a Regulator

As is attested to throughout the book, the methods and extent of government regulation of fund-raising are controversial. This section provides the viewpoint of a seasoned regulator, including a perspective on the future of this aspect of the law.[50]

The latter half of the decade of the 1980s brought fundamental change to the regulation by states of charitable solicitation. The changes were precipitated by U.S. Supreme Court decisions that gave broad First Amendment protection to charities and by a major restructuring of accounting standards that charities follow in the preparation of financial statements. These events have influenced contemporary state regulation in different ways. On the one hand, it is more difficult to prosecute the burgeoning number of organizations that annually take in a huge number of tax-exempt dollars from a trusting citizenry but provide little or no public benefit in return. On the other hand, regulation has the potential for being more effective because states are focusing on alternative regulatory options that could, in the years ahead, prove to be better at controlling practices inimical to true philanthropy.

Before the U.S. Supreme Court decisions in 1980[51] and 1984,[52] the states' efforts to protect the public from those using the guise of charity for personal enrichment focused almost exclusively on the fund-raising cost ratio. It was a simplistic approach that was not always fair. To be sure, the amount an organization spends on fund-raising and management as a percentage of revenue is often a reliable indicator of whether the organization exists to serve the public or as a vehicle for private gain. Yet, as the Supreme Court correctly pointed out, that is not necessarily the case. There is sometimes good reason why a charity must incur seemingly high fund-raising costs. While government regulation, not only of charity but of any industry, is rarely free of some unfairness, the Supreme Court's opinion that charitable solicitation is among the types of speech deserving fullest protection, makes all but the most benign unfairness intolerable under the law. Thus, states had to abandon enforcing laws that made a low fund-raising percentage the litmus test for legitimacy.

In the years immediately following 1984, the states tried a new approach. Under legislation adopted by several key states, a professional fund-raiser hired by a charity had to disclose to the person being solicited the minimum percentage of the gross contributions that the charity

---

[50] This analysis was prepared by David E. Ormstedt, Esq., assistant attorney general of the state of Connecticut. His contribution is gratefully acknowledged by the author.

[51] *Schaumburg* v. *Citizens for a Better Environment*, 444 U.S. 618 (1980).

[52] *Maryland Secretary of State* v. *Joseph H. Munson Co.*, 467 U.S. 947 (1984).

would receive from the fund-raising campaign. From years of experience, the states knew that telephone soliciting conducted by professional fund-raising firms was enormously expensive for the charities that were supposed to benefit. Whether this was because of high (or inflated) expenses, or because of the generous profits reaped by the fund-raising firms, the bottom line for donors was the same—their contributions were not going very far. Yet donors had no reason to suspect that this was the case and, if they did suspect it, had no practical way to determine in any specific case whether their donation would benefit charity or some commercial operation. Thus, it seemed a reasonable regulatory objective to provide the potential donor with this information at the point of solicitation, when the donor is most in need of it. The Supreme Court ended this short-lived approach by its decision in a 1988 case, in which the Court held that it is unconstitutional to compel those raising money in the name of charity to say something they do not want to say.[53] And certainly few charities or fund-raisers want to talk about fund-raising costs with a prospective donor.

The second event that helped determine the contemporary environment for state regulation was a change in the accounting standards that govern financial reporting by charities. The primary purpose rule, established in the 1960s in response to widely publicized scandals, required, with a limited exception, that the entire cost associated with making a fund-raising appeal had to be reported as fund-raising costs in a charity's financial statements.[54] Thus, if the primary purpose of a particular activity was to solicit contributions, virtually all costs of that activity were considered fund-raising even if the appeal contained material that could be construed as having an educational value.

With the advent of state percentage limits on fund-raising costs and the growth in the number of nontraditional charities whose programs were to advocate causes and affect public opinion, often using the same direct mail vehicle that contained their fund-raising appeal, some charities sought a rescue from what they perceived as an overly restrictive accounting rule. In response, the American Institute of Certified Public Accountants changed the rule so that much of what used to be a fund-raising cost

[53] *Riley v. National Federation of the Blind of North Carolina, Inc.*, 108 S. Ct. 2667 (1988).

[54] *Standards of Accounting and Financial Reporting for Voluntary Health and Welfare Organizations* (New York: National Health Council, National Assembly of Voluntary Health and Welfare Organizations, and United Way of America, 1964).

could not be credited as a program cost.[55] The new rule contains purported criteria to determine whether there is a bona fide program component to an activity that also contains a request for money and, if there is, then the basis upon which an allocation of costs should be made. However, the criteria are vague and subject to wide variations in interpretation. In practice, the criteria serve only to discourage the most absurd allocation—not the merely bizarre.

The confluence of the line of court cases with the destabilizing of the accounting standards has created fertile ground for those who are more interested in personal gain than in serving society. One or more individuals (including a professional fund-raiser in need of a client) can now establish a purported charity, obtain tax exemption by claiming it will engage in public education and advocacy on any one of myriad health and social welfare problems, prepare and mail millions of appeals annually that contain heart-wrenching stories about the extent of the problem, emphasize how contributions are desperately needed to solve it, and then use most of the revenue generated to pay the fund-raiser to send out more of the same mailings and the rest to pay themselves a salary. The process is then repeated every few months. This scenario also works for telephone solicitation.

To a state regulator who may challenge this conduct, the organization points to the Supreme Court decisions to excuse its payment of virtually all of the contributions to the fund-raiser. Moreover, the charity points to the heart-wrenching stories as evidence that the payments were not just for fund-raising but also for implementing the organization's public education program. Any citizen who wants to examine the organization's financial statement before deciding whether to give will find that the organization reports having spent a significant portion of its revenue on program services. What the prospective donor will not know is that the program service was the mailing he received requesting a contribution and that his donation will be used to produce more talk about the problem. If the donor is lucky, a token amount will be used to actually help victims.

Another outgrowth of the court decisions is the phenomenal rise in the amount of telephone soliciting by paid soliciting firms on behalf of small to midsize charities and, most notably, police- and firefighter-related groups. In Connecticut, the number of registered soliciting firms

---

[55] Statement of Position 87-2, Accounting for Joint Costs of Informational Materials and Activities of Not-for-Profit Organizations that Include a Fund-Raising Appeal (New York: American Institute of Certified Public Accountants, 1987).

nearly tripled in the years following the 1984 Supreme Court opinion. In 1989, Connecticut residents and businesses contributed $10.7 million in response to telephone solicitations offering tickets to a show or advertising space in a publication, a 24 percent increase over 1987. Only $2.8 million, or 26 percent, ever reached the intended beneficiaries.[56] The victims are not the groups that hire the solicitors; the victims are the donors. The telephone pitch is structured to lead the call recipients to believe that they are speaking to a volunteer member of the group. In the fast-paced sales pitch, little useful information is imparted, and the solicitor either avoids any discussion or lies about how much of the donation the group will actually see.

A standard defense to criticism by legislators, regulators, and the media is that fund-raising costs of new, or small, or unpopular charities will necessarily be high, especially in the first few years of operation as they work to build a donor base. While this may be true, it is too often just a convenient excuse that conceals self-dealing and profiteering. It buys about five years of protection, which is plenty of time in which to do considerable damage. Before enough time has passed to prove that the organization's managers never had any intention of developing a bona fide charity, or that the professional fund-raiser was merely milking the organization for all it could get, they have moved on to a new cause and started the cycle all over again. For those that have enjoyed enough success and remain in business after the "start-up phase," a liberal allocation of fund-raising costs to the program function keeps the organization competitive in the marketplace.

To be sure, the number of organizations engaging in these practices do not constitute the majority of all organizations soliciting for charitable purposes. Beyond question, most charities adhere to high fund-raising standards and provide valuable, indispensable services. However, organizations engaged in these practices are also not the exception. The numbers are significant enough to cause great concern not only for the protection of the gifts of well-intentioned donors, but also for the deleterious effect the practices are having on the credibility of the nonprofit sector as a whole.

---

[56] Paid Telephone Soliciting in Connecticut During 1989 for Charitable, Civic, Police and Firefighter Organizations (a report to Clarine Nardi Riddle, Attorney General, and Mary M. Heslin, Commissioner of Consumer Protection; prepared by The Public Charities Unit, a joint program of the Dept. of Consumer Protection and the Office of the Attorney General), (Apr. 9, 1990).

For state regulators, who are probably in the best position to observe the fund-raising and financial reporting practices of charities across the board, and who daily receive complaints and inquiries from the public, the question is how to meet these challenges and maintain accountability by all charities without interfering with the ability of bona fide charities to raise funds and carry out their programs. The answer is not readily apparent, as evidenced by the spate of widely different legislative proposals across the country, including in the U.S. Congress, in the wake of the 1988 Supreme Court decision.

It would be ideal if state regulators and responsible leaders of the independent sector could work together to create a more healthy climate for charitable giving. They could cooperate on legislation (although additional laws are not always needed or wise) or on programs to educate the public on the realities of fund-raising and how to distinguish the wheat from the chaff. Unfortunately, real cooperation is unlikely to emerge as long as the independent sector is unwilling to acknowledge that there are problems in the sector that call for remedial action. The usual reactions of sector leaders to regulators' concerns are disbelief, denial, and charges that regulators are, either out of ignorance or on purpose, creating a destructive regulatory environment. In public, at least, they say that the problems are aberrations, perpetrated by a tiny few fly-by-night operators. The solution, they often say, lies in sector self-policing and less government interference. To regulators, who know that the problems are well entrenched and too widespread to tolerate, and who have over the years heard a lot of talk about self-regulation but seen little evidence that the self-policers are willing to tackle the hard issues, the reaction of the sector appears perplexing and disingenuous. No doubt, some regulators do overreact and could benefit from the advice of the sector. But until regulators and the sector achieve a common frame of reference, productive cooperation will be difficult.

In the meantime, states are refining existing regulatory programs and exploring new ones. In the foreseeable future, state regulation will be characterized by the systematic dissemination of financial and programmatic information about soliciting charities, together with stepped up enforcement and stiffer penalties for charities and professional fund-raisers that engage in misrepresentation and self-dealing, or that fail to file timely and accurate financial reports. To achieve those ends, states will be concentrating on several key areas.

Registration and financial reporting remains the bedrock of any regulatory scheme. Despite their inadequacies, financial reports provide a good overview of individual charities as well as aggregate data on the sector. They are a valuable source of information to the public and for the detection of abuses. States must be vigilant to assure the accuracy and timeliness of these reports. The public is not well served when states do not devote sufficient resources to monitor compliance with periodic reporting requirements.

No doubt financial reporting requirements place some burden on national charities that must file reports with up to 40 states. Most states accept a copy of IRS Form 990 as the basic financial document, which at least partially addresses this issue. Many states, however, still require their own separate registration forms and supplemental financial schedules. This is one area in which an atmosphere of cooperation between the independent sector and the states could pay dividends in the nature of greater uniformity. Absent that, states should examine their requirements to determine whether they are asking for more than what they can reasonably expect to use in their regulatory programs.

In 1988, the Supreme Court suggested to the states that they could achieve their interest of informing donors how their contributions are spent by publicizing the information obtained from charities. Some states have taken this suggestion seriously, and more can be expected to do so. The systematic and timely release of accurate and comprehensive financial and programmatic information on charities and/or professional fund-raisers is an extremely useful regulatory tool. The public is hungry for this information, which is not readily available from any other source. When done properly, it is a powerful form of disclosure that is far more effective than the difficult-to-enforce disclosure provision declared unconstitutional in 1988. Minnesota and Connecticut, for example, have published reports about paid telephone soliciting. New York has published key financial data on charities registered there. Maryland has by statute mandated a state public information program. Sophisticated data processing techniques will enable more states to institutionalize a public education program.

To protect the public from misleading and fraudulent solicitations, states are increasingly relying on statutory and common law authority in addition to that granted under traditional solicitation statutes. Consumer protection laws, patterned after but not identical to the Federal Trade Commission Act, are well suited to combat deceptive practices of for-profit fund-raisers. Although the FTC Act does not generally apply to nonprofit organizations, court decisions in Connecticut and Pennsylvania have upheld the use of similar state laws against charity defendants, relying on crucial differences between those state laws and the FTC Act with respect to the definition of trade and commerce.[57] These statutes often offer a broader range of remedies than do solicitation laws and, importantly, there is usually extensive reported case law interpreting them.

Statutes requiring the disclosure of specific financial information by charities and professional fund-raisers at the point of solicitation are highly suspect after the 1988 Supreme Court opinion. However, the Court made it clear that not all mandated disclosures are unconstitutional per se. For example, the Court observed that states could require professional fund-raisers to clearly identify themselves as such during a solicitation. Seizing on this, legislation has been proposed in some states to require a charity to disclose in its solicitations if the primary purpose of the solicitation or the primary program of the charity is to conduct public education.

Whether these new regulatory approaches will be effective remains to be seen. What is certain is that the states feel compelled to try. In this period of regulatory transition, the opportunity is there for the independent sector to recognize the legitimate concerns of the states and to take steps to meet them. Whether that will happen also remains to be seen.

§ 2.7   Viewpoint of a Regulated Professional

Most fund-raising professionals do not believe that their practices in assisting charities to acquire charitable gifts are in any way abusive to potential donors or other citizens. It is no surprise, then, that they find government regulation of philanthropy to be unduly restricting and a misdirection of resources. What follows is the view of one of these regulated professionals.[58]

The nonprofit organizations that collectively comprise the "third sector" of the U.S. economy are a loose and unorganized delivery system for services that are generally not profitable, are too cumbersome, or are

---

[57] *Connecticut v. Cancer Fund of America*, Conn. L. Trib., March 5, 1990, at 27 (Conn. Super. Ct., Feb. 22, 1990) (order denying motion to strike); *Pennsylvania v. Watson & Hughey Company*, No. 44 Misc. Docket (Pa. Commw. Ct., June 9, 1989) (order overruling demurrer).

[58] This analysis was prepared by Delmar R. Staecker, CFRE, who is president of the Saint Thomas Foundation, Nashville, Tennessee, and currently chair of the Board of the National Society of Fund Raising Executives.

too partisan for business or government to support. Our societal response is to fund such endeavors through private financial support of philanthropy. The impetus to modern philanthropy is the still rather vague and developing discipline of fund-raising (also called development and/or financial resource development).

For the most part, the third sector is populated by well-intentioned, hardworking individuals whose dedication to a particular cause or goal takes precedence over personal gains and rewards. This description also includes the majority of fund-raisers, particularly those whose careers are encompassed by employment solely as staff of nonprofit organizations.

The thinking of the majority of practitioners is that the regulation of fund-raising practices is similar to "preaching to the choir." Although no precise sources of data are available concerning the verifiable amount of fraud or other abuse in fund-raising, it can safely be said that the actual level is far lower than the general perception holds, and quite laudable when compared with other forms of activity in our society. By and large, the fund-raising activities engaged in to benefit nonprofit organizations are conducted with an exceptionally high degree of honesty and professionalism.

Regardless of their intent or reason for being enacted, regulations are perceived by practitioners of fund-raising as a breach of the public's trust in the operation of nonprofit organizations or, at the very least, regulations are a nuisance. It is generally felt by the members of the third sector that well-run, well-intentioned nonprofit organizations do not abuse the public's trust. Existing accounting and audit procedures, along with other routine guards against fraud and the like, are seen as adequate to protect fund-raising activities, by and large. To be regulated is to be insulted by the "public" which the nonprofit organization and the fund-raiser are working to assist. The real abuses are performed by "those other guys," the unprofessionals who will do anything for a buck. That is the perception.

Of course, this perception of selfless service does not exempt fund-raisers from scrutiny, nor should it. However, such a perception, coupled with the decentralized and diverse nature of the third sector, creates a perfect environment for miscommunication, misunderstanding, and distrust with regard to fund-raising regulation.

While the regulated and the regulators have the same goal—the protection of the public from fraud and deception—the reality is that practitioners are generally unsupportive of regulation, and regulators are generally unaware of the third sector's nature and operations (concerning resource development), and the impact that regulation has on delivery of service(s). In general, there is considerable confusion and too little action based on consistent dialogue and the understanding built by mutual respect.

Cumulative and consistent efforts by the third sector to communicate with regulators have been insufficient and, therefore, ineffective in educating regulators about the issues and outcomes of fund-raising regulation. Cooperative efforts made to date by professional fund-raising associations and some regulators have been partly successful, but short-lived.

According to current estimates, the $100 billion plus annually contributed to finance the third sector will double by the turn of the century. If so, this amount will equal approximately one-ninth of federal government expenditure predictions. Considering the amount's size, intended purpose, and source, it is amazing that the relative level of consistent dialogue between all interested parties is so low. No area of our society is so poorly regulated.

Both too much and too little regulation is bad. However, to engage in any level of regulation with so little dialogue between concerned and affected parties is like running in the dark. Rather than spend precious resources and valuable time highlighting specific shortcomings and failures of regulation from either perspective, those who perceive a need for regulation and those who are to be regulated should develop simple and consistent communication. This communication could take several forms, such as annual or biannual meetings of representatives from fund-raising professional associations and legislators and/or enforcement entities; testimony or position papers delivered during the regulatory development process; meetings, conferences, and symposia sponsored by philanthropic foundations interested in the health and well-being of the third sector; and the like.

The specific means of communications are not important if they are effective in stimulating and maintaining the much needed dialogue. The real value lies in their ability to produce outcomes that answer some rather simple questions, such as:

- Are donors protected and is philanthropy nurtured?
- Are funds used to support those purposes for which they are solicited?
- Are the regulations fair to all nonprofit organizations?
- Can the regulations be evaluated for effectiveness?

Often regulations are a reaction to a perceived form and level of abuse. The perception may be correct or incorrect; that is not the issue. The issue is that the enacted regulation rarely benefits from the type of exchanges described above. Less or more regulation is not important, better regulation is.

§ 2.8 Coping with Regulation: A System for the Fund-Raising Charity

Monitoring of Compliance Requirements

An organization subject to a substantial number of the charitable solicitation laws—and that undertakes to register and report under them—should design a system by which it can remain abreast of its varied compliance responsibilities.

The state charitable solicitation laws are published as part of each state's code of statutes.[59] County, city, and town ordinances are similarly published. Other "law" with respect to these statues and ordinances will appear as administrative regulations and rules, administrative and court decisions, and instructions with regard to applications and report forms.

Therefore, the first step is to ascertain which of the 51 jurisdictions (50 states and the District of Columbia) do not (as yet) have a charitable solicitation act. At the present, there are 8 such jurisdictions: Alaska, Arizona, Delaware, Idaho, Mississippi, Montana, Vermont, and Wyoming.

The second step is to identify the municipal ordinances that are applicable. No one has identified them all, but assuredly there are several in each state.[60] (Probably the most well-known and stringently enforced of these ordinances is the one in effect in the city of Los Angeles.)

The third step is to identify the jurisdictions in which, for one reason or another, the organization *voluntarily* refrains from conducting a solicitation.

The fourth step is to identify the status of the organization's compliance with the applicable solicitation laws. A typical evaluation would utilize this analysis of jurisdictions:

1. States in which the organization is registered.

2. States in which the organization is exempt from one or more requirements.

---

[59] These laws are summarized in Ch. 3.
[60] The balance of this analysis is confined to state laws but it is equally applicable to a system of local law compliance.

3. States in which the organization is pursuing initial registration.

4. States in which the organization does not know its status but is investigating its status.

5. States in which the organization is registered but where one or more questions are being raised that may lead to revocation or modification of the registration.

6. States in which the organization is registered but is operating under some type of condition or temporary or probationary status.

The fifth step is to identify any jurisdictions in which the organization has been prohibited from soliciting contributions.

The sixth step is to make an inventory of due dates for the filing of renewals of registration and reports.

The seventh step (an ongoing one) is to persist in all reasonable endeavors to remedy the organization's difficulties as reflected in the fourth (subsections 5, 6) and fifth steps.

Any professional fund-raiser or professional solicitor retained by a charitable organization has independent registration and reporting responsibilities. Therefore, the organization's compliance efforts should be carefully coordinated with those of its fund-raiser(s), solicitor(s), or both.

Public Relations

To responsibly, accurately, and promptly respond to inquiries from the general public, an organization should be prepared to disseminate an annual report upon request. (This may also be sent to others, without waiting for a request, such as members, donors, community leaders, and other organizations.) A form letter from the organization's president or executive director may be effectively used to transmit the report.

With today's heavy emphasis on the issue of fund-raising costs, the annual report or like document should discuss the organization's fund-raising program and costs.

Record Keeping and Financial Data

A principal focus of this field of government regulation is fund-raising costs. Therefore, management should make a substantial effort to accurately ascertain and record both direct and indirect fund-raising costs. This process will require careful analysis of individuals' activities (so as to isolate the portion of their compensation and related expenses that are attributable to fund-raising) and careful allocation of expenditures (where an outlay is partially for fund-raising and partially for something else, such as program).

Fund-raising costs must be reflected in the annual information return filed by tax-exempt organizations with the IRS.[61] Although percentage limitations on fund-raising costs are unconstitutional,[62] some state laws require disclosure of these costs in a variety of ways.[63]

In any event, most organizations wish to be able to consider their fund-raising costs "reasonable," particularly in response to inquiries from donors or the media. Therefore, a fund-raising organization should be prepared to demonstrate the reasonableness of its fund-raising costs.[64]

---

[61] See Ch. 6 § 6.6.
[62] See Ch. 5 § 5.3.
[63] See Ch. 8 § 8.7.
[64] Ch. 5 § 5.1 contains principles an organization may utilize in explanation of the reasonableness of its fund-raising costs.

3

The State Charitable Solicitation Acts: Comprehensive Summaries

Fund-raising for charitable purposes in the United States is a heavily regulated activity. This regulation comes in many forms and is manifested at the federal, state, and local level. Most of the states regulate charitable fund-raising and do so principally by means of statutes known as "charitable solicitation acts."

These laws are, in many instances, extremely intricate. In addition to their complexity, there is a considerable absence of uniformity. This combination of intricacy and nonuniformity makes this a body of law with which it is quite difficult to comply—a problem aggravated by a disparity in intensity of enforcement. There are, nonetheless, some relatively common features of these laws.

Thirty states have adopted what may be termed "standard" charitable solicitation acts. To date, 8 states have not enacted a charitable solicitation statute. The remaining 12 states (including the District of Columbia) have elected to regulate charitable fund-raising by differing approaches. The comparisons and analyses of these charitable solicitation laws in subsequent chapters (particularly Chapter 4) focus primarily on the various standard charitable solicitation acts. Synopses of the principal components of all 42 state (and District of Columbia) charitable solicitation acts follow.

ALABAMA

Introduction

Comprehensive statute: No
Regulatory office(s): Attorney general
Citation: Act No. 87-605

Registration or Licensing Requirements

Charitable Organizations.   This statute does not contain any registration requirements for charitable organizations.

Professional Fund-Raisers.   This statute does not contain any registration requirements for professional fund-raisers.

Professional Solicitors.   This statute does not contain any registration requirements for professional solicitors.

Annual Reporting Requirements

Charitable Organizations.   This statute does not contain any reporting requirements for charitable organizations.

Professional Fund-Raisers.   This statute does not contain any reporting requirements for professional fund-raisers.

Professional Solicitors.   This statute does not contain any reporting requirements for professional solicitors.

Exemptions

This statute does not contain any exemptions.

Commercial Co-ventures

This statute does not regulate commercial co-ventures.

Unique Provisions

Disclosures.   Every individual in the process of soliciting funds must identify himself or herself. If the individual is being paid for soliciting, he or she must inform the prospective donor of that fact.
Also see Percentages, below.

Percentages.   If less than all of the funds solicited is going to the charity involved, the solicitor must inform the prospective donor of the percentage of the collected monies that will be transferred to the charity.

Prohibited Acts.   A person (other than an officer, director, or trustee of the charitable organization involved in the solicitation) may not, for the purpose of soliciting contributions in the state, use the name of a charitable organization without the consent of the organization. An organization's name is deemed used for this purpose if the name is listed on any stationery, advertisement, brochure, or correspondence used in the solicitation of gifts. However, this rule does not prevent the publication of names of contributors without their consent in a report issued by a charitable organization for the purpose of reporting its operations to its membership or reporting contributions to contributors.

A charitable organization or professional fund-raiser "soliciting contributions" may not use a name, symbol, or statement so closely related or similar to that used by another charitable organization or governmental agency where the use would tend to confuse or mislead the public.

Other.   A solicitor who knowingly represents that he or she is soliciting funds for a charitable organization, where the organization has not consented to the solicitation, and the solicitor receives contributions that are not delivered to the organization, within the earlier of 30 days after receipt or 10 days after the request by the organization for the gifts, is guilty of "theft of property by charitable fraud."

Anyone who violates any other provision of this law is also guilty of theft of property by charitable fraud.

It is an "absolute defense" to a criminal prosecution under this law if the solicitor has, prior to the issuance of an arrest warrant or grand jury indictment, given all funds raised to the charitable organization "for whom he represented he was soliciting funds."

Sanctions

A theft of property by charitable fraud is a felony where the value of the property is in excess of $100; otherwise, the theft is a misdemeanor.

The attorney general of the state, the district attorneys of the counties in the state, or an affected charitable organization may enforce this law by applying for relief by injunction, mandamus, or any other appropriate remedy in order to prevent any solicitor from using a charitable organization's name without its consent.

ALASKA

No statute.

ARIZONA

No statute.

ARKANSAS

Introduction

Comprehensive statute: Yes
Regulatory office(s): Secretary of state
Citation: Arkansas Acts 251–253 (1959)

Registration or Licensing Requirements

Charitable Organizations.   A charitable organization, unless exempt from the requirement, may not solicit contributions in the state of Arkansas unless, prior to any solicitation, the organization has submitted certain information to the state's secretary of state.

The information submitted must include the following: (1) the identity of the charitable organization by or for whom the solicitation is to be conducted; (2) the address of the organization; (3) the purpose or purposes for which the contributions solicited are to be used; (4) the individual or officer who will have custody of the contributions; (5) the individuals responsible for the distribution of the contributions; (6) the period of time during which the solicitation is to be conducted; (7) a description of the method or methods of solicitation "in such detail as may from time to time be determined by the Secretary of State"; (8) whether the solicitation is to be conducted by voluntary unpaid solicitors, by paid solicitors, or both; and (9) if the solicitation is to be conducted, in whole or in party by paid solicitors, the name and address of "each professional fund-raiser supplying such solicitors, the basis of payment and the nature of the arrangement."

Professional Fund-Raisers.   A person acting as a professional fund-raiser for a charitable organization must register with the secretary of state. This registration is effective for a period of one year and may be renewed for additional one-year periods.

A professional fund-raiser must file, and have approved by the secretary of state, a bond in the amount of $5,000.

Professional Solicitors.   Every professional solicitor employed by or retained by a professional fund-raiser required to register under this law (see above) must, before accepting employment by the professional fund-raiser, register with the secretary of state. This registration is effective for a period of one year and may be renewed for additional one-year periods.

Annual Reporting Requirement

Charitable Organizations.   Every charitable organization that is required to submit information to the state, as above-described, which has received contributions during the preceding calendar year must file a report with the secretary of state. For calendar-year organizations, this report is due on or before March 31. Other organizations may, as the result of permission from the secretary of state, file the report within 90 days after the close of their fiscal year.

This annual report must include (1) the gross amount of the contributions pledged or collected; (2) the amount of the contributions given or to be given to the charitable purpose represented; (3) the aggregate amount paid and to be paid for the expenses of the solicitation; and (4) the aggregate amount paid to and to be paid to professional fund-raisers and solicitors.

As discussed below, a charitable organization, the total contributions to which during any year are $1,000 or less, is exempt from this filing requirement. Nonetheless, an organization initially in this position must file the requisite information with the secretary of state within 30 days after the date it receives, during a calendar year, contributions in excess of $1,000.

The secretary of state is empowered to require that, within 90 days after the close of any special period of solicitation, a charitable organization conducting a solicitation must file a "special report" of the required information for the period involved.

Professional Fund-Raisers.   There is no separate reporting requirement in the statute for professional fund-raisers. However, the annual registration obligation is the equivalent of annual reporting.

Professional Solicitors.   There is no separate reporting requirement in the statute for professional solicitors. However, the annual registration obligation is the equivalent of annual reporting.

Exemptions

This law does not apply to any solicitation made by the members of a charitable organization where the solicitations are solicited solely from persons who are members of the organization at the time of the solicitation. Also, this law does not apply to solicitations made solely for church, missionary, or religious purposes. Further, this law does not apply to any charitable organization that does not intend to solicit and receive and does not actually receive contributions in excess of $1,000 during a calendar year, provided all of its functions, including its fund-raising functions, are carried on by volunteers and provided that no part of its assets or income inures to the benefit of or is paid to any officer or member.

The law pertaining to unauthorized use of names in connection with the solicitation of charitable contributions is inapplicable to solicitations made solely for "evangelical, missionary or religious" purposes.

Commercial Co-ventures

This state's charitable solicitation act does not regulate commercial co-venturing.

Other Requirements

Contracts. A contract entered into by a charitable organization soliciting in the state and a professional fund-raiser must be in writing. Copies of the agreement must be kept on file in the offices of the charitable organization and the professional fund-raiser for a period of three years from the date the solicitation of contributions provided for in the contract actually commences. These contracts must be available for inspection by the secretary of state and "other authorized agencies."

Record Keeping and Accounting. Every charitable organization that is subject to this law must keep a "full and true" record in such form as will require the organization to accurately provide the required information.

All records required by this law are open to inspection "at all times" by the secretary of state.

Unique Provisions

Prohibited Acts. A charitable organization, professional fund-raiser, or professional solicitor seeking to raise funds for charitable purposes may not use the name of any other person (except that of an officer, director, or trustee of the charitable organization involved) for the purpose of soliciting contributions in the state without the written consent of the person. This rule is said to not prevent the publication of names of contributors, without their written consent, in an annual or other periodic report issued by a charitable organization for the purpose of reporting to its membership or for the purpose of reporting contributions to contributors.

It is a violation of this law to use the name of a person for the purpose of soliciting contributions, including listing the person's name on any stationery, advertisement, brochure, or correspondence in or by which a contribution is solicited by or on behalf of a charitable organization, or listing or referring to his or her name in connection with a request for a contribution as one who has contributed to, sponsored, or endorsed the charitable organization or its activities.

Other.   A nonresident charitable organization desiring to solicit contributions in the state must file, in addition to the above-summarized information, an irrevocable written consent that in suits, proceedings, and actions growing out of the violation of any provision of this law, or as a result of any activities conducted within the state, giving rise to a cause of action, service on the secretary of state shall be as valid and binding as if service had been made on the charitable organization. Similar rules apply with respect to professional fund-raisers and professional solicitors.

The secretary of state is empowered to enter into reciprocal agreements with a like authority of any state or states for the purpose of exchanging information made available to the secretary of state under this law. Pursuant to such agreements, the secretary of state may accept information filed by a charitable organization with another state in lieu of the information required to be filed by a charitable organization under this law, if the information is substantially similar.

Sanctions

A person conducting a solicitation in violation of, or filing false information under, these laws must be punished by a fine not in excess of $500 or by imprisonment for not more than six months, or both. Every officer or agent of a charitable organization who authorizes or conducts such a solicitation is jointly and severally liable for the fine.

Upon complaint of any person, or other information coming to the attention of the prosecuting attorney that a charitable organization is violating or intends to violate the provisions of this law, the prosecuting attorney may institute action in the proper chancery court to enjoin the solicitation of contributions by or on behalf of the organization. A similar rule applies with respect to professional fund-raisers and professional solicitors.

As to the rules pertaining to professional fund-raisers and professional solicitors, any person violating those rules shall be punished by a fine not to exceed $500 or by imprisonment for up to six months, or both.

CALIFORNIA

Introduction

Comprehensive statute: No
Regulatory office(s): Attorney general
Citation: Business and Professions Code § 17510.3 et seq.;
         Government Code § 12580 et seq.

Registration or Licensing Requirements

Charitable Organizations.   The statute does not contain any registration requirements for charitable organizations.

Professional Fund-Raisers.   The statute does not contain any registration requirements for professional fund-raisers.

Professional Solicitors.   The statute does not contain any registration requirements for professional solicitors.

Annual Reporting Requirements

Charitable Organization.   Every charitable organization that is subject to this law that has received property for charitable purposes must file with the attorney general a copy of the document by which the organization was established. This report is due within six months "after any part of the income or principal is authorized or required to be applied to a charitable purpose."

Professional Fund-Raisers.   The statute does not contain any reporting requirements for professional fund-raisers.

Professional Solicitors.   The statute does not contain any reporting requirements for professional solicitors.

Exemptions

The provisions of these laws (other than those pertaining to sales solic- itations for charitable purposes) are inapplicable to religious organizations, educational institutions, hospitals, and licensed "health care service plans."

The law pertaining to sales solicitations for charitable purposes does not apply to solicitations, sales, offers, or attempts to sell within the membership of a charitable organization or upon its "regular occupied premises," nor does it apply to funds raised pursuant to the state's penal code.

Commercial Co-ventures

See Disclosures, below.

Other Requirements

Record Keeping and Accounting. The attorney general is directed to maintain a register of charitable organizations that are subject to this law.

The financial records of a soliciting organization must, under the sales solicitation for charitable purposes rules, be maintained on the basis of generally accepted accounting principles as defined by the American Institute of Certified Public Accountants and the Financial Accounting Standards Board. The disclosure requirements of the fourth item of the third paragraph and of the fourth paragraph under Disclosures (see below) must be based upon the same accounting principles used to maintain the financial records of the soliciting organization.

Unique Provisions

Disclosures. This statute requires a solicitor of a charitable gift to provide to the prospective donor certain information prior to the solic- itation. The statute also imposes this disclosure requirement in the context of sales solicitations for charitable purposes.

An individual who is a principal, staff member, or officer of the soliciting organization must display to a prospective donor or purchaser a Solicitation or Sale for Charitable Purposes Card, signed and dated, under penalty of perjury. The card must provide the name and address of the soliciting organization or of the individual who signed the card, and the name and business address of any paid solicitor. As an alternative, the solicitor or seller may distribute during the course of the solicitation other printed material, as long as the prospective donor or purchaser is informed of the presence of certain information (see below).

The card or other printed material must contain the following: (1) the name and address of the combined campaign, each organization, or fund on behalf of which all or any of the money collected will be utilized for charitable purposes; (2) if there is no charitable organization or fund, the manner in which the money collected will be utilized for charitable purposes; (3) the amount, stated as a percentage of the total gift or purchase price, that will be used for charitable purposes; (4) if a paid fund-raiser is paid a fixed fee rather than a percentage of the total amount raised, the total cost that is estimated will be used for direct fund-raising expenses; (5) if the solicitation is not a sale solicitation, the material may state, in place of the amount of fund-raising expenses, that an audited financial statement of the expenses may be obtained by contacting the organization; (6) if the organization or fund is not recognized as a charitable entity under both federal and state law, the non-tax-exempt status of the organization or fund; (7) the percentage of the total gift or purchase price which may be deducted as a charitable contribution under both federal and state law, or, if there is no deduction, the material must state that fact; and (8) if the entity making the solicitation represents a nongovernmental organization with a name that would reasonably be understood to imply that the organization is composed of law enforcement personnel, the total number of members in the organization and the number of members working or living within the county where the solicitation is being made, and, if the solicitation is for advertising, the statewide circulation of the publication in which the solicited advertisement will appear.

"Knowing and willful noncompliance" by a volunteer solicitor or seller for a charitable organization subjects the individual to the penalties of this law. Where the solicitation is not a sales solicitation, a volunteer may comply with the disclosure provisions of this law by providing the name and address of the charitable organization involved, by stating the charitable purposes for which the solicitation is made, and by stating to the person solicited that information as to the revenues and expenses of the organization (including its administrative and fund-raising costs) may be obtained by contacting the organization's office; the organization must provide the information to the person solicited within seven days after receipt of the request.

However, a volunteer in connection with a solicitation or sales solicitation, serving on behalf of an organization recognized as a charitable one under federal law and who is 18 years of age or younger, is not required to make any disclosures pursuant to this law.

If the initial solicitation or sales solicitation is made by radio, television, letter, telephone, or any other means not involving direct personal contact with the person solicited, the solicitation must clearly disclose the required information (see above). However, the disclosure requirement does not apply to any radio or television solicitation of 60 seconds or less. If the gift is subsequently made or the sale is subsequently consummated, the solicitation or sale for charitable purposes card or material must be mailed or otherwise delivered to the donor or to the buyer with the item or items purchased.

Other.   Compliance with an ordinance of a city or county within the state which provides for disclosure of information relating to solicitations or sales solicitations for charitable purposes substantially similar to and no less than the disclosure requirements of this law shall be deemed to satisfy the requirements of this law. The provisions of this law are not intended to preempt any city or county ordinance.

The sales solicitation for charitable purposes statute is preceded by the following recitation of "legislative findings":

The Legislature finds that there exists in the area of solicitations and sales solicitations for charitable purposes a condition which has worked fraud, deceit, and imposition upon the people of the state which existing legal remedies are inadequate to correct. Many solicitations or sales solicitations for charitable purposes have involved situations where funds are solicited from the citizens of this state for charitable purposes, but an insignificant amount, if any, of the money solicited and collected actually is received by any charity. The charitable solicitation industry has a significant impact upon the well-being of the people of this state. The provisions of this . . . [law] relating to solicitations and sales solicitations for charitable purposes are, therefore, necessary for the public welfare.

The Legislature declares that the purpose of this . . . [law] is to safeguard the public against fraud, deceit, and imposition, and to foster and encourage fair solicitations and sales solicitations for charitable purposes, wherein the person from whom the money is being solicited will know what portion of the money will actually be utilized for charitable purposes. This . . . [law] will promote legitimate solicitations and sales solicitations for charitable purposes and restrict harmful solicitation methods, thus the people of this state will not be misled into giving solicitors a substantial amount of money which may not in fact be used for charitable purposes.

COLORADO

Introduction

Comprehensive statute: Yes
Regulatory office(s): Secretary of state
Citation: Colorado Revised Statutes, Title 6, Section 1

Registration or Licensing Requirements

Charitable Organizations.   A charitable organization that uses a paid solicitor may not solicit contributions in the state of Colorado unless, prior to any solicitation, the organization has filed, with the state's secretary of state, a completed solicitation notice.

This solicitation notice must contain the following information: (1) a copy of any contract between the paid solicitor and any charitable organization; (2) the full legal name and address of the paid solicitor who will be conducting the solicitation campaign; (3) the address where records and accounting concerning the solicitation campaign are being kept and will be kept; (4) a statement of the nature of the intended solicitation campaign, including the means of communication to be used in the campaign, the projected commencement and conclusion dates, and a description of "any event the solicitation campaign will lead up to"; (5) a statement of the charitable purpose for which the solicitation campaign is being carried out; and (6) a certification statement by the charitable organization, on behalf of which the paid solicitor is acting, certifying that the solicitation notice and accompanying material are true and complete to the best of its knowledge.

Professional Fund-Raisers.   There is no registration requirement under this statute for professional fund-raisers, as such. However, the definition of "paid solicitor" (see below) was amended in 1989 so as to cause it to also explicitly apply to professional fund-raisers.

Professional Solicitors.   Professional solicitors (under this law, termed "paid solicitors") must register with the secretary of state. A paid solicitor must file a completed solicitation notice (see above).

A "paid solicitor" is defined as a person who, for monetary compensation, performs any service in which contributions will be solicited in the state by the compensated person or by any compensated person he employs, procures, or engages, directly or indirectly, to solicit for contributions. The term does not include (1) a person whose sole responsibility is to print or mail fund-raising literature; (2) a lawyer, investment counselor, or banker who, in a professional capacity, advises a person to make a charitable contribution; (3) a bona fide volunteer; or (4) a director, officer, or compensated employee who is directly employed by a charitable organization which, at the time of the solicitation, had received a determination letter from the IRS recognizing the organization as one that is charitable in nature, that promotes social welfare, that is a fraternal beneficiary organization, that is a domestic fraternal organization, or that is a veterans' organization, although the determination letter may not have retroactive effect.

Annual Reporting Requirements

Charitable Organizations.   Every charitable organization required to file a solicitation notice (see above) must, within 90 days after the conclusion of a solicitation campaign, file a financial report for the campaign with the secretary of state. This report must include the gross proceeds, and an itemization of all expenses or disbursements for any purpose. The report must be signed by an authorized representative of the charitable organization and the paid solicitor.

Professional Fund-Raisers.   Paid solicitors (as defined, see above) must file the financial report that is required of charitable organizations (see above).

Professional Solicitors.   Paid solicitors (as defined, see above) must file the financial report that is required of charitable organizations (see above).

Exemptions

This statute does not provide any general exemption from its registration and annual reporting requirements, other than the exceptions from the term "paid solicitor" (see above).

Commercial Co-ventures

This law regulates commercial co-venturing. However, it applies only when a commercial co-venturer reasonably expects that more than one-half of all proceeds of a solicitation campaign will be derived from transactions within the state.

Other Requirements

Record Keeping and Accounting.   During each solicitation campaign, a paid solicitor must create and maintain, for at least two years after the completion of the campaign, the following records: (1) copies of all written confirmations provided (see above); (2) the name and residence address of every person involved in the solicitation; (3) the locations and account numbers of all financial institution accounts into which the paid solicitor has deposited receipts from the solicitation; (4) records indicating the quantity of donated tickets or sponsorships which were actually used or received by donees or beneficiaries (see below); (5) a complete record and accounting of the receipts and disbursements of funds derived from the campaign; (6) all written records relating to "pitches," sales approaches, or disclosures used during the campaign and all instructions provided to paid solicitors concerning the content of solicitations; (7) all contracts made with charitable organizations or other represented beneficiaries of solicitations; and (8) for each contribution, records indicating the name and address of the contributor, the amount of the contribution (if monetary), and the date of the contribution, as well as the name of the individual paid solicitor who solicited the contribution.

A person involved in solicitations who claims to be exempt from the definition of "paid solicitor" because he or she is a director, officer, or employee of a qualified tax-exempt organization (see above) must maintain records of ruling letters and other communications from the IRS regarding this exempt status. In the case of a charitable organization, failure to produce the records on written demand of the appropriate district attorney gives rise to a rebuttable presumption that the organization involved is not tax-exempt as a charity.

All notices and reports filed pursuant to this law must be available for public inspection.

Unique Provisions

Confirmations.   A paid solicitor who makes an oral solicitation must furnish to every contributor, prior to the gift, a written confirmation of the expected contribution. This confirmation must contain the following information "clearly and conspicuously": (1) the full legal name, address, and telephone number of the employer of the paid solicitor who directly communicated with the contributor; (2) a disclosure that the contribution is not tax deductible (if that is the case); (3) a disclosure, in capital letters of at least 10-point bold-faced type, identifying the paid solicitor as a paid solicitor (or professional fund-raiser); (4) the address and telephone number of the location from which the solicitation has been or is being conducted if that information is different from that provided in (1), except that this information is not required to be provided if telephone solicitations are being conducted from more than one location and from the residence of the paid solicitor (or professional fund-raiser); (5) the name, address, and telephone number of any charitable organization connected with the solicitation or any organization the name or symbol of which has been used "in aid of or in the course of" the solicitation; (6) the amount of any expected monetary contribution; (7) the name and address of the contributor, as well as the date of the solicitation, or spaces where this information may be filled in by the contributor.

If the contributor is absent when the contribution is to be collected, the paid solicitor may comply with these requirements by furnishing the written confirmation in a manner previously agreed upon between the paid solicitor and the contributor.

A written solicitation must contain the same information as is required of oral solicitations, except for the amount of the expected contribution.

Accounts.   Each monetary contribution in the custody of a paid solicitor must be deposited in an account at a federally insured financial institution in its entirety within 10 days following its receipt.

Prohibited Acts.   A person may not, in the course of a charitable solicitation, represent that a contribution will be used to purchase a ticket or tickets to be donated for use by another, sponsor the attendance of another at an event, or sponsor the receipt of a benefit of another while knowing that the donated tickets or sponsorships will not actually be used or received by the donees or beneficiaries in the quantity represented.

Other.   A contributor has the right to cancel his or her agreement or pledge to contribute, by delivering notice of the cancellation to the paid solicitor. In a situation where the paid solicitor knowingly fails to comply with this law, a contributor can cancel the gift at any time. Otherwise, the cancellation must occur within one business day for nonmonetary gifts or three business days for monetary gifts.

A foreign corporation performing a prohibited act through a "salesman or agent" is subjected to service of process either upon the registered agent specified by the corporation or upon the secretary of state.

This statute is preceded by the following "legislative declaration":

The general assembly hereby finds that fraudulent charitable solicitations are a widespread practice in this state which results in millions of dollars of losses to contributors and legitimate charities each year. Legitimate charities are harmed by such fraud because the money available for contributions continually is being siphoned off by fraudulent charities, and the goodwill and confidence of contributors continually is being undermined by the practices of unscrupulous solicitors. The general assembly therefore finds that the provisions of this article, including those involving disclosures to be made by paid solicitors, are necessary to protect the public's interest in making informed choices as to which charitable causes should be supported.

Sanctions

The sanctions pursuant to this statute are cast as acts of "charitable fraud," which are either felonies (items (2), (3), (4), (7), and (8) below) or misdemeanors (items (1), (5), and (6) below). These acts are as follows: (1) a knowing solicitation of a contribution where an act or omission is a knowing violation of this law; (2) a knowing solicitation of a contribution where the person uses the name or symbol of another person without written authorization; (3) a solicitation where there is use of a name, symbol, or statement that is similar to that of another where there is intent to mislead the prospective donor as to the identity of the solicitor; (4) a knowing solicitation, with intent to defraud, where the person assumes or allows to be assumed a "false or fictitious identity or capacity"; (5) a knowing failure to create and maintain all required records; (6) a knowing failure to make these records available for examination and photocopying at the office of the appropriate district attorney on a timely basis; (7) a knowing misrepresentation of a material fact in any notice, report, or record required to be filed, maintained, or created by this law; or (8) an act, with the intent to defraud, where the person devises or executes a scheme or artifice to defraud by means of a solicitation or obtains money, property, or services by means of a false or fraudulent pretense, representation, or promise in the course of a solicitation.

CONNECTICUT

Introduction

Comprehensive statute: Yes
Regulatory office(s): Department of Consumer Protection
Citation: Chapter 419d, Solicitation of Charitable Funds Act

Registration or Licensing Requirements

Charitable Organizations.   A charitable organization, unless exempt from the requirement, may not solicit contributions in the state of Connecticut unless, prior to any solicitation, the organization has registered with the state's department of consumer protection.

A chapter, branch, or affiliate in the state of a registered parent organization is not required to register, as long as the principal office of the parent organization is located in the state and a consolidated annual report is filed.

Professional Fund-Raisers.   Professional fund-raisers (under this law, termed "fund-raising counsel") that at any time have custody or control of contributions from a solicitation must register with the department. Each registration is valid for one year and may be renewed.

An applicant for registration or renewal of registration must file, and have approved by the department, a bond in the amount of $20,000.

Professional Solicitors.   Professional solicitors (under this law, termed "paid solicitors") must register with the department. Each registration is valid for one year and may be renewed.

A paid solicitor must file, and have approved by the department, a bond in the amount of $20,000.

Annual Reporting Requirements

Charitable Organizations.   Every charitable organization required to register (see above) must annually file a report with the department. This report must include a financial statement. A copy of financial statements filed with the IRS or under a similar state law is acceptable.

A charitable organization with gross revenue in excess of $100,000 in a year must include with the financial statement an audit report of a certified public accountant.

This report must be filed within five months following the close of the fiscal year. Extensions up to three months are authorized.

Professional Fund-Raisers.   While there is no separate annual reporting requirement as such for fund-raising counsel, the effect of the annual registration requirement (see above) is the same as annual reporting.

Professional Solicitors.   A paid solicitor must file a financial report for the campaign with the department within 90 days after completion of the solicitation, and annually where the campaign extends longer than one year.

Any material change in any information filed with the department by a paid solicitor must be reported in writing by the paid solicitor within seven days of the change.

Exemptions

The registration and annual reporting requirements are inapplicable to a (1) duly organized religious, corporation, institution, or society; (2) a parent-teacher association; (3) an accredited educational institution; (4) a nonprofit hospital; (5) a governmental unit or instrumentality of a state or the United States; (6) a person who solicits solely for the benefit of organizations described in (1) to (5); and (7) a charitable organization that normally receives less than $25,000 in contributions annually and does "not compensate any person primarily to conduct solicitations."

However, an organization must submit information as required by the department to substantiate an exemption.

Commercial Co-ventures

This law regulates commercial co-venturing by use of the concept of the charitable sales promotion.

Other Requirements

Contracts.   A contract between a charitable organization and a fund-raising counsel must be in writing and filed by the fund-raising counsel with the department at least 15 days prior to the performance by the counsel of "material services" under the contract. This agreement must contain such information "as will enable the department to identify the services the fund-raising counsel is to provide and the manner of his compensation."

A contract between a charitable organization and a paid solicitor must be in writing and filed by the paid solicitor with the department at least 20 days prior to the commencement of the solicitation. This agreement must "clearly state the respective obligations" of the parties and state the "minimum amount which the charitable organization shall receive" as the result of the solicitation, "which minimum amount shall be stated as a percentage of the gross revenue."

Record Keeping and Accounting.   Every charitable organization required to file an annual report (see above) and that is exempt under the $25,000 limitation (see above) must keep accurate fiscal records for at least three years. These records must be made available to the department for inspection upon request.

A paid solicitor must maintain for at least three years records concerning each solicitation pertaining to (1) the name and address of each contributor, (2) the date and amount of the contribution, (3) the name and residence of each person involved in the solicitation, and (4) all income received and expenses incurred in the course of the solicitation. These records must be available to the department upon request.

A commercial co-venturer must keep a final accounting for a charitable sales promotion for three years. This accounting must be made available to the department upon request.

Unique Provisions

Disclosures.   At least 20 days prior to the commencement of the solicitation, a paid solicitor must file with the department a written "completed solicitation notice." This notice must include a description of the solicitation event or campaign, the location and telephone number from which the solicitation is to be conducted, the names and residence addresses of those who are to solicit, and the account number and location of all bank accounts where the solicitation receipts are to be deposited. The charitable organization involved must certify as to the accuracy of the notice and accompanying material.

A paid solicitor must disclose at the point of solicitation the fact that he or she is a paid solicitor and the percentage of gross revenue which the charitable organization is to receive.

Confirmations.   In the case of an oral solicitation, a paid solicitor must, within five days, send a written confirmation to each pledgor. This information must include a "clear and conspicuous" disclosure of 'the percentage of gross revenue destined for charity and the fact that the person is a paid solicitor.

Percentages.   See Disclosures (above).

Accounts.   All funds collected by a paid solicitor must be deposited in a bank account, in the name of the charitable organization in control of the account.

Prohibited Acts.   There are 12 prohibited acts: (1) misrepresentation of the purpose or beneficiary of a solicitation; (2) misrepresentation of the purpose or nature of a charitable organization; (3) a financial transaction by a charitable organization which is not related to the accomplishment of its charitable purpose or which jeopardizes or interferes with the ability of the charitable organization to accomplish its charitable purpose; (4) the expenditure by a charitable organization of an "unreasonable amount of money" for fund-raising or management; (5) use or exploitation of the fact of registration so as to lead the public to believe that the registration constitutes an endorsement by the state; (6) misrepresentation that another person sponsors or endorses a solicitation; (7) the use of the name of a charitable organization, or to use material of a charitable organization, without the written consent of the organization; (8) use by a charitable organization of a name that is similar to the name of another charitable organization absent the written consent of the latter; (9) the making of a false or misleading statement on a document required by this law; (10) the failure to comply with any requirement of this law; (11) the use by a charitable organization of the services of an unregistered fund-raising counsel or paid solicitor; and (12) the performance of services by a fund-raising counsel or paid solicitor on behalf of an unregistered charitable organization.

Also, a paid solicitor may not represent that contributions received will be given to a charitable organization unless the organization has consented, in writing and in advance of the solicitation, to the use of its name.

Tickets.   A paid solicitor may not represent that tickets to an event are to be donated for use by another, unless the solicitor has first obtained a written commitment from a charitable organization stating that it will accept donated tickets and specifying the number of tickets that it is willing to accept and provided "no more contributions for donated tickets shall be solicited than the number of ticket commitments received from the charitable organization."

If a paid solicitor sells tickets to an event and represents that tickets will be donated for use by another, the paid solicitor shall maintain, for at least three years, records of (1) the name and address of contributors of tickets; (2) the number of tickets donated by each contributor; and (3) the name and address of all organizations receiving donated tickets for use by others, including the number of tickets received by each organization. These records must be available to the department upon request.

Other.   A person may not act as a paid solicitor if the person (or any officer or director of it, any person with a controlling interest in it, or any person the solicitor procures to solicit) has been convicted by a court of any felony or any misdemeanor involving "dishonesty or arising from the conduct of a solicitation for a charitable organization or purpose."

Sanctions

The department is authorized to conduct investigations to determine whether there have been violations of this law.

The commissioner of consumer protection is empowered to deny, suspend, or revoke the registration of a charitable organization, fund-raising counsel, or paid solicitor that has violated this law.

The attorney general is empowered to seek injunctions to enforce this law, as well as seek an appointment of a receiver, an order of restitution, and an accounting to "ensure the due application of charitable funds."

Any person who violates any provision of this law may be fined up to $1,000 or imprisoned up to one year, or both.

DELAWARE

No statute.

DISTRICT OF COLUMBIA

Introduction

Comprehensive statute: No
Regulatory office(s): District of Columbia Department of Economic
                     Development
Citation: District of Columbia Code, Title 2, Chapter 7

Registration or Licensing Requirements

Charitable Organizations.   A charitable organization, unless exempt from the requirement, may not solicit contributions in the District of Columbia unless, prior to any solicitation, the organization has procured a certificate of registration. The application for the certificate must be filed at least 15 days prior to the time when the certificate of registration applied for is to become effective. The certificate must be issued within

10 days of the application for it, as long as "sufficient information" is provided.

Each certificate of registration is valid for the period of time that is stated on it.

Any changes in the information filed in application for a certificate of registration must be reported within 10 days of the change.

Professional Fund-Raisers.   There is no specific registration requirement for a "person" soliciting in the jurisdiction.

Professional Solicitors.   There is no specific registration requirement for professional solicitors. However, the statute applies to any "person" soliciting in the jurisdiction.

Annual Reporting Requirements

Charitable Organizations.   Each registrant must, unless exempt from the requirement (see below), within 30 days after the period for which a certificate of registration has been issued or within 30 days after a demand from the department, file a report. This report must state the contributions received, the expenses of the solicitation "in detail," and "showing exactly for what use and in what manner all such contributions were or are intended to be dispensed or distributed."

Professional Fund-Raisers.   See Reporting Requirement, above.

Professional Solicitors.   See Reporting Requirement, above.

Exemptions

The statute is inapplicable to any person making solicitations solely for a church, religious corporation, or a corporation or an unincorporated association under the supervision and control of a church or religious corporation, as long as the entity has been granted tax-exempt status under federal law.

The registration, solicitor information card, and reporting requirements, and the prohibition on telephone solicitation (see below), are not applicable to (1) the American National Red Cross, (2) solicitations exclusively among the membership of the soliciting organization, and (3) a solicitation that may be excluded by regulation of the District of Columbia Council (although any such exemption cannot exceed for any calendar year $1,500 in money or property).

Commercial Co-ventures

This statute does not regulate commercial co-ventures.

Unique Provisions

Disclosures.   An individual soliciting contributions in the District of Columbia must, unless exempt from the requirement (see above), exhibit a "solicitor information card" or a copy of it and read it to the person being solicited or present it to a potential donor "for his perusal, allowing him sufficient opportunity to read such card before accepting any contribution so solicited." Where the solicitation is by printed matter, radio, television, telephone, or telegraph, the "publicity" must contain the information required on the card. In the case of a telephone solicitation, each person who indicates an intent to contribute must be furnished the card, or a copy of it, prior to making the gift.

Prohibited Acts.   A person may not make, or cause to be made, any representation that the issuance of a certificate of registration or of a solicitor information card is a finding by the department that (1) the statements contained in the registrant's application are "true and accurate," (2) the application does not omit a material fact, or (3) the department passed upon the merits or given approval to the solicitation.

A person may not, for "pecuniary compensation or consideration," conduct or make any solicitation by telephone for or on behalf of any actual or purported charitable use.

A person who is required to obtain a certificate of registration may not, for the purpose of soliciting contributions, use the name of another person (except that of an officer, director, or trustee of the soliciting organization) without the written consent of the other person. Use of another's name occurs where it is listed on stationery or a brochure used to solicit gifts and where the person's name is listed as one who has donated to or endorsed the organization. However, names of contributors can be printed in an organization's annual report without their written consents.

Other.   The statute authorizes the appointment of an advisory committee to advise the department with respect to matters related to the enforcement of this law.

Sanctions

The department has the authority to investigate the allegations of an application for a certificate of registration, to investigate the methods of making or conducting a solicitation, and to suspend or revoke any certificate of registration or solicitor information card.

Prosecutions for violation of this law are pursued by the District of Columbia Corporation Counsel.

Punishment for violation of this law, or for making a false or fraudulent statement in an application or report, is a fine of no more than $500 and/or imprisonment of no more than 60 days.

FLORIDA

Introduction

Comprehensive statute: No
Regulatory office(s): Department of Agriculture, Division of Consumer Services
Citation: Chapter 496, Florida Statutes

Registration or Licensing Requirements

The statute does not contain any registration or licensing requirements for charitable organizations, professional fund-raisers, or professional solicitors.

Annual Reporting Requirements

There are no reporting requirements for charitable organizations, professional fund-raisers, or professional solicitors.

Exemptions

This law does not apply to churches, ecclesiastical or denominational organizations, or established physical places for worship in the state at which nonprofit religious services and activities are regularly conducted and carried on, and to bona fide religious groups that do not maintain specific places of worship. The law also does not apply to separate groups or corporations that form an integral part of the institutions described in the previous sentence, where they are tax-exempt as charitable or religious organizations under federal law and where they are "not primarily supported by funds solicited outside their own membership or congregation."

Further, the law does not apply to educational institutions, state agencies or other governmental agencies, and the solicitation of political contributions in accordance with the election laws of the state.

Commercial Co-ventures

This law does not regulate commercial co-venturing.

Unique Provisions

Disclosure.   Upon the request of any person being solicited in the state, each person to whom this law applies must furnish to the potential donor, prior to the time of the gift, an annual financial report, or other written statement or summary for the immediate past fiscal year or period of fund-raising activity, which shall include at a minimum the following information: (1) the purpose for which the funds are being raised, (2) the total amount of all contributions raised, (3) the total costs and expenses incurred in raising contributions, (4) the total amount of contributions dedicated to the stated purpose or disbursed for the stated purpose, and (5) a statement as to whether the services of another person have been contracted to conduct a solicitation for contributions.

If an annual financial report, statement, or summary, as required under the preceding paragraph, is unavailable, the person must furnish, prior to the time of the gift, a financial report, statement, or summary for its current fund-raising activity which must include at a minimum the following information: (1) the purpose for which funds are raised, (2) the anticipated amount of contributions to be raised, (3) the anticipated total costs and expenses to be incurred in raising contributions, (4) the anticipated amount of contributions to be dedicated or disbursed for the stated purpose, and (5) a statement as to whether the services of another person have been or will be contracted to conduct fund-raising solicitations.

Accounts.   Contributions solicited for or accepted by or on behalf of a named individual must be deposited in a trust account opened by a trustee named in a "properly established" trust document or must be deposited in a qualified depository. Disbursements of contributions may be properly made from a trust account only upon written verification from the trustee that the disbursement is in furtherance of the purpose for which the funds were solicited, with documentation reflecting the identity of the proposed payee and the justification for the proposed payment.

Prohibited Acts.   In connection with the solicitation of charitable gifts, a person may not make misrepresentations or misleading statements to the effect that any other person sponsors or endorses the solicitation, approves of its purpose, or is connected with the solicitation, when the person has not given written consent to the use of his, her, or its name.

Other prohibited acts are (1) failure of a person to identify his, her, or its professional relationship to the person for whom the solicitation is made; (2) a solicitation using any name other than the legal name or names for the organization for which the solicitation is made; (3) the making of a misrepresentation or misleading statement to the effect that the person on whose behalf the solicitation is being conducted is a charitable organization or that the proceeds or part thereof will be used for charitable purposes when that is not the fact; (4) the making of a misrepresentation or misleading statement to the effect that a contribution or the display of any sticker, emblem, or insignia offered to contributors will entitle the other person to any special treatment by "emergency service employees" (firefighters, ambulance drivers, emergency medical technician, or paramedic) or law enforcement officers in the performance of their official duties; (5) the solicitation of contributions on behalf of another person by implying that failure to make a contribution shall result in a reduced level of law enforcement services being provided to the public or the person solicited; and (6) the employment in any solicitation of contributions any device, scheme, or artifice to defraud or to obtain a contribution by means of any false pretense.

Further, an individual may not solicit contributions from a person while wearing the uniform of an emergency service employee or law enforcement officer, or while on duty as an emergency service employee or law enforcement officer, except where the solicitation is for a charitable organization recognized as such under the federal tax law or except when soliciting contributions to benefit an emergency service employee or law enforcement officer who has been injured in the line of duty, or to benefit the family or dependents of an emergency service employee or law enforcement officer who has been killed in the line of duty.

Other

Except for the costs of fund-raising, no person or organization may expend funds raised for purposes other than those stated in the solicitation.

Contributions that were donated under express conditions regarding their disposition must be used solely for the conditions specified.

If the solicited funds received exceed the amount needed for the specific purpose, or if funds remain when the person or organization soliciting ceases to exist, the excess funds must be dedicated to a "like or similar" purpose.

The provisions of this law are not to be construed to preempt any more stringent county or municipal provisions or to restrict local units of government from adopting more stringent provisions and, should these provisions be adopted, they must be complied with if the registrant desires to solicit within the geographic district of the local unit of government.

The division is mandated to undertake a "public information campaign" to further the purposes of this law.

The state used to have one of the most comprehensive of the charitable solicitation acts. This law was repealed in 1989, with the legislature stating that it "recognizes[s] the rights of persons or organizations to conduct fundraising activities for charitable purposes." However, it was written that "[i]t is also the intent of the Legislature to prohibit fundraising solicitation activities which are fraudulent or misleading" and that "[t]his can best be accomplished by allowing the public to be informed as to how solicited funds are being expended, by providing penalties for the failure to disclose such information upon request, and by prohibiting certain solicitation activities."

Sanctions

The division has the power to conduct investigations where there is an "appearance" of violation or potential violation of this law. It has the power to issue subpoenas, and to pursue them and injunctive relief in court. The state's department of legal affairs also has the authority to conduct investigations and to issue subpoenas.

The department of legal affairs has the authority to initiate a civil action against a person, including an officer of an organization, that is soliciting funds in violation of this act. The maximum civil penalty for a violation found as a result of this litigation is $10,000.

A person who violates the rules summarized under Accounts (above) commits a felony, as is the case with respect to any person who "willfully and knowingly" violates any provision of this law. A felony is committed by one who willfully fails to maintain adequate records from which to prepare the information required under the rules summarized under Disclosure (above) or who willfully fails to timely disclose this information.

GEORGIA

Introduction

Comprehensive statute: Yes
Regulatory office(s): Secretary of state
Citation: Title 43, Chapter 17, Official Code of Georgia

Registration or Licensing Requirements

Charitable Organizations.   A charitable organization, unless exempt from the requirement, may not solicit contributions in the state of Georgia unless, prior to any solicitation, the organization has filed a registration statement with the state's secretary of state.

This registration statement must contain the following information: (1) the name under which the charitable organization intends to solicit contributions; (2) the names and addresses of its officers, directors, trustees, and "executive personnel"; (3) in the case of a statewide parent organization, the communities in which the chapters, branches, or affiliates are located and their directors; (4) the name and address of any professional fund-raiser who acts or will act on behalf of the charitable organization; (5) a statement "setting forth the terms of the arrangements for salaries, bonuses, commissions, or other remuneration" to be paid to a professional fund-raiser; (6) the general purposes for which the charitable organization is organized; (7) the purposes for which the contributions to be solicited will be used; (8) the period of time during which the solicitation will be made; (9) the method of solicitation; and (10) "[s]uch other information as may be necessary or appropriate in the public interest or for the protection of contributors."

A registration of a charitable organization is effective either for a prescribed period or on "a continuing basis, without limitation as to time."

Professional Fund-Raisers.   A professional fund-raiser, acting on behalf of a charitable organization that is required to be registered under this law (see above), must register with the secretary of state. This registration is effective for a period of one year or a part thereof, expiring on August 31, and may be renewed for additional one-year periods.

A professional fund-raiser must file, and have approved by the secretary of state, a bond in the amount of $10,000 or in an amount equal to 50 percent of the total income of the professional fund-raiser for the preceding reporting period, whichever is greater.

Professional Solicitors.   There is no requirement under Georgia law for the registration of professional solicitors (although the statute contains a definition of the term).

Annual Reporting Requirements

Charitable Organizations.   Generally, every charitable organization that is required to file a registration statement (see above) and that has received contributions during the preceding year, may be required to file a report with the secretary of state. Thereafter, an annual report must be filed within 180 days after the close of the fiscal year.

This annual report must include a financial statement covering the preceding fiscal quarter or year of operation. The report must set forth the gross income, expenses, and net amount inuring to the benefit of the charitable organization.

The report must state the names of any professional fund-raisers used by the organization during the year and the amounts of compensation received by them.

A report of a charitable organization must be accompanied by a certified financial statement prepared in accordance with generally accepted accounting principles and examined in accordance with generally accepted auditing standards by an independent certified public accountant, if the charitable organization has received or collected more than $50,000 during the reporting period.

The report of a statewide parent charitable organization must include the combined reports of all of its chapters, branches, or affiliates. This total state report of chapters, branches, or affiliates or their managers to the parent organization need not be made separately to the secretary of state but must be made to the parent organization after being verified by an independent local audit.

Professional Fund-Raisers.   A professional fund-raiser required to register under this law (see above) and who received contributions during the preceding year may be required to file, with the secretary of state, a report for the first year of operation. Thereafter, an annual report must be filed within 180 days after the close of the fiscal year of the professional fund-raiser.

This report must include a financial statement covering the preceding fiscal quarter or year of operation, setting forth the gross income, expenses, and net amount inuring to the benefit of the charitable organization.

This report must be accompanied by a certified financial statement prepared in accordance with generally accepted accounting principles and examined in accordance with generally accepted auditing standards by an independent certified public accountant if the professional fund-raiser has received or collected more than $50,000 during the reporting period.

Professional Solicitors.   There is no separate reporting requirement in the statute for "professional solicitors."

Exemptions

Generally, the registration and annual reporting requirements are inapplicable to (1) religious agencies and organizations; and charities, agencies, and organizations operated, supervised, or controlled by or in connection with a religious organization; (2) nonprofit educational institutions and those organizations, foundations, associations, corporations, charities, and agencies operated, supervised, or controlled by or in connection with nonprofit educational institution; (3) business, professional, and trade associations and federations that do not solicit members or funds from the general public; (4) fraternal, civic, benevolent, patriotic, and social organizations, when solicitation of contributions is confined to their membership or when contributions are solicited only from persons who reside within the county in which the organization is located; (5) persons requesting any contributions for the relief of any other individual, specified by name at the time of the solicitation, if all of the contributions collected, without any deductions, are turned over to the named beneficiary; (6) any charitable organization the total income of which is less than $15,000 in each calendar year; and (7) any local or statewide organization of hunters, fishermen, and target shooters that has been recognized as a charitable or social welfare organization.

To be exempt under the sixth category, a charitable organization must file an affidavit with the secretary of state each calendar year, representing that the organization received less than $15,000 in total income during the preceding calendar year.

Local community organizations or local fund-raising campaign managers affiliated with or acting for a statewide parent organization by contract or agreement need not separately register. The single registration of the statewide parent organization is considered to include all of its chapters, branches or affiliates, and individuals, which will be identified by listing the communities in which they are located and their directors, as referenced above.

Commercial Co-ventures

This statute does not regulate commercial co-venturing.

Other Requirements

Contracts.   All contracts entered into by professional fund-raisers and charitable organizations must be in writing. True and correct copies of the contracts must be kept on file in the offices of the charitable organization and the professional fund-raiser for a period of three years from the date the solicitation of contributions provided for therein actually commences. These contracts must be available for inspection and examination by the secretary of state and other authorized agencies.

Record Keeping and Accounting.   Reports filed by charitable organizations and professional fund-raisers become part of the public record.

Unique Provisions

Disclosures.   In connection with a charitable solicitation, the name and address of the charitable organization must be disclosed, along with (1) the name and address of the person soliciting the contributions, and (2) a description of the charitable purpose for which the solicitation is being made.

Prohibited Acts.   The act prohibits inappropriate use of names, for the purpose of suggesting endorsements or sponsorships or by one charitable organization of the name of another charitable organization.

Other.   A charitable solicitation is deemed to be a consumer act, practice, or transaction for purposes of the state's Fair Business Practices

Act, thereby bringing into play in this context the state's law concerning unfair and deceptive acts or practices.

A person who suffers injury or damages as a result of acts or practices in violation of this charitable solicitation act may bring a lawsuit against the charitable organization, professional fund-raiser, or professional solicitor that is engaged in the offending acts or practices. If successful, the person bringing the suit may recover general damages, as well as, in the case of intentional violations, exemplary damages and lawyer's fees. Class actions are also authorized.

Provision is made for the deemed appointment of the secretary of state as agent for service of process on behalf of a charitable organization or professional fund-raiser that solicits in the state.

Counties, municipalities, and consolidated governments within the state of Georgia are allowed to pass ordinances, rules, and regulations to regulate further the solicitation of funds within the jurisdiction but may not alter any of the obligations of the state law.

Sanctions

The state's secretary of state has the authority to initiate investigations as part of enforcement of this charitable solicitation act. In this connection, he or she may obtain statements from any person, publish information, conduct hearings, and bring actions to restrain or enjoin activities that violate this law.

Whenever the secretary of state determines that a charitable organization or professional fund-raiser has violated or refused to comply with this law, the secretary of state may revoke its registration. Once the registration is revoked, the charitable solicitation is no longer authorized.

Upon issuance of a notice of revocation, the secretary of state is required to send a "notice of opportunity for hearing." A hearing must be held in conformance with the state's administrative procedure act. The statute provides for the reinstatement of registrations.

In any civil action brought under this law, if the court finds that intentional violations have occurred, the state, upon petition to the court, may recover a civil penalty not exceeding twice the amount collected in violation of this law.

Generally, any person who violates this law is guilty of a misdemeanor. However, a person who solicits funds for charitable purposes, without complying with the requirements of this law, is guilty of a felony and, upon conviction, may be punished by imprisonment for not less than one nor more than five years, by a fine of not less than $1,000 nor more than $5,000, or by both. Nonetheless, a violator of this law may be sentenced as for a misdemeanor.

HAWAII

Introduction

Comprehensive statute: Yes
Regulatory office(s): Department of Commerce and Consumer Affairs
Citation: Hawaii Statutes, Chapter 467B

Registration of Licensing Requirements

Charitable Organizations.   A charitable organization, unless exempt from the requirement, may not solicit contributions in the state of Hawaii unless, prior to any solicitation, the organization has filed a registration statement with the state's Department of Commerce and Consumer Affairs.

The information submitted must include the following: (1) the name of the charitable organization; (2) the purpose for which it was organized; (3) the principal address of the charitable organization and the addresses of any office in the state or, otherwise, the name and address of any office in the state or, otherwise, the name and address of the person having custody of its financial records; (4) the name and address of any chapter, branch, or affiliate in the state; (5) the date and place when the organization was legally established; (6) the form of its organization; (7) a reference to any determination of its tax-exempt status under federal law; (8) the names and addresses of all officers, directors, trustees, and the principal salaried staff officer; (9) a copy of a financial statement audited by an independent certified public accountant where contributions are in excess of $10,000 during the preceding accounting period, or otherwise a copy of an unaudited financial statement; (10) whether the charitable organization intends to solicit contributions directly from the public or have the solicitation done on its behalf by others; (11) whether the charitable organization is authorized by any other governmental authority to solicit contributions; (12) whether the organization is or has ever been enjoined by a court from soliciting contributions; (13) the general purpose for which the contributions to be solicited are to be used; (14) the name under which it intends to solicit contributions; and (15) the name of the individual of the organization who has final responsibility for the custody of the contributions.

In lieu of the filing of the audited financial statement, the charitable organization can substitute the annual information return (Form 990) filed with the IRS for the same period.

This registration is valid for one year and may be renewed for additional one-year periods.

Professional Fund-Raisers. A person acting as a professional fund-raiser (termed "professional fund-raising counsel") for a charitable organization that is subject to this law must register with the department. A partnership or corporation that is a professional fund-raising counsel may register on behalf of its members, officers, and employees.

This registration is effective for a period of a one year and may be renewed for additional one-year periods.

A professional fund-raising counsel must file, and have approved by the department, a bond in the amount of $5,000. A partnership or corporation that is a professional fund-raising counsel may file a consolidated bond on behalf of its members, officers, and employees.

Professional Solicitors. A person acting as a professional solicitor for a charitable organization that is subject to this law must register with the department. A partnership or corporation that is a professional solicitor may register on behalf of its members, officers, and employees.

This registration is effective for a period of one year and may be renewed for additional one-year periods.

A professional solicitor must file, and have approved by the department, a bond in the amount of $5,000. A partnership or corporation that is a professional solicitor counsel may file a consolidated bond on behalf of its members, officers, and employees.

Annual Reporting Requirements

Charitable Organizations. There is no separate requirement for charitable organizations under this law. However, the annual registration requirement (see above) operates as an annual reporting requirement.

Professional Fund-Raisers. There is no separate reporting requirement for professional fund-raisers under this law. However, the annual registration requirement (see above) operates as an annual reporting requirement.

Professional Solicitors. There is no separate reporting requirement for professional solicitors under this law. However, the annual registration requirement (see above) operates as an annual reporting requirement.

Exemptions

This law does not apply to (1) a religious organization, including organizations that "serve religion by the preservation of religious rights and freedom from persecution or prejudice or by fostering religion, including the moral and ethical aspects of a particular religious faith"; (2) an organization established for charitable, hospital, or educational purposes that is affiliated with a religious organization; (3) educational institutions that are recognized by the department or that are accredited; (4) a foundation having an "established identity" with a recognized or accredited educational institution; (5) any other educational institution confining its solicitation of contributions to its student body, alumni, faculty, and trustees, and their families; (6) a library established under the state's law; (7) persons requesting contributions for the relief of any individual specified by name where all of the contributions are turned over to the named beneficiary; (8) a charitable organization that does not receive contributions from the general public that are in excess of $4,000 during a calendar year or do not receive contributions from more than 10 persons during a calendar year, if all of their functions (including fund-raising) are carried on by volunteers and if there is no private inurement of net assets or income of the organization; (9) charitable hospitals that file annual financial reports with the state; (10) organizations that solicit only within their membership by their members; and (11) any nonprofit corporation that has been on record with the department for at least five years, is in good standing as respects compliance with the laws of the state, and carries on fund-raising activities solely through the use of volunteers.

An exemption must be applied for and obtained annually. If eligible, an organization will receive a letter of exemption from the department.

Commercial Co-ventures

This law does not regulate commercial co-venturing.

Other Requirements

Contracts. A contract between a charitable organization and a professional fund-raising counsel must be in writing and filed with the department within 10 days after the agreement is concluded.

A contract between a charitable organization and a professional solicitor must be in writing and filed with the department within 10 days after the agreement is concluded. Solicitation activity may not commence prior to 10 days after the date of filing of the contract.

A contract involving a professional solicitor must "disclose the percentage distribution between the parties to the contract of all funds raised or received as a result of the agreed upon solicitation activity."

Record Keeping and Accounting. Charitable organizations must keep "true and accurate" fiscal records as to their activities in the state. These records, which must be retained for three years, must be made available to the department upon request.

Registration statements and applications, reports, professional fund-raising counsel contracts, professional solicitor contracts, and other documents required by this law are public records.

Other. The department is authorized to enter into a reciprocal agreement with other states for the purpose of exchanging information with respect to charitable organizations, professional fund-raising counsel, and professional solicitors. Pursuant to these agreements, the department may accept information filed by a charitable organization, professional fund-raising counsel, or professional solicitor with other states in lieu of the information required to be filed under this law, if the information is substantially similar to the information required under this law. The department is empowered to grant an exemption from the annual registration requirement to a charitable organization operating in another state, where the other organization is exempt from the registration requirements of the law of the other state, as long as the other state law is similar to this law.

A charitable organization, professional fund-raiser, professional solicitor, or "resident," having his, her, or its principal place of business outside the state or organized under the law of another state, that solicits contributions in the state, is deemed to have appointed the director of the department as his, her, or its agent for purposes of service of process.

Unique Provisions

Disclosures. See Contracts (above).

Percentages. See Contracts (above).

Prohibited Acts. A person may not, for the purpose of soliciting contributions, use the name of another (except that of an officer, director, or trustee of the charitable organization involved) without the written consent of the other person. A person is deemed to have used the name of another for solicitation purposes if the other person's name is listed on stationery, advertisements, brochures, or correspondence in or by which a contribution is solicited by or on behalf of a charitable organization, or the other person's name is listed or referred to in connection with a request for a contribution as one who has contributed to, sponsored, or endorsed the charitable organization or its activities.

A charitable organization or professional fund-raiser soliciting contributions may not use a name, symbol, or statement so closely related or similar to that used by another charitable organization or governmental agency where the use would tend to confuse or mislead the public.

A person may not, in connection with the solicitation of contributions for or the sale of goods or services of a person other than a charitable organization, misrepresent or mislead anyone to believe that the person on whose behalf the solicitation or sale is being conducted is a charitable organization or that the proceeds of the solicitation or sale will be used for charitable purposes, if that is not the fact.

A professional solicitor may not solicit in the name of or on behalf of any charitable organization unless the solicitor has proper written authorization from the organization, has the authorization with him or her when making solicitations, and exhibits the authorization on request to persons solicited, police officers, or agents of the department.

A charitable organization, professional fund-raising counsel, or professional solicitor may not use or exploit the fact of registration so as to lead the public to believe that the registration constitutes an endorsement or approval by the state of the purposes or goals for the solicitation by the organization.

A person may not, in soliciting contributions or the sale of goods for a charitable organization, "impede or obstruct, with the intent to physically inconvenience the general public or any member thereof in any public place or in any place open to the public."

Sanctions

Where a charitable organization, professional fund-raising counsel, or professional solicitor fails to file a required registration application or other information, or otherwise violates this law, and a correction is not timely made, the department is empowered to cancel, suspend, or refuse to accept the registration or other required information.

The department has the authority to conduct investigations of charitable organizations, professional fund-raising counsel, and professional solicitors to determine if this law has been violated. The department is empowered to seek injunctions against ongoing or potential violations of this law.

The statute authorizes the imposition of fines up to $1,000 and/or imprisonment for up to one year for violation of this law.

IDAHO

No statute.

ILLINOIS

Introduction

Comprehensive statute: Yes
Regulatory office(s): Attorney general
Citation: Title 14, Subtitle B, Chapter II, Part 400; Illinois Revised
Statutes, Chapter 23, paragraphs 5101–5114

Registration or Licensing Requirements

Charitable Organizations.   A charitable organization, unless exempt from the requirement, may not solicit contributions in the state of Illinois unless, prior to any solicitation, the organization has registered with the state's attorney general.

To register, a charitable organization must file a completed registration statement and the appropriate attachments, including a copy of any contract with a professional fund-raiser.

Any change in registration information must be communicated to the state within 10 days of the change.

The foregoing is a summary of the state's charitable solicitation act registration requirements. There are separate registration requirements under the state's solicitation act.

Professional Fund-Raisers.   A professional fund-raiser may not be employed by a charitable organization without prior registration with the state. This registration is accomplished by filing a registration statement, copies of all fund-raising contracts involving solicitations in the state, and a bond in the amount of $5,000.

Any change in registration information must be communicated to the state within 20 days of the change.

This registration expires on June 30 and is renewable.

The solicitation act also provides a registration requirement for professional fund-raisers.

Professional Solicitors.   A professional solicitor may not act in the state without prior registration. A person may not register as a professional solicitor without being employed by a registered professional fund-raiser.

Any change in registration information must be communicated to the state within 10 days of the change.

This registration expires on June 30 and is renewable.

The solicitation act also provides a registration requirement for professional solicitors.

Annual Reporting Requirements

Charitable Organizations.   Every charitable organization must file an annual financial report. An organization that solicits more than $4,000 during its fiscal year can file a copy of its federal annual information return (Form 990). An organization that solicits contributions of more than $50,000 (not including bequests, community fund receipts, or government grants) or that employs a professional fund-raiser must provide a financial report certified by an independent public accountant. This report is due six months after the close of the organization's fiscal year, although an extension of up to three months may be granted.

The solicitation act also provides reporting requirements for soliciting organizations.

Professional Fund-Raisers.   There is no separate annual reporting obligation for professional fund-raisers. However, the annual registration obligation is the equivalent of annual reporting.

Professional Solicitors.   There is no separate annual reporting obligation for professional solicitors. However, the annual registration obligation is the equivalent of annual reporting.

Exemptions

This law exempts a religious organization from its coverage, as long as the organization is exempt from the state's solicitation act, which is a separate statute (Ill. Rev. Stats., Ch. 23, ¶¶ 5101–5114).

To be exempt from that law, an organization must be (1) established for religious purposes; (2) established for and engaged in charitable, hospital, or educational purposes and be affiliated with, operated by, or supervised or controlled by a religious organization; or (3) otherwise an organization that "serve[s] religion by the preservation of religious rights and freedom from persecution or prejudice or by fostering religion, including the moral and ethical aspects of a particular religious faith." However, an organization seeking this exemption must initially file a registration statement and be determined by the attorney general that its purposes are "actual and genuine."

The attorney general can issue an exemption for a single religious organization or a "blanket" exemption to a church and its affiliated entities.

By reason of the state's solicitation act, the following organizations are exempt from the registration requirement: (1) a charitable organization that solicits less than $4,000 annually and does not employ a professional fund-raiser; (2) a charitable organization that receives its funds from a united or community fund and does not independently solicit more than $4,000 or employ a professional fund-raiser; (3) educational institutions and foundations having an "established identity" with an education institution, where the institution (a) is the University of Illinois, Southern Illinois University, Eastern Illinois University, Illinois State University, Northern Illinois University, or Western Illinois University, (b) is recognized by the state's board of education, (c) is accredited by a regional or national accrediting association or by an organization affiliated with the National Commission on Accrediting, or (d) confines its solicitations to students, faculty, trustees, and their families; (4) libraries established under state law and that file annual reports; (5) fraternal, patriotic, and similar organizations that confine their solicitation to their membership; (6) persons conducting a charitable benefit for a particular person, as long as they are unpaid for their services and the contributions, less reasonable expenses, are turned over to the named beneficiary; (7) volunteer firefighters and their auxiliaries, as long as the solicitations are conducted by their members and the members are not paid for their services; (8) nurseries for infants awaiting adoption and their affiliates, as long as the solicitations are conducted by their members and the members are not paid for their services; (9) a charitable organization organized by and reporting annually to the U.S. Congress, as long as its annual financial report is audited by the federal government; and (10) the Boys' Club of America and its affiliates, as long as they file the annual reports required by the national organization and the national organization makes the reports required by its charter.

Similar exemptions are provided in the solicitation act.

Commercial Co-ventures

This law does not regulate commercial co-venturing.

Other Requirements

Contracts.   Charitable organizations and professional fund-raisers must, as part of the registration process (see above), file copies of their contracts with each other with the state.

All charitable organizations and professional fund-raisers must retain copies of their contracts with each other for at least three years following completion of the contract.

The solicitation act requires that contracts between a charitable organization and professional fund-raisers be in writing. A "true and correct" copy of the contract must be filed by the professional fund-raiser with the attorney general within 10 days of its execution.

Record Keeping and Accounting.   All registrations and reports are public records and are available for inspection in the office of the attorney general.

The solicitation act provides that registration statements, annual reports, financial statements, professional fund-raisers' contracts, bonds, applications for registration and reregistration, and other documents required to be filed with the attorney general are open to public inspection.

The solicitation act also provides that every person subject to it must maintain "accurate and detailed books and records" at the principal office of the organization.

Also see Contracts (above).

Unique Provisions

Percentages.   The attorney general is empowered, under the solicitation act, to enjoin a solicitation where less than 75 percent of the gross receipts (excluding testamentary bequests) of a charitable organization are used for charitable purposes.

Prohibited Acts.   A charitable organization, professional fund-raiser, or professional solicitor may not, in connection with a solicitation, make any representation that it has registered under or has otherwise complied with this law. A similar rule is in the solicitation act.

Under the solicitation act, a person may not, for the purpose of soliciting contributions, use the name of another (other than that of an officer, director, or trustee of the soliciting organization) without the written consent of the other person. Use of a person's name on stationery or a brochure is subject to this rule, as is a listing of donors.

Under the solicitation act, a charitable organization or professional fund-raiser soliciting contributions may not use a name, symbol, or statement so closely related or similar to that used by another charitable organization or governmental agency where the use would tend to confuse or mislead the public.

Other.   The attorney general is authorized to enter into reciprocal agreements with a like authority of other states for the purpose of exchanging information

Sanctions

The registration of a charitable organization is subject to cancellation for failure to file a timely and complete financial report.

The state has the authority to immediately cancel the registration of any person that violates the rule concerning registration as an endorsement by the state (see Prohibited Acts, above).

Violations of some of the sections of the solicitation act are misdemeanors.

INDIANA

Introduction

Comprehensive statute: No
Regulatory office(s): Attorney general
Citation: Indiana Statutes, Title 23, Chapter 8

Registration or Licensing Requirements

Charitable Organizations.   There are no registration requirements for charitable organizations under this statute.

Professional Fund-Raisers.   A person may not act as a professional fund-raiser (termed "professional fundraiser consultant") for a charitable organization unless the person has first registered with the state's attorney general (consumer protection division).

This registration entails provision of the following information: (1) the names and addresses of all officers, employees, and agents who are "actively involved in fundraising or related activities"; (2) the names and addresses of all persons who own a 10 percent or more interest in the registrant; (3) a description of any other business related to fund-raising conducted by the registrant or any other person who owns at least a 10 percent interest in the registrant; (4) the name or names under which it intends to solicit contributions; and (5) whether the organization has ever had its registration denied, suspended, revoked, or enjoined by any court or other governmental authority.

Any change in this information must be communicated to the state within 180 days of the change.

Each registration is valid for one year and is renewable.

Professional Solicitors.   A person may not act as a professional solicitor for a charitable organization unless the person has first registered with the attorney general. The registration requirements are the same as those for professional fund-raisers (see above).

Also see Disclosures, below.

Annual Reporting Requirements

Charitable Organizations.   There are no reporting requirements for charitable organizations under this law.

Professional Fund-Raisers.   There are no reporting requirements as such for professional fund-raisers under this law. However, the requirement of annual registration is the equivalent of annual reporting.

Professional Solicitors.   There are no reporting requirements as such for professional solicitors under this law. However, the requirement of annual registration is the equivalent of annual reporting.

Exemptions

There are no exemptions under this law.

Commercial Co-ventures

This statute does not regulate commercial co-venturing.

Other Requirements

Contracts.   Before acting as a professional fund-raiser for a charitable organization, the consultant must enter into a written contract with the organization and file the contract with the state. This contract must identify the services that the consultant is to provide.

Before a professional solicitor engages in a solicitation, the solicitor must have a contract, which is filed with the state. This contract must specify the "percentage of gross contributions which the charitable organization will receive or the terms upon which a determination can be made as to the amount of gross revenue from the solicitation campaign that the charitable organization will receive." This amount must be expressed as a fixed percentage of gross revenue or as a reasonable estimate of the gross revenue.

Record Keeping and Accounting.   Registration statements and other information required to be filed under this law are public records. These records must be maintained for at least two years.

Every professional fund-raiser and professional solicitor required to register under this law must keep accurate fiscal records regarding their activities in the state. These records must be maintained for at least three years.

Unique Provisions

Disclosures.   If requested by the charitable organization, the person who solicits must, at the conclusion of a charitable appeal, provide to the organization the names and addresses of all contributors, the amount of each contribution, and a final accounting of all expenditures. This information may not be used in violation of any trade secret laws.

Before beginning a solicitation campaign, a professional solicitor must file a solicitation notice with the state. This notice must include (1) a copy of the contract, (2) the projected dates when soliciting will begin and end, (3) the location and telephone number from where the solicitation will be conducted, and (4) the name and residence address of each person responsible for directing and supervising the conduct of the campaign.

A professional solicitor subject to registration, or a person employed to solicit or act on behalf of a professional solicitor, must disclose at the time of the solicitation and before a contribution is made (1) the charitable organization that is being represented; (2) the fact that the person soliciting the gift is, or is employed by, a professional solicitor; and (3) the fact that the professional solicitor is compensated. If the solicitation is by telephone, the disclosures must be made orally; otherwise, the disclosures must be in writing. These disclosures must be "clear and conspicuous."

Confirmations.   A written confirmation must be mailed within 10 days after each solicitation in which a contribution has been given.

Percentages.   See Contracts, above.

Prohibited Acts.   A person who solicits charitable contributions may not (1) use the fact of registration as an endorsement by the state; (2) use the name "police," "law enforcement," "trooper," "rescue squad," "firemen," or "firefighter" unless a bona fide police, law enforcement, rescue squad, or fire department authorizes its use in writing; (3) misrepresent that the contribution will be used for a charitable purpose if the person "has reason to believe" the contribution will not be used for a charitable purpose; (4) misrepresent that another person endorses the solicitation unless that person has consented in writing to the use of the person's name for the purpose of endorsing the solicitation; or (5) misrepresent that the contribution is solicited on behalf of anyone other than the charitable organization that authorized the solicitation.

Tickets.   A person who solicits charitable contributions may not represent that tickets to events will be donated for use by another, unless (1) the paid solicitor has commitments, in writing, from charitable organizations stating that they will accept donated tickets and specifying the number of tickets they are willing to accept; and (2) no more contributions for donated tickets are solicited than the number of ticket commitments received from charitable organizations.

Other.   A professional fund-raiser or professional solicitor who has his, her, or its principal place of business outside of the state, or who has organized under the laws of another state, and who solicits contributions from persons in the state, is subject to this law and is considered to have appointed the secretary of state as his, her, or its agent.

In the administration of this law, the attorney general may accept an "assurance of voluntary compliance" with respect to any violation of the law. This assurance of voluntary compliance may include a stipulation for the voluntary payment by the person of the costs of the investigation and payment of an amount to be held in escrow pending the outcome of an action or as restitution to aggrieved persons. This assurance of voluntary compliance is not considered an admission of a solicitation or failure to register in violation of this law.

Sanctions

The attorney general is empowered to receive, investigate, and prosecute complaints concerning the activities of professional fund-raisers and professional solicitors. He or she can seek injunctions to enjoin violations of this law.

IOWA

Introduction

Comprehensive statute: No
Regulatory office(s): Secretary of state
Citation: Chapter 122, Iowa Code

Registration or Licensing Requirements

Charitable Organizations.   A charitable organization, unless exempt from the requirement, may not solicit contributions in the state of Iowa unless, prior to any solicitation, the organization has obtained a permit from the state's secretary of state. The permit expires on December 31 of each year.

Professional Fund-Raisers.   There is no permit requirement for professional fund-raisers, as such.

Professional Solicitors.   There is no permit requirement for professional solicitors, as such.

Annual Reporting Requirements

Charitable Organizations.   A charitable organization having a permit under this law must file an annual report with the secretary during December of each year. This report must contain, in accordance with generally approved accounting methods, the following: (1) the names and addresses of its officers, (2) whether any change has been made during the year previous to the filing of the report, (3) a "detailed statement" of all moneys received during the year previous to the filing of the report, and (4) a "detailed statement" of moneys disbursed during the year previous to the filing of the report and for what purpose.

Professional Fund-Raisers.   There is no reporting requirement for professional fund-raisers.

Professional Solicitors.   There is no reporting requirement for professional solicitors.

Exemptions

This law does not prohibit any person, as representative or agent of any local organization, church, school, or any recognized society or branch of any church or school, from publicly soliciting donations from within the county in which the person resides or the institution is located, or within an adjoining county if the residence or location is within six miles of the adjoining county.

Commercial Co-ventures

This law does not regulate commercial co-venturing.

Unique Provisions

The state's consumer fraud statute (a separate law) provides that the act, use, or employment by a person of an unfair practice, deception, fraud, false pretense, false promise, or misrepresentation or the concealment, suppression, or omission of a material fact with intent that others rely upon the concealment, suppression, or omission, in connection with the lease, sale, or advertisement of any merchandise or the solicitation of contributions for charitable purposes, whether or not a person has in fact been misled, deceived, or damaged, is an unlawful practice.

Sanctions

In the enforcement of this law, the secretary may use the services of the attorney general, the county attorney of any county, and any peace officer in the state for the purpose of investigation and prosecution. The secretary may call upon the extension division of the University of Iowa and the commissioner of the department of human services for assistance.

A person who violates the provisions of this law or who solicits funds without a permit, or if under a permit diverts funds to purposes other than that for which the gifts were made, is guilty of a misdemeanor.

General state law, concerning investigations, injunctive relief, and penalties, applies.

KANSAS

Introduction

Comprehensive statute: Yes
Regulatory office(s): Secretary of state
Citation: Chapter 17, Sections 1759–1774, Kansas Statutes

Registration or Licensing Requirements

Charitable Organizations.   A charitable organization, unless exempt from the requirement, may not solicit contribution in the state of Kansas unless, prior to any solicitation, the organization has filed a registration statement with the state's secretary of state.

This registration statement must contain the following information: (1) the name of the organization; (2) the purpose for which the organization was organized; (3) the principal mailing address and street address of the organization and the mailing addresses and street addresses of any offices in the state; (4) the names and mailing addresses and street addresses of any subsidiary or subordinate chapters, branches, or affiliates in the state; (5) the place where and the date when the organization was legally established; (6) the form in which the organization is organized; (7) a reference to the organization's tax-exempt status, if any; (8) the names and mailing addresses and street addresses of the officers, directors, trustees, and the principal salaried executive staff officer; (9) the name and mailing address and street address of the person having custody of the organization's financial records; (10) the names of the individuals or officers of the organization who will have responsibility for custody of the contributions; (11) the names of the individuals or officers of the organization who will have responsibility for the distribution of the contributions; (12) the names of the individuals or officers of the organization who will have responsibility for the conduct of solicitation activities; (13) the general purposes for which the organization intends to solicit contributions; (14) a statement indicating whether the organization intends to solicit contributions directly or have the solicitation done on the organization's behalf by others and naming any professional fund-raiser the organization intends to use; (15) a statement indicating whether the organization is authorized by any other governmental authority to solicit contributions and whether the organization is or has ever been enjoined by a court from soliciting contributions; (15) the cost of fund-raising incurred or anticipated to be incurred by the organization, including a breakdown of all expenses and a statement of fund-raising costs as percentage of contributions received; and (16) a financial statement covering complete disclosure of all of the fiscal activities of the organization during the preceding year.

A successful registration leads to the issuance of a charitable solicitation license and an identification number.

As discussed below, a charitable organization, the total contributions to which during any year are $10,000 or less, can be exempt from this registration requirement. Nonetheless, an organization initially in this position must file a registration statement with the secretary of state within 30 days after the close of the year in which the organization's total contributions exceeded $5,000.

Professional Fund-Raisers.   A professional fund-raiser, for a charitable organization that is required to register or for a religious organization that is exempt from the registration requirement (see below), must register with the secretary of state. The registration is for a period of one year, expiring at the end of June.

A professional fund-raiser must file a bond in the amount of $5,000.

Professional Solicitors.   A person may not act as a professional solicitor in the employ of a professional fund-raiser without first registering with the secretary of state. The registration is for a period of one year, expiring at the end of June. The secretary of state is to issue a professional solicitor's license and an identification number.

Annual Reporting Requirements

Charitable Organizations.   There is no reporting requirement for charitable organizations. However, the annual registration requirement is the equivalent of an annual report.

Professional Fund-Raisers.   There is no reporting requirement for professional fund-raisers. However, the annual registration requirement is the equivalent of an annual report.

Professional Solicitors.   There is no reporting requirement for professional solicitors. However, the annual registration requirement is the equivalent of an annual report.

Exemptions

Generally, the registration requirements are inapplicable to (1) the state's colleges and universities; the state's unified school districts; "educational interlocals"; "educational cooperatives"; area vocational-technical schools; all accredited educational institutions; a foundation having an "established identity with any of the aforementioned educational institutions"; and any other educational institution confining its solicitation of contributions to its student body, alumni, faculty, and trustees, and their families; (2) a library established under the laws of the state; (3) fraternal, patriotic, social, educational, and alumni organizations, historical societies, and subsidiaries of these organizations, when solicitations are confined to their membership; (4) persons requesting contributions for the relief or benefit of any named individual, where the contributions collected are turned over to the named beneficiary, less reasonable expenses for costs of any banquets or other social gatherings, as long as the fund-raising is conducted only by volunteers; (5) any charitable organization that does not intend to solicit and receive, and does not actually receive, contributions in excess of $10,000 during its year, as long as the fund-raising is conducted only by volunteers; (6) any charitable organization receiving an allocation from an incorporated community chest, united fund, or united way; (7) a bona fide organization of volunteer firefighters, or a bona fide auxiliary or affiliate of the organization, as long as the fund-raising is carried on only by the members of the organization(s) and no one is compensated for fund-raising services; (8) any charitable organization operating a nursery for infants awaiting adoption, as long as the fund-raising is carried on only by members of the organization (or an affiliate) and no one is compensated for fund-raising services; (9) a corporation established under federal law that must annually report to a federal department; (10) a boys' club affiliated with the Boys' Club of America, or a girls' club affiliated with the Girls' Club of America, that properly files annual reports with that national organization; (11) an organization established for religious purposes; or that is established for charitable, hospital, or educational purposes, and is affiliated with a religious organization; or any other "religious agency or organization which serves religion by the preservation of religious rights and freedom from persecution or prejudice or by fostering religion, including the moral and ethical aspects of a particular religious faith"; (12) the Boy Scouts of America and the Girl Scouts of America, and their affiliates; (13) the Young Men's Christian Association and the Young Women's Christian Association, and their affiliates; (14) any licensed medical care facility organization as a nonprofit organization under the state's law; (15) any licensed community mental health center or licensed mental health clinic; (16) any licensed community mental retardation center and its affiliates (as determined by the state's department of social and rehabilitation services); (17) any charitable organization of employees of a corporation, the principal gifts of which are made to an incorporated community chest, united fund, or united way, and the solicitation of which is limited to the employees; (18) any community foundation or community trust that is qualified as a publicly supported charitable organization under federal tax law; (19) a charitable organization that does not intend to or does not actually solicit or receive contributions from more than 100 persons; (20) any charitable organization the funds of which are used to support an activity of a municipality of the state; and (21) the Junior League, including any local community organization affiliated with it.

Commercial Co-ventures

This act does not regulate commercial co-venturing.

Unique Provisions

Disclosures. A solicitation by a professional solicitor must contain the following disclosures at the point of solicitation: (1) the name, address, and telephone number of the charitable organization; (2) the identification number of the charitable organization; (3) the identification number of the professional solicitor; and (4) the fact that an annual financial report (see registration statement information item (16)) is on file with the secretary of state.

Prohibited Acts. The act prohibits the following practices, in connection with the planning, conduct, or execution of a charitable solicitation: (1) operating in violation of, or otherwise failing to comply with, this law; (2) utilizing a deceptive act or practice, as defined in the statute, and including the use of "undue pressure" in soliciting; (3) utilizing any representation that implies that the contribution is for or on behalf of a charitable organization without securing written authorization from the organization; (4) utilizing any emblem, device, or printed matter belonging to or associated with a charitable organization without securing written authorization from the organization; (5) utilizing a name, symbol, or statement so closely related or similar to that used by another charitable organization that the use would tend to confuse or mislead a solicited person (whether or not anyone has in fact been misled); (6) misrepresenting or misleading any person in any manner to believe that the person on whose behalf a solicitation is being conducted is a charitable organization; (7) using contributions for purposes other than those stated in the organization's articles of incorporation, current registration statement, or solicitation materials; (8) using contributions for purposes other than charitable ones; (9) misrepresenting or misleading any person in any matter to believe that any other person or governmental unit sponsors, endorses, or approves a charitable solicitation when that other person has not given written consent to the use of the other person's name for these purposes; and (10) utilizing or exploiting the fact of registration to lead any person to believe that the registration in any manner constitutes an endorsement or approval by the state.

Other.   Provision is made for the manner in which service of process may be made upon a charitable organization, person, professional fund-raiser, or professional solicitor that solicits, but is not required to be registered under this law and does not maintain an office, in the state.

The state is authorized to enter into reciprocal agreements with other states for the purpose of exchanging information.

Sanctions

The state's attorney general, and the appropriate county or district attorney, has the authority to initiate investigations as part of enforcement of this charitable solicitation act.

The attorney general and the appropriate courts may seek to enjoin a charitable solicitation or cancel a registration statement of a charitable organization, professional fund-raiser, or professional solicitor.

A person who violates this law may be found liable to the "aggrieved contributor" or to the state or appropriate county in a sum not to exceed $2,000 per violation. A person who willfully violates the terms of an injunction or other court order issued pursuant to this law must pay a penalty not in excess of $10,000 per violation.

KENTUCKY

Introduction

Comprehensive statute: Yes
Regulatory office(s): Attorney general

Citation: Sections 367.650-367.670, Solicitation for Charitable and Civic
Purposes

Registration or Licensing Requirements

Charitable Organizations.   An organization that is exempt from federal
income taxation as a "charitable" organization is deemed to fulfill reporting
requirements if it files a copy of the federal annual information return
(Form 990) with the attorney general.

Professional Fund-Raisers.   Prior to acting for a charitable organization,
a professional fund-raiser must file a "complete and detailed statement"
with the attorney general. This statement is open to public inspection.
The statement must contain (1) the name of the professional fund-
raiser; (2) the address of the professional fund-raiser, (3) the names and
addresses of any chapters, branches, affiliates, or others who will share
the charitable contributions received; (4) the place and date the professional
fund-raiser was legally established, "if applicable"; (5) the names, addresses,
and occupations of those who are directly in charge of the fund-raising
activities and of those who have custody of the financial records or
contributions; (6) a statement as to whether anyone embraced by (5) has
been convicted of a felony; (7) a copy of a financial statement audited
by an independent public accountant for the immediately preceding
fiscal year or portion of the present year; if total profits exceed $250,000,
the report must be audited by an independent certified public accountant;
(8) a statement as to whether the professional fund-raiser is authorized
by any other governmental authority to solicit contributions; (9) a statement
as to whether it, any officer, professional fund-raising counsel, or employee
has ever been enjoined by any court or otherwise prohibited from soliciting
contributions in any jurisdiction; (10) the names of all charitable organizations on behalf of which solicitations are to be conducted; (11) the
location of the records of the professional fund-raiser; (12) the method
by which the solicitation is to be made, including the use of volunteers
and employees, a "narrative description of the promotional plan," copies
of advertising material, and the location of telephone solicitation facilities;
(13) the names and addresses of any professional fund-raising counsel
and employees of the professional fund-raiser who are acting on behalf
of the charitable organization, along with information as to the terms
of the arrangements for remuneration; (14) the period of time during
which the solicitations are made and, if less than statewide, the areas
in which the solicitation generally takes place; (15) the purposes for
which the contributions solicited are to be used; (16) the total amount

of funds proposed to be raised; (17) the use or disposition to be made of the charitable contributions received; (18) the names under which the person solicits contributions; (19) a sample copy of the authorization issued to individuals soliciting by means of personal contact; (20) the name and address of an agent authorized to accept service of process in the state; (21) a statement indicating whether an agreement exists permitting another to use the name of a charitable organization in a "charitable sales promotion" and a copy of any accounting of the promotion; and (22) any other information as may be reasonably required by the attorney general "for the public interest or for the protection of contributors."

Professional Solicitors. Prior to acting for a charitable organization, a professional solicitor must file a "complete and detailed statement" with the attorney general. This statement is open to public inspection.

The statement must contain essentially the same information as is required of the statement of a professional fund-raiser (see above).

Annual Reporting Requirements

Charitable Organizations. There is no annual reporting requirement for charitable organizations, other than the above-referenced filing of the federal annual information return.

Professional Fund-Raisers. There is no annual reporting requirement for professional fund-raisers.

Professional Solicitors. There is no annual reporting requirement for professional solicitors.

Exemptions

The following solicitations are exempt from this law: (1) solicitations by an organization of contributions from its members and their families, as long as membership is not included in a solicitation to avoid application of this law, is not granted upon the basis of contributions alone, and is supported by the payment of authentic dues; (2) solicitations by a religious organization for funds for religious purposes, as distinguished from other charitable purposes of nonreligious organizations; (3) solicitations by licensed educational institution from the alumni, faculty, and student body of the institution, and their families, and from corporations, for the "continuance of an established educational program"; and (4) local solicitations by a student group or parent-teacher association for its "campus or group-connected activities with the approval of the educational institution."

Sanctions

The remedies, powers, and duties generally accorded to the attorney general are applicable in the charitable solicitation context.

LOUISIANA

Introduction

Comprehensive statute: No
Regulatory office(s): Governor's Consumer Protection Division
Citation: Chapter 24, Deceptive Practices in Soliciting Charitable Contributions

Registration or Licensing Requirements

Charitable Organizations. The statute states that a charitable organization must provide, upon request, to any district attorney, the state's attorney general, or the state's office of consumer protection certain information. However, the governor's consumer protection division has promulgated rules mandating registration in connection with a charitable solicitation at least 10 days prior to the commencement of a solicitation.

The statute states that this information is (1) that "relevant to or as substantiation for" the claim that the organization is charitable; (2) the information required in certain "disclosure statements" (see below); and (3) the names and residential addresses of the organization's incorporators, shareholders, directors, officers, "sales persons," and employees.

However, the rules of the consumer protection division make the failure of a charitable organization using a professional solicitor to register an "unfair and deceptive act or practice." The information required under this registration process is (1) the name of the charitable organization; (2) the purpose for which it was organized; (3) its principal address and the address of any offices in the state or, if there is no office, the name and address of the person having custody of its financial records; (4) the estimated amount of funds to be raised by professional solicitors and all related expenses, including "publicity costs," overhead costs, and salaries or fees of the professional solicitors; (5) notification as to whether any professional solicitor used by the organization has ever been enjoined by a court from soliciting contributions; (6) the purposes for which the contributions solicited shall be used; (7) the name or names under which the organization intends to solicit contributions; (8) the name or names of the individuals who shall be responsible for the disbursement of contributions; (9) the names and addresses of all professional solicitors to be used in the solicitation; (10) notification as to whether the organization is incorporated and, if so, in what state; (11) notification as to whether the charitable organization has federal tax exemption; and (12) notification as to whether the organization has state tax exemption.

Professional Fund-Raisers.   There is no requirement for registration of professional fund-raisers.

Professional Solicitors.   There is no requirement for registration of professional solicitors.

Annual Reporting Requirements

There is no annual reporting requirement for charitable organizations, professional fund-raisers, or professional solicitors.

Exemptions

Under the rules, this law is inapplicable to (1) "ecclesiastical or denominational organizations, churches, or established physical places for worship in this State at which nonprofit religious services and activities are regularly conducted and carried on"; (2) "bona fide religious groups which do not maintain specific places of worship"; (3) separate organizations which form an integral part of religious institutions that are tax-exempt under federal law and "which are not primarily supported by funds solicited outside its own membership or congregation"; (4) institutions soliciting contributions for the construction and maintenance of a "house of worship or clergyman's residence"; (5) educational institutions "recognized and/or approved" by a state educational board; (6) a hospital organized under the state's law; and (7) any voluntary health organization organized under the state's law or federal law.

Commercial Co-ventures

This law does not regulate commercial co-venturing.

Unique Provisions

Disclosures.   Under the statute, any person soliciting contributions or payments for goods or services to organizations which "hold themselves out to be law enforcement organizations, publications of law enforcement organizations, or promoters of activities to benefit law enforcement organizations or law enforcement officers" must disclose, at the "outset of the solicitation," (1) the "actual name" of the caller; (2) the city, town, or parish and state from which he or she is calling; (3) the "exact name" and principal business address of the "soliciting organization or publication"; (4) the total number of active or retired law enforcement personnel who are members of each "beneficiary organization or subscribers, in the case of a publication," and the percentage of those who are residents of the state; and (5) in the case of a publication, the total number of copies of the most recently published issue individually addressed and mailed to law enforcement officers.

A similar rule applies with respect to "fire fighting organizations, publications of fire fighting organizations, or promoters of activities to benefit fire fighting organizations or fire fighting officers."

Prohibited Acts.   Under the rules, it is an unfair and deceptive practice to misrepresent to prospective contributors or to the general public the purpose of an organization and the purpose for which the funds are solicited.

Under the rules, it is an unfair and deceptive practice to imply, when soliciting funds or otherwise, that the charitable organization is incorporated under this state's law and/or has a federal income tax exemption when that is not the case.

Sanctions

Generally, a violation of any of the provisions of this law constitute an "unfair practice."

Anyone who violates the law pertaining to law enforcement or fire-fighting solicitations (see above) may be fined up to $500 or imprisoned for up to six months, or both.

MAINE

Introduction

Comprehensive statute: Yes
Regulatory office(s): Commissioner of Business Regulation
Citation: Chapter 385, §§ 5001–5016

Registration or Licensing Requirements

Charitable Organizations.   A charitable organization, unless exempt from the requirement, may not solicit contributions in this state unless, prior to any solicitation, the organization has filed a registration statement with the state's commissioner of business regulation.

The registration statement must contain (1) the name of the organization; (2) the purpose for which it was organized; (3) the principal address of the organization and the address of any offices in the state or, if there is no office, the name and address of the person having custody of its financial records; (4) the names and addresses of any chapters, branches, or affiliates in the state; (5) the place where and the date when the organization was legally established; (6) the form of the organization; (7) a reference to any determination of its tax-exempt status under federal tax law; (8) the names and addresses of the officers, directors, or trustees, and the "principal salaried executive staff officer"; (9) a statement as to whether the organization intends to solicit contributions from the public directly or by others; (10) the name and address of any professional fund-raising counsel, professional solicitor, or commercial co-venturer who is to act on behalf of the charitable organization and the terms of their compensation; (11) a statement as to whether the organization is authorized by any other governmental authority to solicit contributions; (12) a statement as to whether it is or has ever been enjoined by any court from soliciting contributions; (13) the purpose or purposes for which the contributions to be solicited shall be used; (14) the estimated percentage of each dollar contributed that will be expended for program services, fund-raising, and management; (15) the name or names under which it intends to solicit contributions; (16) the names of the individuals of the organization who will have final responsibility for the custody of the contributions; (17) the names of the individuals of the organization responsible for the final distribution of the contributions; (18) the organization's fiscal year; (19) the total amount of contributions received during the preceding fiscal year; and (20) the estimated percentage of each dollar contribution to be expended in the state.

As noted below, a charitable organization that does not receive more than $10,000 in contributions need not register under this law. However, a charitable organization that intends that result but in fact receives contributions in excess of $10,000 in a calendar year must, within 30 days after the date contributions reach $10,000, register and report under this law.

A parent organization may file a consolidated registration statement for its affiliates, chapters, and branches in the state.

The registration statement must be filed at least 30 days prior to solicitation in each year in which the organization is engaged in solicitation activities in the state.

Professional Fund-Raisers.   Professional fund-raisers (under this law, termed "professional fund-raising counsel") must register with the commissioner of business regulation. A registration is effective for one year.

A professional fund-raising counsel must file, and have approved by the commissioner, a bond in the amount of $10,000.

Professional Solicitors.   Professional solicitors must register with the commissioner. A registration is effective for one year.

A professional solicitor must file, and have approved by the commissioner, a bond in the amount of $10,000.

Commercial Co-venturers.   Commercial co-venturers must register with the commissioner. A registration is effective for one year.

A commercial co-venturer must file, and have approved by the commissioner, a bond in the amount of $10,000.

Annual Reporting Requirements

Charitable Organizations.   Generally, a charitable organization must file an annual "financial report." The filing requirement applies to (1) every charitable organization that is required to register (see above) and that receives more than $30,000 in contributions during the fiscal year, and (2) any chapter, branch, or affiliate of a parent organization which receives, separate from contributions to the parent organization, more than $30,000 in contributions during the fiscal year.

The annual reports are to be "based upon" the "audit guides" published by the American Institute of Certified Public Accountants and must set forth "in detail" the financial activities of the charitable organization in the state. The reports must be prepared by an independent public accountant. The report must contain either (1) a copy of a financial statement reflecting the preceding year's fund-raising activities, showing the balance sheet, changes in fund balances, kind and amount of funds raised, fund-raising expenses, allocation or disbursement of funds raised, and notes to the audit and opinion if an audit, opinion, or statement has been prepared as to the fairness of the presentation by the accountant; or (2) a copy of the organization's annual information return (Form 990) filed with the IRS, along with other information describing how funds were spent or raised to substantiate the figures in the return, including an accountant's statement, and to prove that the return was in fact submitted to the IRS.

This annual report is due within six months after the close of the organization's fiscal year.

Professional Fund-Raiser.   A professional fund-raising counsel must file an annual report. This report must state the names and addresses of all charitable organizations for which a solicitation was conducted, the total amount raised, and the amount paid to the charitable organization.

Professional Solicitors.   A professional solicitor must file an annual report. This report must state the names and addresses of all charitable organizations for which a solicitation was conducted, the total amount raised, and the amount paid to the charitable organization.

Commercial Co-venturers.   A commercial co-venturer must file an annual report. This report must state the names and addresses of all charitable organizations for which a solicitation was conducted, the total amount raised, and the amount paid to the charitable organization.

Exemptions

This law does not apply to any organization "established for and serving bona fide religious purposes."

The following are not required to register under this law: (1) organizations that solicit primarily within their membership, where the solicitation activities are conducted by the members; (2) persons requesting contributions for the relief of an individual, where all of the contributions collected are turned over to the named beneficiary; (3) charitable organizations that do not intend to solicit and receive and do not actually solicit or receive contributions from the public in excess of $10,000 during a calendar year or do not receive contributions from more than

10 persons during a calendar year, if all fund-raising activities are carried on by persons who are unpaid for their services and if no part of the assets or income of the organization inures to the benefit of or is paid to any officer or member; (4) educational institutions, the curricula of which are registered or approved by a recognized accrediting body; (5) organizations operated by the student bodies of exempt educational institutions; and (6) nonprofit and charitable hospitals.

A charitable organization that claims to be exempt from the registration requirements and which solicits contributions must submit to the commissioner a statement of the name, address, and purpose of the organization and a statement setting forth the reason for the claim for exemption. However, this requirement is inapplicable to exempt persons—item (2) above—who are organized for a limited time for the sole purpose of providing immediate relief to a named beneficiary.

Commercial Co-ventures

This act regulates commercial co-venturing.

Other Requirements

Contracts. A contract between a professional fund-raising counsel, a professional solicitor, or a commercial co-venturer, and a charitable organization (whether or not exempt from the registration requirement) must be in writing, and a true and correct copy of the contract must be filed, by the party other than the charity, with the commissioner in advance of the performance of services under the contract. True and correct copies of the contract must be kept in the offices of the parties for three years.

Record Keeping and Accounting. A professional fund-raising counsel, professional solicitor, or commercial co-venturer must maintain accurate and complete books and records of activities. These records must be kept available for inspection, for three years, by the state's attorney general.

All information filed under this law is part of the public records of the state and thus is available to the public.

Other. A charitable organization, professional fund-raising counsel, professional solicitor, or commercial co-venturer having its principal place of business outside the state and functioning in the state is deemed to have irrevocably appointed the commissioner as its agent for purposes for purposes of service of process.

Unique Provisions

Disclosures.   A professional fund-raising counsel, professional solicitor, commercial co-venturer or any other person, when soliciting contributions in the state, must disclose to the prospective donor at the time of solicitation the estimated percentage of each dollar contributed to be expended for program services, fund-raising, and management, where less than 70 percent of the amount contributed will be expended for program services.

Any person required to register under this law or its agents, who solicits contributions, must disclose to the prospective donor at the time of the solicitation the percentage of the gross contribution that will constitute its compensation and all fund-raising expenses connected with the solicitation.

Prohibited Acts.   No person shall, for the purpose of soliciting contributions in the state, use the name of any other person without the written consent of the other person.

The names of contributors may be published without their consent in an annual or other periodic report issued by a charitable organization for the purpose of reporting on its operations and affairs to its membership or for the purpose of reporting contributions to contributors.

Other.   The registration fee and bond otherwise required by this law is waived for an auctioneer, when he or she engages in conduct for which he or she is already bonded, who is licensed by the state's department of business regulation, and who has otherwise complied with state law.

A violation of this law constitutes a violation of the state's unfair trade practices law.

The commissioner must annually make a report to the governor and the legislature on the activities of charitable organizations within the state.

Sanctions

An intentional violation of this law is a crime.

MARYLAND

Introduction

Comprehensive statute:Yes
Regulatory office(s): Secretary of state
Citation: Code of Maryland, Article 41, §§ 3-201–3-219

Registration or Licensing Requirements

Charitable Organizations. A charitable organization, unless exempt from the requirement, may not solicit contributions in the state of Maryland unless, prior to any solicitation, the organization has filed a registration statement with the state's secretary of state. This rule also applies to a charitable organization in the state intending to solicit contributions within or without the state.

The registration statement must include the following information: (1) the name(s) and address(es) of the organization and any chapter, branch, or affiliate in the state; (2) the names and addresses of its officers, principal salaried executive staff officers, and the person(s) who have final responsibility for the custody and final distribution of the contributions or, if there is no office in the state, the name and address of the person having custody of its financial records; (3) the purpose for which it was organized; (4) a copy of its current articles of incorporation or other governing instrument; (5) its tax-exempt status under federal law; (6) whether it intends to solicit contributions from the public directly or have the solicitations made on its behalf by either a professional solicitor or a fund-raising counsel; (7) the purpose or purposes for which the contributions to be solicited will be used; (8) other information as prescribed by the secretary of state; and (9) (*a*) a copy of its federal annual information return or comparable information on forms provided by the secretary or (*b*) an audit or audit review of the financial information by an independent certified public accountant if the amount of gross income received from contributions in the most recent fiscal year equals or exceeds $100,000.

The secretary of state is empowered to require an audit or audit review if the amount of gross income of a charitable organization is less than $100,000.

A chapter, branch, or affiliate of a registered parent charitable organization must either file a separate registration statement or report the information to the parent which shall then file a consolidated registration statement.

The president, chairman, or other principal officer of the charitable organization is personally responsible for the timely filing of the registration statement.

A charitable organization may commence fund-raising once a registration statement has been filed. However, a charitable organization may not solicit the public for contributions if its registration has been denied (see Sanctions, below).

Professional Fund-Raisers.   A professional fund-raiser (under this law, termed "fund-raising counsel") acting on behalf of a charitable organization must first register with the secretary of state. Each registration is valid for one year and may be renewed for additional one-year periods.

If the registration is not approved or denied within 30 days of its receipt by the secretary of state, it is deemed approved.

Professional Solicitors.   Professional solicitors acting on behalf of a charitable organization must first register with the secretary of state. Each registration is valid for one year and may be renewed for additional one-year periods.

If the registration is not approved or denied within 30 days of its receipt by the secretary of state, it is deemed approved.

A professional solicitor must file with, and have approved by the secretary, a bond in the amount of $25,000.

There is a separate annual registration requirement for "solicitors," who are persons who for compensation solicit or receive contributions for or on behalf of a professional solicitor.

Annual Reporting Requirements

Charitable Organizations.   Every charitable organization required to register (see above) must annually file a report with the secretary. This report, which must be filed within six months of the close of the organization's fiscal year, must contain any changes to its registration statement and any previous annual reports and shall include a financial statement. A copy of the annual information return filed with the IRS is acceptable for this purpose.

The president, chairman, or other principal officer of the charitable organization is personally responsible for timely filing the annual report.

The fee that must be paid with the annual report is dependent upon the level of public contributions collected or the use of the services of a professional solicitor.

Every charitable organization that intends to discontinue solicitation in the state must file a statement of its intention to terminate solicitation and a final annual report within six months of the close of its fiscal year.

Professional Fund-Raisers.   While there is no separate annual reporting requirement as such for fund-raising counsel, the effect of the annual registration requirement (see above) is the same as annual reporting.

Professional Solicitors.   A professional solicitor must annually file a report with the secretary of state. Where the gross receipts of any fund-raising drive or event exceed $25,000, the report must be prepared by a certified public accountant according to "generally accepted auditing and accounting standards."

A professional solicitor must also provide to the secretary, within three months from the end of each fund-raising campaign or event, an accounting of all funds received and disbursed.

Exemptions

The registration and reporting requirements are inapplicable to the following persons (as long as they do not employ a professional solicitor): (1) persons requesting contributions for the relief of individuals specified by name in the solicitation as long as the gross amount of the contributions collected are turned over the the named beneficiaries for their use; (2) a charitable organization that does not receive contributions for the public in excess of $25,000 during the year for which a registration statement and annual report would otherwise be required, as long as (a) all of the fund-raising activities are carried on by persons who are volunteers and (b) no part of its assets or income inures to the benefit of or is paid to any officer or member of the organization; (3) an organization that solicits only from among its members, including the normal constituency of a school or university; and (4) a bona fide religious organization, its parent, or a school affiliated with it, if the entity has received a determination of its tax-exempt status from the IRS.

Under the authority to enter into reciprocal agreements with other states (see below), the secretary may grant an exemption from the requirement for the filing of a registration statement or annual report to charitable organizations organized under the laws of another state and having their principal place of business in another state, the funds of which are derived principally from sources outside the state, and which have been granted an exemption from the filing of registration statements under the other state's law.

Commercial Co-ventures

This law does not regulate commercial co-venturing.

Other Requirements

Contracts.   A contract between a charitable organization and a fund-raising counsel or a professional solicitor must be in writing, contain the names and addresses of the parties, and be filed with the secretary within 10 days after it is entered into or no later than the commencement of any solicitation.

As to the contract with fund-raising counsel, the agreement must contain provisions addressing the services to be provided, the number of persons to be involved in providing the services, the time period over which the services are to be provided, and the method and formula for compensation for the services. Fund-raising counsel may not receive compensation that is dependent in whole or in part upon the number or value of contributions made as a result of the efforts of the fund-raising counsel.

As to the contract with a professional solicitor, the agreement must include a statement of the minimum percentage of the gross receipts from fund-raising which will be realized by the charitable organization "exclusively to advance its programmatic charitable purposes." The contract must be accompanied by the wording to be used by the professional solicitor (or solicitors) when conducting verbal solicitations and which must include a statement of the charitable purposes to be advanced with the funds raised, disclosure of the percentage (if any) that is the basis for the compensation of the professional solicitor, and a statement that a copy of the charitable organization's financial statement is available and will be provided upon request.

A professional solicitor may not enter into an agreement with a charitable organization to raise funds on its behalf in the state unless the charitable organization is currently registered in the state.

Record Keeping and Accounting.   Every charitable organization must keep accurate fiscal records of its activities in the state for at least three years. These records must be made available to the secretary for inspection upon request.

A professional solicitor must maintain for a period of at least three years, from the date of a fund-raising campaign or event, records that contain the name, address, and telephone number of each person solicited, the date of the solicitation, the amount pledged or contributed, the date any refund was made, the name and address of each solicitor, the amount paid to each solicitor, and the dates on which payments were made to solicitors. These records must also accurately reflect all compensation received for services rendered and all fund-raising expenses incurred. These records must be made available to the secretary for inspection upon request.

All registration statements, annual reports, fund-raising counsel contracts, professional solicitor contracts, and other documents and information field in accordance with this law are public records. These records must be maintained by the secretary for at least two years.

Other.   Provision is made for the appointment of the secretary as agent for service of process on behalf of charitable organizations, fund-raising counsel, professional solicitors, or solicitors having the principal place of business outside of the state or organizations organized under the laws of another state, where there is a solicitation of contributions in the state.

The secretary is authorized to enter into reciprocal agreements with regulators in other states for the purpose of exchanging information with respect to charitable solicitations. By these agreements, the secretary may accept information filed in another state in lieu of the information required to be filed under this law, if the information is "substantially similar" to the information required under this law.

Unique Provisions

Disclosures.   A written solicitation must contain a disclosure statement, which must be conspicuously displayed. However, a disclosure statement is not required for any written solicitation by an accredited school, college, or university to their students, parents of students, alumni, board members, or school personnel.

Upon request for a financial statement, a charitable organization must mail the statement without charge within 30 days of the receipt of the request.

A professional solicitor must file with the secretary 10 days before, or no later than upon commencement of, any public solicitation, fund-raising drive, event, or campaign, a "fund-raising notice." This notice must contain certain information, including the fund-raising methods to be used and the dates scheduled for specific fund-raising drives, events, or campaigns.

When a contribution is received as a result of a telephone solicitation, a professional solicitor must, within 30 days after receiving the contribution, send the contributor a written receipt containing the professional solicitor's name and address, a disclosure statement, and other information as prescribed by the secretary.

Accounts.   All funds received by a professional solicitor as contributions must be deposited in a bank account, established by the charitable organization involved. The professional solicitor may not be authorized to draw funds from the account.

Prohibited Acts.   Prohibited acts include: (1) use or exploitation of the fact of registration so as to lead the public to believe that the registration constitutes an endorsement by the state; (2) the solicitation of contributions for a noncharitable organization in a manner so as to lead one to believe that the contributions will be used for charitable purposes; (3) misrepresentation that another person sponsors or endorses a solicitation; (4) a representation that a contribution is being requested for a charitable organization, or the use of material of a charitable organization, without the authorization of the organization; (5) use of a name, symbol, emblem, device, service mark, or printed matter of another charitable organization so as to confuse or mislead the public; or (6) the solicitation by a professional solicitor or a solicitor on behalf of a charitable organization absent the written authorization of two officers of the charitable organization and where the professional solicitor or solicitor fails to exhibit it and personal identification on request to persons solicited.

In addition, in connection with a charitable solicitation, a charitable organization, fund-raising counsel, professional solicitor, or solicitor may not use a "deceptive act or practice." This is defined as a practice which (1) "[h]as a capacity to mislead whether by affirmative representation or omission," and (2) "[i]s misleading in a material respect in that it concerns information that is important to a person's decision to make a contribution or concerns information that is likely to affect a person's decision to make a contribution."

Still other rules concern the use, in connection with a charitable solicitation, of offers of prizes or awards, other contests, sweepstakes, and other promotional efforts. These rules include extensive disclosure requirements. Other prohibited acts include a ban on "false or materially misleading advertising or promotional material" in connection with a charitable solicitation and the mandate that a person "may not fail to apply contributions in a manner substantially consistent with the solicitation for charitable purposes."

Other.   A charitable organization may not solicit funds from the public or expend them except for the charitable purposes stated in its registration statement and most recent annual report.

A professional solicitor may not use the services of an individual to conduct solicitations unless that individual is currently registered with the secretary as a "solicitor."

This law established a "Charitable Giving Information Program" for the purpose of educating the public about charitable organizations and solicitations to enable the public to "[r]ecognize unlawful, misleading, deceptive, or fraudulent solicitations" and "[m]ake knowledgeable and informed decisions concerning donations to charitable organizations." This program provides information to the public concerning:

1.   "The laws and regulations dealing with charitable organizations and solicitations, including registration requirements, prohibited acts and penalties, and the availability of information through the Secretary of State's office."

2.   "The importance of reporting alleged unlawful, misleading, deceptive, or fraudulent solicitations to the Secretary of State's office."

3.   "A toll-free number and address that may be used by the public to obtain information about charitable organizations or to report alleged violations of the law concerning charitable organizations and solicitations."

4.   "Precautions a person may take before making a donation to a charitable organization."

5.   "Any other information the Secretary of State believes will assist the public in making knowledgeable and informed decisions concerning donations to charitable organizations"

The program is to make available to the public (1) written materials concerning charitable solicitations in locations easily accessible to the public (such as public libraries, buildings, and schools); (2) individuals to speak about charitable solicitations to community groups and other organizations; and (3) public information material for broad distribution or media use.

The statute creates liability to donors on the part of charitable organizations, fund-raising counsel, professional solicitors, solicitors, or officers, directors, or trustees of charitable organizations. This liability can arise where any of these "willfully fails to comply with any requirement" imposed by this law "with respect to a contribution made as a result of a charitable solicitation." The damages can be the amount of actual damages sustained by the donor, punitive damages (not to exceed three times actual damages), and the costs of the litigation (including lawyers' fees). Where liability arises because the person was "grossly negligent" in failing to comply with this law, the resulting liability cannot exceed actual damages and costs. There is no liability where the person can establish, by a "preponderance of the evidence," that "reasonable procedures" were followed.

The statute prohibits "conflicts of interest" in the fund-raising setting. The law states that an officer, director, "partner," or trustee of a charitable organization cannot vote for the "authorization, approval, or ratification of a contract or transaction involving a matter related to a charitable solicitation in which the officer, director, partner, or trustee has a material financial interest or a material conflicting interest."

This statute makes fund-raising counsel, professional solicitors, and solicitors "fiduciaries" with respect to the charitable contributions that are collected. The statute extends the status of "fiduciary" to charitable organizations and their officers, directors, and trustees. This law also makes officers and directors of fund-raising counsel, professional solicitors, and solicitors fiduciaries with respect to the gifts.

Sanctions

The secretary of state is empowered to deny the registration of a charitable organization that has failed to correct deficiencies in its registration materials within 30 days of notification or a reasonable time of longer duration or has engaged in any practice that is unlawful under these rules. Also, the secretary may deny the registration of a charitable organization that fails to file, in a timely manner, a registration statement required under these rules.

A charitable organization, fund-raising counsel, professional solicitor, or solicitor which willfully fails to file a registration statement, report, or other information with the secretary or willfully files such a document or information that is materially false is guilty of a misdemeanor. The same is true of any other violation of this law, whether by an organization or by an officer or director who causes the organization to commit a willful violation of this law. Conviction of the misdemeanor can lead to a fine of up to $5,000, imprisonment for one year, or both.

The secretary is authorized to investigate alleged violations of this law. If a violation is found, the secretary is authorized to cancel a registration, refer the matter to the attorney general for civil enforcement, and refer the matter to the appropriate state's attorney for prosecution.

The attorney general is empowered to seek injunctions to enforce this law, as well as seek a restraining order as to further fund-raising activities in the state.

MASSACHUSETTS

Introduction

Comprehensive statute: Yes
Regulatory office(s): Attorney general
Citation: Chapter 68 of the General Laws

Registration or Licensing Requirements

Charitable Organizations.   A charitable organization, unless exempt from the requirement, may not solicit contributions in the commonwealth of Massachusetts unless, prior to any solicitation, the organization has filed a registration statement with the division of public charities in the department of the attorney general. The division is to issue a certificate of registration to a charitable organization within 10 days of the receipt of the registration statement, where the organization is in compliance with the law. A charitable organization may not lawfully solicit contributions without a valid certificate of registration.

This registration statement must contain the following information: (1) the name of the organization; (2) the purpose of the organization; (3) the address of the organization and the address of any offices in the commonwealth or, if there is no office, the name and address of the person having custody of its financial records; (4) the date and place of its formation; (5) the form of the organization; (6) the tax-exempt status of the organization for federal income tax purposes; (7) the names and addresses of its officers, directors, and trustees and the principal salaried executive staff officers; (8) a copy of the annual report for the organization's immediate preceding fiscal year as required under another law (see below); (9) whether the organization intends to solicit contributions from the public; (10) whether the organization is authorized by any other governmental authority to solicit contributions, and whether it is or has ever been enjoined by any court from soliciting contributions; (11) the charitable purpose or purposes for which the solicited contributions will be used; (12) the name or names under which it intends to solicit contributions; (13) the names of the individuals of the organization who shall have final responsibility for the custody of the contributions; and (14) the names of the individuals of the organization responsible for the final distribution of the contributions. As discussed below, a charitable organization, the total contributions to which during a calendar year are no more than $5,000, is often exempt from this registration requirement. Nonetheless, an organization initially in this position must file a registration statement with the division within 30 days after the date on which the organization's total contributions exceeded $5,000.

Every charitable organization having one or more chapters, branches, or affiliates in the commonwealth and filing on behalf of these entities may pay a single registration fee.

Under other law, every "public charity" (an undefined term), with exceptions, must, prior to engaging in a charitable solicitation, register filing copies of its governing instruments and other information with the division.

Professional Fund-Raisers.   A professional fund-raiser (termed "professional fund-raising counsel"), acting on behalf of a charitable organization that is required to have a certificate of registration, must register with the division of public charities. This registration is effective for a period of one calendar year or a part thereof and may be renewed for additional one-year periods. A partnership or corporation that is a professional fund-raising counsel may register for its members, officers, agents, and employees.

Professional Solicitors.   A professional solicitor, acting on behalf of a charitable organization that is required to have a certificate of registration, must register with the division. This registration is effective for a period of one calendar year or a part thereof and may be renewed for additional one-year periods. A partnership or corporation that is a professional solicitor may register for its members, officers, agents, and employees.

A professional solicitor must file with and have approved by the division a bond in the amount of $10,000. This bond must run to the division and to any charitable organization that may have a cause of action against the solicitor for any "malfeasance or misfeasance in the conduct of solicitation activities." A partnership or corporation which is a professional solicitor may file a consolidated bond on behalf of its members, officers, and employees.

Commercial Co-venturers.   A commercial co-venturer, acting on behalf of a charitable organization that is required to have a certificate of registration, must register with the division. This registration is effective for a period of one calendar year or a part thereof and may be renewed for additional one-year periods. A partnership or corporation that is a commercial co-venturer may register for its members, officers, agents, and employees.

A commercial co-venturer must file with and have approved by the division a bond in the amount of $10,000. This bond must run to the division and to any charitable organization that may have a cause of action against the co-venturer for any "malfeasance or misfeasance in the conduct of solicitation activities." A partnership or corporation that is a commercial co-venturer may file a consolidated bond on behalf of its members, officers, and employees.

Annual Reporting Requirements

Charitable Organizations.   There is no annual report requirement, under the solicitation law, for charitable organizations. However, an annual reporting requirement is imposed inasmuch as the registration statement, referenced above, must be filed with the division of charities annually.

However, under another law, a public charity must file an annual report with the division of public charities. Where the public charity receives more than $100,000 during a fiscal year, its annual report must be accompanied by a "complete audited financial statement."

Professional Fund-Raisers.   There is no annual report requirement for professional fund-raising counsel. However, the registration requirement, referenced above, is applicable annually.

Professional Solicitors.   For each calendar year, a professional solicitor must file with the division a report stating, with respect to each contract with a charitable organization, the name of the charitable organization, the gross receipts collected pursuant to the contract, the amount paid to the charitable organization for its charitable purposes as described in the solicitation, the amount paid to the professional solicitor, all additional expenses not otherwise stated, and such other information that the director of the division may require.

Commercial Co-venturers.   For each calendar year, a commercial co-venturer must file with the division a report stating, with respect to each contract with a charitable organization, the name of the charitable organization, the gross receipts collected pursuant to the contract, the amount paid to the charitable organization for its charitable purposes as described in the solicitation, any amount paid to the commercial co-venturer, all additional expenses not otherwise stated, and such other information that the director of the division may require.

Exemptions

The following organizations are not required to file registration statements with the division: (1) any organization established for religious purposes; (2) any organization organized and operated for charitable purposes that is affiliated with a religious organization; (3) any other religious organization which serves religion "by the preservation of religious rights and freedom from persecution or prejudice or by fostering religion, including the moral and ethical aspects of a particular religious faith"; and (4) charitable organizations that do not receive contributions in excess of $5,000 during a calendar year or do not receive contributions from more than 10 persons during a calendar year, if all of their functions, including fund-raising activities, are carried on by volunteers and if no part of their assets or income inures to the benefit of any officer or member.

Certain named organizations are exempt from the separate registration requirement imposed on public charities.

Also, the reporting requirement imposed upon public charities is inapplicable with respect to "property held for any religious purpose by any public charity, incorporated or unincorporated."

Commercial Co-ventures

This act regulates commercial co-venturing.

Other Requirements

Contracts.   Every contract between a professional fund-raising counsel, commercial co-venturer, or professional solicitor and a charitable or-ganization required to have a certificate of registration must be in writing, signed by two officers of the charitable organization. The contract must be filed with the division within 10 days of execution. A charitable solicitation may not be conducted prior to the filing of the contract.

Every contract between a professional solicitor or a commercial co-venturer and a charitable organization must include a statement of the charitable purposes to be described in the solicitation and a statement of the "guaranteed minimum percentage of the gross receipts from fund-raising which will be utilized exclusively for the charitable purposes described in the solicitation."

Record Keeping and Accounting.   Every public charity required to file annual reports with the division must keep "true fiscal records" as to its activities within the commonwealth "in such form as will enable it accurately to provide the information required."

Registration statements, applications, reports, contracts, and agreements of professional fund-raising counsel, commercial co-venturers, and professional solicitors, and other filed documents become public records. Likewise, under the other statute, registration statements, annual reports, and other information required of public charities become public records.

Every professional fund-raising counsel, commercial co-venturer, professional solicitor, and charitable organization required to have a certificate of registration must keep true fiscal records. These records, which must be retained for a period of at least three years, must be made available to the division for inspection.

Other.   Provision is made for the manner in which service of process may be made upon a charitable organization, professional fund-raising counsel, commercial co-venturer, or professional solicitor that solicits, but does not maintain an office, in the state. Under this provision, the secretary of state is deemed appointed agent for service of process.

The division is authorized to enter into reciprocal agreements with other states and the United States for the purpose of exchanging information with respect to charitable solicitations. A charitable organization may file with the commonwealth information filed with another state if the laws are substantially similar.

Unique Provisions

Disclosures.   Every solicitation by a professional solicitor or commercial co-venturer must contain, at the time of solicitation, the following: (1) the name, address, and telephone number of the charitable organization, or if there is no charitable organization the name, address, and telephone number of the professional solicitor or commercial co-venturer; (2) a description of how the contributions raised by the solicitation will be utilized for charitable purposes; (3) a statement that the solicitation is being conducted by a "paid fund-raiser"; (4) the "guaranteed minimum percentage of the gross receipts from fund-raising [see below] that will be utilized exclusively for the charitable purposes described in the solicitation"; and (5) such other disclosures as may be required by regulations promulgated by the division. If the solicitation is for advertising, the disclosure must also include the geographic distribution and the circulation of the publication in which the advertising will appear.

Any person who solicits contributions for charitable (or civic or political) purposes and who receives, for the service, compensation (including a percentage of the contributions received) must inform each person being solicited, in writing, that the solicitation is a "paid solicitation." However, this rule is inapplicable to the "finance chairman, accountant, treasurer or auditor" of an organization, unless he or she is "directly soliciting," nor does this law apply to any "ordained clergyman, minister, priest, rabbi, officer or any duly authorized member of any religious order or any other tax-exempt religious organization."

Percentages.   A professional solicitor or commercial co-venturer, or its agents, servants, or employees, may not receive "compensation which in the aggregate amounts to a total in excess of 25 per cent of the total moneys, pledges or other property raised or received by reason of any solicitation activities or campaigns, including reimbursement for all expenses incurred in the solicitation."

Also, see Contracts (above).

Prohibited Acts.   The law prohibits (1) inferences, by a charitable organization, professional fund-raising counsel, professional solicitor, or commercial co-venturer, that the state endorses a solicitation; (2) any representation that funds will be used for charitable purposes when that is not true; and (3) any representation that a person sponsors or endorses a solicitation when that is not true. A person may not represent that he or she is soliciting contributions for a charitable organization without authorization to do so. A commercial co-venturer or professional solicitor may not solicit on behalf of a charitable organization unless he or she possesses the written authorization of two officers of the organization; this authorization must be exhibited on request to a person being solicited, any police officer, or any agent of the division.

Every person soliciting, collecting, or expending, for charitable purposes, contributions from the public, and every officer and employee of this type of person, is deemed to be acting in a fiduciary capacity.

Pursuant to the other statute, a gift made for a "public charitable purpose shall be deemed to have been made with a general intention to devote the property to public charitable purposes, unless provided in a written instrument of gift."

Sanctions

The attorney general has the authority to initiate investigations as part of enforcement of this charitable solicitation act. In this connection, he or she may take testimony, examine documents, and require the attendance of any person during an examination of documents. The attorney general also has the authority to pursue injunctions to restrain a violation of this law, as well as any "unfair or deceptive acts or practices" or attempt to obtain money or property by means of any "false pretense, representation or promise." The attorney general also has, under the other statute, investigative powers that may be invoked whenever he or she "believes that charitable funds have not been or are not being applied to charitable purposes or that breaches of trust have been or are being committed in the administration of a public charity."

A failure to file a registration application, report, or other required information can lead to cancellation or suspension of the registration. A filing of false or misleading information can lead to cancellation, suspension, or revocation of the registration.

A person who knowingly violates any provision of this law, or knowingly gives false information to the division, may be fined up to $1,000 dollars, imprisoned up to one year, or both.

A person who violates the rule concerning "paid solicitations" must be punished by a $100 fine for each violation.

If a public charity willfully fails to comply with the registration requirements, each officer and agent of the organization is subject to a penalty of up to $500. The same penalty is applicable with respect to the reporting requirements for public charities. Moreover, any public charity, or any officer or agent of a public charity, who willfully makes, executes, or files a report that is "false in any material representation" shall be punished by a fine of up to $5,000 or by imprisonment for up to one year, or both.

MICHIGAN

Introduction

Comprehensive statute: Yes
Regulatory officials: Attorney general
Citation: Public Act 169, as amended by Public Act 368

Registration or Licensing Requirements

Charitable Organizations.   A charitable organization, unless exempt from the requirement, may not solicit contributions in the state of Michigan unless, prior to any solicitation, the organization has filed an application for a license with the state's attorney general.

This application for a license must contain the following information: (1) the name of the organization; (2) the name under which it intends to solicit contributions; (3) the principal address of the organization (or, if none, the name and address of the person having custody of its financial records) and the address of any office in the state; (4) the names and addresses of the officers, directors, trustees, chief executive officer, and state agent; (5) where and when the organization was legally established; (6) the form of its organization; (7) the tax-exempt status of the organization; (8) the purpose for which it was organized; (9) the purposes for which contributions to be solicited will be used; (10) the fiscal year of the organization; (11) whether the organization is or has ever been enjoined from soliciting contributions; (12) all methods by which solicitations will be made; (13) copies of contracts between charitable organizations and professional fund-raisers "relating to financial compensation or profit to be derived by the professional fund raisers"; and (14) other information "as required by rule."

An application for a license "in proper form and supported by material information required" is examined by the attorney general. If the application and supporting material is in conformity with the law, the attorney general must issue a license to the charitable organization within 30 days. This license is valid for one year and is renewable. A charitable organization must notify the attorney general within 30 days of any change in the information required by the application.

A charitable organization, in support of its application for a license or renewal, must file with the attorney general a financial statement covering the immediately preceding 12-month period of operation.

If a local, county, or area division of a charitable organization is directly supervised and controlled by a "superior or parent" organization, which is incorporated, qualified to do business or doing business in the state, the local, county, or area division is not required to obtain a license if the superior or parent organization files an application on behalf of the local, county, or area division in addition to or as part of its application.

This license is required for more than the solicitation of gifts, in that it is required to "sell memberships or otherwise raise moneys from the public for the specified charitable purpose."

As discussed below, a charitable organization that generally does not receive more than $8,000 in contributions annually is not required to procure this license. However, should an organization under this exemption receive more than $8,000 during a year, it must file for a license within 30 days after the date the gifts exceeded $8,000.

Professional Fund-Raisers.   A person may not act as a professional fund-raiser for a charitable organization before filing an application for a license with the attorney general. This license is valid for one year, expires on June 30, and is renewable.

The applicant must file with and have approved by the attorney general a bond in the amount of $10,000.

Professional Solicitors.   A person may not act as professional solicitor in the employ of a professional fund-raiser required to be licensed before registering with the attorney general. This registration is valid for one year, expires on June 30, and is renewable.

Annual Reporting Requirements

Charitable Organizations.   A charitable organization must file an annual report with the attorney general, in the form of a financial statement.

Where an application for a license has been filed by a superior or parent organization (see above), it must file an annual report on behalf of the local, county, or area division.

Professional Fund-Raisers.   There is no separate annual report for professional fund-raisers. However, as noted, an application for a license must be made annually.

Professional Solicitors.   There is no separate annual report for professional solicitors. However, as noted, an application for a license must be made annually.

Exemptions

The licensing and financial statement requirements do not apply to (1) a person who is soliciting contributions for the benefit of a specified individual, where the contributions are turned over to the beneficiary less reasonable solicitation costs and where all fund-raising functions are carried on by volunteers; (2) a person who does not intend to solicit and receive and does not actually receive contributions in excess of $8,000 during a 12-month period, where the organization makes publicly available a financial statement for its most recent year and where all fund-raising functions are carried on by volunteers; (3) an organization that does not invite the general public to become members and confines solicitation activities to fund-raising drives among its members and their immediate families, as long as the drives are not held more frequently than quarterly; (4) an educational institution certified by the state board of education; (5) a veterans' organization incorporated under federal law; (6) an organization that receives funds from an organization licensed under this law, where there is no solicitation from persons other than charitable organizations, where the organization makes publicly available a financial statement for its most recent year; (7) licensed hospitals, hospital-based foundations, and hospital auxiliaries that solicit funds solely for one or more licensed hospitals; (8) a nonprofit service organization that is not a charitable entity under the federal tax law but nonetheless occasionally solicits funds for a charitable purpose, where the solicitation is performed by members of the organization who are acting as volunteers, where the funds are wholly used for the charitable purpose, and where the organization files with the attorney general a copy of the federal annual information return (Form 990); (9) a nonprofit corporation the stock of which is wholly owned by a religious or fraternal society which owns and operates facilities for the aged and chronically ill, in which no part of the net income from the operation of the corporation inures to the benefit of a person other than the residents; and (10) charitable organizations, licensed by the state's department of social services, which serve children and families.

Commercial Co-ventures

This statute does not regulate commercial co-venturing.

Other Requirements

Contracts.   As noted, the application by a charitable organization for a license must be accompanied by a copy of any contract between the organization and professional fund-raisers. If such a contract is executed after the filing of the application, a copy of the contract must be filed within 10 days of execution.

Copies of a contract between a charitable organization and a professional fund-raiser must be kept in the offices of both entities during the term of the contract and for six years thereafter.

Record Keeping and Accounting.   A person subject to this law must maintain accurate and detailed books and records at its principal office or office of its resident agent. These records must be open to inspection at all reasonable times by the attorney general.

Documents required to be filed with the attorney general are open to public inspection.

Unique Provisions

Disclosures.   A charitable organization, whether or not exempt under this law, must supply to each solicitor and each solicitor must have in immediate possession identification that states the name of the solicitor and the name of the charitable organization.

Prohibited Acts.   A person may not use the name of another (other than that of an officer, director, or trustee of the charity) for the purpose of soliciting contributions without consent. However, the names of contributors can be published without consent in a report.

A charitable organization or professional fund-raiser soliciting contributions may not use a name, symbol, or statement that is so closely related or similar to that of another charitable organization or governmental agency that the general public would be confused or misled.

Other.   Provision is made for the service of process on charitable organizations, professional fund-raisers, or professional solicitors who function within the state but do not maintain an office within the state.

An application for a license will not be accepted from a charitable organization located outside the state unless it first designates a registered agent in the state.

Once a charitable organization has filed an application for a license, it may petition the attorney general to suspend for a "reasonable, specifically designated time" the filing of reports. The attorney general may grant the request after a determination that the "interest of the public will not be prejudiced thereby."

The attorney general may continue under conditions the license of a charitable organization, professional fund-raiser, or professional solicitor that fails to comply with this law.

Sanctions

The attorney general is authorized to investigate the operations or conduct of charitable organizations, professional fund-raisers, or professional solicitors that are subject to this law. He or she can produce individuals for testimony and/or to produce documents.

A person is guilty of a misdemeanor, which is punishable by a fine of up to $500 and/or imprisonment for up to six months, if (1) this law is violated; (2) public donations or memberships are solicited and received on behalf of an organization that is subject to this law and is not duly licensed; or (3) there is a solicitation of funds under a license where the funds are diverted to purposes other than those for which the funds were contributed.

The attorney general has the authority to decline to issue a license to a charitable organization that has materially misrepresented or omitted information that is required by this law or that is or has acted in violation of this law. He or she also is empowered to suspend or revoke a license issued under this law, following reasonable notice and an opportunity to be heard, although there is provision for suspension of a license on an emergency basis.

The attorney general is empowered to seek a preliminary or permanent injunction against any person who is violating this law or who is using a scheme or artifice to defraud or to obtain money or property under false pretenses or deception.

The attorney general may exercise the authority of that office against a person that is not a charitable organization but operates under the pretense of being one. The same is the case for a charitable organization that is not exempt under this law but operates under the guise of an exemption.

MINNESOTA

Introduction

Comprehensive statute: Yes
Regulatory office(s): Attorney general
Citation: Chapter 309, Social and Charitable Organizations

Registration or Licensing Requirements

Charitable Organizations.   A charitable organization, unless exempt from the requirement, may not solicit contributions in the state unless, prior to any solicitation, the organization has filed a registration statement with the state's attorney general.

This registration statement must contain (1) the organization's legally established name; (2) the name or names under which it solicits contributions; (3) the form of the organization; (4) the date and place of its formation; (5) the address of its principal office in the state or, if none, the name and address of the person having custody of its books and records in the state; (6) the names and addresses of its officers, directors or trustees, and chief executive officer; (7) its federal and state tax-exempt status; (8) any denial by any governmental agency or court of the organization's right to solicit contributions; (9) the date on which its accounting year ends; (10) the general purposes for which the organization was organized; (11) the general purposes for which the solicited contributions will be used; (12) the methods by which the solicitation will be made; (13) copies of contracts between the organization and any professional fund-raisers "relating to financial compensation or profit to be derived by" the latter; (14) "[b]oard, group or individual having final discretion as to the distribution and use of contributions received"; (15) the amount of total contributions received during the accounting year last ended; and (16) "[s]uch other information as the attorney general may by rule or order require to promote fairness of the solicitation and to assure full and fair disclosure of all material information to the attorney general."

As discussed below (see Exemptions), a charitable organization, the total contributions to which during any year are $25,000 or less, is often exempt from this registration requirement. Nonetheless, an organization initially in this position must file a registration statement with the attorney general within 30 days after the date on which the organization's total contributions exceeded $25,000. The first registration statement filed by a charitable organization must include a financial statement of its operation for its most recent 12-months' period immediately preceding the filing of the first registration statement.

Where any chapter, branch, area office of similar affiliate of a charitable organization is supervised and controlled by a parent organization located within or outside the state, the affiliate may file a registration statement on behalf of the parent organization in addition to or as part of its own registration statement, or the parent organization may file a registration statement on behalf of the affiliate in addition to or as part of its own registration statement.

The registration of a charitable organization may not continue in effect after the date the organization should have filed, but has failed to file, an annual report (see below). An organization, if in such default, is not eligible to file a new registration statement until it has filed the required annual report(s).

The law provides special rules for organizations that are organized and operated "primarily for the purpose of offering and paying rewards for information leading to the apprehension or conviction of criminal suspects."

Professional Fund-Raisers.   Professional fund-raisers must register with the attorney general. This registration is effective for a period of no more than 12 months from the date of issuance and, in any event, expires on the July 30 next following the date of issuance.

When a professional fund-raiser, or anyone employed or otherwise engaged by a professional fund-raiser, has custody of or access to charitable contributions derived from a solicitation, it must file a bond in the amount of $20,000.

If a professional fund-raiser, or any person employed or otherwise engaged by a professional fund-raiser, solicits in the state, the registration statement must include a completed "solicitation notice." This notice must include a copy of the contract between the parties (see below), the projected dates of the solicitation, the location of and telephone number for the place of the solicitation, the name and residence address of each person responsible for supervising the solicitation, a statement as to whether the professional fund-raiser will have custody of contributions, and a description of the charitable program of the soliciting organization.

A professional fund-raiser must, as part of the registration process, submit a copy of the contract between the charitable organization and the professional fund-raiser. Also, the financial report for previous campaigns conducted by the professional fund-raiser in the state must be submitted.

A professional fund-raiser may not solicit in the name of or on behalf of a charitable organization unless it has written authorization from two officers of the organization, a copy of which must be filed with the attorney general.

The same rules as to denial of applications, and revocations and censures, as summarized above, apply in this registration context.

This law does not utilize the traditional definition of the term "professional fund-raiser." This law defines a professional fund-raiser as one who, for financial compensation or profit, "performs for a charitable organization any service in connection with which contributions are, or will be, solicited in this state by the compensated person or by any compensated person the person employs, procures, or engages to solicit; or any person who for compensation or profit plans, manages, advises, consults, or prepares material for, or with respect to, the solicitation in this state of contributions for a charitable organization." Thus, a professional fund-raiser (as generically known), a professional fund-raising counsel, or a professional solicitor is likely to be subject to this rule.

Professional Solicitors.   There is no requirement under this law for the registration of professional solicitors, using that term. However, as noted, the meaning of the term "professional fund-raiser" under this law embraces professional solicitors.

Annual Reporting Requirements

Charitable Organizations.   Generally, every charitable organization that is required to file a registration statement, as discussed above, must file an annual report with the attorney general. This report is due, for calendar year organizations, on or before June 30 of each year; for other organizations, the report is due within six months after the close of the fiscal year. The attorney general has the authority to extend the annual report filing due date for up to three months.

A charitable organization is not required to file an annual report if it (1) did not receive total contributions in excess of $25,000 from the public (both within and without the state) during its most recent fiscal year; (2) does not plan to receive total contributions in excess of $25,000 from the public during any fiscal year; and (3) does not employ a professional fund-raiser.

This annual report must include a financial statement covering the most recent 12-month period of operation. The report must be accompanied by a copy of the annual information return (Form 990) filed by the organization with the IRS for the period.

The financial statement must include a balance sheet, a statement of income and expenses, and a statement of functional expenses, all prepared in accordance with generally accepted accounting principles. There must be "full disclosure" of the following, including necessary allocations between each item and the basis of the allocations: (1) total receipts and income; (2) cost of management and general; (3) cost of fund-raising; (4) cost of public education; (5) funds or properties transferred out of state, with an explanation as to recipient and purpose; (6) total net amount disbursed or dedicated within the state, "broken down into total amounts disbursed or dedicated for each major purpose, charitable or otherwise"; and (7) names of professional fund-raisers used during the accounting year and the financial compensation or profit resulting to each.

A financial statement of a charitable organization that has solicited from the public, within or outside the state, contributions in excess of $100,000 for the 12-month period covered by the statement must be accompanied by an audited financial statement prepared in accordance with generally accepted accounting principles by a certified public accountant. The statute also provides that the certified public accountant shall, in preparing the audit, "take into consideration capital, endowment or other reserve funds, if any, controlled by the charitable organization."

The federal annual return (Form 990) may be filed in lieu of other financial statements if it is prepared in accordance with generally accepted accounting principles and meets other requirements for financial statements set forth in the statute.

This statute allows parent and affiliate organizations to file combined annual reports. It also provides special rules for charitable organizations that are organized and operated primarily for the purpose of offering and paying rewards for information leading to the apprehension or conviction of criminal suspects.

Professional Fund-Raisers.   Within 90 days after completion of a solicitation campaign, and on the anniversary of the commencement of a solicitation campaign lasting more than one year, the professional fund-raiser who solicited contributions in the state in conjunction with a charitable organization must file, with the attorney general, a financial report for the campaign. This report, which must include gross revenue and an itemization of expenses, must be signed by an authorized official of the professional fund-raiser and of the charitable organization.

Professional Solicitors.   By reason of the definition of the term "professional fund-raiser," the above rules concerning reporting by professional fund-raisers are equally applicable to those generically classified as professional solicitors.

Exemptions

Generally, the registration and annual reporting requirements are inapplicable to charitable organizations (1) which did not receive total contributions in excess of $25,000 from the public during its most recent accounting period; (2) which do not plan to receive total contributions in excess of \$25,000 from the public during any year; (3) the functions and activities of which (including fund-raising) are performed wholly by persons who are volunteers; and (4) none of the assets or income of which inure to the benefit of or are paid to any officer.

These requirements also are inapplicable to (1) a federally tax-exempt religious society or organization that is exempt from the federal reporting requirements; (2) an accredited educational institution; (3) a fraternal, patriotic, social, educational, alumni, professional, trade, or learned society that limits solicitation of contributions to persons who have a right to vote as a bona fide member; (4) a charitable organization soliciting contributions for a named person, where all of the contributions are transferred to the named person "with no restrictions on the person's expenditure of it [sic] and with no deductions whatsoever"; and (5) a private foundation which did not solicit from more than 100 persons during the most recent year.

Notwithstanding the foregoing, where a group, association, or person soliciting for the benefit of a group or association that is an otherwise exempt charitable organization, religious society or organization, or fraternal or like organizations soliciting only among their memberships employs a professional fund-raiser to solicit or assist in the solicitation of contributions, the registration and annual reporting requirements become applicable.

Commercial Co-ventures

This law does not regulate commercial co-venturing.

Other Requirements

Contracts. A contract between a charitable organization and a professional fund-raiser must (1) be in writing; (2) contain information to enable the attorney general to identify the services the professional fund-raiser is to provide, including whether the fund-raiser will at any time have custody of contributions; and (3) if the professional fund-raiser, or any person the fund-raiser employs or otherwise engages, solicits in the state, disclose the "percentage or a reasonable estimate of the percentage of the total amount solicited from each person which shall be received by the charitable organization for charitable purposes."

Record Keeping and Accounting. Registration statements, annual reports, and other filed documents become public records. Requisite books and records must be maintained by charitable organizations and professional fund-raisers; these are open to inspection by the state's attorney general.

Other.   Provision is made for the manner in which service of process may be made upon a charitable organization or professional fund-raiser that solicits, but does not maintain an office, in the state.

The state is authorized to enter into reciprocal agreements with other states for the purpose of exchanging information.

Unique Provisions

Disclosures.   Prior to an oral charitable solicitation or contemporaneously with a written solicitation, the following information must be "clearly" disclosed: (1) the name and location by city and state of each charitable organization on behalf of which the solicitation is made; (2) the percentage of the contribution which may be deducted as a charitable gift under both federal and state income tax laws; and (3) a description of the charitable program for which the solicitation is being carried out and, if different, a description of the programs and activities of the charitable organization. Where the solicitation is made by "direct personal contact," the required information must be disclosed "prominently" on a written document that must be exhibited to the prospective donor. If the solicitation is made by radio, television, letter, telephone, or any other means not involving personal contact, the required information must be clearly disclosed in the solicitation.

In addition to the foregoing point-of-solicitation disclosure requirement, a professional fund-raiser soliciting contributions in the state must disclose the name of the professional fund-raiser as on file with the attorney general and that the solicitation is being conducted by a "professional fund raiser."

Prohibited Acts.   The act prohibits inappropriate use of names, inferences that the state endorses a solicitation, solicitation of contributions by uniformed personnel of governmental agencies (other than firefighters), use of fraud or deception in seeking gifts, and inappropriate use of one charitable organization as a gift solicitor for another. A person may not use the name of a charitable organization for "financial compensation or profit" unless the organization has consented to use of the name in a written contract with the person.

Other.   Special rules apply for the regulation of so-called "registered combined charitable organizations."

In the administration of the powers to "appropriate appreciation," to make and retain investments, and to delegate investment management of institutional funds, members of the governing board of a charitable organization must "consider long- and short-term needs of the institution in carrying out its educational, religious, charitable, or other eleemosynary purposes, its present and anticipated financial requirements, expected total return on its investments, price level trends, and general economic conditions."

Sanctions

The state's attorney general has the authority to initiate investigations as part of enforcement of this charitable solicitation act. In this connection, he or she may obtain discovery from any person "regarding any matter, fact, or circumstance, not privileged, that is relevant to the subject matter involved in the investigation."

The attorney general may seek a court order restraining and enjoining violations of this law. He or she may accept an "assurance of discontinuance" of any method, act, or practice in violation of this law from any person alleged to be engaged or to have been engaged in the method, act, or practice.

Any person who "willfully and knowingly" violates any of the provisions of this law, or who willfully and knowingly gives false information to a state governmental agency, is guilty of a misdemeanor.

MISSISSIPPI

No statute.

MISSOURI

Introduction

Comprehensive statute: Yes
Regulatory office(s): Attorney general
Citation: Charitable Organizations and Solicitations Law, Sections 407.450–407.478

Registration or Licensing Requirements

Charitable Organizations. A charitable organization, unless exempt from the requirement, may not solicit contributions in the state of Missouri unless, prior to any solicitation, the organization has registered with the state's attorney general.

This law does not specify the information that must be submitted as part of the registration process.

A charitable organization may not lawfully employ a professional fund-raiser to solicit funds in the state until the organization has complied with the registration requirement.

Professional Fund-Raisers.   Professional fund-raisers must register with the state's attorney general. Each registration is valid for one year and may be renewed.

Professional Solicitors.   This law does not contain a separate registration requirement for professional solicitors. However, the definition of the term "professional fundraiser" under this law is sufficiently broad as to embrace most professional solicitors.

Annual Reporting Requirements

Charitable Organizations.   Every charitable organization required to register (see above), except those noted below, must annually file a report with the attorney general. This report is due within 75 days of the close of the organization's fiscal year.

The following do not have to file these reports: an organization that (1) receives an allocation of money from an incorporated community chest or united fund, provided that the community chest or united fund is complying with the registration and filing requirements of this law; (2) does not receive contributions (including those in goods or services) in excess of an amount established by the attorney general (which must be at least $10,000) during the reporting period; or (3) is a local affiliate of a statewide or national charitable organization if all local fund-raising expenses are paid by the statewide or national organization and the statewide or national organization files the required annual reports.

Professional Fund-Raisers.   While there is no separate annual reporting requirement as such for professional fund-raisers, the effect of the annual registration requirement (see above) is the same as annual reporting.

Professional Solicitors.   While there is no separate annual reporting requirement as such for paid solicitors, the effect of the breadth of the definition of the term "professional fundraiser" and the annual registration requirement (see above) is to generally cause a reporting obligation for professional solicitors.

Exemptions

The registration and annual reporting requirements are inapplicable to (1) religious organizations (as defined); (2) educational institutions (as defined) and their authorized and related foundations; (3) fraternal, benevolent, social, educational, alumni, and historical organizations, and any auxiliaries associated with any of these organizations, as long as the solicitation of contributions is confined to the membership of the organizations or auxiliaries; (4) hospitals and auxiliaries of hospitals, as long as all fund-raising activities and solicitations of contributions are carried on by employees of the hospital or members of the auxiliary and not by any professional fund-raiser who is employed as an independent contractor; and (5) any organization that has obtained an exemption from the payment of federal income taxes as a charitable organization if no part of its net earnings inures to the benefit of any private person associated with the organization.

As noted (see above), additional types of organizations are exempt from the reporting requirements.

Commercial Co-ventures

This law does not regulate commercial co-venturing.

Other Requirements

Record Keeping and Accounting.   The attorney general is directed to maintain a register of all documents filed by charitable organizations in compliance with this law. Generally, this register is open to public inspection.

Unique Provisions

Disclosures.   All charitable organizations required to submit an annual report must, upon request, disclose the percentage of funds solicited which were expended for fund-raising in the most recent 12-month period for which an annual report was filed. For this purpose, fund-raising costs include "all money directly expended on fund-raising and that portion of all administrative expenses and salaries of the charitable organization attributable to fund-raising activities."

Whenever a solicitation of funds on behalf of a charitable organization is undertaken by a professional fund-raiser, the professional fund-raiser must disclose that fact to prospective contributors.

Percentages.   See Disclosures, above.

Accounts.   All registration and reporting fees must be deposited in a "merchandising practices revolving fund."

The provisions of this law apply "regardless of any contrary provisions contained in any contract, agreement, instrument or other document."

This law is not to be construed to preclude any person or group of persons from asserting any private cause of action they might have against a charitable organization.

Sanctions

The attorney general is empowered to issue a "civil investigative demand" in conjunction with an investigation concerning a violation or potential violation of this law. Under these circumstances, the attorney general is also authorized to bring an action in pursuit of an injunction prohibiting the continuation of unlawful methods, uses, acts, or practices.

MONTANA

No statute.

NEBRASKA

Introduction

Comprehensive statute: No
Regulatory office(s): County attorney and secretary of state
Citation: Article 14, Sections 28–1440

Registration or Licensing Requirements

Charitable Organizations.   Any person (including any organization, association, or institution), whether resident or nonresident of the state, which solicits funds (for charitable purposes or otherwise) in any county of the state other than the county where its "home office" is located, must first obtain a letter of approval from the county attorney of the country in which its home office is located, which letter must be forwarded to the state's secretary of state. Upon receipt of that letter, the secretary of state is required to issue a certificate granting the person the "privilege" of soliciting throughout the state for the balance of the calendar year.

A person that does not have a home office in the state must file with the secretary of state, in lieu of a letter from the county attorney, a certified copy of its articles of incorporation or of its constitution and bylaws, or other evidence of existence and evidence of good standing as the secretary of state may deem necessary before issuing the certificate.

A person soliciting funds in the state must have copy of the certificate from the secretary of state in his, her, or its possession.

Professional Fund-Raisers.   The registration and licensing requirements applicable to professional fund-raisers are described above.

Professional Solicitors.   The registration and licensing requirements applicable to professional solicitors are described above.

Annual Reporting Requirements

Charitable Organizations.   A "voluntary health and welfare organization" soliciting funds in the state, whether individually or with other organizations, must file an annual financial report, certified by the chief executive officer and the treasurer, with the secretary of state. This report is due on or before the last day of the sixth month following the close of the organization's fiscal year.

This report may comply with the publication entitled *Forms and Instructions Recommended to State and Local Regulatory Bodies for Uniform Financial Reporting by Voluntary Health and Welfare Organizations.* The secretary of state is obligated to furnish a copy of this publication at cost to a charitable organization that is subject to the provisions of this law.

Any organization that has adopted its own standard or uniform report or audit can file it with the secretary of state in satisfaction of this requirement. The secretary will accept the IRS annual information return (Form 990) in compliance with this requirement.

Professional Fund-Raisers.   There are no reporting requirements for professional fund-raisers.

Professional Solicitors.   There are no reporting requirements for professional solicitors.

Exemptions

There are no exemptions from this law.

Commercial Co-ventures

This law does not regulate commercial co-venturing.

Unique Provisions

Disclosures.   Before any person may receive any funds by solicitation, he or she must display to the prospective donor a copy of the letter from the secretary of state with the solicitor's photograph attached.

Confirmations.   Once a gift is received, the donor must be provided a receipt in duplicate where the amount of the gift is in excess of two dollars. The original of the receipt must be given to the donor and the copy to the charitable organization involved.

Prohibited Acts.   The letter of approval from the county attorney and the certificate issued by the secretary of state does not constitute an endorsement of any person, organization, corporation, or institution making the solicitation, and that fact must be printed in "bold type" on the certificate.

Sanctions

An organization failing to file a required annual report may be enjoined from further solicitations of funds in the state in an action brought by the state's attorney general or any county attorney at the request of the secretary of state.

Any person soliciting that has not complied with the provisions of this law shall be guilty of a misdemeanor.

NEVADA

Introduction

Comprehensive statute: No
Regulatory office(s): Secretary of state
Citation: Revised Statutes, Chapter 86, Section 86-190

Registration or Licensing Requirements

Charitable Organizations.   There are no registration or licensing requirements for charitable organizations in this law.

Professional Fund-Raisers.   There are no registration or licensing requirements for professional fund-raisers in this law.

Professional Solicitors.   There are no registration or licensing requirements for professional solicitors in this law.

Annual Reporting Requirements

Charitable Organizations.   A charitable organization, national or statewide, operating in the state and receiving its "major support" from contributions from the public must file a report by July 1 of each year with the state's secretary of state showing receipts and expenditures realized through operation in the state during the preceding year.

Professional Fund-Raisers.   There are no reporting requirements for professional fund-raisers in this law.

Professional Solicitors.   There are no reporting requirements for professional solicitors in this law.

Exemptions

There are no exemptions from the above reporting requirement.

Commercial Co-ventures

This law does not regulate commercial co-venturing.

NEW HAMPSHIRE

Introduction

Comprehensive statute: Yes
Regulatory office(s): Attorney general
Citation: Revised Statutes 7:19–7:25

Registration or Licensing Requirements

Charitable Organizations.   This law does not contain any registration or licensing requirements for charitable trusts or other forms of charitable organizations. The law is only applicable with respect to solicitations on behalf of charitable trusts.

Professional Fund-Raisers.   Professional fund-raisers (under this law, termed "fund raising counsel") that at any time have custody of contributions from a solicitation must register with the state's attorney general. Each registration is valid for one year and may be renewed. The attorney general must examine this application for registration to determine compliance with this law; lack of notification by the attorney general of any deficiencies in the document within 20 days of its receipt is deemed to constitute acceptance of it.

An applicant for registration or renewal of registration must file, and have approved by the attorney general, a bond in the amount of $10,000.

A person may not act as a fund-raising counsel without first complying with these requirements.

Professional Solicitors.   Professional solicitors (under this law, termed "paid solicitors") must register with the attorney general prior to the commence of any solicitation. Each registration is valid for one year and may be renewed.

The attorney general is to examine each paid solicitor registration application to determine compliance with this law. The registration is deemed approved as filed, unless the attorney general notifies the solicitor, within 20 days of receipt of the application, of any deficiencies in it.

An applicant for registration or renewal of registration must file, and have approved by the attorney general, a bond in the amount of $10,000.

Annual Reporting Requirements

Charitable Organizations.   Every charitable trustee must file with the attorney general "periodic" written reports, setting forth information as to the nature of the assets held for charitable purposes, the receipts and expenditures in connection with administration of the trust, the names and addresses of the beneficiaries of the trust, the conduct of any charitable solicitation, the conduct of any commercial co-venturing, and such other information as may be required by the attorney general.

In addition, where a charitable trust utilizes the services of a paid solicitor, within 90 days after completion of a solicitation, and on the anniversary of the commencement of a solicitation lasting more than one year, a charitable trust and its paid solicitor must jointly file a financial report for the campaign with the attorney general. This report must include gross revenue and an itemization of all expenses.

Professional Fund-Raisers.   While there is no separate annual reporting requirement as such for fund-raising counsel, the effect of the annual registration requirement (see above) is the same as annual reporting.

Professional Solicitors.   As indicated above, paid solicitors must file, jointly with the charitable trust involved, financial reports for solicitation campaigns with the attorney general.

Also, the effect of the annual registration requirement (see above) is the same as annual reporting.

Exemptions

This law is inapplicable to (1) religious organizations which hold property for charitable or religious purposes or their integrated auxiliaries, (2) conventions or associations of churches, (3) operating educational institutions, (4) hospitals, or (5) persons soliciting for these organizations.

Commercial Co-ventures

This law regulates commercial co-venturing by use of the concept of the charitable sales promotion.

Other Provisions

Contracts.   There must be a written contract between a charitable trust and a fund-raising counsel. This contract must be filed by the fund-raising counsel with the attorney general prior to the performance by the fund-raising counsel of any "material" services pursuant to it. This contract must contain information that will enable the attorney general to identify the services the fund-raising counsel is to provide, including whether the fund-raising counsel will at any time have custody of contributions. The attorney general must examine this contract to determine compliance with this law; lack of notification by the attorney general of any deficiencies in the document within 10 days of its receipt is deemed to constitute acceptance of it.

There must be a written contract between a paid solicitor and a charitable trust. This contract must clearly state the respective obligations of the parties, as well as the amount of the gross revenue from the solicitation that the charitable trust will receive.

Record Keeping and Accounting.   Within 90 days after a solicitation campaign has been completed, and on the anniversary of the commencement of a solicitation campaign lasting more than one year, the fund-raising counsel must account to the charitable trust involved for all contributions collected and expenses paid. This accounting must be in writing, must be retained by the charitable trust for three years, and must be available to the attorney general upon request.

A fund-raising counsel must maintain during each solicitation campaign, and for not less than three years after its completion, the following records: (1) a record of all contributions at any time in the custody of the fund-raising counsel, including the name and address of each contributor and the date and the amount of the contribution; and (2) the location and account number of all financial institution accounts in which the fund-raising counsel has deposited revenue from the solicitation campaign.

A paid solicitor must maintain during each solicitation campaign, and for not less than three years after its completion, the following records: (1) the name and address of each pledgor, (2) the date and amount of every pledge, (3) the name and residence address of any person involved in the solicitation, (4) a record of all contributions at any time in the custody of the paid solicitor, (5) a record of all expenses incurred by the paid solicitor for which the charitable trust is liable for payment, and (6) the location and account number of all financial institution accounts in which the paid solicitor has deposited revenue from the solicitation.

If a paid solicitor sells tickets to an event and represents that tickets will be donated for use by another, the solicitor must maintain, during the solicitation campaign and for not less than three years after its completion, the following records: (1) the name and address of those donating tickets, (2) the number of tickets donated by each contributor, (3) the name and address of all organizations receiving donated tickets for use by others, and (4) the number of tickets received by each organization.

The records required to be maintained by paid solicitors must be made available to the attorney general upon request. Any material change in information filed with the attorney general must be reported in writing to the attorney general within seven days following the change.

Unique Provisions

Disclosure.   Prior to the commencement of a solicitation campaign, a paid solicitor must file with the attorney general a completed "solicitation notice." This notice must include a copy of the contract between a charitable trust and the paid solicitor, the projected dates when soliciting will commence and terminate, the location and telephone number from where the solicitation will be conducted, the name and residence address of each person responsible for directing and supervising the conduct of the campaign, a statement as to whether the paid solicitor will at any time have custody of contributions, and a full description of the charitable program for which the campaign is being carried out. The charitable trust involved must certify as to the accuracy of the notice and accompanying material.

The attorney general is to examine each solicitation notice to determine compliance with this law. The notice is deemed approved as filed, unless the attorney general notifies the solicitor, within 20 days of receipt of the notice, of any deficiencies in it.

Prior to an oral request for a contribution or contemporaneously with a written request for a contribution, the following must be "clearly and conspicuously" disclosed at the point of solicitation: the (1) name of the paid solicitor, (2) fact that the solicitation is being conducted by a paid solicitor, and (3) fixed percentage of the gross revenue or the reasonable estimate, expressed as a percentage of the gross revenue, to be received by the trust (see above). In the case of an oral solicitation, a written confirmation must be sent to each donor or pledger within five days after the solicitation, including a clear and conspicuous disclosure of these three items of information.

Percentages.   If the compensation of the solicitor is contingent upon the number of contributions or the amount of revenue received from the solicitation, the gross amount must be expressed as a fixed percentage of the gross revenue. If the compensation of the solicitor is not contingent upon either element, the amount must be stated as a reasonable estimate, expressed as a percentage of the gross revenue; the contract must clearly disclose the assumptions upon which the estimate is based (which reflect all the relevant facts known to the solicitor). Where a reasonable estimate is used, the contract must also provide that the charitable trust "is guaranteed a percentage of the gross revenue which is no less than the reasonable estimate less 10 percent of the gross revenue." These stated percentages must exclude any amount which the charitable trust is to pay as expenses of the solicitation campaign, including the cost of merchandise or services sold or events staged.

Prohibited Acts.   These acts and practices are unlawful: (1) operating in violation of, or failing to comply with, any of the requirements of this law; utilizing any "unfair or deceptive acts or practices"; (3) utilizing any representation that implies that the contribution is for or on behalf of a charitable trust without first obtaining written authorization to do so by the charitable trust; (4) utilizing any emblem, device, or printed matter belonging to or associated with a charitable trust without first obtaining written authorization to do so by the charitable trust; (5) utilizing a name, symbol, or statement so closely related or similar to that used by another charitable trust that the use would tend to confuse or mislead a solicited person; (6) misrepresenting or misleading anyone to believe that a solicitation or commercial co-venture is for charitable purposes when that is not true; (7) misrepresenting or misleading anyone to believe that a person sponsors, endorses, or approves the endeavor when that is not true; (8) utilizing or exploiting the fact of registration to lead a person to believe that the state endorses or otherwise approves the solicitation; and (9) representing that a charitable trust will receive a fixed or estimated percentage of the gross revenue from a solicitation in an amount greater than that identified to the donor or pledger (see above).

A paid solicitor may not represent that contributions received will be given to a charitable trust unless the trust has consented, in writing and in advance of the solicitation, to the use of its name.

Accounts.   Each contribution in the custody of a paid solicitor must, in its entirety and within five days of its receipt, be deposited in an account at a federally insured financial institution. The account must be in the name of the charitable trust involved and the trust must have sole control over all withdrawals from the account.

Tickets.   A paid solicitor may not represent that tickets to an event are to be donated for use by another, unless the solicitor has first obtained a written commitment from one or more charitable trusts stating that it or they will accept donated tickets and specifying the number of tickets which it or they are willing to accept, and provided "[n]o more contributions for donated tickets shall be solicited than the number of ticket commitments received from charitable trusts."

Other.   There is a director of charitable trusts, who is an assistant attorney general. This individual shall have and exercise all of the common law and statutory rights, duties, and powers of the attorney general in connection with the supervision, administration, and enforcement of charitable trusts, charitable solicitations, and commercial co-venturing.

The attorney general is authorized to prepare and maintain a register of all charitable trusts established or active in the state. This register is open to public inspection at reasonable times and for "legitimate purposes."

Every person soliciting, collecting, or expending contributions for charitable purposes, and every officer, director, trustee, and employee of any such person concerned with the solicitation, collection, or expenditure of contributions, is deemed to be a fiduciary and acting in a fiduciary capacity.

A charitable trust may not indemnify an officer, employee, or director for any costs, fees, restitution, fines, or penalties assessed against that individual by a court (see below) unless the court determines that the individual "conducted himself [or herself] in good faith and reasonably believed the conduct was in or not opposed to the best interests of the charitable trust."

Sanctions

The attorney general may investigate charitable trusts, charitable solicitations, and commercial co-ventures to ascertain whether they are administered and conducted in conformance with this law.

The attorney general is empowered to suspend or revoke any registration, by a charitable trust, fund-raising counsel, or paid solicitor, where a registration statement, report, or other filing contains a false statement.

The attorney general is empowered to seek injunctions against and to otherwise prosecute all acts or practices declared a violation of this law. The attorney general is authorized to accept an "assurance of discontinuance" of any act or practice in violation of the law, which must be filed with the court, in lieu of seeking an injunction or otherwise proceeding with prosecution.

Upon finding a violation of this law, a court may order or award injunctions, restitution, reasonable lawyers' fees, costs of investigation and litigation, and civil penalties.

Civil penalties are provided for violation of the terms of an injunction or other order entered in conjunction with this law.

NEW JERSEY

Introduction

Comprehensive statute: Yes
Regulatory office(s): Attorney general
Citation: Chapter 469, New Jersey Statutes

Registration or Licensing Requirements

Charitable Organizations.   A charitable organization, unless exempt from the requirement, may not solicit contributions in the state of New Jersey unless, prior to any solicitation, the organization has registered with the state's attorney general.

The registration form must contain (1) the name of the organization; (2) the name or names under which it intends to solicit contributions; (3) the names and addresses of its officers, directors, trustees, and "executive personnel"; (4) the addresses of the organization and of any offices in the state, or otherwise the name and address of the person having custody of its financial records; (5) where and when the organization was legally established; (6) the form of its organization; (7) the tax-exempt status of the organization; (8) the purposes of the organization; (9) the purpose or purposes for which the contributions to be solicited will be used; (10) the date on which the fiscal year of the organization ends; (11) whether the organization is authorized by any other governmental authority to solicit contributions; (12) whether the organization is or has ever been enjoined by any court from soliciting contributions; and (13) the names and addresses of any professional fund-raisers who are acting or have agreed to act on behalf of the organization.

This registration remains in effect unless it is canceled (see Sanctions, below) or withdrawn by the attorney general. Any changes in the information provided are to be communicated to the attorney general within 10 days of the change. A registration will not continue in effect where the organization is delinquent in the filing of the requisite annual report (see below).

As discussed below (see Exemptions), a charitable organization, the total contributions to which during any year are $10,000 or less, is often exempt from this registration requirement. Nonetheless, an organization initially in this position must register with the attorney general within 30 days after the date on which the organization's total contributions exceeded $10,000.

Professional Fund-Raisers.   A person acting as a professional fund-raiser for a charitable organization that is subject to this law must register with the attorney general. This registration is effective for a period of one year and may be renewed for additional one-year periods.

A professional fund-raiser must file, and have approved by the attorney general, a bond in the amount of $10,000.

Professional Solicitors.   A person acting as a professional solicitor in the employ of a professional fund-raiser that is subject to this law must register with the attorney general. This registration is effective for a period of one year and may be renewed for additional one-year periods.

Annual Reporting Requirements

Charitable Organizations.   Every charitable organization that is registered under this law (see above) that receives more than $10,000 in any year, and every charitable organization that does not conduct its fund-raising solely by means of volunteers must annually report to the department. This report is due within six months of the close of the organization's fiscal year.

This annual report must include a financial statement, a balance sheet, and a schedule of activities. While these reports generally must be accompanied by an opinion of an independent public accountant, the attorney general has the authority to waive this requirement in the case of organizations that receive less than $50,000 annually.

A less comprehensive annual report is required of all other registered charitable organizations. An affidavit can be filed by organizations that are registered but that qualify for an exemption from the registration requirement (see above). A consolidated report can be filed by a parent organization and its chapters.

Professional Fund-Raisers.   A professional fund-raiser must file a report with the attorney general within 20 days after the completion of a "fund-raising event" (or at periodic intervals) for which the fund-raiser was retained.

Professional Solicitors.   There is no separate reporting requirement as such for professional solicitors.

Exemptions

The statute is inapplicable to religious corporations organized under state law, other religious agencies or organizations, and charities, agencies, and organizations operated, supervised, or controlled by or in connection with a religious organization.

The registration requirements are inapplicable to (1) accredited educational institutions or educational institutions otherwise approved by the state; (2) educational institutions that confine their solicitation of contributions to their student body, alumni, faculty, and trustees, and their families; (3) registered libraries; (4) fraternal, patriotic, social, alumni organizations, historical societies, and similar organizations organized under state law, where the solicitation is confined to their membership; (5) persons requesting any contributions for the relief of a specified individual, where all of the contributions are turned over to the beneficiary; (6) a charitable organization that does not receive contributions in excess of $10,000 during its fiscal year, where all of the fund-raising functions are carried on by volunteers; (7) certain charitable organizations that receive an allocation from an incorporated community chest or united fund; (8) state veterans' organizations, where all of the fund-raising is carried on by uncompensated members; (9) volunteer firefighter organizations, ambulance or rescue squads, or their affiliates, where all of the fund-raising is carried on by uncompensated members; and (10) organizations created under state law that operate for the care and treatment of invalid or crippled children.

Commercial Co-ventures

This law does not regulate commercial co-venturing.

Other Requirements

Contracts.   A contract between a professional fund-raiser or professional solicitor and a charitable organization must be filed with the attorney general within 10 days after the contract is concluded.

Record Keeping and Accounting. Registration applications (of charitable organizations, professional fund-raisers, and professional solicitors), financial reports, professional fund-raisers' contracts, bonds, and other documents required to be filed are public records in the office of the attorney general.

All records, books, and reports maintained by a charitable organization registered or required to register under this law must at all times be available for inspection by the attorney general.

A professional fund-raiser must maintain "accurate and current" books and records of activities. These materials must be retained for at least three years and made available for examination by the attorney general.

Other. A charitable organization, professional fund-raiser, or professional solicitor having his, her, or its principal place of business outside the state or organized under the law of another state, that solicits contributions in the state, is deemed to have appointed the secretary of state as its agent for purposes of service of process.

Unique Provisions

Percentages. See Sanctions, below.

Prohibited Acts. A person may not, for the purpose of soliciting contributions, use the name of another person (except that of an officer, director, or trustee of the charitable organization involved) without the written consent of the other person. A person is deemed to have used the name of another for solicitation purposes if the other person's name is listed on stationery, advertisements, brochures, or correspondence in or by which a contribution is solicited by or on behalf of a charitable organization or the other person's name is listed or referred to in connection with a request for a contribution as one who has contributed to, sponsored, or endorsed the charitable organization or its activities. However, a charitable organization can publish the names of contributors without their written consent, in an annual or other periodic report, issued for the purpose of reporting on its operations to its membership or for the purpose of reporting contributions to contributors.

A charitable organization that is required to be registered pursuant to this law may not employ a professional fund-raiser until the fund-raiser is registered under this law. A professional fund-raiser that is required to be registered pursuant to this law may not contract with or raise funds for a charitable organization that is required to be registered pursuant to this law until the charity is registered under this law. A professional fund-raiser that is required to be registered pursuant to this law may not employ a professional solicitor who is not registered under this law.

The failure of a person to immediately discontinue solicitation or to register in accordance with this law, following notification to do so from the attorney general, is deemed to be a "continuing fraud" upon the people of the state.

Sanctions

The attorney general is empowered to cancel the registration of a charitable organization, professional fund-raiser, or professional solicitor who fails to timely comply with the registration requirements or other provisions of this law (see above). Cancellation of a registration may also occur where (1) a solicitation involves any device, scheme, or artifice to defraud or for obtaining money or property by means of a false pretense, representation, or promise; (2) there is a material false statement in an application, registration, or statement required to be filed pursuant to this law; and (3) there is a solicitation of funds by mail where the solicitation includes the sending of goods, wares, or merchandise not ordered or requested by the recipient and less than 50 percent of the total amount of the funds so raised is or will be devoted to the purported purposes of the charitable organization.

The attorney general is empowered to bring legal actions to enjoin any violations of this law.

NEW MEXICO

Introduction

Comprehensive statute: No
Regulatory office(s): Attorney general
Citation: New Mexico Code, Title 57, Article 22

Registration or Licensing Requirements

Charitable Organizations.   A charitable organization, unless exempt from the requirement, may not solicit contributions in the state of New Mexico unless, prior to any solicitation, the organization has registered with the state's attorney general. This filing must include a copy of the document creating the organization and defining its purposes.

Professional Fund-Raisers.   There is no registration requirement for professional fund-raisers.

Professional Solicitors.   There is no registration requirement for professional solicitors.

Annual Reporting Requirements

Charitable Organizations.   Every charitable organization subject to this law must file an annual report.

Professional Fund-Raisers.   There is no reporting requirement for professional fund-raisers.

Professional Solicitors.   There is no reporting requirement for professional solicitors.

Exemptions

This law is inapplicable to religious organizations; universities, colleges, schools, and similar educational organizations; and charitable organizations that do not receive contributions in excess of $2,500 annually.

The registration and reporting requirements of this law are inapplicable to a local affiliate of a statewide or national organization for which all local fund-raising expenses are paid by the parent organization if the parent organization files the required report.

Commercial Co-ventures

This law does not regulate commercial co-venturing.

Other Requirements

Record Keeping and Accounting.   The attorney general is directed to maintain a register of all documents filed by charitable organizations in accordance with this law. This register is open to public inspection, although the attorney general may withhold from public inspection information obtained in the course of an investigation.

Unique Provisions

Disclosures.   When a solicitation is undertaken by a professional fund-raiser, that fact must be disclosed to prospective contributors.

Percentages.   A charitable organization subject to this law must disclose upon request the percentage of the funds solicited that are expended for fund-raising.

Prohibited Acts.   A solicitation of funds for charitable purposes may not use the fact or requirement of registration or the filing of a report under this law with the intent to cause or in a manner tending to cause any person to believe that the solicitation, the manner in which it is conducted, its purposes, any use to which the proceeds will be applied, or the person conducting it has been or will be in any way endorsed, sanctioned, or approved by any governmental agency.

Other.   All officers, directors, managers, trustees, or other persons having access to the funds of a charitable organization intended for use for charitable purposes is held to the standard of care defined for fiduciary trustees under common law.

Sanctions

The attorney general is authorized to examine and investigate a charitable organization that is subject to this law to "ascertain the conditions of its affairs and to what extent, if at all, it fails to comply with the trusts it has assumed or has departed from the purposes for which it is formed."

The attorney general has the authority to seek an injunction to enjoin a solicitation of funds where this law is being violated. He or she is also authorized to initiate appropriate proceedings to seek compliance with this law.

This law does not preclude any person or group of persons from asserting any private cause of action against a charitable organization.

NEW YORK

Introduction

Comprehensive statute: Yes
Regulatory office(s): Secretary of state
Citation: Article 7-A of the Executive Law

Registration or Licensing Requirements

Charitable Organizations. A charitable organization, unless exempt from the requirement, may not solicit contributions in the state of New York unless, prior to any solicitation, the organization has registered with the state's secretary of state.

This registration must contain the following information: (1) the name of the organization; (2) the names or names under which the organization intends to solicit contributions; (3) the names and addresses, "where each can regularly be found," of the organization's officers, directors, trustees, and executive personnel; (4) the addresses of the organization and the addresses of any offices in the state or, if an office is not maintained, the name and address of the person having custody of its financial records; (5) the date and place of its formation; (6) the form of the organization; (7) the tax-exempt status of the organization for federal income tax purposes; (8) copies of its certificate of incorporation, bylaws, other "operative organizational documents," and the determination from the IRS recognizing the organization's tax exemption; (9) a "clear description of the specific programs" of the organization, whether in existence or planned, for which the contributions to be solicited will be used; (10) the date on which the fiscal year of the organization ends; (11) whether the organization is authorized by any other governmental authority to solicit contributions, whether it (or any of its present officers, directors, trustees, or executive personnel) is or has ever been enjoined by any court from soliciting contributions, and whether its registration or license has been suspended or canceled by any governmental agency and, if so, the reasons for the suspension or cancellation; (12) the names and addresses of any professional fund-raisers, fund-raising counsels, and/or commercial co-venturers who are acting or have agreed to act on behalf of the organization; (13) a copy of its annual report, as required by this law, for the immediately preceding fiscal year; and (14) the names and addresses of any chapters, branches, affiliates, or organizations that share in the revenue raised in the state. A charitable organization must notify the secretary of state within 30 days of any material change in the information required to be furnished.

As discussed below, a charitable organization, the total contributions to which during a fiscal year are no more than $25,000, is often exempt from this registration requirement. Nonetheless, an organization initially in this position must register with the secretary of state within 30 days after the date on which the organization's total contributions exceeded $25,000.

A registration remains in effect unless it is canceled by the secretary of state (see below) or withdrawn by the organization. Nonetheless, a registration of a charitable organization may not continue in effect after the date the organization should have filed, but did not, an annual report (see below).

Professional Fund-Raisers.   A professional fund-raiser, acting on behalf of a charitable organization that is required to register, must register with the secretary of state. This registration is effective for a period of one year or a part thereof, expiring on August 31, and may be renewed for additional one-year periods. Any material change in the information required to be provided as part of this registration must be communicated to the secretary of state within 20 days.

A professional fund-raiser must file with and have approved by the secretary of state a bond in the amount of $10,000. This bond must run to the secretary of state and to any person that may have a cause of action against the fund-raiser for any "malfeasance or misfeasance in the conduct of" a solicitation.

A registration (but no bond) requirement is also imposed upon "fund-raising counsel."

Professional Solicitors.   A professional solicitor, in the employ of a professional fund-raiser that is required to register, must register with the secretary of state. This registration is effective for a period of one year or a part thereof, expiring on August 31, and may be renewed for additional one-year periods.

Annual Reporting Requirements

Charitable Organizations.   A charitable organization (1) that is registered under this law and that receives in any fiscal year total revenue in excess of $150,000 and (2) the fund-raising functions of which are not carried on solely by volunteers must file an annual written report with the secretary of state.

The report must include a financial statement for the year, setting forth gross income, expenses, and net income; a balance sheet as of the close of the year; a schedule of the activities carried on by the organization in the performance of its purposes; and the amounts expended for its purposes during the year. An organization must file its annual financial statement in accordance with "standards and classifications of accounts prescribed by the secretary to effect uniform reporting by organizations having similar activities and programs." These standards must be in accordance with generally accepted accounting principles.

This report must be executed by the president or other authorized officer, and the chief financial officer, of the organization. The report must be accompanied by an opinion signed by an independent public accountant that the financial statement and balance sheet "present fairly the financial operations and position of the organization."

An organization that is registered under this law and that receives in any fiscal year total revenue of at least $75,000 but not more than $150,000 must file an annual financial statement accompanied by an independent certified public accountant's review report. This statement must be prepared in accordance with generally accepted accounting principles. The report must include a statement of any changes in the information required to be contained in the registration form filed by the charitable organization.

An organization that is registered under this law and that receives in any fiscal year total revenue not in excess of $75,000 must file an unaudited financial report with the secretary. The report must include a statement of any changes in the information required to contained in the registration form filed by the charitable organization.

For any fiscal year of any organization registered under this law in which it was eligible for an exemption from registration, or in which it did not solicit or receive contributions, the organization must file, in lieu of the applicable report referenced above, a report stating the basis for the exemption or that contributions were not received or solicited. The report must include a statement of any changes in the information required to be contained in the registration form filed by the charitable organization.

Provision is made for the filing of combined reports for parent organizations and their affiliate organizations.

The secretary of state is authorized to accept a copy of a current annual report filed by a charitable organization with another government agency, in compliance with this law, as long as the report is "substantially similar in content" to the report required under this law.

Professional Fund-Raisers.   There is no annual report requirement for professional fund-raisers and fund-raising counsel. This is because the registration requirement, referenced above, is applicable annually.

Professional Solicitors.   There is no annual report requirement for professional solicitors. This is because the registration requirement, referenced above, is applicable annually.

Commercial Co-venturers.   There is no annual report requirement for commercial co-venturers. This is because the registration requirement, referenced above, is applicable annually.

Exemptions

Religious organizations are not required to comply with this law, nor are charities, agencies, and organizations operated, supervised, or controlled by or in connection with a religious organization.

The following persons are not required to register under this statute: (1) an educational institution confining its solicitation of contributions to its student body, alumni, faculty and trustees, and their families; (2) fraternal, patriotic, social, alumni organizations and historical societies chartered by the state's board of regents as long as solicitation of contributions is confined to their membership; (3) persons requesting any contributions for the relief of a named individual as long as all of the contributions collected are turned over to that individual; (4) charitable organizations that do not receive contributions in excess of $25,000 during a fiscal year as long as none of the fund-raising functions are carried on by professional fund-raisers or commercial co-venturers; (5) a charitable organization receiving an allocation from a federated fund, incorporated community appeal, or united way, as long as (a) the organization providing the allocation is in compliance with this law, (b) the organization does not receive, in addition to the allocation, contributions in excess of $25,000 during the fiscal year, and (c) all of the fund-raising functions of the organization are carried out by volunteers; (6)(a) a local post, camp, chapter, or similarly designated element, or a county unit of such elements, of a bona fide veterans' organization which issues charters to such local elements throughout the state, (b) a bona fide organization of volunteer firefighters, (c) an organization providing volunteer ambulance service, or (d) a bona fide auxiliary or affiliate of any of the foregoing organizations, as long as all of its fund-raising activities are carried on by its members, or an affiliate thereof, and the members do not receive any compensation for fund-raising services; (7) an educational institution that files annual financial reports with the regents of the University of the State of New York or with an agency having similar jurisdiction in another state; (8) a library which files annual financial reports as required by the state education department; and (9) a charitable organization that receives all or substantially all of its funds from a single governmental agency and reports annually to that agency, as long as (a) the reports contain financial information substantially similar in content to that which would otherwise be required under this law and (*b*) the organization does not receive more than $25,000 from sources other than the government agency to which it reports.

Commercial Co-ventures

This act regulates commercial co-venturing.

Other Requirements

Contracts.   A person may not act as a professional fund-raiser, fund-raising counsel, or commercial co-venturer without having a written contract with the charitable organization. Copies of contracts involving professional fund-raisers and fund-raising counsel must be filed with the secretary within 10 days of execution. In the case of a professional fund-raiser, services may not be performed until the contract is on file with the secretary for at least 15 days. Within 90 days after the termination of a contract, the professional fund-raiser must file with the secretary a "closing statement" disclosing gross receipts and all expenditures incurred in the performance of the contract.

Every contract between a professional fund-raiser or fund-raising counsel and a charitable organization must contain a clear statement of the financial arrangement, including (if applicable) a statement of the percentage of the total funds collected on behalf of the charitable organization to be retained by the professional fund-raiser for noncharitable purposes.

Whenever a charitable organization contracts with a professional fund-raiser or fund-raising counsel, the charitable organization has the right to cancel the contract, without any cost or penalty, for a period of 15 days. A copy of a notice of cancellation must be sent to the secretary of state. These rights and responsibilities as to cancellation must be conspicuously stated in the contract. Funds collected in violation of this rule are deemed to be held in trust for the charitable organization "without deduction for costs or expenses of any nature."

Record Keeping and Accounting.   Every charitable organization required to register under this law, and every professional fund-raiser, fund-raising counsel, and commercial co-venturer, must keep books and records for at least three years. These records must be open to inspection by the state's attorney general or secretary of state.

Applications for registration, financial reports, professional fund-raisers' contracts, and other filed documents become public records.

Other.   Provision is made for the manner in which service of process may be made upon a charitable organization, professional fund-raiser, fund-raising counsel, commercial co-venturer, or professional solicitor that solicits, but does not maintain an office, in the state. Under this provision, the secretary of state is deemed appointed agent for service of process.

Unique Provisions

Disclosures.   Every solicitation by a charitable organization that is required to file annual reports under this law must include a conspicuously placed statement that, upon request, a person may obtain from the organization or from the secretary of state a copy of the most recent annual report it has filed. A request must be responded to within 15 days.

Every solicitation used by or on behalf of a charitable organization must provide a clear description of the programs and activities for which it has requested or expended contributions or must include a statement that, upon request, a person may obtain the description from the organization. A request must be responded to within 15 days.

Accounts.   Every contract between a charitable organization and a professional fund-raiser must contain, or is deemed to contain, a provision that, within five days of receipt, all funds received from a solicitation shall be deposited in a bank account under the exclusive control of the charitable organization.

Prohibited Acts.   This law contains 18 categories of "prohibited activities." These include making untrue material statements in documents; engaging in a fraudulent or otherwise illegal act in connection with the solicitation of charitable gifts; failing to apply contributions in a manner "substantially consistent" with a solicitation; implying that the state endorses a solicitation; using the name or symbol of another charitable organization during a solicitation; soliciting contributions in a manner or with words that are "coercive"; and violating several of the provisions of this law.

Also, the law prohibits the use of the name of another person in conjunction with a charitable solicitation (other than that of an officer or director of the organization) without the written consent of the person.

It is further considered a "prohibited activity" to vote or use personal influence as an officer or member of the board of directors of a charitable organization, a majority of whose members are professional fund-raisers or their designees, on matters on which the officer or member has a financial or material conflicting interest.

Other. If a person violates a registration provision of this law and fails to comply after being notified by the attorney general, the ongoing failure to register or to solicit contributions is deemed to be a "continuing fraud upon the people of the state of New York." Another such continuing fraud occurs when a professional fund-raiser or commercial co-venturer fails to discontinue a solicitation once the charitable organization cancels the contract.

There is an advisory council on charities registration, which advises the secretary and makes recommendations with respect to the operation and administration of this law "with the objective of assuring maximum simplicity in the conformance of charitable organizations with" this law.

Sanctions

The state's attorney general has the authority to initiate investigations as part of enforcement of this charitable solicitation act. In this connection, he or she may take testimony, examine documents, and require the attendance of any person during an examination of documents. The attorney general also has the authority to pursue an injunction to restrain a violation of this law, as well as bring a cause of action in the state's supreme court.

The secretary of state is empowered to enforce a variety of provisions of this law, by revoking, suspending, or denying a registration or by denying a claim of exemption. The secretary may assess a civil penalty against a violator up to $1,000 for each act or omission constituting a violation, and an additional penalty of $100 per day for ongoing violations.

As noted, the attorney general also has enforcement responsibilities under this law and is empowered to initiate a variety of actions, including injunctive proceedings.

A violation of several of the provisions of this law is a misdemeanor.

NORTH CAROLINA

Introduction

Comprehensive statute: Yes
Regulatory office(s): Department of Human Resources, Social Services
                               Commission

Citation: General Statutes Chapter 108, Article 3, Part 1A, Chapter
        131C

Registration or Licensing Requirements

Charitable Organizations.   A charitable organization, unless exempt
from the requirement, may not solicit contributions in the state of North
Carolina unless, prior to any solicitation, the organization has obtained
a license from the state's department of human resources. This license
must be acquired annually.

An application for licensure must contain (1) the name and address
of the applicant; (2) the name and addresses of any other organizations,
including chapters and affiliates, that are to share in the solicitation
proceeds; (3) the date and place the organization was legally established;
(4) a reference to the organization's federal tax-exempt status; (5) copies
of the articles of incorporation, constitution, and/or bylaws; (6) copy of
the determination letter of tax exemption from the IRS; (7) copies of
any agreements of affiliation; (8) the names, addresses, and occupations
of the organization's officers, directors, trustees, other persons directly
in charge of the fund-raising activities, and persons who have custody
of the financial records or custody of the contributions; (9) a statement
indicating whether any of these individuals has been convicted of a
felony; (10) a copy of an audited financial statement (by a certified public
accountant where total revenue for the year exceeds $250,000); (11) a
statement indicating whether the organization is authorized to solicit
contributions in any other governmental jurisdiction; (12) a statement
indicating whether the organization, or any officer, professional fund-
raising counsel, or professional solicitor has ever been enjoined from
soliciting contributions; (13) a statement indicating whether the organization solicits gifts directly from the public or has solicitations done
on its behalf by others; (14) the location of the organization's financial
records; (15) the method by which the solicitation is made; (16) a narrative
description of the "promotional plan"; (17) copies of all "advertising
material"; (18) the location of all telephone solicitation activities; (19)
the names and addresses of any professional fund-raising counsel and
professional solicitors involved; (20) a statement of the terms of compensation of professional fund-raising counsel and professional solicitors;
(21) the period of time during which the solicitations are made and, if
less than statewide, the areas in which the solicitation will generally
take place; (22) the purposes for which the solicited contributions will
be used; (23) the total amount of funds proposed to be raised; (24) the

disposition to be made of the solicitation proceeds; (25) the name or names under which the organization solicits contributions; (26) a sample copy of the authorization issued to individuals soliciting for the organization by means of personal contact; (27) the name and address of an agent authorized to accept service of process in the state; (28) a statement indicating whether the organization has agreed to have its name used in a commercial co-venture; (29) a copy of any accounting of the outcome of the venture; and (30) such other information as may be reasonably required by the state's Social Services Commission.

Any changes in this information must be communicated to the department within 30 days of the change.

Once a application for a license has been filed, the solicitation can commence until and unless the department notifies the applicant that the application has been denied. If a license is denied, a solicitation may not commence until a new license is issued.

Professional Fund-Raisers. A professional fund-raiser (termed "professional fund raising counsel") must annually obtain a license from the department.

The application for this license must include (1) the name and address of all officers, employees, and agents, (2) the name and address of all persons who own at least a 10 percent interest in the applicant; and (3) a description of any other business conducted by the applicant or by any person who owns at least a 10 percent interest in the applicant. Any change in this information must be communicated to the department within seven days of the change.

A professional fund-raising counsel must obtain a bond in the amount of $10,000, unless counsel "does not personally receive any of the contributions collected and . . . does not personally handle any of the contributions expended."

Professional Solicitors. A professional solicitor must annually obtain a license from the department. The application for this license must contain the information required of applications filed by professional fund-raising counsel (see above).

The bonding requirements for professional solicitors are the same as those for professional fund-raising counsel (see above).

Annual Reporting Requirements

Charitable Organizations. There is no reporting requirement as such for charitable organizations. However, there is an annual reporting requirement in the sense that the license must be applied for annually (see above).

Professional Fund-Raisers.   There is no reporting requirement as such for professional fund-raising counsel. However, there is an annual reporting requirement in the sense that the license must be applied for annually (see above).

Professional Solicitors.   A professional solicitor must file with the department, within 20 days of conclusion of a solicitation, an accounting of all funds received, pledged, and disbursed.

Also, the license must be renewed annually (see above).

Exemptions

The requirement that a license be annually obtained is inapplicable to (1) a person soliciting contributions for a religious purpose or a religious organization; (2) solicitations by the federal, state, or local government, including agencies such as government-funded fire department or rescue squads; (3) a person receiving less than $10,000 in charitable contributions in a calendar year, as long as compensation is not provided to any officer, trustee, organizer, incorporator, fund-raiser, or professional solicitor; (4) an accredited educational institution; (5) an educational institution that is otherwise in compliance with state law; (6) a foundation or department having any "established identity" with either category of educational institution; (7) a state-licensed hospital, as long as its governing board authorizes the solicitation and receives an accounting of the collection and expenditure of the funds; and (8) a noncommercial radio or television station.

Commercial Co-ventures.   This law does not regulate commercial co-ventures, although it does require disclosure of a charitable organization's participation in a commercial co-venture (see above) (using the concept of a charitable sales promotion).

Other Requirements

Contracts.   A contract between a professional fund-raising counsel or professional solicitor and a charitable organization must be in writing and filed with the department within 10 days of its execution.

Record Keeping and Accounting.   Any person subject to licensure under this law must maintain accurate fiscal records.

Unique Provisions

Disclosures.   Any person subject to licensure under this law, or its state agent if the person subject to licensure is not a resident of the state, must disclose in writing the percentage of fund-raising expenses and the purpose of the organization, upon receipt of a written or oral request from the department or any citizen of the state.

Percentages.   See discussion under Disclosures (above).

Prohibited Acts.   A person soliciting contributions may not (1) use the fact of licensure as an endorsement by the state; (2) use the words "police," "law enforcement," "firemen," or "firefighter" unless a bona fide agency authorized use of the phraseology; (3) misrepresent or mislead anyone to believe that a contribution will be used for charitable purposes if that is not the case; (4) misrepresent or mislead anyone to believe that another person sponsors or endorses the solicitation unless that person has provided written consent; (5) misrepresent or mislead anyone to believe that the contribution is solicited on behalf of anyone other than the person for whose benefit the contribution is solicited; or (6) spend the contributions solicited for purposes other than those stated in the application or, if not subject to licensure, for purposes other than those stated at the time of the solicitation.

Other.   The department is authorized to enter into reciprocal agreements with other states and the federal government in connection with the administration of this law.

Sanctions

The department has the power to investigate anyone soliciting charitable contributions in the state. The department has the authority to compel examinations and to inspect documents. The department is empowered to seek injunctive relief in the courts.

The department has the authority to revoke or deny a license. Denial or revocation must occur if (1) the application is incomplete, (2) the application fee has not been paid, (3) the application contains one or more false statements, (4) the charitable contributions are not being applied for the purposes stated in the application, and/or (5) the application or licensee has failed to comply with this law. A notification process is provided where a denial or revocation of a license is contemplated.

Anyone who willfully violates any provision of this law is guilty of a misdemeanor.

NORTH DAKOTA

Introduction

Comprehensive statute: Yes
Regulatory office(s): Secretary of state, attorney general
Citation: Century Code, Chapter 50-22

Registration or Licensing Requirements

Charitable Organizations.   A charitable organization, unless exempt from the requirement, may not solicit contributions in the state of North Dakota unless, prior to any solicitation, the organization has obtained a license from the state's secretary of state.

The application for a license must include the following information: (1) the name and address of the charitable organization; (2) the purposes for which the contributions are to be used; (3) the individuals who will have custody of the contributions; (4) the individuals responsible for the distribution of the solicitation proceeds; (5) the period of time during which the solicitation is to be conducted; (6) a description of the methods of solicitation; (7) the name and address of any professional fund-raiser or professional solicitor, and the nature of the arrangement between the parties (including the basis of payment); and (8) such additional information as may be deemed necessary by the secretary of state.

Issuance of this license must be preceded by an investigation of the applicant's "financial responsibility, experience, character and general fitness" by the secretary of state. If the applicant satisfies the secretary that these criteria are met, that the solicitations are for a "worthy charitable purpose," that any professional fund-raiser or solicitor will act in con-formance with this law, and that the applicant will comply with this law, a license will be issued.

A license is valid for one year. The annual fee is dependent upon the amount raised and whether the services of a professional fund-raiser or professional solicitor are used.

Professional Fund-Raisers.   A person may not act as a professional fund-raiser for a charitable organization subject to this act unless the person has first registered with the secretary of state. This application process is annual.

The names and addresses of all officers, agents, and employees employed to work under the direction of a professional fund-raiser must be listed in the application.

Professional Solicitors.   The registration requirements for professional solicitors are the same as for professional fund-raisers (see above).

Annual Reporting Requirements

Charitable Organizations.   A charitable organization receiving contributions and subject to this law must, within 60 days following the close of its year, file an annual report. This report must contain the following information: (1) the gross amount of the contributions pledged or collected; (2) the amount of the solicitation proceeds given or to be given to the charitable programs involved; (3) the aggregate amount paid and to be paid for the expenses of the solicitation; and (4) the aggregate amount paid and to be paid to professional fund-raisers and professional solicitors.

Professional Fund-Raisers.   There are no reporting requirements as such for professional fund-raisers. However, there is a reporting requirement in the sense that licenses must be annually renewed.

Professional Solicitors.   There are no reporting requirements as such for professional solicitors. However, there is a reporting requirement in the sense that licenses must be annually renewed.

Exemptions

This law is inapplicable to (1) an organization soliciting funds for institutions of higher learning; (2) an organization soliciting funds for churches operating and having a place of worship in the state; and (3) a duly constituted religious organization or any group affiliated with and forming an integral part of the organization, as long as there is no private inurement of net earnings and the organization has received a determination letter as to tax-exempt status from the IRS (unless it is covered by a group exemption letter).

Commercial Co-ventures

This law does not regulate commercial co-venturing.

Other Requirements

Contracts.   Every contract between a professional fund-raiser or a professional solicitor and a charitable organization must be filed by the professional fund-raiser and charitable organization within 10 days after it is executed.

Record Keeping and Accounting.   Applications for licenses filed by charitable organizations are a matter of public record.

A charitable organization subject to this law must keep a "full and true record" so as to enable it to comply with this law.

Unique Provisions

Prohibited Acts.   No charitable organization, professional fund-raiser, or professional solicitor, or agent or employee of them, may use any deceptive act or practice, fraud, false pretense, false promise, or mis-representation, with the intent that others rely on it in connection with the solicitation of a contribution for or on behalf of a charitable organization.

Sanctions

The secretary of state has the authority to make a "detailed examination" of the accounts of a charitable organization soliciting funds in the state, and to deny or suspend applications for licenses or revoke licenses.

The secretary of state can seek the assistance of the attorney general in enforcing this law. The attorney general has the authority to seek injunctive relief to terminate acts or practices that are in violation of this law.

A person conducting a solicitation in violation of this law shall be guilty of a misdemeanor.

OHIO

Introduction

Comprehensive statute: No
Regulatory office(s): Attorney general, county clerk of courts
Citation: Revised Code, Chapter 1716

Registration or Licensing Requirements

Charitable Organizations. A person, unless an individual or exempt from the requirement, may not solicit contributions in the state of Ohio unless, prior to any solicitation, the person has registered with the state's attorney general or the county clerk of courts. If the solicitation is to be made in more than one county, the person has the option of filing with the attorney general or the county clerk of courts.

The application for registration must include the following information: (1) the name under which contributions are to be solicited; (2) the names and addresses of officers, directors, trustees, and executive personnel; (3) the names and addresses of any professional fund-raisers and professional solicitors who act or will act on behalf of the person; (4) a statement of the terms of the arrangements for salaries, bonuses, commissions, or other remunerations to be paid a professional fund-raiser or professional solicitor; (5) the general purposes for which the person is organized; (6) the purposes for which the contributions to be solicited will be used; (7) the period of time during which the solicitation is to be conducted; and (8) the written consent of any existing person for which the solicitation is made.

A registration is effective as long as the information on file remains complete, accurate, and current. However, a registration must be effective for at least one year.

A charitable organization directing and conducting a joint campaign with the consent of and for the benefit of two or more charitable organizations in which it is contemplated that the organization will participate in the proceeds may file a consolidated registration and report for the participating charitable organizations.

Professional Fund-Raisers. A person may not act as a professional fund-raiser for a person that is required to register (see above) until he, she, or it has first registered with the attorney general. Registration is for a period of one year, or a part thereof, expiring at the end of March, and may be renewed annually.

The applicant must file, and have approved by the attorney general, a bond in the amount of $5,000.

Professional Solicitors. Every professional solicitor employed or retained by a professional fund-raiser that is required to register (see above) must, before accepting employment by the fund-raiser, register with the attorney general. This registration is for a period of one year, or a part thereof, expiring at the end of March, and may be renewed annually.

Annual Reporting Requirements

Charitable Organizations.   Every person that is required to register (see above), which has received contributions during the preceding calendar year, must, within 90 days following the close of each year, file a written report with the clerk of courts of each county where the solicitation was conducted, or with the attorney general if the solicitation was made in more than one county, at the option of the person.

This report must include (1) a financial statement covering the preceding fiscal year of operation; (2) the gross income, expenses, and net amount accruing to the charitable organization involved; (3) the names of professional fund-raisers and professional solicitors used during the year; and (4) the amounts of compensation received by professional fund-raisers and solicitors.

Professional Fund-Raisers.   In addition to the above requirement, the annual registration requirement for professional fund-raisers (see above) is the equivalent of an annual reporting mandate.

Professional Solicitors.   In addition to the above requirement, the annual registration requirement for professional solicitors is the equivalent of an annual reporting mandate.

Exemptions

This law does not apply to religious organizations or to charitable organizations operated, supervised, or controlled by a religious organization.

The registration requirements are not applicable to (1) an educational institution, when solicitation is confined to alumni, faculty, trustees, or the student membership and their families; (2) an organization where a solicitation for a charitable purpose is confined to its membership; (3) a person requesting any contributions for the relief of a specified individual, if all of the contributions collected, without any deductions, are distributed to the named beneficiary; (4) any person, when contemplated fund-raising expenses of a solicitation will not exceed $500 in a year; (5) an individual acting as an agent of a person required to register or a person exempt from registration; or (6) any other individual.

Commercial Co-ventures

This law does not regulate commercial co-venturing.

Other Requirements

Contracts.   A contract entered into by a professional fund-raiser with persons required to register (see above) must be in writing. This contract must be available for inspection and examination by the attorney general.

Record Keeping and Accounting.   A true and correct copy of a contract between a professional fund-raiser and a person required to register (see above) must be kept on file in the offices of the professional fund-raiser for a period of three years from the date of the report of the solicitation.

Other.   The reports filed by those required to register (see above) are public records.

Sanctions

Whoever violates a provision of this law may be fined up to $500 or imprisoned for six months, or both.

OKLAHOMA

Introduction

Comprehensive statute: Yes
Regulatory office(s): Tax commission
Citation: Title 18, §§ 552.1–552.18, Oklahoma Statutes

Registration or Licensing Requirements

Charitable Organizations.   A charitable organization, unless exempt from the requirement, may not solicit contributions in the state of Oklahoma unless, prior to any solicitation, the organization has registered with the state's tax commission. This registration is valid for one year and may be renewed.

The application for registration must include the following: (1) the name under which the charitable organization intends to solicit or accept contributions; (2) the identity of the charitable organization by or for whom the solicitation is to be conducted; (3) the address of the charitable organization; (4) the names and addresses of the organization's officers, directors, trustees, and executive personnel; (5) the purposes for which the contributions solicited or accepted are to to used; (6) the person who will have custody of the contributions; (7) the persons responsible for the distribution of funds collected; (8) the period of time during which the solicitation is to be conducted; (9) a description of the method or methods of solicitation; (10) whether the solicitation is to be conducted by voluntary unpaid solicitors, by paid solicitors, or both; (11) if the solicitation is to be conducted, in whole or in part, by paid solicitors, the name and address of each professional fund-raiser supplying the solicitors, the basis of payment and the nature of the arrangement (including a copy of the contract between the charitable organization and the professional fund-raiser), the specific amount or percentage of compensation, or property of any kind or value to be paid or paid to the professional fund-raiser, and the percentage value of the compensation as compared (*a*) to the total contributions received; and (*b*) to the net amount of the total contributions received; and (12) such additional information as may be deemed "necessary and appropriate" by the commission in the public interest or for the specific protection of contributors.

A charitable organization (or a professional fund-raiser or professional solicitor) may not be registered under this law where the board of directors of the charitable organization would not have "full control" of all funds collected.

Professional Fund-Raisers.   A person may not act as a professional fund-raiser for a charitable organization, including those that are exempt (see below), until he or she has first registered with the commission. Registration is for a period of one year and is renewable.

The applicant must file with and have approved by the commission a bond in the amount of $2,500.

Professional Solicitors.   A professional solicitor employed or retained by a professional fund-raiser required to register must, before accepting employment by the fund-raiser, register with the commission. Registration is for a period of one year and is renewable.

Annual Reporting Requirements

Charitable Organizations.   Every charitable organization that has received contributions during the previous calendar year must, unless exempt from the requirement (see below), file a report with the commission. This report must contain (1) the gross amount of the contributions pledged or collected; (2) the amount of the contributions given or to be given to the charitable purpose involved; (3) the aggregate amount paid and to be paid for the expenses of the solicitation; and (4) the aggregate amount paid to and to be paid to professional fund-raisers and professional solicitors. This report is due within 90 days following the close of the organization's fiscal year.

The commission is empowered to require that, within 90 days after the close of any "special period of solicitation," an organization file a "special report" with the commission.

Professional Fund-Raisers.   There is no separate reporting requirement for professional fund-raisers. However, registration must be accomplished annually, so that, in effect, there is a reporting requirement.

Professional Solicitors.   There is no separate reporting requirement for professional solicitors. However, registration must be accomplished annually, so that, in effect, there is a reporting requirement.

Exemptions

The registration and reporting requirements of this law are inapplicable to (1) organizations incorporated for religious purposes and "actually engaged" in bona fide religious programs; (2) other organizations directly operated, supervised, or controlled by a religious organization; (3) educational institutions that have a faculty, regularly enrolled students, and offer courses of study leading to the granting of recognized degrees, when solicitations are confined to the institution's student body and their families, alumni, faculty, and trustees; (4) fraternal organizations when soliciting from their own members and where the solicitation is managed by their own membership without paid solicitors; (5) patriotic and civic organizations when soliciting from their own members and where the solicitation is managed by their own membership without paid solicitors; (6) persons soliciting contributions for a named person when the person is specified by name at the time of solicitation, the purpose for the contribution is clearly stated, and if the gross contributions solicited, without any deductions whatsoever for the benefit of the solicitor or any other person, be deposited to an account in the name of the beneficiary established for that purpose at a licensed local bank, and if the contributions are used for the direct benefit of the named individual person as beneficiary; and (7) any organization that collects from charitable solicitations less than $10,000 per year.

Commercial Co-ventures

This law does not regulate commercial co-venturing.

Other Requirements

Contracts. All contracts entered into by charitable organizations and professional fund-raisers must be in writing. "True and correct" copies of the agreement must be kept on file in the offices of the parties for at least three years. Contracts must be available for inspection and examination by the commission and other authorized agencies. Contracts are a matter of public record. A contract is not valid until prior approval of it is given by the commission.

Record Keeping and Accounting. Every charitable organization must keep a "full and true" record as will enable it to accurately provide the information required by this law. All records mandated by the law must be open to inspection at all times by the commission.

The information filed as part of the registration process is available to the general public as a matter of public record, as is the information filed as annual or special reports.

Also, see Contracts, above.

Other. The commission is authorized to enter into reciprocal agreements with like authorities in other states for the purpose of exchanging information concerning fund-raising charities. The commission may accept information filed by a charitable organization with another state in lieu of the information required under this law where the information is substantially similar to the information required to be filed under this law.

Provision is made for the designation of the secretary of state as agent for service of process in the case of out-of-state charitable organizations, professional fund-raisers, or professional solicitors.

Unique Provisions

Percentages. A charitable organization, professional solicitor, or professional fund-raiser may not be registered under this law where the professional fund-raiser or professional solicitor would receive more than 10 percent of the net receipts from the solicitation of contributions, nor where the charitable organization involved would receive less than 90 percent of the receipts.

Also, see Registration Requirements, above.

Prohibited Acts.   A person seeking to raise funds for charitable purposes may not use the name of another person (except that of an officer, director, or trustee of the charity involved) for the purpose of soliciting contributions without the written consent of the other person. However, a charitable organization may, without consent, publish the names of contributors in an annual or other periodic report for the purpose of reporting to its membership or for the purpose of reporting contributions to contributors.

A charitable organization soliciting or accepting contributions may not use a name so closely related or similar to other charitable organizations or governmental bodies that the use would tend to confuse or mislead the public.

A person may not use the name of any other person (except that of an officer, director, or trustee of the charity involved) for the purpose of soliciting contributions if the other person's name is listed on any stationery, advertisement, brochure, or correspondence in or by which a contribution is solicited by or on behalf of a charitable organization or his or her name is listed or referred to in connection with a request for a contribution as one who has contributed to, sponsored, or endorsed the charitable organization or its activities.

No contribution or any portion thereof may inure to the private benefit of any voluntary solicitor.

Registration under this statute may not be deemed to constitute endorsement by the state of the registered charitable organization.

Other.   A person soliciting or accepting funds for charitable purposes must issue a receipt in duplicate when the amount of the contribution is in excess of two dollars. The original of the receipt must be given to the donor and the copy to the charitable organization, which must retain it for at least three years.

This law does not exempt any person from any ordinances and restrictions of political subdivisions of the state regulating solicitations for charitable purposes.

Sanctions

An action for violation of this law may be prosecuted by a district attorney of the state or by the state's attorney general. The district attorneys and attorney general are empowered to seek injunctions to restrain violations of this law, as well restrain the employment of any device, scheme, or artifice to defraud or an attempt to obtain money or property by means of any false pretense, representation, or promise.

The commission must immediately revoke the registration of any person who directly or indirectly misrepresents the effect of registration under this law to any donor or prospective donor.

A person who solicits or attempts to solicit any contributions as a charitable organization, or for a charitable purpose by means of knowingly false or misleading representation, advertisement, or promise, or any person violating the provisions of this law, including the filing of false information, must lose its status as a tax-exempt organization and shall upon conviction be punished by a fine not in excess of $1,000 or imprisonment for not more than two years, or both. Every officer or agent of a charitable organization who authorizes or conducts illegal solicitations must be jointly and severally liable for the fine.

OREGON

Introduction

Comprehensive statute: Yes
Regulatory office(s): Attorney general
Citation: Revised Statutes §§ 128.801–128.898

Registration or Licensing Requirements

Charitable Organizations.   There is no registration requirement for charitable organizations under this law.

Professional Fund-Raisers.   There is no registration requirement for professional fund-raisers (termed "professional fund raising counsel").

Professional Solicitors.   A person may not engage in a solicitation for contributions for or on behalf of a professional solicitor (termed "professional fund raising firm") unless the solicitor (firm) is registered with the attorney general. A registration is valid for one year and is renewable.

The application for registration must include the following information: (1) the address of the principal place of business of the applicant and any local addresses if the principal place of business is not located within the state; (2) the form of the applicant's organization; (3) the names and personal addresses of all principals of the organization, including all officers and those who own at least a 10 percent interest in the organization; (4) the name of any person who is in charge of any solicitation activities; and (5) the account number and location of all of the organization's bank accounts.

Any change in the information contained in the application must be communicated to the attorney general within seven days of the change.

Annual Reporting Requirements

Charitable Organizations. A charitable organization, unless exempt from the requirement, that solicits contributions in the state must file a "detailed report" to the attorney general. The report must be filed within 4½ months of the organization's financial year.

This report must show (1) the amount of funds received from fund-raising activities; (2) all expenditures for supplies, equipment, goods, services, or other expenses; (3) a "detailed list" of all salaries and wages paid and expenses allowed to any officer, employee, or agent, each of whom must be identified by name; and (4) the disposition of the net proceeds received from fund-raising activities.

Professional Fund-Raisers. There is no reporting requirement for professional fund-raising counsel.

Professional Solicitors. Within 90 days after the completion of a solicitation campaign, a professional fund-raising firm must file with the attorney general a financial report for the campaign, including gross receipts and all expenditures incurred in the campaign. A similar report must be filed one year after the start of a solicitation in the case of a campaign still in progress on that date.

In addition, the annual registration requirement (see above) is the substantive equivalent to annual reporting.

Exemptions

This law is inapplicable to the United States, any state, territory, or possession of the United States, the District of Columbia, the commonwealth of Puerto Rico, or to any of their agencies or governmental subdivisions.

The following categories of organizations need not comply with the reporting requirement: (1) an educational institution, hospital, historical society, museum, church, or other religious organization soliciting funds solely for its own use; (2) an educational institution, community college, higher education foundation, hospital, historical society, museum, church, other religious organization, or "similar [religious] society" soliciting funds, including membership fees or dues, solely from its members, or persons otherwise presently affiliated with the church, religious organization, or society; (3) an institution of higher education, community college, or foundation supporting higher education; (4) a local affiliate of a statewide or national organization, when all local fund-raising expenses are paid by the parent organization, if the parent files the requisite report; or (5) an organization that solicits contributions of $5,000 or less in any 12-month period.

Commercial Co-ventures

This law does not regulate commercial co-venturing, although it contains a definition of the term.

Other Requirements

Contracts. A contract between a charitable organization and a professional fund-raising firm must be in writing. The agreement must provide for a minimum percentage of the gross receipts of the campaign to be paid to the charity. This percentage must exclude any amount which the charitable beneficiary is to pay as expenses of the fund-raising campaign pursuant to the contract, including all costs of merchandise or services sold or fund-raising events staged.

At least 10 days before the commencement of a solicitation, the professional fund-raising firm involved must file with the attorney general a copy of the contract between the firm and the charity (see above).

Record Keeping and Accounting. A professional fund-raising firm must maintain for a period of at least three years from the completion of a fund-raising campaign the following records: (1) the name and address of each contributor, (2) the date and the amount of each contribution, (3) the name and address of any paid solicitor, (4) the dates and amount of compensation paid to any solicitor, and (5) records of all fund-raising expenses incurred in the course of the fund-raising campaign.

These records and those pertaining to tickets (see below) must be available for inspection by the attorney general upon request.

Unique Provisions

Disclosures.   A person may not engage in solicitations for contributions for or on behalf of a professional fund-raising firm unless, prior to an oral solicitation and simultaneously with a written solicitation, the solicitor or solicitation discloses (1) the name of the professional fund-raising firm, (2) that it is being paid to conduct the solicitation on behalf of the charitable organization, and (3) that each charitable beneficiary will receive the appropriate percentage of gross receipts (see Contracts, above).

In the case of a solicitation conducted orally, all contributors must receive, within 10 days after making a pledge to contribute, a written statement which shall include a "clear and conspicuous" disclosure of the foregoing information.

Percentages.   See Contracts (above) and Prohibited Acts (below).

Accounts.   All funds collected by a professional fund-raising firm shall be deposited in a bank account. The bank account must be in the name of the charitable organization involved and the charity must have sole or joint control of the account.

Prohibited Acts.   A person may not make a false or misleading representation in the course of a solicitation of contributions. A misleading representation includes a solicitation of contributions by a charitable organization when it knows or should know that less than 50 percent of the net proceeds will be used by it for program activities, unless it discloses in the solicitation (see above) the estimated percentage of the net proceeds that will be used in its program activities.

A person soliciting for or on behalf of a professional fund-raising firm may not represent that any part of the contributions received will be given to a charitable organization unless the organization has consented in writing to the use of its name prior to the solicitation.

No solicitation for contributions may in any way use the fact or requirement of registration, or the filing of any report, with the intent to cause or in a manner tending to cause any person to believe that the solicitation, the manner in which it is conducted, its purposes, any use to which the proceeds will be applied, or the person conducting it have been or will be in any way endorsed, sanctioned, or approved by the attorney general or any other governmental agency or office.

Tickets.   A professional fund-raising firm may not represent, in the course of its solicitation activities, that tickets to events will be donated for use by another unless it has complied with the following requirements: (1) the firm must obtain commitments, in writing, from beneficiaries stating that they will accept donated tickets and specifying the number of tickets they are willing to accept; (2) the firm may not solicit and accept more contributions of tickets than the number of ticket commitments it has received from beneficiaries; and (3) a ticket commitment alone may not constitute written consent to use the organization's name (see above).

If a professional fund-raising firm sells tickets to an event and represents that tickets will be donated for use by another, the firm must maintain, for at least three years, the following records: (1) the name and address of those who donate tickets, (2) the number of tickets donated by each contributor, and (3) the name and address of all organizations receiving donated tickets, including the number of tickets received by each organization.

Other.   At least 10 days prior to the commencement of a solicitation, the professional fund-raising firm involved must file with the attorney general a completed "fund raising notice." This notice must include (1) a description of the fund-raising event or campaign; (2) the projected starting and ending dates of the campaign; and (3) the location (address and telephone number) where the campaign will be conducted, and must require that copies of campaign solicitation literature (including solicitation scripts) be attached and that the professional fund-raising firm affirm that the solicitation material has been approved by all beneficiaries.

Any written or oral statement made in connection with a solicitation of contributions that the person conducting the solicitation is registered or has filed, will file, or is required to file any report with the attorney general, or any statement of similar import, must be immediately followed by a statement of "equal prominence" that the registration or report does not constitute or imply any endorsement, sanction, or approval of the solicitation, its purposes, the manner in which it is conducted, or the person conducting it, by the attorney general or any other governmental agency or officer.

Sanctions

The attorney general may deny or revoke a registration if it is found that there is a material misrepresentation or false statement in any statement filed with the attorney general or a material violation of the provisions concerning registration of a professional fund-raising firm, the content and filing of contracts between a charitable organization and a professional fund-raising firm, the filing of fund-raising notice by a professional fund-raising firm, the disclosures required of a professional fund-raising firm, the financial reports required of a professional fund-raising firm, the maintenance of records by a professional fund-raising firm, the bank account requirements, the written consent requirements, and prohibited acts.

The attorney general is empowered to obtain an injunction against a solicitation of contributions until the charitable organization or professional fund-raising firm has complied with all of the registration and reporting requirements of this law.

A violation of the registration requirement imposed upon those who solicit contributions for or on behalf of a professional fund-raising firm or the filing or assisting in preparing or filing a statement or report required by this law that is false or fraudulent is a misdemeanor.

PENNSYLVANIA

Introduction

Comprehensive statute: Yes
Regulatory office(s): Department of state
Citation: Act No. 1983-36

Registration or Licensing Requirements

Charitable Organizations.   A charitable organization, unless exempt from the requirement, may not solicit contributions in the state of Pennsylvania unless, prior to any solicitation, the organization has registered with the state's department of state.

The requisite registration statement must contain (1) the name of the organization; (2) the purpose for which the organization was organized; (3) the principal address of the organization and the address of any offices in the state or, if there is no office, the name and address of the person having custody of its financial records; (4) the names and addresses of any chapters, branches, or affiliates in the state; (5) the place where and date when the organization was legally established; (6) the form of its organization; (7) a reference to any recognition of its tax-exempt status by the IRS; (8) the names and addresses of the officers, directors, trustees, and the principal salaried executive staff officer; (9) a copy of the financial statements of the charitable organization's immediate preceding fiscal year; (10) information about whether the organization intends to solicit contributions from the public directly or have the fund-raising done on its behalf by others; (11) information about whether the organization is authorized by any other governmental authority to solicit contributions; (12) information about whether the organization is or has ever been enjoined by any court from soliciting contributions; (13) the general purpose or purposes for which the contributions to be solicited shall be used; (14) the name or names under which the organization intends to solicit contributions; (15) the names of the individuals of the organization who will have final responsibility for the custody of the contributions; and (16) the names of the individuals responsible for the final distribution of the contributions.

A chapter, branch, or affiliate may separately report the required information or report the information to the parent organization which shall furnish the information in a consolidated form to the department.

As to the financial statements, where the gross contributions of the organization are in excess of $15,000 but are less than $50,000, the financial statements must be audited or reviewed by an independent public accountant or an independent certified public accountant. Where the gross contributions exceed $50,000, the financial statements must be audited by an independent public accountant or an independent certified public accountant. The financial statements must be completed in accordance with accounting standards promulgated by the department. All audits and reviews must be performed in accordance with the American Institute of Certified Public Accountants standards.

The department has the discretion to require the submission of an audit or review by a charitable organization when it files a registration statement. It also has the discretion to accept the organization's financial statements in lieu of an audit or review in the event of "special facts and circumstances."

This registration is in effect for one year and may be renewed.

Professional Fund-Raisers. A person may not act as a professional fund-raiser (termed "professional fund-raising counsel") for a charitable organization subject to this law unless he, she, or it has first registered with the department. A partnership or corporation that is a professional fund-raiser may register on behalf of all its members, officers, agents, and employees. This registration is valid for one year and is renewable.

The fund-raiser must file with and have approved by the department a bond in the amount of $10,000. A partnership or corporation that is a professional fund-raiser may file a consolidated bond on behalf of all its members, officers, and employees.

Professional Solicitors.   The reporting and bonding requirements for professional solicitors are the same as those for professional fund-raising counsel (see above).

Annual Reporting Requirements

Charitable Organizations.   There are no separate annual reporting requirements for charitable organizations. However, the annual registration requirement operates as an annual reporting requirement.

Professional Fund-Raisers.   There are no separate annual reporting requirements for professional fund-raisers. However, the annual registration requirement operates as an annual reporting requirement.

Professional Solicitors.   There are no separate annual requirements for professional solicitors. However, the annual registration requirement operates as an annual reporting requirement.

Exemptions

This statute is inapplicable to a duly constituted religious organization or any group affiliated with and forming an integral part of such an organization, where no part of the net income of the organization inures to the direct benefit of any individual and where the organization has received recognition of tax-exempt status from the IRS.

The following organizations are exempt from the registration requirements of this law: (1) educational institutions, the curriculums of which in whole or in part are properly accredited; (2) hospitals that are charitable and that are required to file financial reports with the state's auditor general; (3) a local post, camp, chapter, or "similarly designated element" or a "country unit" of such elements of a bona fide veterans' organization which issues charters to the local elements throughout the state, as long as the fund-raising is conducted by volunteer members; (4) a bona fide organization of volunteer firefighters, as long as the fund-raising is conducted by volunteer members; (5) a bona fide ambulance association, as long as the fund-raising is conducted by volunteer members; (6) a bona fide rescue squad association, as long as the fund-raising is conducted by volunteer members; (7) a bona fide auxiliary or affiliate of an organization referenced in (3), (4), (5), or (6), as long as the fund-raising is conducted by volunteer members; (8) public nonprofit library organizations that receive financial aid from municipal and state governments and file an annual fiscal report with the state's library system; (9) charitable senior citizen centers that are tax-exempt under federal law, where all fund-raising activities are carried on by volunteer members or officers of the organization; and (10) bona fide parent/teacher associations or organizations as recognized in a notarized letter from the school district in which they are located.

Certain organizations file a "short form annual registration statement." These are (1) persons requesting contributions for the relief of any individual specified by name at the time of solicitation when all of the contributions collected are turned over to the named beneficiary; (2) charitable organizations that do not intend to solicit and do not actually receive contributions from the public in excess of $15,000 during a calendar year and if no part of their assets or income inures to the benefit of or is paid to any officer or member (with registration required within 30 days where that threshold is exceeded); and (3) organizations that solicit only within their membership by the members of the organization.

Commercial Co-ventures

This statute does not regulate commercial co-venturing.

Other Requirements

Contracts. A contract between a charitable organization and a professional fund-raiser must be filed with the secretary within 10 days after the contract is executed.

A contract between a charitable organization and a professional solicitor must be filed with the secretary within 10 days after the contract is executed. If the contract does not provide for compensation on a percentage basis, the department must examine the contract to ascertain whether the compensation to be paid is likely to exceed 15 percent of the contributions received; if the "reasonable probabilities" are that the compensation will exceed 15 percent of contributions received, the secretary must disapprove the contract. A registered charitable organization or professional solicitor may not carry out or execute a disapproved contract or receive or perform services, or receive or make payments, pursuant to a disapproved contract.

Record Keeping and Accounting.   Registration statements and applications, reports, contracts, and all other documents and information required to be filed under this law become public records.

Every charitable organization subject to this law must keep "true fiscal records" as to its activities in the state in such form as will enable it accurately to provide the required information. These records are available to the state for inspection upon demand and must be maintained for at least three years.

Unique Provisions

Percentages.   A charitable organization may not pay or agree to pay to a professional solicitor or the solicitor's agents, servants, or employees in the aggregate a total amount in excess of 15 percent, including reimbursement for expenses incurred and direct payment of expenses incurred, of the contributions received.

Generally, a charitable organization may not incur solicitation and fund-raising expenses in excess of 35 percent of contributions received. The department has the discretion to allow higher fund-raising expenditures where "special facts and circumstances" are presented. For this purpose, fund-raising expenses do not include the amount expended for postage. The department is empowered to review applications for registration and to disapprove them where this percentage limitation is exceeded.

Also see Contracts (above).

Prohibited Acts.   A charitable organization, professional fund-raising counsel, or professional solicitor, subject to this law, may not use or exploit the fact of registration so as to lead the public to believe that registration constitutes an endorsement or approval by the state.

A person may not, in connection with the solicitation of contributions for or the sale of goods or services of a person other than a charitable organization, misrepresent to or mislead anyone to believe that the person on whose behalf the solicitation or sale is being conducted is a charitable organization or that the proceeds of the solicitation or sale will be used for charitable purposes, if that is not the fact.

A person may not, in connection with the solicitation of contributions for or the sale of goods or services for charitable purposes, represent to or lead anyone to believe that any other person sponsors or endorses the solicitation of contributions, sale of goods or services for charitable purposes, or approves of the charitable purposes or the charitable organization, when that other person has not consented to use of his, her, or its name for these purposes. A member of the governing board of a charitable organization or a volunteer in the solicitation campaign is deemed to have given this consent.

A person may not make a representation that he, she, or it is soliciting contributions for or on behalf of a charitable organization, or may not use any emblem, device, or printed material belonging to a charitable organization for the solicitation of contributions, without first being authorized to do so by the charitable organization.

A charitable organization, professional fund-raiser, commercial co-venturer, professional solicitor, or other person soliciting gifts for a charitable organization may not use a name, symbol, or registered service mark that is closely similar to that used by another charitable organization, either registered in the state or a national organization with a chapter or affiliate in the state, or a governmental agency, where the use would tend to confuse or mislead the public.

Other.   A charitable organization may not solicit funds from the public except for charitable purposes and may not expend funds raised for charitable purposes for noncharitable purposes.

A professional solicitor may not solicit in the name of a charitable organization unless the solicitor has (1) written authorization from the organization, a copy of which is filed with the department, and which may not extend beyond one year; and (2) the authorization at the time of making solicitations and exhibits it on request to those solicited, police officers, or agents of the department.

A person soliciting contributions for the benefit of a named individual who receives gifts in excess of $5,000 must hold the funds in trust and is subject to the state's law concerning trust estates.

The department is authorized to enter into reciprocal agreements with other states for the purpose of exchanging information with respect to charitable organizations, professional fund-raising counsel, and professional solicitors. The department can accept information filed with another state in lieu of information required under this act, where the information is substantially similar to the information required under this act. The department can grant exemption from the annual registration requirement (see above) to charitable organizations organized under the law of another state having their principal operations outside this state, the funds of which are derived principally from sources outside the state and which have been granted the exemption under the other state's law, if the other state has a statute similar in substance to this law.

This law establishes within the department a bureau of charitable operations which has the responsibility for effectuating this law. The law also establishes an advisory board to "offer advice or consultation regarding registration and/or regulation of charitable organizations" in the state.

Sanctions

The department is authorized to investigate an applicant. An applicant may not be approved if (1) one or more of the statements in it are not true; (2) the applicant is or has engaged in a fraudulent transaction or enterprise; (3) the solicitation would be a fraud upon the public; (4) the fund-raising expenses are too high (see Percentages, above); or (5) the activities to be financed will be incompatible with the health, safety, or welfare of the citizens of the state.

The department also is authorized to investigate a registered person and may cancel, suspend, or refuse to accept the registration of a charitable organization, professional fund-raising counsel, or professional solicitor that fails to timely file information with the department. A registration that contains false information may be revoked.

The attorney general or a district attorney who believes a person is operating in violation of this law or where fraudulent fund-raising is to occur or is occurring is authorized to bring court action to enjoin the violation or other practice.

A person who willfully and knowingly violates a provision of this law or who willfully and knowingly provides false information to the department is guilty of a misdemeanor. The punishment for a first offense is a fine of at least $100 and not more than $500 and/or six months' imprisonment. The punishment for any subsequent offense is a fine of at least $500 and no more than $1,000 and/or imprisonment for one year.

RHODE ISLAND

Introduction

Comprehensive statute: Yes
Regulatory office(s): Department of Business Regulation, attorney general
Citation: General Laws, Title 5, Chapter 53

Registration or Licensing Requirements

Charitable Organizations.   A charitable organization, unless exempt from the requirement, may not solicit contributions in the state of Rhode Island unless, prior to any solicitation, the organization has registered with the state's department of business regulation. This rule expressly also embraces solicitations on behalf of a charitable organization by a professional fund-raiser, professional solicitor, or one or more other charitable organizations. This registration is valid for one year and may be renewed by filing a registration statement within 90 days subsequent to the end of its fiscal year.

A registration statement must contain the following information: (1) the name of the organization; (2) the purpose for which it was organized; (3) the principal address of the organization and the address of any offices in the state or, if the organization does not maintain an office, the name and address of the person having custody of its financial records; (4) the names and addresses of any chapters, branches, or affiliates in the state; (5) the place where and the date when the organization was legally established; (6) the form of the organization; (7) a reference to any determination of its tax-exempt status under federal law; (8) the names and addresses of the officers, directors, trustees, and the principal salaried executive staff officer; (9) a copy of the annual financial statement of the organization audited by a certified public accountant (with more modest statements of organizations with annual gross budgets of no more than $100,000); (10) a description of the methods of solicitations, including whether the organization intends to solicit contributions directly from the public or have the solicitation done on its behalf by others; (11) information about whether the organization is authorized by any other governmental authority to solicit contributions and whether it is or has ever been enjoined by any court from soliciting contributions; (12) the general purpose or purposes for which the contributions to be solicited will be used; (13) the name or names under which it intends to solicit contributions; (14) the names of the individuals of the organization who will have final responsibility for the custody of the contributions; (15) the names of the individuals of the organization responsible for the final distribution of the contributions; and (16) a listing of the names, addresses, and compensation of all directors, officers, agents, servants, employees, and/or other individuals who receive an annual compensation, commission, or other remuneration in excess of $12,500.

The director of business regulation must examine each initial application of a charitable organization for the right to solicit funds and each renewal application and, if found to be in "conformity" with this law, it must be approved for registration.

Each chapter, branch, affiliate, or member agency of a federated fund-raising agency may report the information required by this law to its parent organization and, when that is done, the parent organization must furnish the information as to its state chapters, branches, affiliates, or member agencies in consolidated form to the department or each chapter, branch, affiliate, or member agency of a federated fund-raising agency may report this information separately to the department.

Both the branch, chapter, "area office," or similar affiliate soliciting in the state, as well as the parent of a charitable organization that has its principal place of business outside of the state, are subject to the provisions of this law.

The department must investigate an applicant charitable organization. The department must certify to the secretary of state its approval or disapproval of the application. An applicant may not be approved if it is found that (1) one or more of the statements in the application are false; (2) the applicant is engaging or has engaged in a fraudulent transaction or enterprise; (3) a solicitation would be a fraud upon the public; (4) the solicitation and fund-raising expenses of the organization during any of the three years immediately preceding the date of application have exceeded 50 percent of the total moneys, pledges, or other property received by reason of any fund-raising activities (with the department empowered to waive this restriction in the event of "special facts and circumstances"); (5) the expected cost of solicitation and fund-raising expenses for the year in which the application is submitted will exceed 50 percent of the total moneys, pledges, or other property received by reason of any fund-raising activities (with the department empowered to waive this restriction in the event of "special facts and circumstances"); or (6) the activities to be financed will be "incompatible with the health, safety or welfare" of the citizens of the state.

Professional Fund-Raisers.   A person may not act as a professional fund-raiser (termed "professional fund-raising counsel") for a charitable organization subject to the provisions of this law unless he, she, or it has first registered with the department. A partnership or corporation, that is a professional fund-raising counsel, may register for and pay a single fee on behalf of its members, officers, agents, and employees. However, the names and addresses of all officers, agents, and employees of a professional fund-raising counsel must be listed in the application.

Each registration is valid throughout the state for a period of one year and may be renewed.

An applicant for registration must file, and have approved by the department, a bond in the amount of $10,000. A partnership or corporation that is a professional fund-raising counsel may file a consolidated bond on behalf of its members, officers, and employees.

The director of the department of business regulation is to examine each application and, if it is in conformity with this law and if the registrant is in compliance with this law, the registration must be approved. An applicant who is denied approved registration may, within 15 days from the date of notification of the denial, request a hearing before the department; this hearing must be held within 15 days from the date of the request.

Professional Solicitors.   The rules with respect to registration and bonding for professional fund-raising counsel (see above) are the same for professional solicitors.

Annual Reporting Requirements

Charitable Organizations.   There is no reporting requirement as such for charitable organizations. However, the annual renewal of the registration (see above) is the functional equivalent of an annual report.

Professional Fund-Raisers.   There is no reporting requirement as such for professional fund-raising counsel. However, the annual renewal of the registration (see above) is the functional equivalent of an annual report.

Professional Solicitors.   There is no reporting requirement as such for professional solicitors. However, the annual renewal of the registration (see above) is the functional equivalent of an annual report.

Exemptions

This law is inapplicable to "duly constituted" religious organizations, societies and institutions, or any group affiliated with and forming an integral part of such an organization, provided that no part of the net income of the organization inures to the direct benefit of any individual and that the organization has received a recognition of tax-exempt status from the IRS. An affiliated group is not required to obtain this recognition if the parent or principal organization has received it.

The following are exempt from the requirement of filing an annual registration statement: (1) educational institutions, including parent-teacher associations, the curriculums of which are registered or approved by the state's board of regents for education either directly or by acceptance of accreditation; (2) churches of "recognized denominations" and religious organizations, societies, and institutions operated, supervised, or controlled by a religious organization that solicit from other than their own membership; (3) persons requesting contributions for the relief of an individual specified by name where all of the contributions are turned over to the beneficiary; (4) charitable organizations that do not intend to solicit and receive and do not actually receive contributions from the public in excess of $3,000 during a calendar year or do not receive contributions from more than 10 persons during a calendar year, if all of their functions, including fund-raising activities, are carried on by volunteers and if no part of their assets or income inures to the benefit of or is paid to any officer or member; (5) charitable hospitals; (6) organizations that solicit only from their own membership; (7) public libraries; (8) persons soliciting contributions solely from corporations and foundations; (9) foundations or associations operating exclusively for the benefit of religious organizations, educational institutions, charitable hospitals, and public libraries; (10) veteran's organizations and their auxiliaries; (11) grange organizations and their auxiliaries; (12) historical societies organized under the state's law; and (13) "[f]ree nonprofit public" art museums.

A charitable organization claiming to be exempt from the registration requirement and which solicits contributions must annually submit to the department the name, address, and purpose of the organization and a statement setting forth the reason for the claim of exemption. If exempt, the department is to annually issue a letter of exemption.

Commercial Co-ventures

This law does not regulate commercial co-venturing.

Other Requirements

Contracts. Every contract between professional fund-raising counsel and a charitable organization must be filed with the department within 10 days after the contract is executed. This rule is also applicable with respect to a contract between a professional solicitor and a charitable organization.

If a contract between a professional solicitor and a charitable organization does not provide for compensation on a percentage basis, the department must examine the contract to ascertain whether the compensation to the solicitor is likely to be in excess of the 25 percent standard (see Percentages, below). If there is a reasonable probability that this standard will be exceeded, the department must disapprove the contract. The parties to a disapproved contract may not perform services or receive payments pursuant to it. A party to a disapproved contract is authorized to seek a hearing on the matter before the department.

Record Keeping and Accounting.   Every charitable organization required to file a registration statement (see above) must maintain a record of each contribution in excess of $50, including the name and address of the contributor, the amount of the contribution, and the date the contribution was received. These records must be maintained in "good order" and available to the department for inspection. However, in the case of periodic contributions from an employer that has automatically withheld contributions from the compensation of its employees, the charitable organization is required to only maintain a record of the name and address of the employer and the total amount received.

Every charitable organization must keep true fiscal records as to its activities in the state as may be covered by this law in such form as will enable it accurately to provide the information required by this law. Upon demand, the records must be made available to the department for inspection. These records must be kept for at least three years.

Other.   Registration statements and applications, reports, professional fund-raising counsel contracts, professional solicitor contracts, and all other documents and information required to be filed must become public records in the office of the department. These records are open to the general public for inspection.

Unique Provisions

Disclosures.   Upon payment of the registration fee, a charitable organization that submits a proper registration that has been approved by the department must issue an identification card to each professional solicitor. This card must include the name and address of the charitable organization, the purpose for which the contribution is solicited, the tax-exempt status of the charitable organization, and the percentage of the contribution that is deductible for income tax purposes.

The professional solicitor must present his card for each solicitation that is made in person. In the event of a telephone solicitation, the professional solicitor must prepare and execute an affidavit stating that the information contained on the card has been given to the potential contributor.

Confirmation.   A professional solicitor must provide each contributor with a receipt for the contribution. This receipt must include the purpose for which the contribution is to be used and the percentage of the funds contributed by the donor to be used for the charitable purpose.

Percentages.   A charitable organization may not pay or agree to pay to a professional solicitor or his, her, or its agents, servants, or employees in the aggregate a total amount in excess of 25 percent (including reimbursement for expenses incurred and direct payment of expenses incurred) of the total moneys, pledges, or other property raised or received by reason of any solicitation activities.

A charitable organization may not incur solicitation and fund-raising expenses in excess of 50 percent of total moneys, pledges, or other property raised or received by reason of any solicitation activities. Nonetheless, the department has the discretion to allow a higher expenditure for fund-raising expenses in the event of "special facts or circumstances"; in the event an exemption is granted, it may be accompanied by the imposition of such conditions as the department or the attorney general of the state may deem necessary.

Also, see the discussion of the application process for charitable organizations.

Prohibited Acts.   A charitable organization, professional fund-raising counsel, or professional solicitor may not use or exploit the fact of registration to lead the public to believe that the registration constitutes an endorsement or approval by the state.

A person may not, in connection with the solicitation of contributions for or the sale of goods or services of a person other than a charitable organization, misrepresent to or mislead anyone to believe that the person on whose behalf the solicitation or sale is being conducted is a charitable organization or that the proceeds of the solicitation or sale will be used for charitable purposes, if that is not the fact.

A person may not, in connection with the solicitation of contributions or the sale of goods or services for charitable purposes, represent to or lead anyone to believe that another person sponsors or endorses a solicitation of contributions, sales of goods or services for charitable purposes, or approves of the charitable purposes or a charitable organization involved when the other person has not given consent to the use of his, her, or its name for these purposes.

A person may not make any representation that he, she, or it is soliciting contributions for or on behalf of a charitable organization or use or display any emblem, device, or printed matter belonging to or associated with a charitable organization for the purpose of soliciting or inducing contributions from the public without first being authorized to do so by the charitable organization.

A professional solicitor may not solicit in the name of or on behalf of any charitable organization unless (1) the solicitor has written authorization of two officers of the organization, a copy of which must be filed with the department; (2) the authorization is carried with the solicitor when making solicitations; and (3) the authorization is upon request exhibited to prospective donors, police officers, or agents of the department.

Other.   A charitable organization may not solicit funds from the public except for charitable purposes and may not expend funds raised for charitable purposes for noncharitable purposes.

The department is empowered to enter into reciprocal agreements with other states to exchange information with respect to charitable organizations, professional fund-raising counsel, and professional solicitors. Pursuant to these agreements, the department may accept information filed by a charitable organization, professional fund-raising counsel, or professional solicitor in another state in lieu of the information required under this law, if that information is "substantially similar" to the information required under this law. The department can also grant exemption from the registration requirement to charitable organizations that principally derive their gift support from sources outside the state and that are granted exemption under the laws of another state where the statutes are "similar in substance."

A charitable organization, professional fund-raising counsel, or professional solicitor having his, her, or its principal place of business in another state or organized under the laws of another state, that solicits contributions in the state, is deemed to appoint the director of the department of business regulation as agent for service of process.

Sanctions

The department has the authority to cancel, suspend, or refuse to accept a registration where the party involved (charitable organization, professional fund-raising counsel, or professional solicitor) fails to file a registration statement, report, or other information required by this law or otherwise violates this law. The department is accorded the authority to conduct investigations in this regard.

A registration must be revoked where the party knowingly makes a false or misleading statement in any filing with the department.

A person who violates this law may be liable for a civil penalty of up to $500 for each violation.

A person who willfully and knowingly violates any provision of this law or provides false information to the department must, upon conviction, be sentenced for the first offense to pay a fine of up to $1,000 or undergo imprisonment for up to one year, or both, and for the second and any subsequent offense to pay a fine up to $5,000 or undergo imprisonment for up to five years, or both.

The attorney general is empowered to bring legal action in the event of a violation of this law, including the pursuit of injunctions.

SOUTH CAROLINA

Introduction

Comprehensive statute: Yes
Regulatory office(s): Secretary of state
Citation: Chapter 35, South Carolina Code, §§ 33-55-10–33-55-230

Registration or Licensing Requirements

Charitable Organizations.   A charitable organization, unless exempt from the requirement, may not solicit, or have solicited on its behalf, contributions in the state of South Carolina unless, prior to any solicitation, the organization has filed a registration statement with the state's secretary of state. This registration is effective for one year and may be renewed.

The registration statement must contain the following information: (1) the name of the organization; (2) the purpose for which it was organized; (3) the principal address of the organization and the address of any offices in the state or, if there is no office, the name and address of the person having custody of the financial records; (4) the names and addresses of any chapters, branches, or affiliates in the state; (5) the place where and the date when the organization was legally established; (6) the form of the organization; (7) a reference to any recognition of its tax-exempt status by the IRS; (8) the names and addresses of the officers, directors, trustees, and the principal salaried executive staff officer; (9) whether the organization intends to solicit contributions from the public directly or by means of others; (10) whether it is "certified" as a tax-exempt organization; (11) whether it is authorized by any other governmental authority in the state to solicit contributions; (12) whether it is or has ever been enjoined by any court of the state from soliciting contributions; (13) the general purpose for which the contributions to be solicited are to be used; (14) the name under which it intends to solicit contributions; (15) the names of the individuals of the organization who will have final responsibility for the custody of the contributions; and (16) the names of the individuals of the organization responsible for the final distribution of the contributions.

Each chapter, branch, or affiliate, except an independent member agency of a federated fund-raising organization, must report the required information to its parent organization, which shall then furnish the information as to its state affiliates, chapters, and branches in a consolidated from to the secretary of state.

As noted below (see Exemptions), organizations that receive contributions that are not in excess of $2,000 are not required to register with the state. However, once an organization receives contributions in excess of that amount, it is required to register with the state within 30 days after the date the $2,000 threshold is exceeded.

Professional Fund-Raisers.   A person may not act as a professional fund-raiser (termed "professional fund-raising counsel") for a charitable organization subject to this law unless the person has first registered with the secretary of state. A partnership or corporation may register for and pay a single fee on behalf of its members, officers, agents, and employees. However, the names and addresses of all officers, agents, and employees of the professional fund-raising counsel must be listed in the application. A registration is valid for one year and is renewable.

The applicant must file with, and have approved by, the secretary a bond in the sum of $5,000. A partnership or corporation may file a consolidated bond on behalf of all its members, officers, and employees.

Professional Solicitors.   A person may not act as a professional solicitor for a charitable organization subject to this law unless the person has first registered with the secretary of state. A partnership or corporation may register for and pay a single fee on behalf of its members, officers, agents, and employees. However, the names and addresses of all officers, agents, and employees of the professional solicitor must be listed in the application. A registration is valid for one year and is renewable.

The applicant must file with, and have approved by, the secretary a bond in the sum of $5,000. A partnership or corporation may file a consolidated bond on behalf of all its members, officers, and employees.

Annual Reporting Requirements

Charitable Organizations.   A charitable organization subject to this law must file an annual report with the secretary of state. This report must be filed within six months of the close of the organization's fiscal year. This report must be prepared in conformance with the current version of the publication *Forms and Instructions Recommended to State and Local Regulatory Bodies for Uniform Financial Reporting by Voluntary Health and Welfare Organizations.*

Professional Fund-Raisers.   There is no reporting requirement as such for professional fund-raisers, although the annual registration requirement is the functional equivalent of an annual reporting requirement.

Professional Solicitors.   There is no reporting requirement as such for professional solicitors, although the annual registration requirement is the functional equivalent of an annual reporting requirement.

Exemptions

This law does not apply to duly constituted religious organizations or any group affiliated with and forming an integral part of a religious organization, no part of the net income of which inures to the direct benefit of any individual and which has received recognition of tax-exempt status from the IRS. However, an affiliated group is not required to obtain this recognition of tax-exempt status if the parent or principal organization has obtained it.

The following organizations do not have to file registration statements: (1) religious organizations, religious societies, and institutions affiliated with them that are under their supervision or control, or which are indirectly affiliated with them and which own, maintain, and operate homes for the aged for its membership in which are contained a house of worship, when solicitation is confined to members, families of members, corporations, foundations, trustees, or employees of the organizations; (2) educational institutions that are registered or accredited (although they must file with the state copies of the annual reports filed with the state's department of education); (3) persons requesting contributions for the relief of any individual specified by name at the time of the solicitation when all of the contributions are turned over to the beneficiary; (4) charitable organizations that do not intend to solicit and receive and do not receive contributions in excess of $2,000 during a calendar year or do not receive contributions from more than 10 persons during a calendar year, if all of their functions, including fund-raising activities, are carried on by volunteers and if no part of their assets or income inures to the benefit of or is paid to any officer or member; (5) charitable hospitals; (6) organizations that solicit only within their membership by the members; and (7) a veterans' organization that has a national charter.

A charitable organization claiming to be exempt from these registration requirements and which solicits charitable contributions must submit annually to the secretary the name, address and purpose of the organization and a statement setting forth the reason for the claim for exemption. If exempted, the state's division of public charities (within the office of the secretary of state) is to issue annually a letter of exemption.

This statute exempts from the requirement of payment of an annual registration fee (1) any individual chapter, branch, or affiliate of a parent organization or a federated fund-raising organization that raises money by the sale of merchandise or any other thing of value for which a reasonable return is received by the purchaser; (2) the Children's Trust Fund of South Carolina; and (3) an organization that is exempt from the registration requirement.

Commercial Co-ventures

This law does not regulate commercial co-venturing.

Other Requirements

Contracts. A contract between a professional fund-raiser and a charitable organization must be in writing and filed with the secretary within 10 days after the contract is executed.

A contract between a professional solicitor and a charitable organization must be filed with the secretary within 10 days after the contract is executed.

Record Keeping and Accounting.   Every charitable organization subject to this act must keep true fiscal records as to its activities in the state, in accordance with the standards set out in *Standards of Accounting and Financial Reporting for Voluntary Health and Welfare Organizations.* These records must be retained for a period of at least three years.

Registration statements, applications, reports, contracts, and other information required to be filed under this law are public records in the office of the secretary of state and are available to the public.

Other.   A charitable organization, professional fund-raiser, or professional solicitor having a principal place of business outside the state or organized under the laws of another state that solicits contributions in the state is deemed to have appointed the secretary of state as agent for service of process.

Unique Provisions

Percentages.   A charitable organization may not pay or agree to pay to a professional solicitor, or his, her, or its agents, servants, or employees, an aggregate amount in excess of a reasonable percent. Also see Sanctions.

Prohibited Acts.   A charitable organization, professional fund-raiser, or professional solicitor, subject to the provisions of this law, may not use or exploit the fact of registration so as to lead the public to believe that the registration constitutes an endorsement by the state.

A person may not, in connection with the solicitation of contributions for or the sale of goods or services of a person other than a charitable organization, mislead anyone to believe that the person on whose behalf the solicitation or sale is being conducted is a charitable organization or that the proceeds of the solicitation or sale will be used for charitable purposes, if that is not the case.

A person may not, in connection with the solicitation of contributions or the sale of goods or services for charitable purposes, represent to or lead anyone to believe that any other person sponsors, endorses, or approves of the solicitation or sale, where the other person has not given consent for these purposes. However, any member of the board of directors or trustees of a charitable organization or any other person who has agreed to serve or to participate in a voluntary capacity in a solicitation campaign is deemed to have given consent to the use of his or her name in the campaign.

A person may not make any representation that he, she or it is soliciting contributions for or on behalf of a charitable organization, or display or otherwise use any emblem, device, or printed matter belonging to a charitable organization for the purpose of soliciting contributions without first being authorized to do so by the charitable organization.

A professional solicitor may not solicit in the name of or on behalf of a charitable organization unless the solicitor has written authorization from the charity (which must be filed with the secretary) and displays it to prospective donors, police officers, and agents of the secretary upon request.

A person may not, for the purpose of soliciting contributions, use the name of another person, except that of an officer, director, or trustee of the charitable organization involved, without the written consent of the other person. A person is deemed to have used the name of another if the other person's name is listed on any stationery, advertisement, brochure, or correspondence in or by which a contribution is solicited by or on behalf of a charitable organization if the person's name is listed or referred to in connection with a request for a gift as one who has contributed to, sponsored, or endorsed the charitable organization or its activities.

A charitable organization is permitted to publish the names of contributors, without their written consent, in a report issued for the purpose of reporting on its operations and affairs to its membership or for the purpose of reporting contributions to contributors.

Other.   Where a registration has been refused, canceled, or suspended, the organization involved may file another application for registration for the following year, where (1) the subject of the refusal, cancellation, or suspension of the registration and the reasons for it have been submitted to the organization's governing board and placed on the agenda for consideration at its next meeting; (2) an extract of the minutes of the meeting is submitted to the secretary, including a statement of all corrective measures to be taken in order to gain compliance that have been agreed to by the board; and (3) a letter signed by the principal officer of the organization, transmitting the extract and indicating willingness to attend a hearing for the purpose of providing any additional information regarding the organization's operations program.

The secretary is authorized to enter into reciprocal agreements with other states to exchange information about charitable organizations, professional fund-raisers, and professional solicitors. The secretary, under these agreements, may accept information filed with another state in lieu of the information required to be filed in accordance with this law, if that information is "substantially similar" to information required under this law. The secretary may also grant exemption from the registration requirement to charitable organizations organized under the laws of another state and having their principal place of business outside the state, where their funds are derived principally from sources outside the state and are exempt from the registration requirements of the other state's law, if the other state has a statute similar in substance to the provisions of this law.

This law creates, within the office of the secretary of state, a division of public charities. The law also creates a commission on charitable organizations, which has the power to promulgate and prescribe rules and forms to accompany, and to hold hearings in enforcement of, this law.

Sanctions

The secretary of state has the authority to deny approval of an application for registration, on the ground that the application is not in conformity with this law.

The secretary has the authority to request the attorney general to bring an action to attempt to enjoin the activities of a charitable organization, professional fund-raiser, or professional solicitor that is operating in contravention of this law, is making false statements, or is engaging in fraudulent fund-raising, or enjoin the devotion of contributions to noncharitable purposes. The secretary may also proceed against a charitable organization that is operating under the pretense of being an exempted organization (see above) but is not in fact entitled to an exemption. A charitable organization that fails to file the required annual report may be enjoined from the solicitation of funds in the state.

If a charitable organization, professional fund-raiser, or professional solicitor fails to timely file any information required to be filed under this law or otherwise violates this law, the secretary may cancel or suspend the registration or refuse to accept the registration of the party. This action may be appealed to the commission (see above), which must hold a public hearing on the matter.

The secretary has the authority to investigate the activities of any charitable organization, professional fund-raiser, or professional solicitor. Upon a finding of violation of this law, the secretary may suspend or cancel the appropriate registration. A charitable organization that fails to file an annual report (see above) may be enjoined from further solicitation of funds in the state by reason of an action brought by the attorney general at the request of the secretary of state.

If the secretary concludes that a contract between a charitable organization and a professional solicitor will involve an "excessively high" fund-raising cost, he or she must request the parties to provide "satisfactory explanation" and may, if not satisfied, request renegotiation of the arrangement. Otherwise, the secretary may disapprove the contract. A charitable organization or a professional solicitor may not perform services or make payments pursuant to a disapproved contract.

The filing by a charitable organization, professional fund-raiser, or professional solicitor, with the secretary, of information that knowingly contains a false or misleading statement must lead to revocation of the appropriate registration. This action may be appealed to the commission (see above), which must hold a public hearing on the matter.

Where a registration has been refused, canceled, or suspended, the party involved may file another registration statement for the following year as long as it provides certain "assurances."

Any person who willfully and knowingly violates any provision of this law, or willfully and knowingly provides false information to the secretary, is deemed guilty of a misdemeanor. Punishment for the first offense is by fine of between $10 and $100 or imprisonment for up to 30 days; punishment for subsequent offenses is by fine of between $100 and $1,000 or imprisonment for up to one year, or both.

TENNESSEE

Introduction

Comprehensive statute: Yes
Regulatory office(s): Secretary of state
Citation: Article 48, Tennessee Code, §§ 48-3-501–48-3-519

Registration or Licensing Requirements

Charitable Organizations.   A charitable organization, unless exempt from the requirement, may not solicit contributions in the state of Tennessee or have funds solicited in the state on its behalf unless, prior to any solicitation, the organization has filed a registration statement with the state's secretary of state.

The registration statement must contain the following information: (1) the name of the organization; (2) the purpose for which it was organized;

(3) the principal address of the organization and any other address(es) in the state or, if there is no office in the state, the name and address of the person having custody of its financial records; (4) the names and addresses of any chapters, branches, or affiliates in the state; (5) the place where and the date when the organization was legally established; (6) the form of the organization; (7) its federal law tax-exempt status (if any); (8) the names and addresses of the officers, directors, trustees, and the principal salaried executive staff officer; (9) a copy of a financial statement audited by an independent public accountant or of the annual information return (Form 990) filed with the IRS or form filed with any other federal agency disclosing the same or substantially similar data required in the financial statement; (10) a statement as to whether the organization intends to solicit contributions directly from the public or have the solicitation done by others; (11) a statement as to whether the organization is authorized by any other government agency to solicit contributions; (12) a statement as to whether the organization is or has ever been enjoined by any court from soliciting contributions; (13) the general purpose or purposes for which the contributions solicited are to be used; (14) the name or names under which it intends to solicit contributions; (15) the names of the individuals of the organization who will have final responsibility for the custody of the contributions; and (16) the names of the individuals of the organization responsible for the final distribution of the contributions.

As discussed below, a charitable organization that does not solicit and receive contributions in excess of $5,000 annually is exempt from this statute. However, in any year in which that level of giving is exceeded, the charitable organization must, within 30 days after contributions exceed $5,000, register with the secretary of state.

A chapter, branch, or affiliate of a parent organization or independent member agency of a federated fund-raising organization may register separately or on a consolidated basis.

Where the application for registration is complete, the secretary of state will issue a certificate of registration. The last day of the sixth month following the month in which the fiscal year of the organization ends is the "anniversary date" of the organization. Certificates of registration expire on this anniversary date.

Professional Fund-Raisers.   There is no registration requirement for professional fund-raisers under this statute. However, the definition of "professional solicitor" is sufficiently broad to embrace most professional fund-raisers, so that the registration requirement for professional solicitors under this statute will likely be applicable with respect to professional fund-raisers.

Professional Solicitors.   Professional solicitors must register with the secretary of state and receive a certificate of registration. Employees of professional solicitors must be separately certified by the secretary. Each of these certificates expires on December 31 of the year in which issued.

A person who has been convicted within the past five years for a violation of this law and a person convicted of a felony under any state's law is ineligible for a certificate of registration and cannot serve as an employee, member, officer, or agent of any professional solicitor "until his civil rights have been restored."

A professional solicitor must file, and have approved by the secretary, a bond in the amount of $10,000. A solicitor may file a consolidated bond on behalf of its members, officers, and employees.

Annual Reporting Requirements

Charitable Organizations.   Every charitable organization required to register (see above) that is soliciting funds in the state must annually reapply for a certificate of registration.

Professional Fund-Raisers.   There are no annual reporting requirements for professional fund-raisers. However, the requirements applicable with respect to professional solicitors may apply.

Professional Solicitors.   A professional solicitor must file a financial report for a solicitation with the secretary within 90 days after the solicitation has been completed and/or on the anniversary date of the commencement of a solicitation of more than one year's duration. This report must be audited by an independent accountant. If the solicitation is conducted regionally or nationally, the financial information that must be filed "shall be inclusive of" the regional or national campaign.

Exemptions

This law is not applicable to a (1) bona fide religious institution, including (a) "ecclesiastical or denominational organizations, churches, or established physical places for worship in this state, at which nonprofit religious services and activities are regularly conducted and carried on" and "bona fide religious groups which do not maintain specific places of worship," (*b*) separate groups or corporations that form an integral part of a religious organization, as long as they are tax-exempt and "are not primarily supported by funds solicited outside their own membership or congregation," and (*c*) institutions soliciting contributions for the construction and maintenance of a house of worship or clergyman's residence; (2) educational institutions that are accredited by a recognized accrediting agency; (3) organizations composed of parents of students and other persons connected with an educational institution that are organized and operated for the purpose of conducting activities in support of the operations or extracurricular activities of the institution; (4) foundations soliciting contributions exclusively for educational institutions; and (5) charitable organizations that do not receive contributions from the public in excess of $5,000 during a year.

The secretary is empowered to grant exemption from the requirement of filing an annual registration statement to charitable organizations organized under the law of another state and having their principal place of business outside the state, where their funds are derived principally from sources outside the state and where they have been granted exemption from the filing of registration statements by the law of the state in which they are organized, if the state has a statute that is similar in substance to this law.

Commercial Co-ventures

This law does not regulate commercial co-venturing.

Other Requirements

Contracts.   See Disclosures (below).

Record Keeping and Accounting.   Every charitable organization and professional solicitor required to have a certificate of registration (see above) must keep true fiscal records as to its activities in the state for at least three years. These records must be made available to the secretary of state or appropriate district attorney general for inspection upon demand.

A professional solicitor must maintain a record of the names of donors, their addresses, and the date on which their donations were received. This record must be maintained for one year, and must be produced to the secretary of state or attorney general upon demand (with some protections for donor lists).

Registration statements and applications, reports, and other documents required by this law are matters of public record. The secretary has the discretion to compile, summarize, publish, or otherwise release to the public any information contained in applications and other documents received by the secretary pursuant to this law.

The secretary of state is required to prescribe a uniform system of accounting to determine "fund raising costs" and "gross contributions."

Other.   The secretary of state is authorized to enter into reciprocal agreements with other states for the purpose of exchanging information with respect to charitable organizations. Pursuant to these agreements, the secretary may accept information from a charitable organization filed in another state, in lieu of information required under this law, where the information is substantially similar to the information required under this law.

Charitable organizations and professional solicitors having their principal place of business outside the state or organized under the law of another state, and which solicits contributions in the state, are deemed to have appointed the secretary of state as agent for service of process.

Unique Provisions

Disclosures.   A professional solicitor may not solicit in the name of or on behalf of a charitable organization unless (1) he, she, or it has first obtained written authorization of two officers of the charity, which may not be for a period longer than one year; (2) the solicitor exhibits the authorization upon request to persons solicited, to agents of the secretary of state, or to law enforcement officials; and (3) prior to the solicitation, the solicitor has filed with the secretary a true copy of any written agreement with the charitable organization. Where there is no written contract, a written statement of the terms and conditions of the relationship, including the solicitor's compensation, must be filed with the secretary.

A professional solicitor, or agent, servant, or employee of a solicitor, may not solicit a person for a charitable contribution without identifying himself or herself as a professional solicitor to the person being solicited.

It is the responsibility of a charitable organization, whether or not exempt under this law, to furnish identification to persons who solicit on its behalf, including professional solicitors, indicating that the solicitor is authorized to solicit contributions for it. This identification, which must include the name of the holder of the identification and the name and number of the certificate of the charitable organization, must be displayed by the solicitor on demand.

Prior to the commencement of a solicitation, the professional solicitor involved must file a "solicitation notice" with the secretary. This notice must include a description of the solicitation event, the location and telephone number from which the solicitation is to be conducted in the state, the names and residence addresses of all employees or other persons who are to participate in the solicitation, and the account number and location of all bank accounts where receipts from the solicitation are to be deposited. Any changes in the required information must be transmitted to the secretary within 72 hours.

Within five days after the commencement of a solicitation, a professional solicitor must file copies of campaign solicitation literature, including the text of any solicitation made orally which is utilized in the solicitation, with the secretary. Any changes in this literature must be transmitted to the secretary within 72 hours.

Percentages.   A professional solicitor, or his, her, or its agents, servants, or employees, must disclose upon request by the prospective donor the percentage of gross contributions raised by the professional solicitor that will be received by the charitable organization after the deduction of solicitation expenses or otherwise disclose the "guaranteed contract amount" that the charitable organization will receive as a result of the solicitation.

Prohibited Acts.   It is unlawful to use unfair, false, misleading, or deceptive acts and practices affecting the conduct of solicitations for contributions.

A charitable organization may not use or exploit the fact of registration to lead the public to believe that the registration constitutes an endorsement or approval by the state.

In the case of a solicitation of contributions for or the sale of goods or services of a noncharitable organization, a person may not lead another to believe that the organization is a charitable one or that the contributions will be used for charitable purposes, if that is not the case.

In connection with the solicitation of contributions or the sale of goods or services for professional purposes, a person may not lead another to believe that anyone sponsors or endorses the solicitation or sale, or approves of the charitable purposes or charitable organization, where the person has not given written consent for the use of his, her, or its name for these purposes. A member of the board of directors of a charitable organization or any other person who has agreed to serve or to participate in any voluntary capacity in the solicitation is deemed to have consented to the use of his or her name.

A person may not represent that he, she, or it is soliciting contributions for or on behalf of a charitable organization, or use or display any device or printed matter belonging to or associated with a charitable organization for the purpose of soliciting contributions from the public, without being first authorized to do so by the charitable organization.

A charitable organization may only solicit contributions in the state from the public for charitable purposes. A charitable organization may not expend funds raised for charitable purposes for noncharitable purposes.

A person may not, while soliciting contributions or selling goods, magazines, newspaper advertising, or any other service, use the words "police," "firefighter," or "firemen" without authorization from a bona fide police or firefighter organization or police or fire department.

A person may not use the words "charity" or "charitable" as part of its name unless registered or exempt under this law.

No employee of a nonprofit corporation organized in the state or of any nonprofit foreign corporation having a certificate of authority to transact business in the state, may own or operate or have any pecuniary interest, directly or indirectly, with any business enterprise relating to the product, aims, goals, or purposes of the corporation.

A charitable organization or professional solicitor that fails to file a registration application, statement, report, or other information required pursuant to this law as a prerequisite to registration may not engage in any of the activities permitted duly registered persons under this law.

Other.   An applicant who is denied approval of registration or an exemption may, within 20 days of notification of the denial, request a hearing before the secretary of state. This hearing generally must be held within a reasonable time from the date of the request.

The statute is not to be construed to preempt more stringent county or municipal laws regulating charitable fund-raising. Municipalities are authorized to require information in addition to that required by this law.

The conduct of a raffle is considered a solicitation for charitable purposes. Generally, organizations may not conduct raffles where the gross proceeds exceed $5,000. However, a charitable organization may, no more than three times a year, conduct a raffle where the gross proceeds exceed that limitation. At least 50 percent of the gross proceeds from such raffles must be used for charitable purposes.

An organization failing to renew its registration or an exemption by the time of its expiration is automatically suspended from the right to operate under this law until the registration is renewed.

Sanctions

The secretary of state is empowered to make "such individual investigations of all applicants for certificates of registration as he may deem necessary."

The secretary of state is empowered to issue, deny, suspend, or revoke certificates of registration to organizations that obtain contributions for charitable purposes and to professional solicitors.

The secretary of state may, where there are reasonable grounds to suspect a violation, investigate a charitable organization or professional solicitor to determine whether this law has been violated or whether false or misleading statements have been made. The latter can lead to a suspension or revocation of a certificate of registration and the imposition of a $5,000 civil penalty.

The secretary of state is empowered to seek injunctions to enforce this law, as well as appear in court in pursuit of warrants of arrest in criminal cases.

This law authorizes a prospective donor or a person who "suffers an ascertainable loss of money or property" as the result of the use of an unfair, false, misleading, or deceptive practice to bring a lawsuit to recover actual damages. Where the violation was willful, the court involved may award punitive damages up to three times the amount of actual damages.

Any person who willfully and knowingly violates any provision of this law, or who provides false or incorrect information to the secretary of state, may be punished for the commission of a misdemeanor or a felony and/or fined up to $5,000.

TEXAS

Introduction

Comprehensive statute: No
Regulatory office(s): Attorney general
Citation: Texas Code, Title 132, Article 9023

Registration or Licensing Requirements

Charitable Organizations.   There are no registration requirements for charitable organizations.

Professional Fund-Raisers.   There are no registration requirements for professional fund-raisers.

Professional Solicitors. Before beginning a solicitation in the name of a law enforcement organization (as defined; see Disclosure, below), a solicitor must have on file with the attorney general for public disclosure the following: (1) the name, street address, and telephone number of the solicitor; (2) the name, street address, and telephone number of each organization on behalf of which all or part of the contributions will be used or, if there is no organization, the manner in which the contributions will be used; (3) a statement as to whether the organization involved has federal and/or state tax-exempt status as a charity; (4) the name and law enforcement agency of each peace officer who serves on the board of directors or other governing body of the organization involved, if any; (5) the number of members of each organization involved, as determined on December 31 of the year preceding the year in which the solicitation is made, if any; and (6) the name of each local, chapter, lodge, association, or group of peace officers that are members of the organization for which contributions are solicited, if any.

Annual Reporting Requirements

Charitable Organizations. There are no reporting requirements for charitable organizations.

Professional Fund-Raisers. There are no reporting requirements for professional fund-raisers.

Professional Solicitors. There are no reporting requirements for professional solicitors.

Exemptions

There are no exemptions provided in this law. As discussed below, however, its scope is such that most charitable organizations are not subject to the requirements of this statute.

Commercial Co-ventures

This law does not regulate commercial co-venturing.

Unique Provisions

Disclosures. A person who makes a solicitation of contributions in person, by telephone, or by mail, representing a "nongovernmental organization" that uses in the name or in a publication the term "officer," "peace officer," "police officer," "police," "law enforcement," "reserve officer," "deputy," "deputy sheriff," "constable," "deputy constable," or any other term that "reasonably implies that the organization is composed of law enforcement or public safety personnel," must notify the person solicited that the person may contact the attorney general to examine the information required to be disclosed under this law. If the solicitation is in person, the disclosure must be verbal; otherwise, the disclosure must be in writing.

Prohibited Acts. It is unlawful under this statute for a person to solicit a charitable gift by telephone and (1) "intentionally or knowingly" make a materially false or misleading statement of fact during the course of the solicitation that "would lead a reasonable person to believe that proceeds of the solicitation would go to an organization benefiting or composed of police or fire fighters," and (2) fail to state whether or not the solicitation is authorized by this type of organization.

Sanctions

A violation of this law is a misdemeanor.

UTAH

Introduction

Comprehensive statute: Yes
Regulatory office(s): Department of Commerce, Division of Consumer
                     Protection
Citation: Code 1987-88, Sections 13-22-1–13-22-14

Registration or Licensing Requirements

Charitable Organizations. A charitable organization, unless exempt from the requirement, may not solicit contributions in the state of Utah unless, prior to any solicitation, the organization has secured a permit from the state's division of consumer protection.

The application for a permit must include (1) the organization's name and address; (2) the "specific legal nature of the organization" (such as a corporation); (3) the names and residence addresses of the officers and directors of the organization; (4) the purpose of the solicitation; (5) the use of contributors to be solicited; (6) the method by which the solicitation will be conducted; (7) the projected length of time the solicitation is to be conducted; (8) the anticipated expenses of the solicitation (not including expenses paid with funds other than those obtained as charitable gifts); (9) "a statement of what percentage of the contributions collected as the result of the solicitation are projected to remain available for application to the charitable purposes declared in the application, including a satisfactory statement of the factual basis for the projected percentage"; (10) a statement of total contributions collected or received by the organization within the calendar year immediately preceding the date of the application, including a description of the "expenditures made from or use made of" the contributions; (11) a list of any agreements with any professional fund-raiser involved with the solicitation; (12) a copy of each written agreement with a professional fund-raiser; and (13) any additional information the division may require by rule.

The permit expires one year from the date of its issuance and is renewable.

Professional Fund-Raisers.   A person may not, without first obtaining a professional fund-raiser's permit, solicit a contribution for a charitable purpose on behalf of any organization (whether or not it holds a permit) in exchange for compensation. However, this rule does not apply to an individual who is a bona fide officer or employee of a charitable organization that holds a permit if the solicitation is solely for the benefit of that organization.

To obtain a permit as a professional fund-raiser, an applicant must provide (1) his or her (or its) name, residence, and business address, and residence and business telephone numbers; (2) all other residence addresses of the applicant for the three-year period immediately prior to the application; (3) a complete set of fingerprints; (4) a recent photograph; (5) the applicant's business, occupation, or employment for the three-year period immediately preceding the date of the application; (6) "the applicant's history as a professional fund raiser or in any similar business or occupation, including, if applicable, under what circumstances, in previously operating in this or another state under permit or license, he has had his permit or license revoked or suspended, stating the reason therefore [sic], and disclosing his business activity or occupation subsequent to the suspension or revocation"; (7) the applicant's criminal record, if any (other than misdemeanor traffic violations); (8) the name of the operator or manager of the applicant's operations and, if the operator or manager is not the applicant, all of the information required of applicants as it regards the operator or manager; (9) the "general plans and method by which the applicant proposes to conduct his business" as a professional fund-raiser; and (10) any additional information the division may require by rule.

This permit expires one year from the date of issuance and is renewable. An applicant must secure a bond in the amount of $10,000.

Professional Solicitors.   There is no separate registration requirement for professional solicitors. However, the term "professional fund raiser" is defined to include what is generally defined as a professional solicitor.

Also see Disclosures, below.

Annual Reporting Requirements

Charitable Organizations.   There is no separate reporting requirement for charitable organizations. However, the requirement of an annual permit is the equivalent of an annual reporting requirement.

Professional Fund-Raisers.   There is no separate reporting requirement for professional fund-raisers. However, the requirement of an annual permit is the equivalent of an annual reporting requirement.

Professional Solicitors.   See the above summaries for professional fund-raisers.

Exemptions

The registration requirement does not apply to (1) a "bona fide" religious organization; (2) a political party authorized to function within the state; (3) an organization with annual gross receipts that are less than $5,000; and (4) a school accredited by the state or any accredited institution of higher education. However, the third exemption is inapplicable to an organization that "has no reasonably documented record of gross receipts from solicitations" or "that has, as one of its substantial purposes, the objective of circumventing compliance" with this law.

The registration requirement is also inapplicable, as long as a professional fund-raiser is not involved, to a solicitation (1) that an organization conducts among its membership through the efforts of the donated services of its members; (2) in the form of a collection or contribution made at a "regular assembly or service"; (3) by a licensed radio or television station; (4) made upon premises owned or occupied by the organization on behalf of which the solicitation is made; (5) for a specified individual where the entire amount collected is remitted to the named person; (6) on behalf of an established bona fide youth organization, including a youth sports organization, with a membership in the state exceeding $1,000, as long as the solicitation is made by members of the organization who are identified at the time of solicitation through uniforms, insignia, or membership cards; (7) on behalf of an established bona fide parent-teacher organization, with a membership in the state exceeding 100, as long as the solicitation is made by members of the organization who reasonably identified as such at the time of solicitation; or (8) on behalf of an established bona fide veterans' organization, as long as the solicitation is made by members of the organization who are identified at the time of solicitation through uniforms, insignia, or membership cards.

Commercial Co-ventures

This statute does not regulate commercial co-venturing.

Other Requirements

Contracts.   A contract between a charitable organization and a professional fund-raiser must be in writing.

Unique Provisions

Disclosures.   A person other than a professional fund-raiser who solicits a contribution for a charitable organization holding a permit must first obtain an "information card" from the organization. This card must be on an official form supplied to the organization by the division.

Each permit and information card issued by the division must "set forth such information as will assist any person solicited to determine the purpose for which the contribution is solicited," including (1) the percentage of contributed funds projected to remain available for application to the charitable purpose represented in the solicitation; (2) if the permit is for a professional fund-raiser, the form and amount of compensation the professional fund-raiser receives from any contributed funds; (3) if it is an information card or a professional fund-raiser permit, the identity of the person making the solicitation; (4) if the permit is for a charitable organization, the identity of the organization; (5) if it is an identification card, the identity of the organization for which the contribution is solicited; (6) an official acknowledgement or seal that the permit is issued by the division or, in the case of an information card, that the card is on a form supplied by the division; (7) a statement that the state does not warrant the truthfulness of the information contained on the card; (8) the expiration date of the permit or information card; and (9) any other information that the division may prescribe by rule.

In an in-person solicitation, each holder of a permit or information card must maintain in his or her possession the permit or card and display it, on request, to any person solicited. In a solicitation by telephone, the information on the permit or card must be "distinctly and clearly repeated" as part of the solicitation.

An information card expires 180 days from the date of issuance by a charitable organization.

Percentages.   See Registration or Licensing Requirements (for Charitable Organizations) and Disclosures, above.

Other.   A professional fund-raiser must maintain all contributed funds separate from his, her, or its own.

Sanctions

The division may refuse to issue or renew, and may suspend or revoke, a permit or information card of any person that (1) violates this law; (2) has been convicted of a crime involving moral turpitude; (3) has obtained or attempted to obtain a permit by misrepresentation; (4) in connection with a solicitation, materially misrepresents the purpose and manner in which contributed funds and property will be used; and (5) violates any rule of the division respecting the use and display of a permit or information card.

A person violating this law, either by failing to comply with a requirement or by doing an act prohibited in the law, is guilty of a misdemeanor.

A person damaged as a result of a charitable solicitation can maintain a civil action for damages or injunctive relief.

The division may maintain an action for damages or injunctive relief on behalf of itself or any other person to enforce compliance with this law.

VERMONT

No statute.

VIRGINIA

Introduction

Comprehensive statute: Yes
Regulatory office(s): Board of Agriculture and Consumer Services
Citation: Code of Virginia, Title 57, Chapter 5

Registration or Licensing Requirements

Charitable Organizations.   A charitable organization, unless exempt from the requirement, may not solicit, or have solicited on its behalf, contributions in the state of Virginia unless, prior to any solicitation, the organization has filed an initial registration statement with the state's commissioner of agriculture and consumer services.

The registration statement includes the following information: (1) the name of the organization; (2) the purpose for which it was organized; (3) the principal address of the organization and the address of any offices in the state or, if none, the name and address of the person having custody of the financial records; (4) the organization's agent for service of process (if none, the organization is deemed to have designated the secretary of state as its agent); (5) the names and addresses of any chapters, branches, or affiliates in the state; (6) the place where and date when the organization was legally established; (7) the form of its organization; (8) a reference to any determination of its federal tax-exempt status; (9) the names and addresses of the officers, directors, trustees, and the principal salaried executive staff officer; (10) a financial statement prepared by an independent public accountant; (11) a statement showing the computation of fund-raising costs as a percentage (see below); (12) a statement indicating whether the organization intends to solicit contributions from the public directly or have it done on its behalf by others; (13) a statement indicating whether the organization ia authorized by any other jurisdiction to solicit contributions; (14) a statement as to whether the organization, or any officer, professional fund-raiser, or professional solicitor associated with it, is or has ever been enjoined by any court or otherwise prohibited from soliciting contributions in any jurisdiction; (15) the general purpose or purposes for which the contributions solicited are to be used; (16) the name or names under which the organization intends to solicit contributions; (17) the names of the individuals who will have final responsibility for the custody of the contributions; (18) the names of the individuals responsible for the final distribution of the contributions; and (17) a statement as to whether the organization, an officer, professional fund-raiser, or professional solicitor associated with it, has ever been convicted of a felony and, if so, a description of the pertinent facts.

Thereafter, a registration statement must be filed on or before the 15th day of the fifth month of each subsequent year in which the organization is engaged in solicitation activities in the state.

Each chapter, branch, or affiliate of a charitable organization may separately register or report the information to the parent organization which must then register for the organizations in consolidated form. Federated fund-raising organizations report in consolidated form.

Professional Fund-Raisers.   A person may not act as a professional fund-raiser (termed "professional fund-raising counsel") for a charitable organization without having first registered with the commissioner. This registration is valid for one year and is renewable. Any change in information must be reported to the commissioner within seven days. A partnership or corporation that is a professional fund-raising counsel may register on behalf of all its members, officers, agents, and employees.

Professional Solicitors.   A person may not act as a professional solicitor for a charitable organization without having first registered with the commissioner. This registration is valid for one year and is renewable. Any change in information must be reported to the commissioner within seven days. A partnership or corporation that is a professional solicitor may register on behalf of all its members, officers, agents, and employees.

A professional solicitor must file with and have approved by the commissioner a bond in the amount of $20,000. A partnership or corporation that is a professional solicitor may file a consolidated bond on behalf of all its members, officers, and employees.

Annual Reporting Requirements

Charitable Organizations.   There are no reporting requirements for charitable organizations.

Professional Fund-Raisers.   There are no reporting requirements for professional fund-raisers.

Professional Solicitors.   At least 10 days prior to the commencement of a solicitation, the professional solicitor must file with the commissioner a copy of the contract entered into with a charitable organization. The solicitor must also file a completed written "Solicitation Notice," which must include a description of the solicitation event or campaign, the projected starting and ending dates of the solicitation, and the location and telephone number from where the solicitation will be conducted. Copies of all campaign solicitation literature, including the text of any solicitation to be made orally, must be attached to the solicitation notice.

A professional solicitor must file with the commissioner, within 90 days after completion of a solicitation campaign, a report showing all funds collected and other information as the commissioner may require.

Exemptions

This law is inapplicable to any church or convention or association of churches, primarily operated for nonsecular purposes, no part of the net income of which inures to the direct benefit of any individual.

The law also is inapplicable to political parties, political campaign committees, labor unions, trade associations, and the American Red Cross and its local chapters.

The following persons are exempt from the registration and record-keeping requirements generally imposed upon charitable organizations: (1) appropriately accredited educational institutions; (2) foundations related to these educational institutions; (3) other educational institutions confining solicitation of contributions to their student body, alumni, faculty, trustees, and their families; (4) persons requesting contribution for the relief of any individual specified by name at the time of the solicitation, when all of the contributions collected are turned over to the individual; (5) charitable organizations that do not intend to solicit and receive, during a calendar year, and have not actually raised or received, during any of the three next preceding calendar years, contributions from the public in excess of $5,000, if all of their functions (including fund-raising) are carried on by volunteers and if no part of their assets or income inures to the benefit of or is paid to any officer or member (with registration required within 30 days following the date contributions exceed the threshold); (6) organizations that solicit only within the membership of the organization by the members of it; (7) organizations that do not have an office in the state, which solicit in the state from outside the state solely by means of telephone, telegraph, direct mail, or advertising in national media, and which have a chapter, branch, or affiliate within the state that is registered; (8) health care institutions that have been recognized by the IRS as tax-exempt charitable organizations; (9) supporting organizations that exist solely to support an exempt health care institution; and (10) civic organizations.

A charitable organization may be subject to the ban on prohibited acts (see below) and to the penalties provisions (see below), and otherwise be exempt from this statute for any year in which it confines its solicitations in the state to no more than five cities and counties, and in which it has registered under the charitable solicitations ordinance (if any) of each such city and county. However, an organization may not be exempt under this rule if, during its next preceding fiscal year, more than 10 percent of its gross receipts were paid to any person or combinations of persons located outside the boundaries of these cities and counties other than for the purchase of real property or tangible personal property or personal services to be used within these localities. An organization which is otherwise qualified for exemption under this rule that solicits by means of a local publication, or radio or television station, is not disqualified solely because the circulation or range of the medium extends beyond the boundaries of the cities or counties.

An organization cannot be exempt from this law unless it submits to the commissioner its name, address, and purpose, along with a statement setting forth the reason for the claim for exemption. If the organization qualifies, a letter of exemption will be issued, which will remain in effect as long as the organization remains in compliance with the rules for the exemption.

Commercial Co-ventures

This statute does not regulate commercial co-venturing.

Other Requirements

Contracts.   A contract between professional fund-raising counsel and a charitable or civic organization must be in writing and filed with the commissioner within 10 days after it is executed. The same rule applies with respect to contracts involving professional solicitors.

Record Keeping and Accounting.   A charitable organization must keep true fiscal records in accordance with (1) the *Standards of Accounts and Financial Reporting for Voluntary Health and Welfare Organizations*, (2) the standards and practices for hospitals as published by the American Hospital Association, or (3) other uniform standards of accounting as the commissioner may find to be appropriate.

A professional solicitor must maintain during the solicitation, and for at least three years thereafter, the following records: (1) the name and address of each contributor and the date and amount of the contribution;

(2) the name and residence address of each employee, agent, or other person involved in the solicitation; (3) records of all expenses incurred in the course of the solicitation; (4) the account number and location of all bank accounts where receipts from the solicitation will be deposited; and (5) all records required to be maintained under the rules concerning donations of tickets (see below).

If a professional solicitor sells tickets to an event and represents that tickets will be donated for use by another, the solicitor must maintain, for the period described in the preceding paragraph, (1) the names and addresses of those who donate tickets, (2) the number of tickets donated, and (3) the names and addresses of all organizations receiving donated tickets for use by others, including the number of tickets received by each organization.

All information required to be filed under this law becomes public records in the office of the commissioner.

Unique Provisions

Disclosures.   A professional solicitor may not solicit contributions without (1) identifying himself, herself, or itself and the employer; (2) disclosing that he, she, or it is a paid solicitor; and (3) disclosing in writing the fact that a financial statement for the most recent fiscal year is available from the Office of Consumer Affairs.

Also see Percentages (below).

Percentages.   A charitable organization must, as part of its registration statement, compute the percentage that its fund-raising expenses for its preceding fiscal year bore to its support received directly from the public during the year.

A professional solicitor may not solicit contributions without disclosing to the prospective donor at the time of solicitation the minimum percentage of any amount contributed that will be received by the organization for its own use. However, this disclosure need not be made where the percentage is at least 70 percent.

Accounts.   All funds collected by a professional solicitor must be deposited in a bank account. This account must include the name of the charitable organization with which the solicitor has contracted. The solicitor must provide to the organization a copy of all monthly bank statements "forthwith."

Prohibited Acts.   A charitable organization may not use the fact of registration to lead the public to believe that the registration constitutes an endorsement or approval by the state.

A person may not, in connection with the solicitation of contributions or the sale of tangible personal property or services, represent or lead anyone to believe that the person on whose behalf the solicitation or sale is being conducted is a charitable organization or that the proceeds of the solicitation or sale will be used for charitable purposes, if that is not the case.

A person may not, in connection with the solicitation of contributions or the sale of tangible personal property or services, represent or lead anyone to believe that another person sponsors or endorses the solicitation or sale, or approves of the charitable organization or its purposes, where the other person has not given written consent to the use of his, her, or its name. A member of the board of directors or trustees of a charitable organization or any other person who has agreed to participate in a voluntary capacity in the campaign is deemed to have given his or her consent to the use of his or her name in the campaign. A charitable organization may publish the names of contributors without their consents in a report issued by it for the purpose of reporting on its operations to its membership or for the purpose of reporting contributions to contributors.

A person may not denominate a membership fee or purchase price of goods or services sold as a contribution or otherwise imply that the member or purchaser will be entitled to an income tax deduction for any portion of the payment unless the organization has obtained an opinion of a lawyer or a ruling from the IRS holding that a deduction is available or the member or purchaser is informed in writing that there is no deduction. A similar rule applies with respect to contributions.

A person may not make any representation that he or she is soliciting contributions for or on behalf of a charitable organization or use or display an emblem, device, or printed matter associated with a charitable organization for the purpose of soliciting contributions without first being authorized to do so by the charitable organization.

A professional solicitor may not solicit in the name of or on behalf of any charitable or civic organization unless the solicitor has written authorization from the organization and exhibits the authorization to prospective donors, police officers, or agents of the commissioner.

A charitable or civic organization may not accept any contribution in excess of five dollars without providing, at the request of the donor, a written receipt for the gift.

An individual and an organization of which he or she is an officer, professional fund-raising counsel, or professional solicitor, may not solicit in the state if (1) the individual has been convicted of a crime involving the obtaining of money or property by false pretenses or the misapplication of funds impressed with a trust unless the person has received a pardon for the offense or the public is informed of the conviction in advance of the solicitation; or (2) the individual has been prohibited from soliciting gifts in any jurisdiction, unless the commissioner first determines in writing that the individual is entitled to solicit in the jurisdiction at the time of the solicitation in the state or that the reason for the prohibition does not involve "moral turpitude."

A person may not solicit in the state for the benefit of a person located outside the state if the other person refuses to supply any information which the commissioner deems necessary to assure himself or herself that this law is complied with. A solicitation is deemed to be on behalf of a person who or which receives, directly or indirectly, more than 10 percent of the gross amount collected.

A charitable or civic organization may not allow a professional solicitor to solicit on its behalf where the solicitor has not registered (see above). A charitable or civic organization, professional fund-raising counsel, or professional solicitor may not solicit in the state without being registered under this law (see above).

A person may not employ in any solicitation of contributions any device, scheme, or artifice to defraud or obtain money or property by any misrepresentation or misleading statement.

An officer, agent, director, or trustee of any charitable or civic organization, professional fund-raising counsel, or professional solicitor may not refuse to produce to the commissioner any books and records of the organization.

A person may not use or permit the use of the funds raised by a charitable solicitation for a purpose other than the solicited purpose or the general purposes of the charitable or civic organization involved.

A person may not knowingly and willfully make any false statements in any registration application, report, or other disclosure required by this law.

Tickets. A professional solicitor may not represent that tickets to events will be donated for use by another unless it has (1) obtained written commitments from persons or charitable organizations stating that they will accept donated tickets and specifying the number of tickets they are willing to accept, and (2) accepted no more contributions for donated tickets than the number of ticket commitments it has received from persons or charitable organizations.

Also see Record-Keeping Requirements (above).

Other. An unregistered charitable organization, professional fund-raising counsel, or professional solicitor having its principal place of business in another state or organized under the law of another state which solicits contributions in the state is deemed to have appointed the secretary as agent for service of process.

The commissioner is authorized to enter into reciprocal agreements with other states for the purpose of exchanging information with respect to charitable organizations, professional fund-raising counsel, and professional solicitors. Pursuant to these agreements, the commissioner may accept information filed by a party with another state in lieu of the information required by this law, if the information is "substantially similar" to the required information. The commissioner may also grant exemption from the requirement of filing an annual registration statement to charitable organizations organized under the laws of another state, having their principal place of business in the other state, having funds derived principally from sources outside the state, and having been granted exemption from the filing of registration statements by the other state, if the other state has a statute "similar in substance" to this law and participates in a reciprocal agreement with the state.

A charitable organization that has no place of business in the state and solicits in the state solely by telephone, telegraph, direct mail, or national media advertising, and any professional fund-raising counsel or professional solicitor engaged by the organization, must file with the commissioner any report that would otherwise be required of it or request the commissioner to determine that it is exempt from the requirement (see above).

This statute expressly authorizes the adoption of charitable solicitation ordinances by cities, towns, and counties, as long as these laws are not inconsistent with the state law. This law provides for certain exemptions from these ordinances.

Sanctions

If the commissioner determines that a charitable or civic organization that is not registered and is not exempt from the requirement is soliciting in the state, he or she may, following notice, cause to be printed in one or more newspapers a notice to that effect, cautioning donors that their contributions may be used for noncharitable purposes.

If the commissioner determines that a charitable or civic organization has contracted with a professional solicitor and that the solicitor is soliciting in the state without having first registered under this law, the commissioner may, following notice, cause to be printed in one or more newspapers a notice to that effect and cautioning donors that their contributions may be used for noncharitable purposes.

The commissioner has the authority to suspend or revoke a registration where a charitable organization has failed to comply with the registration rules or there is a violation of the rule concerning contracts, disclosures by solicitors, or prohibited acts.

A person who willfully and knowingly violates any provision of this law, or who willfully and knowingly provides false or incorrect information to the commissioner, is guilty of a misdemeanor. The punishment for the first offense is a fine of at least $100 and no more than $500 and/or imprisonment for no more than six months. The punishment for any subsequent offenses is a fine of at least $500 and no more than $1,000 and/or imprisonment for no more than one year.

The commissioner is authorized to undertake investigations, subpoena witnesses, hold hearings, and pursue injunctive relief in the courts.

The attorney general, any state's attorney, or the attorney for a city, county, or town is empowered to bring court action to enjoin a charitable organization, professional fund-raising counsel, or a professional solicitor from violating any provision of this statute.

WASHINGTON

Introduction

Comprehensive statute: Yes
Regulatory office(s): Secretary of state, attorney general, county prosecutors
Citation: Chapter 19.09

Registration or Licensing Requirements

Charitable Organizations.   A charitable organization, unless exempt from the requirement, may not solicit contributions in the state of Washington unless, prior to any solicitation, the organization has registered with the state's secretary of state.

An application for registration as a charitable organization must contain (1) the name, address, and telephone number of the charitable organization; (2) the name(s) under which the organization will solicit contributions; (3) the names, addresses, and telephone numbers of the organization's officers; (4) the names of the three officers or employees receiving the greatest amount of compensation from the organization; (5) the purpose of the organization; (6) information indicating whether the organization is exempt from federal income tax; (7) information indicating whether the financial affairs of the organization are audited by an independent entity and, if so, the name and address of the entity; (8) a solicitation report of the organization for the preceding year, including (a) the number and types of solicitations conducted, (b) the total dollar value of support received from solicitations and from all other sources received on behalf of the charitable purpose of the charitable organization, (c) the total amount of money applied to charitable purposes, fund-raising costs, and other expenses, and (d) the name, address, and telephone number of any independent fund-raiser used by the organization; and (9) an irrevocable appointment of the secretary to receive service of process in noncriminal proceedings.

The requirements of (8)(b) and (c), above, may be satisfied by the submission of such federal tax forms as may be approved by the secretary.

This registration is effective for one year and is renewable. Reregistration must be received by the secretary no later than the 15th day of the fifth month after the organization's accounting period ends. Changes in information must be filed within 30 days.

A charitable organization that utilizes the services of an independent fund-raiser must complete another registration form prior to contracting for fund-raising services. This registration must be filed within five working days of execution of the contract, containing (1) the name and registration number of the fund-raiser; (2) the name of the surety or sureties issuing the bond required (see below), the aggregate amount of the bond or bonds, the bond number(s), original effective date(s), and termination date(s); (3) the name and registration number of the charitable organization; (4) the name of the representative of the fund-raising entity who will be responsible for the conduct of the fund-raising; (5) the type(s) of service(s) to be provided by the fund-raiser; (6) the dates on which the fund-raising service(s) will begin and end; (7) the terms of the agreement between charitable organization and the fund-raiser relating to (a) the amount or percentages of amounts to inure to the charitable organization, (b) any limitations placed on the maximum amount to be raised by the fund-raiser, if the amount to inure to the charity is not stated as a percentage of the amount raised, (c) the costs of fund-raising that will be the responsibility of the charity, regardless of whether paid as a direct expense, deducted from the amounts disbursed, or otherwise, and (d) the manner in which contributions received directly by the charitable organization, and not the result of services provided by a fund-raiser, will be identified and used in computing the fee owed to the fund-raiser; (8) the names of any entity to which more than 10 percent of the total anticipated fund-raising cost is to be paid; and (9) whether any principal officer or owner of the fund-raiser or relative by blood or marriage is an owner or officer of an entity that receives more than 10 percent of the fund-raising costs.

Professional Fund-Raisers.   Professional fund-raisers (termed "independent fund raisers" under this law) must register under this statute. The application for registration must include (1) the name, address, and telephone number of the fund-raiser; (2) the name(s), address(es), and telephone number(s) of the owner(s) and principal officer(s) of the fund-raising entity; (3) the name, address, and telephone number of the individual responsible for the activities of the fund-raiser in the state; (4) a list of states and Canadian provinces in which fund-raising has been performed; (5) the names of the three officers or employees receiving the greatest amount of compensation from the fund-raising entity; (6) a statement indicating whether the financial affairs of the fund-raiser are audited by an independent entity and, if so, the name and address of the entity; (7) a solicitation report of the fund-raiser for the preceding accounting year including (a) the number and types of fund-raising services conducted, (b) the names of charitable organizations required to register under this law for which fund-raising services have been performed, (c) the total value of contributions received on behalf of charitable organizations required to register under this law by the fund-raiser or any affiliate of or any entity retained by the fund-raiser, and (d) the amount of money disbursed to charitable organizations for charitable purposes, net of fund-raising costs paid by the charitable organization as stipulated in any agreement between charitable organizations and the fund-raiser; (8) the name, address, and telephone number of any fund-raiser that was retained in the conduct of the provision of fund-raising services; and (9) an irrevocable appointment of the secretary to receive service of process in noncriminal proceedings.

This registration is effective for one year and is renewable. A reregistration must be received by the secretary no later than the 15th day of the third month after the organization's accounting period ends. Changes in information must be filed within 30 days.

A separate registration is required of a nonprofit organization that solicits contributions on behalf of a charitable organization (this soliciting organization termed a "nonprofit fund raiser"). This registration is effective for one year. Reregistration must be received by the secretary no later than the 15th day of the fifth month after the organization's accounting period ends. Changes in information must be filed within 30 days.

An independent fund-raiser who (1) directly or indirectly receives contributions from the public on behalf of a charitable organization; (2) is compensated based upon funds raised or to be raised, number of solicitations made or to be made, or any other similar method; (3) incurs or is authorized to incur expenses on behalf of a charitable organization; or (4) has not been registered as an independent fund-raiser for the preceding year must execute and provide a $15,000 bond.

Professional Solicitors.   There is no separate registration requirement for "professional solicitors." However, the definition of "independent fund raiser" encompasses persons generally referenced as professional solicitors, thus the foregoing registration and reregistration requirements are also applicable to solicitors.

Annual Reporting Requirements

Charitable Organizations.   There are no separate reporting requirements for charitable organizations. However, the annual registration requirement is the equivalent of a reporting requirement.

Nonetheless, at the request of the attorney general or appropriate county prosecutor, a charitable organization is required to submit a financial statement containing (1) the gross amount of the contributions pledged and collected; (2) the amount given or to be given to charitable purposes represented, together with details as to the manner of distribution as may be required; (3) the aggregate amount paid and to be paid for the expenses of the solicitation; (4) the amounts paid and to be paid to independent fund-raisers; (5) copies of any annual or periodic report of its activities, furnished by the charitable organization to its parent organization, subsidiaries, or affiliates, during or for the same fiscal period.

Professional Fund-Raisers.   There are no separate reporting requirements for fund-raisers. However, the annual registration requirement is the equivalent of a reporting requirement.

Professional Solicitors.   There are no separate reporting requirements for professional solicitors. However, the annual registration requirement (for those that are considered "independent fund raisers") is the equivalent of a reporting requirement.

Exemptions

This statute is inapplicable with respect to solicitations for religious, evangelical, or missionary activities under the direction of a religious organization duly organized and operating in good faith that are entitled to receive recognition of tax-exempt status from the IRS.

Bingo games, raffles, and amusement games expressly are not considered solicitations for these purposes.

The registration requirements of this law (see above) are not applicable to (1) a charitable organization raising less than $5,000 in a year, where all of the activities of the organization (including fund-raising) are carried on by volunteers and where no part of the charitable organization's assets or income inures to the benefit of or is paid to any officer or member of the organization; and (2) a charitable organization located outside of the state if the charity files with the secretary (a) the registration documents required under the law of the state in which the charitable organization is located, (b) the registration required under the charitable solicitation laws of the states of California and New York, and (c) such federal "income tax forms" as may be required by the secretary.

A charitable organization that is supervised and controlled by a superior or parent organization that is incorporated, qualified to do business, or is doing business in the state is not required to register under this law if the superior or parent organization files an application, on behalf of the subsidiary, in addition to or as part of its own application.

Commercial Co-ventures

This statute does not regulate commercial co-venturing.

Other Requirements

Contracts.   A contract between a charitable organization and an independent fund-raiser must be in writing. A true and correct copy of the agreement must be kept on file in the offices of the charity and fund-raiser for at least three years. These records must be available for inspection by the attorney general of the state or appropriate county prosecuting attorney.

Record Keeping and Accounting.   Charitable organizations and independent fund-raisers must maintain accurate, current, and readily available books and records as their usual business locations for at least three years.

Information provided to the secretary pursuant to this law becomes part of the public record.

Unique Provisions

Disclosures.   A person soliciting charitable contributions must disclose orally or in writing to each prospective donor (1) the name of the individual making the solicitation; (2) the name of the charitable organization; (3) the purpose of the solicitation; (4) the name of the organization that will receive the funds contributed; (5) whether the charitable organization is or is not properly registered under this law; and (6) if registered, that information relating its financial affairs is available by contacting the secretary of state, giving the secretary's toll-free telephone number (if available).

A person soliciting charitable contributions also must conspicuously disclose in writing to each person solicited (1) if the solicitation is conducted by a charitable organization, the percentage relationship between the total amount of money applied to charitable purposes and the dollar value of support received from solicitations and from all other sources "received on behalf of the charitable purpose of the organization," and (2) if the solicitation is conducted by an independent or nonprofit fund-raiser, the percentage relationship between the amount of money disbursed to charitable organizations for charitable purposes and the total value of contributions received on behalf of charitable organizations by the independent or nonprofit fund-raiser.

A person soliciting charitable contributions by telephone must make the disclosures as described in the preceding paragraph in writing within five days of the receipt of a contribution. If the organization sends any materials to a prospective donor, the materials must include the appropriate disclosures.

If the charitable organization is associated with, or has a name that is similar to, a unit of government, each person soliciting contributions must disclose to each prospective donor whether the organization is or is not part of any unit of government and the "true nature" of its relationship to the unit of government.

The advertising material and the "general promotional plan" for a solicitation may not be false, misleading, or deceptive, and must afford "full and fair" disclosure.

Percentages.   See Disclosures (above).

Prohibited Acts.   A person soliciting charitable contributions may not represent, orally or in writing, that (1) a contribution is deductible unless the organization involved has received recognition of tax-exempt status from the IRS; (2) the individual soliciting the contribution is a volunteer, if that is not the case; or (3) the individual soliciting the contribution is a member, staffer, helper, or employee of the organization involved, if that is not the case.

A charitable organization, independent fund-raiser, or other entity may not knowingly use the name of any other person for the purpose of soliciting contributions from persons in the state without the written consent of the solicited person. Directors, trustees, officers, employees, agents, and independent fund-raisers are deemed to have given this consent. A person's name is deemed used for solicitation purposes if the person's name is listed on stationery, advertisement, brochure, or correspondence of the charitable organization or if the name is listed or represented to anyone who has contributed to, sponsored, or endorsed the charitable organization or its activities.

A charitable organization, independent fund-raiser, or other person soliciting contributions for or on behalf of a charitable organization may not use a name, symbol, or statement so closely related to that used by another charitable organization or governmental agency that the use would tend to confuse or mislead the public.

Registration under this law may not be considered or represented as an endorsement by the secretary or the state.

Other.   A charitable organization must comply with all local governmental regulations applying to solicitations for or on behalf of charitable organizations.

Solicitations may not be conducted by a charitable organization or independent fund-raiser that has, or if a corporation, its officers, directors, or principals have, been convicted of a crime involving solicitations for or on behalf of a charitable organization in the state, the United States, or any other state or foreign country within the past 10 years or has been subject to certain permanent injunctions or administrative orders within the past 10 years, or of restraining a false or misleading promotional plan involving solicitations for charitable organizations.

When an individual or organization registered under this law, or its president, treasurer, or comparable officers, cannot be found after "reasonably diligent effort," the secretary becomes the agent of the individual or organization upon whom process may be served.

The commission by any person of an act or practice prohibited by this law is an unfair act or practice or unfair method of competition in the conduct of trade or commerce for the purpose of application of the state's consumer protection law.

Sanctions

A person who willfully and knowingly violates any provision of this law or who willfully and knowingly gives false or incorrect information to the secretary, attorney general, or county prosecuting attorney in filing statements required by this law, whether or not the statement or report is verified, is guilty of a gross misdemeanor.

A person who violates any provisions of this law or who gives false or incorrect information to the secretary, attorney general, or county prosecuting attorney in filing statements required by this law, whether or not the statement or report is verified, is guilty of a misdemeanor.

A charitable organization, nonprofit fund-raiser, or independent fund-raiser who, after notification by the secretary, fails to properly register under this law by the end of the first business day following issuance of a notice, is liable for a late filing fee of five dollars per day from the date of the notice until the registration is properly completed and filed.

WEST VIRGINIA

Introduction

Comprehensive statute: Yes
Regulatory office(s): Secretary of state
Citation: Title 29, Article 19, Sections 1–15

Registration or Licensing Requirements

Charitable Organizations.   A charitable organization, unless exempt from the requirement, may not solicit contributions in the state of West

Virginia unless, prior to any solicitation, the organization has registered with the state's secretary of state.

The registration statement must contain (1) the name of the organization; (2) the purpose of the organization; (3) the principal address of the organization and the address of any offices in the state or, if there is no office, the name and address of the person having custody of its financial records; (4) the names and addresses of any chapters, branches, or affiliates in the state; (5) the place where and the date when the organization was legally established; (6) the form of its organization; (7) the names and addresses of the directors, trustees, officers, and the principal salaried executive staff officer; (8) a balance sheet and income and expense statement or financial statement for the organization's immediately preceding fiscal year (audited by an independent public accountant where the organization receives contributions in excess of $50,000 annually); (9) a copy of any determination from the IRS recognizing the tax-exempt status of the organization; (10) a copy of the annual information return (Form 990) most recently filed with the IRS; (11) information indicating whether the organization intends to solicit contributions directly or have the fund-raising done by others; (12) information indicating whether the organization is authorized by any other governmental authority to solicit contributions; (13) information indicating whether the organization is or has ever been enjoined by any court from soliciting contributions; (14) the general purpose or purposes for which the contributions to be solicited shall be used; (15) the name or names under which it intends to solicit contributions; (16) the names of the individuals who will have final responsibility for the custody of the contributions; and (17) the names of the individuals responsible for the final distribution of the contributions.

A chapter, branch, or affiliate may separately register or report the information to its parent organization who must thereafter furnish the information in consolidated form to the secretary of state.

This registration is effective for one year and is renewable.

Professional Fund-Raisers.   A person may not serve as a professional fund-raiser (termed "professional fund-raising counsel") for a charitable organization subject to this law without first registering with the secretary. A partnership or corporation that is a professional fund-raising counsel may register on behalf of all its members, officers, agents, and employees.

Fund-raising counsel must file with and have approved by the secretary a bond in the amount of $10,000. A partnership or corporation that is a professional fund-raising counsel may file a consolidated bond on behalf of all its members, officers, agents and employees.

This registration is effective for one year and is renewable.

Professional Solicitors.   The registration and bonding requirements for professional solicitors are the same as those for professional fund-raising counsel (see above).

Annual Reporting Requirements

Charitable Organizations.   There are no separate reporting requirements as such for charitable organizations. However, this annual registration requirement serves as the equivalent of a reporting requirement.

Professional Fund-Raisers.   There are no separate reporting requirements as such for professional fund-raising counsel. However, the annual registration requirement serves as the equivalent of a reporting requirement.

Professional Solicitors.   There are no separate reporting requirements as such for professional solicitors. However, the annual registration requirement serves as the equivalent of a reporting requirement.

Exemptions

The following charitable organizations are exempt from the registration requirement: (1) properly accredited educational institutions; (2) "auxiliary associations, foundations, and support groups" related to exempt educational institutions; (3) persons requesting contributions for the relief of any individual specified by name at the time of the solicitation, when all of the contributions are turned over to the named beneficiary; (4) hospitals; (5) organizations that solicit only within the membership of the organization by its members; and (5) churches, other religious organizations, or any group affiliated with and forming an integral part of one of these organizations, where no part of the net income of the organization inures to the direct benefit of any individual and where the organization has received recognition of tax-exempt status from the IRS.

The following charitable organizations are exempt from the filing of an annual registration statement, as long as they do not employ professional fund-raising counsel or a professional solicitor and do not receive more than $10,000 in contributions during a calendar year: (1) local youth athletic organizations; (2) community civic clubs; (3) community service clubs; (4) fraternal organizations; (5) labor unions; (6) local posts, camps, chapters, or similarly designated elements or "country units" of these elements of bona fide veterans' organizations or auxiliaries that issue charters to the local elements throughout the state; (7) bona fide organizations of volunteer firefighters or auxiliaries; (8) bona fide ambulance associations or auxiliaries; and (9) bona fide rescue squad associations or auxiliaries. If any of these organizations raises more than $10,000 in a year, it must register with the secretary within 30 days.

Commercial Co-ventures

This law does not regulate commercial co-venturing.

Other Requirements

Contracts. A contract between a charitable organization and a professional fund-raising counsel and/or a professional solicitor must be filed with the secretary within 10 days of its execution. If there is no contract with a professional solicitor, a written statement of the nature of the arrangement (including the amount, percentage, or other method of compensation to the solicitor) must be filed.

Record Keeping and Accounting. Registration statements, applications, reports, contracts, and other documents and information required by this law become public records.

A charitable organization subject to this law must keep "true fiscal records" as to its activities in the state and must make these records available to the state upon demand. These records must be retained for at least three years.

Unique Provisions

Disclosures. A registered charitable organization, professional fund-raising counsel, or professional solicitor must disclose in writing (1) the name of a representative of the person to whom inquiries may be made; (2) the name of the charitable organization; (3) the purpose of the solicitation; (4) upon request of the person solicited, the estimated percentage of the money collected that will be applied for fund-raising and administration, or how much of the money collected will be applied directly to the charitable purpose; and (5) if applicable, the number of the raffle, bingo, or other state permit used for fund-raising. This disclosure statement must be conspicuously displayed on any written solicitation.

Charitable organizations must include in each solicitation a "clear description" of programs for which funds are requested and source from which written information is available.

A written solicitation must include a statement that the charitable organization's registration and supporting documents are available from the secretary.

Percentages.   See Disclosures (above).

Prohibited Acts.   A charitable organization, professional fund-raising counsel, or professional solicitor may not solicit contributions in the state where their registration has been cancelled, suspended, or refused.

A person may not use the fact of registration under this law to lead the public to believe that the registration constitutes an endorsement or approval by the state.

A person may not, in connection with the solicitation of contributions for or the sale of goods or services of a person other than a charitable organization, mislead anyone to believe that the solicitation is for a charitable organization or for charitable purposes, if that is not the case.

A person may not, in connection with the solicitation of contributions, use a name, symbol, or statement so closely similar to that used by another charitable organization or governmental agency that the use would tend to mislead the public.

A person may not, in connection with the solicitation of contributions or the sale of goods or services for charitable purposes, lead anyone to believe that any other person sponsors or endorses the solicitation or sale, or approves of the charitable purposes of the organization, when the other person has not given consent to the use of his, her, or its name for this purpose. A member of the organization's governing body or a volunteer in the solicitation campaign is deemed to have given consent for these purposes.

A person may not make any representation that he, she, or it is soliciting contributions for a charitable organization, or may not use any emblem, device, or printed material belonging to a charitable organization for the purpose of soliciting gifts, without first being authorized to do so by the charitable organization.

Other.   A charitable organization subject to this law must solicit contributions only for charitable purposes and may not expend funds raised for charitable purposes for noncharitable purposes.

Expenditures by a charitable organization "must be related in a primary degree to stated purpose (programs and activities) described in solicitations and in accordance with reasonable donor expectations."

A charitable organization must "establish and exercise controls over fund-raising activities conducted for the organization['s] benefit[,] including written contracts and agreements, and assurance of fund-raising activities without excessive pressure."

A charitable organization must "substantiate a valid governing structure" and its members must comply with the state's conflict-of-interest statute.

A professional solicitor may not solicit for a charitable organization unless the solicitor (1) has obtained written authorization from the charity, a copy of which must be filed with the secretary, that is effective for no longer than one year; and (2) carries the authorization on his or her person when soliciting gifts and exhibits the authorization on request to those solicited, police officers, or agents of the secretary.

A charitable organization, professional fund-raising counsel, or professional solicitor having its principal place of business outside the state or organized under the law of another state, that solicits contributions in the state, is deemed to have appointed the secretary as its agent for purposes of service of process.

The secretary is authorized to enter into reciprocal agreements with other states for the purpose of exchanging information with respect to charitable organizations, professional fund-raising counsel, and professional solicitors. The secretary may accept information filed by a person with another state in lieu of the information required to be filed by this law, if that information is substantially similar to the information required by this law. The secretary may grant exemption from the registration requirement (see above) to charitable organizations organized under the law of another state having their principal operations in the other state, where the funds are derived principally from sources outside the state and where the organization has been granted exemption from the filing of registration statements by the other state's law, if the other statute is similar in substance to this law.

This statute creates a commission on charitable organizations, which advises and makes recommendations to the secretary as to the effectuation of this law, holds hearings, and is authorized to request the attorney general and the appropriate county prosecuting attorney to take action to enforce this law or protect the public from any "fraudulent scheme or criminal act."

Sanctions

The secretary is empowered to cancel, suspend, or refuse to accept the registration of a charitable organization, professional fund-raising counsel, or professional solicitor where the person fails to timely file information with the secretary.

The secretary is authorized to initiate investigations to determine if there is any violation of this law, which can lead to the suspension or cancellation of a registration. A registration that knowingly contains a false or misleading statement must be revoked.

The attorney general or any prosecuting attorney who has reason to believe that a person is operating in violation of this law, or has knowingly and willfully made any false statement in information filed with the secretary, is empowered to bring court action to enjoin the violation.

A person who willfully and knowingly violates a provision of this law or who willfully and knowingly provides false or incorrect information to the secretary is guilty of a misdemeanor. The punishment for the first offense is a fine of at least $100 and no more than $500 and/or imprisonment for no more than six months. The punishment for any subsequent offense is a fine of at least $500 and no more than $1,000 and/or imprisonment for no more than one year. The willful and knowing employment of a device, scheme, artifice, false representation, or promise with intent to defraud or obtain money or other property, by a charitable organization, professional fund-raising counsel, or professional solicitor, also is a misdemeanor and is so punishable.

In the case of these violations, there is a procedure for returning to contributors the gifts that were wrongfully obtained.

WISCONSIN

Introduction

Comprehensive statute: Yes
Regulatory office(s): Department of Regulation and Licensing
Citation: Section 440.41

Registration or Licensing Requirements

Charitable Organizations.   A charitable organization, unless exempt from the requirement, may not solicit contributions in the state of Wisconsin unless, prior to any solicitation, the organization has registered with the state's department of regulation and licensing.

The application for registration must contain (1) the name under which the charitable organization intends to solicit contributions; (2) the names and addresses of directors, trustees, officers, and executive personnel; (3) the names and addresses of any professional fund-raiser and professional solicitor who will act on behalf of the charity; (4) copies of contracts stating the arrangements (including compensation) between a charitable organization and a fund-raiser or solicitor; (5) the general purposes for which the charitable organization is organized; (6) the purposes for which the contributions to be solicited will be used; (7) the period of time during which the solicitation will be made; (8) the addresses of the organization and the addresses of any offices in the state or, if the organization does not maintain a principal office in the state, the name and address of any person in the state having custody of any of its financial records; (9) where and when the organization was legally established; (10) the tax-exempt status of the organization; (11) a copy of its annual information return (Form 990) most recently filed with the IRS; (12) information indicating whether the organization is authorized by any other governmental authority to solicit contributions; (13) information indicating whether the organization is or has ever been enjoined by any court from soliciting contributions or has lost its authorization to solicit contributions; (14) the name of the board, group, or individual having final discretion as to the distribution and use of contributions received; and (15) such other information as may be "necessary or appropriate in the public interest or for the protection of contributors."

This registration remains in effect until cancelled by the department or withdrawn by the organization. However, a registration may not continue beyond the date the organization should have filed an annual report (see below) but failed to do so. Once the due date for the report has passed, a new registration may not be filed until the delinquent report is filed.

Any change in this information must be sent to the department within 10 days.

Professional Fund-Raisers.   A person may not act as a professional fund-raiser for a charitable organization required to register under this law until the person has first registered with the department. This registration is effective for one year and is renewable.

The fund-raiser must file with and have approved by the department a bond in the amount of $5,000.

Professional Solicitors.   A professional solicitor employed or retained by a professional fund-raiser required to register under this law must, before accepting employment, register with the department. This registration is effective for one year and is renewable.

Annual Reporting Requirements

Charitable Organizations.   A registered charitable organization that receives in any calendar year contributions in excess of $50,000, and every charitable organization the fund-raising functions of which are carried on by one who is compensated for the services, must annually file a report with the department. This report must include a financial statement for the preceding 12 months and a statement of any changes in the information contained in the registration statement (see above), and be the subject of an opinion of an independent certified public accountant. Other registered charitable organizations must likewise annually file a report, although this report need not be accompanied by the opinion of an accountant. However, a report with an accountant's opinion is due from any charitable organization that receives more than $500 from a "solicitation project" or special event where more than 25 percent of the gross receipts are expended for solicitation costs.

Where a registration statement has been filed by a superior or parent organization (see above), it must file the annual report on behalf of the local, county, or area division in addition to or as part of its own report.

An organization that qualifies for an exemption or that has not solicited or received contributions during the year can file an affidavit stating that situation in lieu of the annual report.

Professional Fund-Raisers.   There is no annual reporting requirement as such for professional fund-raisers. However, the annual registration is the equivalent of annual reporting.

Professional Solicitors.   There is no annual reporting requirement as such for professional solicitors. However, the annual registration is the equivalent of annual reporting.

Exemptions

This law is inapplicable to veterans' organizations incorporated under state law or chartered under federal law.

The following persons are exempt from the registration requirement: (1) religious corporations and other religious agencies and organizations, and charities, agencies, and organizations operated, supervised, or controlled by or in connection with a religious organization; (2) educational institutions, where the solicitation is confined to the student body and their families, alumni, faculty, and trustees; (3) a charitable organization that does not receive contributions in excess of $4,000 during a calendar year, as long as all of its fund-raising functions are carried on by volunteers (with registration required within 30 days once that threshold is exceeded); (4) fraternal, civic, benevolent, patriotic, and social organizations, as long as they solicit contributions solely from their membership; (5) persons requesting contributions for the relief of an individual specified by name at the time of the solicitation, where all of the contributions are turned over to the named beneficiary; (6) any local, county, or area division of a charitable organization supervised and controlled by a superior or parent organization that is incorporated, qualified to do business, or doing business in the state, where the superior or parent organization files a registration statement on behalf of the local unit in addition to or as part of its registration statement; and (7) any state agency, city, village, town, or school board.

Commercial Co-ventures

This statute does not regulate commercial co-venturing. However, the state has a separate fraudulent advertising law that contains a provision (sec. 100.18(4)), which regulates commercial co-venturing and similar forms of fund-raising.

Other Requirements

Contracts.   A contract entered into by a charitable organization and a professional fund-raiser must be in writing. "True and correct" copies must be filed with the department, and kept on file in the offices of the charitable organization and the professional fund-raiser for a three-year period. The contract must be made available for inspection by any authorized agency.

A contract between a charitable organization and a professional fund-raiser or professional solicitor must be filed with the department within 10 days of its execution (unless filed with the charity's registration application).

Unique Provisions

Percentages.   The department must semiannually compile and make public lists of the charitable organizations registered, indicating the gross receipts and total solicitation costs for each organization and each project or special event of each organization in "dollar values and percentages."

Prohibited Acts.   A person who is required to register under this law may not use the name of any other person for the purpose of soliciting contributions in the state without the written consent of the other person. A person is deemed to have used the name of another person for this purpose if the other person's name is listed on any stationery, advertisement, brochure, or correspondence of the charitable organization, or his or her name is listed or referred to as one who has contributed to, sponsored, or endorsed the charitable organization or its activities.

Other.   A charitable organization, professional fund-raiser, or professional solicitor that is a resident or has his, her, or its principal place of business outside the state or is organized under the law of another state, and that solicits contributions in this state, is deemed to have irrevocably appointed the secretary as agent for service of process.

Sanctions

The department, with the advice and consent of the attorney general, must cancel the registration of any organization that fails to timely comply with the applicable reporting requirement(s) or fails to furnish additional information as is requested by the department or attorney general within the required time.

An action for violation of this law may be prosecuted in court by the attorney general, who has the power to seek court injunctions to enjoin violations of this law or to prevent fund-raising fraud.

A violation of this law is punishable by a fine not to exceed $1,000 and/or imprisonment for six months.

WYOMING

No statute.

A summary of the principal components of each state's charitable solicitation act appears as Appendix A.

4

The State Charitable Solicitation Acts: A Comparative Analysis

Because of the diversity of the contents of the various state charitable solicitation acts, it is, to understate the problem, somewhat difficult to generalize about their terms and requirements.[1] Nonetheless, as reflected in Chapter 3, there are 30 more or less "standard" state charitable solicitation acts in the United States,[2] and thus there are some basic commonalities among them.[3]

In essence, these fundamental features are (1) a series of definitions; (2) registration, licensing, or similar requirements for charitable organizations; (3) annual reporting requirements for charitable organizations; (4) exemptions for certain charitable and other organizations from all or a portion of the statutory requirements; (5) registration and/or reporting requirements for professional fund-raisers; (6) registration and/or reporting requirements for professional solicitors; (7) regulatory requirements for commercial co-venturers; (8) record-keeping and public information requirements; (9) mandatory contract requirements; (10) point-of-solicitation disclosure requirements; (11) limitations on fund-raising expenses;[4] (12)

---

[1] Of even greater variance are the requirements imposed by the many regulations, rules, and forms promulgated to accompany the various state statutes, the enforcement efforts among the states, and the requirements imposed by the hundreds of county and city ordinances.

[2] Also see Appendix A.

[3] See Ch. 8 § 8.22 for an overview of the state laws and § 8.11 of that chapter for a discussion of a prototype state charitable solicitation act.

[4] Most, if not all, of these limitations and prohibitions are unconstitutional. See Ch. 5 § 5.3.

a variety of so-called prohibited acts; (13) registered agent requirements; (14) investigatory and injunctive authority vested in enforcement officials; and (15) civil and criminal penalties, and other sanctions. Each of these characteristics are discussed next.

§ 4.1 Definitions

Most state charitable solicitation acts open with a glossary of many of the important terms used in the laws.

Charitable

Inasmuch as the purpose of the states' solicitation statutes is to regulate the process of fund-raising for "charitable" purposes, the definition of the term "charitable" is a major factor in establishing the parameters of the reach of these laws. (The boundaries of these laws are also somewhat set by the scope of the terms "solicit" and "contribution.") The meaning of the term "charitable" in this context is usually considerably broader than that used in the federal tax setting in defining terms such as "charitable," "educational," "religious," and "scientific."[5]

In general, the law of charity emanates from the common law treatment of the term, derived largely from the law pertaining to charitable trusts. The meaning of the term "charitable" under the law of the United States has been developed largely through interpretations, by the courts and the IRS, of the meaning of the term for purposes of the tax exemption and charitable contribution deductions.

The term "charitable" as used in the state charitable solicitation act context is extremely broad and sufficiently encompassing to embrace all categories of organizations that are regarded as "charitable" entities for federal tax purposes, including churches, and conventions, associations, integrated auxiliaries, and the like, of churches; other religious organizations; schools, colleges, universities, libraries, and museums; other educational organizations; hospitals, clinics, homes for the aged, and medical research organizations; other health care organizations; publicly supported charitable organizations; and certain organizations that are supportive of public charities.[6]

However, the states, in defining the term "charitable" for purposes of regulating charitable fund-raising, also sweep within the ambit of

---

[5] See Ch. 2 § 2.1.
[6] IRC §§ 501(c)(3), 509(a)(1) (IRC § 170(b)(1)(A)(i)–(vi)), 509(a)(2), 509(a)(3), & 509(a)(4).

these laws some or all of the following purposes, actual or purported: "benevolent," "philanthropic," "eleemosynary," "patriotic," "humane," "social service," "civic," "fraternal," "voluntary," "public interest," "cultural," "artistic," "environmental," "social advocacy," "recreation," and/or "welfare."

Moreover, some state's laws expressly incorporate within the reach of the statute purposes that would normally not be covered. For example, the law of one state includes within its purview solicitations for "police" and "labor" purposes.[7] The statute in another state includes as a charitable activity the "purposes of influencing legislation or influencing the actions of any public official or instigating, prosecuting, or intervening in litigation."[8] The law of another state[9] includes "legal defense activities."[10]

As discussed below, the typical state charitable solicitation statute exempts some "charitable" organizations from all or a portion of its requirements. The blanket exemption from these laws often accorded religious organizations is frequently achieved by carving them out of the ambit of the term "charitable."

Some solicitations for gifts by nonprofit organizations lie outside the scope of a state's charitable solicitation act because the gifts are not to be used for "charitable" purposes. An illustration is solicitation of contributions by political action committees. For the most part, these unreached solicitations are implicit from a facial reading of the statute. Sometimes the statute itself expressly recognizes this type of exclusion, such as one[11] that excludes solicitations for political, trade, or labor purposes.[12] Six of these laws are expressly not applicable to political parties, committees, or clubs.[13]

---

[7] Rhode Island.

[8] Virginia.

[9] Washington.

[10] Solicitations for an individual's legal defense fund are not normally regarded as solicitations for a charitable purpose. The Virginia statute (see the text accompanying *supra* note 8) includes within the concept of charity the instigation of, prosecution of, and intervention in litigation but not the defense against litigation. The exemptions for solicitations for specified individuals (see text accompanying *infra* notes 132–35) may be applicable in this context.

[11] Virginia.

[12] A problem with this form of statutory exclusion is that it invites the argument that solicitations of these types would be embraced by the statute absent the statutory exception. Simply because a type of solicitation is excluded by one state's law obviously does not mean it is excluded from the law of another.

[13] Florida, Maryland, Minnesota, Virginia, Utah (registration only), and Washington.

Some fund-raising is undertaken for the benefit of a named individual. As discussed, it is common for this type of solicitation to be excluded from regulation.[14] Although state regulators disagree on the point, a quite respectable argument can be made that fund-raising for one person is not fund-raising for "charity," because of the private benefit involved. (Certainly, for federal income tax purposes, an organization benefiting only one individual cannot be a charitable one.)[15]

There is no court opinion delinating the ultimate scope of these laws. As a general rule, the government officials enforcing these statutes accord the term "charitable" great latitude when determining their jurisdiction over fund-raising regulation matters.

Charitable Organization

A "charitable organization" is usually defined for these purposes as including any "person" organized and operated for a "charitable" purpose. The term "person" is, then, usually very broadly defined as, in the language of one statute, any "individual, organization, trust, foundation, association, partnership, corporation, society, or other group or combination acting as a unit."[16] Another state adds to the definition a "firm, copartnership, . . . company . . . or league, and . . . any trustee, receiver, assignee, agent, or other similar representative thereof."[17]

Often, the term "charitable organization" also includes a person that "holds itself out" as a charitable organization or one that solicits or obtains contributions solicited from the public.

Solicitation

Another key term associated with a charitable solicitation act is the word "solicitation."

The term is generally broadly defined. This fact is evidenced, not only by the express terms of the definition, but also by application of these acts to charitable solicitation conducted "by any means whatsoever." Thus, a solicitation can take place by an in-person request, mail, other publishing, television, radio, telephone, or other medium.

As an illustration, pursuant to one statute, the term "solicit" means "to request, directly or indirectly, money, credit, property, or other

---

[14] See *infra* § 4.4.

[15] E.g., *Wendy L. Parker Rehabilitation Foundation, Inc.* v. *Commissioner*, 52 T.C.M. 51 (1986).

[16] Virginia.

[17] Minnesota.

financial assistance in any form on the plea or representation that the money, credit, property, or other financial assistance will be used for a charitable purpose."[18] This is, obviously, a most encompassing definition of the term, yet it is a typical definition.

This statute (unlike many) amplifies the definition by stating types of solicitations that are included within the definition. Nonetheless, even if not expressly provided for in a state's law, these activities are undoubtedly "solicitations" in every jurisdiction. These categories of solicitations are the following:

1.   Both oral and written requests for contributions.

2.   An "announcement to the news media for further dissemination by it of an appeal or campaign seeking contributions from the public for one or more charitable purposes."

3.   The "distribution, circulation, posting, or publishing of any handbill, written advertisement, or other publication which, directly or by implication, seeks contributions by the public for one or more charitable purposes."

4.   The "sale of, or offer or attempt to sell or secure, any advertisement, patron listing, advertising space, book, card, tag, coupon, device, magazine, membership, subscription, ticket, admission, chance, merchandise, or other tangible item in connection with which (i) an appeal is made for contributions to one or more charitable purposes, or (ii) the name of a charitable organization is used or referred to, whether express or implied, as an inducement to make such a purchase, or (iii) a statement is made that the whole or any part of the proceeds from the sale is to be used for one or more charitable purposes."

The term "solicitation" may embrace the pursuit of a grant (as opposed to a contract) from a private foundation, other nonprofit organization, or a governmental unit. Thus, a charitable organization seeking this type of financial assistance should explore the need to register pursuant to the charitable solicitation act (if any) in effect in the state in which the prospective grantor is located before submitting the grant proposal. As noted below, for example, the statute in one state expressly excludes government grants from the term "contribution."[19] By contrast, the law

[18] Maryland.
[19] Virginia.

in another state defines the word "contribution" to include a "grant or other financial assistance from any agency of government."[20]

One state's law, like others, also provides—probably unnecessarily—that a solicitation "is deemed to have taken place when the request is made, whether or not the person making it actually receives a contribution."[21] Another state's law provides that its charitable solicitation act is not to be construed as prohibiting an organization from receiving an unsolicited contribution.[22]

Sale

A few charitable solicitation acts include a definition of the term "sale" (or "sell" or "sold").

For example, one state's statute provides that a "sale" means the "transfer of any property or the rendition of any service to any person in exchange for consideration, including any purported contribution without which such property would not have been transferred or such services would not have been rendered."[23]

In those states that define a commercial co-venture as a charitable sales promotion,[24] the term "sale" is usually defined in that context.

Contribution

In contrast to a "sale," a "contribution" is a transfer of money or property in the absence of "consideration" (consideration being the elements of the bargain between the contracting parties). Thus, one charitable solicitation act defines the word "contribution" as any "gift, bequest, devise or other grant of any money, credit, financial assistance or property of any kind or value, including the promise to contribute . . . ," the latter being, of course, a pledge.[25]

This statute excludes three types of payments from the scope of the term "contribution." The first of these presumably is the case with respect to every state charitable solicitation act; the other two are unique. These exclusions are the following:

[20] New York.
[21] Maryland.
[22] Utah.
[23] Virginia.
[24] See *infra* § 4.4.
[25] Virginia.

1. "[P]ayments by the membership of an organization for membership fees, dues, fines, or assessments, or for services rendered to individual members. . . ."

2. "[M]oney, credit, financial assistance or property received from any governmental authority" (this includes grants).

3. "[A]ny donation of blood or any gift made pursuant to the Uniform Anatomical Gift Act."

Essentially, the concept in this context is that a gift is a payment to a charitable organization where the donor receives nothing of material value in return. This is why the payment of bona fide dues—which is the purchase of one or more services—is not the making of a gift. In some instances, a payment to a charitable organization is partially a gift and partially the purchase of a product or service.[26]

Membership

In the foregoing and other connections, these laws occasionally define the term "membership" or "member." The principal purpose of this definition is to define the term in relation to the exclusion for solicitations that are confined to the membership of the soliciting organization.[27]

Thus, the law of one state defines the term "membership" as being "[t]hose persons to whom, for payment of fees, dues, assessments, etc., an organization provides services and confers a bona fide right, privilege, professional standing, honor or other direct benefit, in addition to the right to vote, elect officers, or hold offices."[28]

This statute adds, as is the case with most of these definitions, that the concept of "membership" does "not include those persons who are granted a membership upon making a contribution as the result of solicitation."

Professional Fund-Raiser

The phrase "professional fund-raiser" is usually defined as, such as in the language of one state's law, "[a]ny person who for a flat fixed fee under a written agreement plans, conducts, manages, carries on, advises

---

[26] See Ch. 6 §§ 6.1 & 6.2.
[27] See the discussion in Ch. 5 § 5.8.
[28] Virginia.

or acts as a consultant, whether directly or indirectly, in connection with soliciting contributions for, or on behalf of, any charitable organization, but who actually solicits no contributions as a part of such services."[29] This definition, or a similar version of it, is utilized in 25 states.[30]

This definition of the term "professional fund-raiser" usually provides one or more exclusions from the embrace of the term, such as:

1.   In the language of one state's law, a "bona fide salaried officer or employee of a registered or exempt charitable organization or the bona fide salaried officer or employee of a registered parent organization. . . ."[31]

2.   In the language of another state's law, an "attorney who renders professional legal advice" or an "attorney, investment counselor, or banker who advises a client or customer to contribute to a charitable organization."[32]

In 12 states, the term used is "professional fund-raising counsel."[33] In three states, the term is "fund-raising counsel."[34] In one state, the term is "professional fund raiser consultant."[35] In another state, the phraseology is "independent fund raiser" or "independent fund raising entity."[36]

As discussed, there presently is in the law considerable confusion as to the meaning of the term "professional fund-raiser" in relation to the term "professional solicitor."[37] Some state laws so broadly define "professional fund-raiser" that they include a "professional solicitor," such as that in one state, where the term "professional fund-raiser" is defined

---

[29] *Ibid.*

[30] Alabama, Arkansas, Connecticut, Hawaii, Indiana, Kansas, Kentucky, Maine, Maryland, Massachusetts, Minnesota, New Hampshire, New Jersey, New York (which defines both "fund-raising counsel" and "professional fund-raiser"), North Carolina, North Dakota, Oklahoma, Oregon, Pennsylvania, Rhode Island, South Carolina, Virginia, Washington, West Virginia, and Wisconsin.

[31] Virginia.

[32] Maryland.

[33] Connecticut, Hawaii, Maine, Maryland, Massachusetts, North Carolina, Oregon, Pennsylvania, Rhode Island, South Carolina, Virginia, and West Virginia.

[34] Maryland, New Hampshire, and New York.

[35] Indiana.

[36] Washington.

[37] See Ch. 5 § 5.9; Ch. 8 § 8.3.

as "any person who for financial compensation or profit performs for a charitable organization any service in connection with which contributions are, or will be, solicited in this state by the compensated person or by any compensated person the person employs, procures, or engages to solicit; or any person who for compensation or profit plans, manages, advises, consults, or prepares material for, or with respect to, the solicitation in this state of contributions for a charitable organization."[38] In two other states, the term "professional fund-raising firm" is used to describe what is usually defined, in other states, as a "professional solicitor."[39]

Professional Solicitor

The term "professional solicitor" is usually defined in a state charitable solicitation act in one of two ways.

One of these definitions, as typified by the language of one state's statute, is that a "professional solicitor" is any "person who, for a financial or other consideration, solicits contributions for, or on behalf of, a charitable organization, whether such solicitation is performed personally or through his agents, servants, or employees or through agents, servants, or employees specially employed by, or for a charitable organization, who are engaged in the solicitation of contributions under the direction of such person, or any person who, for a financial or other consideration, plans, conducts, manages, carries on, advises, or acts as a consultant to a charitable organization in connection with the solicitation of contributions but does not qualify as a professional fund-raising counsel."[40]

This definition, or a similar version of it, is followed in 17 states.[41] In one state, the term used is "paid solicitor."[42]

This definition is usually accompanied by the same exclusions as noted above for professional fund-raisers, relating to officers, employees, lawyers, and the like.

The other definition of the term "professional solicitor," as illustrated by one state's statute, is "any person who is employed or retained for

---

[38] Minnesota.
[39] Oregon and Utah.
[40] Virginia.
[41] Colorado, Connecticut, Hawaii, Indiana, Maine, Maryland, Massachusetts, New Hampshire, North Carolina, North Dakota, Oregon, Pennsylvania, Rhode Island, South Carolina, Tennessee, Virginia, and West Virginia.
[42] New Hampshire.

compensation by a professional fund-raiser to solicit contributions for charitable purposes in this state."[43]

This latter definition is used in nine states.[44]

As noted, there currently is considerable confusion in the law as to the appropriate line of demarcation between the terms "professional fund-raiser" and "professional solicitor."[45] For example, one state's law uses the prevailing definition of the term "professional solicitor"[46] to define the term "professional fund-raiser."[47]

Commercial Co-venturer

Commerical co-venturing occurs when a business announces to the general public that a portion (a specific amount or a specific percentage) of the purchase price of a product or service will, during a stated period, be paid to a charitable organization. This activity usually results in a charitable gift, the amount of which is dependent on consumer response to the promotion by, and positive publicity for, the business sponsor.

One state's law defines the term "commercial co-venturer" as any "person who for profit is regularly and primarily engaged in trade or commerce other than in connection with the raising of funds or any other thing of value for a charitable organization and who advertises that the purchase or use of goods, services, entertainment, or any other thing of value will benefit a charitable organization."[48]

The term "commercial co-venture" is, in some respects, unfortunate terminology. First, it suggests that the charitable organization involved is engaged in a co-venture (joint venture) with the participating for-profit organization.[49] Second, the term implies that the charitable organization involved is doing something that is "commercial." Both connotations have potential adverse consequences in law, particularly in the unrelated business income setting.[50]

---

[43] Kansas.
[44] Alabama, Arkansas, Illinois, Kansas, Kentucky, New Jersey, New York, Oklahoma, and Wisconsin.
[45] See *supra* note 37.
[46] See *supra* note 40.
[47] Utah.
[48] New York.
[49] See Ch. 8 § 8.5.
[50] See Ch. 6 § 6.4.

Other Definitions

Other terms are defined, sometimes frequently and sometimes not, in state charitable solicitation acts.

For example, one state's law defines the phrase "fund-raising expenses" as being the "expenses of all activities that constitute or are an integral and inseparable part of a solicitation."[51]

The term "parent organization," as defined under this law, means "[t]hat part of a charitable organization which coordinates, supervises or exercises control over policy, fund raising, and expenditures, or assists or advises one or more chapters, branches or affiliates."

This law defines a "federated fund-raising organization" as any "federation of independent charitable organizations which have voluntarily joined together, including but not limited to a United Fund or Community Chest, for purposes of raising and distributing money for and among themselves and where membership does not confer operating authority and control of the individual agencies upon the federated group organization."

One state defines the term "volunteer" as "a person who renders services to a charitable organization or for a charitable purpose and who neither receives nor is expressly or impliedly promised financial remuneration for said services."[52]

The enumeration of definitions also includes reference to the state agency, department, or official having the responsibility for administration of the charitable solicitation act, as well as to any related commission. In 15 states, the administrative authority is the Department of State,[53] while in 14 states, the authority is the Office of the Attorney General.[54]

In Connecticut, the regulatory agency is the Department of Consumer Protection. In the District of Columbia, the authority is the Department of Economic Development. In Florida, it is the Department of Agriculture and Consumer Services. In Hawaii, it is the Department of Commerce and Consumer Affairs. In Louisiana, it is the Governor's Consumer Protection Division. In Maine, it is the Commission of Business Regulation.

---

[51] Virginia.

[52] Colorado.

[53] Arkansas, Colorado, Georgia, Iowa, Kansas, Maryland, New York, Nebraska, Nevada, North Dakota, Pennsylvania, South Carolina, Tennessee, Washington, and West Virginia.

[54] Alabama, California, Illinois, Indiana, Kentucky, Massachusetts, Michigan, Minnesota, Missouri, New Hampshire, New Jersey, New Mexico, Ohio, and Oregon.

In Massachusetts, it is the Division of Public Charities. In Minnesota, it is the Department of Commerce. In North Carolina, it is the Department of Human Resources. In Oklahoma, it is the Tax Commission. In Rhode Island, it is the Department of Business Regulation. In South Dakota, it is the Department of Commerce and Consumer Affairs. In Utah, it is the Division of Consumer Protection of the Department of Commerce. In Virginia, it is the Board of Agricultural and Consumer Services. Indeed, for years, in the state of Washington, the regulatory authority in this field was housed in the Department of Motor Vehicles. (Today, the authority is, conventionally, in the secretary of state.) In Wisconsin, it is the Department of Regulation and Licensing.

In some states, the authority to enforce a charitable solicitation act is vested in the attorney general, even though the administrative or regulatory authority, or both, may be lodged elsewhere.

§ 4.2   Preapproval

A fundamental requirement, express or implied, of nearly every state charitable solicitation act mandates a charitable organization (as defined in that law and not exempted from the obligation) that intends to solicit—by any means—contributions from persons in that state to first apply for and acquire permission to undertake the solicitation. The permission, which must be secured by both domestic (in-state) and foreign (out-of-state) charitable organizations, is characterized as a "registration" in 25 states[55] and a "license" in three states.[56] Two states characterize the permission as a "permit,"[57] and one as a "certificate."[58] Two states do not provide any characterization of this nature.[59] If successful, the result is authorization to conduct the solicitation. As noted, application for the registration, license, or other permit is most frequently made to a secretary of state or an attorney general.

A typical provision in this regard is that of one state's statute, which provides that "[e]very charitable organization which intends to solicit

---

[55] Connecticut, District of Columbia, Georgia, Hawaii, Illinois, Kansas, Kentucky, Maine, Maryland, Massachusetts, Minnesota, Missouri, New Jersey, New Mexico, New York, Ohio, Oklahoma, Pennsylvania, Rhode Island, South Carolina, Tennessee, Virginia, Washington, West Virginia, and Wisconsin.

[56] Michigan, North Carolina, and North Dakota.

[57] Iowa and Utah.

[58] Nebraska.

[59] Arkansas and Colorado.

contributions within this Commonwealth, or have funds solicited on its behalf, shall, prior to any solicitation, file a registration statement with the department upon forms prescribed by the department. . . ."[60]

Generally, the law requires a principal officer of the charitable organization to certify the accuracy of and to execute the registration statement, license, application, or the like.

The statute usually enumerates the categories of information about the charitable organization and the solicitation that must be in the registration statement or application for a license or permit. These categories of information generally are some or all of the following:

1.   The name of the organization.

2.   The name in which the organization intends to solicit contributions.

3.   The principal address of the organization and the address of any office in the state involved or, in the absence of an office, the name and address of the person having custody of its financial records.

4.   The names and addresses of any chapters, branches, or affiliates in the state involved.

5.   The names and addresses of its trustees, directors, officers, executive staff, and registered agent.

6.   The place where and the date when the organization was legally established.

7.   The form of the organization (corporation, trust, or unincorporated entity).

8.   The organization's classification as a tax-exempt organization under federal law.[61]

9.   The purpose or purposes for which the organization was founded.

10. A balance sheet and income and expense statement for the organization's immediately preceding tax year (perhaps audited), showing, among other items, the kind and amount of funds raised, expenses incidental to fund-raising, and expenditures of funds raised.

---

[60] Pennsylvania.

[61] In most instances, this will be as an organization that is tax-exempt under IRC § 501(a) because it is described in IRC § 501(c)(3).

11. The methods by which solicitations will be made, including use of a professional fund-raiser and/or professional solicitor.

12. The purpose or purposes for which the contributions to be solicited will be used.

13. The names of the individuals who will have final responsibility for the custody of the contributions.

14. The names of the individuals responsible for the final distribution of the contributions.

15. A statement indicating whether the organization is or has ever been enjoined by one or more states from soliciting contributions.

16. Copies of contracts between the charitable organization and professional fund-raisers and/or professional solicitors.

It is common for the statute to authorize the state's administrative agency to require, by regulations, the submission of additional information.

The states' laws either expressly provide or contemplate that the administrative authorities will examine the application and, where the application is legally sufficient, issue the registration, license, permit, or whatever the authorization is termed. The review authority at this stage is very broad. At a minimum, the governmental authorities have the discretion to determine if the application is in conformity with all legal requirements. Until recently (when the provision was repealed), the most expansive authority delegated in this regard was in Iowa, where the secretary of state was accorded "full discretion" as to which organizations will be issued permits, as well as had the duty to see to it that each applicant is "reputable" and that the contributions raised will be applied solely to "legitimate and worthy" purposes.

Certainly an investigation can ensue at this stage (as well as at any time thereafter). Most states vest plenary investigative power in the administrative and enforcement authorities, particularly the attorney general. Again, the Iowa statute reposes considerable authority in this regard in the secretary of state and perhaps assumes the worst of outcomes, as it empowers the secretary, in enforcing the act, to "call to his aid the attorney general, the county attorney of any county, and any peace officer in the state," as well as seek the assistance of the "extension division of the State University of Iowa and the commissioner of the Department of Social Services."

Sometimes, a chapter, branch, or affiliate (other than an independent member agency of a federated fund-raising organization) has the option of separately reporting the information to the state or reporting the information to the parent organization, which then is required to furnish the information in a consolidated form to the state.

The license or permit will not be issued where the administrative authorities find that the charity has omitted or materially misrepresented required information or if the organization would be acting in violation of one or more provisions of the state's charitable solicitation law. For example, one state's law provides that a permit to solicit will not be issued where a person, among other transgressions, violated the law, attempted to obtain the permit by misrepresentation, or materially misrepresented the purpose and manner in which contributions would be used.[62]

Usually the state levies a registration fee, which is either a fixed amount or an amount correlated with the level of contributions received, administrative or fund-raising outlays, or the like. Some states, however, issue the permit or license without charge.

The specifics of the state laws regarding fees are as follows: 14 states' statutes provide for a fixed fee[63] and four states charge a fee that is dependent upon annual receipts.[64]

State laws differ as to the duration of the registration or license. In 15 states, the permit or license expires one year after the date of issuance, or at the close of the calendar year, or at the close of the organization's fiscal year.[65] Renewal of the permit or license is made by filing an updated application within a certain period prior to the expiration date. These statutes also require a supplemental filing during the license or permit period where there is a material change in the information initially submitted with the application.

In five states, the registration or permit remains in effect until withdrawn by the charity or suspended or revoked by the state.[66]

The statutory law in the other jurisdictions does not address the point.

---

[62] Utah.

[63] Connecticut, Hawaii, Iowa, Kansas, Maryland, Minnesota, New Jersey, New York, North Dakota, Oklahoma, Rhode Island, South Carolina, Washington, and Wisconsin.

[64] Pennsylvania, Virginia, Tennessee, and West Virginia.

[65] Hawaii, Iowa, Kansas, Massachusetts, Nebraska, North Carolina, North Dakota, Pennsylvania, Rhode Island, South Carolina, Tennessee, Utah, Virginia, Washington, and West Virginia.

[66] Kansas, Minnesota, New Jersey, New York, and Wisconsin.

These laws usually provide that, where there is a finding that the charity has violated a provision of its charitable solicitation act, the enforcement authorities are to suspend or revoke the registration, license, or permit. The statute usually provides for some form of due process in this type of situation, including a hearing.

§ 4.3 Annual Reporting

Most state charitable solicitation acts require a soliciting charity (unless exempted) to annually file information with the appropriate governmental agency. This is done either by an annual updating of the registration, license, or the like, as is the case in the above-referenced 15 states,[67] and/or by the separate filing of an annual report, as is the case in 27 states.[68] The categories of charitable organizations exempted from reporting are usually those exempted from the registration or licensing requirement.

The solicitation statute usually mandates the contents of the annual reports. The information requested frequently includes the following:

1. The gross amount of contributions pledged to and collected by the charity—not just in the particular state but throughout the United States and any other countries.

2. The amount from the solicitation that was or is to be devoted to charitable purposes, as well as the amounts paid or to be paid for fund-raising (including the fees of professional fund-raisers) and for administration.

3. Identification of professional fund-raisers and/or professional solicitors used.

4. Net receipts disbursed or dedicated for disbursement within the particular state, by category of expenditure.

In addition, a reporting charitable organization usually must file a financial statement covering the preceding accounting period, prepared in conformance with appropriate accounting standards. Four states require,

---

[67] See *supra* note 65.

[68] Arkansas, California, Colorado, Connecticut, District of Columbia, Florida, Georgia, Illinois, Iowa, Maine, Maryland, Massachusetts, Michigan, Minnesota, Missouri, Nebraska, Nevada, New Hampshire, New Jersey, New Mexico, New York, North Dakota, Ohio, Oklahoma, Oregon, South Carolina, and Wisconsin.

by statute, that the reports be based upon the accounting standards and reporting procedures promulgated by the American Institute of Certified Public Accountants,[69] while two states authorize or require by statute use of the standards and procedures set forth in the *Standards for Uniform Financial Reporting by Voluntary Health and Welfare Organizations.*[70] Presumably, the regulators in other states have the discretion to select the accounting principles with which charities must comply or to develop their own. For example, the law in one state[71] states that each reporting charity "shall report its expenditures in accordance with standards and classifications of accounts as prescribed by the attorney general to effect uniform reporting by organizations having similar activities and programs."

These reports may have to be accompanied by an opinion of a certified public accountant.

The annual report is due at varying times as required by the states' statutes, namely, within 30 days after the close of the accounting period in one state,[72] within 60 days of that period in two states,[73] within 90 days of the period in two states,[74] within 4½ months of the period in two states,[75] within 5 months in one state,[76] and within 6 months of the period in five states.[77] The regulators in one state are expressly authorized by statute to require the filing of a report by a charity with respect to some other period.[78]

In two states, the annual report filing requirement, or the extent of it, is dependent upon the level of annual contributions received and/or use of a professional fund-raiser and/or professional solicitor.[79] In three states, a registration or license may be cancelled or not be renewed until the required annual report is filed.[80]

The report of a parent charitable organization must include the reports of all of its fund-raising affiliated groups.

---

[69] California, Maine, Massachusetts, and New York.
[70] Nebraska and South Carolina.
[71] New Jersey.
[72] District of Columbia.
[73] California and North Dakota.
[74] Arkansas and Oklahoma.
[75] New York and Oregon.
[76] Connecticut.
[77] Illinois, Minnesota, New Jersey, South Carolina, and Wisconsin.
[78] New Hampshire.
[79] Kansas and Oregon.
[80] Kansas, New Jersey, and New York.

Three states provide, by statute, the fee to be paid with the filing of a report.[81] In other states, the fees, if any, are set administratively.

The state charitable solicitation acts frequently also provide for annual reporting for professional fund-raisers, professional solicitors, and/or commercial co-venturers.

§ 4.4 Exemptions

The state charitable solicitation acts vary widely with respect to the exemptions available for eligible organizations and solicitations. As noted, the basic definition of the term "charitable" is sufficiently broad to initially encompass all categories of charitable and some other organizations.[82] Therefore, these statutes are applicable to soliciting religious, educational, health care, and other charitable organizations unless an exemption is expressly available or constitutional law principles mandate an exemption.

These statutory exemptions may be available for an organization as such or for an organization to the extent it engages in a particular type of solicitation. The exemption may be from the entirety of the statute or only a portion of it.

Churches

Churches and their closely related entities are frequently exempted from the entirety of the states' charitable solicitation acts.[83] For example, one state's statute accords total exemption to "any church or convention or association of churches, primarily operated for nonsecular purposes and no part of the net income of which inures to the direct benefit of any individual."[84] This exemption for churches and their affiliated entities is part of the law in 19 states.[85]

---

[81] Connecticut, Illinois, and New York.

[82] See the discussion of charitable organizations in *supra* § 4.1.

[83] Because of constitutional law considerations and as a practical matter, the law does not normally attempt a definition of the term "church." See *Law of Tax-Exempt Organizations* at 198–206. If an organization is classified as a church or a closely related organization for federal income tax purposes (IRC § 170(b)(1)(A)(i)), it presumably is treated the same for state fund-raising regulation purposes.

[84] Virginia.

[85] Arkansas, District of Columbia, Florida, Hawaii, Illinois, Iowa, Kentucky, Louisiana, Nebraska, New Hampshire, New Jersey, New Mexico, New York, North Dakota, Pennsylvania, Rhode Island, South Carolina, Virginia, and Washington.

In many of these states, this exemption is not found within the section of the statute providing for exemptions but instead is located in the definition of "charitable" entities.

Other Religious Organizations

Some state statutes do not make express provision for churches but instead embrace these institutions, for purposes of exemption, within a general reference to religious organizations.

Twenty-one states provide an exemption for religious organizations in general from the totality of their charitable solicitation acts.[86] In this category is the state law provision that so excludes "a corporation sole or other religious corporation, trust or organization incorporated or established for [a] religious purpose, . . . to any agency or organization incorporated or established for charitable, hospital or educational purposes and engaged in effectuating one or more of such purposes, that is affiliated with, operated by, or supervised or controlled by a corporation sole or other religious corporation, trust or organization incorporated or established for religious purposes, . . . [and] other religious agencies or organizations which serve religion by the preservation of religious rights and freedom from persecution or prejudice or fostering religion, including the moral and ethical aspects of a particular religious faith."[87]

It is less common for the exemption for religious organizations to be confined to the registration or licensing requirements. Thus, for example, one state's law exempts from its registration requirements "[a]ny person who solicits charitable contributions for a religious purpose."[88] Seventeen states provide exemption for religious organizations only from their registration or licensing requirements.[89]

Where an organization is exempt from the registration requirement, it usually is exempt from any reporting requirement.

---

[86] Arkansas, California, District of Columbia, Florida, Hawaii, Illinois, Iowa, Kentucky, Louisiana, Maine, Nebraska, New Hampshire, New Jersey, New York, North Dakota, Ohio, Pennsylvania, Rhode Island, South Carolina, Tennessee, and Washington.

[87] Hawaii.

[88] North Carolina.

[89] Connecticut, Georgia, Kansas, Maryland, Massachusetts, Michigan, Minnesota, Missouri, North Carolina, Oklahoma, Oregon, Rhode Island, South Carolina, Tennessee, Utah, West Virginia, and Wisconsin.

Educational Institutions

Ten states exempt at least certain types of educational institutions from the entirety of their charitable solicitation acts.[90] Usually, this exemption applies where the educational institution is accredited.

The more common practice is to exempt educational institutions from only the registration or licensing, and reporting, requirements. Twenty states have adopted this approach, as typified by the provision of one state[91] that exempts from that state's charitable solicitation act's licensing requirement "any educational institution, the curriculum of which in whole or part, is registered, approved or accredited by the Southern Association of Colleges and Schools or an equivalent regional accrediting body."[92]

Nine states, either as an alternative to or in addition to the foregoing approach, exempt from the registration and reporting requirements educational institutions that confine their solicitations to their "constituency."[93] Thus, for example, one state's law provides an exemption from registration for "any other educational institution confining its solicitation of contributions to its student body, alumni, faculty and trustees, and their families."[94]

Two states exempt solicitations by educational institutions of their constituency from the entirety of their charitable solicitation laws.[95]

Many schools, colleges, and universities undertake their fund-raising by means of related "foundations."[96] Ten states expressly provide exemption, in tandem with whatever exemption their laws extend to ed-

---

[90] California, District of Columbia, Florida, Hawaii, Iowa, Louisiana, New Hampshire, New Mexico, North Dakota, and Tennessee.

[91] North Carolina.

[92] Connecticut, Georgia, Illinois, Kansas, Maine, Michigan, Minnesota, Missouri, New Jersey, New York, North Carolina, Oklahoma, Oregon, Pennsylvania, Rhode Island, South Carolina, Tennessee, Utah, Virginia, and West Virginia.

[93] Kansas, Maryland, New Jersey, New York, Ohio, Oklahoma, Oregon, Virginia, and Wisconsin.

[94] Virginia.

[95] Hawaii and Kentucky.

[96] Foundations functioning on behalf of educational institutions that are operated by governments are expressly recognized, as concerns public charity and charitable donee classifications, in IRC § 170(b)(1)(A)(iv). See *Law of Tax-Exempt Organizations* at 441. Foundations functioning on behalf of other educational institutions are also public charities. See *Law of Tax-Exempt Organizations* at 442–72.

ucational institutions, to these supporting foundations.[97] Six states exempt, from the registration requirements, "parent-teacher associations" affiliated with an educational institution,[98] five states so exempt alumni organizations,[99] and one state so exempts "student groups."[100]

Libraries

While one state exempts nonprofit libraries from the entirety of its solicitation act,[101] six states exempt them from the registration requirements.[102]

Even where a charitable solicitation act fails to make express provision for exemption for libraries, these institutions may be able to secure an exemption as educational institutions.

Museums

Two states exempt nonprofit museums from the registration requirements of their charitable solicitation act.[103] One state exempts museums from the totality of its charitable solicitation act.[104]

As is the case with libraries, museums may be able to receive exemption as educational institutions where no express provision has been made for them in the exemption clauses.

Health Care Institutions

Twelve states exempt nonprofit hospitals from the registration or reporting requirements of their charitable solicitation acts.[105] Three states similarly exempt hospital-related foundations.[106]

---

[97] Hawaii, Illinois, Kansas, Missouri, North Carolina, Oregon, Rhode Island, Tennessee, Virginia, and West Virginia.

[98] Connecticut, Kentucky, Pennsylvania, Rhode Island, Tennessee, and Utah.

[99] Kansas, Minnesota, Missouri, New Jersey, and New York.

[100] Kentucky.

[101] Hawaii.

[102] Illinois, Kansas, New Jersey, New York, Pennsylvania, and Rhode Island.

[103] Oregon and Rhode Island.

[104] Oregon.

[105] Connecticut, Kansas, Maine, Michigan, Missouri, North Carolina, Oregon, Pennsylvania, Rhode Island, South Carolina, Virginia, and West Virginia.

[106] Michigan, Rhode Island, and Virginia.

Four states exempt nonprofit hospitals from the entirety of their charitable solicitation acts.[107]

Other Health Care Provider Institutions

Two state charitable solicitation acts exempt volunteer ambulance organizations from their registration provisions.[108] Two state laws provide exemption from registration for volunteer rescue squad associations.[109]

One state exempts from the registration requirements "medical care facilities," "community mental health centers," and "mental health clinics," as long as they are licensed.[110] One state's charitable solicitation act exempts from its registration requirements any nonprofit "licensed medical care facility" incorporated under its law,[111] while another state exempts from registration "licensed nursing care facilities."[112] One state's law totally exempts "volunteer hospital organizations."[113] Another law totally exempts licensed "health care service plans."[114]

Membership Organizations

Charitable solicitation acts are designed to apply to solicitations of the general public so as to protect members of the public from fund-raising fraud and other misuses of charitable dollars. This body of law is intended to ward off misrepresentation in charitable giving by ensuring an appropriate flow of information to donors to prevent their being duped into giving in circumstances where the gifts are diverted to noncharitable ends.

Consequently, when a charitable organization solicits its own "constituency" (such as a church soliciting its congregation or a college soliciting its alumni), it is appropriate to regard the solicitation as being a "private" one and thus exempt from the regulatory requirements.[115] This exemption

---

[107] California, Hawaii, Iowa, and New Hampshire.
[108] Pennsylvania and West Virginia.
[109] *Ibid.*
[110] Kansas.
[111] *Ibid.*
[112] South Dakota.
[113] Washington.
[114] California.
[115] As to this point, an analogy may be made to the federal securities laws, which differentiate between (regulated) sales of securities to the public and (somewhat unregulated) private offerings of securities.

is based upon the proposition that the regulatory protections are unnecessary because the donor's relationship with the charitable organization, by means of the membership status, is such that he, she, or it can easily obtain the requisite information without need of the force of law.

In conformity with this rationale, 20 states exempt organizations (or, in some instances, some organizations)—but only from the registration or licensing requirements—that confine their solicitation to their membership.[116] Typical is the provision of one state's statute, which provides this exemption to "[o]rganizations which solicit only within the membership of the organization by the members thereof."[117] As noted earlier, the scope of this exemption is confined by the definition given the term "member" or "membership."

Four jurisdictions exempt organizations soliciting only their membership from the entirety of the charitable solicitations act.[118]

As the quotation from the above state statute indicates, these exemptions are often unavailable where the charitable organization uses professional assistance in the solicitation. Thus, for example, the exemption referenced in the preceding paragraph is, in one state,[119] contingent upon the conduct of the solicitation solely by the organization's officers and employees acting as volunteers.

Small Solicitations

For administrative convenience and to alleviate the regulatory burdens otherwise imposed, nearly all state charitable solicitation acts exempt small solicitation efforts from the registration, licensing, or permit requirements. However, the definition as to what is "small" varies from state to state.

Typical is the clause in one state's charitable solicitation act, that provides an exemption for "[c]haritable organizations which do not intend to solicit and receive and do not actually solicit or receive contributions from the public in excess of $10,000 during a calendar year or do not receive contributions from more than 10 persons during a calendar year. . . ."[120] While there are variations on the phraseology of these

---

[116] District of Columbia, Georgia, Illinois, Kansas, Maine, Maryland, Michigan, Minnesota, Missouri, New Jersey, New York, Ohio, Oklahoma, Oregon, Rhode Island, South Carolina, Utah, Virginia, West Virginia, and Wisconsin.

[117] Tennessee.

[118] Arkansas, California, Hawaii, and Kentucky.

[119] Washington.

[120] Maine.

clauses, four states provide for this exemption with the threshold set at
$25,000,[121] one state has this type of provision with the threshold at
$15,000,[122] four states have this type of clause with the threshold of
$10,000,[123] one state has the limitation set at $8,000,[124] seven states have
this limitation set at $5,000,[125] three states have the limitation at $4,000,[126]
one state has the limitation at $3,000,[127] one state has the limitation set
at $2,000,[128] and one state finds a small charitable solicitation to be one
that is capped at $1,000.[129] Often, this exemption is accompanied by a
provision that triggers applicability of the registration requirements should
contributions exceed the threshold amount. Thus, the state statute adds:
"If a charitable organization which does not intend to solicit or receive
contributions from the public in excess of $10,000 during a calendar
year does actually solicit or receive contributions in excess of such amount,
whether or not all such contributions are received during a calendar
year, the charitable organization shall, within 30 days after the date of
[sic] contributions reach $10,000, register with and report to the Secretary
of State as required by this Act."[130]

This exemption may be confined to organizations that conduct their
fund-raising wholly by volunteers.

Five states make provision for this exemption from the entirety of
the solicitation act.[131]

Solicitations for Specified Individuals

Many states exempt from the registration requirements of their charitable
solicitation acts solicitations that are solely for the benefit of specified
individuals. This is the case, with variations, in 17 states.[132]

---

[121] Connecticut, Maryland, Minnesota, and New York.

[122] Georgia.

[123] Maine, New Jersey, North Carolina, and Oklahoma.

[124] Michigan.

[125] Kansas, Massachusetts, Oregon, Tennessee, Utah, Virginia, and Washington.

[126] Hawaii, Illinois, and Wisconsin.

[127] Rhode Island.

[128] South Carolina.

[129] Arkansas.

[130] Maine.

[131] Arkansas, Georgia, New Mexico, North Carolina, and Washington.

[132] Georgia, Illinois, Kansas, Maine, Maryland, Michigan, Minnesota, New
Jersey, New York, Ohio, Oklahoma, Rhode Island, South Carolina, Utah, Virginia,
West Virginia, and Wisconsin.

As an illustration, the charitable solicitation statute in the law of one state[133] makes this exemption available for "[p]ersons requesting contributions for the relief of any individual specified by name at the time of the solicitation when all of the contributions collected without any deductions whatsoever are turned over to the named beneficiary for his use."

As this quotation indicates, this exemption is usually voided where professional fund-raising assistance is used.

As discussed, this type of exemption is often in conflict with the concept of solicitations for charitable purposes.[134]

One state exempts these solicitations from the totality of its charitable solicitation act.[135]

Veterans' Organizations

Seven states exempt veterans' organizations from the registration requirements of their charitable solicitation acts.[136] One state exempts veterans' organizations from the entirety of its charitable solicitation act.[137]

Named Organizations

Some state charitable solicitation acts provide exemption—usually only from the registration requirements—for organizations identified by name.[138]

This practice is evidenced in provisions such as those granting this type of exemption to the American Red Cross in two states,[139] boys' clubs in two states,[140] named educational institutions in two states,[141] Boy and Girl Scout organizations in one state,[142] girls' clubs in one

---

[133] South Carolina.

[134] See *supra* § 4.1.

[135] Hawaii.

[136] Michigan, New Jersey, New York, Pennsylvania, Rhode Island, Utah, and West Virginia.

[137] Wisconsin.

[138] As noted in Ch. 5 § 5.5, these provisions are of questionable legality.

[139] District of Columbia and Virginia (complete exemption).

[140] Illinois and Kansas.

[141] Illinois and Minnesota.

[142] Kansas.

state,[143] the Junior League in one state,[144] and Young Men's and Young Women's Christian Associations in one state.[145] In one state, the Children's Trust Fund of South Carolina is exempt from payment of the annual registration fee.[146]

Other Categories of Exempted Organizations

State charitable solicitation acts contain exemptions—usually from the registration requirements—for a variety of categories of organizations other than those referenced above. The scope of these exceptions is myriad, with some expressly mandating a filing requirement for the exemption, solicitations only by volunteers, no private inurement,[147] solicitations only of members, and other limitations.

This type of exemption, albeit with some restrictions in some states, is extended to include fraternal organizations in 11 states,[148] volunteer fire companies in seven states,[149] patriotic organizations in seven states,[150] historical societies in six states,[151] social groups in six states,[152] civic organizations in five states,[153] nonprofit nurseries or other children's groups in four states,[154] certain organizations receiving an allocation from community chests, united funds, and the like, in three states,[155] federally chartered organizations (without limitation as to category) in two states,[156] community service organizations in two states,[157] youth organizations in

---

[143] *Ibid.*

[144] *Ibid.*

[145] *Ibid.*

[146] South Carolina.

[147] See *Law of Tax-Exempt Organizations* at 239–64.

[148] Georgia, Illinois, Kansas, Maryland, Minnesota, Missouri, New Jersey, New York, Oklahoma, West Virginia, and Wisconsin.

[149] Illinois, Kansas, Maryland, New Jersey, North Carolina, Pennsylvania, and West Virginia.

[150] Illinois, Kansas, Minnesota, New Jersey, New York, Oklahoma, and Wisconsin.

[151] Kansas, Missouri, New Jersey, New York, Oregon, and Rhode Island.

[152] Kansas, Minnesota, Missouri, New Jersey, New York, and Wisconsin.

[153] Georgia, Oklahoma, Virginia, West Virginia, and Wisconsin.

[154] Illinois, Kansas, Michigan, and New Jersey.

[155] Kansas, New Jersey, and New York.

[156] Illinois and Kansas.

[157] Michigan and West Virginia.

two states,[158] business and professional associations in two states,[159] organizations for the care and treatment of invalid or crippled children in one state,[160] labor unions in one state,[161] senior citizen centers in one state,[162] and persons seeking contributions and grants only from corporations and private foundations in one state.[163]

The law in two states expressly states that a noncommercial radio or television station is exempt from that state's charitable solicitation act's licensing requirements.[164] The law of another state exempts from the registration and reporting requirements a private foundation that does not solicit contributions from more than 100 persons annually.[165] Another state exempts from its registration requirements a solicitation in the "form of a collection or contribution made at a regular assembly or service" and a solicitation made upon the premises of the charitable organization.[166] Another state exempts from its registration requirements organizations that do not have an office within the jurisdiction; that solicit in the state solely by means of telephone, telegraph, direct mail, or advertising in national media; and that have a chapter or affiliate in the state that has registered. Still another state exempts from its registration requirements any charitable organization located outside the state if the organization files the registration documents required under the charitable solicitation laws of the state in which it is located, the registration documents required under the laws of two specified states[167] (if applicable), and such federal forms[168] as may be required by rule.[169] Finally, in one state, the exemption is available where the organization's fund-raising expenses do not exceed $500 annually.[170]

---

[158] Utah and West Virginia.
[159] Georgia and Minnesota.
[160] New Jersey.
[161] West Virginia.
[162] Pennsylvania.
[163] Rhode Island.
[164] North Carolina and Utah.
[165] Minnesota.
[166] Utah.
[167] California and New York.
[168] Principally, the federal annual information return (Form 990). See Ch. 6 § 6.6.
[169] Washington.
[170] Ohio.

In one state, certain fraternal, patriotic, and civic organizations are exempted from the entirety of the charitable solicitation act.[171] This blanket exemption is extended in one state to historical societies,[172] and to organizations of hunters, fishermen, and target shooters in one state.[173] Another state exempts from the entirety of its charitable solicitation act corporations that have been "on record" with its authorities for at least five years, where they are in good standing with respect to compliance with the laws of the state, as long as all fund-raising is conducted by volunteers.[174]

Obviously, there is a wide range of nonprofit, tax-exempt organizations that are exempt from the states' charitable solicitation acts because these entities are not "charitable" as that term is defined in the applicable statutes.[175]

The foregoing exemptions are not necessarily absolute or automatic. That is, in five states, a charitable organization (but not necessarily all categories of them) must first secure a determination from the state authorities as to its status as an organization exempt from some or all of the charitable solicitation act's requirements,[176] in five states some or all of the exemptions are precluded or lost where a charitable organization uses the services of a professional fund-raiser,[177] and in four states the exemption is precluded or lost where a charitable organization uses the services of a professional solicitor.[178] In one state,[179] an exemption is lost if an organization mails more than 500,000 solicitations for contributions in any year.

§ 4.5 Regulation of Professional Fund-Raisers

The state charitable solicitation statutes often require a professional fund-raiser, acting on behalf of a charitable organization that is subject

---

[171] Maryland.
[172] Oregon.
[173] Georgia.
[174] Hawaii.
[175] See Ch. 2 § 2.1; also *supra* § 4.1.
[176] Hawaii, Maine, Rhode Island, South Carolina, and Virginia.
[177] Minnesota, North Carolina, Utah, Washington, and West Virginia.
[178] Maryland, North Carolina, Washington, and West Virginia.
[179] Maryland.

to the particular statute, to register with or secure a license from (hereafter referenced as a registration requirement) the appropriate state agency. This is the law in 31 states.[180] This registration must be completed before the professional fund-raiser commences to act in that capacity for a charitable organization soliciting funds in the state.

This registration is usually effective for a period of one year, with expiration of the registration set to occur on a stated date, and is renewable.

Often, these laws also impose reporting requirements for professional fund-raisers.

An applicant for this registration is usually required to file with and have approved by the appropriate state officials a bond in a statutorily set sum. The bond coverages are as follows: $10,000 in 11 states,[181] $5,000 in seven states,[182] $20,000 in two states,[183] $15,000 in one state,[184] and $2,500 in one state.[185]

These bonds inure to the benefit of the state in reimbursement for any losses resulting from malfeasance, nonfeasance, or misfeasance in the conduct of charitable solicitation activities.

Most of these statutes require professional fund-raisers to maintain accurate books and records, and to do so for a stated period of time (frequently, three years).

Of course, the scope of this registration requirement is largely governed by the reach of the definition, under a state's charitable solicitation law, of the term "professional fund-raiser."[186]

---

[180] Arkansas, California, Connecticut, Georgia, Hawaii, Illinois, Indiana, Iowa, Kansas, Kentucky, Maine, Maryland, Massachusetts, Michigan, Minnesota, Missouri, New Hampshire (where the professional fund-raiser has custody of contributions), New Jersey, New York, North Carolina, North Dakota, Ohio, Oklahoma, Pennsylvania, Rhode Island, South Carolina, Utah, Virginia, Washington, West Virginia, and Wisconsin.

[181] Georgia, Maine, Michigan, New Hampshire, New Jersey, New York, North Carolina, Pennsylvania, Rhode Island, Utah, and West Virginia.

[182] Arkansas, Hawaii, Illinois, Kansas, Ohio, South Carolina, and Wisconsin.

[183] Connecticut and Minnesota.

[184] Washington.

[185] Oklahoma.

[186] See Ch. 5 § 5.9; Ch. 8 § 8.3.

§ 4.6   Regulation of Professional Solicitors

Generally, the states' charitable solicitation acts require professional solicitors to register in accordance with the statute. This is the case in 27 states.[187] Often, these laws also impose reporting requirements.

The bonding requirements for professional solicitors are as follows: $10,000 in eight states,[188] $20,000 in two states,[189] $5,000 in two states,[190] and $25,000 in one state.[191]

Again, of course, the scope of this registration requirement is largely governed by reach of the definition, under a state's charitable solicitations law, of the term "professional solicitor."[192] In one state, the matter is even more confusing in that the statute differentiates between "professional solicitors" and "solicitors."[193]

§ 4.7   Regulation of Commercial Co-venturers

Nine states require registration of and/or otherwise regulate commercial co-venturers.[194] The registration and record maintenance requirements for them are generally the same as those applicable to professional fund-raisers and professional solicitors.

The bonding requirements for commercial co-venturers are in the law of two states, with the amount set at $10,000.[195]

---

[187] Arkansas, Colorado, Connecticut, Hawaii, Illinois, Indiana, Kansas, Kentucky, Maine, Maryland, Massachusetts, Michigan, New Hampshire, New Jersey, New York, North Carolina, North Dakota, Ohio, Oklahoma, Oregon, Pennsylvania, Rhode Island, South Carolina, Tennessee, Virginia, West Virginia, and Wisconsin.

[188] Maine, Massachusetts, New Hampshire, North Carolina, Pennsylvania, Rhode Island, Tennessee, and West Virginia.

[189] Connecticut and Virginia.

[190] Hawaii and South Carolina.

[191] Maryland.

[192] See *supra* note 182.

[193] Maryland.

[194] California, Colorado, Connecticut, Maine, Massachusetts, New Hampshire, New York, North Carolina, and Wisconsin (separate statute). Two states, Oregon and Pennsylvania, define the term but do not provide for any regulation.

[195] Maine and Massachusetts.

In some states, the concept of the commercial co-venture is stated as a "sales solicitation for charitable purposes"[196] or a "charitable sales promotion."[197]

§ 4.8 Limitations on Fund-Raising Costs

One of the most controversial issues in the field of fund-raising for charitable purposes is the matter of fund-raising costs. While nearly everyone agrees that charitable fund-raising costs should be "reasonable," there is much disagreement about what is, in fact, a reasonable fund-raising cost. There also is disagreement about how to determine the "reasonableness" of fund-raising costs. As discussed, ascertainment of the reasonableness of a fund-raising cost often is dependent upon the particular facts and circumstances.[198]

The states have long tried to prevent charitable organizations with (allegedly) "high" or "unreasonable" or "excessive" fund-raising costs from soliciting contributions within their jurisdictions. The mechanism for doing this has been a refusal to allow a charity with fund-raising costs in excess of a particular percentage of total contributions or revenues received to solicit in the state. This percentage ceiling comes in two forms: an "absolute" limitation (that is, one with no exceptions) and a "rebuttable" limitation (where the prohibition may be overcome by a showing that the fund-raising costs are reasonable, notwithstanding their percentage of total receipts). As discussed, this mechanism has been repeatedly found to be unconstitutional under federal and state law, as a violation of the free speech rights of soliciting charitable organizations.[199]

Nonetheless, while some states consequently have repealed this type of percentage limitation, a few persist in retaining the prohibition in their statutes. Four states' charitable solicitation laws still contain some form of percentage limitation on annual fund-raising outlays that is absolute or rebuttable.[200] (Occasionally, the print of the statute will indicate that the particular provision is not being enforced, due to constitutional

---

[196] California.

[197] E.g., Colorado. In general, see Ch. 8 § 8.5.

[198] See Ch. 5 §§ 5.1 & 5.3.

[199] See Ch. 5 § 5.3.

[200] Massachusetts, Oklahoma, Pennsylvania, and Rhode Island. South Carolina law provides for a "reasonable" percentage limitation on payment of compensation by a charity to a professional solicitor. Tennessee law uses a similar approach in the disclosure context.

infirmities.)[201] The restriction means that a charitable organization with annual fund-raising costs (as a total, for professional fund-raisers' fees, or for professional solicitors' fees) in excess of the percentage is forbidden to solicit contributions in the state. These prohibitions are so blatantly unconstitutional, however, that charitable organizations, and their fund-raising consultants and agents, can safely ignore them.

Summarized next are are those provisions that are still in the law, without notation as to their unconstitutionality. One state prohibits a professional solicitor from being compensated by a charitable organization in an amount in excess of 30 percent of the contributions raised by reason of the fund-raising campaign.[202] Another state has a similar provision (also applicable to commercial co-venturers), with the limitation set at 25 percent.[203]

In one state, a charitable organization, professional fund-raiser, or professional solicitor cannot become registered where the fund-raiser or solicitor would receive more than 10 percent of the net receipts from the solicitation of contributions.[204] A similar provision in the law of another state sets the percentage limitation at 30 percent, with compensation in excess of that percentage presumed to be unreasonable.[205]

In one state, a charitable organization cannot pay a professional solicitor more than 15 percent of contributions received and cannot, as a general rule, incur fund-raising expenses in excess of 35 percent of contributions received.[206] Another like statute sets the limitations at 25 and 50 percent, respectively.[207] Another of these provisions fixes the limitations at 15 and 25 percent, respectively, with the latter percentage a rebuttable presumption.[208] Still another state requires that payments to a professional solicitor be "reasonable," without use of any specific percentage.[209]

Some of the states that have abandoned or foregone the use of the percentage mechanism as a basis for preventing fund-raising for charity utilize the percentage approach in a disclosure setting. Several states, for example, require charitable organizations to make an annual reporting,

---

[201] E.g., the New Jersey statute.
[202] Maryland.
[203] Massachusetts.
[204] Oklahoma.
[205] Minnesota.
[206] Pennsylvania.
[207] Rhode Island.
[208] Tennessee.
[209] South Carolina.

either to update a registration or as part of a separate report, to the authorities as to their fund-raising activities in the prior year, including a statement of their fund-raising expenses. Some states[210] require a disclosure of a charity's fund-raising costs, stated as a percentage, to donors at the time of the solicitation—although this requirement is of dubious constitutionality.[211] In a few states, solicitation literature used by a charitable organization must include a statement that, upon request, financial and other information about the soliciting charity may be obtained directly from the state.

Some states require a statement as to any percentage compensation in the contract between the charitable organization and the professional fund-raiser and/or the professional solicitor.[212] Two states require the compensation of a paid solicitor to be stated in the contract as a percentage of gross revenue;[213] another state has a similar provision with respect to a professional fund-raiser.[214] One state wants a charitable organization's fund-raising cost percentage to be stated in its registration statement.[215]

§ 4.9 Availability of Records

The information filed in accordance with a state's charitable solicitation act, whether contained in an application for registration, annual report, contract, or other form, becomes a matter of public record. This requirement encompasses information filed by charitable organizations, professional fund-raisers, professional solicitors, and commercial coventurers.

For example, the law in one state states: "Registration statements and applications, reports, professional fund-raising counsel contracts or professional solicitor contracts and all other documents and information required to be filed under this chapter or by the director shall become public records in the department, and shall be open to the general public for inspection at the time and under the conditions as the director

---

[210] E.g., Alabama, Connecticut, New Mexico, Utah, and Washington.
[211] See Ch. 5 § 5.3.
[212] E.g., Hawaii.
[213] Indiana and New Hampshire.
[214] Oregon.
[215] Virginia. In general, see Ch. 5 § 5.3.

may prescribe."[216] This type of provision is in the charitable solicitation laws of 29 states.[217]

Many of these laws require that the information be maintained, by the regulators and/or the regulated, for a stated period of time, usually at least three years. Where the records must be maintained by a regulated entity (such as the charitable organization or professional fund-raiser), the law usually requires that the information be open to inspection at all reasonable times by officials of the state. Most of these laws also require a charitable organization, and/or related professional fund-raisers, professional solicitors, and commercial co-venturers, to keep "true and complete" records to ensure compliance with the law requiring disclosure of information and the availability of records.

§ 4.10   Contractual Relationships

Many of the state charitable solicitation acts require that the relationship between a charitable organization and a professional fund-raiser, and/or between a charitable organization and a professional solicitor, be evidenced in a written agreement. This agreement is required to be filed with the state soon after (usually within 10 days) the contract is executed.

These requirements, in whole or in part, involving professional fund-raisers are in the law in 27 states,[218] and involving professional solicitors are in the law in 19 states.[219] Five of the states with laws pertaining to

---

[216] Hawaii.

[217] Arkansas, Colorado, Connecticut, Georgia, Hawaii, Illinois, Indiana, Kansas, Maine, Maryland, Massachusetts, Michigan, Minnesota, New Hampshire, New Jersey, New Mexico, New York, North Carolina, North Dakota, Ohio, Oklahoma, Oregon, Pennsylvania, Rhode Island, South Carolina, Tennessee, Virginia, Washington, and West Virginia.

[218] Arkansas, Connecticut, Georgia, Hawaii, Illinois, Indiana, Kansas, Maine, Maryland, Massachusetts, Michigan, New Hampshire, New Jersey, New York, North Carolina, North Dakota, Ohio, Oklahoma, Oregon, Pennsylvania, Rhode Island, South Carolina, Utah, Virginia, Washington, West Virginia, and Wisconsin.

[219] Connecticut, Hawaii, Indiana, Maine, Maryland, Massachusetts, New Hampshire, New Jersey, New York, North Carolina, North Dakota, Oregon, Pennsylvania, Rhode Island, South Carolina, Tennessee, Virginia, West Virginia, and Wisconsin.

commercial co-venturers have a like requirement with respect to contracts entered into between charitable organizations and business enterprises.[220]

The states that make these requirements applicable to charitable organizations and professional fund-raisers, but not to charitable organizations and professional solicitors, are usually the states that define a professional solicitor as being an employee of a professional fund-raiser (see above).

§ 4.11   Registered Agent Requirements

A state charitable solicitation act usually contemplates that a charitable organization, professional fund-raiser, and/or a professional solicitor will appoint a registered agent in the state where contributions are being solicited.

Where the charitable organization, fund-raiser, or solicitor is incorporated under a state's law or has its principal place of activity or business in a particular state, it will have appointed a registered agent in conformity with the requirements of that state.[221]

However, where the charitable organization, fund-raiser, or solicitor has its principal place of activity or business in a state other than that in which the solicitation is being conducted, it likely will not have appointed a registered agent in that state.[222] In this situation, the charitable solicitation act in 19 states provides that where the foreign charitable organization, fund-raiser, and/or solicitor participates in a charitable solicitation in a state, the administrator of the act (usually, the secretary of state) is deemed, by virtue of the solicitation activity, to have been irrevocably appointed its agent for service of process and similar functions.[223]

§ 4.12   Prohibited Acts

Thirty-three state charitable solicitation acts contain a list of one or more acts in which a charitable organization (and perhaps a professional fund-

---

[220] Maine, Massachusetts, New Hampshire, New York, and Wisconsin.

[221] The typical state nonprofit corporation act requires an organization incorporated pursuant to it or authorized to do business in the state to appoint a registered agent, which will be an individual domiciled in the state or a corporation authorized to serve as a registered agent in the state.

[222] See the observation in *infra* note 251, that a charitable solicitation does not amount to "doing business" in a state.

[223] Arkansas, Colorado, Georgia, Hawaii, Indiana, Kansas, Maine, Maryland, Massachusetts, Michigan, New Jersey, New York, Oklahoma, Rhode Island, South Carolina, Tennessee, Virginia, West Virginia, and Wisconsin.

raiser and/or professional solicitor) may not lawfully engage.[224] These acts may be some or all of the following:

1. A person may not, for the purpose of soliciting contributions, use the name of another person (except that of an officer, director, or trustee of the charitable organization by or for which contributions are solicited) without the consent of the other person.[225] This prohibition extends to the use of an individual's name on stationery or in an advertisement or brochure, or as one who has contributed to, sponsored, or endorsed the organization.

2. A person may not, for the purpose of soliciting contributions, use a name, symbol, or statement so closely related or similar to that used by another charitable organization or governmental agency that it would tend to confuse or mislead the public.[226]

3. A person may not use or exploit the fact of registration with the state so as to lead the public to believe that the registration in any manner constitutes an endorsement or appeal by the state.

4. A person may not misrepresent to or mislead anyone, by any manner, means, practice, or device, to believe that the organization on behalf of which the solicitation is being conducted is a charitable organization or that the proceeds of the solicitation will be used for charitable purposes, where that is not the case.

5. A person may not represent that the solicitation is for or on behalf of a charitable organization or otherwise induce contributions from the public without proper authorization from the charitable organization.[227]

---

[224] Alabama, Arkansas, Colorado, Connecticut, District of Columbia, Florida, Georgia, Hawaii, Illinois, Indiana, Kansas, Louisiana, Maine, Maryland, Massachusetts, Michigan, Minnesota, Nebraska, New Hampshire, New Jersey, New York, North Carolina, North Dakota, Oklahoma, Oregon, Pennsylvania, Rhode Island, South Carolina, Tennessee, Virginia, Washington, West Virginia, and Wisconsin.

[225] This type of provision has been upheld in the courts (e.g., *People* v. *Caldwell*, 290 N.E. 2d 279 (1972)).

[226] This type of provision has been upheld in the courts (e.g., *People ex rel. Brown* v. *Illinois State Troopers Lodge No. 41*, 286 N.E. 2d 524 (1972); *American Gold Star Mothers, Inc.* v. *Gold Star Mothers, Inc.*, 191 F.2d 488 (D.C. Cir. 1951)).

[227] In general, see Ch. 8 § 8.6.

Twenty-two states prohibit a professional solicitor from soliciting for a charitable organization unless the solicitor has a written and otherwise valid authorization from the organization, has the authorization in his or her possession when making solicitations, and displays the authorization upon request to the person being solicited, police officers, or agents of the state.[228]

§ 4.13 Regulatory Prohibitions

Some states have provisions in their charitable solicitation acts that go beyond the usual regulation of the fund-raising process.

In six states, it is unlawful for a charitable organization to solicit and/or expend funds raised for noncharitable purposes or for purposes not referenced in the application for registration.[229]

Thirteen states have disclosure rules as part of their charitable solicitation acts, as a condition to a lawful fund-raising effort.[230]

Five states have rules concerning the solicitation of gifts of tickets to be used at promotional or fund-raising events.[231]

§ 4.14 Reciprocal Agreements

As the foregoing indicates, the requirements of the state charitable solicitation acts can vary widely, as can the regulations, rules, and forms promulgated to accompany and expand these laws, and the enforcement activities with respect to them. This makes it very difficult and expensive for a charitable organization soliciting contributions nationwide to lawfully comply with all of the varying requirements. Some state authorities are attempting to remedy this situation by pursuing methods to bring their

---

[228] California, Connecticut, District of Columbia, Florida, Georgia, Hawaii, Louisiana, Maine, Maryland, Massachusetts, Michigan, Minnesota, Missouri, Nebraska, New Hampshire, North Carolina, Oregon, Rhode Island, Tennessee, Utah, Virginia, and Washington.

[229] Florida, Maryland, Rhode Island, Tennessee, Virginia, and West Virginia.

[230] District of Columbia (solicitor information card), Florida, Indiana ("solicitation notice"), Maryland (disclosure statement), Minnesota (card sometimes required), Nebraska (display of certificate of authority), New Hampshire ("solicitation notice"), New Mexico (when soliciting for law enforcement organization), North Carolina, Rhode Island (identification card), Virginia (solicitation notice), Washington, and West Virginia (disclosure statement).

[231] Colorado, Connecticut, New Hampshire, Oregon, and Virginia.

laws, and the interpretations and enforcement of them, into some basis of conformity with other state requirements.

For the most part, state regulators have the inherent authority (where revision of the statutory law is not necessary) to promulgate regulations, rules, forms, and enforcement policies that are comparable to similar requirements in other states. Nonetheless, some states' charitable solicitation acts contain a provision that, if earnestly followed, could somewhat alleviate this lack of consistency. This provision authorizes the appropriate state official to enter into reciprocal agreements with his or her counterparts in other states to (1) exchange information about charitable organizations, professional fund-raisers, and professional solicitors; (2) accept filings made by these persons in the other states where the information required is substantially similar; and (3) grant exemptions to organizations that are granted exemption under the other state's statute where the laws are substantially similar.

This type of provision is in the law of 15 states.[232]

§ 4.15　Powers of Attorney General

Frequently, a state charitable solicitation statute invests the state's attorney general (or, occasionally, some other official) with specific powers in connection with administration and enforcement of the statute.[233] Usually, the attorney general is authorized to investigate the operations or conduct of charitable organizations, professional fund-raisers, or professional solicitors subject to the statute, with the authority to issue orders having the same force and effect as a subpoena. The attorney general is often expressly empowered to institute an action in court to enjoin, preliminarily or permanently, a charitable organization, professional fund-raiser, professional solicitor, or other person who (1) engages in a method, act, or practice in violation of the statute or a rule or regulation promulgated in connection with the statute; or (2) employs or uses in a solicitation of charitable contributions a device, scheme, or artifice to defraud, or to obtain money or property by means of any false pretense, deception, representation, or promise.

---

[232] Arkansas, Hawaii, Illinois, Kansas, Maryland, Massachusetts, Minnesota, North Carolina, Oklahoma, Pennsylvania, Rhode Island, South Carolina, Tennessee, Virginia, and West Virginia.

[233] An excellent discussion of the role of an attorney general in overseeing charities appears in *Attorney General's Guide for Charities* 39 (1988) (California Department of Justice).

Occasionally, the attorney general is collaterally granted some or all of this authority with respect to individuals or organizations masquerading as a charity or as a charitable organization entitled to an exemption from the statutory requirements. For example, the statute of one state[234] empowers the state's attorney general to institute legal action "against a charitable organization or person which or who operates under the guise or pretense of being an organization or person exempted by this act and is not in fact an organization or person entitled to such an exemption."

These state statutes usually include the obligatory provision that they shall not be construed to limit or restrict the exercise of powers or performance of duties of the attorney general that he or she otherwise is authorized to exercise or perform under any other provision of law. The charitable solicitation act in one state[235] states the matter more positively: "The attorney general shall enforce the due application of funds given or appropriated to public charities within the commonwealth and prevent breaches of trust in the administration thereof."

§ 4.16 Miscellaneous Provisions

In 21 states, the regulators are expressly granted the authority to promulgate rules and regulations to accompany the particular state's charitable solicitation act.[236]

In eight states, the law provides that county or municipal units of government may adopt other and/or more stringent requirements regarding charitable solicitations and, expressly or impliedly, that these requirements will not be preempted by the state law.[237]

In three states, a provision states that the charitable solicitation law may not be construed to restrict the exercise of authority generally accorded to the state's attorney general.[238]

---

[234] Michigan.

[235] Massachusetts.

[236] California, Connecticut, District of Columbia, Hawaii, Kansas, Maryland, Massachusetts, Minnesota, New Hampshire, New Jersey, New Mexico, New York, North Carolina, Oregon, Pennsylvania, Rhode Island, South Carolina, Tennessee, Utah, Virginia, and Washington.

[237] California, Florida, Georgia, Indiana, Nebraska, Oklahoma, Tennessee, and Virginia.

[238] New Jersey, New York, and Oklahoma.

In two states, the regulators must make an annual report to the governor and the legislature on the activities of charitable organizations in the state.[239]

The law in five states authorizes a commission or council to serve, in an advisory capacity and/or otherwise, as part of the administration of the state's charitable solicitation act.[240]

In some states, the solicitation of contributions in the state is deemed to be "doing business" in the state.[241]

In one jurisdiction, persons are prohibited by statute from using the telephone for charitable solicitation purposes, if they are compensated for the service.[242]

§ 4.17 Sanctions

The means of enforcing a state charitable solicitation act are manifold. The principal enforcement mechanisms, which come into play upon the occasion of one or more violations of the act, are the following: 24 states authorize the revocation, cancellation, or denial of a registration,[243] 24 states expressly authorize an investigation by the appropriate authorities,[244] 31 states authorize injunctive proceedings,[245] 21 states authorize the

---

[239] Maine and Pennsylvania.

[240] District of Columbia, New York, Pennsylvania, South Carolina, and West Virginia.

[241] E.g., Kansas and Michigan. See text accompanying *supra* notes 221–22.

[242] District of Columbia.

[243] Connecticut, District of Columbia, Hawaii, Illinois, Kansas, Maryland, Massachusetts, Michigan, Minnesota, New Hampshire, New Jersey, New York, North Carolina, North Dakota, Oklahoma, Oregon, Pennsylvania, Rhode Island, South Carolina, Tennessee, Utah, Virginia, West Virginia, and Wisconsin.

[244] Connecticut, District of Columbia, Florida, Georgia, Hawaii, Indiana, Iowa, Kansas, Maryland, Massachusetts, Michigan, Minnesota, Missouri, New Hampshire, New Mexico, New York, North Carolina, North Dakota, Pennsylvania, Rhode Island, South Carolina, Tennessee, Virginia, and West Virgnia.

[245] Alabama, Arkansas, Connecticut, District of Columbia, Florida, Georgia, Hawaii, Indiana, Iowa, Kansas, Maryland, Massachusetts, Michigan, Minnesota, Missouri, Nebraska, New Hampshire, New Jersey, New York, North Carolina, North Dakota, Oklahoma, Oregon, Pennsylvania, Rhode Island, South Carolina, Tennessee, Virginia, Utah, West Virginia, and Wisconsin.

levying of fines and other penalties,[246] and 18 states authorize the imposition of criminal penalties (including imprisonment).[247] Many states characterize violations of these statutes as misdemeanors, with specific penalties referenced elsewhere in the state's code of laws. One state mandates loss of tax-exempt status as a sanction,[248] while five states expressly recognize private actions.[249]

In nine states, a violation of the state's charitable solicitation act simultaneously constitutes a violation of the state's unfair trade practices law.[250]

§ 4.18   Other Laws

In addition to the panoply of state charitable solicitation acts, charitable organizations soliciting gift support from the public may have to face other state statutory or regulatory requirements, including:

1. A state's nonprofit corporation act, which has registration and annual reporting requirements for foreign (out-of-state) corporations that "transact business" within the state. It is not clear whether, as a matter of general law, the solicitation of contributions in a state constitutes "doing business" in the state.[251] As noted, some states, by statute, treat fund-raising as the doing of business. If the solicitation of contributions is a business transaction in the states, the reporting consequences would be enormous, considering the fact that nearly every state has a nonprofit corporation act. Such a requirement would cause a charity that is soliciting gifts

---

[246] Arkansas, Connecticut, District of Columbia, Florida, Georgia, Hawaii, Louisiana, Maryland, Massachusetts, Michigan, New Hampshire, New York, Ohio, Oklahoma, Pennsylvania, Rhode Island, South Carolina, Tennessee, Virginia, West Virginia, and Wisconsin.

[247] Arkansas, Connecticut, District of Columbia, Florida, Hawaii, Louisiana, Maryland, Massachusetts, Michigan, Ohio, Oklahoma, Pennsylvania, Rhode Island, South Carolina, Tennessee, Virginia, West Virginia, and Wisconsin.

[248] Oklahoma.

[249] Georgia, Kansas, New Mexico, Tennessee, and Utah.

[250] Georgia, Massachusetts, Iowa, Louisiana, Maine, New Hampshire, Tennessee, Washington, and Wisconsin.

[251] One court has observed: "It is doubtful . . . whether the solicitation of funds for a charitable purpose is, to use the statutory words, the 'carrying on, conducting or transaction of business.'" (*Lefkowitz* v. *Burden*, 254 N.Y.S. 2d 943, 944–945 (1964)).

in every state to register and report over 90 times each year, not taking into account federal and local laws!

2. A state's insurance law (such as that in New York), which may embody a requirement that a philanthropic organization writing charitable gift annuity contracts obtain a permit to do so and subsequently file annual statements.

3. A state's "blue sky" statute regulating securities offerings, which may be applicable to offers to sell and to sales of interests in, and operation of, pooled income funds.[252] These laws may also apply with respect to charitable remainder annuity trusts and unitrusts.[253]

4. A state's law prohibiting fraudulent advertising or other fraudulent or deceptive practices.

5. A state's enactment of the Uniform Supervision of Trustees for Charitable Purposes Act, which requires a charitable trust to file with the state's attorney general a copy of its governing instrument, an inventory of the charitable assets, and an annual report. Of similar scope and effect is an enactment, such as the Ohio Charitable Trust Act, which invests the state's attorney general with plenary investigative power over charitable groups.

6. State law concerning charitable contribution deductions and eligibility for tax-exempt status.

---

[252] See *Starting and Managing a Nonprofit Organization* at 197–98.
[253] *Id.* at 196–97.

5

State Regulation
of Fund-Raising:
Legal Issues

There are several issues of law that arise concerning the application of state charitable solicitation acts. The purpose of this chapter is to survey and analyze these issues.

These issues stand in stark contrast to the general administration of the state charitable solicitation acts. They are reflective of what one court described as the "direct conflict [between] the power of a government to license and regulate those who wish to pursue a professional calling [that is, professional fund-raisers] with the rights of free speech protected by the First Amendment."[1] Another court stated the dilemma more broadly: "It is no easy task to draft a facially neutral and neutral-content ordinance consistent with the first and fourteenth amendments that will protect the public from fraud and harassment in solicitation of funds."[2]

§ 5.1 Regulation of Fund-Raising Costs

State regulation of charitable solicitations is clearly on the rise, and all indications are that this trend will continue. The single most important issue arising out of this regulation, and the intense focus of the regulatory attention, is the matter of annual fund-raising costs incurred by charities—both internal expenses and fees paid to professional fund-raisers, professional solicitors, or to both.

[1] *Heritage Publishing Company* v. *Fishman*, 634 F. Supp. 1489, 1499 (D. Minn. 1986).
[2] *International Society for Krishna Consciousness of Houston, Inc.* v. *City of Houston, Texas*, 689 F.2d 541, 543 (5th Cir. 1982).

There have been well-publicized abuses—and more may be anticipated—of "charitable" entities with excessive fund-raising costs, and this exposure has tainted the thinking of many on the subject: the general public, state legislators, and state and local regulators.

Several research projects have been undertaken to examine the matter of fund-raising costs experienced by charitable organizations, including the issue of the elements that should be taken into account in assessing the "reasonableness" of fund-raising costs and how to appropriately report such costs.[3] Presumably all agree that the fund-raising costs of every charitable institution and organization should be "reasonable," yet there is not much of a consensus as to how to evaluate the "reasonableness" of fund-raising costs.

In the meantime, however, the attitude of many state legislators and regulators is hardening—to the detriment of charitable organizations that have what some may regard as "above average" fund-raising costs. State regulatory patterns are becoming fixed, and some legislatures in states with charitable solicitation acts presently in place are beginning to rewrite their laws in more stringent fashion. Clearly, a solution is called for, and some proposals are discussed below. But first, consideration must be given to the fundamental elements underlying the issue.

The Disclosure Dilemma

One of the essential functions of most of the state charitable solicitation acts is to promote disclosure of information to the public. A matter of principal concern among charitable groups, and thoughtful legislators and regulators, is the appropriate mode by which to effect public disclosure by organizations soliciting support for philanthropic purposes. This issue basically has revolved around two conflicting positions, represented by the catch phrases "point-of-solicitation disclosure" and "disclosure-on-demand."

Under the point-of-solicitation disclosure concept, certain information must be stated as part of the solicitation materials. The solicitation-on-demand approach generally requires that a soliciting charity provide information to the public upon request; in some instances, the solicitation materials must bear notice of the availability of this information.

Proponents of the point-of-solicitation disclosure rule insist that it is the only effective way to ensure that the general public has at least

---

[3] E.g., "Fund Raising Costs—A Progress Report," XII *The Philanthropy Monthly* (No. 10) 19 (1979).

minimal information about a charity at the time the decision as to whether to contribute is made. They assert that most people will not bother to write for information from charities, with the result being little, if any, authentic disclosure. These advocates view the matter as one akin to consumer protection, with analogy made to existing labeling requirements on containers of food, medicine, and the like.

Opponents of the point-of-solicitation disclosure approach (including proponents of the disclosure-on-demand approach) insist that meaningful and balanced information about a charitable organization (particularly financial data) cannot be presented as part of the solicitation process. They note that the purpose of a solicitation is to raise funds, and they contend that cluttering a solicitation mailing or broadcast with statistical and other information makes the solicitation more confusing and less appealing and, hence, generates fewer dollars, while at the same time making the solicitation more costly to undertake. They also assert that true disclosure cannot be effected by the mere provision of snippets of data and that such a requirement would be counterproductive to the law by enhancing the likelihood that misleading information will be transmitted.

At any rate, this line of reasoning continues, authentic public disclosure is not derived as the result of one-on-one correspondence between a charity and a potential donor but rather from access to and publication of the pertinent information by the independent watchdog agencies, government agencies, the media, and other interested groups. Finally, they reject the analogy to federal packaging disclosure requirements on the ground that making a charitable contribution is a voluntary act, which affords ample time to secure information if it is wanted, while buying and ingesting food and medicine are done out of necessity and without a reasonable opportunity to write the producer or manufacturer for data about the contents of a foodstuff, drug, or similar item that will likely be consumed before any response is forthcoming.

Thus, in designing or evaluating a charitable solicitation law, the mode of disclosure is a threshold issue. In part, the dispute between the two basic disclosure approaches can be resolved or mitigated by the outcome of the decision as to the items of information to be disclosed at the point of solicitation. For example, even the most vehement opponents of general point-of-solicitation disclosure would not object to a requirement that the solicitation literature include a statement about the purpose of the soliciting charitable organization and the intended use of the contributions solicited. Presumably, most solicitation materials contain such information in any case and, therefore, such a requirement, by itself, should pose scant cause for concern (other than the fact that it is mandated by law). By contrast, any requirement that the solicitation materials state the organization's fund-raising costs, and perhaps require that such costs be expressed as a percentage of contributions or other receipts, generates considerable controversy and opposition.

The Fund-Raising Cost Percentage Approach

One observer has correctly stated that "in the field today, there is no agreed-upon base for determining fund-raising cost percentages."[4] However, irrespective of the context (governmental or nongovernmental), the most common practice is to express a charitable organization's fund-raising costs in terms of a single percentage. These costs are usually expressed as a function of total receipts or of charitable contributions, using the prior year's financial data.

This approach is popular because of the ease of ascertaining a percentage and using it as a base of comparison of charitable groups. For example, a person might look at one organization's financial data and see annual gifts of $100,000 and fund-raising costs of $15,000, and another organization with gifts of $100,000 and fund-raising costs of $20,000, and conclude that the organization with fund-raising costs of 15 percent is more "efficient" or "well-managed," or even "better" (and thus more deserving of charitable support), than the organization with fund-raising costs of 20 percent. Moreover, this use of a percentage readily lends itself to the disclosure-at-point-of-solicitation approach, since a simple percentage can be easily displayed on the solicitation literature and, as noted, used by potential donors to evaluate and compare the various soliciting groups.

The percentage approach is roundly attacked on two fundamental bases: (1) there is no universal standard for computing fund-raising costs, thereby precluding meaningful comparisons of organizations, and (2) a single percentage is a misleading factor to use in evaluating an organization's fund-raising practices and overall eligibility for charitable dollars. For example, in reference to the above illustrations, the organization showing fund-raising costs at 15 percent may not be including some outlays (perhaps allocable shares of indirect costs) in the calculation, while the other organization with fund-raising costs of 20 percent may do so, so that in fact both organization's fund-raising expenses are identical (or,

[4] Grimes, "The Fund-Raising Percent as a Quantitative Standard for Regulation of Public Charities," Report to Commission on Private Philanthropy and Public Needs (1975).

perhaps, were the same system used, the 15-percent organization may have higher fund-raising costs than the 20-percent organization). This is not a matter of fraud or cheating but rather a lack of uniformity and understanding about the expense elements to take into account in constructing the ratio. Also, there may be quite valid reasons, even assuming identity of means of determining the percentages, as to why one organization's fund-raising costs exceed another's—reasons that have nothing to do with "efficiency," "cost effectiveness," or program "merit." In fact, the 20-percent organization may be better managed than the 15-percent organization.

Another difficulty with the fund-raising cost percentage approach is that it gives undue emphasis and prominence to fund-raising costs, by the starkness of a percentage and by stating it in isolation from other financial information. Thus, an organization with annual fund-raising expenditures of 10 percent, general administrative and management expenses of 10 percent, charitable outlays of 5 percent, with the remaining 75 percent of its funds expended for speculative land investments, would appear under this approach just as qualified for public support as an organization with the same fund-raising and administrative costs but that devoted the remaining 80 percent of its outlays to charitable ends.

Still another concern relates to the fact that fund-raising practices are diverse and unique to various types of tax-exempt organizations. Therefore, fund-raising costs stated as a single percentage may not be a meaningful indicator of anything or—worse yet—be so misleading as to be counterproductive to the disclosure motive and be unfair to certain categories of charitable groups.

An institution such as a school, college, university, or hospital is likely to have an established donor base and a wide range of fund-raising (in this context, termed "development") methods, including annual giving, planned giving, and charitable bequest programs. Such an institution is therefore likely to have a relatively low fund-raising cost percentage, as may an organization enjoying extensive volunteer assistance. By contrast, another type of organization competing for charitable dollars may be spending most of its money to acquire a donor base, such as a new organization just commencing a direct mail fund-raising effort, or may be required to rely heavily on costly fund-raising techniques, such as special events. This latter type of organization is therefore likely to have a very high fund-raising cost percent, such as 80 or 90 percent, or even in excess of 100 percent.

The relative merit of these varying categories of organizations cannot be measured by their respective fund-raising cost percentages. As noted, a high fund-raising cost percentage is by no means indicative of inefficient operation or lack of a worthy purpose. Conversely, it can be shown that an organization that is poorly managed and/or expending excessive sums on fund-raising can nonetheless have a low fund-raising cost percentage, perhaps attributable to one or more large charitable bequests or unexpected lifetime gifts, or low fund-raising costs in one area to offset excessive fund-raising costs in another. Also, the fund-raising costs for a multiyear capital campaign, which are normally incurred in the initial months of the campaign, or in relation to the establishment of a planned giving program, will introduce additional distortions relative to a single fund-raising cost percentage based on a lone year's experience.

As discussed,[5] a once-employed device appearing in state and municipal charitable solicitation laws was the fund-raising cost percentage used as a ceiling on permissible outlays. In some instances, the ceiling was an absolute one, barring the solicitation where the maximum was exceeded; it may have been imposed on total fund-raising expenses, on fees paid to professional fund-raisers, and/or on fees paid to professional solicitors. In other cases, the percentage was used to create a presumption as to whether a fund-raising cost was "reasonable"; an organization could rebut a presumption of "unreasonable" fund-raising costs by demonstrating special facts and circumstances. However, percentage-based limitations have been declared unconstitutional, as being violations of free speech.

The realities of the costs of fund-raising for charitable purposes are poorly understood by the general public, and in some instances by government regulators and legislators. The maxim that "it takes money to raise money" is frequently incompatible with the typical individual's view of how a charitable dollar should be spent. Many groups understandably fear that the fund-raising cost percentage approach will be used by the public as a ranking system by which to evaluate charities for giving purposes. Those holding this view insist that, at least until a uniform and equitable method for calculating the fund-raising cost percentage is in place, such a "batting average" approach is an inappropriate way to assess the relative worth of charitable groups. Many are convinced that heavy utilization of this basis of comparison will touch off a "price war" among charitable organizations, igniting unnecessary and unproductive competition among philanthropic entities as to which organizations' fund-raising costs are the "lowest."[6]

---

[5] See Ch. 4.

[6] Analyses of the impact of percentage limitations on charities' fund-raising costs appear in Boyle & Jacobs, "Fund-Raising Costs," XII *The Philanthropy Monthly* (No. 4) 5 (1979); and Gross, "Fund-Raising and Program Cost Ratios," VIII *The Philanthropy Monthly* (No. 5) 28 (1975).

The Fund-Raising Cost Line Item Approach

Opponents of the fund-raising cost percentage approach generally contend that the only suitable manner in which to present a charitable organization's fund-raising costs is as part of its financial statements. This approach thus envisions an income and expense statement that displays fund-raising costs as a line item, treated no differently from any other category of expenses.

Proponents of line-item treatment of fund-raising costs assert that mere fairness dictates this approach: (1) it enables an organization to present its fund-raising costs in the context of its overall range of costs, and thus does not place undue emphasis on fund-raising expenses by causing them to be evaluated in isolation, as is the case with the percentage approach, and (2) it avoids the unfair and misleading aspects, as discussed above, of the percentage approach.

Again, this matter of the proper method of fund-raising costs disclosure becomes inextricably entwined with the point-of-solicitation-disclosure versus disclosure-on-demand conflict. This is because it is much more difficult to convey graphically the amount of an organization's fund-raising costs using the line item approach rather than the percentage approach, even if a meaningful financial statement is provided at the point of solicitation (which itself may prove impracticable). It is also more difficult to make easy comparisons of organizations' fund-raising costs when readers have only aggregate sums to consider (although readers can, of course, construct their own fractions and percentages).

Advocates of the line item approach say that this is as it should be, because fund-raising cost computations are a complex and intricate matter, that fast and easy fund-raising expense calculations are not appropriate, and that fund-raising cost disclosure cannot meaningfully be achieved at the point of solicitation.

Proposed Floating Average Approach

Those who are aware of the deficiencies of the fund-raising cost percentage approach, yet believe its virtues (principally, its usage in conjunction with point-of-solicitation disclosure) outweigh those of the fund-raising cost line item approach, often seek a means to mitigate the excesses of the percentage approach by proposing a floating or moving average in lieu of a percentage based on only one year's experience. Such an average would reflect fund-raising expense performance over a three- or four-year period. Thus, for example, an organization that raised $100,000 in contributions in each of four consecutive years and incurred fund-raising costs of $70,000 in the first year, $50,000 in the second year, $30,000 in the third year, and $10,000 in the fourth year, could, while disclosing its costs during its fifth year, report that its fund-raising costs during its previous four years averaged 40 percent rather than have to disclose in year two that its fund-raising costs for the prior year were 70 percent; in year three, its prior year's costs were 50 percent; and so forth.

In this fashion, the same essential facts would be disclosed but in a manner that would eliminate the adverse consequences (such as a shortfall in giving) of disclosing only the initial months' costs. This approach would iron out the distortions that appear in a year-by-year evaluation, such as high start-up costs, unexpected and/or large gifts, and unanticipated gains or failures in the solicitation unique to a single year.

There is ample precedent for this approach in the law at the federal level. Congress at present requires the utilization of such a computation in assessing a charitable organization's eligibility for nonprivate foundation status[7] and for compliance with the annual information return (Form 990) filing requirements[8] and the elective legislative activities rules for charitable, educational, religious, and similar categories of organizations.[9]

However, a fundamental deficiency separates the moving average idea from actual usage: a rule that did not require an organization to report fund-raising costs until after two or three years of existence would be an open invitation for abuse by those who would simply create a new soliciting organization every few months and thus never report actual fund-raising performance. Moreover, a rule that required annual percentage reporting until a moving average period was achieved (that is, after three or four years of existence) would defeat its purpose, particularly for new organizations.

Proposed Pluralization Approach

Much contemporary thinking has been devoted to this question of the proper method of measuring and reporting fund-raising costs. Among the more impressive of the concepts to emerge is the idea that fund-raising costs must be "pluralized" to be meaningful.[10] This approach does not find fault so much with the idea of utilizing a percentage to display

---

[7] IRC §§ 509(a)(1) & 170(b)(1)(A)(vi), & 509(a)(2).

[8] IRC § 6033(a)(2)(A)(ii).

[9] IRC § 501(h)(1).

[10] E.g., Smallwood & Levis, "The Realities of Fund-Raising Costs and Accountability," X *The Philanthropy Monthly* (No. 9) 3 (1977). Also Smallwood, "Measuring Fund-raising Costs," V *Case Currents* 18 (January 1979).

fund-raising costs as it does with the idea that a true measure of fund-raising costs can be captured in a single percentage. According to those who support this concept, "The only way to fairly and productively understand the fund-raising costs of an organization that utilizes more than one . . . [fund-raising method] is not to look at the total of such costs for a particular period but to look at the total of such costs for each fund-raising activity over a period of several years."[11]

In truth, there is no such thing as a single expense for something called "fund-raising," because there is no lone activity that represents "fund-raising." There are many types of fund-raising efforts and, while research has yet to document the precise parameters, each effort carries with it a range of costs expressed as a percentage that may be termed "reasonable." Also, a fund-raising cost that is considered "reasonable" for one fund-raising method is not necessarily "reasonable" for another. The pluralization doctrine calls for a fund-raising cost percentage to be assigned to each of the fund-raising methods and for abandonment of reliance on the bottom-line ratio or percentage.

The pluralization approach is predicated on the fundamental fact that there are at least six categories of fund-raising methods: donor acquisition by direct mail, donor renewal by direct mail, the capital campaign, special events, planned giving and bequest programs, and indirect campaigns.[12]

The pluralization approach postulates that these fund-raising methods may involve associated costs in the following maximum but reasonable amounts: donor acquistion, about 120 percent; donor renewal, about 10 percent; special events, about 20 percent; capital programs, about 15 percent; planned gifts and bequests programs, about 15 percent; and indirect campaigns, about 5 percent.[13] An organization's fund-raising costs, where all are "reasonable," might be pluralized as shown in Table 5.1.

As noted, one of the great distortions perpetuated by the use of a single percentage to reflect fund-raising costs is the fact that the bottom-line percentage can easily camouflage "high" or "inefficient" fund-raising

[11] Smallwood & Levis, *supra* note 10, at 5.

[12] See Ch. 2 § 2.2.

[13] It must be stressed, as do Smallwood and Levis, that these fund-raising activities and figures are not based on actual data; thus the percentage figures should not be construed to represent industry standards or norms for reasonable fund-raising costs. The charts reproduced herein originally appeared in their article cited in *supra* note 10.

TABLE 5.1. ABC INSTITUTION FUND-RAISING COST-EFFECTIVENESS
ANALYSIS FOR THE YEAR ENDED DECEMBER 31, 19X1

	Revenue	Expenses	Net	Percentage of Expenses to Revenue
New donor acquisition	$ 116,000	$135,000	$ (19,000)	116.4%
Donor renewal	3,650,000	359,000	3,291,000	10.0
Special events	104,000	18,000	86,000	17.3
Capital programs	692,000	78,000	614,000	11.3
Planned gifts and bequests	481,000	56,000	425,000	11.6
Indirect campaigns	275,000	8,000	267,000	2.9
Total	$5,318,000	$654,000	$4,664,000	12.3%

costs—which is the very element that this approach is designed to highlight. An organization with fund-raising costs expressed on a pluralized basis, as in Table 5.2, illustrates the point.

The deficiency in the bottom-line percentage approach is that it can shelter unreasonable fund-raising costs. Certainly, by any known measurement technique, a total fund-raising cost percentage of 12.3 percent is "reasonable," yet the fact of unreasonably high donor acquisition costs

TABLE 5.2. ABC INSTITUTION FUND-RAISING COST-EFFECTIVENESS
ANALYSIS FOR THE YEAR ENDED DECEMBER 31, 19X1

	Revenue	Expenses	Net	Percentage of Expense to Revenue
New donor acquisition (direct mail)	$ 116,000	$245,000	$ (129,000)	211.2%
Donor renewal (direct mail)	3,650,000	249,000	3,401,000	6.9
Special events	104,000	18,000	86,000	17.3
Capital programs	692,000	78,000	614,000	11.3
Planned gifts and bequests	481,000	56,000	425,000	11.6
Indirect campaigns	275,000	8,000	267,000	2.9
Total	$5,318,000	$654,000	$4,664,000	12.3%

is hidden in Table 5.2 by offsetting savings in other fund-raising outlay areas.

Another deficiency of the single fund-raising cost percentage is its unworkability with respect to a new fund-raising organization or an organization newly commencing a fund-raising effort. Such an organization lacks a constituency of donors, and its efforts must be concentrated on acquiring that constituency (donor acquisition), a much more expensive undertaking than acquiring contributions from those constituting an established donor base (donor renewal). Table 5.3 shows how an organization in this position might show its fund-raising costs, all of which are "reasonable," on a pluralized basis. Without question, many in the general public, in legislative bodies, and in regulatory agencies would regard fund-raising costs of 90 percent to be "excessive" or "unreasonable."

The pluralization approach also exposes costs of one method of fund-raising, other than direct mail, that are high, even though the bottom-line percentage denotes total fund-raising costs that would be generally recognized as "reasonable." For example, the costs of an institution's capital programs may be high, yet be offset by other, reasonable fund-raising costs, as Table 5.4 illustrates.

Charitable institutions that rely heavily on large gifts of property, where the size and timing of receipt of the contribution bear little relationship to the associated fund-raising cost outlays and the timing of the expenditures, can show total fund-raising costs at a level of rea-

TABLE 5.3. ABC INSTITUTION FUND-RAISING COST-EFFECTIVENESS ANALYSIS FOR THE YEAR ENDED December 31, 19X1

	Revenue	Expenses	Net	Percentage of Expense to Revenue
New donor acquisition (direct mail)	$250,000	$245,000	$ 5,000	98.0%
Donor renewal (direct mail)	47,000	9,000	38,000	19.2
Special events	18,000	13,000	5,000	72.2
Capital programs	· · ·	· · ·	· · ·	· · ·
Planned gifts and bequests	· · ·	15,000	(15,000)	NA
Indirect campaigns	· · ·	· · ·	· · ·	· · ·
Total	$315,000	$282,000	$33,000	90.0%

TABLE 5.4.   ABC INSTITUTION FUND-RAISING COST-EFFECTIVENESS
ANALYSIS FOR THE YEAR ENDED DECEMBER 31, 19X1

	Revenue	Expenses	Net	Percentage of Expense to Revenue
New donor acquisition (direct mail)	$ 150,000	$ 160,000	$ (10,000)	106.7%
Donor renewal (direct mail)	1,678,000	178,000	1,500,000	10.6
Special events	85,000	22,000	63,000	25.9
Capital programs	12,350,000	1,791,000	10,559,000	14.5
Planned gifts and bequests	780,000	32,000	748,000	4.1
Indirect campaign	. . .	. . .	. . .	. . .
Total	$15,043,000	$2,183,000	$12,860,000	15.0%

sonableness, notwithstanding excessive costs with respect to other fund-raising methods. This point is illustrated by Table 5.5 In this instance, the hypothetical institution was fortunate to receive in the year involved substantial planned gifts and charitable bequests, which sheltered high costs being expended in its other fund-raising efforts. Thus, despite the fact that three categories of fund-raising costs were excessive, the institution's total fund-raising costs appear—when expressed as a single percentage—"reasonable."

Consequently, the singular contribution of the pluralization method of stating fund-raising costs is that it exposes the fallacy of the bottom-line ratio. That is, the single percentage approach, while regarded by many as an essential element of complete "disclosure," can make the fund-raising costs of certain organizations appear "unreasonable" when in fact they are "reasonable" and—in an outcome perversely counter-productive to the objective of disclosure—can make the fund-raising costs of some organizations appear "reasonable" when in fact they are "unreasonable." As has been stated, "Where more than one fund-raising technique is being practiced, the bottom-line ratio measurement device can be misleading, manipulated, and counterproductive to and defeating of the principal purposes of the focus on fund-raising costs: meaingful and informative disclosure and accurate measurement of fund-raising effectiveness."[14]

[14] Smallwood & Levis, *supra* note 10, at 8.

TABLE 5.5.   ABC INSTITUTION FUND-RAISING COST-EFFECTIVENESS
ANALYSIS FOR THE YEAR ENDED DECEMBER 31, 19X1

	Revenue	Expenses	Net	Percentage of Expense to Revenue
New donors acquisition (direct mail)	$ 115,000	$230,000	$ (115,000)	200.0%
Donor renewal (direct mail)	650,000	195,000	455,000	30.0
Special events	225,000	135,000	90,000	60.0
Capital programs	· · ·	· · ·	· · ·	· · ·
Planned gifts and bequests	1,850,000	6,400	1,843,000	0.3
Indirect campaign	· · ·	· · ·	· · ·	· · ·
Total	$2,840,000	$566,400	$2,273,600	19.94%

To date, the pluralization approach of reporting fund-raising costs, while a major contribution to the theory of the matter, has not been widely adopted in practice. However, the pluralization approach has facilitated much greater understanding of the complexities of measuring and evaluating the fund-raising costs of charitable organizations. It is a useful technique by which an organization can make an internal assessment of its fund-raising performance. Perhaps of greatest importance, as discussed below, is the availability of this approach as a method for demonstrating to those concerned about the matter why a charitable organization's fund-raising costs are "reasonable" in the face of a seemingly high single fund-raising percentage.

Average Gift Size Factor

The problem of fairly measuring the "reasonableness" of charitable organizations' fund-raising costs is, of course, a particularly acute one for those organizations that, for one reason or another, have relatively high fund-raising cost bottom-line ratios. These organizations are all too frequently perceived by regulators, legislators, standards enforcers, donors, media representatives, and others as being ill intentioned, poorly managed, or both.

One study has shown that a well-intentioned and well-managed charitable organization that is adversely and unfairly affected by application of set percentage limitations on fund-raising costs is likely to have very low cost-per-gift and cost-per-solicitation factors.[15] However, this type of organization is also likely to be dependent on comparatively small contributions. Thus an unfair comparison results when the fund-raising cost ratios of this type of organization are compared with those of another charitable organization whose average gift size is much higher but whose cost ratios are relatively smaller when measured by the overall percentage of fund-raising costs in relation to contributions. Thus the former organization appears to have "high" costs of fund-raising while in fact the latter organization has higher costs per gift.

In illustration of this point, envision two charitable organizations, Charity A and Charity B, both of which received $1 million in contributions in the year under comparison. However, while A's total fund-raising costs were $450,000, B's were only $150,000. Thus, B's single percentage fund-raising outlay would be 15 percent, and A's would be 45 percent, perhaps putting it in considerable difficulty with prospective donors, the media, and the independent watchdog agencies. But, this comparison is lacking because it fails to reveal one additional and essential factor: the number of gifts, from which can be determined the average gift size and the cost per gift. For Charity A and Charity B, this information is hypothesized as follows:

Charity	Number of Gifts	Average Gift Size	Cost per Gift
A	200,000	$ 5.00	$2.25
B	30,000	33.33	5.00

This example shows that it is inappropriate to compare Charity A with Charity B. That is, using the fund-raising cost percentage factor as the basis of comparison, B appears more cost-effective than A, but this conclusion is misleading and unfair to A because it has a lower average gift. Conversely, a comparison on the basis of the cost-per-gift factor shows A as being more cost-effective, but this result is unfair to B because it has a higher average gift. Thus, it can be contended that disclosure of a charitable organization's number of gifts—by category—is essential for a complete and fair evaluation of fund-raising costs, and that any comparisons of fund-raising performance should occur only between

[15] Unpublished paper by Wilson C. Levis (Nov. 28, 1979).

organizations with similar constituencies, based on a number of factors, particularly average gift size.

This approach could lead to a form of point-of-solicitation disclosure that would be an incentive to donors to make larger (more cost-effective) gifts to the disclosing organization. For example, an organization with a fund-raising cost percentage of 45 percent and an average gift size of $5 could utilize the following statement in its solicitation literature:

> We believe an educated donor is our best donor. Because fund-raising costs are a major point of discussion in the press and elsewhere, we want you to know exactly how much of your gift will be used for fund-raising.
>
> In 1990, we spent an average of $2.25 per gift on fund-raising overhead.
>
> The following gift table is provided for your information. Please review it when considering your gift.

			Fund-Raising Expense	
Check One	Gift Categories	Amount of Your Gift	Cost of Your Gift	Percent of Your Gift
—	Average gift	$ 5.00	$ 2.25	45%
—	General gift	10.00	3.00	30
—	Special gift	25.00	5.00	20
—	Advanced gift	50.00	7.50	15
—	Major gift	100.00	10.00	10
—	Leadership gift	250.00	12.50	5
		or more $ _____	more than $12.50	less than 5%

This approach does not necessarily supplant the need for reporting fund-raising costs on a pluralized basis, and highlights the unsuitability of the bottom-line percentage as a measurement of fund-raising performance. Indeed, the two approaches can be merged so that an organization exceeding the applicable administrative percentage would be required to report on a pluralized basis and display supplemental data concerning its fund-raising activity in a manner that might resemble Table 5.6.

Regulated Disclosure Approach

For many, the existing manner of the state statutory approaches for regulating fund-raising for charity has proven to be unsatisfactory and perhaps even counterproductive. The varying state laws are, pursuant to this view, encumbered with arbitrary requirements, needlessly penalize (in terms of cost of compliance and other burdens on the right to solicit)

TABLE 5.6. ILLUSTRATIVE FUND-RAISING COST-EFFECTIVENESS COMPARISON BY TYPE OF FUND-RAISING ACTIVITY

Type of Fund-Raising Activity	Number of Volunteers	Number of Prospects	Budget or Cost	Cost per Prospect	Number of Gifts	Revenue	Fund-Raising Ratio	Average Gift	Cost per Gift
Direct mail—acquisition	1	100,000	$ 15,000	$ 0.15	3,000	$ 15,000	100%	$ 5.00	$ 5.00
Direct mail—renewal	1	50,000	25,000	0.50	20,000	100,000	25	5.00	1.25
Volunteer solicited	2,000	20,000	40,000	2.00	10,000	100,000	40	10.00	4.00
Volunteer solicited—general gifts	250	2,500	15,000	6.00	2,000	100,000	15	50.00	7.50
Volunteer solicited—special gifts	100	1,000	20,000	20.00	800	200,000	10	250.00	25.00
Special event—general	30	3,000	3,750	1.25	300	7,500	50	25.00	12.50
Special event—major	200	10,000	30,000	3.00	1,000	100,000	30	100.00	30.00
Capital project	200	2,000	400,000	200.00	500	5,000,000	8	10,000.00	800.00
Corporation and foundation solicitation	10	300	60,000	200.00	50	600,000	10	12,000.00	1,200.00
Government agency solicitation	10	30	60,000	2,000.00	15	750,000	8	50,000.00	4,000.00
Bequests and trusts	—	400	40,000	100.00	50	500,000	8	10,000.00	500.00
Federated allocations	—	1	5,000	5,000.00	1	200,000	3	200,000.00	6,000.00

well-intentioned charitable organizations, and improperly substitute the judgment of the state for the judgment of the giving public. This view perceives a desperate need for a new and enlightened approach to government regulation of fund-raising for charity in the face of the ever-expanding scope of governmental involvement in this area. (This approach was expounded prior to developments in the law that found fund-raising cost percentage limitations to be unconstitutional.) Advocates of this approach argue that the states should not under any circumstances deny charities the right to solicit contributions, that both rebuttable percentage limitations and tests of what fund-raising performances are "reasonable" are arbitrary because of the variation in interpretation from regulator to regulator, and that even a mandated set of factors to be utilized in assessing the reasonableness of an organization's fund-raising costs is an arbitrary approach because of the possibility that different regulators may interpret the same factors so as to arrive at different conclusions. In an effort to establish the proper regulatory role of the states in this area, and to preserve an effective level of charitable giving, a model charitable solicitation act has been devised.[16]

This proposal contains many of the provisions common to most charitable solicitation statutes: a listing of definitions, a registration requirement for charitable organizations (with no exemptions), a registration and bonding requirement for professional fund-raisers, record-retention and contract-filing requirements, an annual reporting obligation imposed on fund-raisers, a reciprocal agreement clause, and an enumeration of penalties. However, the core of this proposal lies in the reporting requirement that would be imposed on soliciting charitable organizations, the frequency of which, unlike any existing approach, would vary in inverse proportion to the level of the organization's fund-raising costs.

Under the proposal, a charitable organization with relatively low fund-raising costs would be "rewarded" by having to report less often than a charitable organization with relatively high fund-raising costs. This entails reporting according to a tripartite timetable, as follows:

1. An organization whose fund-raising costs are less than 35 percent of its total gross income for the preceding fiscal year would report biennially.

2. An organization whose fund-raising costs are between 35 and 50 percent of gross income would report annually.

[16] Stevenson, "Regulation in the 80's: A New Approach," XIII *The Philanthropy Monthly* (No. 1) 34 (1980).

3.   An organization whose fund-raising costs are in excess of 50 percent of gross income would report semiannually, once following the close of its fiscal year and again following the close of the first six months of its subsequent fiscal year.

All reports would have to be prepared in conformance with the accounting principles and reporting procedures established by the American Institute of Certified Public Accountants.

The regulator in each state would be required to prepare and publish biennially a "Donor's Directory of Financial Information," made available to the general public at cost. This directory would include an enumeration of registered charities, the total amount of contributions received by each, the amounts of outlays for program and fund-raising experienced by each, and an enumeration of registered fund-raisers and their compensation.

This proposal would, it is thought, benefit each state, charities and donors by "(1) elimination of the state's unpopular role as judge and jury in deciding the worthiness of a particular charitable cause; (2) adoption of the concept of a self-supporting regulatory program, thereby lessening the financial burden on the general tax paying public; (3) staggered financial reporting which rewards a charitable organization with low fund-raising costs by lessening its administrative burden; [and] (4) readily available and easily understood financial information on which to evaluate the performance of charitable organizations and professional fund-raisers."[17]

Contemporary Perspective

Along with recent developments in the law that have made percentage restrictions on fund-raising costs unconstitutional[18] has come an easing of pressure to develop law and/or regulatory practice that mandates a system for fairly ascertaining fund-raising costs. Nonetheless, the fundamental problem persists, inasmuch as some of the state laws force disclosure of fund-raising costs;[19] the IRS is displaying renewed interest in the subject;[20] and prospective donors and the media consistently focus on the matter, particularly because annual information returns of tax-exempt organizations, which contain fund-raising costs, are public documents.[21]

[17] *Id.* at 40.
[18] See *infra* § 5.3.
[19] See Ch. 4 § 4.8.
[20] See Ch. 6 § 6.1.
[21] See Ch. 6 § 6.6.

Despite this, charitable organizations adversely affected by the focus of government regulators and the general public on levels of annual fund-raising costs have yet to undertake a coordinated effort to obtain fair and effective rules concerning determination of the expenses of fund-raising for charitable purposes. Yet these groups, and others sympathetic to their plight, are positioned to support an endeavor that could achieve an appropriate resolution to this plaguing regulatory dilemma. Because of the constitutional law aspects, this matter is less of a regulatory problem and more of an educational effort. Clearly, everyone from the media to judges needs help in understanding the realities of costs of fund-raising.

The ideal would be to develop some consensus between the well-intentioned regulated and the regulators concerning the most effective means for determining fund-raising costs and for determining the reasonableness of these costs. This objective should be achieved soon, if only because of the present swirl of regulatory and legislative developments at the federal level.[22]

The law is filled with requirements that something be "reasonable." How the term is defined in practice is dependent upon the particular facts and circumstances. With respect to fund-raising, there is no general agreement on the circumstances and factors to be evaluated in ascertaining "reasonableness." (In the past, before these percentage limitations were found unconstitutional, this caused situations in which charities were denied the authority to solicit contributions in some states because regulators found the fund-raising costs to be "too high.")[23] From the

---

[22] See Ch. 7 § 7.2.

[23] Traditionally, the courts have been quite strict in the evaluation of percentage levels of fund-raising for charity, guided perhaps by the philosophy expressed by one state court: "[P]hilanthropy should be as free as possible from the hard and sometimes avaricious bargains of the market place." *People* v. *Stone*, 197 N.Y.S. 2d 380, 383 (1959). In that case, the court concluded that, "absent special circumstances to justify it, . . . the [fee] charge made by the defendant [a fund-raiser], of 45 cents for every dollar collected, is grossly excessive and . . . his failure to inform the contributing public of this percentage arrangement is a fraud upon that public." *Ibid.* Also *Lefkowitz* v. *Burden*, 254 N.Y.S. 2d 943 (1964) ($34,651 collected from solicitations and $1,495 expended for charitable purposes). A federal court refused to exempt a fund-raising effort (sale of bonds by a nonprofit hospital) from the securities laws, in part because a "substantial purpose" of the bond offering "is to enrich the promoters by providing them with large profits from the enterprise;" the "promotors" were to receive as compensation 10 percent of the proceeds. *Securities and Exchange Commission* v. *Children's Hospital*, 214 F. Supp. 883, 889 (D. Ariz. 1963).

charities' point of view, it is difficult to frame a presentation that fund-raising costs are reasonable where the organization lacks knowledge of the factors to be used in assessing the costs—or where there is no agreement as to the factors.

The factors to be considered in determining the reasonableness of the annual fund-raising expenses of a charitable organization include the following:

Period of Existence.   The period of time a charitable organization has been in existence should be taken into consideration in determining the reasonableness of its fund-raising expenses. A new organization, or an organization newly undertaking a solicitation, may incur fund-raising expenses in the initial years of the solicitation that are higher, in relation to total annual receipts, than the costs incurred in subsequent years. Part of this aspect of the matter pertains to the development of an organization's donor base or "constituency" (see below).

Programs and Purposes.   The nature of a charitable organization's programs and purposes should be taken into consideration in this regard, with particular emphasis on whether the organization advocates one or more causes and disseminates substantive information to the general public as part of the same process by which the organization solicits contributions. Consideration should also be given to whether a charitable organization's programs and purposes involve a subject matter with general public appeal or are sufficiently controversial or unpopular that public support may not readily be forthcoming.

Constituency.   The nature of and extent to which a charitable organization has an established constituency of donors should be taken into account in determining the reasonableness of its fund-raising expenses. This factor looks to whether the organization has established a broad base of support throughout the general public or whether the organization must create such a base as part of its solicitation process.

Methods of Fund-Raising.   The methods selected by a charitable organization or available to it to implement its fund-raising program should be taken into consideration in this regard. Consideration should be given to those organizations that, for one or more reasons, must conduct their fund-raising by means of only one method of solicitation (such as direct mail).

Average Gift Size.   The size of the average annual contribution received by a charitable organization should be taken into consideration in determining the reasonableness of its fund-raising expenses. The object of this factor is to ascertain the dependency of the organization on small contributions and whether it is nonetheless cost effective in the management and expenditure of its receipts.

Unforeseen Circumstances.   The extent to which the expenses of the solicitation effort or efforts of a charitable organization are dependent upon or otherwise materially affected by unforeseen circumstances should be taken into consideration in this regard.

Other Factors.   The estimate by a charitable organization of its fund-raising expenses, and moneys and property to be raised or received during the immediately succeeding 12-month period, and its reasons for the estimate, including any program for reducing its annual fund-raising expenses, should be a factor in this regard. Also of relevance is the extent to which an organization is organized and operated to attract new and additional public or governmental support on a continous basis.[24]

A related subject warrants mention, if only because of the proposal for point-of-solicitation disclosure of fund-raising costs. This subject is the accounting standards and reporting procedures used to determine these costs. At present, there is substantial variation throughout the philanthropic community about the accounting principles that are followed. Some state laws prescribe use of the *Standards of Accounting and Financial Reporting for Voluntary Health and Welfare Organization* rules, some the AICPA Audit Guide rules, some authorize the regulators to develop their own rules, and some fail to address the subject. These variations can have significant consequences as to the fund-raising cost figure that is ascertained, as evidenced, for example, by the conflict over the extent to which certain costs can be allocated to program and fund-raising.[25]

---

[24] Also Solomon, "12 factors in determining 'reasonable' fund-raising costs," XII *The Philanthropy Monthly* (No. 11) 30 (1979).

[25] Among the most controversial issues in the accounting field relating to fund-raising is whether or to what extent certain costs can be allocated part to program and part to fund-raising. For example, many charities understandably consider the costs of mailings or other information activities as being allocable part to educational efforts and part to solicitation efforts. This matter is not resolved in the accounting profession, as illustrated by the fact that where the allocation is "reasonable" it is countenanced by the AICPA Statement of Position and the federal standards as embodied in the revised Form 990 requirements, while the *Standards of Accounting and Financial Reporting for Voluntary Health*

§ 5.2 The Police Power

Each state and municipality inherently possesses the "police power."[26] This power enables a state or like political subdivision to regulate— within the bounds of constitutional law principles—the conduct of its citizens and others, so as to protect the safety, health, or welfare of its people.

Generally, it is clear that a state can enact and enforce, in the exercise of its police power, a charitable solicitation act that requires a charity planning on fund-raising in the jurisdiction first to register with (or secure a license or permit from) the appropriate regulatory authorities and subsequently to render periodic reports about the results of the solicitation. Certainly there is nothing inherently unlawful about such a law that also requires professional fund-raisers and professional solicitors similarly to register and report, that empowers the regulatory authorities to investigate the activities of such organizations and persons in the presence of reasonable cause to do so, and that imposes injunctive remedies, fines, and imprisonment for violation of the statute. It appears clear that a state can regulate charitable fund-raising notwithstanding the fact that the solicitation occurs in interstate commerce, utilizes the federal postal system, or does both.

The rationale is that charitable solicitations may be reasonably regulated to protect the people from deceit, fraud, unreasonable annoyance, or

---

and Welfare Organizations (the "Black Book") require the costs to be treated largely as fund-raising expenses.

This matter came to the fore in 1979 when the New York Department of State, Office of Charities Registration, restated a rule concerning "multiple purpose information activities," a code phrase for direct mail endeavors whereby charities regard (or would like to regard) the effort as part program and part fund-raising. The state of New York opted to continue with the Black Book standards. Thus, the New York rule remains that where an appeal for funds is included as an "essential element" of the activity, nearly all of the costs must be regarded as fund-raising expenses. The only exception—other than cases of "non-essential elements"—is that direct costs of educational material included in a multipurpose activity (such as drafting, design, and printing costs) may be charged to program. But all other costs (such as postage and consultant's fees) must be allocated wholly to fund-raising. However, expenses for multipurpose information activities, other than fund-raising costs, may be "appropriately allocated and reported."

[26] E.g., *Thomas* v. *Collins*, 323 U.S. 516 (1945).

the unscrupulous obtaining of money under a pretense that the money is being collected for a charitable purpose.[27]

One court stated this rationale as follows:

> And the utmost limit of reasonable regulation in the matter is reached by acts protecting the public from charlatans and imposters, insuring knowledge on the part of the donors of the purposes to which their contributions may be put, coupled with adequate safeguards against malversation as to the funds received.[28]

In like vein, one commentator observed:

> The occupation of soliciting for charities is subject to the police power so far as relates to a reasonable supervision over the persons so engaged and for the application and use of the contributions received to the purposes intended, in order to prevent unscrupulous persons from obtaining money or other things under the pretense that they are to be applied to charity, and to prevent the wrongful diversion of such funds to other uses, or to secure them from waste. Measures reasonably tending to these ends are unquestionably valid.[29]

A state supreme court characterized a city's authority to regulate charitable solicitations as follows:

> The city has the power to enact an ordinance to protect itself from charlatans and imposters and insuring knowledge on the part of donors to charities of the purposes to which their contributions may be put, coupled with adequate safeguards against the misuse or diversion of the funds raised by the charities. The city may by general and nondiscriminatory legislation regulate the time, place, and the manner of soliciting, and may protect

---

[27] *Village of Schaumburg* v. *Citizens for a Better Environment* ("*Schaumburg*"), 444 U.S. 620 (1980); *American Cancer Society* v. *City of Dayton* ("*American Cancer Society*"), 114 N.E.2d 219, 224 (1953). However, the federal postal laws have been interpreted as restricting regulation of charitable fund-raising at the local level, as evidenced by the text of a decision by the Controller's Office in the city of Indianapolis on March 17, 1980: "Please be advised that it is held that where a charitable solicitation is conducted solely through the use of the U.S. Mail and such charity has no agents or employees operating or transacting business within the City of Indianapolis, the County of Marion or the State of Indiana, that no jurisdiction or authority to require licensure exists."

[28] *In re Dart*, 155 P. 63, 66 (1916).

[29] *McQuillin on Municipal Corporations* (3d ed.) § 19.32.

its citizens from fraudulent solicitation by requiring a stranger in the community, before permitting him publicly to solicit funds for any purpose, to establish his identity and his authority to act for the cause which he purports to represent, and may require information which will insure that the purposes of the solicitation will be free from any element of deceit and fraud.[30]

Still another court held:

A city has the right to regulate the use of its streets and may protect its citizens from the fraud and abuse to which charitable solicitations are susceptible when in the hands of unscrupulous persons seeking personal and selfish profit.[31]

Despite the inherent police power lodged in the states and municipalities (to regulate the charitable solicitation process and otherwise), and the general scope of the power, principles of law operate to confine its reach. Most of these principles are based upon constitutional law precepts, such as freedom of speech, procedural and substantive due process, and equal protection of the laws, as well as the standards usually imposed by statutory law, which bars the exercise of the police power in a manner that is whimsical, indiscriminate, or arbitrary.[32]

Courts usually indulge a strong presumption in favor of the constitutionality of legislation. Thus, a court generally will not pass upon the constitutionality of a statute or ordinance unless or until it becomes necessary to do so to dispose of the case before it. This means that one challenging a law on constitutional grounds has the substantial burden of convincing a court that constitutional law principles are to govern the outcome of the case.

The Fourteenth Amendment to the U.S. Constitution provides that a state may not "deprive any person of life, liberty, or property, without due process of law; nor deny to any person within its jurisdiction the equal protection of the laws." Most state constitutions contain comparable provisions. The term "liberty," as used in the Fourteenth Amendment, includes the liberties of freedom of speech and of the press, as well as

---

[30] *American Cancer Society, supra* note 27, at 224.

[31] *National Foundation* v. *City of Fort Worth, Texas* ("*National Foundation*"), 307 F. Supp. 177, 186 (N.D. Tex. 1967), aff'd, 415 F.2d 41 (5th Cir. 1969), cert. den., 396 U.S. 1040 (1970). Also *Seattle* v. *Rogers*, 106 P.2d 598 (1940).

[32] E.g., *Hornsby* v. *Allen*, 326 F.2d 605 (5th Cir. 1964).

the general right of liberty of action, as guaranteed by the First Amendment and similar state constitution provisions.[33]

In addition to these fundamental constitutional law protections, there is at least one other pertinent precept of law. This is that the basic regulatory policy must be established by the legislature, including the general standards to be adhered to by the enforcement agency in the performance of its functions, and that the administrative agency, in its rule-making or fact-finding role, must function within the boundaries of the legislatively devised policy and in conformance with it.

In many instances, a solicitation by a charity for contributions is part fund-raising and part dissemination of information, the latter being an educational activity. It is indisputable that such a charitable solicitation is action that is sheltered by the constitutional law guarantees and protections as above discussed, particularly as respects the rights of free speech.[34]

Consequently, the laws that regulate charitable solicitations are by no means constitutionally deficient per se. They are, instead, legitimate utilizations of the states' police power, and those who vociferously complain about the states' regulation in this field must face this basic fact. At the same time, these laws must, like all legislation, conform to certain basic legal standards or face challenges in the courts. As one court stated, while "the government may regulate solicitation in order to protect the community from fraud, . . . [a]ny action impinging upon the freedom of expression and discussion . . . must be minimal, and intimately related to an articulated, substantial government interest."[35] The Supreme Court has stated that, while government has "legitimate interests" in this field, it must serve these interests "by narrowly drawn regulations" that do not unnecessarily interfere with First Amendment freedoms.[36] Another court characterized this right of "freedom of action" to fund-raise for authentic charity as follows:

> [S]ince every person has the right to solicit contributions for charity if he acts in good faith and makes an honest application of the funds so obtained,

[33] *Cantwell* v. *Connecticut*, 310 U.S. 296 (1940).

[34] See § 5.3 *infra*.

[35] *Citizens for a Better Environment* v. *Village of Schaumburg* (N.D. Ill. 1979).

[36] *Schaumburg, supra* note 27. In this case, the Supreme Court suggested the type of laws that would be suitable: proscription on fraud by solicitors, disclosure of finances of charities to the public, registration and reporting pursuant to state charitable solicitation acts, and antitrespass ordinances. See discussion beginning at *infra* note 41.

regulations of this character which are arbitrary and which assume to say what person or what institution may or may not engage in charitable work are objectionable, as a denial of a common right. The police power cannot be used in such an arbitrary, unreasonable and oppressive manner.[37]

The lawsuits against enforcement of these laws that are currently prevailing are not those that confront the statutes broadside but those that focus on one or more aspects of specific applicability, such as these laws' impact on the practice of religious beliefs, alleged violations of free speech rights caused by refusals to allow solicitations by organizations with fund-raising costs in excess of a set percentage, or alleged violations of equal protection rights stemming from exemptions or preferences shown to certain organizations.

§ 5.3   Restraint on the Regulators: Fund-Raising as Free Speech

As a result of significant action by the U.S. Supreme Court throughout the 1980s, in the form of three major opinions, it is now amply clear that fund-raising for charitable purposes is an exercise of the right of free speech, under both federal and state law principles. This application of the First and Fourteenth Amendments to the U.S. Constitution stands as the single most important bar to more stringent government regulation of the process of soliciting charitable contributions.

As discussed, government has the police power to regulate the process of soliciting contributions for charitable purposes.[38] However, it cannot exercise this power in a manner that unduly intrudes upon the rights of free speech of the soliciting charities and their consultants and solicitors.

The most significant clash between a government's police power to regulate for the benefit of its citizens and the free speech rights associated with charitable solicitations involves the application of percentage limitations on fund-raising costs as a basis for determining whether a charity may lawfully solicit funds in a jurisdiction.[39] These percentage limitations are, by application of contemporary Supreme Court pronouncements, blatantly violative of charities' free speech rights or, more formally stated, are unconstitutionally overbroad in violation of the First and Fourteenth Amendments to the U.S. Constitution.

---

[37] *American Cancer Society, supra* note 27, at 224. Also *City of Fort Worth* v. *Craik*, 411 S.W. 3d 541, 542 (1967).

[38] See *supra* § 5.2.

[39] See *supra* § 5.1.

The First Amendment to the Constitution states that "Congress shall make no law . . . abridging the freedom of speech. . . ." This prohibition is made applicable to the states through application of the Fourteenth Amendment.

The law makes a distinction between protected speech and "commercial" speech. The latter is treated as the subject of economic regulation, the scope of which must be tested only for rationality. Laws regulating protected speech, however, must be narrowly tailored to an appropriate governmental interest. In the three Supreme Court decisions in this field in the 1980s, the dissenters argued that the fund-raising regulation statutes are only limiting commercial speech and that they do so in a reasonable manner.

State of Law Prior to 1980 Supreme Court Decision

As noted, three Supreme Court decisions during the 1980s spoke directly to the matter of the status of charitable fund-raising in relation to free speech rights. The first of these decisions, concerning a town ordinance, enacted to regulate the activities of "peddlers and solicitors," was handed down in 1980.

Prior to 1980, however, the law on the point was not as settled as it is today. It is true that the Supreme Court observed in 1977 that "our cases long have protected speech even though it is in the form of . . . a solicitation to pay or contribute money."[40] In 1980, the Supreme Court embellished this conclusion: "Prior authorities . . . clearly establish that charitable appeals for funds, on the street or door to door, involve a variety of speech interests—communication of information, the dissemination and propagation of views and ideas, and the advocacy of causes—that are within the protection of the First Amendment."[41]

There was authority for the proposition that the states, through the exercise of their police power, cannot exercise this power in such a manner as to unduly intrude upon the rights of free speech.[42] An impressive line of Supreme Court cases relevant to canvassing and soliciting by charitable organizations buttresses this conclusion.

For example, one of the early opinions from the Supreme Court in this area held that a state statute, requiring labor organizers to register with and procure an organizer's card from a designated state official

---

[40] *Bates* v. *State Bar of Arizona*, 433 U.S. 350, 363 (1977), citing *New York Times Co.* v. *Sullivan*, 376 U.S. 254 (1964).

[41] *Schaumburg, supra* note 27, at 632.

[42] E.g., *Hynes* v. *Mayor of Oradell*, 425 U.S. 610 (1976).

before soliciting memberships in labor unions, imposed a previous restraint upon the organizers' rights of free speech and free assembly, in violation of the First and Fourteenth Amendments to the U.S. Constitution.[43]

Another early opinion from the Court held that a city ordinance, forbidding as a nuisance the distribution, by hand or otherwise, of literature of any kind without first obtaining written permission from the city manager, violates the Fourteenth Amendment by subjecting freedom of the press to license and censorship.[44]

In another illustration, the Court held that a municipal ordinance, prohibiting solicitation and distribution of circulars by house-to-house canvassing, unless licensed by the police following an inquiry and decision amounting to censorship, is void as applied to those who delivered literature and solicited contributions house to house in the name of religion.[45]

Likewise, a state statute which forbids any person to solicit contributions for a religious cause, unless a certificate for the solicitation is first procured from a designated official, who is required to determine whether the cause is in fact a religious one and who may withhold approval if it is determined that it is not, was held unconstitutional by the Court as a prior restraint upon the free exercise of religion and a deprivation of liberty without due process of law in violation of the Fourteenth Amendment.[46]

Thereafter, the Court held that the streets are proper places for the exercise of the freedom of communicating information and disseminating opinion, and that, though the states and municipalities may appropriately regulate the privilege in the public interest, they may not unduly burden or proscribe its employment in these public thoroughfares.[47]

The Court has held that a state may not, consistent with the Fourteenth Amendment, prohibit the distribution of handbills in the pursuit of a clearly religious activity merely because the handbills invite the purchase of books for the improved understanding of the religion or because they seek to promote the raising of funds for religious purposes.[48]

---

[43] *Thomas* v. *Collins*, *supra* note 26.

[44] *Lovell* v. *Griffin*, 303 U.S. 444 (1938).

[45] *Schneider* v. *Irvington*, 308 U.S. 147 (1939).

[46] *Cantwell* v. *Connecticut*, *supra* note 33.

[47] *Valentine* v. *Chrestensen*, 316 U.S. 52 (1942). Cf. *Breard* v. *Alexandria*, 341 U.S. 622 (1951).

[48] *Jamison* v. *Texas*, 318 U.S. 413 (1942). Also *Largent* v. *Texas*, 318 U.S. 418 (1942).

The Court has also held that a municipal ordinance which, as construed and applied, requires religious corporations to pay a license tax as a condition to the pursuit of their activities is invalid under the U.S. Constitution as a denial of freedom of speech, press, and religion.[49]

To the extent that the constitutionality of percentage limitations in the fund-raising context were analyzed by the courts, it was thought that the so-called rebuttable percentage limitation[50] passed constitutional law muster.[51] The Court upheld a law by which regulators can determine the reasonableness of fund-raising costs by use of this type of limitation. Nonetheless, future developments in this area of the law were somewhat anticipated in this opinion, with the Court observing that a "fixed percentage limitation on the costs of solicitation might be undesirable and inapplicable if applied to all types of charitable organizations."[52] But the Court added: "The ordinance before us . . . permits a determination of the reasonableness of the ratio between the cost of solicitation and the amount collected."[53]

Despite the foregoing body of law, it was not until the series of decisions in the 1980s that the Supreme Court so starkly laid down the pertinent legal principles that govern today and so forcefully applied them to void fund-raising regulation laws as being unconstitutionally overbroad in transgression of free speech principles.

Free Speech Principles in Fund-Raising Context

The three Supreme Court opinions in this area in the 1980s laid down these fundamental constitutional law precepts:

1. The solicitation of charitable contributions is not commercial speech but protected speech.

2. Any restrictions on charitable fund-raising must be narrowly tailored to advance a legitimate governmental interest.

3. Where the issue is the constitutionality of the use of percentages to assess the legality or other consequences in law of fund-raising expenses and the state's interest is the prevention of fraud, the

---

[49] *Murdoch* v. *Pennsylvania*, 319 U.S. 105 (1943).
[50] See § 5.1.
[51] *National Foundation*, *supra* note 31.
[52] *National Foundation*, 415 F.2d, *supra* note 31, at 46.
[53] *Ibid.*

use of percentages will be voided because such a use is unconstitutionally overbroad.

4. Where a state has a sufficient interest to regulate charitable fund-
    raising, the nexus between the mode of regulation and the fur-
    therance of that interest must be substantial.

5. A fund-raising regulation law cannot constitutionally burden a
    charitable speaker or a speaker for a charity with unwanted speech
    during the course of a solicitation.

6. A state can constitutionally regulate charitable fund-raising by
    means of antifraud laws, antitrespass laws, and disclosure laws.

7. Overregulation of charitable solicitations leads to the chilling of
    speech in direct contravention of free speech principles.

A summary and analysis of each of these three opinions from the U.S.
Supreme Court follows.

THE SCHAUMBURG CASE

The first of these three Supreme Court opinions emanated from its
consideration of a municipal ordinance that prohibited door-to-door or
on-street solicitations by charitable organizations that expend more than
25 percent of their receipts for fund-raising and administration. Thus,
that law forced the requirement that, for a lawful charitable solicitation
to occur, the fund-raising charity devote at least 75 percent of receipts
for charitable program purposes. This percentage limitation was absolute,
in that it did not permit a charitable organization to demonstrate the
reasonableness of its nonprogram expenses, notwithstanding the fact
that the costs exceed the limitation.

The ordinance was that of the village of Schaumburg, Illinois. The
village denied a fund-raising permit to the Citizens for a Better Environment (CBE) because the CBE could not demonstrate that 75 percent
of its receipts would be used for charitable purposes. The CBE is a
nonprofit, environmental protection organization, characterized by the
Supreme Court as one of a category of organizations that are "advocacy-
oriented."[54] It employs "canvassers" who travel door to door distributing
literature and answering questions on environmental topics, soliciting
contributions, and receiving complaints about environmental matters
for which the CBE may afford assistance.

[54] *Schaumburg, supra* note 27, at 627.

Unable to secure a permit to solicit in the village, the CBE sued, alleging that the ordinance violates free speech principles, specifically, the First and Fourteenth Amendments to the U.S. Constitution. The CBE prevailed in the trial court, in the federal court of appeals, and in the U.S. Supreme Court, with all three courts finding the ordinance to be unconstitutionally overbroad as unwarranted transgression of free speech rights.

The village claimed that it was merely exercising its police powers in an attempt to prevent fraud, and to protect public safety and residential privacy. The Supreme Court agreed that the village has a substantial governmental interest in so protecting the public but concluded that this interest is "only peripherally promoted by the 75-percent requirement and could be sufficiently served by measures less destructive of First Amendment interests."[55] Thus, in this conflict between the police power and free speech rights, the latter predominate. As the Court stated the matter, "The Village may serve its legitimate interests, but it must do so by narrowly drawn regulations designed to serve those interests without unnecessarily interfering with First Amendment freedoms."[56]

The Supreme Court wrote that "charitable appeals for funds, on the street or door to door, involve a variety of speech interests—communication of information, the dissemination and propagation of views and ideas, and the advocacy of causes—that are within the protection of the First Amendment."[57] Thus, the Court in this opinion did not expressly hold that all types of charitable solicitations are forms of protected speech; rather, this constitutional law shelter was provided only for the form of solicitation that is "characteristically intertwined with informative and perhaps persuasive speech seeking support for particular causes or for particular views on economic, political or social issues."[58] Consequently, this opinion left open the question as to whether protected solicitations are only those that are intermixed with program functions, as opposed to fund-raising efforts, such as annual giving appeals and planned gift solicitations, where little or no "advocacy" is present.

Also, just as there was lack of clarity as to whether every charitable solicitation is an act involving free speech, the Court's opinion can be interpreted to mean that its holding is not applicable to every type of charitable organization. The Court cited, but did not discuss, the appellate

[55] *Id.* at 636.
[56] *Id.* at 637.
[57] *Id.* at 632.
[58] *Ibid.*

court's observation that the 75-percent limitation might be enforceable against the "more traditional charitable organizations" or "where solicitors represent themselves as mere conduits for contributions."[59] Rather, the Court said that the 75-percent rule cannot constitutionally be applied to "advocacy" groups, defined as "organizations whose primary purpose is not to provide money or services for the poor, the needy or other worthy objects of charity, but to gather and disseminate information about and advocate positions on matters of public concern."[60] Quoting from the appellate court's discussion of this point, the Court added that these groups characteristically use paid solicitors who "necessarily combine" the solicitation of financial support with the "functions of information dissemination, discussion, and advocacy of public issues."[61]

Having defined this class of charities, the Court recognized that, even though the salaries they pay are reasonable, they would necessarily expend more than 25 percent of their receipts on salaries and administrative expenses.[62] Then, as observed, the Court proceeded to conclude that a bar on charitable solicitations applied to these types of charitable organizations by means of the 75-percent limitation is an unjustified infringement of the First and Fourteenth Amendments to the U.S. Constitution.

One of the principal consequences of this case is the Court's rejection of the absolute percentage limitation on fund-raising and administrative costs as a basis for prohibiting charitable solicitations. The Court observed that the "submission [by the village] is that any organization using more than 25% of its receipts on fund-raising, salaries and overhead is not a charitable, but a commercial, for-profit enterprise and that to permit it to represent itself as a charity is fraudulent."[63] The Court wrote that this is not the proper conclusion to be drawn and that "this cannot be true of those organizations that are primarily engaged in research, advocacy or public education and that use their own paid staff to carry out these functions as well as to solicit financial support."[64] Likewise, the Court could not find a substantial relationship between the 75-percent limitation and the protection of public safety or of residential privacy.

[59] *Id.* at 620.
[60] *Ibid.*
[61] *Ibid.*
[62] *Ibid.*
[63] *Id.* at 636.
[64] *Id.* at 636–37.

The opinion concerning the village of Schaumburg ordinance clearly states that an *absolute* percentage limitation on fund-raising costs as applied to *advocacy* organizations that solicit *door to door* is unconstitutional. However, the opinion left open these significant questions: (1) Is a *rebuttable* percentage limitation on fund-raising costs likewise a violation of free speech rights? (2) Are these protections available to charitable organizations *other than* advocacy groups? (3) Are these protections available to types of fund-raising *other than* door-to-door (or on-street) appeals? and (4) What is the validity of percentage limitations that apply, not directly to a charity, but to the compensation of a professional fund-raiser or professional solicitor? As discussed next, these questions (and others) were resolved in subsequent Supreme Court pronouncements.

THE MUNSON CASE

Four years later, the U.S. Supreme Court again considered a charitable solicitation law, this one a statute enacted as part of the law of the state of Maryland.[65] The law generally prohibited the solicitation of contributions in the state for a charitable organization where the organization has paid or will pay as expenses more than 25 percent of the amount raised. However, this law, unlike the rigid ordinance of the village of Schaumburg, contained a provision authorizing a waiver, pursuant to rules to be developed by the secretary of state, of the percentage limitation "in those instances where the 25% limitation would effectively prevent a charitable organization from raising contributions." Because of this challenge of the law by the Joseph H. Munson Co., Inc., a professional fund-raiser, this was the first time that the Court considered the so-called rebuttable percentage limitation in the fund-raising context.

Prior to reviewing the Maryland statute, the Court revisited its rationale for striking down the Schaumburg ordinance. The Court noted its earlier pronouncement that the absolute percentage limitation was a "direct and substantial" limitation on protected activity that could not be upheld because it was not a "precisely tailored means of accommodating" the legitimate interests of the village in protecting the public from fraud, crime, and undue annoyance.[66] The Court again noted that the fundamental

---

[65] *Secretary of State of Maryland* v. *Joseph H. Munson Co., Inc.* ("*Munson*"), 467 U.S. 947 (1984), aff'g, 448 A.2d 935 (Md. Ct. App. 1982), rev'g, 426 A.2d 985 (Md. Ct. Spec. App. 1981), aff'g decision of Circuit Court for Anne Arundel County, Maryland.

[66] *Munson*, 467 U.S. at 961.

flaw underlying the municipal ordinance was the assumption that a charity with fund-raising expenses in excess of a fixed percentage was operating in a commercial manner; the Court observed that "there is no necessary connection between fraud and high solicitation and administrative costs."[67]

In answer to the question as to "whether the constitutional deficiencies in a percentage limitation on funds expended in [charitable] solicitation are remedied by the possibility of an administrative waiver of the limitation for a charity that can demonstrate financial necessity," the U.S. Supreme Court concluded that the "waiver provision does not save the statute."[68] Once again, the law deploying a percentage limitation was found inherently defective because "it operates on a fundamentally mistaken premise that high solicitation costs are an accurate measure of fraud."[69]

The Court seemed to concede that the Maryland statute may be somewhat more effective at repelling fraud than the Schaumburg ordinance, due to the waiver provision. But it added that the fact that "the statute in some of its applications actually prevents the misdirection of funds from the organization's purported charitable goal is little more than fortuitous."[70] The Court posited these examples: the statute may well restrict free speech that "results in high costs but is itself a part of the charity's goal or that is simply attributable to the fact that the charity's cause proves to be unpopular," yet "if an organization indulges in fraud, there is nothing in the percentage limitation that prevents it from misdirecting funds."[71] "In either event," the Court concluded, "the percentage limitation, though restricting solicitation costs, will have done nothing to prevent fraud."[72]

"[I]n all its applications," wrote the Court, "the [Maryland] statute creates an unnecessary risk of chilling free speech."[73] The Court reasserted its theme in these contexts: "The possibility of a waiver may decrease the number of impermissible applications of the statute, but it does nothing to remedy the statute's fundamental defect."[74]

The state of Maryland offered reasons in the nature of characteristics of its law, other than the waiver provision, as to why its statute should

[67] *Ibid.*
[68] *Id.* at 962.
[69] *Id.* at 966.
[70] *Id.* at 967.
[71] *Ibid.*
[72] *Ibid.*
[73] *Id.* at 968.
[74] *Ibid.*

be salvaged in contradistinction with the Schaumburg ordinance. The Court was unmoved by these features: (1) a charity's ability to solicit funds without having to first prove compliance with the percentage limitation, (2) the limitation applies only to fund-raising expenses and not to a variety of other noncharitable expenditures (such as postage), (3) a charity's ability to elect to apply the percentage limitation on a campaign-by-campaign basis, and (4) the applicability of the statute to all forms of fund-raising for charitable purposes, not just door-to-door solicitation.

As to the first of these propositions, the Court found elements of a "before-the-fact" prohibition on solicitation, such as the requirement that a contract between a charity and a professional fund-raiser must be filed with the state in advance of a solicitation and the fact that the registration of a professional fund-raiser will be approved by the state only where the application is in conformity with the statute. But more importantly, the Court decided that this distinction about restraint before or after the commencement of fund-raising makes little difference, in that "[w]hether the charity is prevented from engaging in First Amendment activity by the lack of a solicitation permit or by the knowledge that its fund-raising activity is illegal if it cannot satisfy the percentage limitation, the chill on the protected activity is the same."[75]

As to the second and third points, the Court dismissed the distinctions as meaning "only that the statute will not apply to as many charities as did the [Schaumburg] ordinance . . ." and added that they "do nothing to alter the fact that significant fund-raising activity protected by the First Amendment is barred by the percentage limitation."[76]

The fourth point was rejected on the ground that the broader scope of the statute "does not remedy the fact that the statute promotes the State's interest only peripherally."[77] Dryly, the Court wrote that the "statute's aim [in attempting to attack fraud] is not improved by the fact that it fires at a number of targets."[78]

Thus, the percentage limitation enacted in the state of Maryland was voided by the U.S. Supreme Court on the same ground as that of the Schaumburg ordinance: it was unconstitutionally overbroad in transgression of free speech rights.

[75] *Id.* at 969.
[76] *Ibid.*
[77] *Ibid.*
[78] *Id.* at 970.

Regarding the four questions left unanswered by the Supreme Court in 1980 when considering the municipal ordinance, it is clear that the Court in 1984 answered the first question in the affirmative: a rebuttable percentage limitation is just as constitutionally deficient as an absolute one.

The second and third questions basically went unaddressed in this second opinion. Yet there is nothing in the opinion concerning the Maryland statute that suggests that free speech rights are extended only to advocacy groups. Indeed, throughout most of the opinion, reference is only to charities, with the Court observing that advocacy groups are the "organizations that were of primary concern to the Court" in its prior opinion.[79] The only instance of an attempt to bifurcate the charitable world in these regards by the Court in 1984 came when it made reference to "organizations that have high fund-raising costs not due to protected First Amendment activity"; this distinction was dismissed with the observation that "this statute cannot distinguish those organizations from charities that have high costs due to protected First Amendment activities."[80] Consequently, there should be little doubt that free speech rights in these regards are extended to all charities, either because the law treats all charitable organizations as protected when fund-raising or because the law has yet to contemplate a statute that can constitutionally distinguish between the two categories of charitable entities.

Moreover, there is nothing in the opinion concerning the Maryland statute that suggests that free speech protections are available only for fund-raising that occurs door to door. Indeed, the opinion specifically notes, without comment as to the distinction, that the statute "regulates all charitable fund-raising, and not just door-to-door solicitation."[81] Again, there should be little doubt that free speech rights in these regards are extended to all forms of fund-raising for charitable purposes.

The fourth question was not fully answered in the opinion concerning the Maryland statute. Yet the ultimate outcome was subtly hinted at in the 1984 opinion. In the case construing the Maryland statute, the plaintiff was not a charitable organization but a professional fund-raiser. This generated a number of legal problems, principally the question of standing, but the merits of the opinion implicitly stated that free speech rights in the charitable fund-raising context extended beyond rights asserted directly by or on behalf of charitable organizations.

[79] *Id.* at 963.
[80] *Id.* at 966.
[81] *Id.* at 969.

THE RILEY CASE

Surprisingly, during the decade of the 1980s, the U.S. Supreme Court elected to revisit the charitable fund-raising/free speech issue a third time. By this time, the principal author of the dissents in the previous two cases (see below) had become the Chief Justice of the Supreme Court, and it is fairly obvious that he orchestrated the taking of the case in one last attempt to trim the reach of the prior two opinions. But he failed.

In 1988, the U.S. Supreme Court rendered still another opinion addressing the constitutionality of a charitable fund-raising regulation law.[82] At issue in this instance were provisions of the North Carolina charitable solicitation act. Just as the Maryland statute attempted to sidestep constitutional law infirmities by being more sophisticated than the Schaumburg ordinance, the North Carolina statute tried to be constitutional by being more sophisticated than the Maryland law. Part of the problem with the North Carolina statute is that it read as a near parody of the previous Supreme Court rulings and as a too-obvious attempt to stay within the boundaries of fund-raising regulation circumscribed by the law of free speech rights.

The North Carolina charitable solicitation law did not place a limitation on fund-raising expenses by charitable organizations. Rather, it endeavored to constitutionally place a limitation on the amount or extent of fees paid by a charitable organization to professional fund-raisers or professional solicitors. The general rule as articulated by this law was that a professional fund-raiser or solicitor could not lawfully charge a charitable organization a fee that is "excessive and unreasonable." This law established a three-tiered schedule, using percentage-based mechanical presumptions, for determining whether a particular fee is in fact excessive and unreasonable.

Under the North Carolina statute, a fee that is not in excess of 20 percent of the gross receipts collected was deemed "reasonable and nonexcessive." Where a fee is between 20 and 35 percent of gross receipts collected, the law deemed the fee to be excessive and unreasonable upon a showing that the solicitation at issue "did not involve the dissemination of information, discussion, or advocacy relating to public issues as directed by the . . . [charitable organization] which is to benefit from the solicitation." A fee in excess of 35 percent was presumed to

---

[82] *Riley v. National Federation of the Blind of North Carolina, Inc.* ("*Riley*"), 108 S.Ct. 2667 (1988), aff'g, 817 F.2d 102 (4th Cir. 1987), aff'g, 635 F. Supp. 256 (E.D.N.Car. 1986).

be excessive and unreasonable, although the fund-raiser or solicitor could rebut the presumption by showing that the amount of the fee was necessary because (1) the solicitation involved the dissemination of information or advocacy on public issues directed by the charity, or (2) otherwise the ability of the charity to raise money or communicate its ideas and positions to the public would be seriously diminished. The Court went on to describe an additional feature of the North Carolina statute, in that "even where a prima facie showing of unreasonableness has been rebutted, the fact-finder must still make an ultimate determination, on a case by case basis, as to whether the fee was reasonable—a showing that the solicitation involved the advocacy or dissemination of information does not alone establish that the total fee was reasonable."[83]

The U.S. Supreme Court concluded that the three-tiered, percentage-based definition of a "reasonable" fund-raising fee in the North Carolina law failed to pass constitutional muster, as being unduly burdensome of free speech. It rejected the rationale that the statute is constitutional because it was designed to ensure that the maximum amount of funds reaches the charity on the ground that the law is overbroad and in violation of the "First Amendment's command that government regulation of speech must be measured in minimums, not maximums."[84] The Court likewise dismissed the thought that the North Carolina law's flexibility more narrowly tailors it to the state's asserted interests than was the case with the Maryland statute or the Schaumburg ordinance, noting that "[p]ermitting rebuttal cannot supply the missing nexus between the percentages and the State's interest."[85]

The Court considered other justifications offered by the state of North Carolina for regulating the reasonableness of fund-raisers' fees, portraying them as resting on one or both of two premises: "(1) that charitable organizations are economically unable to negotiate fair or reasonable contracts without governmental assistance; or (2) that charities are incapable of deciding for themselves the most effective way to exercise their First Amendment rights."[86] Rejecting both premises, the Court wrote that there is no constitutional law basis for the claim by the state of "the power to establish a single transcendent criterion by which it can bind

---

[83] *Riley*, 108 S.Ct. at 2672.
[84] *Id.* at 2674.
[85] *Id.* at 2675.
[86] *Ibid.*

the charities' speaking decisions," finding the state's position "paternalistic."[87]

The Court observed that the "First Amendment mandates that we presume that speakers, not the government, know best both what they want to say and how to say it."[88] "To this end," continued the Court, "the government, even with the purest of motives, may not substitute its judgment as to how best to speak for that of speakers and listeners; free and robust debate cannot thrive if directed by the government."[89] On this point, the Court then administered this coup de grace: "We perceive no reason to engraft an exception to this settled rule for charities."[90]

The Court in this case also attacked the general concept of forcing fund-raising charities to prove "reasonableness" of fees on the basis of the size of the fund-raiser's fee. That fee, wrote the Court, may be one of many factors affecting fund-raising expenses; others include the type of fund-raising involved and the integration of a non-fund-raising event with a fund-raising effort.[91] Moreover, added the Court, the law is "impermissibly insensitive to the realities faced by small or unpopular charities, which must often pay more than 35% of the gross receipts collected to the fundraiser due to the difficulty of attracting donors" and thus its "scheme must necessarily chill speech in direct contravention of the First Amendment's dictates."[92]

In this case invalidating this aspect of the North Carolina statute, the Court returned to a theme articulated in its opinion concerning the Maryland law: the ability of the states to combat fund-raising fraud by means of antifraud statutes and general disclosure requirements. The Court acknowledged that these laws may not be the most efficient methods of preventing fraud, but added that "the First Amendment does not permit the State to sacrifice speech for efficiency."[93]

Having dispensed with this aspect of the North Carolina law (by voiding it), the Court turned to a somewhat comparable feature: another provision requiring that professional fund-raisers disclose to potential donors, before an appeal for funds, the percentage of charitable contributions collected during the previous 12 months that were expended

[87] Ibid.
[88] Ibid.
[89] Id. at 2674–75.
[90] Id. at 2675.
[91] Ibid.
[92] Id. at 2676.
[93] Ibid.

for charitable purposes. While the state contended that this was a limitation only on commercial speech, in that it relates only to the fund-raiser's profits from a solicitation, the Court wrote that, even if that is true, "we do not believe that the speech retains its commercial character when it is inextricably intertwined with otherwise fully protected speech."[94] Deciding that "we cannot parcel out the speech, applying one test to one phrase and another test to another phrase,"[95] the Court held that this "prophylactic, imprecise, and unduly burdensome rule" is unconstitutional.[96]

These three U.S. Supreme Court opinions have set the stage for more litigation over the permissible reach of state charitable solicitation laws. The essence of these opinions appears at the outset of this section. Aside from the specific rules to be gleaned from these three decisions, the one basic principle of law that is most important is that these fund-raising regulation laws may not "burden a speaker [be it a charity or a fund-raising professional] with unwanted speech during the course of a solicitation."[97]

THE DISSENTS

Each of these three U.S. Supreme Court opinions was followed by a dissenting opinion. The fundamental theme of the dissents was that charitable fund-raising is a type of commercial speech and that the provisions limiting fund-raising expenses are merely forms of economic regulation with no First Amendment implication. The corollary to this view is that the percentage ceilings are permissible as being "reasonable" approaches to regulation.

The essence of the dissent in the opinion concerning the ordinance of the village of Schaumburg is that "a simple request for money lies far from the core protections of the First Amendment. . . ."[98] In this context, the dissenting view is that "the community's interest in insuring that the collecting organization meet some objective financial criteria is indisputably valid," so that the community can insulate itself "against panhandlers, profiteers, and peddlers."[99]

---

[94] *Id.* at 2677.
[95] *Ibid.*
[96] *Id.* at 2679.
[97] *Ibid.*
[98] *Schaumburg, supra* note 27, at 644.
[99] *Ibid.*

The dissents distinguish the pre-1980 law in this area by stating that the laws were struck down because of the amount of discretion vested in the regulators to grant or deny permits on the basis of vague or nonexistent criteria, or because the matter involved the distribution of information (as opposed to requests for contributions). The view embodied in the dissents is that the law should be different when the rule "deals not with the dissemination of ideas, but rather with the solicitation of money."[100]

The dissent in the 1980 case summarized its position with the view that the ordinance, "while perhaps too strict to suit some tastes, affects only door-to-door solicitation for financial contributions, leaves little or no discretion in the hands of municipal authorities to 'censor' unpopular speech, and is rationally related to the community's collective desire to bestow its largess upon organizations that are truly 'charitable.' "[101]

The dissent in the case involving the Maryland statute added an argument as a result of the nature of the particular facts of the case. This was the contention that constitutional rights cannot be "asserted vicariously,"[102] namely (in the case), by a professional fund-raiser rather than a charitable organization, leading to the thought that the overbreadth doctrine is inapplicable in the case. This approach was then used to lead into the argument that, again, the speech is commercial speech. Yet, in this latter setting, the underlying premise of the argument reflected a slight shift of view by observing that the "challenged Maryland statute functions primarily as an economic regulation setting a limit on the fees charged by professional fundraisers."[103] This observation seems to indicate an abandonment of the view, for purposes of dissent writing, that fund-raising by charities is commercial speech and to focus instead on the argument that the statute, when applied to fund-raisers, involves commercial speech. Any impact on fund-raising by charities was considered "incidental and indirect,"[104] so that there is no need to subject the law to strict First Amendment scrutiny. The dissent in the case involving the Maryland statute reinvokes the point that the limitations on the fees charged by professional fund-raisers serve a number of legitimate and substantial governmental interests. And, finally, the dissent in the case

---

[100] *Id.* at 641.

[101] *Id.* at 645.

[102] *Munson*, 467 U.S., *supra* note 65, at 977.

[103] *Id.* at 978.

[104] *Id.* at 947.

tries to distinguish the Maryland law from the Schaumburg ordinance on the ground of the various flexibilities inherent in the percentage limitation contained in the latter provision.

The dissent in the case concerning the North Carolina law expectedly repeats the arguments in the prior two dissents. This dissent, however, argues that even if the other two cases were rightfully decided, this one is not because the fee limitations "put no direct burden on the charities themselves."[105] Once again, the contention is advanced that the matter is one of economic regulation only, with the Court majority accused of stretching for applicability of free speech principles: "As far as I know, this Court has never held that an economic regulation with some impact on protected speech, no matter how small or indirect, must be subjected to strict scrutiny under the First Amendment."[106] This dissent also finds that the approach of the statute in ascertaining the reasonableness of fund-raisers' fees "protects against the vices of the fixed-percentage scheme struck down in" 1984, and that "the fee provisions of the statute thus satisfy the constitutional requirement that it be narrowly tailored to serve the State's compelling interests."[107]

As to the professional fund-raisers' disclosure requirement, the dissent contends that the rule survives free speech analysis in that "the required disclosure of true facts in the course of what is at least in part a 'commercial' transaction—the solicitation of money by a professional fund-raiser—does not necessarily create such a burden on core protected speech as to require that strict scrutiny be applied."[108]

SUBSEQUENT LITIGATION

The tenor of the second and third of the above opinions emanating from the U.S. Supreme Court indicates that the free speech principles extended to fund-raising for charitable purposes are not necessarily dependent upon the type of charitable entity involved nor on the type of fund-raising involved. Certainly, subsequent pronouncements indicate that the lower courts are embracing these principles in settings other than considerations of the limitations on fund-raising expenses.

---

[105] *Riley*, 108 S.Ct., *supra* note 82, at 2683.
[106] *Ibid.*
[107] *Id.* at 2684.
[108] *Id.* at 2685.

State of Law Subsequent to Three Supreme Court Decisions

A significant case that developed in the aftermath of these three Supreme Court pronouncements concerned application of the Virginia charitable solicitation act.[109] The opinion involved did not create any new law but reinforced legal principles so articulately promulgated by the Supreme Court during the 1980s.

The litigation was initiated by a corporation that is in the business of providing fund-raising services to police organizations and firefighter unions. The organization contracted with local police fraternal organizations in Virginia to solicit advertising for publications used in a fund-raising campaign.

The opinion pertained to four aspects of the Virginia statute. One of these provisions requires professional solicitors to submit the script of an oral solicitation to the state at least 10 days prior to the commencement of solicitation. The state argued that this section promotes the state's interest in the prevention of fraud and misrepresentation in solicitation, and that it is the only effective regulation of fund-raising by telephone.

The appellate court found, however, that the section is an unconstitutional prior restraint on speech. It held that, while the state has a legitimate interest in preventing fraud and misrepresentation, there "is a thin line between reviewing a script for misrepresentations and reviewing it for content."[110] The court wrote that state officials are able to "recast solicitation scripts so as to reflect their judgment as to how a solicitation can be made."[111] The state attempted to convince the court that its officials properly utilize this section but the court held that none of the state's assurances persuade it that "bureaucratic review of solicitation scripts is not rife with potential for abuse."[112]

As to the thought that this section may be the most effective means of monitoring telephone solicitations, the court quoted Supreme Court pronouncements in observing that "the First Amendment does not permit the State to sacrifice speech for efficiency."[113]

Another provision of the Virginia law requires professional solicitors to disclose in writing that financial statements for the most recent fiscal

---

[109] *Telco Communications, Inc.* v. *Carbaugh,* 885 F.2d 1225 (4th Cir. 1989), aff'g in part and rev'g in part, 700 F. Supp. 294 (E.D. Va. 1988).
[110] *Id.,* 885 F.2d at 1233.
[111] *Ibid.*
[112] *Ibid.*
[113] *Ibid.*

year are available from the state. The state contended that this section promotes its interest in public education regarding charitable organizations and prevents fraud and harassment, and also that the requirement is narrowly tailored to further these interests. To which the court responded: "We agree."[114]

The agreement was based on the thought that informing the public and preventing fraud are substantial state interests, which are fostered by the provision. The court ruled that the state's interest in "adding to the public knowledge of professional solicitations" is not one that is inherently incompatible with free speech rights.[115] The provision was characterized as one that "educates the public generally about the availability of financial information on solicitors."[116]

The information contained in the financial statements was held to be "invaluable," in that a donor can use the information "to learn further about a solicitor's operations," and the provision was held to assist in preventing fraud.[117] The requirement was found to be narrowly tailored and thus a permissible exercise of state authority.

Also at issue was the Virginia rule that a professional solicitor must disclose to potential donors the percentage of their contribution that will be received by the charitable organization for its use. The challenge to the constitutionality of this provision was held moot, on the ground that the state has conceded the fatal flaw of the statute, under free speech law analysis, and that there is no "reasonable expectation" that the state will seek to enforce the requirement.[118] This change of heart on the part of the state was occasioned by the most recent of the three Supreme Court opinions,[119] and the court "decline[d] to indulge any presumption with respect to their conduct other than one of good faith."[120]

The final provision at issue concerned the ability of the state to suspend or revoke the registration of a solicitor if certain provisions of the statute are violated. This aspect of the complaint was dismissed because the pleadings and records underlying the complaint were found to be inadequate.

---

[114] *Id.* at 1231.
[115] *Ibid.*
[116] *Ibid.*
[117] *Ibid.*
[118] *Ibid.*
[119] *Riley*, 108 S.Ct., *supra* note 82.
[120] *Ibid.*

The doctrine laid down by the U.S. Supreme Court, starting in 1980, holding, as noted, that the regulation of the process of fund-raising for charitable purposes must be undertaken only by the most restrictive of means because the solicitation of gifts is a free speech right of the charities, has spawned many subsequent applications of that principle.

The rule has been applied many times in a variety of settings. In 1989 alone there were seven applications of the doctrine, including the decision just discussed, which construed portions of the Virginia charitable solicitation act.

Thus, the Supreme Court struck down a provision of the amended Federal Communications Act, which attempted to impose an outright ban on indecent interstate commercial telephone messages ("dial-a-porn").[121] The government wanted the ban as a way to prevent minors from gaining access to the messages. But the Court found that, notwithstanding the compelling interest in protecting the physical and psychological well-being of minors, the prohibition "far exceeds that which is necessary to limit the access of minors to such messages," and thus the "ban does not survive constitutional scrutiny."[122] That is, the statute was found to be overbroad in relation to the problem to be solved and thus unconstitutional, since free speech is involved. (A similar prohibition involving obscene dial-a-porn recordings was upheld, because the protection of the free speech right does not extend to obscene speech.)

The Supreme Court declined to undertake an overbreadth analysis in another case but only because the statute in question was amended before the Court's review. At issue was a law prohibiting adults from posing or exhibiting minors "in a state of nudity" for purposes of visual presentation in a publication or photograph. The Massachusetts Supreme Judicial Court reversed the conviction of a man who took photographs of his partially nude and physically mature 14-year-old stepdaughter.[123] There is little doubt that the Supreme Court would have reversed this conviction as well, given the opportunity—the Massachusetts court found the posing to be an act of free speech.

The U.S. Court of Appeals for the Eighth Circuit construed the provisions of the Hatch Act, which is the law forbidding partisan political activity by federal employees.[124] The case concerned the solicitation of

---

[121] *Sable Communications of California, Inc.* v. *Federal Communications Commission*, 109 S.Ct. 2829 (1989).

[122] *Id.* at 4924.

[123] *Massachusetts* v. *Oakes*, 57 L.W. 4787 (1989).

[124] *Bauers* v. *Cornett*, 865 F.2d 1517 (8th Cir. 1989).

funds from governmental employees, which is illegal to the extent used for partisan political campaigns; the appellate court ruled, however, that that act cannot constitutionally prohibit solicitations for lobbying because that is protected speech. The court of appeals observed: "Solicitations necessarily involve advocacy and deserve the full protection of the First Amendment."[125]

The U.S. Court of Appeals for the Fourth Circuit found unconstitutional the federal regulation prohibiting solicitations on property of the U.S. Postal Service.[126] The sidewalk in front of the post office involved was held to be a public forum, with the prohibition found to be neither a reasonable manner restriction nor narrowly drawn to accomplish a significant governmental interest. The court observed that the speech at issue was political, not commercial, and endorsed the precept that gift solicitation and substantive, informative speech can be intertwined.[127] Dismissing postal service assertions of obstructions of customers, the court wrote: "Outright prohibition of a medium of expression will always prove the easier and more efficient course. Yet liberty itself is no efficient concept, and the rights of citizens and interests of government are best reconciled not by total bans but through finespun accommodations."[128]

The U.S. Court of Appeals for the Fifth Circuit had occasion to discuss both of these elements—the presence of a compelling governmental interest and the narrowness of a restriction on free speech—in finding that a city's fire department rule was unconstitutionally applied to a firefighter, who, to the unhappiness of his employer, spoke to the media about the department's shortcomings in fighting a fire, in violation of his free speech rights.[129] This rule was found to support governmental interests but held to violate the second test, in that it was too sweeping in its application.

The U.S. District Court for the District of Columbia struck down the record-keeping requirements and certain other provisions of the Child Protection and Obscenity Enforcement Act (enacted in 1988) as being violative of free speech principles.[130] The record-keeping requirements were to be imposed upon categories of material broader than obscene

---

[125] *Id.* at 1520, note 2.

[126] *United States* v. *Kokinda*, 866 F.2d 699 (4th Cir. 1989).

[127] *Id.* at 703.

[128] *Id.* at 704.

[129] *Moore* v. *City of Kilgore, Texas*, 877 F.2d 364 (5th Cir. 1989).

[130] *American Library Association* v. *Thornburgh*, 713 F. Supp. 469 (D.D.C. 1989).

material and, thus, on material protected by free speech rights. Noting that "[l]aws that burden material protected by the First Amendment must be approached from a skeptical point of view and must be given strict scrutiny,"[131] the court concluded that, notwithstanding a legitimate governmental interest—i.e., efforts to eliminate child pornography— the record-keeping requirements burden too heavily the right to produce protected material and are not narrowly tailored to fit the government's interest.

Other applications of the free speech doctrine have been made in the context of fund-raising for charity.

The Supreme Court of Tennessee found unconstitutional a provision in the state's charitable solicitation act forbidding telemarketing for charitable purposes and thus voided the provision.[132] The statute banned telephone solicitations for gifts by professional solicitors, and defined the term "telephone solicitations" sufficiently broad to embrace the activities of many professional fund-raisers. The court held that an outright ban on telephone solicitations is impermissible as violative of charities' rights of free speech. It noted that the state must use the least restrictive means to protect its citizens from charitable fund-raising fraud and observed that the state failed to show that the ban on telephone fund-raising provides any deterrence to fraud.[133] The Tennessee court also found unconstitutional a limitation on the fees paid to professional solicitors (15 percent of contributions solicited).

A federal district court found that the provision of a Massachusetts law that limited a professional solicitor's compensation to 25 percent of moneys raised for charity is unconstitutional because it impermissibly intrudes upon the free speech rights of charitable organizations.[134] Concluding (as is clearly now the law) that "[p]ercentage limitations on charities' fund-raising expenditures are too imprecise a tool to protect the public from fraud,"[135] the court held that the statute was more than merely an allowable economic regulation of professional solicitors, in that it unduly burdened charitable free speech, and that there are less restrictive means available to accomplish the state's interest in protecting

---

[131] *Id.* at 476.

[132] *WRG Enterprises, Inc.* v. *Crowell*, 758 S.W. 2d 214 (Sup. Ct. Tenn. 1988).

[133] Also *Planned Parenthood League* v. *Attorney General*, 464 N.E. 2d 55, cert. denied, 469 U.S. 858 (1984); *Optimist Club of North Raleigh* v. *Riley*, 563 F. Supp. 847 (E.D.N. Car. 1982).

[134] *Bellotti* v. *Telco Communications, Inc.*, 650 F. Supp. 149 (D. Mass. 1986).

[135] *Id.* at 153.

public confidence in charitable solicitations.[136] On appeal, this opinion was affirmed, with the appellate court dismissing the argument differentiating between percentage limitations on charitable organizations and professional solicitors as being "a distinction without a difference."[137]

A similar opinion was issued by another federal district court holding that a percentage limitation on the compensation of professional solicitors serving charitable organizations constitutes a direct and substantial limitation on the free speech interests of solicitors and charities.[138] The same refrain was echoed: "Whether the statute limits what a charity may pay or what a professional fund-raiser may receive simply does not affect the impact that the limitation has on the free speech rights of the charity."[139] Again, the potential of a waiver from the limitation was held to not remedy its fundamental defect, and the means utilized to accomplish the state's objective of preventing fraud was held to be too imprecise.[140]

---

[136] This opinion reflected *Munson* and anticipated *Riley*, in holding that a percentage limit on a professional solicitor unduly burdens fund-raising for charity to the same extent as such a limit imposed directly on a charity's fund-raising costs. The court observed that the percentage limitation in this case "is, in effect, the other side of the same coin that was invalidated in *Munson*" (*id.* at 152). Cf. *Streich* v. *Pennsylvania Commission On Charitable Organizations*, 579 F. Supp. 172 (M.D. Pa. 1984), upholding the constitutionality of a statute imposing a 15 percent compensation limit on professional solicitors (but decided prior to *Munson* and *Riley*).

[137] *Shannon* v. *Telco Communications, Inc.*, 824 F.2d 150, 152 (1st Cir. 1987).

[138] *Heritage Publishing Company* v. *Fishman*, 634 F. Supp. 1489 (D. Minn. 1986).

[139] *Id.* at 1504.

[140] This case involved a challenge to basically the entire Minnesota charitable solicitation act. The court found the main features of the act constitutional, such as the ability of the regulators to deny a registration or license, the procedures for obtaining a license, the investigatory provisions, the cease-and-desist order procedure, the bond requirements, the requirement that a professional fund-raiser have a written authorization from the charity involved, and the rule-making authority.

A similar broad challenge to a fund-raising regulation law, embodied in an ordinance that is part of the law for the city of Houston, Texas, was unsuccessful, in *International Society for Khrishna Consciousness of Houston, Inc.* v. *City of Houston, Texas, supra* note 1, at 541. Cf. *Holy Spirit Association for Unification of World Christianity* v. *Hodge*, 582 F. Supp. 592 (N.D. Tex. 1984), where a challenge to a fund-raising ordinance in Amarillo, Texas, was partially successful.

Still another federal court concluded that, while a law requiring disclosure to prospective donors of a person's status as a solicitor is constitutional, requirements of disclosure of the percentage of contributions to be received by a charity that will be devoted to charitable purposes and sending of confirmation containing this percentage amount are unconstitutional, as violations of the doctrine of free speech.[141]

Related to this field of the law is the constitutionality of ordinances governing the distribution of literature and the raising of funds for charitable purposes in airports. The courts are holding that the terminal buildings are public forums; thus restrictions on charitable fund-raising in these facilities are subject to the restrictions, as discussed above, under the free speech doctrine, which void laws that are overbroad in relation to the furtherance of legitimate governmental interests.[142]

§ 5.4   Due Process Rights

Laws regulating the fund-raising activities of charitable organizations and those who assist them in this regard must afford these persons their due process rights as prescribed by the Fifth and Fourteenth Amendments to the U.S. Constitution. The Fifth Amendment provides that a person may not be "deprived of life, liberty, or property, without due process of law." This principle is made applicable to the states by means of the Fourteenth Amendment.

In the context of the state charitable solicitation acts, the principal due process arguments came with respect to limitations on fund-raising costs. As discussed,[143] these limitations are unconstitutional, as violations of the right of free speech. The free speech transgressions occur irrespective of whether the percentage limitation is absolute (that is, where a charitable organization is not afforded the opportunity to demonstrate to the regulators that its fund-raising costs are reasonable, notwithstanding the fact that the percentage ceiling is exceeded) or rebuttable (where there is no flexible standard but instead a presumption that expenses in excess of a percentage are unreasonable).

---

[141] *Indiana Voluntary Firemen's Association, Inc.* v. *Pearson*, 700 F. Supp. 421 (S.D. Ind. 1988).

[142] E.g., *Fernandes* v. *Limmer*, 663 F.2d 619 (5th Cir. 1981); *International Society for Krishna Consciousness, Inc.* v. *Rochford*, 585 F.2d 263 (7th Cir. 1978).

[143] See *supra* § 5.3.

Nonetheless, in the due process setting, the absolute percentage limitation probably amounted to a violation of due process rights. The rebuttable percentage limitation may well have been in compliance with due process requirements because the charities were afforded the opportunity to demonstrate the reasonableness of their fund-raising costs—and thus become or remain registered in the jurisdiction—notwithstanding the fact that fund-raising costs exceed the rebuttable percentage limitation.

Still, these laws contain ample opportunities for due process rights to be recognized or violated. For example, some states provide for review of contracts between charitable organizations and professional fund-raisers and/or professional solicitors. Thus, in one state, the secretary of state is empowered to undertake this review of contracts between charities and professional solicitors; if the secretary is not satisfied that the agreement does not "involve an excessively high fund-raising cost," he or she can "disapprove" the contract.[144] Yet the statute does not state guidelines or procedures to be followed by the secretary in making that determination.

Another example is a provision embodied in the law of a state, which enables the regulators to withhold the issuance of a fund-raising permit to a charity until it submits a "satisfactory" statement of the factual basis for the projected percentage of contributions that will be devoted to charitable purposes.[145] Again, what are substantive and procedural rules for making that determination?

Some other statutory provisions that are potential due process violations are these: a rule that a charitable organization cannot expend an "unreasonable" amount for management expenses,[146] a rule that a registration can be suspended or revoked where the applicant has engaged in a "dishonest" practice,[147] and a rule that a license can be revoked where the contributions solicited are not being applied for the purposes stated in the application for the license.[148]

Any time a fund-raising regulation statute contains requirements that are buttressed upon subjective findings by the regulators, a potential for a due process abuse exists.

[144] South Carolina.
[145] Utah.
[146] Connecticut.
[147] Minnesota.
[148] North Carolina.

§ 5.5   Equal Protection Rights

A charitable solicitation act must be in conformance with the guarantee of equal protection of the laws as provided by the Fourteenth Amendment to the U.S. Constitution. This means that such an act may not contain a discriminatory classification of organizations.

An equal protection argument is most frequently raised in connection with the exceptions from coverage provided for in a charitable solicitation act. For example, many of these laws exempt from the registration and/ or reporting requirements organizations (such as churches and fraternal organizations) that solicit funds solely from their members.[149]

The conventional wisdom has been that there is nothing unreasonable or arbitrary in exempting from these requirements organizations that solicit only from their memberships, in that the considerations in such solicitations are different from solicitations from the general public.[150] This approach has been seen to be in conformance with the general rule that states have the power, as part of the police authority, to exercise wide discretion in classifying organizations in the adoption of laws, as long as the basis for doing so is not arbitrary.[151] In the charitable solicitations field, the traditional rule has been that "the high standard of the organizations released from the license [or registration] requirement, their known capacity for effective labor in the realms of benevolence, clearly justifies the exemption accorded them."[152]

However, more recent decisions question the constitutionality of these exemptions.[153] Nonetheless, organizations already accountable to government (such as colleges, universities, and hospitals) or to their membership may validly be granted exemption, if only as a matter of administrative convenience simply because a state may lack the resources to monitor solicitations by every charitable entity.

Another equal protection argument—as yet unadvanced in the courts—is that these laws that treat an organization differently (such as with respect to registration or the consequences of fund-raising costs), depending upon whether or not it is using a professional fund-raiser, are constitutionally deficient in relation to the equal protection clause.

---

[149] See *infra*, § 5.7.

[150] See *National Foundation, supra* note 31.

[151] E.g., *Lindsley* v. *Natural Carbonic Gas Co.*, 220 U.S. 61 (1911).

[152] *Commonwealth* v. *McDermott*, 145 A. 858, 860 (1929).

[153] E.g., *Heritage Village Church and Missionary Fellowship, Inc.* v. *North Carolina*, 40 N.C. App. 429 (1979), aff'd, 263 S.E.2d 726 (1980).

§ 5.6 Delegation of Legislative Authority

It is a cardinal principle of administrative law that an administrative agency may find facts and issue regulations but must do so in the context of a policy established by a legislative body, which has fixed standards for the guidance of the agency in the performance of its functions. Administrative enforcement of charitable solicitation acts is subject to this principle.

This principle of law was employed by the Supreme Court of Ohio to void a charitable solicitation ordinance adopted by the city of Dayton. The ordinance empowered a board with the authority to deny to a charity the right to solicit funds in that city, upon a finding that the objective of the charity is "adequately covered" by another charity previously issued a solicitation permit. Pursuant to this ordinance, the board rejected an application to solicit funds in the city that was submitted by a unit of the American Cancer Society, on the ground that a hospital with an existing permit and the local community chest were adequately covering the object of the unit's proposed solicitation, namely, a drive to generate funds to combat cancer. The board also concluded that the solicitation by the unit would be an unwarranted burden upon the persons to be solicited, that it would hinder the activity of other organizations to which a permit had been granted, and that the solicitation would be incompatible with the public welfare.

In invalidating the Dayton charitable solicitation ordinance, the state supreme court observed:

> The law which separates the lawful vesting of power for administrative purposes and the delegation of legislative, discretionary and unreasonable power is frequently a thin one obscured in a twilight zone, but a legislative body cannot vest powers in a commission which restrict persons or organizations unless in the legislation there is set up some standards of action which relate to legitimate objects for the exercise of the police power and which operate equally upon all persons and organizations. A law which operates arbitrarily and with discrimination upon those engaged in the same enterprises cannot be valid, nor can one which gives arbitrary powers to a commission which are in no way related to the public health, safety or welfare.

> Although the board and the commission doubtless acted in good faith, it is obvious from what we have said that sections 638-4 and 638-5 are invalid as not reasonably related to the public welfare and grant powers to a commission giving it a right to restrict privileges of organizations and persons, without standards, properly within the police power, to guide

it, thus enabling it to exercise arbitrary powers in conflict with constitutional guaranties.[154]

Thus, the state supreme court upheld the findings of the lower courts and the issuance of an injunction against the city from enforcing the ordinance against the American Cancer Society unit.

In the charitable solicitation act context, then, the regulators do not have unfettered authority to determine which charities may solicit funds within the jurisdiction.[155] The flaw of the Dayton ordinance was the arbitrary power vested in the enforcement authorities to make such judgments as whether the applicant for a permit proposes to serve an object, purpose, or movement in a field not adequately covered. Even where it is permissible for the regulators to make a determination involving an appraisal of facts, an exercise of judgment, and the formation of an opinion, the process must occur in reference to legislatively derived standards that are properly within the police power. The following observation of the court remains applicable today:

> We know of no law which authorizes reasonable regulation to include the power to determine which of two equally charitable organizations may be permitted to solicit in a particular field or which gives a legislative body the authority to give the power to decide, without standards or rules properly within the police power, whether one worthy charity shall have an opportunity to present its case to the public and another shall not be entitled so to do.[156]

A similar case involved a statute in Connecticut which provided that no person shall solicit money for any alleged religious, charitable, or philanthropic cause unless such cause was first approved by the secretary of the state's Public Welfare Council. The conviction of some of the members of Jehovah's Witnesses under the statute was reversed, with such reversal upheld by the U.S. Supreme Court, because the statute was held to be in violation of the First and Fourteenth Amendments to the U.S. Constitution. The Supreme Court there stated that, while the state generally may regulate charitable solicitations in the interest of

---

[154] *American Cancer Society, supra* note 27, at 225.

[155] E.g., *Ex Parte Williams*, 139 S.W. 2d 485 (1940), cert. denied sub. nom., *Williams* v. *Golden*, 311 U.S. 675 (1940); *Ex Parte White*, 41 P. 2d 488 (1935); *Commonwealth* v. *Everett*, 170 A. 720 (1934).

[156] *American Cancer Society, supra* note 27, at 226–27.

public safety, peace, or convenience, it cannot condition the solicitation upon a license, the granting of which rests on the determination by a state authority as to what is a religious cause.[157] The Court characterized the secretary's role and its conclusion as follows:

> He is not to issue a certificate as a matter of course. His decision to issue or refuse it involves appraisal of facts, the exercise of judgment, and the formation of an opinion. He is authorized to withhold his approval if he determines that the cause is not a religious one. Such a censorship of religion as the means of determining its right to survive is a denial of liberty protected by the First Amendment and included in the liberty which is within the protection of the Fourteenth.[158]

Some state statutes continue to authorize the regulators to act with a breadth of discretion that raises questions as to the arbitrariness of their actions and whether legislative power has been unconstitutionally delegated. For example, a charitable solicitation act once granted "full discretion" to the secretary of state in allowing a solicitation, and the secretary had the authority to decide if a charitable organization was "reputable" and that the purposes involved were "legitimate and worthy."[159] Another authorizes the state to permit solicitations by "bona fide" charitable groups.[160]

§ 5.7   Treatment of Religious Organizations

Basic Concepts

The First Amendment provides, in the so-called religion clauses, that "Congress shall make no law respecting an establishment of religion, or prohibiting the free exercise thereof. . . ." While most First Amendment cases involve either the establishment clause or the free exercise clause, both of these religion clauses are directed toward the same goal: the maintenance of government neutrality with regard to affairs of religion. Thus, the Supreme Court has observed that "the First Amendment rests upon the premise that both religion and government can best work to

---

[157] *Cantwell* v. *Connecticut, supra* note 33. Also *Jones* v. *City of Opelika*, 316 U.S. 584 (1942).
[158] *Cantwell* v. *Connecticut, supra* note 33, at 305.
[159] Iowa (now repealed).
[160] New Hampshire.

achieve their lofty aims if each is left free from the other within its respective sphere."[161]

Free exercise clause cases generally arise out of conflict between secular laws and individual religious beliefs. The free exercise clause has been characterized by the Supreme Court as follows:

> The door of the Free Exercise Clause stands tightly closed against any governmental regulation of religious beliefs as such. [citations omitted] Government may neither compel affirmation of a repugnant belief, [citation omitted] nor penalize or discriminate against individuals or groups because they hold religious views abhorrent to the authorities. . . . On the other hand, the Court has rejected the challenges under the Free Exercise Clause to governmental regulations of certain overt acts prompted by religious beliefs or principles, for "even when the action is in accord with one's religious convictions, [it] is not totally free from legislative restrictions."[162]

The Court added that "in this highly sensitive constitutional area, '[o]nly the gravest abuses, endangering paramount interest, give occasion for permissible limitation.' "[163]

The more significant free exercise cases include the clash between the secular law prohibiting polygamy and the precepts of the Mormon religion,[164] military service requirements and conscientious objectors' principles,[165] state unemployment compensation laws requiring Saturday work and the dictates of the Seventh Day Adventists' religion,[166] compulsory school attendance laws and the doctrines of the Amish religion,[167] and a license tax on canvassing and the missionary evangelism objectives of Jehovah's Witnesses.[168] Where there is to be government regulation, notwithstanding free exercise claims, there must be a showing by the government of "some substantial threat to public safety, place or order."[169] Thus, courts have upheld a compulsory vaccination requirement,[170] pros-

---

[161] *Illinois ex rel. McCollum* v. *Board of Education*, 333 U.S. 203, 212 (1948).

[162] *Sherbert* v. *Verner*, 374 U.S. 398, 402–403 (1963).

[163] *Id.* at 406, quoting from *Thomas* v. *Collins, supra* note 26, at 530.

[164] *Reynolds* v. *United States*, 98 U.S. 145 (1878).

[165] *Gillette* v. *United States*, 401 U.S. 437 (1971).

[166] *Sherbert* v. *Verner, supra* note 162.

[167] *Wisconsin* v. *Yodor*, 406 U.S. 205 (1972).

[168] *Murdock* v. *Pennsylvania*, 319 U.S. 105 (1943).

[169] *Sherbert* v. *Verner, supra* note 162, at 403.

[170] *Jacobson* v. *Massachusetts*, 197 U.S. 11 (1905).

ecution of faith healers practicing medicine without a license,[171] and a prohibition of snake handling as part of religious ceremonies.[172]

Short of such a "substantial threat," however, the government may not investigate or review matters of ecclesiastical cognizance. This principle frequently manifests itself in the realm of alleged employment discrimination in violation of the Civil Rights Act of 1964.[173] Thus, there must be a compelling governmental interest in regulation before an organization's free exercise rights may be infringed.[174]

While the free exercise clause cases usually involve alleged unwarranted intrusions of government into the sphere of individuals' religious beliefs, the establishment clause cases usually involve governmental regulation of religious institutions. These cases frequently arise as attacks on the propriety of state aid (often to religious schools) or special treatment (such as tax exemption) to religious organizations.[175] This clause is designed to prohibit the government from establishing a religion, or aiding a religion, or preferring one religion over another. Thus, the Supreme Court has observed that the establishment clause is intended to avoid "sponsorship, financial support, and active involvement of the sovereign in religious activity."[176]

The Supreme Court has repeatedly held that the First Amendment is intended to avoid substantial entangling church-state relationships. In one case, where state aid to religious schools, conditioned on pervasive restrictions, was held to be excessive entanglement, the Court stated:

> . . . [a] comprehensive, discriminating, and continuing state surveillance will inevitably be required to ensure that these restrictions are obeyed

---

[171] *People* v. *Handzik*, 102 N.E. 2d 340 (1964).

[172] *Kirk* v. *Commonwealth*, 44 S.E.2d 409 (1947).

[173] E.g., *McClure* v. *Salvation Army*, 460 F.2d 553 (5th Cir. 1972); *Catholic Bishop of Chicago* v. *NLRB*, 559 F.2d 1112 (7th Cir. 1977), aff'd, 440 U.S. 490 (1979).

[174] In general, see Clark, "Guidelines for the Free Exercise Clause," 83 *Harv. L. Rev.* 327 (1969).

[175] E.g., *Committee for Public Education* v. *Nyquist*, 413 U.S. 756 (1973); *Lemon* v. *Kurtzman*, 403 U.S. 602 (1971); *Walz* v. *Tax Commission*, 397 U.S. 664 (1970); *Eagle* v. *Vitale*, 370 U.S. 421 (1962); *Abington School District* v. *Schempp*, 374 U.S. 203 (1953); *Zorach* v. *Clausen*, 343 U.S. 306 (1952); *Illinois ex rel. McCollum* v. *Board of Education*, supra note 161; and *Everson* v. *Board of Education*, 330 U.S. 1 (1946).

[176] *Lemon* v. *Kurtzman*, supra note 175, at 612.

and the First Amendment otherwise respected. . . . This kind of state inspection and evaluation of religious content of a religious organization is fraught with the sort of entanglement that the Constitution forbids. It is a relationship pregnant with dangers of excessive government direction of church schools and hence of churches . . . and we cannot ignore here the danger that pervasive modern governmental power will ultimately intrude on religion and thus conflict with the Religion Clauses.[177]

Thus, where there is significant government investigation and/or surveillance, particularly analysis of the sincerity or application of religious beliefs, or a religious institution, there is likely to be a violation of the establishment clause.[178]

In a posture of particular significance to the law of tax-exempt organizations, the Supreme Court has articulated the possibility of permissible government involvement with religious organizations, but in a manner that furthers neutrality. Thus, the Court, in a case concerning an attack on tax exemption for religious properties as being violative of the establishment clause, has said that the government may become involved in matters relating to religious organizations so as "to mark boundaries to avoid excessive entanglement" and to adhere to the "policy of neutrality that derives from an accommodation of the Establishment and Free Exercise Clauses that has prevented that kind of involvement that would tip the balance toward government control of Church or government restraint on religious practice. . . ."[179] Consequently, the current stance of the law as articulated by the Supreme Court is that tax exemption for religious organizations is not violative of the First Amendment since it promotes neutrality, inasmuch as the alternative of nonexemption would necessarily lead to prohibited excessive entanglements (such as valuation of property, imposition of tax liens, and foreclosures).

As regards nonprofit organizations seeking tax exemption as religious entities, it is difficult to mark the boundary between proper government regulation and unconstitutional entanglement. Not infrequently, for example, a religious organization will claim a violation of its constitutional rights when the IRS probes too extensively in seeking information about it in the context of evaluation of an application for recognition of exemption. However, the courts appear agreed that the IRS is obligated, when processing an application for recognition of tax exemption, to make

---

[177] *Id.* at 619–20.

[178] E.g., *Presbyterian Church* v. *Hull Church*, 393 U.S. 440 (1969); *Caulfield* v. *Hirsh*, 95 L.R.R.M. 3164 (E.D. Pa. 1977).

[179] *Walz* v. *Tax Commission*, *supra* note 175, at 669–70.

inquiries and gather information to determine whether the organization's purposes and activities are in conformance with the statutory requirements, and that such an investigation is beyond the pale of the First Amendment's guarantee of freedom of religion.[180]

It is against this constitutional law backdrop that the efforts by government to regulate the fund-raising practices of religious entities may be viewed.

Constitutionality of Exemption

Many of the state charitable solicitation acts provide some form of exemption for religious organizations.[181] Presumably, this traditional exemption derives from the belief that the First and Fourteenth Amendments to the U.S. Constitution (and comparable provisions of state constitutions) prohibit such regulation of religious groups. Nonetheless, in the face of some fund-raising abuses committed in the name of religion, some states have attempted to expand applicability of their charitable solicitation acts to religious organizations. In response, some organizations are challenging these new requirements, claiming that they are laws respecting an establishment of religion and a prohibition on the free exercise of religion. Successful challenges would, of course, stem any tide toward greater regulation of fund-raising by religious groups, while a general upholding of this form of regulation of religious entities could prompt other states' legislatures to repeal the exemptions for religious organizations in their charitable solicitation acts.

Some states that have expanded their regulatory authority in this field have done so by attempting to distinguish between religious groups that generally solicit only their constituency and those that solicit the general public. For example, the South Carolina law exempts religious organizations from registration only when their solicitations are confined to their members and their families.

A line of Supreme Court cases extending back to the 1940s bears on the matter of state and local regulation of solicitations by religious organizations.[182] In one case, three members of a religious group were convicted, under a state statute that forbade the solicitation of contributions

---

[180] *United States et al.* v. *Toy National Bank et al.*, 79-1 U.S.T.C. ¶ 9344 (N.D. Ia. 1979); *General Conference of the Free Church of America*, 71 T.C. 920, 930–32 (1979); *Coomes* v. *Commissioner*, 572 F.2d 554 (6th Cir. 1978).

[181] See Ch. 4 § 4.4.

[182] A fuller analysis of this subject appears at 76 ALR 3d 924 (1977).

by religious or other philanthropic causes without obtaining government approval, for selling books, distributing pamphlets, and soliciting donations. While the state courts upheld the law on the ground that it was valid as an attempt to protect the public from fraud, the Supreme Court set aside the convictions.[183] The Court held that "a general regulation, in the public interest, of solicitation, which does not involve any religious test and does not unreasonably obstruct or delay the collection of funds is not open to any constitutional objection."[184] However, the Court went on to state that to condition the solicitation of aid for the perpetuation of religious views or systems upon a license, the grant of which rests in the exercise of a determination by state authority as to what is a religious cause" is an invalid prior restraint on the free exercise of religion.[185]

Subsequently, the Court struck down a tax on the sale of religious literature, holding that the sale of such literature by itinerant evangelists in the course of spreading their doctrine was not a commercial enterprise beyond the protection of the First Amendment.[186] Likewise, a license tax applied against an evangelist or preacher who sold religious books door to door for his livelihood was declared unconstitutional, because the activity, although commercial to some degree, was primarily religious.[187]

Another grouping of cases, however, injects a different perspective. Representative of these cases is the upholding by the Supreme Court of California of a Los Angeles municipal code provision that requires all solicitors for charitable purposes to register with the city and to comply with other general regulation.[188] The court observed that "many activities prompted by religious motives can hardly be differentiated from secular activities."[189] In the case, the funds contributed were used by the organization to "carry on their religious home missionary and evangelical work among the poor and underprivileged," which the court found to be a secular activity.[190] Therefore, the court ruled that the organization's activities were subject to regulation, notwithstanding the fact that the

[183] *Cantwell* v. *Connecticut, supra* note 33.
[184] *Id.* at 305.
[185] *Id.* at 307.
[186] *Murdock* v. *Pennsylvania, supra* note 168.
[187] *Follett* v. *Town of McCormick,* 321 U.S. 573 (1944).
[188] *Gospel Army* v. *City of Los Angeles,* 163 P.2d 704 (1945).
[189] *Id.* at 711.
[190] *Id.* at 706.

ordinance exempted "solicitation made solely for evangelical, missionary, or religious purposes."

A recent case involving members of the Krishna Consciousness Society who solicited contributions, disseminated religious tracts, and sold religious material at Chicago's O'Hare Airport had echoed the early Supreme Court opinions in striking city airport regulations.[191] The regulations at issue required persons to register with airport authorities each day before soliciting or distributing literature, with no exemption for religious groups. The court said that, although conduct cannot be made religious by the zeal of the practitioners, "the mere fact that religious literature is sold, or contributions solicited, does not put this form of evangelism outside the pale of constitutional protection."[192] Because the activity was protected by the First Amendment, the discretionary power granted to municipal officals which allowed them to deny permits was too broad to be upheld.

A summary of the current state of the law on this subject may be as follows. First, where the purpose of the solicitation pursued by a religious organization is primarily religious, regulation of the activity must pass a test of strict scrutiny, showing that (1) the state has a compelling interest in undertaking the regulation, (2) the statute has a secular purpose, (3) the primary effect of the law neither advances nor inhibits religion, and (4) the law does not foster excessive government entanglement with religion.[193] Second, if the state's interest is sufficiently compelling, then, although the law inhibits religion to some degree, it may validly outweigh the religious interest.[194] Third—and this is the element that is the most difficult of certainty—it *may* be that, where the funds solicited are to be used for a secular purpose, the state can regulate—in exercise of its police power—the fund-raising of a religious group to the same degree as a secular group.[195] The Supreme Court indicated such an approach when it upheld the constitutionality of tax exemptions for religious organizations for properties used solely for religious worship, with the exemption viewed as merely sparing the exercise of religion from the burden of property taxation as is done for a broad class of "charitable"

---

[191] *International Society for Krishna Consciousness, Inc.* v. *Rochford,* 425 F. Supp. 734 (M.D. Ill. 1977), aff'd and rev'd, 585 F.2d 263 (7th Cir. 1978).

[192] *Id.*, 425 F. Supp.

[193] See *Lemon* v. *Kurtzman, supra* note 175.

[194] See *Wisconsin* v. *Yoder, supra* note 167.

[195] See *Gospel Army* v. *City of Los Angeles, supra* note 188.

organizations.[196] Similarly, in cases of public aid to church-related schools where the establishment clause is the chief concern, the Supreme Court has found no excessive entanglement even where there is state supervision of such schools, including annual review of expenditures.[197]

Among the most important recent cases raising these issues is that in North Carolina, where a church successfully alleged that application of that state's charitable solicitation act to it would violate the federal and state constitutions in that the statute purports to establish, and deny to it the free exercise of, religion, and otherwise constitute an unreasonable intrusion by the state into the constitutionally protected area of religion.[198]

The church won its case at the trial, appellate, and supreme court levels. The courts found the North Carolina charitable solicitation act as applied to religious groups unconstitutional in a variety of ways, as being violative of both the U.S. and North Carolina constitutions.

Prior to 1977, the North Carolina law, like nearly all such laws, provided a blanket exemption for religious organizations. However, the North Carolina statute was amended, effective July 1, 1977, to require the filing of an application for a license to solicit contributions in the state by a religious organization "if its financial support is derived primarily from contributions solicited from persons other than its own members." This law change caused the plaintiff organization to lose its exemption, and the same fate befell another group that intervened in the case, the Holy Spirit Association for the Unification of World Christianity. Thus, the lawsuit ensued.

The trial court found that the general exemption for religious organizations in the North Carolina law is unconstitutional, in relation to the membership provision, "because it creates an establishment of religion." (The statute defines "religious purposes" in terms of practices carried on "according to the rights of a particular denomination.") Moreover, the court held, without explanation, that this provision denies the plaintiff(s) the equal protection of the laws.

The court struck down as unconstitutional the 1977 provision narrowing the exemption on these grounds: (1) it "arbitrarily discriminates between religious organizations primarily supported by contributions solicited from nonmembers and nonreligious organizations so supported"; (2) it "arbitrarily discriminates between religious organizations supported pri-

---

[196] *Walz* v. *Tax Commission, supra* note 175.

[197] *Roemer* v. *Maryland Public Works Board,* 426 U.S. 736 (1976).

[198] *Heritage Village Church and Missionary Fellowship, Inc.* v. *North Carolina, supra* note 153.

marily by members and religious organizations supported primarily by nonmembers"; and (3) the distinction between the two types of organizations created by the law "is not reasonably related to the purposes of the act." The first of these grounds is puzzling, because the effect of the statute is to treat these organizations alike, not discriminate between them.

However, the court did not stop there. The act was found to be unconstitutionally vague, depriving the organization of due process,[199] because the term "members" is not defined. Portions of the act were ruled unconstitutional because they are "arbitrary and unreasonable, overbroad in their regulation, and delegate excessive authority" to the state regulators.

The statute was found unconstitutional as respects its applicability to religious organizations on still other grounds. The regulation of fundraising by religious groups was held to be a "prior restraint upon the exercise of religious functions." The requirement that religious organizations have to secure a license "with respect to their secular activities" was determined to be an interference with the free exercise of religion. And the discretion in the state to determine what is a "religious purpose" was ruled unconstitutional.

For these and still other reasons, the trial court permanently enjoined and restrained the state regulators from requiring either plaintiff organization to apply for or obtain a license to solicit contributions.

The state of North Carolina tendered the appropriate arguments to the court. It contended that the regulation of charitable solicitations is a reasonable exercise of the police power of the state. It asserted that the regulation imposes no burdens on the free exercise of religion. Rather, it argued, the state legislature sought merely to subject religious organizations that solicit beyond their membership to the same disclosure provisions and fraud-prevention regulations as are applicable to secular charitable organizations. The general rationale for charitable solicitation acts was repeatedly asserted: the public has the right to know how and where their contributions are spent and to be protected from unscrupulous promoters and fraudulent schemes.

The state thus contended that the act is not violative of either the free exercise or establishment clauses. It also took the position that freedom of speech and of press rights is not being abridged, nor is the equal protection clause.

---

[199] See *supra* § 5.4.

The church asserted that the North Carolina charitable solicitation statute, as applicable to it, goes beyond the police power of the state and into areas protected by the federal and state constitutions. The principal argument was that the statute unconstitutionally prefers one mode of worship over another, namely, the traditional denominational church with an established congregation, as opposed to (in the words of the church's brief) "the modern evangelical mode of worship . . . which makes use of electronic communications media on a vast scale" and which is a nondenominational ministry. The solicitation of funds by a religious group was characterized as a religious function in itself.

While not all of the conclusions of law expressed by the trial court in the North Carolina case were fully treated by the higher courts, the three opinions taken together form a clear holding that:

1. The solicitation of funds from the general public by a religious organization is, in and of itself, a religious activity, particularly where the organization practices evangelism.

2. The religion clauses of the First Amendment dictate a policy of neutrality that prevents undue governmental involvement in religious affairs, and this fundamental principle is fully applicable to state charitable solicitation acts.

3. A total exemption for religious organizations from such an act avoids First Amendment problems because its effect is one of benevolent neutrality, partaking of neither sponsorship of nor hostility toward religious affairs.

4. A distinction in such an act between religious organizations on the basis of whether or not they solicit the general public is an impermissible establishment of, and entanglement with, religion.

5. The foregoing does not necessarily mean that the state is powerless to prevent fraud in charitable solicitations by religious organizations.

There may be one exception to the general fact that there is little advocacy for a substantial increase in government regulation of fund-raising, and the outcome of government's response to this exceptional situation may say much about its treatment of all charitable institutions over the coming years. The exception is that group of charitable entities the media have tagged as religious "cults."

The word "cult" does not have what could properly be termed a precise legal meaning. But it captures the public's (and some of the regulators') anger, dismay, confusion, and/or misgivings about religious cults, sects, communal groups, unorthodox churches, and the like. Whatever term may be employed, these organizations can be safely encompassed by the term "nontraditional" religious groups.

Religious organizations, including "conventional" churches, have a multicentury, Western world tradition of immunity from entanglement with governmental regulatory authority. This is manifested in English common law, and has always been reflected in a host of United States statutory laws, including the Internal Revenue Code. Of course, as noted, the U.S. and state constitutions afford organized religion with explicit protections against interference by the state.

With this background and battery of legal shields, it is ironic that it is religious groups that are triggering the clamor for their regulation (and prosecution) by the state.

The record in recent years is starkly dramatic. The nation has watched attempts to shelter drug usage as a religious practice, mail-order ministries spring up as income and real estate tax dodges, and churches and other religious organizations amass great wealth, tax-free.

The affairs of the Unification Church, the Worldwide Church of God, the Church of Scientology, and Hare Krishna sects are given heavy coverage in the media. The public reads of federal and state probes into religious groups' activities and operations, and FBI raids on their premises. Other disparate events further darken public suspicions.

All of these and other doubts about this type of organization surfaced after the revelations about the Peoples Temple and the Jonestown tragedy. In addition to what Jim Jones was doing in Guyana, there is great concern about children in cults, the rising deprogramming industry, and the spread of new consciousness movements. State and local investigations have resulted, and a much-publicized, but largely counterproductive U.S. Senate hearing was held in February 1979.

Then, of course, there have been the fund-raising exposés. The chief one of current times was the direct mail fund-raising abuses conducted in the name of the Pallottine Fathers. Subsequently, it was reported that Pope John Paul II prevented an investigation of the expenditures and investment practices of another order, the Pauline Fathers.

Finally, religious groups have become more active in lobbying activities. These activities have intensified in recent years, in the face of religious groups' inability to elect coverage under the 1976 liberalized legislative efforts rules.[200]

---

[200] See Ch. 6 § 6.7.

The answer to this dilemma—if in fact there is one—is not readily at hand. Even assuming an absence of any constitutional law impediments, the range of options open to Congress is not great. For example, federal law might:

1. Regulate investment practices;

2. Seek to prevent self-dealing, including unreasonable salaries and benefits;

3. Constrict program efforts;

4. More tightly control lobbying practices;

5. Regulate fund-raising activities;

6. Mandate minimal spending on exempt function activities;

7. Direct the composition of boards of directors; and/or

8. Restrict forms of business activity and involvement.

As noted, it is by no means clear whether constitutional law precepts would tolerate such regulation. At a minimum, the current state of the law seems to be that, to the extent that government regulation of religious groups is permissible, it must be undertaken equally with respect to all components of the charitable spectrum.

Thus, whatever government does with respect to the "cults," it presumably must do to all "charitable" groups. If the publicity about these entities subsides, so may the lawmakers' desire—such as it may be— to regulate them. But, if regulation is to be forthcoming, chances are it will not be confined to nontraditional religious organizations.

Notwithstanding the developments in constitutional law, the fact remains that some abusive fund-raising is being perpetrated in the name of religion. Some argue strenuously that the need to protect the public and reputable religious organizations dictates the applicability of disclosure laws to all types of charitable, including religious, groups and that this can be done constitutionally.[201] Others contend that First Amendment (and other constitutional) protections shield religious groups from fund-raising regulation. At the present, it must be conceded that it is an open question whether such regulation as applied to religious organizations

---

[201] E.g., Rakay & Sugarman, "A Reconsideration of the Religious Exemption: The Need for Financial Disclosure of Religious Fund-Raising and Solicitation Practices," 9 *Loyola U. L. J.* 863 (1978).

involves unconstitutional infringements on the free exercise of religion and/or an unconstitutional entanglement of church and state.

§ 5.8   Exemption for Membership Groups

As noted, 20 states provide an exemption in whole or in part, from the requirements of their charitable solicitation act with respect to solicitations by organizations of their members.[202] This is done because these laws are usually designed to apply to solicitations of the general public and because an organization's members are deemed to have a sufficiently intimate relationship with the organization so as not to require the protection afforded by a charitable solicitation act.

Because of the obvious potential breadth of this exemption, the definition of the term "member" becomes crucial in evaluating the availability of the exemption. Many of these state laws contain a provision designed to avert the most transparent abuse of the exemption, which states that a "member" does not include one who is denominated a member upon the making of a solicited contribution.

The concept of a member in this context appears to carry with it three essential elements: (1) the member must pay dues, fees, assessments, or the like, (2) in return, the member receives a right, privilege, standing, honor, services, or other benefit, and (3) the member acquires the right to vote, elect officers, or hold office. Where these elements are present, the person is said to be a "bona fide" member.

Thus, the charitable solicitation act definition of "member" rules out application of the term to "associate" or "affiliate" or any other form of nonvoting member. Otherwise, the general rule pursuant to state nonprofit corporation laws is that a member of such a corporation is one who possesses whatever rights or privileges of membership as are stated in the organization's articles of organization (such as articles of incorporation or constitution) or bylaws.[203] But the typical state charitable solicitation act concept of "bona fide member" is likely to be narrower than the

---

[202] See Ch. 4.

[203] "Membership is based on the regulations of the association and constitutes a contract between the organization and the individual." *Rachford* v. *Indemnity Insurance Co. of North America*, 183 F. Supp. 875, 879 (S.D. Cal. 1960). "[T]he test for determining whether a given person is a member of an organization is internal to that organization." *United Nuclear Corporation* v. *NLRB*, 340 F.2d 133, 137 (1st Cir. 1965). Also *Estate of Freshour*, 345 P.2d 689 (1959).

definition accorded the term by the organization in its own governing instruments.

Two of the above criteria may be relatively easy to satisfy. That is, the facts may readily demonstrate that the member bears the responsibility of financially supporting the organization by means of the payment to it of dues, assessments, or the like (as distinguished from contributions) and that the member has the right to receive one or more tangible benefits of membership, such as a magazine or newsletter, or the ability to attend an annual convention or similar meeting.

In designing a membership with the charitable solicitation act exemptions in mind, however, an organization should consider that the regulators will likely look beyond the agreement of the parties as expressed in the governing instruments in search of evidence of some participation by the members in the planning, activities, or programs of the organization, such as attendance at meetings in a voting capacity, performance of some of the work of the organization, or service as officers and/or directors.[204]

For some groups, satisfaction of all of these tests may not be feasible. For example, an authentic national convention of voting members may be impracticable, as may direct participation in the organization's work or election of an organization's board of directors and/or officers, in whole or in part, by authentic members. Also, those who support the organization may wish to do so in the form of gifts, which are deductible, rather than dues, which (unless they qualify as business expenses) are not.

Thus, at a minimum, the bona fides of membership, in this context at least, require more than merely denominating the maker of every solicited gift a "member." How much more will be required to evidence an authentic membership will depend upon how many of the foregoing factors a state's regulators will demand be present.

§ 5.9   Defining the Terms "Professional Fund-Raiser" and "Professional Solicitor"

The typical state charitable solicitation act defines the terms "professional fund-raiser" (or like term) and "professional solicitor."[205] However, there is confusion as to the application of these terms in actual practice. The distinctions are of more than passing consequence; for example, a profes-

---

[204] For a discussion of the elements of a "membership" relationship, see *Fisher v. United States*, 231 F.2d 99 (9th Cir. 1956).

[205] See Ch. 4.

sional fund-raiser may not care to be regarded as a professional solicitor and the compensation of a professional solicitor may be subjected to more stringent limitations than is the case with a professional fund-raiser. As an illustration regarding the latter point, the charitable solicitation act in effect in the commonwealth of Pennsylvania precludes a charitable organization subject to the act from, as a general rule, incurring fund-raising expenses (including payments to a professional fund-raiser) that are in excess of 35 percent of total soliciation receipts, while such an organization may not compensate a professional solicitor in an amount in excess of 15 percent of the total contributions received.

The term "professional fund-raiser" is frequently defined as a person who "plans, conducts, manages, carries on, advises or acts as a consultant, whether directly or indirectly, in connection with soliciting contributions for, or on behalf of any charitable organization but who actually solicits no contributions as a part of such services." By contrast, a "professional solicitor" is one who "solicits contributions for, or on behalf of, a charitable organization," either personally or through agents or employees, and who does not qualify as a professional fund-raiser.

As a general proposition, a professional fund-raiser is a consultant who plans and advises with respect to a charitable solicitation. In nearly all instances involving a professional fund-raiser, the charitable organization is itself the solicitor of charitable contributions. The professional fund-raiser, functioning in an advisory capacity, does not become involved in the actual pursuit of gifts.

However, a professional solicitor directly participates in the solicitation process. Generally, such persons are those who engage in house-to-house or building-to-building canvassing, placement of and collection from receptacles in public places, and charitable solicitations by means of the telephone.[206]

The distinction between the terms, and unfortunately a growing tendency to blur the distinction, can be seen in cases involving professional fund-raisers who provide counsel in the field of charitable solicitations by direct mail. Typically, the services provided by such a person (either directly or by subcontract) are threefold: the writing, design, and production of literature; the securing of suitable mailing lists; and supervision of the mailing of the solicitation literature. Usually, these services are

---

[206] E.g., 60 Am. Jur. 2d, Peddlers, Solicitors, and Transient Dealers §§ 29, 32, & 35; *Derby* v. *Hiegart*, 325 P. 2d 35 (1958); *City of Shreveport* v. *Teague*, 8 So. 2d 640 (1942); *State* v. *Mauer*, 182 A. 2d 175 (1962).

not provided by the firm acting independently but by working in tandem with the charitable organization at each stage of the solicitation process.

There is a growing tendency by state regulators to regard a firm providing these services as a professional solicitor—largely because of its direct participation in the mailing process.[207] (There is no question but that the act of mailing an appeal for contributions is a solicitation.) However, as a general proposition, classification of such a firm, which is in fact a fund-raiser, as a "professional solicitor" is not reasonable. Where the mailing is done pursuant to the charity's postal permit, the charity's name, logo, signature, and the like are utilized, and there is no use of the firm's name or other identification in the mailing, the charitable organization is the solicitor.

When such a firm places the prepared literature into the postal system—an act of "mailing"—it is acting as agent for the charity. Were this not the case, the charity's preferential postage rates could not be used. The prosecution of this agency function by such a firm should not convert the firm into a professional solicitor. It would make more sense to characterize the persons who actually deliver the charity's mail as solicitors than to treat the firm as such. But, in point of fact and law, both the firm and its employees, and the U.S. Postal Service employees, involved are agents of the charitable organization, which is the solicitor.[208]

The artificiality of treating such a firm as a professional solicitor can be seen in the consequence in law of a change in the facts. That is, the firm can avoid classification as a "professional solicitor" by ceasing to supervise the mailing. This can happen by having the firm design and produce the mailing pieces, and affix the addressee labels, and then ship the millions of pieces (at great cost and inconvenience to the charity) to the charitable organization, so that it in turn could physically insert the literature into the postal system. Surely the drafters of the state charitable solicitation acts intended no such result when they defined the two terms.

One of the flaws of this line of thinking is that it assumes that there must be a professional solicitor in the picture. In the direct mail context,

---

[207] See Opinion and Order of the Commission on Charitable Organizations, Commonwealth of Pennsylvania, dated Aug. 14, 1979, holding that a firm that provides direct mail services and that conceives of itself as a professional fund-raiser "is a professional solicitor because it supervises the mailing."

[208] The U.S. Postal Service functions as agent of those who use the mails. E.g., 17 Am. Jur. 2d, Contracts §§ 49, 51.

with rare exception,[209] only the charity itself can be the solicitor; there is no professional solicitor in this setting. By analogy, a solicitation by means of a television program is that of the persons involved in organizing and producing the solicitation; neither the owners of the theater where the program was presented nor the owners of the television network are thereby converted into professional solicitors.[210]

Finally, as to this matter of treating a fund-raising firm as a professional solicitor, this position would convert every fund-raiser serving a charitable organization where its services involve supervision of the organization's mailings into a professional solicitor. To avoid such a result, mammoth shipments of prepared mailings from fund-raiser to charity would be required, at enormous cost and inconvenience, so that the charity rather than the fund-raiser could physically commence the mailing.

Worse, the states have altered their charitable solicitation acts in recent years to strenuously regulate the activities of individuals and companies termed "professional solicitors." Depending upon the breadth of the definition of the term, many fund-raising professionals, believing themselves to be professional fund-raisers (consultants), could be regarded, with unpleasant results, as solicitors.

The foregoing is a survey of the principal legal issues involved in the state regulation of the process of raising contributions for charitable purposes. There are, of course, still other issues of law that impact on charitable fund-raising.

As the legislation in this field mounts and the states attempt to regulate the fund-raising process in ingenious ways (and without use of percentage limitations), more challenges in the form of litigation can be anticipated. As noted as the outset, there is substantial tension between the general right of the states to legislate in this area and the free speech and other rights of charitable organizations and their fund-raising professionals.[211] This tension is not abating, and thus these and other legal issues associated with the application of state charitable solicitation acts continue to ferment and fester.

---

[209] For example, a charity could compensate a person for soliciting gifts for it on that person's own stationery, and the person would contact prospective donors of that person's sole choosing; such a person would presumably be a professional solicitor.

[210] So held in *People* v. *Framer*, 139 N.Y.S. 2d 331 (1954).

[211] See *supra* notes 1 & 2.

6

Federal Regulation
of Fund-Raising

There is not, today, a federal charitable solicitations law.[1] Nonetheless, the federal government is actively regulating the process of the raising of funds for charitable purposes. Indeed, in a dramatic change of policy,[2] regulation of this type is a high priority at the IRS. Other federal agencies play roles in this regard, including the Department of the Treasury, the U.S. Postal Service, and the Federal Trade Commission.

§ 6.1 IRS Audit Guidelines

The IRS is aggressively using its inherent authority, in conjunction with its task of administering the federal tax laws, to regulate in the field of fund-raising for charitable purposes. In part, this is the result of mandates, to the IRS from Congress, to step up its review of charitable fund-raising, made in the context of enacting a law mandating certain disclosures by noncharitable, tax-exempt organizations that solicit contributions.[3]

---

[1] See Ch. 7 for a summary of efforts over the past years to enact a federal charitable fund-raising regulation law.

[2] For example, in 1974, the IRS seemed reticent about its involvement in the field of regulation of fund-raising by charities. In that year, the then-Commissioner of Internal Revenue stated: "The IRS has little power to do much about the few charitable organizations which seem to be forever skating on thin ice in their fund-raising activities." Remarks by Donald Alexander, National Association of Attorneys General Committee on the Office of Attorney General, *Regulation of Charitable Trust and Solicitations Summary of the Special Meeting of the Subcommittee on Charitable Trusts and Solicitations* 60 (1974). Over the next decade, however, the IRS amassed considerable power in the area and began using it with unusual exuberance.

[3] This law is discussed in *infra* § 6.3.

364

A segment of the legislative history of this law, contained in a report of the Committee on the Budget of the House of Representatives accompanying what was to become the Omnibus Budget Reconciliation Act of 1987,[4] is rather meaningful for charitable organizations. While recognizing that this law is inapplicable to charitable organizations, the committee expressed its concern that "some charitable organizations may not make sufficient disclosure, in soliciting donations, membership dues, payments for admissions or merchandise, or other support, of the extent (if any) to which the payors may be entitled to charitable contributions for such payments."[5] The committee reviewed situations where charities may "suggest or imply" the deductibility of payments where that is not the case, contrasting them with "other charities [that] carefully and correctly advise their supporters of the long-standing tax rules governing the deductibility of payments made to a charitable organization in return for, or with expectation of, a financial or economic benefit to the payor."[6]

The House Committee on the Budget launched this aspect of the IRS regulation of charitable fund-raising with its expression of its "anticipat[ion] that the Internal Revenue Service will monitor the extent to which taxpayers are being furnished accurate and sufficient information by charitable organizations as to the nondeductiblity of payments to such organizations where benefits or privileges are received in return, so that such taxpayers can correctly compute their Federal income tax liability."[7] As will be seen, however, the IRS has considerably expanded this mandate beyond the bounds of "monitoring."

The IRS is expanding its efforts to audit the fund-raising programs of charitable organizations. This is evidenced by documentation issued in early 1990 to IRS agents in the field, including a very extensive "checksheet."

Some History

Prior to a discussion of this checksheet and its implications, a little background is in order. Today's fund-raising regulation initiatives by the IRS can best be appreciated in the light of history.

The fund-raising community has long dreaded the day the IRS began actively to regulate the process of raising funds for charitable purposes.

---

[4] H.R. Rep. No. 100-391, 100th Cong., 1st Sess. 1607–08 (1988).
[5] *Id.* at 1607.
[6] *Id.* at 1607–08.
[7] *Id.* at 1608.

This new activism is directly affecting not only the charities that raise funds but also those fund-raising professionals who assist them.

This occasion did not materialize as most expected. No great exposé of fund-raising fraud by a particular organization was uncovered by the media or IRS audit that led the IRS to act. There was no development of new regulations on the subject at the Department of the Treasury or enactment of a far-reaching statute by Congress.

Instead, fund-raising regulation through the tax system arrived because the IRS decided to act with respect to a long-standing problem—some characterize it as an "abuse." The problem is the casting of a payment to a charitable organization as a deductible gift when in fact the transaction does not involve a gift at all or is only partially a gift.

The IRS position that a payment to a charitable organization is not a gift where the donor receives something of approximately equal value in return is not new. That position was made quite explicit in 1967, when the IRS published an extensive revenue ruling on the point.[8] At that time and since, it has been the view of the IRS that charities have an obligation to notify their patrons when payments to them are not gifts, or are only partially gifts, particularly in the context of a special fund-raising event.[9]

There were, over the years, a few instances of deliberate and blatant wrongdoing in this area. Undoubtedly, there were individuals who wrote a check, for example, to a school for something acquired at the school's annual auction and who could not resist the temptation to report the payment as a deductible gift on their tax returns. The same may be said of raffles, sweepstakes, book sales, sports tournaments, dinner and theater events, dues payments, and the like. But there was not enough "abuse" to warrant a massive IRS regulatory response.

Matters changed somewhat when charities began explicitly or implicitly telling "donors" that their payments to the organizations were deductible as gifts, when in fact they were not or were only partially deductible. This practice became so overt and pervasive that the IRS decided that the time had come to act.

It needs to be said, however, that most charitable organizations that advertised gift deductibility, when deductibility was not present, acted in good faith. They simply lacked an understanding of the rules. Most fund-raising professionals did not contemplate the meaning of the word

---

[8] Rev. Rul. 67-246, 1967-2 C.B. 104.
[9] See *infra* § 6.2.

"gift" and were unaware of the 1967 pronouncement from the IRS or, if they were aware of it, did not fully understand its import.

The distinction between deductible and nondeductible payments to charity is not always clear. Murky questions can and do arise where the payor receives admissions or merchandise, or other benefits or privileges, in return for the payment. Indeed, it was as recent as 1986 when the U.S. Supreme Court wrote: "A payment of money [or transfer of property] generally cannot constitute a charitable contribution if the contributor expects a substantial benefit in return."[10] Essentially the same rule was articulated by the Court in 1989, when it ruled that an exchange having an "inherently reciprocal nature" is not a gift and thus cannot be a charitable gift, where the recipient is a charity.[11]

The seriousness of the IRS's intensity on this subject was revealed when, at the final meeting of the IRS Exempt Organization Advisory Group on January 10, 1989, then-Commissioner Lawrence B. Gibbs opened the session with the charge that charities and their fund-raisers are engaged in "questionable" and "egregious" fund-raising practices, notably suggestions that certain payments are deductible gifts when in fact they are not. Assistant Commissioner for Employee Plans and Exempt Organizations Robert I. Brauer made clear the IRS view that these abuses are not isolated but are "widespread practices that involve quite legitimate charities." Mr. Gibbs stated that charities must "clean up their act in this regard" or face stiff regulation from the IRS.[12]

Special Emphasis Program

The IRS launched its attack on these forms of fund-raising misperformance by inaugurating a Special Emphasis Program. This program came to have two parts: an educational phase and an audit phase.

Phase I of the Special Emphasis Program took place throughout 1989. During this period, the IRS engaged in educational efforts to explain the rules to charities. This aspect of the program consisted of speeches by representatives of the IRS, workshops with charitable groups, and the encouragement of education efforts by national charitable organizations. (Certain aspects of this education phase are continuing.)

---

[10] *United States* v. *American Bar Endowment*, 477 U.S. 105, 116–17 (1986).
[11] *Hernandez* v. *Commissioner*, 109 S.Ct. 2136, 2144 (1989). See VI *The Nonprofit Counsel* (No. 7) 4 (1989).
[12] See VI *The Nonprofit Counsel* (No. 2) 7 (1989).

At this time, the IRS began reviewing annual information returns (Form 990) for 1988 filed by charities. Special emphasis was placed on the returns of organizations that are engaged in gift solicitation. Charitable organizations that were not in compliance with the disclosure rules received letters from the IRS requesting immediate conformance with the requirements. There was also talk of more audits of charities and "donors," review of donor lists, and the imposition of various tax penalties.

The regulation by the IRS of fund-raising for charity became much more serious when the second phase of the Special Emphasis Program was initiated, in early 1990. This aspect of the IRS's involvement and scrutiny is evidenced in the rather extraordinary checksheet sent by the IRS National Office to its agents in the field, to enable them to review the fund-raising practices of charitable organizations.[13]

The Checksheet

The checksheet, bearing the title "Exempt Organizations Charitable Solicitations Compliance Improvement Program Study Checksheet," reflects the beginning of the second phase of the IRS's Special Emphasis Program concerning solicitation practices of charitable organizations.[14] As discussed, the first phase consisted of programs designed to educate charities and their fund-raising professionals about the law governing the extent of deductibility of contributions.

This checksheet requires the auditing agent to review, in conjunction with examinations of annual information returns (principally, Form 990) the fund-raising practices of charities, including the solicitation of gifts where the donor is provided a benefit, the use of special events, the conduct of bingo and other games of chance, travel tours, thrift stores, and the receipt of noncash contributions. A special section inquires about the use of professional fund-raisers. The checksheet consists of 82 questions, plus financial information.

Regarding the use of fund-raising professionals, the checksheet requires the agent to obtain the name and address of the fund-raiser, details about direct mail fund-raising (including the cost of the mailings, the number of donor responses, and the amount of gifts generated from the mailings), a copy of any written agreement between the fund-raiser and the charity, the nature of the fund-raiser's compensation (flat fee or commission), and information about whether the fund-raiser had check-writing or check-cashing authority.

---

[13] See *infra* § 6.2.
[14] This checksheet appears in Appendix B.

One question asks the agent to determine whether the charity met the "commensurate test." This is a test, established by the IRS in 1964,[15] that basically looks to see whether a charitable organization is carrying on charitable works commensurate in scope with its financial resources. In the particular facts underlying the ruling, the charity derived most of its income from rents, yet preserved its tax exemption because it satisfied the commensurate test. This is a somewhat odd application of the test, but presumably the agent is supposed to ascertain whether the charity is engaging in sufficient charitable activity in relation to its available resources, including gifts received through fund-raising campaigns, in relation to the time and expense of fund-raising.

Other questions are asked about the use of fund-raising professionals. Here are two. "Was the charity created by an owner, officer, director, trustee, or employee of the professional fund-raiser?" "Is any officer, director, trustee, or employee of the charity employed by or connected with the professional fundraiser in any ownership of business, investment venture, or family relationship?"

The checksheet focuses on the nature of benefits, goods, or services given to donors. These items include retail merchandise, new and donated merchandise received at an auction, tickets for a game of chance, tuition at an educational institution, travel, tickets to an athletic or other event, discounts, free subscriptions, and preferential seating at a college or university athletic event. The document asks whether the charity made any reference to deductibility of the payment in its solicitation or promotional literature or in any thank-you letter, receipt ticket, or other written receipt.

As to gifts of property, the IRS wants a list of all noncash gifts whose fair market value exceeds $500 during the year under examination. The IRS asks who valued the gift property, whether a proper receipt was provided, whether there is an agreement between the donor and donee as to disposition of the property, and whether the requisite forms were properly completed and filed.[16]

The questions concerning travel tours spotlight IRS concerns in this area. Questions: Did the promotional travel literature and/or other written documentation indicate that the tours were educational? Did the promotional travel literature and/or other written documentation contain discussions of any social or recreational aspects of the tour? Did the charity have a contract or do business with a for-profit travel agency? If yes, did the charity receive any fee from the travel agency?

---

[15] Rev. Rul. 64-182, 1964-1 C.B. (Pt. 1) 186.
[16] See *infra* § 6.11.

The inquiry into the conduct of bingo and other games of chance illustrates the degree of complexity this field of law can stimulate. The first question concerns whether the bingo activity satisfies the tests by which it can be exempted from the definition of unrelated business.[17] If not, the agent is supposed to determine whether a tax return[18] was filed and, if not, to secure the delinquent return. A set of questions pertains to the conduct of games of chance. Another question asks whether the game of chance or income from it is embraced by one of the statutory exceptions (such as a business substantially conducted by volunteers). The checksheet requires the agent to find out if the charity timely filed the proper information returns[19] and withholding returns[20] for the winners of the games. Finally, the IRS wants to know if the charity hired outside contractors to specifically operate bingo and other games of chance.

The agent is requested to report on any penalties he or she assessed against the charity. These include failure to file a tax return,[21] failure to pay a tax,[22] failure to file a complete or accurate exempt organization information return,[23] substantial understatement of liability,[24] promotion of abusive tax shelters,[25] aiding and abetting understatements of tax liability,[26] failure to file certain information returns,[27] failure to file certain payee statements,[28] and failure to include correct information on an information return or payee statement.[29]

Audit Guidance

In directions sent to the field in February 1990 concerning the phase II examinations, the IRS National Office wrote that "it is essential that the examinations be thorough." It continued: "The EO examiner must pursue the examination to a point where he/she can conclude that all areas and data concerning fundraising activities have been considered."[30]

[17] IRC § 513(f)(2). See *infra* § 6.4.
[18] Form 990-T.
[19] Form 1099-MISC.
[20] Form W2-G.
[21] IRC § 6651(a)(1).
[22] IRC § 6651(a)(2).
[23] IRC § 6652(c)(1)(A)(ii).
[24] IRC § 6661.
[25] IRC § 6700.
[26] IRC § 6701.
[27] IRC § 6721.
[28] IRC § 6722.
[29] IRC § 6723.
[30] Internal Revenue Manual Transmittal 7(10)00-164 (Feb. 23, 1990), transmitting Manual Supplement 7(10) G-59, § 11.02.

This guidance stated that the second phase of the program will "focus on all aspects of fund-raising and charitable solicitations."[31] Some of the practices the IRS is looking for are the following:

1. Misleading statements in solicitations literature that "imply deductibility of contributions, where none probably exists."

2. Contracts with professional fund-raisers, where they use "questionable" fund-raising methods to solicit contributions from the general public.

3. Solicitations that mislead donors into thinking that their donations will be used for charitable purposes, when in fact the donations may be used for noncharitable purposes (such as administrative and fund-raising costs that constitute a significant portion of the solicited funds or property).

4. Fund-raising activities that result in other tax consequences (such as the generation of taxable income).

These directions continued: "The scope and depth of the examination should be sufficient to fully disclose the nature of abusive situations involving fund-raising activities that mislead donors to claim the incorrect charitable contribution deduction; misrepresent the use of the solicited funds; engage in questionable fund-raising practices or techniques, etc."[32] There is such an insistence on thoroughness because the results of this study "are to be used in report that will be submitted to Congress."[33]

Thus, what started out in 1967 as concern with overdeductibility in the setting of payments to charities has evolved and blossomed into an examination by the IRS of all "questionable fundraising practices or techniques."

Conclusion

The launching of this Special Emphasis Program, particularly the preparation and dissemination of the checksheet, is a most significant development, illustrating once again the fact that the federal government, particularly the IRS, is heavily monitoring and regulating the charitable fund-raising process. This checksheet represents an extraordinary use of the IRS's resources to investigate charitable fund-raising. One particularly striking aspect of this matter is that some of the information requested, particularly that pertaining to the use of professional fund-

---

[31] *Id.* § 11.09.
[32] *Id.* § 11.03.
[33] *Id.* § 11.02.

raisers, has little or no correlation with any requirements of law—at least at this time.

These last five words warrant some emphasis. Congress may well act in this area if the Special Emphasis Program does not succeed.[34]

This Special Emphasis Program is part of the larger message: The federal government will be regulating charitable fund-raising for years to come. The program, replete with checksheets and IRS educational efforts, is an important component of this new form of government intervention in the philanthropic process.

§ 6.2 Fund-Raising Disclosure by Charitable Organizations

It has long been the position of the IRS that a payment to a charitable organization, where the payor receives something of equivalent value in return, is not a "gift" for charitable deduction purposes.[35] The long-standing position of the IRS in this regard has also been that a payment to a charity, where the payor receives value in return, is deductible as a charitable gift only to the extent that the amount transferred exceeds the value received by the donor. And, it has long been the position of the IRS that it is the responsibility of charitable organizations to inform their patrons of this distinction between deductible and nondeductible payments.[36] The latter includes true dues, payments for admissions or merchandise, and other material benefits and privileges received in return for the payment.

These rules have, on occasion, been honored in their breach. As a consequence, in mid-1988, the Commissioner of Internal Revenue sent this message to the nation's charities: "I . . . ask your help in more accurately informing taxpayers as to the deductibility of payments by patrons of your fund-raising events."[37]

This message from the IRS announced the Special Emphasis Program, whereby the IRS is seeking to "ascertain the extent to which taxpayers are furnished accurate and sufficient information concerning the deductibility of their contributions."[38]

The commissioner's message focused on fund-raising events, where part or all of a payment to a charitable organization is attributable to the purchase of admission or some other privilege. In this context, the

[34] See Ch. 7 § 7.2.
[35] See *supra* § 6.1.
[36] Rev. Rul. 67-246, *supra* note 8.
[37] IRS Publication 1391.
[38] *Ibid.*

law presumes that the total amount paid is equivalent to the benefits received in return. That presumption can be rebutted in appropriate instances, where there is a true gift element in the payment.

This matter has several manifestations. One is the fund-raising event, where something of value is provided to the patron, such as a dinner or entertainment. The charity is expected to determine the fair market value of the event and to notify the patron that only the amount of the payment that is in excess of that value (if any) is deductible as a charitable gift. For example, a fund-raising event may center around a dinner; the ticket is $75, and the dinner is worth $50; in compliance with the IRS position, the patron should be told that only $25 of the $75 is deductible as a charitable gift. (The portion of the total amount paid that is reflective of the purchase of the dinner may be deductible as an ordinary and necessary business expense.)[39]

In determining fair value, a charity must look to comparable circumstances. The cost of the event to the charity is irrelevant. Thus, a charity may have a dinner provided to it without cost (such as a donation from a caterer), yet the dinner still has a value to the recipient.

Another manifestation of this problem occurs when a donor donates and receives something of value in return. A payment of $20 that results in a T-shirt or tote bag worth $10 is a gift of $10, not $20. This distinction is sometimes very difficult to ascertain, for much of it is relative. Is the donor of $1 million supposed to reduce the gift deduction by $10 because he or she is sent a T-shirt? The answer is no, yet it is hard to draw the line in this regard between the $20 donor and the $1 million donor. This is the dilemma, for example, with respect to college and university athletic scholarship programs[40] and the distribution of greeting cards by veterans' organizations.[41]

A third aspect is the payment to a charitable organization that is not deductible at all. Obvious examples of this include payments of tuition to nonprofit schools and payments for health care services to nonprofit hospitals. Other such payments are dues, subscriptions, purchases made at auctions, and purchases of raffle and sweepstakes tickets.

---

[39] IRC § 162.

[40] However, where an individual makes a payment to or for the benefit of a college or university, that would be deductible as a charitable contribution but for the fact that the individual receives the right to purchase seating at an athletic event in the institution's athletic stadium, 80 percent of the payment is treated as a charitable contribution (IRC § 170(m)).

[41] E.g., *Veterans of Foreign Wars, Department of Michigan v. Commissioner,* 89 T.C. 7 (1987); *Veterans of Foreign Wars of the United States, Department of Missouri, Inc. v. United States,* 85-2 U.S.T.C. ¶ 9605 (W.D. Mo. 1984).

Thus, the IRS expects charities, before solicitation, to determine the nondeductible portion of a payment and to clearly state the separate amounts on a ticket or other evidence of payment furnished to the contributor.

The IRS has privately ruled that there are no sanctions for violation of these disclosure rules.[42] However, there has been discussion of application of the aiding and abetting, and other penalties,[43] and of potential litigation in this area. There has also been discussion of the use of the unrelated income rules in this setting,[44] as well as of theories by which an organization's tax exemption could be revoked for failure to comport with these rules.

The IRS also reviewed tax returns for 1988 filed by individual taxpayers, looking for situations where a charitable deduction is being claimed, when in fact only a portion or perhaps none of the payment is deductible as a gift.

§ 6.3 Fund-Raising Disclosure by Noncharitable Organizations

Congress specifically brought the IRS into the field of regulation of fund-raising when it legislated certain fund-raising disclosure rules.[45] These rules are not applicable to charitable organizations,[46] although the legislative history accompanying them strongly hints that this type of statutory law may be extended to charities if they persist in securing payments from individuals that are not gifts (such as dues or payments for raffle tickets or at auctions) under circumstances where the payors think, sometimes because of explicit or implicit suggestions from the charity involved,

---

[42] IRS Priv. Ltr. Rul. 8832003.

[43] See *supra* notes 21–29.

[44] See *infra* § 6.4.

[45] IRC § 6113, which is applicable to solicitations made after Jan. 31, 1988. This section of the Internal Revenue Code, a consequence of hearings before the House Subcommittee on Oversight in 1987, is part of the deficit reduction legislation that was signed into law on Dec. 22, 1987 (Pub. L. No. 100-203, 100th Cong., 1st Sess. (1987)). The measure was initially introduced separately, as the "Tax-Exempt Organizations' Lobbying and Political Activities Accountability Act of 1987" (H.R. 2942, 100th Cong., 1st Sess. (1987)). The IRS published rules to accompany this law in 1988, as IRS Notice 88-120, 1988-2 C.B. 459. See VI *The Nonprofit Counsel* (No. 1) 4 (1989).

[46] That is, this law does not apply to organizations described in IRC § 501(c)(3).

that the payments are gifts and try to deduct them as charitable contributions.[47]

These fund-raising disclosure rules are thus applicable to all types of
tax-exempt organizations, principally social welfare organizations,[48] other
than charitable ones, and are designed to prevent these noncharitable
organizations from engaging in fund-raising activities under circumstances
in which donors will assume that the contributions are tax deductible,
when in fact they are not. However, these rules do not apply to an
organization that has annual gross receipts that are normally no more
than $100,000.[49] Also, where all of the parties being solicited are tax-
exempt organizations, the solicitation need not include the disclosure
statement (inasmuch as these grantors have no need for a charitable
deduction).[50]

Technically, in general, this law applies to any organization to which
contributions are not deductible as charitable gifts and which is (1) tax-
exempt,[51] (2) is a political organization,[52] (3) was either type of organization
at any time during the five-year period ending on the date of the fund-
raising solicitation, or (4) is a successor to one of these organizations at

---

[47] See *supra* notes 4–7.

[48] That is, organizations that are described in IRC § 501(c)(4) and that are tax-
exempt (under IRC § 501(a)).

[49] IRC § 6113(b)(2)(A). In determining this threshold, the same principles that
obtain in ascertaining the annual information return (Form 990) $25,000 filing
threshold apply. Rev. Proc. 82-23, 1983-1 C.B. 687. In general, these rules
utilize a three-year average. The organization must include the required disclosure
statement on all solicitations made more than 30 days after reaching $300,000
in gross receipts for the three-year period of the calculation. (IRS Notice 88-
120, *supra* note 45.)

A local, regional, or state chapter of an organization with gross receipts
under $100,000 must include the disclosure statement in its solicitations if at
least 25 percent of the money solicited will go to the national, or other, unit
of the organization that has annual gross receipts over $100,000, because the
solicitation is considered as being in part on behalf of the unit. Also, if a trade
association or labor union with over $100,000 in annual gross receipts solicits
funds that will pass through to a political action committee with less than
$100,000 in annual gross receipts, the solicitation must include the required
disclosure statement.

[50] IRS Notice 88-120, *supra* note 45.

[51] That is, is described in IRC § 501(a) and IRC § 501(c) (other than, as noted
in *supra* note 46, IRC § 501(c)(3)).

[52] That is, is described in IRC § 527.

any time during this five-year period.[53] The IRS is accorded the authority to treat any group of two or more organizations as one organization for these purposes where "necessary or appropriate" to prevent the avoidance of these rules through the use of multiple organizations.[54]

Under these rules, each "fundraising solicitation" by or on behalf of a tax-exempt noncharitable organization must contain an express statement, in a "conspicuous and easily recognizable format," that gifts to it are not deductible as charitable contributions for federal income tax purposes.[55] (The IRS has promulgated rules as to this statement; these rules are discussed below.) A fund-raising solicitation is any solicitation of gifts made in written or printed form, by television, radio, or telephone (although there is an exclusion for letters or calls not part of a coordinated fund-raising campaign soliciting more than 10 persons during a calendar year).[56] Despite the clear reference in the statute to "contributions and gifts," the IRS interprets this rule to mandate the disclosure when any tax-exempt organization (other than a charity) seeks funds, such as dues from members.

Failure to satisfy this disclosure requirement can result in imposition of penalties.[57] The penalty is $1,000 per day (maximum of $10,000 per year), albeit with a reasonable cause exception. However, in an instance of an "intentional disregard" of these rules, the penalty for the day on which the offense occurred is the greater of $1,000 or 50 percent of the aggregate cost of the solicitations that took place on that day, and the $10,000 limitation is inapplicable. For these purposes, the days involved are those on which the solicitation was telecast, broadcast, mailed, otherwise distributed, or telephoned.

The IRS promulgated rules in amplification of this law, particularly the requirement of a disclosure statement.[58] The rules, which include guidance in the form of "safe-harbor" provisions, address the format of the disclosure statement in instances of use of print media, telephone, television, and radio. They provide examples of acceptable disclosure

---

[53] IRC § 6113(b)(1). For this purpose, a fraternal organization (one described in IRC § 170(c)(4)) is treated as a charitable organization only with respect to solicitations for contributions that are to be used exclusively for purposes referred to in IRC § 170(c)(4) (IRC § 6113(b)(3)).

[54] IRC § 6113(b)(2)(B).

[55] IRC § 6113(a).

[56] IRC § 6113(c).

[57] IRC § 6710.

[58] IRS Notice 88-120, *supra* note 45.

language and methods (which, when followed, amount to the safe-harbor guidelines), and of included and excluded solicitations. They also contain guidelines for determining the $100,000 threshold.

The safe-harbor guideline for print media (including solicitations by mail and in newspapers) is fourfold: (1) the solicitation includes language such as the following: "Contributions or gifts to [name of organization] are not deductible as charitable contributions for federal income tax purposes"; (2) the statement is in at least the same type size as the primary message stated in the body of the letter, leaflet, or advertisement; (3) the statement is included on the message side of any card or tear-off section that the contributor returns with the contribution; and (4) the statement is either the first sentence in a paragraph or itself constitutes a paragraph.

The safe-harbor guideline for telephone solicitations includes the first of the above elements. In addition, the guideline requires that (1) the statement be made in close proximity to the request for contributions, during the same telephone call, by the telephone solicitor, and (2) any written confirmation or billing sent to a person pledging to contribute during the telephone solicitation be in compliance with the requirements for print media solicitations.

Solicitation by television must, to conform with this guideline, include a solicitation statement that complies with the first of the print medium requirements. Also, if the statement is spoken, it must be in close proximity to the request for contributions. If the statement appears on the television screen, it must be in large, easily readable type appearing on the screen for at least five seconds.

In the case of a solicitation by radio, the statement must, to meet the safe-harbor test, comply with the first of the print medium requirements. Also, the statement must be made in close proximity to the request for contributions during the same radio solicitation announcement.

Where the soliciting organization is a membership entity, classified as a trade or business association or other form of business league,[59] or a labor or agricultural organization,[60] the following statement is in conformance with the safe-harbor guideline: "Contributions or gifts to [name of organization] are not tax deductible as charitable contributions. How-

---

[59] That is, is an organization described in IRC § 501(c)(6) and is tax-exempt under IRC § 501(a).

[60] That is, is an organization described in IRC § 501(c)(5) and is tax-exempt under IRC § 501(a).

ever, they may be tax deductible as ordinary and necessary business expenses."

If an organization makes a solicitation to which these rules apply and the solicitation does not comply with the applicable safe-harbor guideline, the IRS will evaluate all of the facts and circumstances to determine whether the solicitation meets the disclosure rule. A "good faith effort" to comply with these requirements is an important factor in the evaluation of the facts and circumstances. Nonetheless, disclosure statements made in "fine print" do not comply with the statutory requirement.

This disclosure requirement applies to solicitations for voluntary contributions as well as solicitations for attendance at testimonials and like fund-raising events. The disclosure must be made in the case of solicitations for contributions to political action committees.

Exempt from this disclosure rule are the billing of those who advertise in an organization's publications, billing by social clubs for food and beverages, billing of attendees of a conference, billing for insurance premiums of an insurance program operated or sponsored by an organization, billing of members of a community association for mandatory payments for police and fire (and similar) protection, and billing for payments to a voluntary employees' beneficiary association as well as similar payments to a trust for pension and/or health benefits.

General material discussing the benefits of membership in a tax-exempt organization, such as a trade association or labor union, does not have to include the required disclosure statement. However, the statement is required where the material both requests payment and specifies the amount requested as membership dues. If a person responds to the general material discussing the benefits of membership, the follow-up material requesting the payment of a specific amount in membership dues (such as a union checkoff card or a trade association billing statement for a new member) must include the disclosure statement. General material discussing a political candidacy and requesting persons to vote for the candidate or "support" the candidate need not include the disclosure statement unless the material specifically requests either a financial contribution or a contribution of volunteer services in support of the candidate.

§ 6.4 The Unrelated Business Rules

One of the ways in which the IRS is regulating fund-raising for charitable purposes is by means of the unrelated business rules. Prior to an analysis of the application of these rules to charitable fund-raising, however, an overview of the rules is appropriate.[61]

Basic Concepts of Unrelated Income Taxation

The law of tax-exempt organizations divides the activities of charitable and other tax-exempt organizations into two categories: those that are related to the performance of tax-exempt functions and those that are not. The latter grouping of activities, termed "unrelated activities," is subject to tax. That is, the revenues associated with unrelated activities are taxable, taking into account the deductible expenses generated by or allocable to these activities.

Therefore, even though a charitable organization generally achieves federal income tax exemption, it nonetheless remains potentially taxable on any unrelated business income.[62] This tax is levied on nonprofit corporations[63] at the corporate rates[64] or on charitable trusts[65] at the individual rates.[66]

INTRODUCTION

The taxation of unrelated income, a feature of the federal tax laws since 1950, is based on the concept that tax-exempt organizations should not be in competition with for-profit organizations. Also, the unrelated income rules are believed to be a more effective and workable sanction for authentic enforcement of the law of tax-exempt organizations than denial or revocation of tax-exempt status.

The unrelated income rules reflect a simple concept: The unrelated business income tax applies only to active business income that arises from activities that are "unrelated" to the organization's exempt purposes. Yet, despite the simplicity of the tax structure, it is not always easy to determine which activities of a tax-exempt organization are related to exempt purposes and which are not.

Of course, if a substantial portion of an organization's income is from unrelated sources, the organization will not qualify for tax exemption.

---

[61] In general, see *Law of Tax-Exempt Organizations* at 702–809.

[62] IRC § 501(b).

[63] IRC § 511(a)(1).

[64] IRC § 11.

[65] IRC § 511(b).

[66] IRC § 1(d).

That is, to be tax-exempt, a nonprofit organization must be organized and operated primarily for exempt purposes. However, an organization may satisfy the requirements for tax exemption as a charitable organization even though it operates a business as a substantial part of its activities, where the operation of the business is in furtherance of the organization's exempt purposes and where the organization is not organized and operated for the primary purpose of carrying on an unrelated business (technically termed a "trade or business"). In determining the existence or nonexistence of this primary purpose, all of the circumstances must be considered, including the size and extent of the business and of the activities that are in furtherance of one or more exempt purposes.[67]

At the other end of the spectrum, incidental business activity will not alone cause a charitable or other type of tax-exempt organization to lose or be denied tax exemption, although the income derived from the activity may be taxable.[68] That is, the federal tax law allows a tax-exempt organization to engage in a certain amount of income-producing activity that is unrelated to exempt purposes.

Business activities may preclude initial qualification of an otherwise tax-exempt organization as a charitable or other entity. This would occur through failure to satisfy the operational test that determines whether the organization is being operated principally for exempt purposes.[69] Likewise, an organization will not meet the organizational test if its articles of organization (the documents by which it was established) empower it, as more than an insubstantial part of its functions, to carry on activities that are not in furtherance of its exempt purpose.[70]

The unrelated business income tax—its coverage extended by enactment of the Tax Reform Act of 1969—applies with respect to all charitable and nearly all other types of tax-exempt organizations.[71] They include religious organizations (including churches), educational organizations (including universities, colleges, and schools), health care organizations (including hospitals), and scientific organizations (including research entities).[72] This tax also applies with respect to any college or university which is an agency or instrumentality of any government or political subdivision of a government, or which is owned or operated

---

[67] Reg. § 1.501(c)(3)-1(e)(1).

[68] E.g., Rev. Rul. 66-221, 1966-2 C.B. 220.

[69] See *Law of Tax-Exempt Organizations* at 87–91.

[70] See *Law of Tax-Exempt Organizations* at 80–87.

[71] IRC § 511(a)(2)(A).

[72] These organizations are encompassed by IRC § 501(c)(3).

by a government or political subdivision, or by any agency or instrumentality of one or more governments or political subdivisions, and further applies to any corporation wholly owned by one or more of these colleges or universities.[73]

Beyond the realm of charitable entities, the rules are applicable with respect to social welfare organizations (including advocacy groups),[74] labor organizations (including unions),[75] trade and professional associations,[76] fraternal organizations,[77] and veterans' organizations.[78] Special rules[79] tax all income not related to exempt functions (including investment income) of social clubs,[80] homeowners' associations,[81] and political organizations.[82]

The few tax-exempt organizations that are excepted from the tax are instrumentalities of the federal government,[83] certain religious and apostolic organizations,[84] farmers' cooperatives,[85] and shipowners' protection and indemnity associations.[86]

Certain organizations are not generally subject to the unrelated business rules simply because they are not allowed to engage in any active business endeavors. This is the case, for example, with respect to private foundations

---

[73] IRC § 511(a)(2)(B).

[74] IRC § 501(c)(4) organizations. See *Law of Tax-Exempt Organizations* at 297–315.

[75] IRC § 501(c)(5) organizations. See *Law of Tax-Exempt Organizations* at 356–60.

[76] IRC § 501(c)(6) organizations. See *Law of Tax-Exempt Organizations* at 316–39.

[77] IRC §§ 501(c)(8) & (10) organizations. See *Law of Tax-Exempt Organizations* at 370–74, 377–79.

[78] IRC § 501(c)(19) organizations. See *Law of Tax-Exempt Organizations* at 393–96.

[79] See *Law of Tax-Exempt Organizations* at 348–53.

[80] IRC § 501(c)(7) organizations. See *Law of Tax-Exempt Organizations* at 340–55.

[81] IRC § 528 organizations. See *Law of Tax-Exempt Organizations* at 409–11.

[82] IRC § 527 organizations. See *Law of Tax-Exempt Organizations* at 404–09.

[83] IRC § 501(c)(1) organizations. See *Law of Tax-Exempt Organizations* at 366–67.

[84] IRC § 501(d) organizations. See *Law of Tax-Exempt Organizations* at 207–09.

[85] IRC § 521 organizations. See *Law of Tax-Exempt Organizations* at 396–404.

[86] IRC § 526. See *Law of Tax-Exempt Organizations* at 404.

(within limitations) and title-holding organizations.[87] As to the former, the operation of an active business (externally or internally) by a private foundation would likely trigger application of the excess business holdings restrictions.[88]

The original concept underlying these rules was that of the "outside" business owned and perhaps operated by a tax-exempt organization. However, in 1969, Congress significantly expanded the reach of these rules by authorizing the IRS to evaluate activities conducted by exempt organizations internally—so-called inside activities.

The primary objective of the unrelated business income tax is to eliminate a source of unfair competition for for-profit businesses by placing the unrelated business activities of tax-exempt organizations on the same tax basis as the nonexempt business endeavors with which they compete.[89] Thus, the report of the Houses of Representatives' Committee on Ways and Means that accompanied the 1950 legislation states that the "problem at which the tax on unrelated business income is directed here is primarily that of unfair competition" and the "tax-free status of . . . [nonprofit] organizations enables them to use their profits tax-free to expand operations, while their competitors can expand only with the profits remaining after taxes."[90] The Senate Finance Committee reaffirmed this position in 1976 when it noted that one "major purpose" of the unrelated income tax "is to make certain that an exempt organization does not commercially exploit its exempt status for the purpose of unfairly competing with taxpaying organizations."[91]

However, the absence or presence of unfair competition is not among the criteria for assessing whether the revenue from a particular activity is subject to the unrelated income tax. Thus, it is possible for an exempt organization's activity to be wholly noncompetitive with an activity of a for-profit organization and nonetheless be treated as an unrelated business. For example, in a case finding that the operation of a bingo game by an exempt organization gives rise to unrelated business income, a court observed that "the tax on unrelated business income is not limited to income earned by a trade or business that operates in competition with

---

[87] IRC §§ 501(c)(2) & 501(c)(25) organizations. See *Law of Tax-Exempt Organizations* at 367–69, 416.

[88] See *Law of Tax-Exempt Organizations* at 544–52.

[89] Reg. § 1.513-1(b).

[90] H.R. Rep. No. 2319, 81st Cong., 2d Sess. (1950) at 36–37. Also S. Rep. No. 2375, 81st Cong., 2d Sess. (1950) at 28–29.

[91] S. Rep. No. 94-938, 94th Cong., 2d Sess. (1976) at 601.

taxpaying entities."[92] Yet, the IRS will likely take the concept of unfair competition into account in application of the unrelated income rules.

The term "unrelated trade or business" is defined to mean any trade or business that is regularly carried on, the conduct of which is not substantially related to the exercise or performance by the exempt organization of its exempt purpose or function.[93] The conduct of a business is not substantially related to an organization's exempt purpose solely because the organization may need the income or because of the use the organization makes of the profits derived from the business.

Therefore, absent an exception, gross income of a charitable or other tax-exempt organization is subject to the tax on unrelated business income where three factors are present: (1) it is income from a trade or business, (2) the business is regularly carried on by the organization, and (3) the conduct of the trade or business is not substantially related to the organization's performance of its exempt functions.[94]

Thus, in adopting these rules in 1950 and in amplifying them in 1969, Congress has not prohibited commercial ventures by nonprofit organizations nor has it levied taxes only on the receipts of businesses that bear no relation at all to the tax-exempt purposes of nonprofit organizations. Instead, it struck a balance between, as the U.S. Supreme Court phrased it, "its two objectives of encouraging benevolent enterprise and restraining unfair competition."[95]

The unrelated business rules are in a peculiar state of affairs these days. Despite the statutory scheme, the courts are simultaneously developing additional and sometimes different criteria for assessing the presence of unrelated business. It is out of this context that the doctrine of "commerciality"[96] is emerging. The result is considerable confusion about the law in this area and the extensive judgmental leeway on the part of the courts and the IRS in applying it.

Moreover, the statutory law concerning the taxation of unrelated income may be on the brink of revision. The House Subcommittee on

---

[92] *Clarence LaBelle Post No. 217* v. *United States*, 580 F.2d 270 (8th Cir. 1978), cert. dis., 439 U.S. 1040 (1978). Cf. IRC § 513(f) (see *infra* note 146).

[93] IRC § 513(a).

[94] Reg. § 1.513-1(a).

[95] *United States* v. *American College of Physicians*, 475 U.S. 834, 838 (1986).

[96] This doctrine emerged in the Internal Revenue Code when Congress developed the concept of "commercial-type" insurance (IRC § 501(m)). See *Law of Tax-Exempt Organizations* at 314–15.

Oversight, a unit of the Way and Means Committee, held five days of hearings on the subject in 1987[97] and another one-day hearing in 1988.[98] The staff of the subcommittee prepared an options paper[99] and subsequently a draft of recommendations.[100] In March 1990, another staff draft of proposals became public.[101] However, the subcommittee has not reported any proposals to the full committee. Nonetheless, some changes in this statutory law seem inevitable.

A large part of the impetus for revision of the law of unrelated income taxation was the charge by the small business community of unfair competition. The difference between the circumstances in the 1950s and the 1990s is that the competing activities of nonprofit organizations in the 1950s were of the unrelated variety, while in the 1990s many of the competing activities are those that are, under existing law, related to exempt functions.

DEDUCTION RULES

Generally,[102] the term "unrelated business taxable income" means the gross income derived by an organization from an unrelated trade or business, regularly carried on by the organization, less business deductions that are directly connected with the carrying on of the trade or business. For purposes of computing unrelated business taxable income, both such gross income and business deductions are computed with certain modifications, as discussed below.

Generally, to be "directly connected with" the conduct of unrelated business, an item of deduction must have a proximate and primary relationship to the carrying on of that business. In the case of an organization which derives gross income from the regular conduct of two or more unrelated business activities, unrelated business taxable income is the aggregate of gross income from all such unrelated business activities less the aggregate of the deductions allowed with respect to all such unrelated business activities.[103] Expenses, depreciation, and similar items attributable solely to the conduct of unrelated business are proximately and primarily

---

[97] See IV *The Nonprofit Counsel* (No. 8) 1 (1987); IV *The Nonprofit Counsel* (No. 7) 1 (1987).

[98] See V *The Nonprofit Counsel* (No. 6) 1 (1988).

[99] See V *The Nonprofit Counsel* (No. 5) 1 (1988).

[100] See V *The Nonprofit Counsel* (No. 7) 4 (1988).

[101] See VII *The Nonprofit Counsel* (No. 5) 1 (1990).

[102] IRC § 512(a)(1).

[103] Reg. § 1.512(a)-1(a).

related to that business and therefore qualify for deduction to the extent that they meet the requirements of relevant provisions of the federal tax law.[104]

Where facilities or personnel are used both to carry on exempt functions and to conduct unrelated trade or business, the expenses, depreciation, and similar items attributable to the facilities or personnel (as, for example, items of overhead) must be allocated between the two uses on a reasonable basis. The portion of any such item so allocated to the unrelated trade or business must be proximately and primarily related to that business, and is allowable as a deduction in computing unrelated business income in the manner and to the extent permitted by the federal tax law.[105] In certain cases, gross income is derived from unrelated trade or business that exploits an exempt function. Generally, in such cases, expenses, depreciation, and similar items attributable to the conduct of the exempt function are not deductible in computing unrelated business taxable income. Since such items are incident to a function of the type which is the chief purpose of the organization to conduct, they do not possess proximate and primary relationship to the unrelated trade or business. Therefore, they do not qualify as being directly connected with that business.[106]

MEANING OF "TRADE OR BUSINESS"

The term "trade or business" includes any activity that is carried on for the production of income from the sale of goods or the performance of services.[107] The law also states that "an activity does not lose identity as trade or business merely because it is carried on within a larger aggregate of similar activities or within a larger complex of other endeavors which may, or may not, be related to the exempt purposes of the organization." Additionally, the law states that "(w)here an activity carried on for profit constitutes an unrelated trade or business, no part of such trade or business shall be excluded from such classification merely because it does not result in profit."

By enactment of these rules in 1969, Congress confirmed the government's contention that income for a particular activity can be taxed as unrelated business income even where the activity is an integral part

---

[104] E.g., IRC §§ 162, 167. Reg. § 1.512(a)-1(b).
[105] Reg. § 1.512(a)-1(c). E.g., *Rensselaer Polytechnic Institute* v. *Commissioner*, 732 F.2d 1058 (2d Cir. 1984), aff'g, 79 T.C. 967 (1982).
[106] Reg. § 1.512(a)-1(d).
[107] IRC § 513(c); Reg. § 1.513-1(b).

of a larger activity that is in furtherance of an exempt purpose. This provision is directed chiefly at, but is not confined to, activities of soliciting, selling, and publishing commercial advertising, even where the advertising is published in an exempt organization publication which contains editorial matter related to the exempt purposes of the organization. With this authority, the IRS is empowered to fragment an exempt organization's operation, run as an integrated whole, into its component parts in search of an unrelated trade or business.

This definition of the term "trade or business" embraces nearly every activity of a tax-exempt organization. In this sense, every tax-exempt organization is viewed as a bundle of activities, each of which is a trade or business. (This definition has nothing to do with whether a particular activity is related or unrelated; there are related businesses and unrelated businesses.)

Thus, the IRS is empowered to examine each of the activities in the bundle of activities constituting an exempt organization in search of unrelated business. Each activity in the bundle can be examined as though it existed wholly independently of the others; an unrelated activity cannot, as a matter of law, be hidden from scrutiny by tucking it in among a host of related activities. This rule is known as the "fragmentation rule."

Nothing in the statutory definition of the term "trade or business" requires the tax-exempt organization to engage in the activity with a profit motive. However, the courts seem to be engrafting the profit motive requirement onto the definition, as the result of a 1987 Supreme Court decision.[108] Thus, for example, the U.S. Tax Court held, in a case involving an activity of a trade association that consistently produced losses, that the ongoing losses are evidence that the activity was not engaged in with the requisite profit motive and therefore is not a business.[109]

Not every activity of an exempt organization that generates a financial return is a "trade or business" for purposes of the unrelated income tax rules. As the U.S. Supreme Court has observed, the "narrow category of trade or business" is a "concept which falls far short of reaching every income or profit-making activity."[110]

---

[108] *Commissioner of Internal Revenue* v. *Groetzinger*, 480 U.S. 23 (1987).

[109] *National Water Well Association, Inc.* v. *Commissioner*, 92 T.C. 75 (1989).

[110] *Whipple* v. *Commissioner*, 373 U.S. 193, 197, 201 (1963). Also *Blake Construction Co., Inc.* v. *United States*, 572 F.2d 820 (Ct. Cl. 1978); *Monfore* v. *United States*, 77-2 U.S.T.C. ¶ 9528 (Ct. Cl. 1977); *McDowell* v. *Ribicoff*, 292 F.2d 174 (3d Cir. 1961), cert. denied, 368 U.S. 919 (1961).

Likewise, it is clear that the management of an investment portfolio composed wholly of the manager's own securities does not constitute the carrying on of a trade or business. For example, the Supreme Court has held that the mere keeping of records and collection of interest and dividends from securities through managerial attention to the investments is not the operation of a business.[111] On that occasion, the Court sustained the government's position that "mere personal investment activities never constitute carrying on a trade or business."[112] Subsequently, the Supreme Court stated that "investing is not a trade or business."[113] Likewise, the Ninth Circuit Court of Appeals has observed that "the mere management of investments . . . is insufficient to constitute the carrying on of a trade or business."[114]

It is also clear that investment activities do not constitute the carrying on of a trade or business in this context. Thus, the IRS ruled that the receipt of income by an exempt employees' trust from installment notes purchased from the employer-settlor is not income derived from the operation of an unrelated trade or business.[115] The IRS noted that the trust "merely keeps the records and receives the periodic payments of principal and interest collected for it by the employer." Consequently, it may be regarded as settled that mere record keeping and income collection for a person's own investments are not to be regarded as the carrying on of a trade or business.

Therefore, income that is "passive income" is generally not taxed, on the ground that it is not income derived from the active conduct of a trade or business. This exception, contained in the modifications discussed below, generally extends to forms of income such as dividends, interest, annuities, royalties, rents, and capital gain. Also, as discussed below, certain other items of income and activities are specifically exempted from the unrelated income tax.

MEANING OF "REGULARLY CARRIED ON"

In determining whether a trade or business from which a particular amount of gross income is derived is "regularly carried on," within the

---

[111] *Higgins* v. *Commissioner*, 312 U.S. 212, 218 (1941).

[112] *Id.* at 215.

[113] *Whipple* v. *Commissioner, supra* note 110, at 202.

[114] *Continental Trading, Inc.* v. *Commissioner*, 265 F.2d 40, 43 (9th Cir. 1959), cert. denied, 361 U.S. 827 (1959). Also see *Van Wart* v. *Commissioner*, 295 U.S. 112, 115 (1935); *Deputy* v. *duPont*, 308 U.S. 488, 499 (concurring opinion) (1940); *Commissioner* v. *Burnett*, 118 F.2d 659, 660-661 (5th Cir. 1941); Rev. Rul. 56-511, 1956-2 C.B. 170.

[115] Rev. Rul. 69-574, 1969-2 C.B. 130.

meaning of the unrelated trade or business rules, regard must be had to the frequency and continuity with which the activities productive of the income are conducted and the manner in which they are pursued. (It is in this context that the statutory law comes the closest to using a general doctrine of commerciality.) This requirement must be applied in light of the purpose of the unrelated business income tax to place exempt organization business activities upon the same tax basis as the nonexempt business endeavors with which they compete. Hence, for example, specific business activities of an exempt organization will ordinarily be deemed to be "regularly carried on" if they manifest a frequency and continuity, and are pursued in a manner, generally similar to comparable commercial activities of nonexempt organizations.[116]

Where income-producing activities are of a kind normally conducted by nonexempt commercial organizations on a year-round basis, the conduct of the activities by an exempt organization over a period of only a few weeks does not constitute the regular carrying on of a trade or business. For example, the operation of a sandwich stand by a hospital auxiliary for only two weeks at a state fair would not be the regular conduct of a trade or business. Similarly, if a charitable organization holds an occasional dance to which the public is admitted for a charge, hiring an orchestra and entertainers for the purpose, such an activity would not be a trade or business regularly carried on.[117] However, the conduct of year-round business activities for one day each week would constitute the regular carrying on of a trade or business. Thus the operation of a commercial parking lot on one day of each week would be the regular conduct of a trade or business. Where income-producing activities are of a kind normally undertaken by nonexempt commercial organizations only on a seasonal basis, the conduct of such activities by an exempt organization during a significant portion of the season ordinarily constitutes the regular conduct of trade or business. For example, the operation of a track for horse racing for several weeks of a year would be considered the regular conduct of trade or business because it is usual to carry on this type of trade or business only during a particular season.[118]

In determining whether or not intermittently conducted activities are regularly carried on, the manner of conduct of the activities must be compared with the manner in which commercial activities are normally pursued by nonexempt organizations. In general, exempt organization

[116] Reg. § 1.513-1(c)(1).
[117] S. Rep. No. 2375, *supra* note 90 at 106-7.
[118] Reg. § 1.513-1(c)(2)(i).

business activities which are engaged in only discontinuously or periodically will not be considered regularly carried on if they are conducted without the competitive and promotional efforts typical of commercial endeavors. For example, the publication of advertising in programs for sports events or music or drama performances will not ordinarily be deemed to be the regular carrying on of business. On the other hand, where the nonqualifying sales are not merely casual but are systematically and consistently promoted and carried on by the organization, they meet the requirement of regularity.[119]

Certain intermittent income-producing activities occur so infrequently that neither their recurrence nor the manner of their conduct will cause them to be regarded as trade or business regularly carried on. For example, income-producing or fund-raising activities lasting only a short period of time will not ordinarily be treated as regularly carried on if they recur only occasionally or sporadically. Furthermore, these activities will not be regarded as regularly carried on merely because they are conducted on an annually recurrent basis. Accordingly, income derived from the conduct of an annual dance or similar fund-raising event for charity would not be income from trade or business regularly carried on.[120]

Meaning of "Substantially Related"

Gross income derives from "unrelated trade or business" within the meaning of these rules if the conduct of the trade or business which produces the income is not substantially related (other than through the production of funds) to the purposes for which exemption is granted. The presence of this requirement necessitates an examination of the relationship between the business activities which generate the particular income in question—the activities, that is, of producing or distributing the goods or performing the services involved—and the accomplishment of the organization's exempt purposes.[121]

Trade or business is "related" to exempt purposes in the relevant sense only where the conduct of the business activity has causal relationship to the achievement of an exempt purpose (other than through the production of income) and it is "substantially related" only if the causal relationship is a substantial one. Thus for the conduct of trade or business

---

[119] Reg. § 1.513-1(c)(2)(ii).
[120] Reg. § 1.513-1(c)(2)(iii). E.g., *Orange County Builders Association, Inc.* v. *United States*, 65-2 U.S.T.C. ¶ 9679 (S.D. Cal. 1965).
[121] Reg. § 1.513-1(d)(1).

from which a particular amount of gross income is derived to be substantially related to the purposes for which exemption is granted, the production or distribution of the goods or the performance of the services from which the gross income is derived must contribute importantly to the accomplishment of those purposes.[122] Where the production or distribution of the goods or the performance of the services does not contribute importantly to the accomplishment of the exempt purposes of an organization, the income from the sale of the goods or the performance of the service does not derive from the conduct of related trade or business. Whether activities productive of gross income contribute importantly to the accomplishment of any purpose for which an organization is granted exemption depends in each case upon the facts and circumstances involved.[123]

In determining whether activities contribute importantly to the accomplishment of an exempt purpose, the size and extent of the activities involved must be considered in relation to the nature and extent of the exempt function which they purport to serve. Thus, where income is realized by an exempt organization from activities that are in part related to the performance of its exempt functions, but which are conducted on a larger scale than is reasonably necessary for performance of such functions, the gross income attributable to that portion of the activities in excess of the needs of exempt functions constitutes gross income from the conduct of unrelated trade or business. Such income is not derived from the production or distribution of goods or the performance of services which contribute importantly to the accomplishment of any exempt purpose of the organization.[124]

Gross income derived from charges for the performance of exempt functions does not constitute gross income from the conduct of unrelated trade or business. This principle encompasses income generated by functions such as performances by students enrolled in a school for training children in the performing arts, the conduct of refresher courses to improve the trade skills of members of a trade union, and the presentation of a trade show (at which sales do not occur) for exhibiting industry products by a trade association to stimulate demand for such products.[125]

---

[122] E.g., Rev. Rul. 75-472, 1975-2 C.B. 208.

[123] Reg. § 1.513-1(d)(2). E.g., *Huron Clinic Foundation* v. *United States*, 212 F. Supp. 847 (D.S. Dak. 1962).

[124] Reg. § 1.513-1(d)(3).

[125] Reg. § 1.513-1(d)(4)(i).

Ordinarily, gross income from the sale of products that result from the performance of exempt functions does not constitute gross income from the conduct of unrelated trade or business if the product is sold in substantially the same state it is in upon completion of the exempt functions. Thus in the case of a tax-exempt organization engaged in a program of rehabilitation of handicapped persons, income from sales of articles made by such persons as a part of their rehabilitation training would not be gross income from conduct of unrelated trade or business. The income in such case would be from the sale of products whose production contributed importantly to the accomplishment of purposes for which exemption is granted the organization—namely, rehabilitation of the handicapped. Conversely, if a product resulting from an exempt function is utilized or exploited in further business endeavors beyond that reasonably appropriate or necessary for disposition in the state it is in upon completion of exempt functions, the gross income derived therefrom would be from the conduct of unrelated trade or business. Thus in the case of an experimental dairy herd maintained for scientific purposes by a tax-exempt organization, income from sale of milk and cream produced in the ordinary course of operation of the project would not be gross income from conduct of unrelated trade or business. However, if the organization were to utilize the milk and cream in the further manufacture of food items such as ice cream, pastries, and the like, the gross income from the sale of such products would be from the conduct of unrelated trade or business unless the manufacturing activities themselves contribute importantly to the accomplishment of an exempt purpose of the organization.[126]

An asset or facility necessary to the conduct of exempt functions may also be employed in a commercial endeavor. In such cases, the mere fact of the use of the asset or facility in exempt functions does not, by itself, make the income from the commercial endeavor gross income from related trade or business. The test, instead, is whether the activities productive of the income in question contribute importantly to the accomplishment of exempt purposes. Assume, for example, that a tax-exempt museum has a theater auditorium that is specially designed and equipped for showing educational films in connection with its program of public education in the arts and sciences. The theater is a principal feature of the museum and is in continuous operation during the hours the museum is open to the public. If the organization were to operate the theater as an ordinary motion picture theater for public entertainment

---

[126] Reg. § 1.513-1(d)(4)(ii).

during the evening hours when the museum was closed, gross income from such operation would be gross income from conduct of unrelated trade or business.[127]

Activities carried on by an organization in the performance of exempt functions may generate goodwill or other intangibles which are capable of being exploited in commercial endeavors. Where an organization exploits such an intangible in commercial activities, the mere fact that the resultant income depends in part upon an exempt function of the organization does not make it gross income from related trade or business. In such cases, unless the commercial activities themselves contribute importantly to the accomplishment of an exempt purpose, the income which they produce is gross income from the conduct of unrelated trade or business.[128]

The law is replete with court cases and IRS rulings providing illustrations of related and unrelated activities. Colleges and universities operate dormitories, cafeterias, and bookstores as related activities but can be taxable on travel tours and sports camps. Hospitals may operate gift shops, snack bars, and parking lots as related activities but may be taxable on sales of pharmaceuticals to the general public or on the sale of laboratory testing services to physicians. Museums may, without taxation, sell items reflective of their collections but be taxable on the sale of souvenirs. Trade associations may find themselves taxable on sales of items and particular services to members, while dues and subscription revenue are nontaxable. Fund-raising events may be characterized as unrelated activities, particularly when compensation is paid or when the activity is regularly carried on.

EXCEPTIONS

Exempt from the scope of unrelated trade or business is a business in which substantially all of the work in carrying on the business is performed for the organization without compensation.[129] An example involving this exception is an exempt orphanage operating a secondhand clothing store and selling to the general public, where substantially all of the work in running the store is performed by volunteers.[130] As to the scope of this

---

[127] Reg. § 1.513-(d)(4)(iii).

[128] Reg. § 1.513-1(d)(4)(iv).

[129] IRC § 513(a)(1).

[130] S. Rep. No. 2375, *supra* note 90, at 108. Also *Green County Medical Society Foundation* v. *United States*, 345 F. Supp. 900 (W.D. Mo. 1972); Rev. Rul. 56-152, 1956-1 C.B. 56.

exception, Congress apparently intended to provide an exclusion from the definition of unrelated trade or business only for those unrelated business activities in which the performance of services is a material income-producing factor in carrying on the business and substantially all such services are performed without compensation.[131]

Also excluded is a business, in the case of a charitable organization or a state college or university, which is carried on by the organization primarily for the convenience of its members, students, patients, officers, or employees.[132] An example involving this exception is a laundry operated by a college for the purpose of laundering dormitory linens and the clothing of students.[133] Further, unrelated trade or business does not include a business which is the selling of merchandise, substantially all of which has been received by the organization as gifts or contributions.[134] This last exception is available for thrift shops that sell donated clothes and books to the general public.[135]

Payments to a tax-exempt organization for the lending of securities to a broker and the return of identical securities are not items of unrelated business taxable income.[136] For this nontaxation treatment to apply, the security loans must be fully collateralized and must be terminable on five business days' notice by the lending organization. Further, an agreement between the parties must provide for reasonable procedures to implement the obligation of the borrower to furnish collateral to the lender with a fair market value on each business day the loan is outstanding in an amount at least equal to the fair market value of the security at the close of business on the preceding day.

There are five additional exceptions, namely, the conduct of entertainment at fairs and expositions and of trade shows by exempt organizations, the performance of certain services for small hospitals, the conduct of certain bingo games, the sale of low-cost articles, and the rental of mailing lists under certain circumstances.

---

[131] H.R. Rep. No. 2319, *supra* note 90, at 37, and S. Rep. No. 2375, *supra* note 90, at 107–08. E.g., Rev. Rul. 78-144, 1978-1 C.B. 168.

[132] IRC § 513(a)(2). E.g., Rev. Rul. 69-268, 1969-1 C.B. 160; Rev. Rul. 55-676, 1955-2 C.B. 266.

[133] S. Rep. No. 2375, *supra* note 90, at 108.

[134] IRC § 513(a)(3). E.g., *Disabled Veterans Service Foundation* v. *Commissioner*, 29 T.C.M. 202 (1970).

[135] Rev. Rul. 71-581, 1971-2 C.B. 236.

[136] IRC § 512(a)(5).

The rule with respect to entertainment at fairs and expositions[137] applies to charitable, social welfare, labor, agricultural, and horticultural organizations that regularly conduct, as a substantial exempt purpose, an agricultural and educational fair or exposition.[138]

The term "unrelated trade or business" does not include qualified "public entertainment activities" of an eligible organization.[139] This term is defined to mean "any entertainment or recreational activity of a kind traditionally conducted at fairs or expositions promoting agricultural and educational purposes, including but not limited to, an activity one of the purposes of which is to attract the public to fairs or expositions or to promote the breeding of animals or the development of products or equipment."[140]

No unrelated income taxation is to occur with respect to the operation of a "qualified public entertainment activity" that meets one of the following conditions: the public entertainment activity is conducted (1) in conjunction with an international, national, state, regional, or local fair or exposition, (2) in accordance with state law which permits that activity to be conducted solely by an eligible type of exempt organization or by a governmental entity, or (3) in accordance with state law which permits that activity to be conducted under license for not more than 20 days in any year and which permits the organization to pay a lower percentage of the revenue from this activity than the state requires from other organizations.[141]

The rule with respect to trade show activities[142] applies to labor, agricultural and horticultural organizations, and business leagues, which regularly conduct, as a substantial exempt purpose, shows which stimulate interest in and demand for the products of a particular industry or segment thereof.

As respects the third of these items, it has been the position of the IRS that income which a tax-exempt hospital derives from providing services to other exempt hospitals constitutes unrelated business income to the hospital providing the services, on the theory that the providing of services to other hospitals is not an activity which is substantially

---

[137] IRC § 513(d)(1) & (2).
[138] IRC § 513(d)(2)(C).
[139] IRC § 513(d)(1).
[140] IRC § 513(d)(2)(A).
[141] IRC § 513(d)(2)(B).
[142] IRC § 513(d)(1) & (3).

related to the tax-exempt purpose of the hospital providing the services.[143] Congress acted to reverse this position in the case of small hospitals.

Where a tax-exempt hospital provides certain services[144] only to other tax-exempt hospitals, there will not be an unrelated business as long as each of the recipient hospitals has facilities to serve not more than 100 inpatients and the services would be consistent with the recipient hospitals' exempt purposes if performed by them on their own behalf.[145]

Bingo game income realized by most tax-exempt organizations is not subject to the unrelated business income tax.[146] This exclusion applies where the bingo game is not conducted on a commercial basis and where the games do not violate state or local laws.

For a charitable, veterans', or other organization, to which contributions are deductible, the term "unrelated business" does not include activities relating to the distribution of low-cost articles if the distribution of the articles is incidental to the solicitation of charitable contributions.[147] A "low-cost article" is one that has a cost, not in excess of five dollars (indexed for inflation), to the organization that distributes, or has distributed for it, the item. A "distribution" qualifies under this rule if it is not made at the request of the distributee, it is made without the express consent of the distributee, and the articles that are distributed are accompanied by a request for a charitable contribution from the distributee to the organization and a statement that the distributee may retain the article whether or not a contribution is made.

Also, for a charitable, veterans', or other organization, to which contributions are deductible, the concept of a business does not include exchanging with another like organization the names and addresses of donors to or members of the organization, or the renting of these lists to another like organization.[148]

MODIFICATIONS

In determining unrelated business taxable income, both gross income derived from an unrelated trade or business and business deductions are computed by taking into account certain "modifications."[149]

---

[143] Rev. Rul. 69-633, 1969-2 C.B. 121.
[144] Those described in IRC § 501(e)(1)(A).
[145] IRC § 513(e).
[146] IRC § 513(f).
[147] IRC § 513(h)(1)(A).
[148] IRC § 513(h)(1)(B).
[149] IRC § 512(b).

Passive income, namely dividends, interest, payments with respect to securities loans, annuities, royalties, certain rents (generally of real estate), and gain from the disposition of property, is generally excluded from unrelated business taxable income, along with directly connected deductions.[150]

The legislative history of these provisions indicates that Congress believed that "passive" income should not be taxed under these rules "where it is used for exempt purposes because investments producing incomes of these types have long been recognized as proper for educational and charitable organizations."[151]

The strict definitional classifications of the types of passive income are not dispositive of the question as to their treatment in relation to the modification rules. Rather, "[w]hether a particular item of income falls within any of the modifications . . . shall be determined by all of the facts and circumstances of each case."[152]

The legislative history of the unrelated business income tax provisions is amply clear on the point that Congress, in enacting these modifications, did not intend and has not authorized taxation of the passive receipt of income by exempt organizations, and that a technical satisfaction of the definitional requirements of the terms used in the statute is not required. Thus, the Senate Finance Committee observed in 1950 that the unrelated income tax was to apply to "so much of . . . [organizations'] income as rises from *active business enterprises* which are unrelated to the exempt purposes of the organizations" (emphasis supplied).[153] The Committee added: "The problem at which the tax on unrelated business income is directed is primarily that of unfair competition."[154] Speaking of the exclusion for passive sources of income, the Committee stated:

> Dividends, interest, royalties, most rents, capital gains and losses and *similar items* are excluded from the base of the tax on unrelated income because your committee believes that they are "passive" in character and are not likely to result in serious competition for taxable business having similar income. Moreover, investment-producing incomes of these types have long been recognized as a proper source of revenue for educational and charitable organizations and trusts (emphasis supplied).[155]

---

[150] IRC § 512(b)(1), (2), (3), & (5); Reg. § 1.512(b)-1(a)-(d).

[151] H.R. Rep. No. 2319, *supra* note 90, at 38. Also S. Rep. No. 2375, *supra* note 90, at 30–31.

[152] Reg. § 1.512(b)-1.

[153] S. Rep. No. 2375, *supra* note 90, at 27.

[154] *Id.* at 28.

[155] *Id.* at 30–31.

It seems unmistakable that passive income, regardless of type, is properly includible within the exclusions provided by the modifications.[156]

The exclusion relating to gains and losses from the disposition of property does not extend to dispositions of inventory or property held primarily for sale to customers in the ordinary course of business.[157]

However, there are important exceptions to this general exemption for passive income. One, income in the form of rent, royalties, and the like from an active business is taxable; that is, merely labeling an item of income as rent, royalty, or the like does not make it tax-free. Second, the unrelated debt-financed income rules[158] override the general exemption for passive income. Third, interest, annuities, rents, and royalties (but not dividends) from a controlled corporation may be taxable.[159]

Income derived from research for government is excluded, as is income derived from research for anyone in the case of a college, university, or hospital and "of fundamental research" units.[160] According to the legislative history, "research" includes "not only fundamental research but also applied research such as testing and experimental construction and production."[161] As respects the separate exemption for college, university, or hospital research, it is clear that "funds received for research by other institutions [do not] necessarily represent unrelated business income," such as a grant by a corporation to a foundation to finance scientific research if the results of the research were to be made freely available to the public.[162]

A specific deduction of $1,000[163] makes the first $1,000 of unrelated business income automatically nontaxable. The purpose of this deduction is to eliminate the need for payments of small amounts of tax.

PARTNERSHIP RULE

Generally, a trade or business regularly carried on by a partnership of which an exempt organization is a member is an unrelated trade or business with respect to the organization. In computing its unrelated business taxable income, the organization must (subject to the modifications rules) include its share (whether or not distributed) of the gross income

---

[156] Also see H.R. Rep. No. 2319, *supra* note 90, at 36–38.

[157] IRC § 512(b)(5); Reg. § 1.512(b)-1(d).

[158] IRC § 514.

[159] IRC § 512(b)(13).

[160] IRC § 512(b)(7), (8), & (9); Reg. § 1.512(b)-1(f).

[161] H.R. Rep. No. 2319, *supra* note 90, at 37.

[162] S. Rep. No. 2375, *supra* note 90, at 30.

[163] IRC § 512(b)(12).

of the partnership from the unrelated trade or business and its share of the partnership deductions directly connected with such gross income.[164]

However, a tax-exempt organization's share (whether or not distributed) of the gross income of a publicly traded partnership must be treated as gross income derived from an unrelated trade or business, and its share of the partnership deductions is allowed in computing unrelated business income.[165]

Unrelated Income Rules as Applied to Fund-Raising

It would be a substantial understatement to say that charitable organizations do not regard their fund-raising activities as unrelated business endeavors. Yet, unknown to most in the philanthropic community, fund-raising practices and the unrelated business rules have been enduring a precarious relationship for years.

Traditionally, the IRS has exercised suitable restraint by refraining from applying the unrelated income rules to charitable gift solicitation efforts. However, this restraint is seemingly being abandoned, with the IRS now beginning to utilize the unrelated income rules to characterize the receipts from certain fund-raising activities as taxable income. This utilization of these rules is one of the chief means by which the IRS is embarking upon regulation of fund-raising for charity.

At the outset, it must be conceded that many fund-raising practices possess all of the technical characteristics of an unrelated trade or business. Reviewing the criteria for unrelated income taxation discussed above, some fund-raising activities are (1) trades or businesses, (2) regularly carried on, and (3) not efforts that are substantially related to the performance of tax-exempt functions. Further, applying some of the tests often used by the IRS and the courts, there is no question but that some fund-raising endeavors (4) have a commercial counterpart and are being conducted in competition with that counterpart, and (5) are being undertaken with the objective of realizing a profit.[166] Treatment of a fund-raising effort as an unrelated business may appear to be a rather absurd

---

[164] IRC § 512(c)(1); Reg. § 1.512(c)-1.

[165] IRC § 512(c)(2).

[166] The fact that the "profits" of an activity are destined for use in furtherance of exempt functions cannot be considered in assessing whether an activity is an unrelated one. IRC § 513(a). One court, addressing an analogous circumstance (application of the "feeder organization" rules of IRC § 502), said of an organization: "That it gave all its profits to an educational institution availeth it nothing in the mundane field of taxation, however much the children in our schools have profited from its beneficence." *SICO Foundation* v. *United States*, 295 F.2d 924, 925 (Ct. Cl. 1961), reh'g denied, 297 F.2d 557 (Ct. Cl. 1962).

result, and certainly is not consistent with the intent of Congress when it enacted the unrelated income rules in 1950, but nonetheless can be a logical and technically accurate application of the rules.

In the past, the IRS appears to have basically avoided application of the unrelated income rules to charitable organizations' fund-raising endeavors. Even if the matter was given much thought, the rationale seems to have been that either the fund-raising activity is not a trade or business or is not regularly carried on.

The rationale that fund-raising activities are not "businesses" was expressed by the Senate Committee on Finance in 1969, when it stated that "where an activity does not possess the characteristics of a trade or business within the meaning of IRC [§] 162, such as when an organization sends out low-cost articles incidental to the solicitation of charitable contributions, the unrelated business income tax does not apply since the organization is not in competition with taxable organizations."[167] However, an examination of this rationale reveals two elements that substantially undermine its widespread application: (1) the funds received by the organization are in the form of gifts, not payments for the articles or services provided, and (2) the activity is not in competition with commercial endeavors. These two elements may be absent in a fund-raising endeavor.

Thus, a tax-exempt organization may well engage in fund-raising efforts that have their commercial counterparts. Some of these activities are sheltered by law from consideration as businesses, such as a business (1) in which substantially all of the work is performed for the organization by volunteers,[168] (2) carried on primarily for the convenience of the organization's members, students, patients, officers, or employees,[169] or (3) which consists of the sale of merchandise, substantially all of which has been received by the organization as gifts.[170] Also, a statute exempts from unrelated business income taxation the receipts from certain types of bingo games.[171]

Perhaps the beginning of serious regard of fund-raising activities as businesses can be traced to the enactment of the Tax Reform Act of 1969, whereby Congress authorized the taxation of revenue from the acquisition and publication of advertising in the magazines of tax-exempt

---

[167] S. Rep. No. 91-522, 91st Cong., 1st Sess. 71 (1969), quoted as part of the IRS *Exempt Organizations Handbook* (IRM 7751, Nov. 14, 1975) at (36)21(2), and Reg. § 1.513-1(b).

[168] IRC § 513(a)(1).

[169] IRC § 513(a)(2).

[170] IRC § 513(a)(3). E.g., Rev. Rul. 71-581, 1971-2 C.B. 236.

[171] IRC § 513(f).

organizations. To accomplish this result, Congress codified two rules previously contained in the income tax regulations: it enacted laws which state that (1) the term "trade or business" includes any activity carried on for the production of income from the sale of goods or the performance of services, and (2) an activity of producing or distributing goods or performing services from which gross income is derived does not lose identity as a trade or business merely because it is carried on within a larger aggregate of similar activities or within a larger complex of other endeavors that may or may not be related to the exempt purposes of the organization.[172]

Needless to say, this definition of the term "trade or business" is extremely encompassing. The IRS, for example, has observed that the definition of the term "is not limited to integrated aggregates of assets, activities, and good will which comprise businesses" for purposes of other tax rules.[173] In addition to the breadth of this definition, the IRS is, as noted, authorized by statute to examine an exempt organization's activities one by one (rather than as a single bundle of activities) and fragment its operations in search of unrelated business endeavors. As the result of both of these rules, the fund-raising practices of charitable organizations are now, more than ever, exposed and thus more vulnerable to the charge that they are unrelated businesses.

The IRS has not been reticent to apply these rules in an expansionist manner. For example, the IRS sought (unsuccessfully) to characterize as an unrelated business the selling by universities of the televising and broadcasting rights in connection with the institutions' athletic events.[174] Also, the IRS has attempted (again unsuccessfully, because of overriding action by Congress) to narrowly interpret the rules (discussed above) portraying certain forms of income as "passive" income to contend that income from the writing of options[175] and from the lending of securities[176] by exempt organizations is taxable as unrelated business income.

More directly, in a somewhat fund-raising context, the IRS has held that the regular sales of membership mailing lists by an exempt educational organization to colleges and business firms for the production of income is an unrelated trade or business.[177] By contrast, the IRS has privately

---

[172] IRC § 513(c); also Reg. § 1.513-1 (b).

[173] *Exempt Organizations Handbook, supra* note 167, at (36)21(1).

[174] See *Law of Tax-Exempt Organizations* at 731–33.

[175] See *Law of Tax-Exempt Organizations* at 776.

[176] See *Law of Tax-Exempt Organizations* at 780–85, 787–88, 803–4.

[177] Rev. Rul. 72-431, 1972-2 C.B. 281.

ruled that the exchange of mailing lists by an exempt organization with similar exempt organizations does not give rise to unrelated business income (namely, barter income of an amount equal to the value of the lists received).[178] In this ruling, the IRS ruled that the activity is not a business because it is not carried on for profit but rather to obtain the names of potential donors. Likewise, this exchange function was held to be substantially related to the organization's exempt function as being a "generally accepted method used by publicly supported organizations to assist them in maintaining and enhancing their active donor files." Nonetheless, where a tax-exempt organization exchanges mailing lists to produce income, it is the position of the IRS that the transaction is economically the same as a rental and thus is an unrelated trade or business.[179] Furthermore, the IRS[180] and the courts[181] have regarded the regular conduct of bingo games by exempt organizations to be unrelated activities. As noted,[182] Congress subsequently developed partial exemptions for these types of activities, but the principal point is that the IRS advanced the positions.

The rationale that fund-raising activities are not taxable businesses because they are not regularly carried on also finds support in the early IRS literature. The basic position of the IRS is that "exempt organization business activities which are engaged in only discontinuously or periodically will not be considered regularly carried on if they are conducted without the competitive and promotional efforts typical of commercial endeavors."[183] As noted earlier, the operation of a sandwich stand by a hospital auxiliary for two weeks at a state fair is not the regular conduct of a trade or business,[184] while the operation of a parking lot for commercial purposes one day each week on a year-round basis is the regular conduct of a trade or business.[185] Thus, the IRS has observed that "[a]n annually recurrent dance or similar fund-raising event for charity would not be regular since it occurs so infrequently."[186]

[178] IRS Priv. Ltr. Rul. 8127019.
[179] IRS Priv. Ltr. Rul. 8216009.
[180] Rev. Rul. 59-330, 1959-2 C.B. 153.
[181] *Clarence La Belle Post No. 217* v. *United States, supra* note 92.
[182] See text accompanying *supra* notes 146 & 148.
[183] *Exempt Organizations Handbook, supra* note 167, at (36)30(2)(d).
[184] *Id.* at (36)30(2)(a).
[185] *Id.* at (36)30(2)(b).
[186] *Id.* at (36)30(2)(f). However, a charity may be found to be engaged in an unrelated business for conducting this type of fund-raising event where it is done for the benefit of another charity (Rev. Rul. 75-201, 1975-1 C.B. 164).

In one case, the U.S. Tax Court concluded that the annual fund-raising activity of a charitable organization, consisting of the presentation and sponsoring of a professional vaudeville show one weekend per year, is not regularly carried on.[187] The court observed: "The fact that an organization seeks to insure the success of its fundraising venture by beginning to plan and prepare for it earlier should not adversely affect the tax treatment of the income derived from the venture."[188] Indeed, the court went on to note that the IRS "apparently believes that all fundraisers of exempt organizations are conducted by amateurs in an amateurish manner. We do not believe that this is, nor should be, the case. It is entirely reasonable for an exempt organization to hire professionals in an effort to insure the success of a fundraiser. . . ."[189]

However, just as many fund-raising practices are technically "trades or businesses," so are many "regularly carried on." Inasmuch as the other rationales for avoiding unrelated income taxation (principally, the contention that the activity is "substantially related" or that the income is "passive") are unlikely to apply in the fund-raising context, it is today quite possible for a fund-raising activity to be deemed a trade or business that is regularly carried on and an undertaking that is not substantially related to the exercise of a charitable organization's exempt purposes.

There are several instances of the assumption by the IRS of this position, and they are multiplying. One is a 1979 private letter ruling, concerning a case involving a religious organization that conducted, as its principal fund-raising activity, bingo games and related concessions.[190] Players were charged a fixed amount for the use of bingo cards, the games were held on three nights each week, and the receipts from and expenses of the games were substantial. The IRS concluded that "the bingo games constitute a trade or business with the general public, the conduct of which is not substantially related to the exercise or the performance by the organization of the purpose for which it was organized other than the use it makes of the profits derived from the games."[191]

---

[187] *Suffolk County Patrolmen's Benevolent Association, Inc.* v. *Commissioner*, 77 T.C. 1314 (1981).

[188] *Id.* at 1324.

[189] *Id.* at 1323.

[190] IRS Priv. Ltr. Rul. 7946001. Also *P.L.L. Scholarship Fund* v. *Commissioner*, 82 T.C. 196 (1984); *Piety, Inc.* v. *Commissioner*, 82 T.C. 193 (1984).

[191] The organization was unable to utilize the exemption from unrelated income taxation afforded by IRC § 513(f) because, under the law of the state in which it is organized (Texas), the bingo games constituted, at that time, an illegal lottery.

Second, a federal court of appeals has held that a solicitation of charitable contributions by means of the mailing of greeting cards to potential contributors does not constitute the conduct of an unrelated trade or business.[192] The case concerned a school that unsuccessfully attempted to raise funds from foundations and other organizations, so it turned to a program of mailing packages of greeting cards to prospective donors, with information about the school and a request for contributions. An outside firm printed, packaged, and mailed the greeting cards and the accompanying solicitation letter. The court rejected the government's contention that the solicitation is a trade or business, finding that the greeting cards were not being sold but were distributed incidentally to the solicitation of charitable contributions. As noted, the income tax regulations provide that "an activity does not possess the characteristics of a trade or business . . . when an organization sends out low-cost articles incidental to the solicitation of charitable contributions."[193] The government argued that this rule was inapplicable in this case because the funds involved are not "gifts," but the court said that to read the law in that narrow manner would "completely emasculate the exception."[194] The court held that the case turned on the fact that the unrelated income rules were designed to prevent nonprofit organizations from unfairly competing with for-profit companies, and that the school's fund-raising program did not give it "an unfair competitive advantage over taxpaying greeting card businesses."[195]

While the decision is undoubtedly a correct one, three troublesome facts must be faced: (1) the IRS pursued the issue in the first instance, even into litigation, (2) the trial court agreed with the IRS position, and (3) the IRS at trial secured a verdict by jury.

Third, the U.S. Court of Claims (now the U.S. Claims Court) subsequently examined application of the unrelated business rules as they relate to certain fund-raising efforts of a national veterans' organization.[196] The case focused on two fund-raising practices of the organization. The

---

[192] *The Hope School* v. *United States*, 612 F.2d 298 (7th Cir. 1980).

[193] *Supra* note 167.

[194] *The Hope School* v. *United States*, *supra* note 192, at 302.

[195] *Id.* at 304. Also *Veterans of Foreign Wars of the U.S., Department of Missouri, Inc.* v. *United States*, *supra* note 41. An appeal of this decision was not authorized, with the IRS believing a preferential vehicle on the issue was *Veterans of Foreign Wars, Department of Michigan* v. *Commissioner*, *supra* note 41, which turned out to be accurate.

[196] *Disabled American Veterans* v. *United States*, 80-2 U.S.T.C. ¶ 9568 (Ct. Cl. 1980).

first was its practice of offering items ("premiums") to potential donors as part of its semiannual direct mail solicitation. The premiums, offered in exchange for contributions of $2.00, $3.00, or $5.00, were maps, charts, calendars, and books. The rationale for this use of premiums was that it gained the attention of the recipients so that more initial responses were obtained or, in instances involving prior donors, the level of contributions was upgraded. The second practice was the rental of names on the organization's mailing list to both tax-exempt and commercial organizations. The court found that certain of the organization's solicitation activities using premiums constituted a trade or business because they were conducted in a competitive and commercial manner. In making the differentiation, the court ruled that "if the contribution required for any one premium was set at an amount greatly in excess of the retail value of the premiums concerned, a competitive situation would not be present."[197] Because the $2.00 premium items were valued at $0.85 to $1.00 and the $3.00 items were valued at $1.50, the court concluded that there was not any unrelated business activity. But, because the $5.00 premium items were valued at $2.95 to $5.45, the court found the requisite trade or business, noting that the sending of a $5.00 contribution "may well have formed a contract binding . . . [the organization] to furnish the premium item."[198] Also finding that the solicitation was regularly carried on, because of "sufficient similarity to a commercial endeavor,"[199] and was not an activity related to the organization's tax-exempt purposes (notwithstanding the utility of the premiums as attention-getting devices), the court declared the presence of an unrelated business. The court also determined that the rental of the organization's donor list is a trade or business that is regularly carried on and that is not substantially related to the accomplishment of its tax-exempt purposes.[200]

It is clear from these two court cases that the use of premium items as part of a fund-raising activity is much less likely to be considered an unrelated trade or business if the items are mailed with the solicitation. That is, where the recipients are informed that the premiums can be retained without any obligation to make a contribution, the activity is not conducted in a competitive manner and hence presumably is not a trade or business. But, as the Court of Claims observed, "When premiums

---

[197] *Id.* at 84, 855.

[198] *Ibid.*

[199] *Id.* at 84, 856.

[200] This determination upholds the IRS position on the point as proclaimed in Rev. Rul. 72-431, 1972-2 C.B. 281.

are advertised and offered only in exchange for prior contributions in stated amounts, the activity takes on much more of a commercial nature."[201]

Subsequently, the full Court of Claims adopted the trial judge's report, with some modifications but none concerning the substantive unrelated business issues. Thus, the position of the entire court in the case is that the amounts received by the veterans' organization from a semiannual soliciations program utilizing premium items constituted unrelated business income and that the amounts received by the organization from the rental of its mailing list also constituted unrelated business income. Consequently, the emerging law appears to be that "when premiums are advertised and offered only in exchange for prior contributions in stated amounts,"[202] the activity becomes a commercial one. However, if the organization "had mailed the premiums with its solicitations and had informed the recipients that the premiums could be retained without any obligation arising to make a contribution,"[203] the activity is not a business because it is not a competitive practice.[204]

Armed with this victory out of the Court of Claims, the IRS has begun to apply the rule concerning premium items to situations where organizations distribute greeting cards for the purpose of raising funds. Some charitable groups have engrafted onto their greeting card distribution program some elements that go beyond the mere sending of cards in the hope that a contribution will result. Some of these factors include "suggesting" a minimum contribution, which is equivalent to the retail value of the cards, and invoicing the recipient of the cards for the amount requested. In one instance, an organization entered into a contract with an independent card distributor which distributed cards to the organization's members. A minimum contribution was requested per box of cards and follow-up notices were sent to nonresponsive recipients requesting either payment for the cards or their return. The distributor was paid a fixed amount for each box of cards mailed. In another instance, an organization solicited orders for cards at the time it mailed its newsletter. In some years, a commercial supplier processed the orders; in other years, the organization fulfilled the requests. In all instances, a "minimum price" was suggested. Persons who returned money that was less than the suggested price were invoiced for the difference.

---

[201] *Disabled American Veterans* v. *United States, supra* note 196.

[202] *Disabled American Veterans* v. *United States*, 650 F.2d 1179, 1187 (Ct. Cl. 1981).

[203] *Id.* at 1186.

[204] Also *Hope School* v. *United States, supra* note 192.

In the first instance, the IRS held that the program involved sale of the cards.[205] The IRS noted that commercial practices were being employed, namely, payment for or return of the cards and the sending of follow-up notices. Because of these practices, the IRS concluded that the payments are not "gifts" because they are not "voluntary" and because the amount paid exceeds the fair market value of the cards. The receipts were thus characterizied as a sale of the cards at their fair market value in a competitive manner. In the second instance, the IRS stressed the same factors. Again, the program was said to be "indistinguishable from normal commercial operations."[206] Therefore, it appears clear that the IRS will treat a greeting card distribution program as an unrelated business where there is a "suggested" price equivalent to the retail value of the cards and where the recipients are invoiced for the payment. However, where the cards are distributed without any obligation to the recipient and where there is no subsequent invoicing, the better view is that the activity is not an unrelated business and any support provided in response to the appeal is a deductible charitable contribution.[207]

This matter developed further when the IRS embarked on litigation characterizing card distribution programs of tax-exempt veterans' organizations as unrelated businesses, in the face of the contention that the programs constitute forms of fund-raising. While the government lost the first case in this series,[208] the U.S. Tax Court subsequently ruled that the revenue derived by a veterans' organization from the distribution of Christmas cards to its members constitutes unrelated business income.[209] While recipients of the boxes of cards were not under any legal obligation to pay for them, the literature was written to convey the impression

---

[205] IRS Priv. Ltr. Rul. 8203134.

[206] IRS Priv. Ltr. Rul. 8232011.

[207] For an unrelated business to give rise to taxable income, the business must, as noted, be regularly carried on. In both of the two instances discussed, the cards distributed are Christmas cards; the IRS determined that the period of time within which to measure "regularity" is the "Christmas season" rather than the full year. Also, in both instances, the organization attempted to cast the greeting card program as a related activity. One organization placed its logo on the cards; the other mailed literature about its programs with the cards. The IRS was not persuaded that either exercise made the card-distribution program a related activity.

[208] *Veterans of Foreign Wars of the United States, Department of Missouri, Inc.* v. *United States, supra* note 41.

[209] *Veterans of Foreign Wars, Department of Michigan* v. *Commissioner, supra* note 41.

that the cards cannot be considered unsolicited. This card program involved the organization for about one week of time per month from September through February of each year. The program produced substantial profits, being the second largest revenue source for the organization (behind dues). The veterans' organization contended that the boxes of cards were gifts to its members (in the nature of premiums) and that the monies sent to it from the members also were gifts. It rejected the thought that it was "selling" the cards and thus that a "business" was involved. The organization also contended that the activity was not regularly carried on (and therefore not taxable) and that the card dissemination was related activity in that it promoted comradeship among its members. In finding the activity to be a business, the court concluded that the organization had a profit motive and that the card program constitutes the "sale of goods," noting that 85 to 90 percent of those who paid for the cards paid precisely the amount requested ($2.00 or $3.00, depending on the year involved). It further found that the exception in the tax regulations for "low-cost articles"[210] is inapplicable, in part because of its rejection of the thought that there was any solicitation of contributions. The card program was held to be regularly carried on because of its extent on a seasonal basis, and taxable because it is not related to the advancement of the organization's purposes.

Thus it is that, since the raising of funds by a charitable organization is not in itself an exempt function, many types of fund-raising activities are vulnerable to the claim that they are unrelated trades or businesses.

The likelihood of this result's occurring is substantially reduced where the activity is more akin to an "administrative" or "management" activity, rather than an active "business enterprise." In this category of fund-raising, efforts somewhat comparable to administrative or management undertakings are the writing of charitable remainder trusts and charitable gift annuity agreements, the offering of participations in pooled income funds, and the administration of charitable bequest programs. Yet a 1978 U.S. Tax Court case raises some questions about these activities as well.

A fundamental precept of the federal tax law concerning charitable organizations is that they may not, without imperiling their tax-exempt status, be operated in a manner that causes persons to derive a private benefit from their operations.[211] Yet the provision of services that amount to personal financial and tax planning—an essential element of the appreciated property and planned gift techniques—may not be considered

---

[210] See text accompanying *supra* note 167.

[211] Reg. §§ 1.501(a)-1(c), 1.501(c) (3)-1(c)(2).

exempt activities but rather the provision of private benefit. While it would seem nearly inconceivable to contend that, when a charitable organization works with a donor to effect a major gift that will generate significant tax savings for the donor by reason of a charitable contribution deduction, the organization is jeopardizing its tax-exempt status because it is providing a "private benefit," such a conclusion is the import of this case.

The case concerned the tax status of an organization that engages in financial counseling by providing tax planning services (including charitable giving considerations) to wealthy individuals referred to it by subscribing religious organizations. The counseling given by the organization consists of advice on how a contributor may increase current or planned gifts to religious organizations, including the development of a financial plan that, among other objectives, results in a reduction of federal income and estate taxes.

The position of the IRS was that this organization cannot qualify for federal income tax exemption because it serves the private interests of individuals by enabling them to reduce their tax burden. The organization's position was that it was merely engaging in activities that tax-exempt organizations may themselves undertake without loss of their tax exemption. The court agreed with the government, finding that the organization's "sole financial planning activity, albeit an exempt purpose furthering . . . [exempt] fund-raising efforts, has a nonexempt purpose of offering advice to individuals on tax matters that reduces an individual's personal and estate tax liabilities."[212] As the court dryly stated, "We do not find within the scope of the word charity that the financial planning for wealthy individuals described in this case is a charitable purpose."[213]

In this opinion, the court singled out the planned giving techniques for portrayal as methods that give rise to unwarranted private benefit. Thus, the court observes:

> For example, when petitioner advises a contributor to establish a charitable unitrust gift, the contributor ultimately forfeits the remainder. Nevertheless, this loss is voluntarily exchanged for considerable lifetime advantages. Unitrusts generate substantial income and estate and gift tax benefits, such as retained income for life, reduced capital gains tax, if any, on the exchange of appreciated investments, favorable tax rates for part or all of the income payments on certain investments, and lower probate costs.

[212] *Christian Stewardship Assistance, Inc.* v. *Commissioner,* 70 T.C. 1037, 1041 (1978).
[213] *Id.* at 1043.

Consequently, there are real and substantial benefits inuring to the contributors by the petitioner's activities.[214]

Concluded the court: "We think the tax benefits inuring to the contributors are . . . substantial enough to deny exemption."[215]

The Tax Court returned to this theme in 1983, holding that an admittedly religious organization is not tax-exempt because it engages in a substantial nonexempt purpose, which is the counseling of individuals on the purported tax benefits accruing to those who become ministers of the organization.[216] The organization went by the name of The Ecclesiastical Order of the Ism of Am. The court found the organization akin to a "commercial tax service, albeit within a narrower field (i.e., tax benefits to ministers and churches) and a narrower class of customers (i.e., petitioner's ministers)," and thus that it serves private purposes.[217] The many detailed discussions, by the organization in its literature, of ways to maximize tax benefits led the court to observe that "although petitioner may well advocate belief in the God of Am, it also advocates belief in the God of Tax Avoidance."[218] In words that have considerable implications for fund-raising for charitable purposes generally, the court wrote that "a substantial nonexempt purpose does not become an exempt purpose simply because it promotes the organization in some way."[219] The court somewhat recognized the larger meaning of its opinion and attempted to narrow its scope by noting that "[w]e are not holding today that any group which discusses the tax consequences of donations to and/or expenditures of its organization is in danger of losing or not acquiring tax-exempt status."[220]

The Tax Court revisited this theme early in 1984, holding that an organization, the membership of which is religious missions, is not entitled to tax-exempt status as a religious organization because it engages in the substantial nonexempt purpose of providing financial and tax advice.[221]

[214] *Id.* at 1044.

[215] *Ibid.*

[216] *The Ecclesiastical Order of The Ism of Am, Inc.* v. *Commissioner*, 80 T.C. 833 (1983), aff. 740 F.2d 967 (6th Cir. 1984), cert. denied, 471 U.S. 1015 (1985).

[217] *Id.* 80 T.C. at 839. Also *Universal Life Church, Inc.* v. *United States*, 87-2 U.S.T.C. ¶ 9617 (Ct. Cl. 1987).

[218] *Id.* at 840.

[219] *Id.* at 841.

[220] *Id.* at 842.

[221] *National Association of American Churches* v. *Commissioner*, 82 T.C. 18 (1984).

Once again, the court was heavily influenced by the recent rush of cases before it concerning, in the words of the court, "efforts of taxpayers to hide behind the cover of purported tax-exempt religious organizations for significant tax avoidance purposes."[222] As the court saw the facts of the case, each member "mission" was the result of individuals attempting to create churches involving only their families so as to convert after-tax personal and family expenses into deductible charitable contributions; the central organization provides sample incorporation papers, tax seminars, and other forms of tax advice and assistance to those creating the missions. Consequently, the court was persuaded that "the pattern of tax avoidance activities which appears to be present at the membership level. combined with . . . [the organization's] admitted role as a tax advisor to its members" justifies the conclusion that the organization is ineligible for tax exemption.

Subsequently, the Tax Court again evinced a lack of understanding of fund-raising for charity and thus issued an opinion that raises anew questions about the imposition of the unrelated income tax in the fund-raising context.[223] At issue was the tax status of a membership organization for citizens' band radio operators that uses insurance, travel, and discount plans to attract new members. The organization contended that it is only doing what many tax-exempt organizations do to raise contributions, analogizing these activities to fund-raising events such as rallies and dinners. The court rejected this argument, defining a "fund-raising event" as "a single occurrence that may occur on limited occasions during a given year and its purpose is to further the exempt activities of the organization." These events were contrasted with activities that "are continuous or continual activities which are certainly more pervasive a part of the organization than a sporadic event and [that are] . . . an end in themselves." Of course, there are a wide variety of fund-raising methods other than special events that are "continuous" and "pervasive," and that are intended "to further the exempt activities of the organization." Also, no legitimate fund-raising activity is an end in itself, yet many tax-exempt organizations and institutions have major, ongoing fund-raising and development programs that are permanent fixtures among the totality of the entities' activities. This decision, then, is another in a series of cases that is forming the foundation for the contention that certain types of fund-raising endeavors are unrelated businesses.

[222] *Id.* at 29–30.
[223] *U.S. CB Radio Association, No. 1, Inc.* v. *Commissioner*, 42 T.C.M. 1441 (1981).

The Tax Court subsequently concluded that a novel "fund-raising" scheme is an unrelated trade or business. A nonprofit school consulted with a tax-shelter investments firm in search of fund-raising methods, with the result being a program in which individuals would purchase various real properties from the school, which the school would simultaneously purchase from third parties; both the sellers and the buyers were clients of the investments firm. There were about 22 of these transactions during the years at issue, from which the school received income reflecting the difference between the sales prices and the purchase prices. Finding the "simultaneous purchase and sale of real estate . . . not substantially related to the exercise or performance of [the school's] . . . exempt function," the court held that the net income from the transactions is unrelated, taxable income.[224]

Part of the dilemma in this area stems from functional accounting, a process adopted by the IRS a few years ago and imposed upon charitable organizations as part of the annual information return preparation and filing process. This method of accounting separates a charitable organization's functions into three categories: program, administration, and fund-raising. The dilemma exists because many people—including some in law and accounting—continue to regard fund-raising as part of program since its purpose is to promote the organization's activities in some fashion. This misunderstanding is in part fueled by the distinctions in law—accounting notwithstanding—simply between exempt functions and nonexempt functions. Because it is inconceivable that fund-raising is a nonexempt function, it must be an exempt function—so the reasoning goes. From that position, it is an easy jump in logic to the conclusion that fund-raising is the same as program (as neither are nonexempt functions). But such a conclusion would be erroneous.

From this perspective, the tax consequences where a small charity holds an annual car wash, a symphony hosts an annual theater party, a hospital sponsors an annual ball, or the university maintains a planned giving program are unclear. In each of these cases, functional accounting dictates that the expenses associated with those activities be allocated to "fund-raising." But do these activities constitute "program" or are they "nonexempt functions"? In the four illustrations, the activities are not "programs" and they are "nonexempt functions," and as to the latter they are "insubstantial" activities. In many cases, then, the tax aspects of fund-raising come down to this: Is the fund-raising activity "substantial" (in relation to the organization's other and overall activities) or is it a

---

[224] *Parklane Residential School, Inc.* v. *Commissioner*, 45 T.C.M. 988 (1983).

"business"? Special-event fund-raising is likely to be the prime candidate for classification as a "business," particularly where the event has its commercial counterpart. Some examples of this include car washes, bake sales, games, theater parties, dinner parties, and dances. As noted, it is the fact that these events are not regularly carried on that spares them taxation.[225]

Consequently, nearly all fund-raising efforts by charitable organizations will escape unrelated income taxation. Those that are taxed are held frequently, are operated in a commercial manner, and utilize paid assistance. Nonetheless, this still leaves the fact that fund-raising is not "program" and is a "nonexempt function." Two other principles of tax law apply in this setting. One is that the existence of a single nonexempt purpose, if substantial in nature, will destroy a tax exemption regardless of the number or importance of truly exempt purposes.[226] The other is that a tax-exempt organization must serve public purposes and will lose its exemption if it serves private purposes.[227] An illustration of the latter principle in the fund-raising context has been discussed.[228]

Thus it is that the IRS may be embarking on a new approach for regulating charitable fund-raising, by characterizing it as unrelated business,[229] while the courts may be trending toward a line of thinking that equates charitable giving and associated tax planning with private benefit, thereby causing denial or loss of tax exemption. Either way, it appears that the basic rules governing federal income tax exemption are being applied in a very restrictive manner in relation to fund-raising endeavors, so that fund-raising charitable groups may be facing a new wave of regulation, with their exempt status or the extent thereof as the government's leverage.

The foregoing analysis notwithstanding, the U.S. Claims Court has become the first court to squarely face and analyze the difference, for tax purposes, between a fund-raising activity and a business activity. The specific issue before this court was whether income, received by a charitable organization as the result of assignments to it of dividends

---

[225] *Supra*, note 183.

[226] See *Law of Tax-Exempt Organizations* 225–38.

[227] See *Law of Tax-Exempt Organizations* 239–64.

[228] *Supra* note 212.

[229] The Internal Revenue Manual §331(2), as amended in 1982, directs internal revenue agents to, as part of their examination of public charities, "[c]onsider the [charities'] method of raising funds and whether such income is subject to unrelated business income tax."

paid in connection with insurance coverages purchased by members of a related professional association at group rates, is to be taxed as unrelated income; the court ruled that the program constitutes fund-raising, not a commercial venture.[230] While, as discussed,[231] this particular holding was subsequently overturned, the opportunity was presented to develop a contrast between fund-raising efforts and business undertakings.

At the outset, the court wrote that, where the tax-exempt organization involved in an unrelated income tax case is a charitable one, "the court must distinguish between those activities that constitute a trade or business and those that are merely fundraising." Admittedly, said the court, this distinction is not always readily apparent, as "[c]haritable activities are sometimes so similar to commercial transactions that it becomes very difficult to determine whether the organization is raising money 'from the sale of goods or the performance of services' [the statutory definition of a "business" activity[232]] or whether the goods or services are provided merely as an incident to a fund-raising activity."[233] Nonetheless, the court held that the test is whether the activity in question is "operated in a competitive, commercial manner," which is a "question of fact and turns upon the circumstances of each case."[234] "At bottom," the court wrote, "the inquiry is whether the actions of the participants conform with normal assumptions about how people behave in a commercial context" and "[i]f they do not, it may be because the participants are engaged in a charitable fund-raising activity."

In the specific case and in application of these rules, the court stressed five elements: (1) the activity under examination was a pioneering idea at its inception, (2) the activity was originally devised as a fund-raising effort and has been so presented since then, (3) the "staggering amount of money" and "astounding profitability" that is generated by the activity, (4) the degree of the organization's candor toward its members and the public concerning the operation and revenue of the program, and (5) the fact that the activity is operated with the consent and approval of

---

[230] *American Bar Endowment* v. *United States*, 84-1 U.S.T.C. ¶ 9204 (Cl. Ct. 1984).

[231] See text accompanying *infra* note 236.

[232] IRC § 513(c).

[233] *American Bar Endowment* v. *United States, supra*, note 230. Indeed, the court observed that, "[o]ver the years, charities have adopted fund-raising schemes that are increasingly complex and sophisticated, relying on many business techniques."

[234] Also *Disabled American Veterans* v. *United States, supra* note 196.

the association's membership. Concerning the third element, substantial profits and consistently high profit margins are usually cited as reasons for determining that the activity involved is a business. However, in this case, the amounts of money involved were so great that they could not be rationalized in conventional business analysis terms; the only explanation that was suitable to the court was that the monies are the result of successful charitable fund-raising.

Despite the findings of the lower courts, the U.S. Supreme Court held that the provision of group insurance policies, underwritten by major insurance companies, by the American Bar Endowment, a charitable organization, to its members constitutes the carrying on of an unrelated trade or business.[235] The Court noted that the organization negotiates premium rates with insurers, selects the insurers that provide the coverage, solicits its membership, collects the premiums, transmits the premiums to the insurer, maintains files on each policyholder, answers members' questions concerning insurance policies, and screens claims for benefits. In finding the activity to be a business, the Court observed that the ABE "prices its insurance to remain competitive with the rest of the market," that the Court "can easily view this case as a standard example of monopoly pricing," and that the case "presents an example of precisely the sort of unfair competition that Congress intended to prevent." The Court concluded that the "only valid argument in ABE's favor, therefore, is that the insurance program is billed as a fund-raising effort." But the Court summarily rejected this contention with a rather peculiar observation: "That fact, standing alone, cannot be determinative, or any exempt organization could engage in a tax-free business by 'giving away' its product in return for a 'contribution' equal to the market value of the product." But that is not the state of the law.[236] The dissent concluded that the provision of insurance to the ABE members is not competitive with commercial enterprises and that the program is "operated as a charitable fund-raising endeavor."[237]

Current popular fund-raising techniques that are beginning to raise questions about application of the unrelated business rules are forms of "commercial co-venturing" and "cause-related marketing." The former involves situations in which a charitable organization consents to be a

---

[235] *United States* v. *American Bar Endowment*, 106 S.Ct. 2426 (1986).

[236] *Disabled American Veterans* v. *United States, supra* note 196.

[237] *United States* v. *American Bar Endowment, supra* note 235. Subsequent revisions in this program led the IRS to conclude that it is no longer an unrelated business (IRS Priv. Ltr. Rul. 8725056).

donee under circumstances where a commercial business agrees to make a gift to the charity, with that agreement advertised, where the amount of the gift is predicated on the extent of products sold or services provided by the business to the public during a particular time period.[238] The latter involves the public marketing of products or services by or on behalf of a tax-exempt organization, or some similar other use of an exempt organization's resources. A manifestation of the latter can be seen in the participation by exempt organizations in affinity card programs, in which an exempt organization is paid a portion of the revenues derived from the use of the cards by the consumers who make up the affinity group. The position of the IRS is that the revenues from affinity card programs are taxable because they arise from the exploitation of mailing lists, and that the special exception for these lists[239] is not available because the lists are provided to noncharitable organizations.[240]

§ 6.5   Exemption Application Process

Under the federal income tax system, every element of gross income received by a person—whether a corporate entity or a human being— is subject to taxation, unless there is an express statutory provision that exempts from tax either that form of income or that type of person.[241]

Many types of nonprofit organizations are eligible for exemption from the federal income tax.[242] But the exemption is not forthcoming merely because an organization is not organized and operated for profit. Organizations are tax-exempt where they meet the requirements of the particular statutory provision that supplies the tax-exempt status.

"Recognition" of Tax-Exempt Status

Whether a nonprofit organization is entitled to tax exemption, on an initial or continuing basis, is a matter of law. It is the U.S. Congress that defines the categories of organizations that are eligible for tax ex-

---

[238] See Ch. 8 § 8.5.

[239] See text accompanying *supra* note 148.

[240] Gen. Couns. Mem. 39727. The initial position of the IRS was that affinity card program revenues are not taxable because they are passive royalty income (IRS Priv. Ltr. Rul. 8747066) but that determination was subsequently withdrawn (IRS Priv. Ltr. Rul. 8823109).

[241] IRC § 61.

[242] See Ch. 2 § 2.1.

emption, and it is up to Congress to determine whether an exemption from tax should be continued, in whole or in part. Except for state and local governmental entities, there is no constitutional right to a tax exemption.

Despite what many think, the IRS does not "grant" tax-exempt status. Congress, by means of sections of the Internal Revenue Code that it has enacted, does that. Rather, the function of the IRS in this regard is to "recognize" tax exemption.

Consequently, when an organization makes application to the IRS for a ruling or determination as to tax-exempt status, it is requesting the IRS to recognize a tax exemption that already exists (assuming the organization qualifies), not to grant tax exemption. Similarly, the IRS may determine that an organization is no longer entitled to tax-exempt status and act to revoke its prior recognition of exempt status.

For many nonprofit organizations that are eligible for a tax exemption, it is not required that the exemption be recognized by the IRS. Whether a nonprofit organization seeks an IRS determination on the point is a management decision, which usually takes into account the degree of confidence the individuals involved have in the eligibility for the exemption and the costs associated with the application process. Most organizations in this position elect to pursue recognition of tax-exempt status.

However, charitable organizations (and certain employee benefit organizations) must, to be tax exempt and to be charitable donees, file (successfully) with the IRS an application for recognition of the exemption.[243] Thus, by contrast, entities such as social welfare organizations, labor organizations, trade and professional associations, social clubs, and veterans' organizations need not (but may) file an application for recognition of tax-exempt status.[244]

Unlike most requests for a ruling from the IRS (which are commenced by a letter to the IRS), a request for recognition of tax exemption is commenced by filing a form, entitled "Application for Recognition of Exemption." Charitable organizations file Form 1023; most other organizations file Form 1024.

Subject only to the authority in the IRS to revoke recognition of exemption for good cause (such as a change in the law), an organization that has been recognized by the IRS as being tax-exempt can rely on

---

[243] IRC § 508(a). The rules for the employee benefit organizations appear in IRC § 505(c)(1).

[244] E.g., Rev. Rul. 80-108, 1980-1 C.B. 119.

the determination as long as there are no substantial changes in its character, purposes, or methods of operation.[245] Should material changes occur, the organization should notify the IRS and may have to obtain a reevaluation of its exempt status.

The Application Procedure

The IRS has promulgated specific rules by which a ruling or determination letter may be issued to an organization in response to the filing of an application for recognition of its tax-exempt status.[246] An organization seeking recognition of exemption must file an application with the office of the "key" district director of the IRS in relation to the district in which the principal place of business or principal office of the organization is located. Usually, the determination of exemption will be issued by the key district director's office. However, if the application presents a matter of some controversy or an unresolved or novel point of law, the application will be sent on to the National Office of the IRS in Washington, D.C., for resolution at that level.

This application process requires the organization to reveal some information about its fund-raising program.

A ruling or determination will be issued to an organization, as long as the application and supporting documents establish that it meets the particular statutory requirements. The application must include a statement describing the organization's purposes, copies of its governing instruments (such as, in the case of a corporation, its articles of incorporation and bylaws), and either a financial statement or a proposed multi-year budget.

The application filed by a charitable organization must also include a summary of the sources of its financial support, its fund-raising program, the composition of its governing body (usually board of directors), its relationship with other organizations (if any), the nature of its services or products and the basis for any charges for them, and its membership (if any).

An application for recognition of exemption should be regarded as an important legal document and prepared accordingly. Throughout an organization's existence, it will likely be called upon to provide its application for recognition of exemption to others for review. Indeed, a

---

[245] Reg. § 1.501(a)-1(a)(2).
[246] Rev. Proc. 90-4, 1990-2 I.R.B. 10. See *Law of Tax-Exempt Organizations* at 615–22.

nonprofit organization is required by federal law to keep a copy of this application available for scrutiny by anyone during regular business hours.[247]

The Application Itself

The application for recognition of tax exemption filed by charitable organizations (Form 1023) comes in a packet.[248] This packet includes instructions for preparation of the form, the form itself (in duplicate), and some Forms 872-C (discussed below). Only one copy of Form 1023 need be filed with the IRS; the other copy may be used in drafting the application.

PART I

Part I of Form 1023 requests certain basic information about the organization, such as its name, address, and date of formation. Every nonprofit organization must have an "employer identification number" (even if there are no employees) and this is obtained by filing a Form SS-4. The Form SS-4 may be filed as soon as the organization is formed and organized or it may be filed with the Form 1023.

The contact person (question 3) may be either someone directly involved with the organization, such as an officer or director, or an independent representative of the organization, such as a lawyer or accountant. If such a representative is being used, he or she must be granted a power of attorney, which is filed with the application on Form 2848.

The organization must state the month in which its annual accounting period ends (question 4). The determination of a fiscal year should be given some thought; probably most organizations use the calendar year (in which case the answer is "December"). Whatever period is selected, the organization should be certain that the same period is stated on Form SS-4 and used when compiling its multi-year budget (see below).

The date of formation is to be provided (question 5). If incorporated, for example, this date will be the date the state agency received the articles of incorporation. This date is significant in relation to the "15-month rule" (see below).

---

[247] IRC § 6104(e).

[248] This analysis is based on Form 1023 dated December 1989, pages 1–9 of which appear in Appendix C.

Question 10 of Form 1023 requires an applicant organization to identify its "type." The organization must be one of three types: nonprofit corporation, trust, or unincorporated association.[249]

If a corporation, the attachments will be the articles of incorporation and bylaws, any amendments thereto, and the certificates of incorporation and amendment (if any) issued by the state. If an unincorporated association, the attachments will be the constitution and bylaws. If a trust, the attachments will be the trust document(s).

PART II

The charitable organization must identify, in order of size, its sources of financial support (question 2). The answers will be something like the following: contributions from the general public, other contributions, grants, dues, other exempt function (fee-for-service) revenue, and/or investment income. Whatever sources of support are identified here, the organization should be careful to be consistent when preparing the multi-year budget and selecting the nonprivate foundation status, if any (see below).

The organization must describe its actual and planned fund-raising program (question 3). Here the organization will summarize its actual use of, or plans to use, selective mailings, fund-raising committees, professional fund-raisers, and the like. Again, the organization should be certain to conform its discussion of financial support with that of its fund-raising plans. The organization can describe a very detailed fund-raising program or it can state that it has yet to develop a semblance of a fund-raising program.

The organization must provide a narrative of its purposes and activities (question 1). Usually, this is an essay that is descriptive of the organization's programs and should be carefully written. Good practice is to open with a description of the organization's purposes, followed by one or more paragraphs summarizing its program activities. This response should be as full as is reasonable and may well occupy more space than is provided, in which case the response can be in the form of a separate exhibit.

The names and addresses of the organization's officers and directors must be provided, along with the amount (if any) of their annual compensation (question 4). As to compensation, this includes all compensation, not just that for serving as an officer or director (or trustee).

---

[249] See *Law of Tax-Exempt Organizations* at 611–14.

Question 5, concerning relationships with other organizations, can be very important for some organizations. As a general rule, it does not matter whether the charitable organization has a special relationship with, or is controlled by, another organization. For example, some charitable organizations are controlled by other types of tax-exempt organizations, such as social welfare organizations or trade associations, or are controlled by for-profit corporations (such as corporation-related foundations).

Question 10, concerning membership groups, is basically self-explanatory. However, it relates to organizations that have a true membership, not merely arrangements where the concept of a "membership" is used as a fund-raising technique.

PART III

Question 13, concerning the date of formation of an organization, can be of no particular importance or it can be of extreme importance, depending upon the circumstances. The basic rule is that the recognition of exemption will be retroactive to the date of formation of the charitable organization where the application is filed with the IRS within 15 months from the end of the month in which it was established.[250] For example, if the organization is created on January 15, 1991, and the application for recognition of exemption is filed on or before April 30, 1992, the recognition of exemption (if granted) will be retroactive to January 15, 1991, irrespective of when the determination is made by the IRS. However, to continue with this example, if the application is filed on or after May 1, 1992, the recognition of exemption would be effective only as of the date the application was received by the IRS.

As to the matter of tax-exempt status, the 15-month rule may not be of any particular importance, in that the charitable organization can qualify as a tax-exempt social welfare organization (which does not require recognition of tax-exempt status) until the date of its classification as a charitable organization.[251] However, this alleviation of the tax-exemption problem does not help with respect to the posture of the organization as a charitable donee or as a nonprivate foundation (if the latter is applicable). Donors making gifts during the interim period will, upon audit, find their charitable deductions disallowed. Private foundations making grants during the interim period may be subject to taxation for

---

[250] IRC § 508(a). See *Law of Tax-Exempt Organizations* at 631–35.
[251] Rev. Rul. 80-108, 1980-1 C.B. 119.

failure to exercise "expenditure responsibility."[252] Thus, it is imperative that an organization desiring to be recognized as a charitable organization from its date of formation file a completed application for recognition of tax exemption prior to the expiration of the 15-month period.

Questions 7 through 9 can be of very large consequence. This is where the public charity/private foundation rules come into play.[253]

If the applicant charitable organization is a private foundation, the answer to question 7 is yes. If the organization is seeking classification as a "private operating foundation," it should so indicate in response to question 8 and complete Part IV.

However, if the applicant organization believes it can avoid private foundation status, it must select either a "definitive" ruling or an "advance" ruling. For new charitable organizations that are seeking to be classified as publicly supported entities, an advance ruling (selected by responding to question 9) is the correct choice. This is because they lack the financial history to demonstrate actual public support, which is required before a publicly supported organization can receive a definition ruling. If the applicant believes it will be supported principally by gifts and grants, it should check the box correlating with question 9(h). The box of question 9(i) is for organizations that are expecting support in the form of a blend of gifts, grants, and exempt function income.

Either type of publicly supported organization (to be) must demonstrate its initial qualification for nonprivate foundation status by convincing the IRS that it will receive the requisite extent of public support. This is done by submitting a proposed budget. This budget summarizes contemplated types of revenue (such as gifts, grants, exempt function revenue, and investment income) and types of expenses (such as expenditures for program, compensation, occupancy, telephone, travel, postage, and fund-raising), for each of five years. For this purpose, a year is a period consisting of at least eight months. (For new organizations, this budget is submitted in lieu of the financial statements reflected in Part IV of Form 1023). The five-year period is the "advance ruling period."

In designing the budget, the five years involved are the fiscal years of the organization. The applicant organization should be certain that the fiscal year used to develop the budget is the same period referenced in the response to question 4 of Part I. Also in this process, the applicant

---

[252] See *Law of Tax-Exempt Organizations* at 574–80.
[253] See *infra* § 6.8.

should be certain that the types of revenue stated in the budget correspond to the types of revenue summarized in the response to question 2 of Part III.

The advance ruling pertains only to the applicant organization's status as a publicly supported entity. That is, it is not an advance ruling as to tax-exempt status or charitable donee status. Thus, the advance ruling period is a probationary or conditional ruling, as to "public" status. Once the advance ruling period expires and the organization has in fact received adequate public support during the five-year period, that fact will be reported to the IRS, which will in turn issue a definitive ruling that it is a publicly supported charity. Just as the advance ruling is conditional, the definitive ruling is permanent (unless upset by a subsequent loss of qualification or change in the law).

The publicly supported charitable organization must, during and after the expiration of the advance ruling period (on an ongoing basis), continue to show that it qualifies as a publicly supported charity, assuming it wants to retain that status. This is done by reporting the financial support information as part of the annual information return.[254]

It does not matter which type of publicly supported organization the charitable entity is at any point in its existence; the principal objective is to, at any one time, qualify under one category or another. Thus, an organization can "drift" from one classification of publicly supported organization to another throughout its duration. Likewise, a charitable organization can, without harm, select one category of publicly supported organization when it completes Part III and only satisfy the requirements of the other category as of the close of the advance ruling period.

If an organization selects a category of publicly supported charitable organization when it prepares Part III, and finds at the close of the advance ruling period that it did not meet either set of requirements for publicly supported status, it will be categorized as a private foundation, unless it can demonstrate eligibility for otherwise avoiding private foundation status. This can be done if the organization qualifies as an entity such as a church, school, hospital, or supporting organization (see below).

If the organization is classified as a private foundation following the close of its advance ruling period, it will have to pay the excise tax on its net investment income[255] for each of the years in the advance ruling period (and thereafter). For the IRS to be able to assess a tax retroactively for five years, the taxpayer must agree to waive the running of the statute

---

[254] See *infra* § 6.6.

[255] See *Law of Tax-Exempt Organizations* at 585–92.

of limitations which otherwise would preclude the IRS from reaching that far back. The waiver is granted by the execution of Form 872-C (in duplicate), which, as noted, is part of the Form 1023 package.

An applicant organization that qualifies as a church, school, hospital, supporting organization, or the like is eligible to receive a definitive ruling at the outset. This is because its financial support is not the factor used in classifying it as a "public" entity. Instead, its public status derives from what it does programmatically.

An organization can receive a definitive ruling that it is publicly supported if it has been in existence for, as noted, a tax year of at least eight months and received the requisite public support during that period. The organization in this situation would submit a completed Part IV for each of these years.

An organization that seeks to be categorized as a supporting organization must complete schedule D of Part III.

Every organization that is requesting a definitive ruling must evidence its selection of nonprivate foundation status by answering questions 11 through 14 of Part III. Questions 11 and 14 are to be answered by organizations seeking an advance ruling.

SUMMARY

This application for recognition of tax exemption as a charitable organization, if properly completed, amounts to a rather complete portrait of the programs, fund-raising plans, and other aspects of the applicant organization. That is why it is important to devote some time and thinking to the preparation of the form. It is, as noted,[256] a public document and, during the course of the organization's existence, the organization probably will be called upon to supply a copy of the application. Since those who request the document are likely to be prospective donors or grantors, or representatives of the media, it is particularly important that it be properly prepared.[257]

§ 6.6 Reporting Requirements

One of the most important aspects of federal regulation of the charitable solicitation process is accomplished by means of the annual reporting

---

[256] *Supra* note 247.

[257] A more detailed analysis of the application for recognition of tax exemption (Form 1023), with sample responses, appears in *Starting and Managing A Nonprofit Organization* at 59–74. Also Blazek, *Tax and Financial Planning for Tax-Exempt Organizations* at 57–160 (New York: John Wiley & Sons, Inc., 1990).

obligations imposed on most charitable and other tax-exempt organizations. That is, with some exceptions, a charitable organization must annually file an information return[258] with the IRS.[259]

Filing Categories

Organizations with gross receipts (as defined) that are normally not in excess of $25,000 need not file annual information returns,[260] although it is the view of the IRS that these organizations should file the identification part of the form. In determining the $25,000, an organization takes into account (1) net rental income (gross rents less expenses); (2) net amounts received from the sale of assets other than inventory (gross amounts from the assets, less basis in assets and expenses of sale); (3) net receipts from special fund-raising events and activities; and (4) gross profit or loss from other sales (gross sales, less returns, allowances, and cost of goods sold).

Organizations with annual gross receipts that are normally in excess of $25,000 but less than $100,000, and that have end-of-year assets with a value below $250,000 may file a two-page annual information return.[261] Thus, tax-exempt organizations generally are classified as being in one of three filing categories: those that need not file at all, those that can file the short form, and those that must file the full return.

Aside from the filing exemption accorded "small" organizations, other categories of tax-exempt entities are excused from the filing requirements. These are churches, interchurch organizations of local units of a church, conventions or associations of churches, certain integrated auxiliaries of churches, and certain internally supported, church-controlled organizations; schools below college level affiliated with a church or operated by a religious order; mission societies sponsored by or affiliated with

---

[258] Form 990. Private foundations, a form of charitable organization (see *infra* § 6.8) that rarely engages in fund-raising, file Form 990-PF. Political organizations file Form 990-POL; black lung benefit trusts file Form 990-BL; religious or apostolic organizations file Form 1065.

[259] IRC § 6033(a)(1). See *Law of Tax-Exempt Organizations* at 643–55. This analysis is based upon the annual information return to be used by most tax-exempt organizations for calendar year 1989 or for fiscal years beginning in 1989. See VII *The Nonprofit Counsel* (No. 4) 1 (1990). This form appears in Appendix D.

[260] IRC § 6033(a)(2)(A)(ii); Reg. § 1.6033-2(g)(1)(iii); Rev. Proc. 83-23, 1983-1 C.B. 687, § 3.01. This exception is not available, however, for private foundations.

[261] Form 990EZ.

one or more churches or church denominations, if more than one-half of the society's activities are conducted in or directed at persons in foreign countries; exclusively religious activities of a religious order; many types of state institutions; and certain instrumentalities of the United States.[262]

Income-Producing Activities

A principal component of Form 990 is Part VII, which consists of an extensive reporting of income-producing activities. The information sought is designed to provide Congress with data needed to assess the impact of current or future unrelated business income rules and to enable the IRS to better administer the present unrelated income laws.[263]

Part VII-A of the form requires a tax-exempt organization to identify each income-producing activity. These activities include various forms of program service revenue, membership dues and assessments, investment income, sales of assets, and special fund-raising events.

The revenue from each reported activity must be categorized as unrelated business income, exempt function (related) income, or income excluded from tax by a particular provision of the Internal Revenue Code. The IRS has devised a system of codes to use in classifying unrelated (taxable) business income and income excludable from taxation because of a particular code section (see below).

When an exempt organization classifies an item of income as related, it must explain (in Part VII-B) how the associated activity contributed importantly to the accomplishment of exempt purposes. (Just because an activity generates funds that are used for tax-exempt purposes does not make that activity a related one.)

The instructions to the return include a chart of the "exclusion codes." There is a code for each rationale for excluding otherwise unrelated income from taxation, such as for an activity that is not regularly carried on or one that is conducted substantially by volunteers.

One exclusion code that is particularly noteworthy is number 40, which is to be used for an activity that is not considered a "business" to begin with because the activity is not carried on with a "profit motive," since there have been losses. Where an activity is so classified, the losses from it cannot be offset against gain from other unrelated activities.

---

[262] Rev. Proc. 83-23, *supra* note 260, § 3.01.
[263] See *supra* § 6.4.

Reporting

An organization is required to report (on line 1 of Part I) all amounts received as contributions and grants. The instructions state that "contributions" means "payments, or the part of any payment, for which the payer (donor) does not receive full consideration from the recipient (donee) organization."

Organizations must attach a schedule listing contributors during the year who gave the organization, directly or indirectly, money or property worth at least $5,000. Gifts of less than $1,000 are not included for this purpose.

Separate reporting is required for program service revenue, membership dues and assessments, investment income, asset sales, revenue from special fund-raising events, and other revenue.

Revenue from special fund-raising activities (such as dinners, door-to-door sales of merchandise, carnivals, and bingo games) generally is, as noted, separately reported (on line 9). However, when the payment is part a purchase for the event or activity and part a contribution, the gift portion is reported separately (on line 1a) from the purchase portion. Direct expenses associated with special fund-raising events are subtracted on the face of the return. A schedule must be attached to the return listing the three largest (in terms of gross receipts) special events conducted by the organization.

Revenue, for these purposes, does not include the value of services donated to an organization or the free use of materials, equipment, or facilities. These items may be reported elsewhere (Part VI, line 82).

In general, expenses must be totaled, and also allocated to three categories: program, management, and fund-raising. However, in practice, far more detail about expense allocation is required. For example, as noted, there are allocations regarding special fund-raising activities. Also, charitable organizations should keep records about legislative activities.

Functional Accounting

The annual information return requires charitable organizations to use the functional method of accounting as the means to report their expenses (Part III).[264] This approach to accounting for an organization's expenses requires not only the identification, line by line, of expenses but also

---

[264] Form 990, Part III.

an allocation of expenses by function, namely, the categories of "program services," "management and general," and "fund-raising" (see Form 990, Part III, in Appendix D).

Proper compliance with the requirements of the functional method of accounting obligates organizations to maintain detailed records as to their fund-raising (and other) expenses, since the fund-raising component of each line-item expenditure must be separately identified and reported. This requirement that the fund-raising elements of all expenditures be separately identified may reveal some indirect fund-raising costs that, when combined with direct fund-raising expenses, result in the reporting of considerably higher total outlays for fund-raising. This, in turn, could have adverse repercussions with respect to the organization's status under state charitable solicitation acts, particularly those that seek to force disclosure of organizations' fund-raising expenses.[265] This approach to the reporting of expenses raises other pertinent accounting issues, not the least of which is the basis to be used in making these allocations among functions[266] and whether the state regulators will accept reports containing the allocations as being in compliance with the states' reporting requirements.

The instructions accompanying the return define the term "fund-raising expense" as "all expenses, including allocable overhead costs, incurred in: (a) publicizing and conducting fund-raising campaigns; (b) soliciting bequests, grants from foundations or other organizations, or government grants . . . ; (c) participating in federated fundraising campaigns; (d) preparing and distributing fundraising manuals, instructions, and other materials; and (e) conducting special fundraising events that generate contributions. . . ." The IRS does not differentiate, when using the term "professional fundraiser," between fund-raising counsel and solicitors, in that it defines the phrase "professional fundraising fees" to mean "the organization's fees to outside fundraisers for solicitation campaigns they conducted, or for providing consulting services in connection with a solicitation of contributions by the organization itself."[267]

---

[265] See Ch. 5 § 5.3.

[266] The instructions accompanying Form 990 state that "[o]rganizations should follow their normal method of accounting in reporting their total expenses paid or incurred," and "any reasonable method may be used to allocate expenses among the three categories," and "[f]igures should be reasonably accurate if precise figures cannot be determined."

[267] See Ch. 5 § 5.9. Also Ch. 8 § 8.3.

Other Information

There are at least four other areas of disclosure, mandated by the annual information return, pertaining to fund-raising. First, the return requires organizations to separately identify their sources of "program service revenue" (Part II). Second, organizations have the option of distinguishing between the reporting of revenue that is restricted and revenue that is unrestricted (Part I). Third, organizations must report their receipts from and expenses of "[s]pecial fundraising events and activities," with information separately provided for each type of event. The regulations state that these events include dinners, dances, carnivals, raffles, bingo games, and door-to-door sales of merchandise. (As noted, an organization uses only the net receipts from these events in computing the $25,000 of receipts that may dictate the extent of the organization's reporting obligations.)

As to special fund-raising events, the IRS observes in the return's instructions that "[i]n themselves, these activities only incidentally accomplish an exempt purpose" and that "[t]heir sole or primary purpose is to raise funds (other than contributions) to finance the organization's exempt activities." "This is done," the instructions continue, "by offering goods or services of more than nominal value (compared to the price charged) in return for a payment higher than the direct cost of the goods or services provided." Thus, an activity that only generates contributions (such as a direct mail campaign) is not a "special fundraising event." However, a special fund-raising event can generate both contributions and revenue, such as when a purchaser pays more than the value of the goods or services furnished.

An organization must attach a schedule to the return, describing and providing financial detail for the three largest (as measured by gross receipts) special events conducted. Summary information must be provided for the other events.

Some or all of the dollar limitations applicable to Form 990 when filed with the IRS may not apply when an organization is using the form in place of state or local report forms.[268] Examples of federal law dollar limitations that do not meet some state requirements are the $25,000 gross receipts minimum that gives rise to the obligation to file with the IRS, the identification-only format for organizations that report revenue of $25,000 or less, and the $30,000 minimum for listing professional fees in Schedule A of Form 990.

---

[268] See Ch. 6 § 6.6.

The contents of the annual information return pertain to the relationship between the federal government and the state regulatory agencies with respect to the regulation of fund-raising for charity. These levels of government are coordinating their respective roles. The IRS has taken a significant step toward implementation of this process by stating, in its summary of its adoption of the present return, that "[s]tates are encourged to use this return as the basic form satisfying State reporting requirements" and adding that "[a]ny additional information needed by a particular State could be provided by that State's own supplemental schedules and by requiring every filer to complete all parts of the Form 990 to be filed with the State." More states than ever before use Form 990 as the form for providing financial information in compliance with the states' charitable solicitation acts; for some reason, the IRS wants to know the states in which the return is filed and expects the organizations to report that information (in Part VII).

Other Fund-Raising Aspects

The instructions to the return point out that some states and local governmental units will accept a copy of Form 990 (and, where applicable, Schedule A) in place of all or part of their own financial report forms. Usually this aspect of the matter pertains to filing compliance under the states' charitable solicitation acts.[269]

The instructions observe that "doing business" in a particular state may entail the filing of returns there. They gratuitously note that the concept of "doing business" may include the solicitation of contributions or grants. This is a matter largely of state law; some charitable solicitation acts expressly regard acts of charitable fund-raising as the doing of business in the state.[270]

The instructions also note that the dollar limitations applicable to Form 990 when filed with the IRS may not apply when filing the form for state use. An example of this is the $25,000 gross receipts minimum that gives rise to the obligation to file a Form 990 with the IRS. Further, the time for filing a Form 990 with the IRS may differ from the time for filing reports with one or more states.

Charitable organizations[271] must keep sample copies of their fund-raising materials, such as dues statements, tickets, and receipts. Also

---

[269] See Chs. 3 & 4.
[270] See Ch. 4 § 4.16.
[271] Organizations described in IRC § 501(c)(3).

to be retained are sample copies of advertising copy and scripts used in soliciting gifts by means of radio and television.

Related Organizations

In their annual returns on Schedule A of Form 990, which is filed only by charitable organizations,[272] these organizations must disclose information with respect to their direct or indirect transfers to, and other direct or indirect relationships with, other tax-exempt organizations (not including other charitable organizations), including political organizations.[273]

The purpose of this provision is, in the language of the instructions, "to help prevent the diversion or expenditure of a . . . [charitable] organization's funds for purposes not intended by" that section. Every charitable entity must maintain records regarding these types of transfers, transactions, and relationships.

Public Inspection

These annual information returns must be made available for public inspection upon request.[274] (Approved applications for exemption from federal income tax also must be made available.)[275] Some information is not publicly accessible, however, such as an organization's list of contributors.

In general, all parts of the return must be made available for public inspection. This includes all required schedules and attachments (again, other than a list of donors). Of particular note is the Schedule A required of most charitable organizations, which contains information about the compensation of organizations' employees. Inspection must be permitted during regular business hours at the organization's principal office and at each of its regional or district offices having three or more employees.

Penalties

Failure of a tax-exempt organization to file the appropriate annual information return can result in penalties. A penalty of $10 a day, not to exceed the lesser of $5,000 or 5 percent of the gross receipts of the

---

[272] IRC § 6033(b).
[273] IRC § 6033(b)(9).
[274] IRC § 6104(e)(1).
[275] IRC § 6104(e)(2).

organization for the year, may be charged where a return is filed late, unless the organization can show that the late filing was due to reasonable cause.[276]

The penalty may also be charged if an incomplete return is filed or incorrect information is furnished.

Further, if a complete return is not filed or correct information is not furnished, and a period of correction has expired, the individual failing to comply will be charged a penalty of $10 per day, not to exceed $5,000, unless he or she is able to show that the noncompliance was due to reasonable cause. If more than one individual is responsible, they are jointly and individually liable for the penalty.[277]

A separate penalty applies with respect to a failure to comply with the public inspection requirement.[278] This is $10 for each day that an inspection was not permitted, up to a maximum of $5,000 per return. A penalty will not be imposed if the failure is due to reasonable cause. A person who willfully fails to comply with the requirement is subject to an additional penalty of $1,000. (There are similar penalties that apply for failure to make proper disclosure of an exemption application.)[279]

§ 6.7 Lobbying Restrictions

In 1990, the federal government—specifically the Treasury Department and the IRS—issued regulations that define the term "fund-raising costs" and spell out rules by which to distinguish such costs from (that is, allocate between) the expenses of administration and program. These regulations have been drawn as part of the effort to promulgate rules to implement the requirements enacted in 1976 governing lobbying by charitable organizations.

Normally, lobbying by charities and fund-raising by charities are separate considerations, and fund-raisers have little interest in the legislative activities of the charitable organizations they serve. Thus, the intricacies of the lobbying tax rules enacted in 1976 would seem of dubious relevance. But, as it turns out, these rules are indeed quite pertinent.

A charitable organization[280] is required by the federal tax laws to ensure that "no substantial part of the activities" of the organization

---

[276] IRC § 6652(c)(1).
[277] IRC § 6652(c)(1)(B)(ii).
[278] IRC § 6652(c)(1)(C).
[279] IRC § 6652(c)(1)(D).
[280] An organization described in IRC § 501(c)(3).

constitutes "carrying on propaganda, or otherwise attempting to influence legislation." Years of considerable and continuing uncertainty as to the meaning and scope of these rules[281] led Congress, in enacting the Tax Reform Act of 1976, to clarify and amplify the proscription. This was done by the enactment of laws that measure the substantiality of lobbying activities as a function of funds expended.

While these rules are extensive and complex, the pertinent provision is that which formulates the lobbying standards in terms of declining percentages of aggregate expenditures. For charitable organizations that elect to come within these rules,[282] the basic permitted annual level of expenditures for legislative efforts is 20 percent of the first $500,000 of an organization's expenditures for exempt purposes, plus 15 percent of the next $500,000, 10 percent of the next $500,000, and 5 percent of any remaining expenditures, with the total amount spent for legislative activities in any one year by an organization not to exceed $1,000,000. No more than one-fourth of these amounts may be expended for "grass-roots" lobbying.[283]

In computing the permissible lobbying amount, the percentages are applied to the organization's tax-exempt expenditures, which, however, do not include fund-raising expenditures. Thus, it becomes necessary for an organization endeavoring to comply with these rules to distinguish between its fund-raising costs and its other costs.

The expenditures against which these percentages are applied are termed "exempt purpose expenditures," which means the amounts paid or incurred to accomplish charitable, educational, religious, scientific, and like purposes. The law expressly allows, as exempt purpose expenditures, administrative expenses associated with exempt functions and expenses for legislative activities. But exempt purpose expenditures do not include amounts paid or incurred to or for (1) a separate fund-raising unit of the organization, or an affiliated organization's fund-raising unit; or (2) one or more other organizations, if such amounts are paid or incurred primarily for fund-raising.[284]

The legislative history of these rules gives very little guidance about the allocation and other accounting aspects. (The only mention of accounting precepts is that amounts properly chargeable to capital account are to be capitalized and that, when a capital item is depreciable, a

---

[281] See *Law of Tax-Exempt Organizations* at 175–79.
[282] IRC § 501(h)(4).
[283] IRC § 4911(c)(2).
[284] IRC § 4911(e)(1)(C).

reasonable allowance for depreciation, computed on a straight-line basis, is to be treated as an exempt-purpose expenditure.) Guided by the regulations, electing organizations must make a reasonable judgment as to the calculation of exempt-purpose expenditures, lobbying expenditures (both direct and grass roots), and fund-raising expenditures.

The first task in computing fund-raising costs must therefore be for an organization to determine its direct fund-raising costs. These costs include such items as payments to fund-raising consultants, salaries to employees principally involved in fund-raising, travel, telephone, postage, and supplies. (These items must also be identified with respect to any lobbying expenses.) Even with respect to these so-called direct items, there may well have to be allocations, such as between the educational (program) aspects and the fund-raising aspects of the expenses of creating and delivering printed material.

Subsequently, an organization must ascertain its indirect costs, to be apportioned to fund-raising, lobbying, and other factors. These costs would include such items as salaries of supportive personnel, rent, and utilities. Here again, the basis by which these costs are allocated to the various components will be crucial in computing permissible lobbying expenses accurately. The regulations indicate that the IRS will be demanding extensive cost allocations—thus, the IRS has promulgated standards by which such allocations are to be made.

Finally, there is the matter of defining the term "fund-raising" which, of course, must be done before costs can be determined and apportioned. For the most part, such costs will be readily ascertainable. However, many organizations actively pursue grant support from foundations, corporations, and/or federal agencies. Using the term in its broadest sense, such activities may be termed "fund-raising," yet they bear little relationship to the solicitations of the general public that generally constitute acknowledged forms of fund-raising. Other questions arise, such as the proper classification of costs of a feasibility study, particularly where the consultant recommends against a campaign or other fund-raising effort.

Strict application of these requirements may be nearly impossible. As an illustration, assume an organization raises its financial support by means of direct mail. The organization takes the position that a portion of the mailings consists of educational material (and thus the costs related to that portion are program expenses) and that the remainder of the literature is an appeal for contributions (and thus the costs related to that portion are fund-raising expenses). Also, as part of the mailings, the organization discusses the pendancy of certain legislative proposals and the need for congressional action, and, as a separately identifiable part of the mailings, specifically asks the recipients to contact their representatives in Congress urging their support of the legislation. In such an instance, the costs of the mailings would have to be allocated to program, general lobbying, grass-roots lobbying, and fund-raising. Needless to say, the internal record-keeping obligations and justifications can become extensive, as can the IRS audit exposure.

So it is that the regulations governing lobbying by charitable organizations are of direct relevance to the fund-raising community.[285] Among the other forms of regulatory authority plaguing charitable organizations and fund-raising these days, then, is the evolving lobbying law, and the fund-raising community is well advised to understand the scope of the regulations and submit comments on the rules where questions arise.

---

[285] The regulations appear at 55 *Fed. Reg.* 35579 (Aug. 31, 1990). A related issue can arise in characterizing a direct mail effort as being grass-roots lobbying rather than being fund-raising, with the IRS perhaps inclined to treat it as the former for purposes of regulation, particularly where the fund-raising literature has a legislative theme. In a technical advice memorandum interpreting the IRC § 501(c)(3) limitation on attempts to influence legislation, the IRS has held that the facts and circumstances of the mail appeal for funds will determine whether it is merely a fund-raising appeal or whether it is a disguised attempt at grass-roots lobbying. Some of the factors the IRS considered important in determining that a direct mail solicitation was not grass-roots lobbying include the use of an outside fund-raising consultant; the consultant's preparation of the text of the letter, its graphics and design, and the type of postage used going out and coming in; the design of the involvement devices included in the mailing; the use of standard fund-raising techniques such as the number of times paragraphs asking for more money were included in the text (usually 30 percent of total text); whether the consultant ever consulted with lobbyists or policy analysts of the soliciting organization to assure uniformity or correctness in the discussion of the legislative topic or theme; whether there was any direct request in the letter that the solicitee do anything other than send money or return a poll card; if a poll card was used involving an opinion on the legislative topic, whether the poll card was disregarded or not used in some legislative format by the soliciting organization; whether the soliciting organization had an institutional point of view, expressed through its publications or otherwise, which publicly favored or opposed pending or proposed legislation consistent with the theme of the solicitation letter; the type of mailing lists used by the fund-raising consultant and whether the mailing lists had a political orientation; and finally, whether or not the fund-raising appeal was a financial success.

§ 6.8 The "Public Charity" Classifications

An organization deemed to be a "charitable" organization[286] must either be categorized as a private foundation or acquire recognition from the IRS that it qualifies as a "public charity."[287] Inasmuch as every charitable organization is rebuttably presumed to be a private foundation,[288] an organization finds public charity classification (if it can) by being described in one or more of the "exceptions" to the statutory definition of the term "private foundation."[289]

Many institutions are automatically exempted from classification as private foundations because of the nature of their tax exemption (such as by being churches,[290] educational institutions,[291] or hospitals[292]) or of the nature of their relationship (a supportive one) to one or more other public charities.[293] However, the nonprivate-foundation status of other types of charitable entities is predicated not on the nature of their operations but on the extent of their financial support. It is in this context that fund-raising and IRS regulation once again entwine.

There are three categories of charitable organizations whose nonprivate-foundation status is wholly dependent upon the type of their financial support. These are the following:

1. One type of publicly supported organization is that which normally receives a substantial part of its financial support (other than income from an exempt function) from a governmental unit or from contributions from the general public.[294] An organization can achieve public charity status pursuant to these rules in one of two ways: (*a*) where the total amount of its support normally derived from governmental or public sources, or both, is at least one-third of the total amount normally received, or (*b*) where a "facts and circumstances" test is met, in which

---

[286] That is, one described in IRC § 501(c)(3).

[287] IRC § 508(b). However, certain organizations are exempted from this requirement by IRC § 508(c). In general, see *Law of Tax-Exempt Organizations* at 643–48.

[288] Rev. Rul. 73-504, 1973-2 C.B. 190.

[289] IRC § 509(a). See Ch. 2 § 2.1.

[290] IRC §§ 170(b)(1)(A)(i), 509(a)(1).

[291] IRC §§ 170(b)(1)(A)(ii), 509(a)(1).

[292] IRC §§ 170(b)(1)(A)(iii), 509(a)(1).

[293] IRC § 509(a)(3).

[294] IRC §§ 170(b)(1)(A)(vi), 509(a)(1).

case the total amount of governmental and/or public support normally received by the organization may be as low as 10 percent of its total support normally received. The amount of requisite public support (the numerator of the support fraction) is composed of contributions from an individual, trust, corporation, or other organization but only to the extent that the total amount of the contributions by any such individual or organization during the computation period does not exceed 2 percent of the charitable organization's total support for the period. This 2 percent limitation does not apply to support received from governmental units or to contributions from certain types of public charities, nor are unusual grants taken into account in computing the applicable percentage. The extent of requisite public support generally is measured over a four-year, floating period.

For example, one of the elements of the facts and circumstances test is the extent to which the organization is attracting public support. This element is satisfied where the organization can demonstrate an active and ongoing fund-raising program, as described as follows:

> An organization must be so organized and operated as to attract new and additional public or governmental support on a continuous basis. An organization will be considered to meet this requirement if it maintains a continuous and bona fide program for solicitation of funds from the general public, community, or membership group involved, or if it carries on activities designed to attract support from governmental units or other organizations described in section 170(b)(1)(A)(i) through (vi). In determining whether an organization maintains a continuous and bona fide program for solicitation of funds from the general public or community, consideration will be given to whether the scope of its fund-raising activities is reasonable in light of its charitable activities. Consideration will also be given to the fact that an organization may, in its early years of existence, limit the scope of its solicitation to persons deemed most likely to provide seed money in an amount sufficient to enable it to commence its charitable activities and expand its solicitation program.[295]

2.   Another type of publicly supported organization is that which normally receives more than one-third of its support in each tax year from any combination of (*a*) gifts, grants, contributions, or membership fees, and (*b*) gross receipts from admissions, sales of merchandise, performance of services, or furnishing of facilities in activities related to

---

[295] Reg. § 1.170A-9(e)(3)(ii). In general, see *Law of Tax-Exempt Organizations* at 442–48.

the organization's tax-exempt functions.[296] Such support must derive from governmental units, certain types of public charities, and persons other than those who have a close relationship with the organization. In computing the amount of support received from gross receipts that is allowable toward the one-third requirement, gross receipts from related activities received from any person or from any bureau or similar agency of a governmental unit are includible in any tax year only to the extent that such receipts do not exceed the greater of $5,000 or 1 percent of the organization's support in such year. The extent of requisite public support generally is measured over a four-year, floating period.[297]

3. The third category of charitable organization that predicates its nonprivate-foundation classification on the degree of its public support is the supporting "foundation" that provides financial assistance to public colleges and universities.[298] This type of organization must normally receive a substantial part of its support (exclusive of income received in the exercise or performance of its exempt activities) from the United States, one or more states, or political subdivisions thereof, or from direct or indirect contributions from the general public. As is the case with the other categories, the extent of requisite public support generally is measured over a four-year, floating period.[299]

A charitable organization that fails to meet one or more sets of these rules (and that cannot otherwise qualify as a type of public charity) is denominated a "private foundation" and thus becomes subjected to the complex and restrictive rules applicable only to foundations. These rules prohibit, in effect, self-dealing, large business holdings, and jeopardizing investments, and mandate annual distributions for charitable ends and a range of requirements concerning program expenditures, and levy a tax on investment income.[300] A charitable organization that can do so is well advised to qualify as an entity other than a private foundation.

To so qualify, the organization's nonprivate-foundation status may well depend upon the extent of its public support. Thus, unlike most forms of federal and state regulation of fund-raising for charity, which inhibit or make more costly the fund-raising function, the type of regulation

---

[296] IRC § 509(a)(2).
[297] See *Law of Tax-Exempt Organizations* at 449–58.
[298] IRC §§ 170(b)(1)(A)(iv), 509(a)(1).
[299] See *Law of Tax-Exempt Organizations* at 441.
[300] *Id.* at 406–518.

embodied in the private foundation definitional rules frequently promotes charitable solicitations of the general public.

Consequently, the IRS may be monitoring the extent of a charitable organization's fund-raising efforts, to ascertain whether the organization qualifies as an entity other than a private foundation.

§ 6.9 The School Record-Retention Requirements

The IRS has long taken the position that private tax-exempt educational institutions may not have racially discriminatory policies. The Secretary of the Treasury and the Commissioner of Internal Revenue have been enjoined from approving any application for exemption for, continuing any current exemption for, or approving charitable contribution deductions to any private school in Mississippi which does not show that it has a publicized policy of nondiscrimination.[301] The court found a "Federal public policy against support for racial segregation of schools, public or private" and held that the code "does not contemplate the granting of special Federal tax benefits to trusts or organizations . . . whose organization or operation contravene Federal public policy."[302] Thus, this position is essentially founded on the principle that the statutes providing tax deductions and exemptions are not construed to be applicable to actions that are either illegal or contrary to public policy. The court concluded: "Under the conditions of today they [the tax exemption and charitable deduction provisions[303]] can no longer be construed as to provide to private schools operating on a racially discriminatory premise the support of the exemptions and deductions which Federal tax law affords to charitable organizations and their sponsors."[304]

The IRS in 1971 stated that it would deny tax-exempt status to any private school that otherwise meets the requirements of tax exemption which "does not have a racially nondiscriminatory policy as to students."[305] Subsequently, the IRS has identified private schools lacking such a policy in several states to which contributions can no longer be assured to be tax deductible.

---

[301] *Green* v. *Connally*, 330 F. Supp. 1150 (D.D.C. 1971), aff'd sub nom *Coit* v. *Green*, 404 U.S. 997 (1971).

[302] *Id.* 330 F. Supp. at 1163, 1162.

[303] IRC §§ 501(c)(3) & 170(c)(2).

[304] *Green* v. *Connally*, *supra* note 301, 330 F.Supp. at 1164.

[305] Rev. Rul. 71-477, 1971-2 C.B. 230.

The IRS initially announced its position on the exempt status of private nonprofit schools in 1967, stating that exemption and deductibility of contributions would be denied if the school is operated on a segregated basis.[306] The position was basically reaffirmed early in 1970, and the IRS began announcing denials of exemption later that year. But a clamor began for stricter guidelines when the granting of exemptions resumed to allegedly segregated schools.

The IRS, in 1972, issued guidelines and record-keeping requirements for determining whether private schools that have exemption rulings or are applying for such exemption have racially nondiscriminatory policies as to students.[307] The definition of such a policy remained that of the 1971 ruling, namely, that the school "admits the students of any race to all the rights, privileges, programs, and activities generally accorded or made available to students at that school" and that the school "does not discriminate on the basis of race in administration of its educational policies, admissions policies, scholarship and loan programs, and athletic and other school-administered programs."

Late in 1975, the IRS promulgated guidelines that superseded the 1972 rules.[308]

Under the 1975 rules, the racially nondiscriminatory policy of every private school must be stated in its governing instruments or governing body resolution, and in its brochures, catalogues, and similar publications. This policy must be publicized to all segments of the general community served by the school, either by notice in a newspaper or by use of broadcast media. All programs and facilities must be operated in a racially nondiscriminatory manner, and all scholarships or comparable benefits must be offered on such a basis. Each school must annually certify its racial nondiscrimination policy.

These guidelines state the information that every school filing an application for recognition of exempt status must provide. Also included are an assortment of record-keeping requirements, mandating the retention for at least three years of records indicating the racial composition of the school's student body, faculty, and administrative staff; records documenting the award of financial assistance, copies of all brochures, catalogues, and advertising dealing with student admissions, programs, and scholarships; and copies of all materials used by or on behalf of the

---

[306] Rev. Rul. 67-325, 1967-2 C.B. 113.
[307] Rev. Proc. 72-54, 1972-2 C.B. 834.
[308] Rev. Proc. 75-50, 1975-2 C.B 587.

school to solicit contributions. Failure to maintain or to produce the required reports and information ostensibly creates a presumption that the school has failed to comply with the guidelines and thus has a racially discriminatory policy as to students.

In general, a private school must be able to demonstrate affirmatively (such as upon audit) that it has adopted a racially nondiscriminatory policy as to students that is made known to the general public and that since the adoption of that policy it has operated in a bona fide manner in accordance therewith.[309]

The position of the IRS that a private educational institution that has racially discriminatory policies cannot qualify as a charitable organization was upheld by the U.S. Supreme Court in 1983.[310] The rationale underlying this conclusion was a "public policy" rationale, in that "entitlement to tax exemption depends on meeting certain common law standards of charity—namely, that an institution seeking tax-exempt status must serve a public purpose and not be contrary to established public policy."[311] The Court wrote that an institution that is to be tax-exempt because it is a charitable entity "must demonstrably serve and be in harmony with the public interest" and its "purpose must not be so at odds with the common community conscience as to undermine any public benefit that might otherwise be conferred."[312]

§ 6.10 Fund-Raising Compensation Arrangements

Organizations that are charitable in nature[313] must, among other requirements of that status, be operated so that they do not cause any inurement of their net earnings to certain individuals in their private capacity or otherwise cause private benefit.[314] Where either of these rules are violated, the organization involved can lose or be deprived of its tax-exempt status.

The private inurement doctrine is the principle of law that essentially separates nonprofit organizations from for-profit organizations. An organization that is operated for "profit" is one where the profits are

---

[309] E.g., *Calhoun Academy* v. *Commissioner*, 94 T.C. No. 17 (1990).

[310] *Bob Jones University* v. *United States*, 461 U.S. 574 (1983), aff'g, 639 F.2d 147 (4th Cir. 1980), rev'g, 468 F. Supp. 890 (D.S.C. 1978).

[311] *Id.*, 461 U.S. at 586.

[312] *Id.* at 592.

[313] That is, organizations that are described in IRC § 501(c)(3).

[314] See *Law of Tax-Exempt Organizations* at 239–64.

destined for those who are the owners of the business, such as shareholders of a corporation who receive the corporate profits (net earnings) by means of dividends (the concept does not relate to profits at the entity level). However, a nonprofit organization is expected to retain its profits at the entity level; to be tax-exempt, a nonprofit organization cannot allow its net earnings to be passed along (inure) to those who are the equivalent of its owners. The private inurement doctrine is basically applicable only with respect to a tax-exempt organization and those who have some special relationship to it ("insiders").[315]

By contrast, the private benefit doctrine derives from the rule that a charitable organization must be primarily organized and operated for the advancement of charitable purposes.[316] Operations for private benefit are not, of course, regarded as operations for tax-exempt ends.[317] This doctrine has greater breadth than the private inurement doctrine, and its application is not confined to those who are insiders with respect to an organization.[318]

There are two aspects of this matter, only one of which is directly related to this analysis. The first is the matter of the fund-raising costs of a charitable organization.[319] The second is the matter of the payment of fees for fund-raising to outside consultants. In either instance, however, the organization needs to be certain that its fund-raising does not unduly dominate in relation to its program activities, inasmuch as the IRS is empowered to assess whether a charitable organization is maintaining a program that is commensurate in scope with its financial resources.[320] Precisely how this "commensurate test" will be applied in the fund-raising setting is unclear, but the IRS has expressed renewed interest in application of the doctrine.[321]

---

[315] E.g., *Sound Health Association* v. *Commissioner*, 71 T.C. 158 (1978).

[316] Reg. § 1.501(c)(3)-1(c)(1).

[317] In one instance, an otherwise charitable organization was denied tax-exempt status because its method of fund-raising (bingo games) attracted individuals to the cocktail lounge where the games were held, thereby privately benefiting the owners of the lounge (*P.L.L. Scholarship Fund* v. *Commissioner, supra* note 190.)

[318] E.g., *American Campaign Academy* v. *Commissioner*, 92 T.C. No. 66 (1989). See VI *The Nonprofit Counsel* (No. 7) 1 (1989).

[319] This aspect of the matter is explored in Ch. 5 § 5.1 & Ch. 8 § 8.7.

[320] Rev. Rul. 64-182, *supra* note 15.

[321] A question in the fund-raising audit checksheet (see *supra* § 6.1) concerns application of this "commensurate test."

The private inurement and/or private benefit doctrines can be triggered when a charitable organization pays excessive or otherwise unreasonable compensation for services.[322] Therefore, a charitable organization may not, without endangering its tax-exempt status, pay a fund-raising professional an amount that is excessive or unreasonable. To a large extent, the matter of excessiveness is one of fact. Whether a particular amount of compensation is excessive or not is essentially dependent upon fees paid in the community for comparable services, the experience of the professional, the type of fund-raising involved, the nature of the charitable cause, and the overall resources of the charitable organization. As noted, in many states, the compensation for fund-raising services must be stated in a contract between the charitable organization and the fund-raising professional, with the agreement filed with the regulatory authorities.[323]

Questions about the propriety of compensation of a fund-raising professional may not have as much to do with the amount being paid as the manner in which it is determined. This is particularly true with respect to compensation that is ascertained on the basis of a commission or percentage.

Although the IRS is rather suspicious of fund-raising compensation that is based on percentages of contributions received,[324] the courts have been rather tolerant of the practice. In one instance, a compensation arrangement based upon a percentage of gross receipts was held by the U.S. Tax Court to constitute private inurement, where the facts were somewhat egregious in nature and there was no upper limit as to total compensation.[325] This opinion suggests that one way to avoid private inurement or private benefit when using percentage compensation arrangements is to place a ceiling on the total amount to be paid—assuming, of course, that the total amount is not excessive.

Nonetheless, the Tax Court in a subsequent opinion restricted the reach of this decision by holding that private inurement does not occur when a tax-exempt organization pays its president a commission determined by a percentage of contributions procured by him. The court held that the standard is whether the compensation is reasonable, not

---

[232] E.g., *Church by Mail, Inc.* v. *Commissioner*, 765 F.2d 1387 (9th Cir. 1985) (where ministers of a church were found to be excessively compensated when their church salaries were aggregated with that from a direct mail company owned by them and hired by the church).

[323] See Ch. 4 § 4.10.

[324] See *supra* § 6.1.

[325] *People of God Community* v. *Commissioner*, 75 T.C. 127 (1980).

the manner in which it is ascertained. Fund-raising commissions that "are directly contingent on success in procuring funds," were held to be an "incentive well-suited to the budget of a fledgling organization."[326] In reaching this conclusion, the court reviewed states' charitable solicitation acts governing payments to professional solicitors,[327] which the court characterized as "sanction[ing] such commissions and in many cases endorse[ing] percentage commissions higher than" the percentage commission paid by the organization involved in the case.[328]

Thereafter, the U.S. Claims Court found occasion to observe that "there is nothing insidious or evil about a commission-based compensation system" and that thus an arrangement, whereby those who successfully procure contributions to a charitable organization are paid a percentage of the gifts received, is "reasonable," despite the absence of any limit as to an absolute amount of compensation.[329]

Attempts have been made from time to time by associations of fund-raising professionals to maintain, in their codes of ethics, prohibitions against compensation based on percentages of funds raised. While these restrictions have considerable merit,[330] they are violations of the antitrust laws as illegal restraints of trade and thus cannot lawfully be enforced.[331]

Aside from the reasonableness of a compensation, there is another fundamental consideration: a charitable or other category of tax-exempt organization may not, without transgressing the private inurement doctrine, pay compensation where services are not actually rendered. For example, an organization was denied tax-exempt status because it advanced funds to telephone solicitors, to be offset against earned commissions, where some of the solicitors resigned before they earned commissions equal to or exceeding their advances.[332]

Future enforcement by the IRS of this aspect of this law is to be expected. Loss of tax-exempt status and/or adverse publicity may be in

---

[326] *World Family Corporation* v. *Commissioner*, 81 T.C. 958, 970 (1983).

[327] See Ch. 4 § 4.8.

[328] *World Family Corporation* v. *Commissioner*, *supra* note 326, at 970.

[329] *National Foundation, Inc.* v. *United States*, 87-2 U.S.T.C. ¶ 9602 (Ct. Cl. 1987).

[330] E.g., Greenfield, "Professional Compensation," *The Journal* 35 (National Society of Fund-Raising Executives, Summer 1990).

[331] E.g., "American Institute of Certified Public Accountants; Proposed Consent Agreement With Analysis To Aid Public Comment," 54 *Fed. Reg.* 13,529 (Apr. 4, 1989).

[332] *Senior Citizens of Missouri, Inc.* v. *Commissioner*, 56 T.C.M. 479 (1988).

the offing for some organizations. As one commentator observed, "Charitable organizations must be very careful in structuring commission arrangements with fund-raisers and solicitors, lest they jeopardize their exempt status."[333]

§ 6.11   Charitable Deduction Rules

The process of raising funds for charitable organizations is further "regulated" by federal law because of the rules pertaining to the allowability of deductions for charitable gifts.

The basic concept of the federal income tax charitable contribution deduction is that individual taxpayers who itemize deductions and corporate taxpayers can deduct, subject to a variety of limitations, an amount equivalent to the value of a contribution to a qualified donee.[334] A "charitable contribution" for income tax purposes is a gift to or for the use of one or more "qualified donees."[335]

Charitable gifts are also the subject of gift tax and estate tax deductions.[336]

Meaning of "Gift"

The federal tax law on the subject of the tax aspects of charitable giving is, of course, contained in the Internal Revenue Code and in the interpretations of that body of law found in court opinions, Treasury Department and IRS regulations, and IRS public and private rulings. This body of law is rather specific on such components of the law of charitable giving as qualification of charitable donees, percentage limitations on a year's deductibility, gifts of particular types of property (such as inventory and works of art), and eligibility of various planned giving vehicles.

Despite this extensive treatment of this aspect of the law, there is an omission in the developed rules concerning charitable giving. That is, the law is very scarce on the meaning of the word "gift." This is highly significant, obviously, because there must be a "gift" before there can be a "charitable gift."

Integral to the concept of the charitable contribution deduction, then, is the fundamental requirement that the cash or property transferred

---

[333] Henske, Jr., "Where the IRS Draws the Line on Payments to Professional Fundraisers," 1 *J. Tax'n Exempt Org.* (No. 2) 11, 15 (1989).

[334] IRC § 170.

[335] IRC § 170(c).

[336] IRC §§ 2522 & 2055, respectively.

to a charitable donee be transferred pursuant to a transaction that is in fact a "gift." Just because cash is paid, or property is transferred, to a charity does not necessarily mean that the payment or transfer is a gift. Consequently, when a university's tuition, a hospital's health-care fee, or an association's dues are paid, there is no gift, and thus no charitable deduction for the payment.

Certainly, there is some law, most of it generated by the federal courts, as to what constitutes a gift. (The Internal Revenue Code and the tax regulations are essentially silent on the subject.) Basically, the meaning of a "gift" has two elements: it is a transfer that is "voluntary" and is motivated by something other than "consideration" (namely, something being received in return for a payment). (Where payments are made to receive something in exchange, the transaction is more in the nature of a contract.) The law places more emphasis on the second element than on the first. Thus, the income tax regulations state that a transfer is not a contribution when made "with a reasonable expectation of financial return commensurate with the amount of the donation."[337] Instead, such a payment is a purchase (of a product or a service). A corollary of this simple rule is that a single transaction can be partially a gift and partially a purchase, so that when a charity is the payee only the gift portion is deductible.[338]

Years ago, the U.S. Supreme Court observed that a gift is a transfer motivated by "detached or disinterested generosity."[339] (This is the factor frequently referred to as "donative intent.") One federal court of appeals put the matter more starkly, succinctly observing that this is a "particularly confused issue of federal taxation."[340] Not content with that, this appellate court went on to portray the existing Internal Revenue Code structure on this subject as "cryptic," with the indictment that "neither Congress nor the courts have offered any very satisfactory definition" of the terms "gift" and "contribution."[341]

These concepts have been revisited many times in recent months. One manifestation of this has been the availability of a charitable deduction for the transfer of money to a college or university, where the transferor is granted preferential access to good seating at the institution's athletic events. While the IRS refused to regard these payments as gifts, finding

---

[337] Reg. § 1.162-15(b).

[338] See *supra* § 6.1.

[339] *Commissioner* v. *Duberstein*, 363 U.S. 278, 286 (1960).

[340] *Miller* v. *Internal Revenue Service*, 829 F.2d 500, 502 (4th Cir. 1987).

[341] *Id.* at 502.

that the payment results in receipt of a "substantial benefit,"[342] Congress enacted a special rule to accomodate these payments for tax purposes.[343] The IRS has struggled with this issue for years (e.g., in the early 1980s, when it was popular for homes to be auctioned with benefits accruing to a charitable organization); the IRS ruled that those who purchase tickets from a charity are not making gifts. Other recent manifestations of this phenomenon include the various "tax shelter" programs involving gifts of artwork and the use of premiums and other items of property to donors in response to their contributions.

The U.S. Supreme Court's 1989 ruling[344] on what a charitable gift is comports precisely with the IRS position, which, for years, has been that, when a "donor" receives some benefit or privilege in return for a payment to charity, the payment may not, in whole or in part, constitute a deductible charitable gift.[345]

Qualified Donees

Qualified donees are charitable organizations (including educational, religious, and scientific entities),[346] certain fraternal organizations, most veterans' organizations, governmental entities, and certain cemetery companies.[347] Regarding charitable organizations, contributions to both private and public charities are deductible, although the law favors gifts to the latter.

Federal, state, and local governmental bodies are, under the tax law, charitable donees. However, other law may preclude a governmental entity from accepting charitable gifts. In many instances, a charitable organization can be established to solicit deductible contributions for and make grants to governmental bodies. This is a common technique for public schools, colleges, universities, and hospitals.[348]

---

[342] Rev. Rul. 84-132, 1984-2 C.B. 55.

[343] IRC § 170(m), which provides that 80 percent of an amount provided to an educational institution, where the payor receives the right to purchase tickets for an athletic event at the institution, is deductible as a charitable contribution.

[344] *Hernandez* v. *Commissioner*, *supra* note 10, at 2136.

[345] See *supra* § 6.1.

[346] Organizations described in IRC § 501(c)(3), other than those that test for public safety.

[347] IRC § 170(c).

[348] IRC § 170(b)(1)(A)(iv).

In some instances, an otherwise nonqualifying organization may be the recipient of a deductible charitable gift, where the gift property is used for charitable purposes or received as agent for a charitable organization. An example of the former is a gift to a trade association that is earmarked for a charitable fund within the association.[349] An example of the latter is an additional amount paid by customers of a utility company, when paying their bills to the company, where the additional amounts are earmarked for a charitable organization that assists individuals with emergency energy-related needs.[350]

Gift Properties

Aside from the eligibility of the gift recipient, the other basic element in determining whether a charitable contribution is deductible is the nature of the property given. Basically, the distinctions are between outright giving and planned giving, and between gifts of cash and gifts of property. In many instances, the tax law of charitable giving differentiates between personal property and real property, and between tangible property and intangible property (the latter being stocks and bonds). The value of a qualified charitable contribution of an item of property often is its fair market value.

The federal income tax treatment of gifts of property is dependent upon whether the property is "capital gain property." The tax law makes a distinction between long-term capital gain and short-term capital gain (although generally such net gain of either type is taxed as ordinary income). Property that is neither long-term capital gain property nor short-term capital gain property is "ordinary income property." Short-term capital gain property is generally treated the same as ordinary income property. These three terms are based on the tax classification of the type of revenue that would be generated upon sale of the property. In general, therefore, the operative distinction is between "capital gain property" (actually long-term capital gain property) and ordinary income property.

Capital gain property is property that is a capital asset that has appreciated in value, which if sold would give rise to long-term capital gain.[351] To result in long-term capital gain, property must be held for

---

[349] Rev. Rul. 54-243, 1954-1 C.B. 92.
[350] Rev. Rul. 85-184, 1985-2 C.B. 84.
[351] IRC § 170(b)(1)(C)(iv).

the long-term capital gain holding period, which generally is 12 months.[352] Most forms of capital gain property are stocks, bonds, and real estate.

The charitable deduction for capital gain property is often equal to its fair market value or at least is computed using that value. Gifts of ordinary income property generally produce a deduction equivalent to the donor's basis in the property. The law provides exceptions to the basis-only rule, such as in the instance of gifts by a corporation out of its inventory.[353]

Percentage Limitations

The deductibility of charitable contributions for a particular tax year is confined by certain percentage limitations, which in the case of individuals are a function of the donor's "contribution base." An individual's contribution base is essentially his or her adjusted gross income.[354] There are five of these percentage limitations. Again, the limitations are dependent upon several factors, principally the nature of the charitable recipient and the nature of the property donated. The examples will assume an individual donor ("Donor") with a contribution base (adjusted gross income) each year in the amount of $100,000.

First, there is a percentage limitation of 50 percent of the donor's contribution base for contributions of cash and ordinary income property to public charities and private operating foundations.[355] Thus, Donor may, in any one year, make deductible gifts of cash to public charities up to a total of $50,000. Where an individual makes a contribution or contributions to one or more public charities (or operating foundations) to the extent that the 50 percent limitation is exceeded, the excess generally may be carried forward and deducted in one or more subsequent years, up to five.[356] Thus, if Donor gave $60,000 to public charities in year one (and made no other charitable gifts), he or she would be entitled to a deduction of $50,000 in year one and $10,000 in year two.

Another percentage limitation is 30 percent of contribution base for gifts of capital gain property to public charities and private operating foundations.[357] Thus, Donor may, in any one year, contribute up to

---

[352] For property acquired after June 22, 1984, and before Jan. 1, 1988, the long-term capital gain holding period is six months.

[353] IRC § 170(e)(3).

[354] IRC § 170(b)(1)(F).

[355] IRC § 170(b)(1)(B).

[356] IRC § 170(b)(1)(B), last sentence, & (d)(1).

[357] IRC § 170(b)(1)(C)(i).

$30,000 in qualifying stocks, bonds, real estate, and like property to one or more public charities and enjoy a charitable deduction for that amount (assuming no other charitable gifts that year). Any excess is subject to the carryforward rule described above.[358] Thus, if Donor gave $50,000 in capital gain property to public charities in year one (and made no other charitable gifts that year), he or she would be entitled to a charitable contribution deduction of $30,000 in year one and $20,000 in year two.

A donor that makes gifts of cash and capital gain property to public charities (and/or private operating foundations) in any one year generally must use a blend of these percentage limitations.[359] For example, if Donor in year one gives $50,000 in cash and $30,000 in appreciated capital gain property to a public charity, his or her charitable deduction in year one consists of the $30,000 of capital gain property and $20,000 of cash (thereby capping the deduction with the overall 50 percent ceiling); the other $30,000 of cash is carried forward for deductibility (depending upon Donor's other circumstances) in year two.

A donor of capital gain property to public charities and/or private operating foundations may use the 50 percent limitation, instead of the 30 percent limitation, where the amount of the contribution is reduced by all of the unrealized appreciation in the value of the property.[360] This election, which is irrevocable,[361] is usually made in situations where the donor wants a larger deduction in the year of the gift and the property has not appreciated in value to a great extent. As discussed below, this election can be useful in avoiding a problem in relation to the alternative minimum tax.

The fourth and fifth percentage limitations apply with respect to gifts to private foundations and certain other charitable donees (other than public charities and private operating foundations). These "other charitable donees" are generally veterans' and fraternal organizations. For contributions of cash and ordinary income property to private foundations and these other entities, the deduction may not exceed 30 percent of the individual donor's contribution base.[362] The carryover rules apply to this type of gift. Thus, if Donor gives $50,000 in cash to one or more private foundations in year one, his or her charitable deduction for that year

---

[358] IRC § 170(b)(1)(C)(ii).
[359] IRC § 170(b)(1)(B).
[360] IRC § 170(b)(1)(C)(iii).
[361] *Woodbury* v. *Commissioner*, 65 AFTR 2d 90-973 (10th Cir. 1990).
[362] IRC § 170(b)(1)(B)(i).

(assuming no other charitable gifts) is $30,000, with the balance of $20,000 carried forward for potential deductibility in subsequent years.

These rules also blend with the percentage limitations applicable with respect to gifts to public charities. For example, if in year one Donor gave $65,000 to charity, of which $25,000 went to a public charity and $40,000 to a private foundation, his or her charitable deduction for that year would be $50,000, consisting of $30,000 of the gift to the private foundation and $20,000 of the gift to the public charity; the remaining $10,000 of the gift to the foundation and the remaining $5,000 of the gift to the public charity would be carried forward and made available for deductibility in year two.

The fifth percentage limitation is 20 percent of contribution base in the case of gifts of capital gain property to private foundations and other charitable donees (other than public charities and private operating foundations).[363] There is a carryforward for any excess deduction in the case of these gifts.[364] For example, if Donor gives appreciated securities, having a value of $30,000, to a private foundation in year one, his or her charitable deduction for year one (assuming no other charitable gifts) is $20,000; the remaining $10,000 would never be deductible. Of course, in this situation, Donor would contribute $20,000 of the securities in year one and postpone the gift of the remaining $10,000 in securities until year two. Or, if the value of the stock may substantially decline and an immediate charitable deduction is of prime concern, Donor could in year one donate $20,000 of the securities to the private foundation and donate $10,000 of the securities to a public charity.

Deductible charitable contributions by corporations in any tax year may not exceed 10 percent of pretax net income.[365] Excess amounts may be carried forward and deducted in subsequent years, up to five.[366] For gifts by corporations, the federal tax laws do not differentiate between gifts to public charities and private foundations. As an illustration, a corporation that grosses $1 million in a year and incurs $900,000 in expenses in that year (not including charitable gifts) may generally contribute to charity and deduct in that year an amount up to $10,000 (10 percent of $100,000); in computing its taxes, this corporation would report taxable income of $90,000. If the corporation instead gave $20,000

---

[363] IRC § 170(b)(1)(D)(i).
[364] IRC § 170(b)(1)(D)(ii).
[365] IRC § 170(b)(2).
[366] IRC § 170(d)(2).

in that year, the foregoing numbers would stay the same, except that the corporation would have a $10,000 charitable contribution carryforward.

A corporation on the accrual method of accounting can elect to treat a contribution as having been paid in a tax year if it is actually paid during the first 2½ months of the following year.[367] Corporate gifts of property are generally subject to the deduction reduction rules discussed below.

Deduction Reduction Rules

A donor (individual or corporate) that makes a gift of ordinary income property to any charity (public or private) must confine the charitable deduction to the amount of the cost basis of the property.[368] That is, the deduction is not based on the fair market value of the property; it must be reduced by the amount that would, if sold, have been gain (ordinary income). As an example, if Donor gave to a charity an item of ordinary income property having a value of $1,000 for which he or she paid $600, the charitable deduction would be $600.

Any donor who makes a gift of capital gain property to a public charity generally can, as noted above, compute the charitable deduction using the property's fair market value at the time of the gift, irrespective of basis and with no taxation of the appreciation (the capital gain inherent in the property). However, a donor who makes a gift of capital gain tangible personal property (for example, a work of art) to a public charity must reduce the deduction by all of the long-term capital gain that would have been recognized had the donor sold the property at its fair market value as of the date of contribution, where the use by the donee is unrelated to its tax-exempt purposes.[369]

Generally, a donor who makes a gift of capital gain property to a private foundation must reduce the amount of the otherwise allowable deduction by all of the appreciation element in the gift property.[370] However, an individual is allowed full fair market value for a contribution to a private foundation of certain publicly traded stock made before 1995.[371]

---

[367] IRC § 170(a)(2).
[368] IRC § 170(e)(1)(A).
[369] IRC § 170(e)(1)(B)(i).
[370] IRC § 170(e)(1)(B)(ii).
[371] IRC § 170(e)(5).

"Twice Basis" Deductions

As a general rule, when a corporation makes a charitable gift of property from its inventory, the resulting charitable deduction is confined to an amount equal to the donor's basis in the donated property. In most instances, this basis amount is rather small, being equal to the cost of producing the property. However, under certain circumstances, corporate donors can receive a greater charitable deduction for gifts out of their inventory. Where the tests are satisfied, the deduction can be equal to cost basis, plus one-half of the appreciated value of the property.[372] Nonetheless, this charitable deduction may not, in any event, exceed an amount equal to twice the property's cost basis.

There are five special requirements that have to be met for this twice-basis charitable deduction to be available: (1) the donated property must be used by the charitable donee for a related use; (2) the donated property must be used solely for the care of the ill, the needy, or infants; (3) the property may not be transferred by the donee in exchange for money, other property, or services; (4) the donor must receive a written statement from the donee representing that the use and disposition of the donated property will be in conformance with these rules; and (5) where the donated property is subject to regulation under the Federal Food, Drug, and Cosmetic Act, the property must fully satisfy the applicable requirements of that statute on the date of transfer and for 180 days prior thereto.

Also, for these rules to apply, the donee must be a public charity. That is, it cannot be a private foundation, including a private operating foundation. Further, an "S corporation"—the tax status of many small businesses—cannot utilize these rules.

A similar rule applies with respect to contributions of scientific property used for research.[373]

Alternative Minimum Tax

The alternative minimum tax is intended to cause an individual or corporate taxpayer, no matter how sophisticated his, her, or its financial affairs are structured from a tax point of view, to pay some tax. The alternative minimum tax is a flat tax of 21 percent, payable on the economic value

---

[372] IRC § 170(e)(3).
[373] IRC § 170(e)(4).

of a variety of "tax preference items," less certain adjustments.[374] This tax is to be paid when it is greater than the regular income tax.

One of the tax preference items used to construct the alternative minimum income tax base is an amount equal to the appreciation element inherent in the contributed capital gain property, to the extent it is included in the allowable charitable contribution deduction for regular income tax purposes.[375] This is termed the "appreciated property charitable deduction." For example, Donor gave $30,000 in appreciated securities to a public charity in a tax year and claimed an income tax deduction in that amount, having made no other charitable gifts that year. The securities had a cost basis of $10,000, so Donor has a tax preference item for alternative minimum tax purposes of $20,000.

However, this tax preference rule is inapplicable where the contributed appreciated property, normally subject to the above-described 30 percent limitation, is the subject of the elective 50 percent limitation.[376]

These rules do not apply with respect to charitable contributions made before August 16, 1986. However, these rules do apply to amounts arising out of such gifts that are carried forward and deducted in subsequent years.

Partial Interest Gifts

Most charitable gifts are of all interests in property, that is, by giving, the donor parts with all right, title, and interest in the property. But it is possible to make a deductible gift in the form of a contribution of less than a donor's entire interest in the property. This is termed a gift of a "partial interest."

As a general rule, charitable deductions for gifts of partial interests in property, including the right to use property, are denied.[377] But, the exceptions, which are many, are gifts made in trust form (using a so-called split-interest trust);[378] gifts of an outright remainder interest in a personal residence or farm;[379] gifts of an undivided portion of one's entire

---

[374] IRC § 55.
[375] IRC § 57(a)(6).
[376] IRC § 57(a)(6)(B), last sentence. This election is referenced in the text accompanying *supra* note 360.
[377] IRC § 170(f)(3)(A).
[378] IRC § 170(f)(2).
[379] IRC § 170(f)(3)(B)(i).

interest in property;[380] and a remainder interest in real property that is granted to a public charity exclusively for conservation purposes.[381]

Contributions of income interests in property in trust are basically confined to the use of charitable lead trusts.[382] Aside from the charitable gift annuity and the above-described gifts of remainder interests, there is no charitable deduction for a contribution of a remainder interest in property unless it is in trust and is one of three types: a charitable remainder annuity trust, a charitable remainder unitrust, or a pooled income fund.[383]

Defective charitable split-interest trusts may be reformed to preserve the charitable deduction where certain requirements are satisfied.[384]

Appraisal Rules

The law contains requirements relating to the proof of most charitable deductions for contributions of property claimed by an individual, a closely held corporation, a personal service corporation, a partnership, or an S corporation. These requirements, when applicable, must be complied with if the deduction is to be allowed.

The requirements apply to contributions of property (other than money and publicly traded securities) if the aggregate claimed or reported value of the property (and all similar items of property for which deductions for charitable contributions are claimed or reported by the same donor for the same tax year whether or not donated to the same donee) is in excess of $5,000.[385] The phrase "similar items of property" means property of the same generic category or type, including stamps, coins, lithographs, paintings, books, nonpublicly traded stock, land, or buildings.

For this type of gift, the donor must obtain a "qualified appraisal" and attach an "appraisal summary" to the return on which the deduction is claimed. However, in the case of nonpublicly traded stock, the claimed value of which does not exceed $10,000 but is greater than $5,000, the donor does not have to obtain a qualified appraisal but must attach a

---

[380] IRC § 170(f)(3)(B)(ii).

[381] IRC §§ 170(f)(3)(B)(iii) & 170(h).

[382] IRC § 170(f)(2)(B).

[383] IRC § 170(f)(2)(A). The concept of partial interest gifts from the standpoint of planned gifts is discussed in *Starting and Managing A Nonprofit Organization* at 193–200.

[384] IRC § 170(f)(7).

[385] IRC § 170(a)(1); Reg. § 1.170A-13(c).

partially completed appraisal summary form to the tax or information return on which the deduction is claimed.

A "qualified appraisal" is an appraisal document that (1) relates to an appraisal that is made no more than 60 days prior to the date of the contribution of the appraised property; (2) is prepared, signed, and dated by a "qualified appraiser" (or appraisers); and (3) does not involve a prohibited type of appraisal fee (see below).

Certain information must be included in the qualified appraisal: (1) a sufficiently detailed description of the property; (2) the physical condition of the property (in the case of tangible property; (3) the date (or expected date) of contribution; (4) the terms of any agreement or understanding concerning the use or disposition of the property; (5) the name, address, and social security number of the appraiser; (6) the qualifications of the qualified appraiser (or appraisers); (7) a statement that the appraisal was prepared for tax purposes; (8) the date or dates on which the property was valued; (9) the appraised fair market value of the property on the date (or expected date) of contribution; (10) the method of valuation used to determine the fair market value; (11) the specific basis for the valuation; and (12) a description of the fee arrangement between the donor and the appraiser.

The qualified appraisal must be received by the donor before the due date (including extensions) of the return on which the deduction for the contributed property is first claimed or, in the case of a deduction first claimed on an amended return, the date on which the return is filed.

A separate qualified appraisal is required for each item of property that is not included in a group of similar items of property. One qualified appraisal is required for a group of similar items of property contributed in the same tax year, as long as the appraisal includes all of the required information for each item. However, the appraiser may select any items the aggregate value of which is appraised at $100 or less, for which a group description—rather than a specific description of each item—is adequate.

The "appraisal summary" must be on IRS Form 8283, signed and dated by the donee and qualified appraiser (or appraisers), and attached to the donor's return on which a deduction with respect to the appraised property is first claimed or reported. The signature by the donee does not represent concurrence in the appraised value of the contributed property.

Certain information must be included in the appraisal summary: (1) the name and taxpayer identification number of the donor; (2) a sufficient description of the property; (3) a summary of the physical condition of the property (in the case of tangible property); (4) the manner and date of acquisition of the property; (5) the basis of the property; (6) the name, address, and taxpayer identification number of the donee; (7) the date the donee received the property; (8) the name, address, and taxpayer identification number of the qualified appraiser (or appraisers); (9) the appraised fair market value of the property on the date of contribution; and (10) a declaration by the appraiser.

The rules pertaining to separate appraisals, summarized above, also apply with respect to appraisal summaries. However, a donor who contributes similar items of property to more than one charitable donee must attach a separate appraisal summary for each donee.

If the donor is a partnership or S corporation, it must provide a copy of the appraisal summary to every partner or shareholder who receives an allocation of a deduction for a charitable contribution of property described in the appraisal summary. The partner or shareholder must attach the appraisal summary to that partner's or shareholder's return.

The term "qualified appraiser" is an individual who includes on the appraisal summary a declaration that (1) he or she holds himself or herself out to the public as an appraiser; (2) because of the appraiser's qualifications as described in the appraisal, he or she is qualified to make appraisals of the type of property being valued; and (3) he or she understands that a false or fraudulent overstatement of the value of the property described in the qualified appraisal or appraisal summary may subject the appraiser to a civil penalty for aiding and abetting an understatement of tax liability, and consequently the appraiser may have appraisals disregarded.

Notwithstanding these requirements, an individual is not a qualified appraiser if the donor had knowledge of facts that would cause a reasonable person to expect the appraiser to falsely overstate the value of the donated property. Also, the donor, donee, or certain other related persons cannot be a "qualified appraiser" of the property involved in the transaction. (In formulating these rules, the government thus rejected thoughts of including in the criteria certain professional standards or the establishment of a registry of qualified appraisers.) More than one appraiser may appraise donated property, as long as each appraiser complies with the requirements.

Generally, no part of the fee arrangement for a qualified appraisal can be based, in effect, on a percentage (or set of percentages) of the appraised value of the property. If a fee arrangement is based in whole or in part on the amount of the appraised value of the property that is allowed as a charitable deduction, it is treated as a fee based on a percentage of the appraised value of the property. (This rule does not

apply in certain circumstances to appraisal fees paid to a generally recognized association that regulates appraisers.)

Record-Keeping Rules

Concerning contributions of money to charity, a corporate or individual
donor must keep some record of the gift. Preferably, this record will
be a cancelled check or a receipt. Otherwise, the record must be "written"
and "reliable." The record must show the name of the donee, the date
of the contribution, and the amount of the contribution.

A letter or other communication from the recipient charity acknowl-
edging receipt of the contribution, and showing the date and amount
of the contribution, constitutes a "receipt." A donor has the burden of
establishing "reliability" of a written record other than a check or receipt.
Factors indicating that such other written evidence is "reliable" include
the contemporaneous nature of the writing that evidences the contribution,
the regularity of the donor's record-keeping procedures, and—in the
case of a contribution of a "small amount"—any other written evidence
from the charity evidencing the making of a gift that would not otherwise
constitute a "receipt" (such as an emblem or a button).

As for contributions of property other than money to charity, a corporate
or individual donor must obtain a receipt from the recipient charitable
organization and a reliable written record of specified information with
respect to the donated property.

This receipt must include the name of the donee, the date and location
of the contribution, and a description of the property in detail that is
reasonable under the circumstances (including the value of the property).
However, a receipt is not required in instances where the gift is made
in circumstances in which it is impractical to obtain a receipt.

Also, the donor of property that has appreciated in value must maintain
a "reliable written record" of specified information with respect to each
item of property. This information must include (1) the name and address
of the charitable donee; (2) the date and location of the contribution; (3)
a description of the property in detail reasonable under the circumstances
(including the value of the property) and, in the case of securities, the
name of the issuing company, the type of security, and whether or not
it is regularly traded on a stock exchange or in an over-the-counter
market; (4) the fair market value of the property at the time of the gift,
the method utilized in determining the value, and a copy of the signed
report of any appraiser; (5) the cost or other basis of the property if it
is "ordinary income property" or other type of property where the de-

duction must be reduced by the gain (see above); (6) where the gift is of a "remainder interest" or an "income interest,"[386] the total amount claimed as a deduction for the year due to the gift and the amount claimed as a deduction in any prior year or years for gifts of other interests in the property; and (7) the terms of any agreement or understanding concerning the use or disposition of the property, such as any restriction on the charity's right to use or dispose of the property, a retention or conveyance of the right to the income from the donated property, or an earmarking of the property for a particular use.

Additional rules apply with respect to charitable gifts of property other than money for which the donor claims a deduction in excess of $500. In this situation, the donor is required to maintain additional records, regarding the manner of acquisition of the property and the property's cost or other basis if it was held for less than six months prior to the date of gift. For property held for six months or more preceding the date of contribution, the cost or other basis information must be maintained by the donor if it is available.

Reporting Rules

A charitable organization donee, that sells or otherwise disposes of gift property within two years after receipt of the property, generally must file an information return (Form 8282) with the IRS.[387] (There is an exception for property that is disposed of as part of the organization's exempt program activity.) A copy of this information return must be provided to the donor and retained by the donee.

This information return must include the following: (1) the name, address, and taxpayer identification number of the donor and the donee; (2) a sufficient description of the property; (3) the date of the contribution; (4) the amount received on the disposition; and (5) the date of the disposition.

A donee that receives a charitable contribution valued in excess of $5,000 from a corporation generally does not have to file a donee information return.

---

[386] See *supra* notes 377–83.
[387] IRC § 6050L; Reg. § 1.6050L-1.

7

Prospective Federal Regulation of Fund-Raising: Proposals and Issues

Federal regulation of fund-raising by and on behalf of charities is a present reality, as discussed in the previous chapter, notwithstanding the absence of a general statute on the subject.

Nonetheless, a federal law monitoring, supervising, and/or regulating interstate fund-raising for charitable organizations appears likely. The question is no longer whether but when this type of law will be enacted—and why. At this point, it appears that such a law will begin with disclosure, expand along the way to regulate fund-raising expenses, and build from there.

There is a remarkable lack of consensus—within and without Congress—about the appropriate features and reach of this type of law. This is probably the single most important factor preventing enactment of a federal fund-raising regulation statute sooner rather than later.

§ 7.1 Introduction

Historically, the responsibility for regulating and otherwise monitoring the process by which organizations solicit contributions for charitable purposes has been left to the states, with some collateral assistance by counties and cities. However, the present manner of state and local regulation of interstate charitable solicitations has produced considerable confusion and has, in many respects, been ineffective. These statutes and ordinances involve a bewildering myriad of different forms, due dates, and accounting requirements. At the same time, state and local regulation of fund-raising has enjoyed some successes in monitoring and curbing abuses in intrastate fund-raising practices.

It is, of course, difficult for a charitable organization that is soliciting financial assistance across the states to comply with or even be aware of each of the various state statutes and local ordinances. As discussed above,[1] the exemptions may be unclear and inconsistent, the requirements for registration and reporting are different, the deadlines are dissimilar and, in general, the compliance effort can be a time-consuming and confusing one. Indeed, the above survey of these state requirements does not disclose what may be the most difficult aspect of the entire process: the multiplicity of varying application, registration, and reporting forms, which contain a wide range of questions, differing accounting requirements, and more.

Frankly, the only factor that may be keeping the present multifarious system of differing requirements from becoming totally impossible to adhere to is the lack of enforcement by a sizable number of regulatory agencies. There are indications, however, that the enforcement attitude is changing, in part because of the more frequently used technique of soliciting funds by mail and the attendant abuses that are finding their way into media exposés. Today it is obviously a calculated risk at best for a charitable organization to ignore a charitable solicitation regulation requirement in the expectation or hope that the activities in violation of the requirement will escape enforcement.

One solution to the present jumble of conflicting and complicated requirements for complying with governmental regulation of fund-raising activities would be to bring uniformity to such requirements. Despite intensive and excellent efforts by the National Health Council and others, state and local governments have been unwilling (with minor exceptions) to voluntarily adopt common reporting requirements, forms, accounting principles, exemptions, and the like. Nor has a model state statute generated any interest, although contributions by the accounting profession and nonprofit organizations such as the National Assembly of National Health and Welfare Agencies and the United Way of America in developing standardized legislative provisions have been extensive.[2] Consequently, a federal statute is being viewed by many as the sole feasible solution, in part because no progress is being made toward the establishment of systems of uniform reporting and perhaps enforcement.

---

[1] See Ch. 4.

[2] An analysis of state laws regulating charitable solicitations, accompanied by a model statute, is available in National Health Council, *Viewpoints on State and Local Legislation Regulating Solicitation of Funds From the Public* (rev. ed. 1976).

As may be expected, many insist that a federal government entry into this field is unwarranted. This position is usually based on the belief that federal regulatory authority over charitable organizations is already too pervasive, or that present state and local law enforcement with respect to charitable solicitations is sufficient, or that the abuses in fund-raising for charitable purposes that have surfaced to date are isolated instances that fail to command remedial action by means of federal law.

These are legitimate and debatable points. The fact is, however, that more and more legislators in the Congress, and regulators in the Department of the Treasury and the IRS, are arriving at the conclusion that a federal statute in this field is now necessary.

A statute at the federal level in the field of fund-raising for charity was one of the recommendations of the Commission on Private Philanthropy and Public Needs.[3] Such a law was also advocated by the Department of the Treasury in the waning days of the Ford Administration.[4] The necessity and parameters of such a law are periodically under examination at the Treasury Department and IRS; a specific proposal may be anticipated should Congress call for these agencies' views on the subject or if there is a public outcry (such as in response to a well-publicized scandal) for remedial action.

Consequently, a working assumption—palatable or not—must be that a federal charitable solicitations statute is forthcoming. Therefore, it is appropriate to consider the components and extent of such a law.

The design of a charitable fund-raising supervision bill necessarily depends upon the motives of those formulating it. Some seek to expose to the public those organizations that are "inefficiently" managed and/or that have "excessive" fund-raising costs. Others have a more encompassing objective, perceiving the appropriate purpose of this type of law to be "consumer protection," which becomes translated into a proposed scheme of disclosure on a much more extensive, and at the same time more specific, scale. For still others, the matter of regulating fund-raising costs, and otherwise regulating fund-raising, is viewed as merely part of a much larger purpose, which is the regulation of public charities (that is, charitable organizations other than private foundations)[5] in relation to the conduct of their programs and other practices. Some of the individuals in this last category, including some in the legislative and executive branches of the federal government, desire not only a national

---

[3] See *infra* § 7.3.
[4] *Ibid.*
[5] See Ch. 6 § 6.8.

charitable solicitations regulation law but also the imposition of the vast panoply of laws at present applicable to private foundations (principally the prohibitions on self-dealing, excess business holdings, and jeopardy investments, and the rules mandating minimum payout of funds and restricting the uses of such funds) on the affairs of public charities.[6]

If it is assumed, then, that a federal charitable solicitations law and disclosure of fund-raising costs as a part thereof is inevitable, consideration may be given to the specific components and scope of such a law.

§ 7.2   Legislative Proposals

In recent years, principally five bills have been introduced in Congress on this subject. These measures are the "Wilson bill," the "Van Deerlin bill," the "Mondale bill," the "Owens bill," and the "Luken bill." The "Metzenbaum bill" has been drafted but not yet introduced.

The Wilson Bill

The Wilson bill, as introduced in various forms by then-Congressman Charles H. Wilson (D-Cal.),[7] would engraft federal fund-raising regulation

---

[6] *Ibid.*

[7] This legislation originated as H.R. 9584, 93d Cong., 1st Sess. (1973), and was reintroduced as H.R. 5269, 94th Cong., 1st Sess. (1975). Following a hearing on July 30, 1975, the measure emerged as H.R. 10922, 94th Cong., 1st Sess. (1975), which was reported by the then-named House Committee on Post Office and Civil Service (H. Rep. No. 94–1135, 94th Cong., 2d Sess. (1976)). The bill was again reintroduced as H.R. 41, 95th Cong., 1st Sess. (1977), and underwent three days of hearings before the House Subcommittee on Postal Personnel and Modernization (of which Mr. Wilson was chairman) on March 24, 29, and 30, 1977. For lack of support in the philanthropic community and in Congress, H.R. 41 (as amended in the subcommittee on July 25, 1977) progressed no further during the 95th Congress and died upon its adjournment in 1978. The measure was again introduced in 1979 as H.R. 875, 96th Cong., 1st Sess. (1979) but no further action was ever taken on it.

A somewhat comparable bill was H.R. 11991, 93d Cong., 2d Sess. (1974), introduced by then-Congressman Lionel Van Deerlin (D-Cal.), and reintroduced as H.R. 1123, 94th Cong., 1st Sess. (1975). Hearings were held on the Van Deerlin legislation on Jan. 14, 1975. This legislation would have vested fund-raising regulation authority in the Department of Commerce.

Legislation titled the "Charitable Solicitation Disclosure Act," that would require disclosure of information in the course of fund-raising by mail, was introduced in 1987, as H.R. 2130, 100th Cong., 1st Sess. (1987), by Congressman onto the postal laws, by investing the U.S. Postal Service with authority to monitor fund-raising for charitable purposes as part of its mail fraud investigative and enforcement functions.

The legislation would be generally applicable to "[a]ny charitable organization which solicits, in any manner or through any means, the remittance of a contribution by mail." An organization to which the proposed law would apply would have to disclose certain specified information in the literature used in the solicitation process, including the amount expended for charitable purposes during its preceding fiscal year, expressed as a single percentage. (However, the percentage rule would not become effective until three years after the effective date of the act.) Comparable rules would apply to audio and visual communications. A soliciting organization would be required, within 30 days after the request, to provide a person with a financial statement for its most recent full fiscal year, prepared in accordance with generally accepted accounting principles.

Exceptions would be available for solicitations of organizations' "constituencies," such as solicitations by bona fide membership groups (including local religious congregations or parishes) exclusively of their members; by schools, colleges, and universities (and their supporting foundations) exclusively of their students, alumni, faculty, trustees, committee members, and family members of these individuals; and by hospitals or other health care facilities (and their supporting foundations) exclusively of their professional staff, other personnel, trustees, committee members, and family members of these individuals.

Although enforcement of this proposed law would be a responsibility of the Postal Service, there was considerable desire by the author of the measure to not create a massive regulatory bureaucracy. Thus, the final versions of the bill expressly prohibited the Postal Service from requiring charitable organizations to furnish it at regular intervals with audit reports, accounts, or other information, or from prescribing any rules or regulations to carry out the provisions of the statutory law.

The Wilson bill basically addressed the matter of federal charitable fund-raising regulation as a consumer protection effort, emphasizing public disclosure by charitable organizations rather than governmental regulation of them.

Major R. Owens (D-N.Y.). The measure was reintroduced in the next Congress as H.R. 1257, 101st Cong., 1st Sess. (1989). Referred to the Subcommittee on Postal Personnel and Modernization of the House Committee on Post Office and Civil Service, the bill has not advanced.

The Mondale Bill

The Mondale bill, as originally authored by then-Senator Walter F. Mondale (D-Minn.),[8] was written with the attitude that charitable organizations and their solicitations need to be strenuously regulated by the federal government.

The Mondale proposal would add requirements to the Internal Revenue Code pursuant to which certain types of "publicly supported charities" and related entities would have to distribute at least 50 percent of their gross revenues each year for charitable purposes. Expenditures for salaries (except for persons performing services in furtherance of charitable programs), outlays for office facilities, administrative expenses, and fund-raising expenses would not qualify as expenditures for charitable purposes.

Public charities subject to the Mondale bill requirements would be those receiving a substantial part of their support from the general public or organizations supportive of them.[9] Thus, the measure would not apply to institutions such as churches, colleges, universities, hospitals, and medical research organizations. Also, the bill's requirements would not apply to any organization with revenues of $25,000 or less in a tax year.

Charitable organizations subject to the Mondale bill provisions would have to annually prepare and file with the IRS information (in addition to that required in the annual information return) for determination by the IRS as to whether this 50 percent payout requirement has been met. These data would have to be prepared by a certified public accountant in accordance with approved uniform accounting principles. This annual report would also have to be filed with the appropriate officials in each state where a solicitation of contributions is made.

A public charity subject to these requirements would be required to furnish prospective contributors with adequate information regarding its revenues and expenditures for charitable purposes and for other

---

[8] This legislation, titled the "Truth in Contributions Act," was originally introduced as S. 1153, 94th Cong., 1st Sess. (1975), following hearings before the Senate Subcommittee on Children and Youth (of which Mr. Mondale then was chairman) on Feb. 4, 5 and 6, and March 11 and 12, 1974. It was introduced in the House of Representatives by now-retired Congressman Joseph E. Karth (D-Minn.) as H.R. 4689, 94th Cong., 1st Sess. (1975), and subsequently by Congressman William Lehman (D-Fla.) as H.R. 478, 95th Cong., 1st Sess. (1977). The measure was not reintroduced in subsequent Congresses.

[9] Specifically, this law would apply to those organizations whose public charity status is derived from IRC § 170(b)(1)(A)(vi), 509(a)(2), or 509(a)(3). See Ch. 6 § 6.8.

purposes during the previous year. This information would have to be disclosed at the time of the solicitation, regardless of the manner or the medium used. A "disclosure statement" would be required, which would have to be approved (or at least not disapproved) by the IRS. This statement would have to be mailed within 15 days to any person upon request and would have to be filed with the appropriate officials in each state where a solicitation is undertaken.

These requirements would be enforced by a system of excise taxes, as is presently the nature of the enforcement scheme underpinning the private foundation rules.[10] The measure would extend the termination rules, now applicable only to private foundations, to this category of public charities and would impose civil and criminal penalties on organizations or persons responsible for a failure to comply with these various requirements.

The bill would direct the Department of the Treasury to develop standard accounting principles for public charities. The department would also be required to encourage state and local governments to accept filings made in compliance with this law in lieu of separate local reports.

Thus, the Mondale bill approached the matter of federal law applicability to charitable solicitations by the proposed establishment of rather stringent regulatory authority.

The Luken Bill

An effort is under way to invest the Federal Trade Commission[11] with authority to investigative and regulate fund-raising for charitable purposes. On July 28, 1989, hearings on this subject were held before the Subcommittee on Transportation, Tourism, and Hazardous Materials of the House Committee on Energy and Commerce. This subcommittee is interested in charitable fund-raising because it has jurisdiction over the FTC, and the chairman of the subcommittee, Congressman Thomas A. Luken (D-Ohio), is of the view that the FTC should investigate and curtail certain direct mail fund-raising efforts, such as the use of misleading sweepstakes.

The regulatory community is showing renewed interest in direct mail sweepstakes as a fund-raising form, in part because, all too often, little of the money raised goes for charitable purposes and in part because the promised prizes rarely materialize. Some states' attorneys general

[10] IRC Ch. 42.
[11] Hereinafter, the FTC.

are suing direct mail promotion firms over the issue and the U.S. Postal Service has become involved. The basis for these actions are allegations of fraud and other deceptive practices.

Recent history of this matter includes an inquiry to the FTC from Congressman Edward F. Feighan (D-Ohio) in December 1987, requesting information about certain fund-raising programs, including a sweepstakes appeal. The FTC response and subsequent action has been less than satisfactory to the House members, thus prompting a more formal inquiry.

The present jurisdiction of the FTC in these regards is not clear. The FTC has some jurisdiction over nonprofit organizations, but the extent of the reach is uncertain. Of course, the FTC has jurisdiction over direct mail companies and other for-profit fund-raising entities.

Under existing law, the FTC must go through the exercise of determining its jurisdiction in the case before it can review the case on its substantive merits. One of the points of the congressional inquiry was to determine whether the FTC's jurisdiction should be clarified in relation to charitable fund-raising, so that the agency's resources would not be depleted in precomplaint investigations.

The ability of the FTC to investigate, make rules, and enforce law in this field is uncertain. Apparently its staff resources are somewhat limited.

At the hearings, the FTC representatives testified that the agency welcomes the clarification as to its jurisdication and responsibility for investigating abuses in the field of fund-raising for charitable purposes.

Thereafter, Congressman Luken introduced legislation that would amend the Federal Trade Commission Act to empower the FTC to regulate the fund-raising activities of charitable organizations.[12] The proposal would accord the FTC jurisdiction over nonprofit organizations. The bill would require a charity that uses a professional fund-raiser[13] in connection with the solicitation of funds to provide at the time of the solicitation to each person solicited a "clear and conspicuous" statement that the fund-raising is "being conducted by" the fund-raising professional, containing the name and address of the fund-raiser. The FTC would be required to promulgate uniform accounting principles governing the costs of fund-raising for charitable purposes. A professional fund-raiser would be required to report annually to "appropriate State agencies the

---

[12] H.R. 3964, 101st Cong., 2d Sess. (1990), titled the "Fair Fund-Raising Act of 1990."

[13] The term "professional fund-raiser" would be defined as "a person who engages in solicitation for a charity for compensation and who is not an employee of the charity for whom the solicitation is made."

amounts charged each charity for its services and the amount raised for each charity." It would prevent a charitable organization[14] from having an individual serve as an officer or director of it where he or she is also an officer, director, or agent of a "professional fund-raising organization" that is employed by the charity. The requirement of a statement to prospective donees and the prohibition on interlocking directorates between charities and professional fund-raisers would preempt any state or local law that is "inconsistent" with the requirements, although a state or political subdivision would be able to secure a waiver of the preemption where the FTC determined that the requirement of state or local law "affords an equal or greater level of protection to the public" than would be afforded by the preemptive requirements.

When introducing the legislation, Congressman Luken said that the measure "will help stamp out modern peddlers of deceit, who use sophisticated technology to raise money in a way that cheats many people, particularly the elderly, and injures legitimate charities by siphoning off much needed money."[15]

The Metzenbaum Bill

The most recent effort in Congress to enact a fund-raising regulation bill has been initiated by Senator Howard Metzenbaum (D-Ohio), who is authoring a "Truth in Fund-Raising Act."

This proposal would utilize the federal tax rules to create a new disclosure requirement.[16] The disclosure rule would be applicable to nearly all tax-exempt organizations. Technically, this law would be applicable to all organizations that are required to file annual information returns[17] with the IRS, other than those that have annual gross receipts that normally are not more than $50,000.[18]

The specific rule underlying this proposed legislation is that a fund-raising solicitation by or on behalf of a tax-exempt organization must contain an "express statement (in a conspicuous and easily recognizable format) setting forth the exempt purpose expenditure percentage."

---

[14] As defined in this legislation, a "charitable" organization is one that has its federal income tax exemption based upon IRC § 501(c)(3) or 501(c)(4).
[15] News Release dated Feb. 6, 1990.
[16] Proposed IRC § 6115.
[17] Form 990.
[18] IRC § 6033.

The term "fund-raising solicitation" would be the same as that under the disclosure rules.[19] That is, it is a solicitation of contributions which is made in written or printed form, by television or radio, or by telephone.

The term "exempt purpose expenditure percentage" would be determined by using the figures for the year immediately preceding the year in which the solicitation took place. For example, if the disclosure was to take place in 1991 and the organization uses the calendar year as its fiscal year, the organization would compute the percentage using 1990 figures. If this organization received $1 million in gifts in 1990 and had a fund-raising cost of $100,000, its exempt purpose expenditure percentage would be 90 percent.

Thus, this organization, in all of its fund-raising during 1991, would be required to conspicuously state that 90 percent of its gift support went to program. The same would be true for an organization that had a 1990 fund-raising cost of 60 percent, except that its exempt purpose expenditure percentage would be 40 percent.

The legislation would not allow for the allocation of costs between program and fund-raising. The draft bill specifically states that "the cost of any solicitation shall include the entire cost of preparing and disseminating the written or printed form, television or radio advertisement, or telephone call of which it is a part." This would prevent the cost of, for example, a direct mail letter from being allocated part to program (education) and part to fund-raising.

In computing gift support, an organization would not be able to include funds derived from a grant from a governmental unit or from any tax-exempt organization.

The penalty for violation of this law would be $1,000 for each day on which a failure to comply occurred.[20]

This legislative proposal was endorsed by some state officials at a hearing held before the Senate Judiciary Subcommittee on Antitrust, Monopolies, and Business Rights on December 15, 1989. The subcommittee is chaired by Senator Metzenbaum.

§ 7.3   The Emerging Issues

The prospects of a federal law regulating charitable solicitations raise a host of questions for philanthropy. These include (1) the extent of the

[19] IRC § 6113(c). See Ch. 6 § 6.3.
[20] IRC § 6710(a),(d).

federal government role, that is, whether it should be confined only to disclosure or more extensive (private foundation-like) regulation; (2) the nature and scope of the disclosure requirements; (3) the appropriate enforcement agency or agencies, for example, the IRS, Department of the Treasury, Department of Commerce, Postal Service, Federal Trade Commission, or some new agency; (4) the extent of any preemption of state and local laws and responsibilities; (5) the appropriate category or categories of charities or other tax-exempt organizations to be encompassed by this type of statute; (6) the impact of such legislation on the already existing pressure for uniform accounting principles for nonprofit organizations; and (7) the nature of the sanctions to be applied. Still another question: When will this new law be enacted?

Necessity of More Rules

As noted, many are skeptical of the need for more law in the charitable solicitations field. However, if the issue concerns the appropriateness of a law requiring the disclosure or availability of pertinent information concerning a charitable organization to those individuals who have been solicited for a charitable contribution to that organization (and who lack another means for obtaining that information, such as a membership status in the organization), it is difficult to find a basis for contending against such a law. It is equally difficult to argue against a law designed to eliminate the criminal, fraudulent, and/or unscrupulous solicitor from the "marketplace" of charitable giving. One can argue against the specifics of such laws but not against the concept; many precedents for such an approach are embedded in the United States legal system, and this approach is being expanded as the consumer protection movement gains momentum.

This assumes, of course, that one can make the case that a sufficient number of charitable solicitations are being conducted by the abusive and the unscrupulous to warrant corrective action. Because of the exploits of a few, many believe that this case can be made. It must also be assumed that self-regulation by the philanthropic community, as valuable as such regulation is, cannot generate the requisite degree of disclosure to the public of the activities and financial practices of charitable organizations.

Assuming, then, that this type of law—as a concept—is necessary, the next question must be whether there should be laws at the state and local level or law on the federal level. For the most part, the answer to this question will depend upon one's view of our system of government and general political philosophy and whether federal law would preempt state and local law.

Many believe that a scheme of well-written uniform state laws fairly and uniformly enforced would be preferable to federal law. Others contend that the existing state and local law picture is one of statutes and ordinances that are poorly conceived, poorly written, and poorly enforced. Thus, some would assert that the entire system should be scrapped as far as solicitations in interstate commerce are concerned and replaced by a well-written effective federal law. By contrast, others would argue that the solution lies with uniform requirements, accounting standards, reporting forms, and the like.

Mode of Disclosure

The previously discussed bills embody the point-of-solicitation disclosure concept. For example, the Wilson bill would require the solicitation to include a statement of the "purpose of the solicitation and the intended use of the contribution solicited." The Wilson bill also would require the information to be included with a written solicitation to be "presented in language which is readily understandable by those persons to whom the solicitation is directed, . . . be located in a conspicuous place on such solicitation, and . . . appear in conspicuous and legible type in contrast by topography, layout, or color with other printed matter on such solicitation." The Metzenbaum bill reflects today's penchant for the use of percentages.

The point-of-disclosure solicitation approach is also frequently accompanied by a requirement that the charity supply additional information (including a financial statement) to the public upon request, with notice of the availability of such information to accompany the solicitation. Under the Wilson bill, this additional information would have to be provided within 30 days after receipt of a request for it. Under the Mondale bill, as noted, a disclosure statement would have to be mailed within 15 days to any person upon request. Provision of information to the federal enforcement agency would be still another disclosure and data dissemination requirement.

Under the disclosure-on-demand approach, the solicitation material would have to contain a statement notifying the recipient of his or her right to information about the soliciting charitable organization. A recipient of a charitable solicitation would have, e.g., 180 days to request the information and the organization would have, e.g., 30 days within which to respond.

One can argue that all that is required is a federal statute mandating every charitable organization to provide to whomever requests it a copy of an annual report containing financial statements which, among other elements, would state fund-raising costs. A notice of the availability of this report could accompany the solicitation. Perhaps this report could be the information return that charitable organizations annually file with the IRS (Form 990), although if so, the contents of that filing would probably have to be expanded.

Disclosure of Fund-Raising Costs

A federal charitable solicitations law will likely provide for disclosure of a charitable organization's fund-raising costs. A principal issue, however, is the appropriate format and method of such disclosure.

The question of format is entangled in the issue of whether disclosure in general is to be accomplished by the point-of-solicitation or disclosure-on-demand approach, as discussed above. As to method, this issue has become narrowed to two positions: presentation of fund-raising costs as a line item as part of a general financial statement or expression of fund-raising costs as a single percentage of receipts. The Mondale bill utilizes the first approach; the Wilson and Metzenbaum bills have as one of their key provisions the second approach.

The Wilson bill would require a charitable organization to state its outlays for charitable purposes as a percentage and do so on the solicitation materials. Such a percentage would be based on the prior year's financial data. The Metzenbaum measure is based upon a comparable approach. The deficiencies of this requirement have been discussed above.

The ultimate resolution of the matter of the method of fund-raising costs disclosure will probably be a by-product of the point-of-solicitation versus disclosure-on-demand conflict. However, if a single fund-raising cost percentage remains a requirement of a federal charitable solicitations law, consideration should be given to the use of a three- or four-year moving average rather than a single year's performance. As noted, Congress at present requires the utilization of such a computation in assessing a charitable organization's eligibility for nonprivate-foundation status.[21]

Uniform Accounting Principles

A federal charitable solicitations law would be a major force for adoption of uniform accounting principles throughout the nonprofit organization

---

[21] IRC §§ 170(b)(1)(A)(vi)/509(a)(1) & 509(a)(2). See Ch. 6 § 6.8.

community. (It may be noted that uniform accounting principles for nonprofit organizations seem inevitable for other reasons.) At present, colleges and universities, hospitals, voluntary health and social welfare organizations, and other organizations observe varying accounting standards.[22]

The issue of the proper method of disclosure of fund-raising costs will likely depend on the requirements of the applicable set of generally accepted accounting principles. This is a matter which transcends current federal legislative developments because of the ferment—which is co-incidental but exceedingly pertinent—taking place at this time within the accounting profession. These developments are far from incidental, inasmuch as federal law may require that the financial statements of covered philanthropic organizations be prepared and/or be the subject of a favorable opinion by a certified public accountant. This means that such statements will have to be prepared in accordance with "generally accepted accounting principles."

The American Institute of Certified Public Accountants promulgates rules by which financial statements are to be prepared if they are to be in conformance with "generally accepted accounting principles." For colleges and universities, hospitals, and voluntary health and welfare organizations, the AICPA has issued such rules in the form of "audit guides."[23] (A fourth audit guide applies to state and local government units.) The AICPA also has developed a set of accounting principles and reporting practices for nonprofit organizations not covered by an existing audit guide (such as private schools, clubs, civic associations, and political

[22] Much has been written on the subject of uniform accounting principles for charitable and other nonprofit organizations. For example, the National Health Council, National Assembly of National Voluntary Health and Welfare Organizations (formerly National Social Welfare Assembly), and the United Way of America have published *Standards of Accounting and Financial Reporting for Voluntary Health and Social Welfare Organizations* (rev. ed. 1976). The National Association of College and University Business Officers has published accounting standards for institutions of higher education, entitled *College and University Business Administration*. In general, see Gross, Jr., & Warshauer, Jr., *Financial and Accounting Guide for Nonprofit Organizations* (3d ed. 1979); Anthony, *Financial Accounting in Nonbusiness Organizations* (1978); Robinson, "The Accounting Revolution Is Coming," XIII *The Philanthropy Monthly* (No. 4) 5 (1980).

[23] *Industry Audit Guide—Audits of Voluntary Health and Welfare Organizations* (1974); *Industry Audit Guide—Audits of Colleges and Universities* (1973); and *Industry Audit Guide—Audits of Hospitals* (1972).

organizations).[24] Many regard these proposed principles and practices as the beginning of development of a single package of accounting standards to be uniformly adhered to by all categories of nonprofit (including philanthropic) organizations.

Congressman Wilson repeatedly stated that it was not the intention of his legislation to have the Postal Service itself design accounting principles for charitable organizations but rather to incorporate by reference existing accounting standards in its enforcement of this law. Such standards would presumably include not only those in the AICPA audit guides and the principles for other nonprofit organizations but also other standards.[25] Thus, the Wilson bill contemplated the retention and use of uniform accounting standards for different categories of charitable organizations.

The Mondale bill would impose much more detailed obligations in this regard. As part of the annual information return (Form 990) filing requirements, a public charity (as defined) would be mandated to report its annual gross income "on a fund accounting basis in which restricted and unrestricted sources of revenue are clearly distinguished, broken down into such categories as are appropriate for their organization." Expenses would be reported "on a functional basis in which program costs, administrative and fund-raising expenses are reported separately, and in which the program expenses are also broken down to show each of the major programs carried out by the organization together with expenses applicable to more than one program or functional category being allocated as appropriate in accordance with generally accepted accounting principles or standards."[26]

This and other information would have to be accompanied by a statement by a certified public accountant that the return was prepared in conformance with generally accepted accounting principles. The Treasury Department would be authorized to require reporting of additional information that is determined to be "necessary to inform prospective contributors of the activities and fiscal policies of the public charity, and to present fairly the financial status of the public charity." Moreover, the Mondale bill, as part of the requirement of a separate annual report, would have mandated preparation of that document in conformance with

---

[24] Statement of Position 78-10 (1978).

[25] See *supra* note 21.

[26] Without waiting for such legislative authority, the IRS has engrafted the functional method of accounting requirements onto the Form 990. See Ch. 6 § 6.2.

generally accepted accounting principles and a statement by a certified public accountant to that effect.

The matter of disclosure of fund-raising costs is, of course, very much intertwined with the matter of the applicable accounting standards. Of great concern must be the manner in which the pertinent accounting standards define the term "fund-raising costs." In many instances, such as with respect to programs and publications of schools, colleges, and universities in relation to their alumni and membership organizations, it may be difficult to ascertain the extent to which the costs of such endeavors are properly regarded as being for fund-raising.

The interplay of fund-raising costs' disclosure and accounting principles becomes crucial when viewed in light of proposals that such costs be displayed as or reflected in a percentage of the charitable organization's annual gross receipts.[27] As noted, the Wilson and Metzenbaum bills would require such a percentage on the solicitation materials, and the Mondale bill would require it as part of the disclosure statement. Obviously, the fund-raising cost percentage is highly dependent upon the accounting rules, for that is how the amounts to be used as the numerator and denominator of the ratio are determined.

For example, the AICPA statement of accounting principles for organizations not covered by an audit guide would require those organizations to report on the accrual basis of accounting. But the Wilson and Mondale proposals appear predicated on use of the cash basis accounting method. The AICPA statement consequently contemplates a category of receipts to be characterized as "deferred revenue," which presumably includes donor support when tendered in the form of pledges, bequests, and perhaps other types of gift transactions. However, the AICPA statement would not permit the deferral of fund-raising expenses that are associated with the deferred gift support. Thus, for many organizations, the result may be mandatory disclosure of a fund-raising cost percentage that is much higher than is actually the case, with a consequent deleterious effect on subsequent giving by the general public.

As discussed, the Mondale measure would have the Department of the Treasury promulgate uniform accounting principles; the Luken bill would have the FTC do this.

The inconsistencies and dilemmas may well be the result of a deficiency in the proposed federal laws rather than in the accounting principles. Nonetheless, as the federal law proposals evolve, the relationship between

---

[27] See Ch. 5 § 5.1.

their requirements and the applicable accounting standards will have to be carefully monitored and closely studied.

Federal Agency Jurisdiction

The prospect of federal government involvement in the establishment or recognition of accounting principles for philanthropic and other types of nonprofit organizations raises still another important question in this area: which agency of the government should assume the responsibility for administering and enforcing the charitable solicitations law?

Many advocates of a federal charitable solicitations law contend that the appropriate agency must be the IRS (specifically, the Office of Employee Plans and Exempt Organizations), because of its experience and expertise in the field of tax-exempt organizations and charitable giving, guided by regulations promulgated by the Department of the Treasury. This is, as noted, the approach of the Mondale bill.

The Postal Service, now engaged in cutting back basic services on a variety of fronts, seems an unlikely candidate for the task. However, the Wilson bill would assign such a role to the Postal Service, specifically the Postal Inspection Service, with its existing investigatory and enforcement authority, the latter including the ability to institute mail stops.

The Department of Commerce does not want the assignment. Some, like Congressman Luken, have proposed the Federal Trade Commission. Others raise the possibility of creation of a new federal agency to regulate solicitations and perhaps other activities of charitable organizations.

The only independent analysis of this subject to date is contained in the Filer Commission report.[28] The commission, in urging the establishment of a system of federal regulation of interstate charitable solicitations, recommended that all charitable organizations be required to disclose solicitation costs to the IRS and that a special office be established somewhere in the federal bureaucracy to oversee and regulate charitable solicitations.[29] However, the creation of such a new agency is not to be reasonably expected any time soon. Evidence of this was manifested in 1977, at the outset of the Carter administration, when then-Treasury Secretary Michael Blumenthal disbanded the Advisory Committee on

[28] *Giving in America—Toward a Stronger Voluntary Sector* (1975).
[29] *Id.* at 176.

Private Philanthropy and Public Needs, only weeks after it was assembled by the Ford administration. The Commission has yet to be reestablished.

In relation to legislation actually introduced in this field to date, the federal agency named in the particular bill as the enforcement agency has been a matter of happenstance: a member of Congress becomes interested in the subject and introduces what he perceives to be a remedial bill, naming therein a federal agency that is subject to the jurisdiction of the legislative committee of which he is a member. Thus it was that Senator Mondale and Congressmen Karth and Lehman picked the Department of the Treasury, that Congressman Wilson opted for the Postal Service, that Congressman Van Deerlin selected the Department of Commerce, and that Congressman Luken chose the FTC.

A possible compromise would be to assign principal jurisdiction in this field to the IRS and Treasury Department, which would develop regulations and to which reporting would be made. Collateral enforcement authority could be vested in the Postal Service, which has available to it sanctions (principally, the mail stop) that could be more effective than those available to the IRS (principally, imposition of subsequent penalties and revocation of tax exemption).

Exemptions

Another controversial question is whether or to what extent one or more categories of charitable organizations should be exempted from coverage by a charitable solicitations regulation law.

One school of thought is that a federal charitable fund-raising law should apply only to those charitable organizations (and their fund-raisers) that extensively engage in fund-raising activities as the principal means of deriving their financial support. (Whenever an abuse in this field surfaces in the media, the charity involved inevitably is heavily engaged in fund-raising, usually by direct mail.) An opposing contention has it that a charitable solicitations law should apply to every philanthropic organization simply because it engages in charitable activities or to the extent it solicits funds from the public irrespective of its other sources of financial support.

If a federal charitable solicitation law is not to apply to all categories of charitable organizations, the question becomes how to distinguish between the charitable organizations that warrant coverage by a fund-raising regulation statute and those that do not. An answer to this question lies in existing federal tax law, inasmuch as Congress has enacted an extensive statutory scheme that categorizes charitable organizations in a way that could be extremely useful for this purpose and adaptable to it. This body of law[30] is that which differentiates private foundations from other categories of charitable organizations.[31] These provisions specifically reference operating institutions (such as churches, schools, colleges, universities, and hospitals)[32] and grant-making charities heavily supported by charitable contributions[33] (so-called publicly supported organizations).

Consequently, in formulating a charitable solicitation law that applies only to organizations that derive most of their financial support from fund-raising campaigns targeted to the general public, application of the law could be confined to these publicly supported organizations. These are charitable entities that, for the most part, receive at least one-third of their support from the general public. (One flaw in this effort to distinguish between publicly supported charities and operating institutions is that the statutory definition of publicly supported charities includes such "operating institutions" as some libraries, museums, orchestras, theaters, and the like.) The Mondale bill utilizes these rules, exempting such organizations from its definition of a "public charity."

By contrast, the Wilson, Metzenbaum, and Luken bills would not exempt any category of charitable organization from all of its requirements. Instead, for example, the Wilson legislation offers only a limited exemption from the point-of-solicitation disclosure requirement and then only where the individuals solicited have a relationship with the organization whereby they already receive or can obtain sufficient information about the organization by reason of that relationship. These partial exemptions are for membership organizations soliciting gifts from among their bona fide members; schools, colleges, and universities soliciting contributions from their alumni, students, faculty, trustees, advisory committee members, and family members of such individuals and supporting foundations of such institutions to the extent they are soliciting those individuals; and hospitals soliciting contributions from their trustees and employees and supporting foundations of such institutions to the extent they are soliciting those individuals.

Institutions such as schools, colleges, universities, and hospitals infrequently solicit the general public for financial support and rarely engage in direct mail appeals, particularly on a nationwide scale. For

---

[30] IRC §§ 170(b)(1)(A) & 509.
[31] See Ch. 6 § 6.8.
[32] See IRC §§ 170(b)(1)(A)(i)-(v), 509(a)(1).
[33] See IRC §§ 170(b)(1)(A)(vi)/509(a)(1) & 170(b)(1)(A)(viii)/509(a)(2).

the most part, these institutions solicit only those individuals who constitute a relatively well-defined group that has an ongoing relationship with the institution. These individuals collectively share two common character-istics: (1) they are already in a position to secure the same information from the institution that any solicitations law could reasonably require, and (2) they are not solicited as members of the "general public." Similar observations may be made as respects the fund-raising practices of other operating institutions.

The Wilson bill's partial exemption for membership organizations would encompass churches, synagogues, and temples soliciting their congregations. (The Wilson bill contains no general exemption for religious organizations.) Also, the Wilson bill would create a total exemption for a written solicitation by an individual of a small number of persons who are presumably personal acquaintances of the correspondent.

A difficult aspect of the exemption question is the unavoidable fact that when one category of charitable organization is granted an exclusion, other categories of organizations immediately lay claim to a comparable exemption, making the issue a divisive one within the philanthropic community. However, the exemption for solicitations of a group of ac-quaintances or an organization's natural constituency is not actually an "exemption" at all but is instead a reflection of the legitimate scope of charitable solicitations regulation. That is, law in this field should be designed to encompass solicitations of the general public and hence need not and should not apply to personal, private, and constituent-oriented types of solicitations. This is a little-discussed aspect of these proposed laws and deserves treatment in the legislative history of any federal statute in this field.

One other aspect of the matter of appropriate classification of orga-nizations for purposes of fund-raising regulation that requires brief mention is the proper treatment of "religious organizations." Of course, First Amendment problems lurk here.[34] It has proved very difficult for any agency of the government to define the terms "church" or "religion." At the same time, some of the most vigorous, remunerative, and abusive fund-raising takes place on behalf of "religious organizations," many of which are not necessarily "churches."

It may be that a fund-raising regulation law that is made applicable to "religious organizations" (as would occur pursuant to the Wilson bill), particularly to "churches," would be unconstitutional as "prohibiting the free exercise" of religion. It may also be that such a law made applicable

----

[34] See Ch. 5 § 5.7.

to charitable organizations but not to religious organizations (solely because of their "religious" orientation) would be unconstitutional as law "respecting an establishment of religion." (A law of the latter variety may also be constitutionally infirm as a denial of "equal protection of the laws" under the Fourteenth Amendment.)

The outcome of this issue may also be of particular consequence to those schools, colleges, hospitals, orphanages, and similar institutions that are operated by direction of a church or church denomination (so-called integrated auxiliaries of churches).

The answer to this dilemma was hinted at by the Supreme Court in 1970[35] when it upheld the constitutionality of tax exemptions for religious organizations for properties used solely for religious worship Such an exemption, said the Court, is "benevolent neutrality"; the exemption was seen as simply sparing the exercise of religion from the burden of property taxation as is done for a broad class of "charitable" organizations. Therefore, the standard for the exemption may be that it is constitutional where the religious organization is treated no differently from its counterparts in the law of tax-exempt organizations. The legal questions on this point may be clarified somewhat if a challenge is mounted against the extension to the churches of the tax on income from an unrelated trade or business. It may also be noted that nearly every state with a charitable solicitation statute exempts religious entities from its requirements.

Federal Preemption of State Law

Another key issue with respect to federal charitable solicitations legislation is whether this type of law should be preemptive of state and local law where solicitations using a means of interstate commerce are involved.

A federal statute cannot preempt state law unless it (or, perhaps its legislative history) explicitly states that it is doing so, assuming such preemption is constitutionally permissible. Rarely does Congress preempt state law on a subject, although it will where circumstances warrant. Most recently, this was done in connection with the expansion of laws governing campaign financing and reporting practices where elections for federal office are involved and the establishment of a regulatory system concerning the trading of commodity futures. In what may serve as a close model to a federal law regulating fund-raising—the federal laws regulating the interstate offers and sales of securities—Congress

[35] *Walz* v. *Tax Commission*, 397 U.S. 664 (1970).

has permitted the states simultaneously to legislate and enforce laws in this field.

Nonetheless, it is the view of some that any federal law regulating solicitations for charitable purposes should expressly preempt comparable state and local law. This means that the federal government would assume the basic responsibility for regulating solicitations for charity where a means of interstate commerce is used. (None of the bills introduced in Congress in this area to date carry with them a preemption feature.) This approach would leave to the states and perhaps local governments the responsibility for monitoring intrastate charitable solicitations and prosecuting cases of charitable (other than mail) fraud involving violations of general civil and criminal laws.

It is clear that the calls for federal law preemption of this field stem not from any belief that federal government responsibilities require expansion but rather as a means of affording relief from the existing hodgepodge of state laws and local ordinances regulating charitable solicitations.

Such a preemptive federal statute would have the virtue of enabling charities and their fund-raisers to have to comply with only one set of requirements: one law, one due date, one form, and the like. Aside from the inherent advantage of having to cope with only one law instead of many, there is a substantial savings of time and money to be achieved in effecting compliance. Also, the danger of running afoul of enforcement authorities is minimized; many philanthropic organizations and their agents seem to be soliciting support across the country without much awareness of the states' and other jurisdictions' legal requirements for doing so. Finally, an obvious virtue of a preemptive federal law in this area would be the substitution of one statute for dozens of varying statutes and ordinances.

Another solution to the problem would be, of course, for the states to adopt uniform laws or, on a less extensive scale, uniform reporting requirements, forms, and due dates. Even the use of standardized registration and reporting forms among the states would go a long way toward easing the costs and other burdens of compliance with these laws. In 13 states, the legislatures have explicitly authorized the regulators to agree reciprocally with their counterparts in other jurisdictions to exchange information for enforcement purposes and to accept filings and grant exemptions on a uniform, multistate basis where the requirements are substantially similar. Unfortunately, this authority has been little utilized.[36] In most instances, express statutory

---

[36] See Ch. 8 § 8.8.

authority to achieve uniformity is not even required, since the enforcement officials (attorneys general, secretaries of state, and the like) have ample authority within the scope of their regulatory powers to work toward and achieve a standardized registration and reporting system. In fact, it would seem that such uniformity would breed an increase in charitable organizations' compliance with these laws, thereby enhancing the regulatory function.

Clearly, a Wilson type bill, emanating from the postal law-writing committee in the House, could be a vehicle for a preemptive law in this field, unless it is sequentially referred to another committee for amendment for this purpose. The same is true for the other proposals discussed above. However, other legislation may be introduced to this end, under the combined jurisdiction of the judiciary, interstate commerce, and/or taxation committees in Congress.

Realistically, however, there is not much likelihood of a preemptive federal statute in this area at this time. The attorneys general of the states covet too greatly their present authority to investigate abuses in charitable solicitations; they can be expected to strongly oppose such a feature.[37] Thus Congress will probably elect to continue to rely on the states as the principal vehicle to monitor charitable fund-raising, with the federal government playing a supervisory but secondary role. If this happens, the provisions of the Mondale bill, whereunder the Secretary of the Treasury would be directed to "encourage the appropriate officers of State and local governments to accept copies of the annual information returns and annual reports [as would be required by the bill] in satisfaction of the requirements of the States and local laws for similar reports from such organizations" (i.e., "public charities"), may represent the extent to which the federal government may reasonably go in securing, by statute, uniformity of reporting in this field.

At a minimum, however, coordination between federal, state, and local law and enforcement in this field is essential. Perhaps, with the cooperation of federal and state officials and representatives of interested organizations, the practical equivalent of preemption can be realized: adoption of a federal reporting form which could be filed, in lieu of

---

[37] During its annual meeting in 1977, the National Association of Attorneys General adopted a resolution stating, *inter alia*, that the "Association unalterably opposes [federal] legislative preemption of the state Attorneys General from enforcement of state charitable trust regulations and fiduciary obligations of charitable trustees and fund-raisers," although it also did express support for a "comprehensive uniform registration and reporting system" as to which the federal and state governments would have concurrent regulatory authority.

separate state reports, in those states where a solicitation is undertaken and made available to the interested public.[38]

Sanctions

Still another major issue with respect to a federal law regulating the solicitation of charitable contributions is the nature of the sanctions to be imposed.

Mention has been made of the possibility of invocation of the "mail stop" by the U.S. Postal Service as a means of circumscribing solicitations by mail that are not in compliance with the federal requirements. Other potential sanctions include those usually levied as part of the federal tax system: monetary penalties, injunctions, and criminal penalties (including imprisonment) for violations of the law. Also, some conceive of a point-of-solicitation disclosure requirement as a type of sanction.

A proposal prepared for the United Way of America[39] suggests fashioning sanctions parallel to those underlying the private foundation rules, namely, a series of excise taxes imposed in the event of the payment of "unreasonable" fund-raising fees. Such an approach would parallel existing tax law,[40] whereunder foundation directors, officers, and other insiders who receive unreasonable compensation are subject to an initial 5 percent excise tax on the amount of compensation in excess of what is reasonable and a 200 percent additional tax if that excessive amount is not timely repaid to the foundation, with additional sanctions available in the case of willful, repeated, or flagrant violations. As the proposal states, "This pattern could be applied to unreasonable fund-raising expenditures,

---

[38] The National Association of State Charity Officials was established in 1978 to improve communications between those who administer and enforce state charitable solicitation acts, and between the regulators and the regulated. An analysis of its genesis appears as Alexander, "State Regulators Seek New Super Organization," XI *The Philanthropy Monthly* (No. 11) 13 (1978). Among its projects is the development of a uniform reporting form for use by all of the states. A discussion draft of such a report, distributed under the auspices of NASCO and the National Association of Attorneys General, appears at XIII *The Philanthropy Monthly* (No. 3) 18 (1980). Another eventual NASCO project is the development of a uniform charitable solicitation act for adoption by the states. A proposed model law on the subject was published by the National Health Council, *supra* note 2.

[39] Troyer, "Proposal for Federal Legislation on Charitable Solicitations," X *The Philanthropy Monthly* (No. 10) 30 (1977).

[40] See IRC § 4941(d)(2)(E).

providing (1) a relatively modest initial excise tax on the recipient of excessive compensation, (2) a much larger excise tax if the excessive amount is not repaid within a correction period, and (3) recourse to the federal district courts for the traditional battery of equitable remedies (injunctions, removal of trustees, surcharge of trustees, and the like) in the case of repeated or serious violations."[41] The proposal also suggests that this same approach could be applied to other types of payments by private foundations where the payments exceed the level of "reasonableness."

In explanation of this proposal, it is pointed out that the term "reasonable" is often employed within the Internal Revenue Code, such as the limitation on the deductibility of salaries and other business expenses. Thus, this approach would look to actual practices and comparable data in assessing whether a particular fund-raising or other expenditure is in fact "reasonable." The principal difficulty with this idea is the absence of meaningful information and understanding as to how to assess the reasonableness of fund-raising costs, although this set of rules could well serve as an incentive for the development of that information.

As an alternative to this excise tax system, the proposal advocates point-of-solicitation disclosure of information, including fund-raising expenses, to prospective donors and others. Pursuant to this approach, charities could report their fund-raising costs as an average of four years' experience (five years for new organizations), and most solicitations for churches would be exempted from the requirements.

Filer Commission Recommendations

One of the recommendations of the Filer Commission was that a "system of federal regulation be established for interstate charitable solicitations and that intrastate solicitations be more effectively regulated by the state governments."[42] The commission's specific recommendations for federal regulation of charitable solicitations are as follows:

> In the Commission's sample survey of taxpayers, 30 per cent of those questioned said they did not like the way their contributions were used and one out of seven respondents specifically complained of excessive fund-raising or administrative costs. This wariness undoubtedly has been heightened in many minds by recent cases, including those uncovered in congressional investigations, where some costs of charitable fund-raising

[41] Troyer, *supra* note 39, at 33.
[42] *Giving in America, supra* note 28.

absorbed most of the funds raised, leaving the impression that some charitable solicitations are more for the benefit of the solicitors than for the charitable causes involved. In some other instances, contributions have been recurrently solicited and raised that are far in excess of the organization's operating outlays.

The Commission believes that the vast majority of charitable solicitations are conscientiously and economically undertaken. Nonetheless, cases of unduly costly or needless fund-raising point to the absence of any focused mechanism for overseeing such activity and, if need be, applying sanctions. One Commission study finds, in fact, that only one half of the 50 states regulated the solicitation of funds and that "the coverage and scope of" those that do regulate "vary widely." State regulation of intrastate solicitations, the Commission believes, should be strengthened, but because many solicitations spread over many states at once, state regulation is inevitably limited in its effectiveness. Clearly, the federal government and federal law must play the major role in assuring the integrity of charitable solicitations, a role that they just as clearly do not play today. The Commission recommends specifically that all charitable organizations should be required by law to disclose all solicitation costs to the Internal Revenue Service, in accordance with accepted accounting principles; that all solicitation literature should be required to carry a notice to the effect that full financial data can be obtained from the soliciting organization on request; that any such requests be required to be rapidly answered; and that a special office be established in the Internal Revenue Service or in some other federal agency or regulatory body, such as the Federal Trade Commission, to oversee charity solicitation and take action against improper, misleading or excessively costly fund-raisings. This special office might be supplemented by and guided by an accrediting organization, which would review the finances of and certify all exempt organizations whose solicitation practices are found to merit approval.

The Commission considered but rejected proposals that solicitation costs be legally limited to a fixed percentage of receipts because, unless such a ceiling were so high as to be an ineffective restraint on most fund-raising, it would risk being too low to account for the often justifiably high costs of solicitation for new or unpopular causes. On the other hand, state as well as federal agencies concerned with regulating solicitations should be required to establish clear qualitative criteria as to what constitutes "excessively costly" fund-raising (or improper or misleading solicitation, as well). Such criteria should be widely publicized so that both soliciting organizations and the contributing public would clearly understand the limits within which fund-raisers operate.[43]

These recommendations, however, drew the following dissent from commission member Raymond J. Gallagher:

---

[43] *Id.* at 176–78.

State governments already adequately police the solicitations of charitable contributions. There is no hard data in the material collected by this Commission that warrants a recommendation that the federal government assume a new policy role in this area. The Commission indicates that it believes that the vast majority of charitable solicitations are conscientiously and economically undertaken. The Commission, however, is concerned about the impression of many taxpayers that charity solicitations cost more than they should. I do not believe that the effective remedy for this impression is the creation of a new federal bureaucracy or the expansion of an existing one. Potential donors who have doubts about the efficiency of charitable solicitations can inquire directly of the organizations they are concerned about; and if they are not satisfied with the answers they are given, they have the most effective remedy of all: not making the contribution.[44]

Ford Administration Treasury Proposals

When outgoing Treasury Secretary William E. Simon, on January 14, 1977, sent a package of legislative proposals to Congress to "improve public accountability and prevent abuses" in private philanthropy, the proposals included a recommendation that interstate solicitations be subject to federal legislation that would be administered by the Treasury Department. The Treasury also recommended disclosure of financial information about the soliciting organization, particularly with respect to its fund-raising and administrative costs.[45]

In assessing the present situation, the Treasury proposals contain the observation that "[t]here is no supervision or monitoring of interstate solicitation [of charitable contributions] by the Federal government, and the State laws affecting it vary considerably, making it easy, particularly for large fund-raising drives, to circumvent tough enforcement by any one state."

This is a curious statement. In fact, the exemption application filed by charitable organizations (Form 1023) requests information concerning charitable solicitation activities. Also, the IRS and Treasury are fully empowered to request more information about solicitation activities in the application for recognition of exemption and in an organization's annual information return (Form 990) than is at present required. Further, it is an understatement to say that the state laws relating to charitable solicitations "vary considerably." In fact, they vary widely, and the accompanying regulations, forms, and enforcement efforts are even more

---

[44] *Id.* at 220–21.
[45] Department of the Treasury News Release, Jan. 18, 1977.

divergent. However, it does not follow from this observation that this variation contributes to lack of enforcement of these laws. Additionally, "large fund-raising drives" are able to "circumvent tough enforcement by any one state" only by refraining from soliciting contributions in that jurisdiction (unless the state law is simply violated); at the same time, the trade-off resulting from such a decision is that the organization deprives itself of the financial support otherwise available to it from the citizens of the particular state.

In connection with its recommendations, the Treasury Department suggested that Congress (specifically, the House Committee on Ways and Means and the Senate Committee on Finance) conduct hearings on the "appropriate methods" for regulating charitable solicitations, with "emphasis" on the following issues:

1.   The extent of financial data concerning the soliciting organization that must be supplied with the solicitation material;

2.   The need for administrative review of solicitation material prior to dissemination (as opposed to relying solely on criminal and equitable sanctions for misleading or incomplete material);

3.   The appropriate method for regulating oral solicitations (e.g., by telephone or television) and the extent of disclosure required for them;

4.   The need for limitations on fund-raising and administrative costs; and

5.   The preemption of varying state reporting requirements for interstate solicitations, with a uniform federal report to be filed with all requesting states.

The Treasury Department recommendations went far beyond the supervision and monitoring of charitable solicitations. In related areas, the recommendations also included a proposal that every private foundation, every public charity that makes grants, and every public charity or social welfare organization with annual gross receipts of at least $100,000 (other than a church or integrated auxiliary thereof or a convention or association of churches) be required to make available to the public an annual report on its finances, programs, and priorities. Also, the Treasury recommended that certain of the restrictions on private foundations be extended to public charities. These restrictions involve the present Internal Revenue Code Chapter 42 requirements with respect to self-dealing, minimum payout, jeopardy investments, and taxable expenditures.

This proposal for an annual report by most public charities has considerable merit. Such a report could be the document which a soliciting charity would have to send to the public upon request and also file with the Postal Service and perhaps in the states where the solicitation is to take place. However, the prospects of preparation of another major document for filing with the federal tax authorities (in addition to the Form 990) are certain to generate protests if only because of the increased costs. Another reason that such a proposal will likely stimulate unhappiness is the scope of further disclosure that will be inevitable, particularly if the reporting requirements extend to the names and amount of compensation paid to top employees, consultants, contractors, and the like.

Regarding other aspects of federal involvement in the private philanthropic processes, the Treasury recommended a variety of revisions of the tax laws with respect to the charitable contribution deduction and an investment of U.S. district courts with equity powers sufficient to remedy any violation of the substantive rules concerning philanthropic organizations in such a way as to minimize any financial detriment to the organization and to preserve its assets for its philanthropic purposes.

Thus it is that, due to a convergence of a number of trends and developments, public charities seem destined for greater governmental involvement in their affairs. To recapitulate: the converging forces are (1) the movements toward increasing "consumer protection," "disclosure," and "public accountability"; (2) those who wish to encompass nearly all types of charitable organizations within the scope of the existing rules governing private foundations; and (3) those who are seeking to expand government regulation of the process of soliciting financial support. The outcome of all this will say much about the nature of philanthropy in this country in the coming years.

8

Overviews, Perspectives, and Commentaries

One purpose of this chapter is to provide some overview of the law by which fund-raising for charitable objectives is regulated. To achieve this end, some material in earlier chapters is restated. In the interest of making each of the chapters of this book "stand alone," overlap is unavoidable.

The other purpose of this chapter is to offer some perspectives and commentaries on the subject of charitable fund-raising. While some of this is done in the previous chapters, this chapter is intended to attract and collect most of the commentary in the book on the matter of regulation of fund-raising today.

§ 8.1 Charitable Fund-Raising and the Law: Overview I

The greatest problem created by the law for the professional fund-raising community in general is the barrage of registration, reporting, disclosure, and other requirements demanded by the various state charitable solicitation acts. Consequently, one of the chief governmental relations challenges for the profession in the 1990s will be to arrest the expansion of this form of regulation, not only because it is antithetical to the legitimate fund-raising process, but also because it imposes additional expense and other burdens on the charitable community.

Despite major successes by the philanthropic world in the courts, the states continue to increase their interventionist roles in this arena as they create new laws and otherwise expand the scope of their involvement in the charitable fund-raising process.

It must be said that some form of regulation in this area is, as a practical matter, unavoidable. There are forms of fraudulent and other bogus fund-raising and fund-raisers in the land. Donors, like consumers, deserve some guidance and protection from misleading fund-raising. Wrongdoers should be aggressively prosecuted and punished. The integrity of the charitable dollar is vital to a strong philanthropic sector. Fund-raising scandals taint the process for everyone.

At the same time, balance is required. Fund-raising is constitutionally protected, principally through the doctrine of free speech. Charitable solicitations are the lifeblood of the sector. It is wonderful for the states to nab the few bad guys, but at what expense to all others in the fund-raising world? Is all this paperwork, bonding, and the like really necessary? Is it doing much good?

Regulation in this area is out of hand. Reasonable people, thinking creatively, must be able to come up with a better system. Or, if that is too grandiose, at least reasonable and creative people can devise some manner of reforming present law to allow the legitimate fund-raising process to prosper (for the benefit of charitable works as well as the profession) while simultaneously protecting the public and punishing the few outlaws.

Constitutional Law Background

Presumably, bona fide fund-raisers do not object to reasonable registration and reporting obligations. Even if they do object, it is irrelevant, because the law is clear that these obligations may be imposed. Each state inherently possesses the "police power," and this power enables it to protect its populace from the unscrupulous if not downright fraudulent charitable solicitation.

At the same time, the fund-raising process, when undertaken for charitable ends, is an act of free speech. In fact, charitable fund-raising is one of the highest forms of free speech, fully protected by the First and Fourteenth Amendments to the U.S. Constitution. This causes great tension and conflict in the writing and enforcement of the state charitable solicitation acts. Once again, the law calls for balance between the exercise of the police power and the restraints on enforcement of these laws as called for in the preservation of free speech rights.

The Supreme Court has made it clear, in three opinions issued during the 1980s,[1] that the regulation of the process of fund-raising for charitable

---

[1] *Village of Schaumburg* v. *Citizens for a Better Environment*, 444 U.S. 620 (1980); *Secretary of State of Maryland* v. *Joseph H. Munson Co., Inc.*, 467 U.S. 947 (1984); *Riley* v. *National Federation of the Blind of North Carolina, Inc.*, 108 S. Ct. 2667 (1988). See Ch. 5 § 5.3.

purposes must be undertaken only by the most restrictive means because the solicitation of gifts is a free speech right of the charities and their advisors.

Two of these cases were launched by fund-raisers for the charities, not by the charities themselves.[2] The High Court has held that free speech and fund-raising are inextricably intertwined, so that the fund-raiser can assert the protection, as well as the charity.

In the first of these cases, the Court wrote that a government may constitutionally limit speech in serving a legitimate interest as long as it does so "by narrowly drawn regulations designed to serve those interests without unnecessarily interfering with First Amendment freedoms."[3] That is, a government may regulate the content of constitutionally protected speech to promote a compelling interest of it if the government chooses the least restrictive means to further the articulated interest. Otherwise, a form of regulation of fund-raising will be voided as being unconstitutionally violative of free speech rights.

In one of the aftermath cases, a federal court of appeals held that a state law requirement that a professional solicitor must submit the script of an oral solicitation to the state at least 10 days prior to the commencement of solicitation was unconstitutional.[4] The court found that the requirement is an inappropriate prior restraint on free speech, being overly broad in its scope. The state contended that the law was the most effective means of monitoring telephone solicitations, but the court dismissed that argument with the observation that the "First Amendment does not permit the State to sacrifice speech for efficiency."[5]

Thus, the position of the law today on the validity of state charitable solicitation acts is that the courts will strike down any provision of these acts that directly impedes the fund-raising process. The courts will uphold general disclosure rules, however, such as a provision for notifying prospective donors that financial statements of charitable organizations and professional solicitors are available.

Fund-Raising Costs Percentages

The most frequent application of this aspect of constitutional law has been the attempt by the states to bar charitable fund-raising where the

---

[2] *Munson, supra* note 1; *Riley, supra* note 1.

[3] *Schaumburg, supra* note 1, at 637.

[4] *Telco Communications, Inc.* v. *Carbaugh*, 885 F.2d 1225 (4th Cir. 1989).

[5] *Id.* at 1233.

fund-raising cost percentage of the charity involved is deemed to be excessive or unreasonable. A more recent variant of this is an attempt to prohibit compensation paid to a professional fund-raiser or professional solicitor where the amount involved exceeds a particular percentage. Both of these types of laws have uniformly been struck down as being blatantly unconstitutional, overbroad, and not serving a legitimate governmental interest.

This subject is addressed elsewhere in this book in greater detail.[6] Nonetheless, a point to be made here is that a charitable organization's fund-raising cost is, in these quarters at least, being held up as a sole means for determining the charity's worth or validity in the eyes of a prospective donor. The fallacy of this underlying premise seems so obvious as to not warrant analysis.

Yet it must be said: The thought that the merits of a charity can be determined by an annual percentage of fund-raising costs is a wholly invalid thought. That is the case because many variables account for the fund-raising expense of a charity in a particular year—variables that have little or nothing to do with the merits of the charity or its cause.

Some fund-raising methods are inherently more expensive than others. Some organizations have controversial programs that impede fund-raising and thus increase costs. Usually, fund-raising costs are higher in the early years of an organization's existence. An organization with a well-developed constituency is likely to have much lower fund-raising costs than one that does not. Legitimate charitable organizations do not deliberately have "high" fund-raising costs. Some have higher costs in the beginning, then strive to reduce them as the years go on. There is no uniform way to measure fund-raising costs. And, there is much controversy over what is fund-raising, and how to (if at all) allocate costs between fund-raising and program activities.

Many factors, other than fund-raising costs, should be taken into account in judging the efficacy of a charitable organization. Fund-raising costs are certainly one factor, but they should be judged in context, not as an isolated element, inflated as to its importance.

Fund-Raisers and Solicitors: Defining the Difference

Another major problem with the state charitable solicitation acts is the failure of the legislators and regulators to divine an adequate definition

---

[6] See Ch. 5 § 5.3; *infra* § 8.7.

of the terms "professional fund-raiser" and "professional solicitor."[7] In the past, the definitions written into the various state acts sufficed; today, they are so out-of-date and unrealistic as to be laughable.

In previous, simpler times, the fund-raising professional was viewed as a consultant, one who helped the charity plan a solicitation campaign, although it was the charity that actually sought the gifts. The professional solicitor, by contrast, was a person who, in lieu of but on behalf of a charity, asked for a gift. The latter had a poor reputation at best, as one who begged door to door or on a street corner, or—worse—solicited by telephone from the proverbial boiler room.

Those days are gone. The bright line distinction between consultants and solicitors has evaporated. It probably started with direct mail fund-raising, where those who consulted about the design of the literature began physically introducing it into the U.S. mails (whereby they became part of the solicitation process). Soliciting by telephone in recent years has come out of the boiler room and become respectable (with the callers regarded as solicitors). The line was irreversibly crossed when tele-marketing came into vogue as a fund-raising medium, and the distinction between the consultants and solicitors was lost forever.

Under contemporary legal precepts, many of those who are—generically—professional fund-raising consultants are considered professional solicitors. This poses two problems. One, despite recent changes in practice, professional solicitors still suffer from the stigma of an image of being in the underbelly of philanthropy. Consequently, professional fund-raising executives are loath to be cast as professional solicitors.

Second, the state charitable solicitation acts almost uniformly treat professional solicitors even more harshly than they do professional fund-raisers. So the latter go through great legalistic contortions and acrobatics to avoid being classified under the law as the former, even though, in reality, they perform functions of both. But the law does not accommodate the hybrid form very well, except to treat consultants and solicitors alike as solicitors, which only compounds the problem. Indeed, some state laws have abandoned the distinction—and regard everyone assisting charities in the fund-raising process as solicitors.

Even if the assumption is granted that the professional solicitor is the bane of the field, certainly somehow reasonable individuals can conjure up a definition that allows the states to prosecute the weekend bandits without defaming and overly regulating the authentic fund-raising consultant.

[7] See Ch. 5 § 5.9; *infra* § 8.3.

Bonding Requirements

Traditionally, state charitable solicitation acts have imposed, on professional fund-raisers and/or professional solicitors, the requirement that they procure a bond before commencing with their services.[8] The purpose of the bond, of course, is to offer some protection to the citizens of the particular state who have donated to "charity" under circumstances in which they may have been bilked.

The problem, obviously, stems from the above-mentioned failure to understand the distinction between fund-raising consultants and solicitors, in that bonding only works when it pertains to those who have access to the donated funds.

Although today's definitions are at best vague on the point, one of the basic generic distinctions between a professional fund-raiser and a professional solicitor is the handling of money. Basically, where the services of a professional fund-raiser are provided to a charity, the charity is the solicitor and the recipient of the gifts. Usually, where a professional solicitor is involved, the monies are transferred to him, her, or it; the solicitor's compensation is paid out of the gifts; and the net is paid to the charity involved. Therefore, a bond makes sense when required of a professional solicitor; it makes no sense when applied to a professional fund-raiser.

Why, then, do some state laws extend the bond requirements to professional fund-raisers? It is because the writers of these laws really do not understand the distinction between a professional fund-raising consultant and a professional solicitor. This is partially a function of the matter discussed above; it is partially a miscomprehension of the charitable fund-raising process, in the sense of understanding who receives the charitable dollars.

Other Features

There are many other features of the states' charitable solicitation act that pose great problems for professional fund-raising consultants.

Many state laws contain several types of "prohibited acts" that can apply to the professional fund-raiser.[9] These prohibitions often go beyond the scope of fund-raising regulation per se. Violations of these rules can bring heavy penalties.

Some laws require onerous disclosures by solicitors.[10] While these laws are designed to drive solicitors out of the states and keep them

---

[8] See Ch. 4 §§ 4.5 & 4.6.
[9] See *id.* § 4.12; *infra* § 8.6.
[10] See Ch. 4 § 4.13; *infra* § 8.7.

out, they often (as noted) apply to professional fund-raisers, thus causing many problems. A few of these states impose burdensome requirements with regard to confirmations of gifts to the donors.

These laws impose hefty registration, reporting, record-keeping, and other accounting requirements on professional fund-raisers.[11] They often dictate the contents of contracts between the fund-raising consultant and the charities.[12] Some even allow private lawsuits against the fund-raising consultants. The statutes are filled with civil and criminal penalties, with the sanctions being fines and/or imprisonment.[13] The attorneys general, secretaries of state, and other officials are given nearly unfettered authority to launch investigations, pursue injunctions, and prosecute.[14]

A growing number of these laws regulate commercial co-venturing.[15] Many go so far as to have elaborate rules concerning the sale of tickets for charitable events.[16] The list goes on and on.

Conclusion

Where all this is going is anyone's guess. All indications are that present trends will continue, which means more strenuous state statutes and more litigation. This analysis does not include the local ordinances. Worse, federal regulation of the charitable fund-raising process is on the rise.

As will be discussed, the laws regulating fund-raising and fund-raisers will multiply and become more egregious, unless something is done to offset these developments.[17]

§ 8.2 Charitable Fund-Raising and the Law: Overview II

The point will be stated as succinctly as possible: The states heavily regulate the process of raising funds for charitable purposes. This is done through the exercise of the states' inherent police power, where they

---

[11] See Ch. 4 § 4.5.
[12] See *id.* § 4.10.
[13] See *id.* § 4.17.
[14] See *id.* § 4.15.
[15] See *id.* § 4.7; *infra* § 8.5.
[16] See Ch. 4 § 4.16.
[17] See *infra* § 8.12.

are looking out for the interests of their citizens who are potential or actual donors.[18]

The problem, as seen by the states, is all too well reflected in the "legislative declaration" that precedes the fund-raising regulation statute in Colorado. That state's legislature has concluded that "fraudulent charitable solicitations are a widespread practice in this state which results in millions of dollars of losses to contributors and legitimate charities each year." This body continues with the observation that "[l]egitimate charities are harmed by such fraud because the money available for contributions continually is being siphoned off by fraudulent charities, and the goodwill and confidence of contributors continually is being undermined by the practices of unscrupulous solicitors." This legislature thus found that the law it enacted is "necessary to protect the public's interest in making informed choices as to which charitable causes should be supported."

These statutes present many issues of law.[19] The purpose of this analysis is to provide an overall summary of the present legislative picture as it relates to state regulation of fund-raising for charity.

The Varying Statutes

There are 30 more or less "standard" charitable solicitation acts in the United States. Twelve states (including the District of Columbia) have some form of fund-raising regulation law. The remaining nine states do not have a charitable solicitation act.[20]

The standard laws (and in some instances the other fund-raising regulation statutes) have some basic commonalities. In essence, there are 15 of these fundamental features. These are (1) a series of definitions; (2) registration, licensing, or similar requirements for charitable organizations; (3) annual reporting requirements for charitable organizations; (4) exemptions for certain charitable and other organizations from all or a portion of the statutory requirements; (5) registration and/or reporting requirements for professional fund-raisers; (6) registration and/or reporting requirements for professional solicitors; (7) regulatory requirements for commercial co-venturers; (8) record-keeping and public information requirements; (9) mandatory contract requirements; (10) point-of-solicitation

---

[18] See Ch. 5 § 5.2.
[19] See Ch. 5.
[20] See Ch. 3.

disclosure requirements; (11) limitations on fund-raising expenses (most, if not all, of which are unconstitutional); (12) a variety of "prohibited acts"; (13) registered agent requirements; (14) investigatory and injunctive authority vested in enforcement officials; and (15) civil and criminal penalties, and other sanctions.

Definitions

The standard charitable solicitation acts contain a series of definitions. Chief among the words that are defined are "charitable," "solicitation," "contribution," "professional fund-raiser" and "professional solicitor," and "commercial co-venturer."

Part of the sweep of these statutes is attributable to the breadth of the definition given the term "charitable" in these laws. The meaning of the term is far broader than that accorded the concept in the federal tax laws, which defines terms such as "charitable," "educational," "religious," and "scientific."[21]

Certainly the term "charitable" as used in the state laws encompasses all categories of organizations that are regarded as "charitable" entities for federal tax purposes.[22] These include churches, and conventions, associations, integrated auxiliaries, and the like, of churches; other religious organizations; schools, colleges, universities, libraries, and museums; other educational organizations; hospitals, clinics, homes for the aged, and medical research organizations; other health care organizations; publicly supported charitable organizations; and certain organizations supportive of public charities.

However, the states, in defining the term "charitable" for purposes of regulating fund-raising, also sweep within the ambit of these laws some or all of the following purposes: "benevolent," "philanthropic," "eleemosynary," "patriotic," "humane," "social service," "civic," "fraternal," "voluntary," "public interest," "cultural," "artistic," "environmental," "social advocacy," "recreation," and/or "welfare."

Moreover, the boundaries are even broader in some jurisdictions. Thus, for example, solicitations in one state[23] for "police" and "labor" purposes are considered "charitable." Lobbying is "charitable" activity in another state,[24] as are "legal defense activities" in still another state.[25]

---

[21] See Ch. 2 § 2.1.
[22] Organizations described in IRC § 501(c)(3).
[23] Rhode Island.
[24] Virginia.
[25] Washington.

The other terms are likewise broadly defined to cast the widest possible reach. For example, the term "solicit" in Maryland law means "to request, directly or indirectly, money, credit, property, or other financial assistance in any form on the plea or representation that the money, credit, property, or other financial assistance will be used for a charitable purpose." In Virginia, a "contribution" is any "gift, bequest, devise or other grant of any money, credit, financial assistance or property of any kind or value, including the promise to contribute . . ." (the latter being, of course, a pledge).

The regulatory authorities vary. In 15 states, it is the secretary of state. In 14 states, it is the attorney general. Twelve states rely on other regulators, such as the Department of Consumer Protection in one state[26] and the Department of Commerce in another state.[27]

Preapproval

A fundamental requirement of nearly every state charitable solicitation act is that a charitable organization must, in advance of a solicitation in the state, obtain permission to undertake the fund-raising.[28] This is cast as a "registration" in 25 states, a "license" in three states, a "permit" in two states, a "certificate" in one state, and a "letter of approval" in one state.

A considerable amount of information is requested of the charity in this process. Usually, the elements of information requested are stated in the statute.

In 14 states, the registration expires after the expiration of one year. In five states, the registration remains in effect until withdrawn by the charity or suspended or revoked by the state. The statutory law in the other jurisdictions does not address the point.

Annual Reporting

Most of the state charitable solicitation acts require a soliciting charity to annually file information with the appropriate governmental agency.[29] In 29 states, a separate annual report is required. In the above-noted 14 states, annual reporting is accomplished through an annual updating of the registration, license, or the like.

---

[26] Connecticut.
[27] Minnesota. See Ch. 4 § 4.1.
[28] See Ch. 4 § 4.2.
[29] See *id.* § 4.3.

The solicitation statute usually mandates the contents of the annual reports. The reports may have to be accompanied by an opinion of a certified public accountant. The due dates vary widely—ranging from six months to 30 days.

The state charitable solicitation acts frequently also provide for annual reporting for professional fund-raisers, professional solicitors, and/or commercial co-venturers.

Exemptions

The state charitable solicitation acts vary widely with respect to the exemptions that are available, from their requirements, for eligible organizations and solicitations.[30] The exemption may be from the entirety of the statute or only a portion of it.

In some states, churches and their affiliated entities are exempt from the entirety of the statute. Other states provide a total exemption for religious organizations in general. Some states provide exemption for religious organizations only from their registration or licensing requirements.

Some states exempt at least certain types of educational institutions from the entirety of their charitable solicitation acts. Other states exempt educational institutions from only the registration and reporting requirements. Some states, either as an alternative to or in addition to the partial exemption approach, exempt from the registration and reporting requirements educational institutions that confine their solicitations to their "constituency," such as students, alumni, faculty, and trustees. Two states exempt solicitations by educational institutions of their constituency from the entirety of their charitable solicitation laws. Ten states provide some form of exemption for "foundations" related to exempted educational institutions.

Some states exempt nonprofit libraries from the registration requirements; one provides exemption for libraries from the entirety of its law. Two states exempt museums from the registration requirements, while one exempts museums from its fund-raising regulation altogether.

Some states exempt nonprofit hospitals from the registration and reporting requirements. A few states similarly exempt hospital-related foundations. Occasionally, states exempt nonprofit hospitals from the entirety of their charitable solicitation acts.

Many states exempt organizations from the registration and reporting requirements where the solicitation is confined to their membership. A

---

[30] See *id.* § 4.4.

few jurisdictions exempt this type of solicitation from all of the statutory requirements.

"Small" organizations are often exempted from the registration and reporting rules of these laws. As is typical of this body of law, the states do not agree, however, as to the meaning of this term. Definitions as to what is "small" for this purpose range from organizations that receive no more than $25,000 annually to those that receive $1,000 annually.

Solicitations for the benefit of specified individuals are frequently exempt. In several states, this exemption is available from the registration and reporting requirements. One state exempts this category of solicitation from the entirety of its law.

Other organizations have total or partial exemptions in the states, although there is little commonality here. Depending upon the jurisdiction, there may be some form of exemption for veterans' organizations, patriotic groups, fraternal organizations, civic groups, historical societies, social groups, and many more entities. Some statutes exempt certain organizations by name.

Professional Fund-Raisers and Solicitors

Although the matter of the regulation of professional fund-raisers and solicitors is addressed elsewhere,[31] it is noted here that many states require registration of fund-raisers and/or solicitors.

Several states require bonds of fund-raisers, with the amounts ranging from $2,500 to $20,000. Bonds of solicitors are required in some states, with the amounts ranging from $5,000 to $25,000.

Other Regulation

Some states regulate in some fashion the practice of commercial co-venturing.[32]

Despite repeated rulings by the courts that the rules are unconstitutional, some states persist in having in their statutes limitations on allowable fund-raising costs.[33] Many states have one or more so-called prohibited acts.[34]

Other forms of rules abound. These include disclosure requirements by professional solicitors and others,[35] rules mandating the contents of

[31] See *id.* §§ 4.5 & 4.6; *infra* § 8.3.
[32] See Ch. 4 § 4.7; *infra* § 8.5.
[33] See Ch. 4 § 4.8; Ch. 5 § 5.3; *infra* § 8.7.
[34] See Ch. 4 § 4.12; *infra* § 8.6.
[35] See Ch. 4 § 4.13.

contracts involving professional fund-raisers and professional solicitors,[36] registered agent requirements,[37] reciprocal agreement provisions,[38] and record-keeping requirements.[39]

Some states expressly allow county or municipal units of government to have other and/or more stringent fund-raising regulation rules.[40] A few states' laws authorize a commission or council to serve in an advisory capacity with respect to the administration and enforcement of these laws.[41]

Sanctions

The means of enforcing state charitable solicitation acts are manifold.[42] The principal enforcement mechanisms are revocation or denial of a registration, investigations of and/or injunctions on fund-raising programs, fines and other penalties, and/or imprisonment.

Two states expressly recognize private actions as an enforcement tool, while one state mandates loss of tax-exempt status as a sanction.

A violation of some charitable solicitation acts simultaneously constitutes a violation of the state's unfair trade practices law.

Conclusion

The foregoing summary and the previous one, not to mention this book as a whole, should serve to convince anyone that the states impose an enormous amount of regulation on the process of raising funds for charitable organizations. The trend in this area is for more state regulation.

When this body of law is combined with fund-raising regulation on the federal and local level, it should be obvious that governmental regulation of fund-raising for charity is of immense proportion and complexity.

§ 8.3 Defining a "Fund-Raising Professional"

The various state charitable solicitation acts—there are 42 at present—pose many problems for the fund-raising professional. Overviews of this understatement can be found throughout this book.[43]

[36] See *id.* § 4.10; *infra* § 8.9.
[37] See Ch. 4 § 4.11.
[38] See *id.* § 4.14.
[39] See *id.* § 4.9.
[40] See *id.* § 4.16.
[41] *Ibid.*
[42] See *id.* § 4.17.
[43] See *id.* § 4.5; *supra* §§ 8.1 & 8.2.

Definitions

Among the headaches is the threshold definitional one: what is a "fund-raising professional"? At a simplistic level (the historical one), a fund-raising professional is a consultant, one who assists charities in planning and implementing a solicitation campaign. The actual asking for gifts is, according to this level of analysis, the province of the charities, who do this using volunteers.

To continue this line of analysis, there are exceptions, of course, and sometimes charities would obtain contributions through paid solicitors. This practice was generally frowned upon by fund-raising professionals. Indeed, it was basically thought throughout the world of philanthropy that "self-respecting" charities did not use paid solicitors and "proper" professional fund-raisers did not associate with them.[44]

The laws among the states were written with this dichotomy in mind: the consultant and the solicitor. Thus, today, the predominant definition of a "professional fund-raiser" is this: "Any person who for a flat fixed fee under a written agreement plans, conducts, manages, carries on, advises or acts as a consultant, whether directly or indirectly, in connection with soliciting contributions for, or on behalf of, any charitable organization, but who actually solicits no contributions as a part of such services."[45] As can be seen, there are two principal elements of this definition: the professional fund-raiser does not solicit gifts and is paid for the service provided (the definition thus excludes volunteers). This definition (or a similar version of it) of the term "professional fund-raiser" is used in 25 states, with 12 of these states using the term "professional fund-raising counsel."[46] (To be different, one state[47] prefers the term "independent fund-raiser.")

The usual definition of the term "professional solicitor"—that found in 17 states[48]—is this: A "person who, for financial or other consideration, solicits contributions for, or on behalf of, a charitable organization, whether such solicitation is performed personally or through his [or her] agents, servants, or employees or through agents, servants, or employees specially employed by, or for a charitable organization, who are engaged in the

---

[44] The author recalls serving on a task force, some years ago, that was drafting a prototype charitable solicitation act. Someone suggested adding a paid solicitor to the group, to gain his or her perspective, but no task force member would confess to knowing one.

[45] This language is from the Virginia statute.

[46] See Ch. 4 § 4.1.

[47] Washington.

[48] See Ch. 4 § 4.1.

solicitation of contributions under the direction of such person, or any person who, for a financial or other consideration, plans, conducts, manages, carries on, advises, or acts as a consultant to a charitable organization in connection with the solicitation of contributions but does not qualify as a professional fund-raising counsel."[49] While a little long-winded, this definition has three principal elements: the solicitor asks for contributions, is paid for the service, and is anyone in the solicitation process (excepting volunteers) other than a "professional fund-raiser." (To be different, one state[50] uses the term "paid solicitor.")

Some states will excuse from the status of either a professional fund-raiser or professional solicitor those who are employees or officers of the soliciting charity, as well as lawyers, investment counselors, and bankers.

Over the years, there have been two problems with these definitions. One, they increasingly do not work. Two, the derogation associated with being a professional solicitor has continued, with the law often being far more stringent with respect to solicitors than fund-raisers. (As to the latter point, this aspect has been somewhat ameliorated, in that courts have struck down some of the harsher provisions as being unconstitutional.)

Before discussing why these definitions do not work very well, it is important to note that there are other definitions of these terms. Consequently, considerable confusion exists in this area of the law at present. Some states so broadly define "professional fund-raiser" that the definition includes a "professional solicitor." For example, one state[51] defines a professional fund-raiser as "any person who for financial compensation or profit participates in public solicitation in this state of contributions for, or on behalf of any charitable organization." In another state,[52] the term "professional fund-raising firm" is used to describe what is usually defined, in other states, as a "professional solicitor"; two other state statutes[53] contain the same anomaly. In one state,[54] the term "professional solicitor" is so broadly defined that it encompasses what is normally defined as a "professional fund-raiser."

Some states define a "professional solicitor" as "any person who is employed or retained for compensation by a professional fund-raiser to

[49] This language is from the Virginia statute.
[50] New Hampshire.
[51] Minnesota.
[52] Oregon.
[53] Those in Louisiana and Utah.
[54] Tennessee.

solicit contributions for charitable purposes in this state."[55] This definition is used in nine states.[56]

In recent times, the relatively easy-to-define dichotomy between "professional fund-raisers" (that is, as consultants) and "professional solicitors" has evaporated. This phenomenon probably started with direct mail fund-raising, where those who consulted about the design of the literature began physically introducing it into the U.S. mails, thereby becoming part of the solicitation process. Soliciting by telephone has come out of the boiler room and become respectable, with the callers regarded as solicitors. The lines of demarcation were further blurred when telemarketing became a mode of fund-raising.[57] The distinctions between consultants and solicitors—somewhat artificial to begin with—are, today, all too antiquated.

Defining "Solicit"

Part of the problem lies in the definition of the term "solicit."[58] (A search of case law on this subject yielded only cases concerning barratry—lawyers illegally soliciting business—or prostitution.) The state charitable solicitation acts define the term broadly. For example, the statute in one state[59] defines the term "solicit" as meaning "to request, directly or indirectly, money, credit, property, or other financial assistance in any form on the plea or representation that the money, credit, property, or other financial assistance will be used for a charitable purpose." This is, obviously, a most encompassing definition of the word, although it is typical.

In part, this becomes a line-drawing exercise, with the question being: At what point does a consulting service become a solicitation service? As referenced above, direct mail fund-raising presents the dilemma. A firm that assists a charity in designing fund-raising literature and does nothing more is a professional fund-raiser. Yet if this firm provides an additional service, such as mailing the literature for the charity, does it become a professional solicitor? Technically, the answer must be yes, since the act of mailing a letter requesting a gift is a "solicitation." However, this is an overly technical application of the term.

---

[55] This language is from the Kansas statute.
[56] See Ch. 4 § 4.1.
[57] See *infra* § 8.4.
[58] See Ch. 4 § 4.1.
[59] Maryland.

The better view is to regard the firm in this instance as the agent of the charity. Some years ago, this issue was before the Pennsylvania Charities Commission. The fund-raising firm involved designed the literature and further assisted the charity by physically introducing the literature into the U.S. mail. The literature was mailed using the charity's preferential postal rate, the envelopes contained the charity's return address, the gifts were returned to the charity, and there was no mention of the firm in the literature. Yet, because the firm had the service of taking the bags of mail to the post office on behalf of the charity, the commission ruled that the entire operation of the firm was that of a professional solicitor.[60] So much for the "better view."

Reasons for Avoiding Solicitor Status

There are several reasons why a firm or individual would prefer to not be regarded as a professional solicitor. One of them is simply that of "image." Solicitors are differentiated from consultants. Solicitors are characterized as those who go door to door, stand on street corners, or telephone during private time, seeking gifts. They are also portrayed as those who consume a very large portion of the contributions intended for charitable ends.

From a law point of view, professional solicitors are frequently treated more harshly under the state charitable solicitation acts than professional fund-raisers. As an extreme example, the statute in one state[61] is only applicable to those who solicit contributions (as noted, this law terms such persons "professional fund-raisers"); apparently persons who function only as consultants are not covered at all by the statute. Another illustration is the law in a state[62] where a "fund-raising counsel" has to register with the state only where he, she, or it "has custody or control of contributions from a solicitation."

In some states, professional solicitors must be bonded, although professional fund-raisers need not be.[63] In various states, professional solicitors are required to adhere to certain requirements about disclosure, confirmations, and receipts that do not apply to professional fund-raisers. For example, in one state,[64] professional solicitors must provide receipts

[60] See Ch. 5 § 5.9, note 207.
[61] Utah.
[62] Connecticut.
[63] E.g., Maryland.
[64] Rhode Island.

to donors. As another illustration, in two states,[65] extensive point-of-solicitation disclosure requirements are applicable to paid solicitors but not to professional fund-raisers.

Amending the Statutes

The most obvious way to resolve this dilemma is to amend the statutes. One would think this a rather reasonable way to proceed. Yet there is nearly total resistance to this approach, out of fear by the regulators that a "loosening" of the definition will allow solicitors, generically defined, to escape regulation. State regulators are so concerned about the weekend solicitors that their mind-set is expansion of the concept of the professional solicitor, rather than a dilution of it.

Nonetheless, there are at least two ways to proceed in this regard. One is to provide certain exceptions to the definition of the term "professional solicitor" to exclude, for example, organizations that mail fund-raising literature where the mailing is in the charity's name and otherwise under its auspices.[66] Another way would be to build the agency concept into the statutory definition.

Probably a more radical approach is needed. This approach would entail abandonment of these traditional definitions and a fresh start. The new definitions would recognize that many individuals and firms are now hybrids of consultants and solicitors. One of the elements to distinguish one from the other would be the matter of which person would receive the charitable gifts. This is not the place to propose specific legislative language, but surely reasonable individuals can conjure up definitions that allow the states to engage in effective regulation of the process of fund-raising for charity without overly regulating the authentic fund-raising consultant.

The law in one state[67] comes the closest to this approach. That statute differentiates among "fund-raising counsel," "professional fund-raiser," and "professional solicitor." Under this law, a fund-raising counsel is one who, for compensation, only consults or otherwise assists charities with respect to fund-raising but "who does not have access to contributions or other receipts from a solicitation or authority to pay expenses associated with a solicitation. . . ." The term "professional fund-raiser" is defined in accordance with the majority approach, and a "professional solicitor"

---

[65] Massachusetts and New Hampshire.
[66] This proposal is in the law in Colorado.
[67] New York.

is one who solicits gifts as an employee of a professional fund-raiser. (Among other things, under this law, a fund-raising counsel is not required to procure a bond.)

There is a project here—members of the fund-raising profession need to develop definitions of those who practice in the field and collateral to it. These definitions could then be submitted to the states in an effort to procure amendments of the state charitable solicitation acts on the point. At present, these definitions (and laws) are too often being written by legislators who do not understand the functions of the fund-raising profession.

§ 8.4   Professional Solicitors: Role of Telemarketing

An aspect of state regulation of charitable fund-raising that borders on foolishness is the impact of the various solicitation acts on telemarketers who assist charitable organizations in fund-raising.

As noted,[68] one of the greatest defects in the usual state charitable solicitation act lies in the section containing the definitions of terms used in the statute. There will be found the meaning of words such as "professional fund-raiser," "professional (or "paid") solicitor," and "solicit."

Most of the fund-raising regulation zealotry is being directed at the quickie promoters, those who roll into town for a weekend with a circus or some other attraction and roll out of town with most of the money collected, leaving the charitable beneficiary with a pittance. (It is a scandal that all of fund-raising, be it capital, annual giving, direct mail, or planned giving programs, is heavily regulated so that purveyors of tickets to vaudeville acts can be monitored.) Yet the statute writers cannot seem to write law regulating only these types. Instead, they rely on the traditional, but out-of-date, definitions of the terms "professional fund-raiser" and "solicitor."

To reiterate, the term "professional fund-raiser" is usually defined as a person who, for compensation, plans, manages, advises, or consults with respect to the solicitation of contributions by a charitable organization, but who does not solicit contributions.[69] In a word, a professional fund-raiser is thought of as a consultant. A "solicitor" is defined as a person who, for compensation, performs for a charitable organization any service in connection with which contributions are solicited.[70] Throw in the fact

[68] See Ch. 4 § 4.5; *supra* §§ 8.1–8.3.
[69] See Ch. 4 § 4.5.
[70] See *id.* § 4.6.

that the term "solicit" is defined to include seeking of contributions over the telephone,[71] and logic seems to lead inextricably to the conclusion that a telemarketer is a solicitor.

The fact is, generically, a telemarketer is not a solicitor because the telemarketer does not receive the funds from the solicitation. That is an important distinguishing characteristic. A true "professional solicitor" is one who requests a contribution on behalf of a charity, receives all of the gifts, retains the fee and the amount to cover expenses, and remits the (perhaps slim) balance to the charity. Frequently, another characteristic of a solicitor is that compensation is fixed as a percentage of funds received. Further, the transactions usually are such that the donor realizes that the solicitor is not an employee of the donee/charity but is functioning in an independent capacity.

Under normal circumstances, when a gift is made to a charity as the result of a telemarketing effort, the gift is—literally—made to the charity. Compensation is usually on a set fee basis, rather than as a function of contributions received. Furthermore, those called usually believe that the caller is a direct representative of the charity, not some independent taker of most of the gift amount. In fact, a telemarketer is such a representative, functioning as an agent of the soliciting charity.

Except for the disparaging connotation usually associated with the term "solicitor," there would be no harm done to telemarketers to be classified as solicitors if it were all a matter of definitions. However, the matter involves much more than definitions simply because, in their zealous efforts to drive out the circus promoters, the statute writers have made life miserable for those who are categorized as solicitors.[72]

Many of these statutory burdens imposed upon telemarketers are silly. They are also stupid because they are based upon unstated assumptions that, in actuality, are not true. Some of these rules are unconstitutional, as an unwarranted burden upon charities' free speech rights.

What is to be done? First, there needs to be adequate recognition of the law warp that the telemarketers are in. (Direct mail consultants are basically in this same spot.) The states are overreacting and overregulating, and the telemarketers are caught up in statutory definitions that, in real life, have no bearing on what they do. Generically, telemarkers are not solicitors.

[71] See *id.* § 4.1.
[72] See *id.* § 4.6; §§ 8.1 & 8.2.

Second, there must be some organized effort to change these laws. A single telemarketing firm is unlikely to do it single-handedly. An association or coalition must spearhead the project. It will be difficult, however, because fund-raisers have no political constituency (at least not like there is for charities), and the presumptions are against them.

Third, any such remedial effort must not repeat the same mistake that many legislatures have recently made. That is, drafting sweeping definitions (or exemptions) will not do. The corrective legislation must be narrow and precise enough to rectify this particular problem but not at the same time excuse the weekend promoters from the light of disclosure and stringent regulation.

As to this third point, a grand opportunity was lost during the course of developing a model fund-raising law.[73] To their discredit, the writers of this proposal perpetuated the problems by sticking with the outmoded definitions instead of crafting real-world ones, despite the fact that specific corrective language was drafted for them.

No one—not donors, donees, telemarketers, regulators, or the public—is served by this present state of affairs. It cries out for correction. Can the industry do it?

§ 8.5 Commercial Co-venturing

Traditionally, the state charitable solicitation acts impose registration and reporting requirements on charitable organizations, professional fund-raisers, and/or professional solicitors. Most of the present-day 42 state fund-raising regulation statutes embody one or more of these elements.

A more recent phenomenon, however, is regulation of "commercial co-venturers."[74] Like professional fund-raisers and solicitors, these co-venturers are almost always for-profit organizations. Unlike fund-raisers and solicitors, they are not paid for their role in the fund-raising process.

The Terminology

In short, a commercial co-venturer is a business. It is a business that, for differing reasons, wishes to help a charity. To this end, therefore, the business agrees to be a part of a promotion—indeed, to be the enervating and principal part—to benefit a charity. The motive may be

---

[73] The Connecticut statute comes the closest to this prototype law. See Ch. 3.
[74] See Ch. 4 § 4.7.

purely charitable; more likely, it is a blend of motives: part charitable intent, part marketing, and part the development of goodwill in the community or across the country.

The enterprise is termed "commercial" because a business is involved. The business is a "co-venturer." The other party to the co-venture is, of course, the charity or charities involved in the promotion.

Commercial co-venturing occurs when a business announces to the general public that a portion (a specific amount or a specific percentage) of the purchase price of a product or service will, during a stated period, be paid to a charitable organization. When properly structured, this activity results in a charitable gift, the amount of which is dependent on consumer response to the promotion, by the business sponsor.

The term "commercial co-venture" is, in some respects, unfortunate terminology. First, it suggests that the charitable organization involved is engaged in a co-venture (joint venture) with the participating for-profit organization. Second, the term implies that the charitable organization involved is doing something that is "commercial." Both connotations have potential adverse consequences in law, particularly in the unrelated business income setting.[75]

Thus, a commercial co-venture works best for all parties concerned when the charity's role in the "venture" is passive. If, however, the charity's participation in the venture is an active one, it could be characterized as a true joint venture, with the charity seen as providing marketing services to the business. The consequence of this could be that the charity is not receiving a tax-free gift but is receiving taxable unrelated business income. Should this be the outcome, the business involved would not be entitled to a charitable contribution deduction (but would be able to deduct the amount paid as a business expense).

Scope of Regulation

A few states regulate commercial co-venturing. Why do these states do this? In substantial part, they engage in this form of regulation as part of a consumer protection mentality. But, another aspect of this regulation of philanthropy exists as an attempt to save charities from themselves.

The usual dismay of a business when facing this type of regulation is understandable. Here is a business, wanting only to do something for charity; and here is a state regulator, insisting that the business register with his or her office, file accountings and other reports, and perhaps

---

[75] See Ch. 6 § 6.4.

even become bonded. The resulting outrage is predictable; one would think that the business would simply decline to be part of the promotion and thus spare itself the burdens of regulation.

And yet this does not happen. The reason is that more is going on here than pure charity. A commercial co-venture is advertising, an opportunity for the business to associate itself with a charitable cause. Its reputation becomes enhanced because of the charity's reputation. The public sees the business doing something for charity and the image of the business is enhanced. In turn, the public purchases the business' products or services, knowing that they are advancing charity in the process. (The consumers receive no charitable contribution deduction, however.) Consequently, charity is benefited and the business is benefited.

But the states want to be certain that the promised monies make it to charitable ends. They want to be certain that the business' promise to make a charitable gift is valid. And they want to protect the charity by making certain that a bad bargain is not struck and that the terms of the arrangement are memorialized in a written contract.

The State Laws' Definitions

Eight states have some form of regulation of commercial co-venturing.[76] Disclosure and the mandated content of contracts are the principal forms of regulation; two states[77] require the business to acquire a bond (face amount of $10,000). In four of these states, the concept of the commercial co-venture is stated as a "sales solicitation for charitable purposes"[78] or a "charitable sales promotion."[79] Oddly, three other states[80] define the term "commercial co-venture" or "charitable sales promotion" in their charitable solicitation acts but do not regulate the practice of commercial co-venturing.

The definitions of the term "commercial co-venture" are not uniform—as befits the general state of this area of law. One of the better definitions appears in the charitable solicitation law of one state.[81] Pursuant to that law, a "commercial co-venturer" is defined as "[a]ny person who for profit is regularly and primarily engaged in trade or commerce other

---

[76] See Ch. 4 § 4.7.
[77] Maine and Massachusetts.
[78] California.
[79] Colorado, Connecticut, and New Hampshire.
[80] North Carolina, Oregon, and Pennsylvania.
[81] New York.

than in connection with the raising of funds or any other thing of value for a charitable organization and who advertises that the purchase or use of goods, services, entertainment, or any other thing of value will benefit a charitable organization."

The law of another state[82] more broadly defines a "commercial co-venturer" as "any person who for profit or other commercial consideration, conducts, produces, promotes, underwrites, arranges or sponsors a performance, event, or sale to the public of a good or service which is advertised in conjunction with the name of any charitable organization or as benefiting to any extent any charitable purpose."[83]

In another state,[84] the statute defines a "commercial co-venturer" as a "person who for profit is regularly and primarily engaged in trade or commerce in this state other than in connection with the raising of funds for charitable organizations or purposes and who conducts a charitable sales promotion." A "charitable sales promotion" is defined as "an advertising or sales campaign, conducted by a commercial co-venturer, which represents that the purchase or use of goods or services offered by the commercial co-venturer are to benefit a charitable organization or purpose."[85] One state[86] takes a slightly different approach, defining a "charitable sales promotion" as "an advertising campaign sponsored by a for-profit entity which offers for sale a tangible item or provides a service upon the representation that all or a portion of the purchase price will be donated to a person established for a charitable purpose."

One state[87] regulates commercial co-venturing, not by its charitable solicitation act, but through application of its fraudulent advertising law. That law relates to the practice of a person who "sell[s] merchandise" or "solicit[s] programs or any other advertising when any part of the proceeds will be donated to any organization or fund." California's rule is found in its business and professions code, where a "sales solicitation for charitable purposes" is detailed as "the sale of, offer to sell, or attempt to sell any advertisement, advertising space, book, card, chance, coupon device, magazine subscription, membership, merchandise, ticket of admission or any other thing or service in connection with which" there

---

[82] Massachusetts.

[83] This definition is also used in Maine.

[84] Connecticut.

[85] Essentially, this same set of definitions is in the law in Colorado, New Hampshire, Oregon, and Pennsylvania.

[86] North Carolina.

[87] Wisconsin.

is an appeal for charitable purposes, or the name of a charity is used "as an inducement" for making the sale, or any statement is made that all or any part of the proceeds of the sale will be used for a charitable purpose.

Forms of Regulation

Once a promotion is defined as a commercial co-venture, then what? In one state,[88] for example, a commercial co-venturer is required to maintain "accurate and current" records during the promotion and for three years thereafter, have a written contract with the charity, and file reports with the state which includes an accounting of the funds received and disbursed. Moreover, in this state, the charity involved must annually report to the state about the commercial co-ventures it has authorized, the terms and conditions of each contract, and a statement about whether it received the requisite accounting.

The law of another state[89] contains similar requirements and adds registration, payment of a fee, and (as noted) a bond. Some states[90] mandate certain elements in the contract.

In one state,[91] disclosure to the public is the principal requirement of the law. (This statute is applicable only where the commercial co-venturer expects that more than half of the proceeds of the solicitation will be derived from transactions within the state.) In this state, where the rule applies, a commercial co-venturer must disclose in each advertisement for the promotion the dollar amount or percent per unit of goods and services purchased or used (or, in some instances, a reasonable estimate) that will be transmitted to charity.

In two states,[92] much of the foregoing applies. That is, there are rules about the content and filing of the agreement between the charity and the commercial co-venturer, record keeping, and public disclosure.

The state laws that force contracts between charitable organizations and commercial co-venturers to contain certain provisions are useful, in that certain requirements are essential in any agreement between these parties. These elements include (1) the goods or services to be offered to the public, (2) the geographic area where the offering is to

[88] New York.
[89] Maine.
[90] E.g., Massachusetts and Wisconsin.
[91] Colorado.
[92] Connecticut and New Hampshire.

be made, (3) the starting and final date of the offering, (4) the representation to be made to the public about the amount or percent per unit of goods or services purchased or used that will benefit the charitable organization, (5) a final accounting by the commercial co-venturer, and (6) the date when and the manner in which the benefit is to be conferred upon the charitable organization. (The foregoing are the requirements in the Connecticut statute.)

Some Practical Problems

State regulators in jurisdictions with charitable solicitation acts frequently do not insist on compliance with their laws in every case. Some fund-raising events or campaigns are so clearly proper that intervention by the regulator is not warranted—even though the fund-raising is not in conformity with the state law requirements. These regulators are often overburdened; if "selective nonenforcement" is the result, so be it. The regulators might regulate in these circumstances if asked (such as by complaint), otherwise the fund-raising is ignored.

This is often the case with a commercial co-venture, particularly a national promotion. With a national campaign, the business involved is often a well-known and respected enterprise; the charity is equally well-known and well-perceived. There is no particular nexus with the state. (Note, for example, that the definition of a commercial co-venturer in one state[93] includes the point that the business involved be one that is primarily functioning "in this state.") Regulation would likely achieve nothing, other than unnecessary paperwork for all parties concerned. So the regulators do not enforce the law, although technically they should.

Sometimes it is not clear whether the promotion is really a commercial co-venture. Perhaps a product is purchased but another company makes the gift. Or, there may be two businesses involved, and one does not comply, thinking that any compliance with state law is the responsibility of the other.

In some situations, there is overregulation. Requiring commercial co-venturers to take out bonds, for example, seems unnecessary.

Some in philanthropy do not care for commercial co-ventures. They believe that co-ventures can be demeaning for the charities and that the businesses are interested only in benefiting by association with the charities rather than having any true charitable motive. While there is

[93] Connecticut.

truth in these beliefs, it is not the entire story. These ventures can be quite advantageous for charities. As is so often the case in this area of the law, if there must be regulation, it should be undertaken in a way that does not discourage the practice of commercial co-venturing.

§ 8.6   Regulation Unlimited: The "Prohibited Acts"

Other portions of this book summarize the more well-known features of the state charitable solicitation acts: the registration, reporting, bonding, and like requirements imposed upon charitable organizations, professional fund-raisers, professional solicitors, and commercial co-venturers, as well as certain other rules pertaining to contents of contracts, record keeping, appointment of registered agents, and disclosure.[94]

There is, however, an element of most of these solicitation statutes— 42 altogether, to be precise—that all too many overlook: the provisions containing the so-called prohibited acts. These provisions, which appear in 33 of these statutes, embody a dimension of charitable fund-raising regulation that can carry this body of law far beyond the bounds of registration and reporting.

These prohibited acts are acts in which a charitable organization (and perhaps a professional fund-raiser and/or professional solicitor) may not lawfully engage. The more common of these several prohibitions will be reviewed first.

Of course, every person with a role in the fund-raising process should check the law of each state involved to be certain that some "prohibited act" is not about to be transgressed.

Basic Prohibitions

In most of these states, a person may not, for the purpose of soliciting contributions, use the name of another person without the consent of that other person. Usual exceptions concern the use of the names of officers, directors, or trustees of the charitable organization by or for which contributions are solicited. This prohibition extends to the use of an individual's name on stationery or in an advertisement or brochure, or as one who has contributed to, sponsored, or endorsed the organization.

A person may not, for the purposes of soliciting contributions, use a name, symbol, or statement so closely related or similar to that used

---

[94] See Ch. 4 and appropriate sections of this chapter.

by another charitable organization or governmental agency that it would tend to confuse or mislead the public.

A person may not use or exploit the fact of registration with the state to lead the public to believe that the registration in any manner constitutes an endorsement or appeal by the state.

A person may not misrepresent to or mislead anyone, by any manner, means, practice, or device, to believe that the organization on behalf of which the solicitation is being conducted is a charitable organization or that the proceeds of the solicitation will be used for charitable purposes, where that is not the case.

A person may not represent that the solicitation is for or on behalf of a charitable organization or otherwise induce contributions from the public without proper authorization from the charitable organization.

Extraordinary Prohibitions

Some state's laws contain prohibitions that go much beyond the foregoing and reach into domains normally covered by other bodies of law, such as those pertaining to tax-exempt status or deductible charitable giving. These prohibitions are extraordinary and, were it not for the fact that they are rarely enforced, would play havoc with the functions of many charitable organizations and the fund-raising professionals that they use. In many instances, these rules apply even in the absence of any fund-raising.

What follows are examples from various state laws. Although specific state statutory provisions are cited, other states may well have the same provisions. As noted above, it is essential that the laws in each applicable state be reviewed in relation to a charitable fund-raising undertaking.

For example, in one state,[95] it is a prohibited act for a charitable organization to "expend an unreasonable amount of money for solicitation or management." While this is probably the rule for tax-exempt status in general, it is, in the state regulation setting, fraught with free speech and due process implications. Every charity should strive for this result but how are "unreasonable" expenses determined and who makes the determination?

As another example, from the law of this state, it is a violation of law for a charitable organization to "engage in any financial transaction which is not related to the accomplishment of its charitable purpose, or which

---

[95] Connecticut.

jeopardizes or interferes with the ability of the charitable organization to accomplish its charitable purpose." This type of prohibition accords the regulators carte blanche authority to scrutinize everything a charity does in the state—and raises due process concerns.

In another state,[96] it is unlawful for any person to "use or permit the use of the funds raised by a charitable solicitation for any purpose other than the solicited purpose or the general purposes of the . . . organization on whose behalf the solicitation was made." Directors, officers, and employees of charitable organizations, take heed.

In this state, it is also illegal for a charitable organization to represent or imply that a contributor to it will be entitled to a charitable contribution deduction for the gift unless the charity has first obtained a determination from the IRS that the gifts are deductible or a letter of opinion from a lawyer on the point. This type of law can be troublesome (and/or perhaps expensive) for a charitable organization that does not need a ruling from the IRS, such as a religious organization or an organization that is tax-exempt pursuant to a group exemption.

It is also contrary to law in this state for anyone to indicate that any portion of a membership fee or sales price paid to a charitable organization is a deductible gift unless the IRS has so ruled. This prohibition does not apply where the payor is notified in writing that the amount is not deductible. Further, in Virginia, a charitable organization violates the law of that state if it accepts a contribution of cash or tangible property with a value exceeding five dollars unless, at the donor's request, a written receipt is provided.

Focus on Solicitors

These state laws often use the concept of the "prohibited act" to further regulate the activities of professional solicitors. (These prohibitions are among the many reasons it is usually important for a company or individual to be classified as a professional fund-raiser rather than a professional solicitor, if at all possible.)[97]

For example, in one state,[98] it is a prohibited act for a professional solicitor to solicit for a charity without written authorization of two officers of the charity and without exhibiting a copy of the authorization, along with "personal identification," to persons solicited. This authorization

---

[96] Virginia.
[97] See *supra* § 8.3.
[98] Maryland.

must state a period of time for which it is valid and a copy of it must be filed with the state.

Unusual Provisions

Given the scope of the states' prohibited acts and the penchant of the states for avoidance of uniformity, it is to be expected that some states will have some rather unusual laws in this field. Here is a sampling.

In one state,[99] a person may not, when soliciting contributions for charitable purposes, "impede or obstruct, with the intent to physically inconvenience the general public or any member thereof in any public place or any place open to the public." Presumably, everyone is a member of the general public, so this rule has universal application (at least in this state). The difference between a "public place" and a "place open to the public" is not clear. Nonetheless, it is clear that this rule, where applicable, is designed to restrain the more aggressive forms of fund-raising.

In another state,[100] a charitable organization or anyone acting on behalf of one may not solicit contributions using any "uniformed personnel of any local, state or federal agency or department." There is, however, an exception for the solicitation in uniform of firefighters. This rule is obviously designed to eliminate the pressure that is inherent when someone in governmental uniform is soliciting charitable gifts. Sometimes the distinction between charitable giving and "protection" is facially difficult to discern.

In another state,[101] it is a violation of the law for a person to "[v]ote or use personal influence" as an officer or director of a charitable organization, where a majority of the board members of the charity are professional fund-raisers or their designees, "on matters on which such officer or member has a financial or material conflicting interest."

In another state,[102] one who solicits charitable contributions may not use the words "police," "law enforcement," "fireman," or "firefighter" unless a "bona fide police, law enforcement, rescue squad or fire department authorized its use in writing."

In yet another state,[103] the law provides that a charitable organization, professional fund-raiser, or professional solicitor may not, in connection

---

[99] Hawaii.
[100] Minnesota.
[101] New York.
[102] North Carolina.
[103] Maryland.

with a charitable solicitation, engage in a "deceptive act or practice." This term embraces an act or practice which "[h]as a capacity to mislead whether by affirmative representation or omission" and "[i]s misleading in a material respect in that it concerns information that is important to a person's decision to make a contribution or concerns information that is likely to affect a person's decision to make a contribution." This law also contains prohibited acts relating to the awarding of prizes, offering of sweepstakes and other promotional efforts, and the use of advertising and promotional material.

In still another state,[104] an employee of a nonprofit corporation organized in the state or of a corporation authorized to do business in the state may not "own or operate or have any pecuniary interest, directly or indirectly, with any business enterprise relating to the product, aims, goals or purposes of the corporation as set forth in its charter." This rule prohibits, among other aspects of this matter, a nonprofit organization to which the rule is applicable, from having a for-profit subsidiary and having individuals work for both organizations. This prohibition flies in the face of the federal unrelated business income tax rules which, under today's law, encourages the "spin-off" of unrelated activities into separate, taxable organizations.

Duplicative Rules

In some states, the list of prohibited acts includes acts that are violations of the charitable solicitation statutes in any event. For example, some states' laws make it a prohibited act for a charitable organization to use the services of an unregistered professional fund-raiser or professional solicitor. Likewise, these states make it a violation of the law for a professional fund-raiser or professional solicitor to provide services for an unregistered charity.

Conclusion

For the most part, there is nothing wrong with the foregoing prohibitions. (As noted, there are some that bump up against constitutional law barriers.) It may be supposed that the general public would agree with these restrictions. Thus, they are politically sound, which explains why many of them appear in several state charitable solicitation acts.

---

[104] Tennessee.

These rules, nonetheless, once again raise the question of uniformity. As fund-raising becomes more and more national (and, for that matter, international), is philanthropy, and thus the country in general, served by these rules? The answer probably is yes, although those involved in the field of charitable giving as "professionals" would likely say no. Impediments to giving to charity are indeed frustrating and are, in many respects, counterproductive.

Yet, the law clearly is not going to tolerate fund-raising for charity that is fraudulent or otherwise manipulative of other charities' successes.

§ 8.7   Fund-Raising Cost Limitations

Despite the fact that it is unconstitutional for a state to prohibit fund-raising for charitable purposes on the basis of a percentage of amounts of contributions received devoted to fund-raising, six states continue to have this type of provision in their statutes.[105]

For example, one state[106] has a provision prohibiting a professional solicitor or a commercial co-venturer from receiving more than 25 percent of the total amounts received in a solicitation. Although the state regulators concede that this law is unconstitutional and is not being enforced,[107] the provision is still in the solicitation statute. Legislation is pending that would remove this limitation and otherwise amend the present statute.

The law of another state[108] prohibits registration by a charitable organization, professional fund-raiser, or professional solicitor where the charity will receive less than 90 percent of the receipts of a solicitation. According to a representative of the state's tax commission, which administers the state's charitable solicitation act, since the provision has not been removed from the statute by the state legislature, it is still being enforced.[109] However, the state's attorney general's office has written an opinion that the provision is unconstitutional,[110] so persons

---

[105] See Ch. 4 § 4.8.

[106] Massachusetts.

[107] Telephone interview with representative of state's Attorney General's Office (May 29, 1990).

[108] Oklahoma.

[109] Telephone interview (May 24, 1990).

[110] Letter to State Rep. James E. Henshaw stating opinion of attorney general (Jan. 6, 1989).

may lawfully ignore this provision because this aspect of the law is unenforceable.

In still another instance, the law of a state[111] provides that a charitable organization may not pay a professional solicitor an amount in excess of 15 percent of the contributions received. This law also asserts a rebuttable presumption in connection with the fund-raising costs of charitable organizations, which places a general limitation on fund-raising costs of 35 percent, albeit with an opportunity for higher expenses in the event of "special facts and circumstances." These provisions are being challenged in court and are not being enforced at the present time.[112]

The law of another state[113] provides that a charitable organization may not pay a professional solicitor more than 25 percent of contributions received and that a charitable organization may not have fund-raising expenses in excess of 50 percent of contributions received, again with an opportunity for the allowance of higher expenses in the case of special facts and circumstances. This provision remains in the statute, there is no pending challenge to it, and there are no present plans to rewrite the statute.[114]

Finally, the law of still another state[115] states that a charitable organization may not pay a professional solicitor for services in connection with the solicitation of contributions in excess of a "reasonable per cent" of gifts raised. This law also authorizes the state's secretary of state to pass judgment on the contract between a charitable organization and a professional solicitor, and cause renegotiation of the agreement or perhaps disapprove it where the contract "will involve an excessively high fund-raising cost." This provision is still in the law, and no challenges to it are pending.[116]

In contrast to the foregoing, some states have removed the fund-raising cost limitations from their statutes. Thus, the law of one state,[117] which provided that a professional solicitor may not request or receive

---

[111] Pennsylvania.

[112] Telephone interview with representative of state's Bureau of Charitable Organizations (May 30, 1990).

[113] Rhode Island.

[114] Telephone interview with representative of state's Department of Business Regulations (May 30, 1990).

[115] South Carolina.

[116] Telephone interview with representative of state's Office of Public Charities (May 30, 1990).

[117] Maryland.

as compensation for services an amount in excess of 30 percent of the total receipts of a solicitation activity, was repealed, following a decision of the U.S. Supreme Court finding it unconstitutional.[118]

Another state[119] had a provision that established a presumption that a fund-raising cost of a charitable organization that is in excess of 30 percent of total revenue is presumed to be unreasonable; a charitable organization with an unreasonable fund-raising cost could not register in the state. However, that limitation was repealed in 1988.

The law of still another state[120] provided that a charitable organization registered under its solicitation statute may not expend, for fund-raising, an "unreasonable" amount of its gross contributions. An amount in excess of 25 percent of total contributions was presumed to be unreasonable, with the secretary of state empowered to, using unstated criteria, approve higher costs. This provision was subsequently removed from the state's charitable solicitation statute.

One state[121] has gone so far as to state on the most recent print of its charitable solicitation act that provisions limiting compensation of professional solicitors to 15 percent of gifts received are unconstitutional.

As discussed,[122] many states are turning to use of percentages, in connection with fund-raising costs, in the disclosure setting rather than as absolute or rebuttable limitations. The thought underlying this shift is, of course, that this use of percentages is constitutional because the U.S. Supreme Court has approved disclosure as a lawful means of regulating charitable fund-raising.[123] This may or may not be an accurate assumption.

The point here is that state regulation of charitable fund-raising continues to focus heavily on the use of percentages, three Supreme Court opinions notwithstanding. Some states have been very slow in altering their statutes to bring them into conformity with constitutional law principles. As discussed, some states still have blatantly unconstitutional limitations on fund-raising costs in their statutes. The charitable organization, professional fund-raiser, and/or professional solicitor who is unaware of current case law in this field may well comply with these rules, not thinking to call the statute authorities for a regulatory update.

---

[118] *Munson, supra* note 1; see also Ch. 5 § 5.1.
[119] Minnesota.
[120] Tennessee.
[121] New Jersey.
[122] See Ch. 4 § 4.8.
[123] See Ch. 5 § 5.3.

Some individuals and organizations are uncomfortable with the idea of operating in violation of a state law, no matter how many lawyers tell them the provision is not enforceable because it is constitutionally infirm. Despite their unhappiness at losing this battle, state legislatures have a responsibility to rid their laws of these unconstitutional provisions, not to mention being more careful in the future about the type of laws they enact in this field.

§ 8.8 Reciprocal Agreement Opportunities

As discussed,[124] 15 states have in their charitable solicitation statutes a provision concerning "reciprocal agreements." While the language varies from state to state, the essential aspect of these provisions is that they authorize the appropriate state official to enter into reciprocal agreements with his or her counterparts in other states to (1) exchange information about charitable organizations, professional fund-raisers, and professional solicitors; (2) accept filings made by these persons in the other states where the information required is substantially similar; and (3) grant exemptions to organizations that are granted exemption under the other state's statute where the laws are substantially similar.

The meaning of the term "substantially similar" in this context is not clear. Of the 42 state charitable solicitation acts, 30 can be said to be "standard" in nature.[125] These 30 laws are substantially similar in the sense that they contain registration and reporting requirements for charitable organizations, professional fund-raisers, and professional solicitors; provide for some exemptions; require the maintenance of records; mandate the use of contracts; contain a list of prohibited acts; and the like. Thus, in that sense, each of these 30 laws is substantially similar to the others. However, no two laws are precisely identical. Consequently, the decision as to which statutes are "substantially identical" is left up to the regulators in each of the affected states.

Judging by contemporary practice, the state regulators believe that no two state charitable solicitation acts are "substantially identical." The reciprocal agreement provisions are essentially unused. While there is informal networking among the state regulators, whereby they share information (usually in the enforcement setting), that type of communication can be accomplished without the formality of a reciprocal agreement provision. In a few instances, a state may enter into a letter

---

[124] See Ch. 4 § 4.14.
[125] See Ch. 4.

agreement with another for the purpose of exchanging information. However, a telephone survey of the 15 states yielded no information about the use of another state's filing in another state or the provision of an exemption based upon the exemptions in another state.[126] Indeed, some of the state regulators were not aware that the provision was in the statute. On the basis of this survey, it can be concluded that no state regulator is aware of any formal executed reciprocal agreement between two or more states concerning sharing of filings or exemptions.

The tenor of the times in this regard was expressed by a representative of one state, who observed that, because of the rapidity with which these state laws are changing, it would be difficult for one state to correlate its statute with others, simply because of the task of keeping up with the status of these laws. Indeed, this individual thought that when the state charitable solicitation statute in the jurisdiction involved next comes up for revision, the reciprocal agreement clause may well be repealed, inasmuch as it has never been used.

There lie the seeds of a partial solution to the problem of burgeoning state regulation in this field. If the state authorities cannot keep up with what their colleagues in the other states are doing, how can they expect charitable organizations and their professional advisors to do it? One answer, then, to this hodgepodge of state regulation is to smooth out compliance and enforcement by introducing some uniformity to the rules. This does not have to occur through the use of model laws but merely through the use of these reciprocal agreements.

At least this approach could be attempted on a trial basis. What would be the harm, for example, if a charitable organization located in the commonwealth of Virginia and registered under that state's charitable solicitation law sent its annual filings with Virginia to the state of Maryland in lieu of separate reporting to that state? This approach need not imply that the Virginia form is superior to the Maryland form; it would reflect a desire to reduce the quantity of compliance and enhance the quality of compliance. The same may be said about exemptions; for example, if a college is exempt from registration in its home state of Maine, what is the harm in providing the same exemption for it when soliciting gifts in the state of Georgia? This use of reciprocity should improve compliance (if only through greater accuracy of information and reduction of costs) and augment enforcement. A more formalized relationship among the states would enable them to deal more effectively with organizations

---

[126] Telephone survey (May 30, 1990).

and individuals who are not part of the problem and focus their energies and resources on those that are.

One hopes that this pathway to some easing of the regulatory burdens in this field is not being blocked solely by jealousies throughout the states. These provisions were inserted in the state solicitation statutes by the legislatures for a reason, and the regulatory authorities have some obligation to attempt to implement and utilize them. Constructive use of the reciprocity provisions could work to the benefit of both the regulated and the regulators.

§ 8.9 The Fund-Raiser's Contract

The term "professional fund-raiser" is specifically defined under the charitable solicitation statutes of many states.[127] However, a one-word generic definition of a professional fund-raiser is "consultant"—or, more formally in legal parlance, "independent contractor." The latter term is used in law to differentiate someone from an "employee." But, a key word in the term is "contractor."

Almost all consultants have a written agreement with their clients. It is axiomatic, then, that a professional fund-raiser should have a written contract with each client. In fact, several state laws require that the relationship between a charitable organization and a professional fund-raiser (and/or professional solicitor) be the subject of a written contract.[128]

The reasons for a written agreement are obvious. The principal one is to try to avoid disagreements later about what each party to the arrangement is to do. And, a written memorialization gives the substantive basis for litigation should that prove necessary.

Basic Elements

What should a contract between a charitable organization and a professional fund-raiser contain? The place to begin in answering that question is to enumerate the nine elements that any contract should contain. These are:

1.   A description of the services to be provided by the party providing the services.

2.   A statement of the fees to be paid by the party receiving the services.

[127] See Ch. 4 § 4.1; *supra* § 8.3.
[128] See Ch. 4 § 4.10.

3. A provision stating who owns what property that may be utilized or created in the contractual relationship.

4. A provision stating the duration of the agreement.

5. A provision stating the parties' ability to terminate the agreement.

6. A provision stating the state's law that governs interpretation of the agreement.

7. An indemnification clause, whereby one party agrees to absorb the costs of certain liabilities found against the other party.

8. A provision stating that the contract memorializes the entire agreement between the parties and cannot be amended except in writing by the parties.

9. A statement of the effective dates of the agreement.

These items should be reflected in any contract between a charitable organization and a professional fund-raiser. Many of the specific clauses will vary, of course, depending upon the type of fund-raising involved. But, irrespective of whether the fund-raising involved will utilize direct mail, special events, annual campaign, planned giving, or whatever, or whether the fund-raising is in the context of a capital campaign, the advice is the same: the professional fund-raiser and the charitable organization are best served by a reasonably detailed statement of services to be provided, and fees to be paid and when.

Specific Elements

A clear statement about the amount and timing of payment of fees to the professional fund-raiser will minimize, if not eliminate, the likelihood of fee disputes. If the fees are to be paid in phases, and the charitable organization is to make payment following the close of a phase, the professional fund-raiser should be certain that the charity's payment obligations along the way are clearly stated. And, if the fund-raiser desires timely payment, some monitoring and prodding of the charitable client may be necessary.

A full statement of services to be performed is the trick to avoiding breach-of-contract litigation. The professional fund-raiser must thread a way between two extremes: not promise to do more than should or can be done, yet not make the statement of services so skimpy as to cause the charitable client to wonder what it is paying for.

The professional fund-raiser must be cautious about verbal statements that may heighten expectations of the client. This type of statement may later arguably become part of the contractual relationship. It is because of the potential validity of oral agreements that a clause confining the agreement to its written form is essential.

As noted earlier, it is important to state in a contract who owns what property that is to be used in connection with, or may be created as the result of, the provision of services. In the specific context of the professional fund-raiser's contract, the ownership of these properties should be addressed: mailing lists, copyrights, artwork, and photographs. Of course, other properties may properly be the subject of an ownership clause.

It is rarely a good idea for a professional fund-raiser to guarantee results to a charitable organization client. If this is done, however, the fund-raiser should be certain that the guarantee—and any accompanying conditions—are well stated.

A charity's contract for professional fund-raising assistance is a contract for what the law terms "specific performance." This is particularly true where the charity is contracting with one or more individuals. The charitable organization involved should insist that the contract be non-transferable. These conditions are generally true where the professional fund-raiser is a company. The charity is contracting with the particular firm and presumably has no interest in having the obligation to perform services transferred to another company (or to an individual). Indeed, the charity may insist that the contract specify the provision of services by one or more named fund-raising professionals who are employed by or otherwise affiliated with the company.

When the fund-raising professional is an individual, the contract should state that he or she is rendering services as an independent contractor, rather than as an employee.

If the agreement states that the charitable organization client is to provide an approval (such as the text of a letter or graphics of a brochure), the agreement should also state that the approval shall be in writing. Of course, the professional fund-raiser should subsequently be certain that the approval is obtained on a timely basis, in writing.

Fee Arrangements

Caution should be exercised by the fund-raising professional in describing the fee arrangement. It is considered, in many quarters, to be un-professional or even unethical for a fund-raiser to be compensated on a contingent, percentage, commission, or like fee basis. However, the antitrust laws prevent enforcement of such a prohibition as a matter of ethics. In general, this type of fee arrangement is by no means illegal, although in extreme instances a contingent fee arrangement may jeopardize the tax-exempt status of the client charity.[129]

Contingent fee arrangements exist in many ways in addition to a stated percentage of contributions received. For example, compensation tied to the number of solicitation letters mailed, where the fund-raiser controls the timing and extent of the mailing, is a form of contingent compensation.[130]

A percentage limitation, in state law, on the amount of compensation that can be paid by a charitable organization to a professional fund-raiser is unconstitutional.[131]

Solicitor Status

Some state laws preclude a fund-raiser from treatment as a "professional fund-raiser" where the compensation is other than a "flat fixed fee" arrangement. If the compensation is otherwise, the result may be classification as a "professional solicitor." This adverse result can, in turn, lead to more stringent governmental regulation.[132] A trend in charitable regulation is to stringently regulate the solicitors. This is being done by means of strenuous precampaign contract reviews, greater disclosure and reporting requirements, and more.

The description of services in the contract should be reviewed from this definitional standpoint, as well. One of the essential elements of the definition of a "professional solicitor" is that the solicitor is an active participant in the solicitation process.[133] A professional fund-raiser can all too easily fall into this trap by agreeing to, for example, mail the solicitation letters or place the solicitation telephone calls.

Another characteristic of a professional solicitor often is that such a person receives the gifts directly from the donors and remits the net amount to the charity. A professional fund-raiser should be paid a fee by the charity, with the charity having received the gifts directly, and

---

[129] See Ch. 6 § 6.10.

[130] However, in the state of Maryland, "[f]und-raising counsel shall not receive compensation from a charitable organization if the consideration or pecuniary benefit depends in whole or in part upon the number or value of contributions made as a result of the efforts of the fund-raising counsel."

[131] See Ch. 5 §§ 5.1 & 5.3.

[132] See Ch. 4 § 4.6.

[133] See Ch. 5 § 5.9.

the contract should make that feature clear, or at least avoid any language contemplating the receipt of gift funds by the professional fund-raiser.

State Laws

It goes without saying that parties to a contract are expected to obey all applicable laws. It is not necessary, however, for the contract to contain language expressly reflecting that general obligation.

Nonetheless, among the laws that directly relate to both the professional fund-raiser and the charitable organization client are the various charitable solicitation acts. These laws impose registration, reporting, bonding, and other requirements on both professional fund-raisers and their charitable clients.[134] Because the registration and reporting forms for both parties cross-reference, the professional fund-raiser should at least contemplate a clause in the contract that requires both parties to notify each other of the states in which they are registered and of any adverse regulatory developments that may arise.

As is the case with all laws, everyone involved is presumed to know them. In the fund-raising context, both the contracting charity and professional fund-raiser are expected to know and conform with the state charitable solicitation acts. Some of these laws mandate the contents of contracts between charities and fund-raisers. These are independent obligations, bearing potential liabilities (for example, civil penalties and/or injunctive relief) for both parties. Neither party should assume that the other is in compliance with these laws.

Conclusion

A professional fund-raiser should have a solid, comprehensive, and professional-looking prototype agreement to present to prospective charitable clients. With a good agreement, a professional fund-raiser can concentrate on development work without fear of the consequences of a defective contract.

§ 8.10   Update on Unrelated Business Revisions

The staff of the House Subcommittee on Oversight, working with the Department of the Treasury staff, has drafted some recommendations for law revision in the unrelated business income area for the members

---

[134] See Ch. 4 §§ 4.2 & 4.5.

of the subcommittee. The precise status of these proposals is unclear at this time. The items summarized here may not be in any final package of proposals; others may be added. Nonetheless, these recommendations appear to reflect the current thinking of many of those working on this project.

Much in the offing in this area is of import to fund-raising professionals.

General Proposal

The package would include retention of the "substantially related" test. It would also retain the exceptions from the unrelated income rules for activities that are not regularly carried on (thereby protecting many fund-raising special events from taxation), for activities conducted by volunteers, and for sales of donated goods. However, there would be a recommendation that the "convenience" exception be repealed.[135]

Fund-Raising Disclosure

The proposal summary states: "Despite an educational campaign by the IRS, some charitable organizations do not disclose that payments made in return for benefits are not deductible by the donor."[136] Thus, the proposal would direct the IRS to conduct a three-year study on the results of its educational efforts and to report to Congress the name of each organization individually contacted and the results of that contact, as well as the results of a "new cautionary instruction to appear on future Forms 1040 (Schedule A) regarding the charitable deduction."

This suggestion reflects the belief of some on Capitol Hill that the Special Emphasis Program of the IRS (whereby it is investigating many aspects of fund-raising for charity) is not working as well or as quickly as they would like.

Sale of Goods

The sale of functional or decorative items of tangible personal property would be deemed to not further an organization's tax-exempt purposes and thus would be subject to the unrelated income tax—as a general rule. For this purpose, "functional" property would generally include clothing, jewelry, furnishings, or common consumer items. However,

---

[135] In general, see Ch. 6 § 6.4.
[136] See *id.* §§ 6.1 & 6.3.

functional property would not include property used primarily in an exempt function (for example, Girl Scout uniforms, votive candles, or goods produced in a sheltered workshop or by craftspersons demonstrating their crafts in a museum). Also, educational material such as textbooks, guidebooks, educational records and toys, and instructional software would not be considered functional items.

"Decorative" property would include original works of decorative art as well as reproductions or adaptations.

Notwithstanding the foregoing, revenue from the sale of functional or decorative items of tangible personal property would not be taxable if it came within one of the proposed "safe harbors" or one of the exceptions contained in present law.

Safe Harbors

Safe harbors would be (1) mementos (for example, a mug bearing the exempt organization's logo) sold by any tax-exempt organization for no more than $25; (2) any item—if not subject to the federal excise tax (that is, other than cigarettes, liquor, and gasoline)—sold by a charitable organization on its premises for no more than $25; (3) reproductions (or adaptations) of any item maintained in the organization's collection or exhibits if sold for no more than $100, regardless of character (that is, as functional or decorative); (4) the sale by an educational institution of computer equipment to bona fide students provided that the institution adopted "strict procedures" to prevent resale; (5) drugs, supplies, or other goods sold to (or for) a patient of the organization as part of the patient's treatment, or nonpatient medical items not available in the immediate geographic area.

Other "Targeted" Rules

No unrelated income tax would result from the provision of laboratory medical testing to patients or to those to whom such testing is not available in the immediate geographic area.

Fitness centers would generate unrelated business income to the extent of 20 percent of "excess" dues, namely, dues from a member that exceed the average dues paid by all "unsubsidized" members.

Generally, travel and tour services would be unrelated businesses. An exception would be made for "local transportation," which would include transportation provided to sites where the organization conducts exempt activities (such as college bus service from campuses). Any exception for educational travel would be available only for a degree program, regardless of the destination or participants.

Off-premises sales (for example, a sidewalk cafe in front of a museum) or after-hours catering for private parties would be taxable. Other on-premises food sales would not be taxable.

Veterinary services would result in unrelated income, except for (1) spaying and neutering, (2) measures to protect public health (for example, rabies shots), and (3) emergency services to save the life of the animal.

Hotel facilities patronized by the general public would be considered unrelated businesses. However, the term "hotel" would not include hospitals, nursing homes, youth hostels, dormitories, emergency shelters and single-room occupancy facilities that fulfill a charitable purpose, away-from-home lodging provided to patients receiving medical treatment at a hospital or to relatives of (or medical personnel attending to) such patients. The proposal would also exclude a hotel operated as part of a degree program by an educational institution. Nonetheless, an educational institution would realize unrelated income when it leases its dormitories to members of the public (other than those using the facilities for an exempt function, such as an alumni reunion).

Retail sales of condominiums by tax-exempt organizations would result in unrelated business income.

In a somewhat surprise development, this proposal would not create statutory law concerning affinity credit card and other affinity merchandising arrangements. Presumably, the staff believes that the IRS position and enforcement on this subject is sufficient.

Generally, the operation of theme and amusement parks (such as Heritage Village) would be regarded as unrelated businesses. However, "living museums" (such as Colonial Williamsburg and Old Sturbridge Village) would continue as related businesses.

Income from testing for public safety certification purposes by organizations "operated for purposes of testing for public safety" would remain exempt but the income derived by these organizations from other testing would be taxable.

Royalties

Net royalties would be treated as unrelated business income, with exceptions for royalties derived from research, minerals, and activities related to the organization's exempt purpose.

The package does not contain any proposal for gross royalties. However, it states that rules would clarify that a gross royalty measured by advertising revenue earned by the licensee would be treated as net advertising income under the proposals concerning the taxation of advertising revenue (see below). Also, income from the use of mailing lists would be treated as rental income rather than royalty income—and thus would be unrelated income.

The Treasury Department would be directed to conduct a five-year study on royalties, including royalties from research, minerals, and self-created property (including the organization's name and logo), as well as arrangements recast into royalty contracts after the enactment of these proposals.

Subsidiaries

The definition of a controlled subsidiary would be reduced from 80 percent to more than 50 percent, with attribution rules, but without an "acting together" rule (for exempt organizations which together have control).

Instead of requiring taxable corporations to determine their tax liabilities based on the activities and purposes of related exempt organizations (as has been proposed), the package would expand the "hobby loss" disallowance rules[137] to reach any activity carried on by a taxable corporation owned more than 50 percent by an exempt organization.

For this purpose, business activities would be separated only to the extent that they represent separate activities under common commercial practice. That is, a loss from a portion of an integrated activity would not be separately calculated. Thus, for example, a taxable manufacturer would not have to separate its research and development activities from its production activities. Likewise, a taxable magazine publisher would not be required to separate the advertising activity from the editorial activity. Further, a taxable hospital subsidiary could offset losses from a trauma center against income from office visits. By contrast, however, a taxable subsidiary could not offset losses from a trauma center against income from manufacturing a line of medical office furniture.

Computational and Other Rules

This proposal would introduce new rules concerning dual-use facilities (for example, a university stadium leased a portion of the time to outside groups). If an exempt organization uses a facility more than 50 percent

[137] IRC § 183.

for unrelated business activities, under this proposal current law would govern. Thus, the present regulations (allowing any reasonable method for allocating expenses) and the court interpretation of these rules (basing the allocation on percentages of actual exempt and taxable use)[138] would apply.

If, however, the organization uses a facility 50 percent or more for exempt purposes, the organization would, pursuant to this proposal, be required to (1) first reduce the gross income received from the unrelated activity by the marginal costs (such as additional security guards) attributable to that activity (the resulting amount being "net receipts"), and (2) further reduce net receipts by appropriate allocation of all other expenses (including direct operating costs, depreciation, and general and administrative expenses), with the limitation that net receipts cannot be reduced by more than 80 percent by these other expenses.

Advertising would be regarded as a per se unrelated business. However, like the dual-use modification, the exempt organization would be permitted to reduce its net advertising income by no more than 80 percent by net nonadvertising costs of the publication or broadcast.

To reduce the filing burdens for small amounts of unrelated business income, the proposal would provide for a $5,000 specific deduction that would be available to all tax-exempt organizations (other than retirement trusts, including individual retirement accounts). Also, the specific deduction would apply to unrelated business income from any source (directly or through a partnership).

The exempt organization tax return[139] filing requirement would have the same threshold, although the organization would have to make a summary disclosure of the activity (including approximate receipts and costs) on any annual information return[140] it might otherwise be required to file. Appropriate aggregation rules would be required to prevent an exempt organization from claiming multiple specific deductions.

An even higher filing threshold—such as $25,000—could be instituted for charitable organizations, particularly since many charities might become subject to the other rules of the proposal, "often with little prospect of a tax liability." This threshold amount "should" be gross receipts from all taxable sources, that is, receipts that would otherwise be reported on the unrelated business income tax return (e.g., not contributions,

---

[138] *Rensselaer Polytechnic Institute* v. *Commissioner*, 732 F.2d 1058 (2d Cir. 1984).
[139] Form 990-T.
[140] Form 990 or 990-PF.

dues or, in general, dividends, interest, or rents from real property, but gross receipts from the sale of goods under the rules described above without regard to safe harbors).

The proposal also does not contain any revisions of the law pertaining to reporting and administration. This is because the IRS is well on the way, with some prodding from Capitol Hill, to implementing most of the original recommendations.[141]

The proposal does not offer any change in the rules concerning the use of for-profit subsidiaries by tax-exempt organizations. The package thus does not contain the so-called aggregation rule, which would have attributed the activities of taxable affiliates to their parent exempt organizations for purposes of determining the exempt parent's continuing entitlement to tax exemption.

Commentary

This proposal is an important step in the evolutionary development of any new unrelated income rules. This matter has come a long way since the five-day hearing in 1987, the draft proposals that surfaced in 1988, and the many aspects of speculation that have meandered along over the past months.

The package is striking in two respects. First, the range of issues is considerably narrower. Second, much of some of the original recommendations have been or are being "enacted" by IRS action or court opinion.

About the first point, it is now clear that Congress will not, for the foreseeable future, attempt any massive rewrite of the unrelated income rules. Thus, the proposal embodies retention of the "substantiality related" test and nearly all of the present exceptions from unrelated business income taxation.

The proposal's approach of using "targeted" rules—heavily endorsed by Treasury—is a logical extension of previous plans. However, even the proposed targets do not include many hot issues of the past, such as for-profit subsidiaries, partnerships, joint ventures, and most royalties.

Concerning the second point, some of the original proposals were already reflective of existing law (such as taxing "royalties" that are in actuality proceeds from the active participation by exempt organizations in joint ventures). A review of this package of proposals yields more of the same. The IRS action in revamping the applications for recognition

---

[141] See Ch. 6 § 6.6.

of tax exemption,[142] the annual information returns,[143] and the appreciated property gift forms,[144] and inauguration of the fund-raising audit check-sheet,[145] has eliminated any proposed statutory recommendations in the fields of reporting and administration. Other IRS action has caused proposals to tax affinity card revenue to disappear.

Much in this package should cheer exempt organizations, particularly charitable ones. The safe harbor rules are the most reasonable yet. Museums should be heartened by the $100 threshold. Colleges and universities would welcome the rule to allow nontaxable sales of computer equipment. The filing thresholds are the most fair and sensible yet.

Regrettably, hysteria continues to play a role when it comes to fund-raising disclosure. It is not clear what good a three-year study would do, except to buy time for the noncompliant; the general rules are crystal clear. What is the point of reporting the names of exempt organizations contacted to Congress? What is that body going to do with them? Or to them? Effective enforcement of current rules should absorb the energy to be devoted to this area.

Even this package does not seem destined for enactment, however. So, the members and staff of the House Subcommittee on Oversight will continue with their labors. Eventually, something in the unrelated income field will be enacted, and Congress can then say it acted to resolve the problem. And those who have watched this process from its beginning will look at the final legislative product and wonder, in relation to the "problem" as originally defined, why Congress bothered.

§ 8.11 A Model Law

Fund-raising regulation is experiencing great surges. More and more states are getting involved in charitable solicitation regulation, imposing registration, reporting, and a myriad of other requirements upon charities and those who assist them in the fund-raising process. States that have formerly foregone the need for a fund-raising law have suddenly decided their citizens now need one. States with fund-raising regulation laws are making them tougher.[146] And those who administer these laws—the state regulators—are applying them with newfound vigor.

[142] See Ch. 6 § 6.5.
[143] See *id.* § 6.6.
[144] See *id.* § 6.11.
[145] See *id.* § 6.1.
[146] Only the state of Florida has bucked this trend by repealing a very stringent regulation statute and substituting a much narrower set of rules. See Ch. 3.

Introduction

These state laws require compliance by charitable organizations that engage in fund-raising. They apply to these charities by the law of the state in which the organization is located and by the law of the other states in which the organization solicits contributions. Further, these laws directly affect charities by reason of the regulation of those who help them raise funds, namely, professional fund-raisers, professional solicitors, and commercial co-venturers.

Without doubt, these charitable solicitation acts are well intentioned. There are fund-raising abuses taking place, and the public needs and deserves a place to lodge complaints and be assured that the frauds are prosecuted and punished. The law is clear that each state, in the exercise of its "police power," has the authority to enact and enforce this type of law.[147] Indeed, the states' attorneys general have considerable inherent ability to regulate in this field even without the statutory backup.

Sometimes, however, the cure is worse than the disease. Fund-raising regulation, as currently written, is one of those instances. The standard contemporary state charitable solicitation acts are unnecessarily complex, onerous, stringent, and burdensome. They are all too often prompted by a motive to "get" someone or are otherwise ill-conceived. The laws are frequently written by legislators with a dim view of what they are doing and administered by bureaucrats with a negative view toward philanthropy. In too many states, the fund-raising regulation zeal is leading to the creation of little regulatory empires, staffed at taxpayers' expense by lawyers and investigators whose skills are sorely needed in far more important governmental service. The paperwork and the costs imposed upon charities and their professional consultants often exceed any value these overreaching laws may provide.

The ridiculousness of this situation can be readily seen when one stops to think about what is being regulated. This is not a matter of public health and safety. This is not drug trafficking or nuclear waste disposal. This is charitable giving! Some public education and disclosure would go a long way toward solving the problems in this area. If individuals are uncertain about a particular charity and cannot obtain some wanted information, they have a very simple solution: do not give.

The shame of it all is that the legislators and regulators have lost sight of what it is they are regulating. Philanthropy is the lifeblood of the American system. Billions of dollars are annually provided for services that government cannot and will not supply. Giving to charity is, obviously,

[147] See Ch. 5 § 5.2.

what fuels this machine. But fund-raising regulation is damaging the legitimate fund-raising process—despite the fact that gift solicitation is a constitutionally protected act of free speech. In short, fund-raising for charity is overregulated—often unnecessarily, harmfully, and counter-productively.

Some believe that one answer to all of this regulation is a model charitable solicitation act.

Model Law Elements

For a variety of reasons,[148] any uniformity and simplicity to be achieved in the field of fund-raising regulation for charity are not likely to be the result of enactment of a model charitable solicitation act. Nonetheless, the idea of a model charitable solicitation act lingers in some quarters. Thus, this concept is worth a brief look.

A prototype charitable fund-raising regulation law is, obviously, a matter of judgment. The preferred scope of these laws is in part dependent upon one's view of the appropriate role of government. One person's thoughts about the components of a fund-raising law are likely to be anathema to someone else. Thus, the elements presented here are simply the views of one person. Having said that, it must be noted that all things are relative—these elements are not presented from the standpoint of what is ideal but from the standpoint of what is realistic. For some, the preferential situation is no regulation of charitable fund-raising at all. However, the fact is that charitable fund-raising regulation will continue, so the question is not whether this type of regulation should exist but what form it should take.

The dual concepts at play in the area of regulation of fund-raising for charitable purposes are preapproval and disclosure.

Preapproval

The core of the typical state charitable solicitation act is preapproval, in the sense that registration in advance of fund-raising is required. This registration may be in the form of a license or permit, but the fundamental principle is the same: a charitable organization must acquire permission from the state before it can engage in fund-raising within the jurisdiction. There is no reason to believe that this basic requirement will be eliminated; indeed, it is a quite reasonable requirement.

[148] See *infra* § 8.12.

The objective to be obtained here is balance, this being the area where one requirement of registration can be more onerous than another because of the complexity of the application process. The number of questions asked and the substance of the answers requested are extremely relevant. Each of the summaries of the state charitable solicitation acts contain an inventory of what the various statutes require in this regard.[149] What is reasonable in this setting is, again, a matter of judgment, but the model act would ask for only basic information needed to assure the state regulators of compliance with the overall statute.

The model charitable solicitation act would likewise require registration of professional fund-raisers and professional solicitors. The model act would not require registration of commercial co-venturers, however, because this type of regulation places unnecessary burdens on the business involved and should be a matter of registration (and reporting) by the charitable organization.[150]

Reporting

The model act would not have reporting separate from the registration requirement. Instead, the prototype law would provide that each registration (whether for charitable organizations, professional fund-raisers, or professional solicitors) have a duration of one year. Reregistration each year would supply the state regulators with ample information required to enforce the statute.

Again, the contents of the reapplication should be reasonable, so as not to overly burden the regulated yet provide adequate and meaningful information to the regulators.

Definitions

The typical state charitable solicitation statute opens with a series of definitions, and the model law would be no different.

However, a model statute in this field would have a definition of the term "charitable organization" that is not so broad as to embrace entities and purposes that, in other law contexts, are not "charitable."[151]

The model statute would also wrestle with and resolve the difficult matter of the proper definition of the terms "professional fund-raiser" and "professional solicitor."[152] These definitions would attempt to dif-

---

[149] See Ch. 3.
[150] See *supra* § 8.5.
[151] See Ch. 2 § 2.1; Ch. 4 § 4.1.
[152] See Ch. 4 §§ 4.5 & 4.6; Ch. 5 § 5.9; *supra* § 8.8.

ferentiate the consultant from the true solicitor, yet simultaneously avoid placing fund-raising counsel in the category of solicitor simply because of incidental use of the telephone and/or the mails in the raising of contributions for charitable purposes.

Contracts and Bonds

The model charitable solicitation act would mandate written contracts between charitable organizations and professional fund-raisers, professional solicitors, and/or commercial co-venturers. This requirement is for the benefit and protection of charitable organizations, if for no other reason. However, the mandatory contents of these contracts would be minimal, trusting the parties to strike a fair bargain.

Entities or individuals that have access to the contributed funds would have to be bonded. Thus, this requirement would not normally be imposed upon professional fund-raisers and commercial co-venturers.

Compensation

The model law would not (indeed, could not) contain a percentage limitation on allowable fund-raising costs incurred by charitable organizations and/or on the amount payable to professional fund-raisers or professional solicitors.[153] Nor would such a provision be made mandatory as part of contracts.

The model law would require the parties to disclose all compensatory arrangements as part of the registration process. However, this law would not require a charitable organization, when soliciting contributions, to disclose fund-raising costs at the point of solicitation, nor would it mandate disclosure of the use of professional fund-raising counsel or a professional solicitor. The law would, nonetheless, require a charity to state on its solicitation materials that additional information is available from the charity on request and would require the charity to promptly respond to this type of inquiry.

Exemptions

The model charitable solicitation act would have exemptions. Bona fide religious organizations; colleges, universities, and schools; most health care organizations; and foundations related to these entities would be exempt from the entirety of the statute. This can be done without

---

[153] See Ch. 5 § 5.1.

becoming entangled in equal protection violations[154] and should be done to eliminate from the regulatory process those charitable organizations that simply are not "part of the problem."

Other types of entities may be exempted from the registration and reporting requirements because information about them is otherwise readily available in other ways. This exemption would extend to fraternal, veterans, and other membership groups that confine the solicitations to their membership.

The model law would not make availability of the exemptions conditioned on not using professional fund-raisers or professional solicitors. This type of limitation is discriminatory, often petty, and in many instances counterproductive, because often these organizations should be encouraged to use, not penalized for using, professional assistance.

Other

The model law should contain other provision that could induce simplicity and uniformity, such as the reciprocal agreement provisions, uniform accounting principles, use of other states' (and perhaps the federal government's) reporting forms, and simultaneous reporting dates.

Prohibited Acts

One of the most difficult aspects of the state's charitable solicitation acts is the growing number of so-called prohibited acts.[155] Some prohibited acts are quite reasonable and would be included in the model law. These include misrepresentation of the purpose of a solicitation, implied assertions of endorsement by the state, implied assertions of endorsement of the charity involved by others when that is not the case, use of names of others without consent, use of the name of a similar charitable organization, and making false or misleading statements.

The prototype statute would not, however, attempt to regulate collateral matters, such as the amount of money expended for fund-raising or management, or the application of the funds raised in ways that may interfere with the ability of the charitable organization to further its charitable purposes. These are matters more appropriate for the inherent investigatory efforts of a state's attorney general or for the process of obtaining and retaining tax-exempt status.

---

[154] See Ch. 4 § 4.4; Ch. 5 § 5.5.
[155] See Ch. 4 § 4.12; *supra* § 8.6.

Sanctions

The model act would authorize the usual panoply of sanctions, including investigations, use of subpoenas, revocation of registrations, injunctions, civil penalties, and criminal penalties. It would not interfere with the usual and other inherent enforcement options for the state's attorneys general. It would not, however, authorize private actions.

Commentary

The objective in constructing a model charitable solicitation act would be to achieve a balance between the exercise of a state's police power (to protect its citizens against fraudulent or otherwise misleading solicitations for gifts) and the free speech right of charitable organizations to solicit contributions for their support (and thus not unduly impede the process of funding programs that are vital to the very same citizens). There is no need to flood charitable organizations with paperwork requirements or to force fund-raising consultants to adhere to rules meant for solicitors, when no useful purpose is achieved by doing so. Fund-raising outlaws must be caught and punished but not at the expense of hobbling bona fide charity.

The fact is that these laws are not, all too frequently, well thought out. The ideal would be a uniform and minimal prototype law in each of the states. The charities could then comply with the rules rather readily, and enforcement could focus on the true bandits.

Unfortunately, a model law does not seem feasible as a practical matter. Resolution of the present-day mess may be achieved through reciprocal agreements, uniform accounting principles, similar registration and reporting forms, and/or a company to facilitate compliance by charitable organizations and others. Still, when legislating in this area, some model framework is important, if only to minimize the more egregious provisions.

§ 8.12   Some Proposals for Relief

One of the purposes of this book is to summarize the vast amount of government regulation of the process of raising funds for charitable objectives. Preceding sections of this chapter, for example, set forth some of the principal elements of this type of regulation.

With most forms of government regulation, a balance is struck between the scope of the regulating and the ongoing health of the regulated. That is, usually the regulating is not so strenuous that it severely retards the very process—and its growth—that is being regulated.

When it comes to state regulation of philanthropic fund-raising, however, the law is pushing to the point where matters are out of balance, where the regulatory process is impeding the fund-raising process. Lack of compliance with and enforcement of these laws is keeping government regulation from consuming, frustrating, and/or discourging fund-raising for charity. This is not a proper state of affairs, for the regulated or the regulators, and it should be remedied.

Model Law

But, what to do? One solution that has been touted over the years is a model charitable solicitation statute.[156] The thought underlying this proposal is that charitable organizations could more easily comply with the laws in all of the states if these laws were the same. There is some truth to this, although many of the compliance burdens would not change and could even increase. As to the latter, a lobbying effort to enact a model law could result in the substitution of a more strenuous statute for a weaker one in some states, or the adoption of a rigorous statute in a state where previously there was none.

The proposal simply has too many flaws, which is why it has not, and probably will not, work. To date, the charitable organizations have not been able to agree on the contents of a model charitable solicitations act because the issue is too divisive (such as the question of exemptions). Furthermore, the state regulators cannot agree on a uniform statute in this area. Thus, there is little likelihood that both the regulated and the regulators will agree on a law.

Also, the lobbying effort involved would be prodigious and enormously costly. It would probably take millions of dollars to formulate a law and then see it through to enactment in every state. Who would coordinate that effort? Where would the funds come from? Would simplicity really result from uniformity, or would it lead to more regulation in more states? These and other questions and dilemmas make unrealistic the enactment of a uniform charitable solicitation act in every state.

Reciprocal Agreements

As discussed, several of these state laws contain reciprocal agreement provisions,[157] and these provisions are considerably underutilized.[158]

---

[156] See *supra* § 8.11.

[157] See Ch. 4 § 4.14.

[158] See *supra* § 8.8.

Here is an opportunity to breathe some uniformity into these laws and reduce the regulatory burdens, while simultaneously inducing more compliance in this area of law. This approach does not require amendment of the statute, only application of it. Pursuant to these provisions, a state regulator can allow a charitable organization to file, as its registration and/or annual report, a copy of the documents as filed in the home state. Many of these provisions also enable regulators to grant exemptions from compliance where the exemptions are part of the law in the home state.

Therefore, it is not so much uniformity of law that is required as it is unification of the process of complying with the law. How much easier it would be on charities that want to comply, but are overwhelmed by the complexity, if they could prepare documents in their home states and file copies of them in other states. The process would also be advanced and enhanced if there were greater uniformity as to exemptions.

Uniform Annual Report

Another proposal—often made but never successful—is the idea of a uniform annual report. This proposal is likewise grounded on the thought that it is not the laws that need changing so much as the process of complying with them. It truly would be simpler for all concerned if a charity required to annually file in the states could file the same document.

Once again, however, reality intrudes and spoils the potential. The fact is that the state regulators cannot agree on the contents of an annual report. Nor can they agree about the use of any particular state's report as an annual report. (An effort was undertaken once to create a uniform annual report that reflected the requirements of every state; the resulting document was so large and unwieldy that the project collapsed, seemingly of its own weight.)

Other Forms of Uniformity

Still other forms of uniformity are possible. The states could strive for uniform rules and regulations by introducing some commonalities into such subjects as definitions and cost allocations. But the regulators cannot agree.

The accounting profession could inject more uniformity into its rules for fund-raising organizations, but they cannot agree on the appropriate principles either.

Even uniformity of enforcement would help. Some states are known to be strict in their enforcement of these laws; others have a reputation for being lackadaisical. This state of affairs creates an atmosphere of cynicism and lawbreaking, where some charities register only in the "tough" states, waiting to register in the others when and if they "get caught."

A Coordinating Company

It thus appears clear that the pathway to the reduction of regulatory burdens on fund-raising charities and their professional assistants is not uniformity of law so much as uniformity of the process of complying. For any proposal to work, it must achieve twin goals: make regulatory life easier for the fund-raising charitable organizations, and not reduce (indeed, should stimulate) compliance with the fund-raising regulation laws.

Given this messy situation, the ultimate answer may well be an intermediary between regulated and regulators. This intermediary would funnel information from the charities to the states, although the states could use the intermediary as a means for disseminating information as well.

This intermediary would be a company, possibly a nonprofit, tax-exempt organization, but more likely a standard for-profit corporation. Its purpose would be to facilitate charities' compliance with the states' charitable solicitation acts. (It could perform the same functions for professional fund-raisers and professional solicitors, of course, but the focus of this proposal will be on the charities themselves.)

This company (say, the Fund-Raising Compliance Center, Inc.) would computerize the registration and reporting requirements of all of the state charitable solicitation acts. Into its data base would go fee amounts, exemptions, filing dates, and the like. A charitable organization would contract with the company for its services. The process would work as follows: the charity would advise the company of the states in which it intends to solicit funds; the company would send a questionnaire to the charity requesting the information needed to facilitate registration in those states; the charity would return the completed questionnaire; the company would generate through its computer the required registration forms and send them to the charity; and the charity would review the forms for accuracy, sign them, and file them with the states with a check for the registration fee. The same process could occur with annual reports.

If the company functions properly, the charities would know that they are in full compliance with these laws, and the states would have the satisfaction of knowing that the reports are accurate. It may well be that charities would be exempt from some requirements in some states; this process would bring those facts to light. This approach would probably stimulate some advances in the use of reciprocal agreements, as discussed above.

Without illegally practicing law, this company could also serve as a source of ongoing information to its clients. Prospective statutory law changes could be monitored and periodically reported to clients. Changes in regulations and forms could likewise be monitored and disseminated. The states could use this information clearinghouse to communicate information to charities. The company could collect information and do analyses that might lead to improvements in the ways these laws are written and administered.

The point is that expected compliance with state fund-raising regulation laws is too great in relation to the ability of charities to comply. Some charities lack the staffing or other resources to adhere to these requirements. Frequently, the state officials lack the ability to enforce the laws they are charged with administering.

The answer, then, may well be to tap into the American tradition of creating business where new needs arise. Necessity is the mother of invention, and today's charities need help in this area. It is worth a try.

§ 8.13   A Look Ahead

It is appropriate to speculate about what is likely to happen in and to the world of fund-raising and philanthropy, in 1991 and beyond, with regard to the development of law and regulation.

Clearly the nonprofit world will, over the coming months and years, be suffering more regulation by government. This will be true at both the federal and state level.

Why is this? In part, it is due to the deficits governments are experiencing. In Washington, D.C., these days tax laws are being written with revenue impact the primary consideration. Good ideas about tax law revision usually do not move very far or very fast unless they generate some tax revenue. Bad tax policy can advance in this environment if there are tax dollars to be produced.

For example, it is the author's view that the above-the-line charitable contribution deduction for nonitemizing taxpayers is a good idea. It represents tax policy nurturing taxpayer behavior that is productive for the whole of society and consonant with the American impulse to solve problems through the nonprofit sector rather than the governmental sector. But this law change (really, restoration) has no chance of enactment in this budgetary setting because of revenue "losses," its virtues as a matter of political philosophy/tax policy notwithstanding.

Another example are the current tax policies that are dramatically harming gifts of property to museums and similar institutions. Some law reforms are needed in this area, such as elimination of the appreciation element in gifts of appreciated property as a tax preference item for alternative minimum tax purposes, and encouragement through a charitable deduction of gifts of artworks by their creators. Yet the current tax law writing climate is hardly conducive to these and like law changes.

By contrast, there is the lurking proposal to impose a tax on the net investment income of all tax-exempt organizations, including endowment and pension funds. While a bad idea—from the standpoint of political philosophy and the adverse impact on the distribution of funds for charitable and other exempt purposes—it is gaining in popularity simply because of the billions of dollars in revenue that such a tax would yield.

It is in this context that proposals to revise the law of unrelated business income taxation must be evaluated.[159] The author and others have been warning about impending revision of the unrelated business income tax rules for months—really, years. And no law changes in this field have emerged.

There are several reasons for this. Successful lobbying by nonprofit organizations is one reason. Inadequate lobbying by the business community is another. Confusion and indecision in Congress is a third. The difficulties inherent in finding rules to curb or eliminate abuses in the use of unrelated businesses without harming charitable and other exempt works is still another.

Nonetheless, revision of the law of unrelated business is coming. At present, the nation's lawmakers are awaiting pronouncements from the Department of the Treasury about the projected revenue impact of the various proposals. Once they become aware of the millions of dollars that these contemplated laws would (allegedly) generate, the proposals will likely become infused with new life.

Essentially, the same phenomenon is being played out at the state (and local) level. There is renewed interest in narrowing the scope of the exemptions from sales, use, and property taxes. It is not that these regulators are suddenly seeking the performance of less charity in their jurisdictions; it is that they are desperate for additional tax revenues.

The scandal factor, while not as important as the deficit factor, is playing a role here. Recent episodes in the field of direct mail fund-

---

[159] See Ch. 6 § 6.4; *supra* § 8.10.

raising (for example, sweepstakes promotions) are involving new and expanded forms of government regulation. Several states are in this picture, strenuously enforcing their charitable solicitation acts and successfully procuring injunctive relief from the courts. The U.S. Postal Service is enjoining mailings. The FTC is advocating an amplification of its jurisdiction to empower it to regulate charitable fund-raising as a matter of consumer protection.[160]

The IRS is seeing "scandal," too, being particularly annoyed at what its officials perceive as "misleading" fund-raising appeals.[161] This largely concerns the practice of some charitable organizations of advising prospective "donors" that "gifts" to them are deductible as charitable gifts when they in fact are not (because they are not "gifts" at all), or when there is only a partial deduction (because, as in the case of special fund-raising events, the payments are in part a gift and part a purchase of a service or product). Although the revenue implications of this are not enormous, these fund-raising practices are causing unhappiness within the IRS and are tainting that agency's attitude about charitable fund-raising in general, with unfavorable consequences for the future.

A third element contributing to this unsettling environment for nonprofit organizations and those who advise them about fund-raising are the fund-raising endeavors of some charities, which tend to offend lawmakers, regulators, and other policymakers. Some aspects of this have already been referenced, such as misleading fund-raising appeals and certain unrelated business endeavors.

The list of practices in these regards is growing. Here are just a few of the practices of nonprofit organizations (in no particular order) that some are finding noxious (or at least taxable): affinity card programs, commercial co-venturing (or charitable sales promotions), product sales, raffles and sweepstakes, bingo, mailing list rentals, consulting services, catalog sales, product endorsements, provision or marketing of insurance benefits, joint venturing with for-profits, participation in partnerships, and use of taxable subsidiaries.

These activities are all permissible under existing law. Some are taxable under present law. But, for the most part, that is not the point. This aspect of the matter involves value judgments—indeed, views of morality.

There are those who intuitively feel that charities should not be doing these things. Some wish the practices would be outlawed; others would settle for taxing them.

---

[160] See Ch. 7 § 7.2.
[161] See Ch. 6 §§ 6.1 & 6.2.

This in turn leads to a fourth element: the perception by many in government of the distinction between nonprofit and for-profit organizations. Or, to put it more precisely, policymakers and regulators are more and more frequently having difficulty identifying that distinction. The difference continues to be readily ascertainable as a matter of law, but it is all too blurry to much of the regulatory community (and, for that matter, to the general public). The point is that it is easier for lawmakers to advocate new statutory law or regulators to advocate a new regulation or rule when they see the task as one of precluding charitable and other nonprofit organizations from doing what they ought not be doing as a matter of principle. There are those who want a system where charities are supported only by gifts (perhaps nondeductible ones), operated solely by volunteers, and expend all of their revenue annually (which is to say no "profit" making or accumulations in the nature of endowments).

This is not, obviously, the best of regulatory climates for charitable organizations and those who assist them in the raising of money. Indeed, it is not the best of climates for nonprofit organizations in general.

What, then, will be happening in the worlds of charity and law, to the extent that they interrelate, in the coming months? While that is not the most important question, the answer is this: more law and more regulation.

Some specifics in this regard are relatively easy to predict. For example, some revision of the unrelated business laws by Congress is quite likely. On this point, the changes will not be massive but they will be important to the organizations that are directly affected by them. Some of these changes will affect fund-raising by charities and the fund-raising profession, such as alteration of the tax law pertaining to revenue received from affinity card programs and rentals of mailing lists.

More likely, however, the changes in the law of unrelated business income taxation that will directly affect fund-raisers will emanate from court opinions rather than from new statutes. This will be the case for two reasons.

One, the law of unrelated business income taxation is presently evolving on a two-track system. That is, Congress is writing some of this law, and the courts are developing some as well. What is both interesting and alarming, however, is that the courts are creating new unrelated business law, rather than simply interpreting the statutory law authored by Congress. The consequence of this is that the law of unrelated business income taxation now includes some fundamental principles that have little or no correlation with any provisions of the Internal Revenue Code.

This makes it very difficult in many instances to divine what the "law" on a point of unrelated business is; the law found in the Code may be different from that found in a judge's opinion. All indications are that this trend in the evolution of the law will continue and probably intensify.

Two, the courts are far ahead of Congress in articulating the emerging precepts of unrelated business income taxation. Thus, the federal judiciary is busily developing doctrines of "commerciality" and "unfair competition," while Congress is still mired in frets over what to do about university bookstore sales of computers and museum sales of reproductions of items in collections. These broad doctrines are far more likely to affect the law of charitable fund-raising than anything Congress is likely to pass any time soon. Indeed, much of what Congress will be doing in the months and years to come in this field will be to codify rules previously invented by the courts.

Another aspect of law development that is fairly easy to predict is increased involvement in the charitable fund-raising process by the IRS. The IRS will continue to interrogate charitable organizations about their fund-raising plans by means of applications for recognition of tax-exempt status.[162] It will continue to pester charities that persist in touting payments to them as being charitable gifts, when in fact they (in whole or in part) are neither. Budgetary cutbacks will reduce the IRS audit capacity in the exempt organizations area, however.

Perhaps the most dramatic development in the federal tax law pertaining to charitable fund-raising in 1991 (and thereafter) will be the impact of the revised annual information return.[163] This new return requires tax-exempt organizations to report income-producing activities by category. These categories include special fund-raising events. These revenue sources must also be identified as related or unrelated activities, with the former accompanied by an explanation as to why the activity is conducted in advancement of exempt purposes. Preparation of this return should involve the participation of the fund-raising executives.

Another easy prognostication is increase in state regulation of fund-raising by charities and of professional fund-raising consultants, by reason of expansion of the contents and enforcement of charitable solicitation acts.

The coming months will probably be witness to some form of federal tax increase and other revisions of the tax law to generate more federal revenues. Charitable organizations will have to be on guard to repel

---

[162] See Ch. 6 § 6.5.
[163] See *id.* § 6.6.

attempts at law change that would, directly or indirectly, threaten bona fide tax exemptions and charitable contribution deductions.

Federal regulation of the charitable fund-raising process will intensify and expand. Fund-raisers must assume enactment, sooner or later, of law mandating disclosures to prospective donors along the lines of present law applicable to fund-raising by noncharitable organizations.[164] Federal preemption of state fund-raising regulation law is not in the offing, but a greater role by the U.S. Postal Service and perhaps the FTC is.

The foregoing has focused on what is coming, in the realm of law and regulation, for fund-raising professionals and the charitable organization they represent. It is written as though all of this new trouble at the hands of the law is wholly unavoidable and/or that the fund-raising world must passively accept this new regulatory environment.

Most certainly, this is not the case. Earlier, it was noted that the most important question is not, What is coming? but What should fund-raisers be doing about it? The fund-raising profession does not have much of a record in the field of government relations. If nothing is done in this area, more adverse law and regulation for fund-raisers and the charities they serve will be the order of the day. But much can be done to forestall or shape these coming changes.

Here are some suggestions:

1. *More Lobbying.* The fund-raising profession must increase its visibility on Capitol Hill and in many of the state legislatures. Most legislators do not understand charitable fund-raising; this ignorance, unless corrected, will be reflected in new laws. The lawmakers need to learn about fund-raising from charitable organizations at the grass-roots level, as well as from coordinated lobbying efforts in Washington, D.C.

A fundamental lobbying tip: Legislators and their staffs need to be contacted and informed at a time when nothing is being requested of them. For example, lawmakers and/or their staffs should be provided tours of the charitable facilities in their districts or states and honored in various ways. They are thereafter likely to be more receptive to pleas for help when the inevitable crisis develops.

An immediate goal for the profession should be the identification and cultivation of members of Congress who are willing to champion the causes of charitable giving and those professionals who help charities receive it.

---

[164] See *id.* §§ 6.2 & 6.3.

2. *More Coordination.*   The fund-raising world needs to construct more effective systems for lobbying federal and state legislative bodies. This includes mechanisms for in-tandem lobbying by the principal national associations with fund-raising professionals as their members.

3. *More Networking.*   Many effective government relations programs are in place and functioning well. Several of these are assembled by coalitions, both transient and permanent. These coalitions need more infiltration and utilization by fund-raising interests.

4. *More Engagement of the IRS.*   The IRS is open to greater understanding of charitable fund-raising and input from fund-raising professionals. Historically, however, the fund-raising professional, as such, has stayed out of this agency's corridors. Hopefully, this will change, because the IRS needs and wants to hear from professional fund-raisers. The regulatory future of the profession will be directly shaped by the extent to which this engagement occurs and is successful.

5. *More Engagement of the Treasury Department.*   What was said about the IRS is equally true for the Department of the Treasury. Here, more policy-making takes place and thus the Treasury Department is another incubator of the law of charitable fund-raising. For example, in the context of development of the regulations concerning lobbying by public charities,[165] Treasury wrote the first federal tax law definition of the term "fund-raising"; however, the fund-raising profession had no communication with Treasury about the content and scope of this very important and encompassing regulatory definition.

6. *Political Action Efforts.*   The fund-raising world should develop a political action committee, either as an adjunct to a qualified membership association or as an independent (freestanding) PAC. Those interested in the cause, and future, of professional fund-raising would, presumably, gladly give in support of positive law changes and the prevention of adverse law changes.

7. *Alteration of State Charitable Solicitation Acts.*   The proliferation of strenuous and, in some instances, absurd charitable solicitation acts is reaching an alarming state. Something must be done to curb these offenses by state legislators, while at the same time curbing abuses by the unscrupulous.[166] A legislative project in this regard is long overdue; who better to spearhead it than fund-raising professionals?

---

[165] *Id.* § 6.7.
[166] See *supra* § 8.11.

So, that is where matters stand, at least to the extent that one can reasonably predict them. We must assume that 1991 and beyond will bring several attempts to regulate, restrain, and retard fund-raising for charitable purposes. Not to inject too much gloom into the forecast, generally the regulatory climate will not be inhospitable to fund-raising for charity. But, much is looming and policymakers' attitudes are not always favorable. Adversity can bring opportunity and, as usual, the extent of new law and regulation is dependent in part on the degree to which the fund-raising profession wishes to exert itself and influence outcomes.

Appendices

Appendix A

At-a-Glance Summary of State Charitable Solicitation Acts

States with "Standard" Acts (30)

Arkansas, Colorado, Connecticut, Georgia, Hawaii, Illinois, Kansas, Kentucky, Maine, Maryland, Massachusetts, Michigan, Minnesota, Missouri, New Hampshire, New Jersey, New York, North Carolina, North Dakota, Oklahoma, Oregon, Pennsylvania, Rhode Island, South Carolina, Tennessee, Utah, Virginia, Washington, West Virginia, and Wisconsin

Other State Laws (13)

Alabama, California, District of Columbia, Florida, Indiana, Iowa, Louisiana, Nebraska, Nevada, New Mexico, Ohio, South Dakota, and Texas

No Statute (8)

Alaska, Arizona, Delaware, Idaho, Mississippi, Montana, Vermont, and Wyoming

Registration Requirement for "Charitable Organizations" (38)

Arkansas, California, Colorado, Connecticut, District of Columbia, Georgia, Hawaii, Illinois, Iowa, Kansas, Kentucky, Louisiana, Maine, Maryland, Massachusetts, Michigan, Minnesota, Missouri, Nebraska, New Hampshire, New Jersey, New Mexico, New York, North Carolina, North Dakota, Ohio, Oklahoma, Oregon, Pennsylvania, Rhode Island, South Carolina, South Dakota, Tennessee, Utah, Virginia, Washington, West Virginia, and Wisconsin

Registration Requirement for "Professional Fund-Raisers" (30)

Arkansas, Colorado, Connecticut, Georgia, Hawaii, Illinois, Kansas, Kentucky, Maine, Maryland, Massachusetts, Michigan, Minnesota, Missouri, New Hampshire, New Jersey, New York, North Carolina, North Dakota, Ohio, Oklahoma, Pennsylvania, Rhode Island, South Carolina, Tennessee, Utah, Virginia, Washington, West Virginia, and Wisconsin

Registration Requirement for "Professional Solicitors" (26)

Arkansas, Colorado, Connecticut, Hawaii, Illinois, Kansas, Kentucky, Maine, Maryland, Massachusetts, Michigan, New Hampshire, New Jersey, New York,

North Carolina, North Dakota, Ohio, Oklahoma, Oregon, Pennsylvania, Rhode Island, South Carolina, Tennessee, Virginia, West Virginia, and Wisconsin

Regulation of Commercial Co-venturing (9)

California, Colorado, Connecticut, Maine, Massachusetts, New Hampshire, New York, North Carolina, and Wisconsin

Bond Requirement for "Professional Fund-Raisers" (21)

Arkansas, Connecticut, Georgia, Hawaii, Illinois, Kansas, Maine, Michigan, New Hampshire, New Jersey, New York, North Carolina, Ohio, Oklahoma, Pennsylvania, Rhode Island, South Carolina, Utah, Washington, West Virginia, and Wisconsin

Bond Requirement for "Professional Solicitors" (11)

Connecticut, Hawaii, Maryland, Massachusetts, North Carolina, Pennsylvania, Rhode Island, South Carolina, Tennessee, Virginia, and West Virginia

Exemptions from Law

Religious Organizations (21)

Arkansas, District of Columbia, Florida, Hawaii, Illinois, Iowa, Kentucky, Louisiana, Maine, Nebraska, New Hampshire, New Jersey, New York, North Dakota, Ohio, Pennsylvania, Rhode Island, South Carolina, Tennessee, Virginia, and Washington

Educational Institutions (7)

Florida, Hawaii, Kentucky, Louisiana, New Hampshire, North Dakota, and Tennessee

Membership Organizations (4)

Arkansas, California, Hawaii, and Kentucky

Small Organizations (4)

Arkansas ($1,000), Hawaii ($4,000), Illinois ($4,000), and Tennessee ($5,000)

Hospitals (3)

Hawaii, Louisiana, and New Hampshire

Named Individual (1)

Hawaii

Exemption from Registration and Reporting

Educational Institutions (22)

Connecticut, Georgia, Illinois, Kansas, Maine, Maryland, Michigan, Minnesota, Missouri, New Jersey, New York, North Carolina, Ohio, Oklahoma, Oregon, Pennsylvania, Rhode Island, South Carolina, Utah, Virginia, West Virginia, and Wisconsin

Small Organizations (20)

Connecticut ($25,000), Georgia ($15,000), Illinois ($4,000), Kansas ($5,000), Maine ($10,000), Maryland ($25,000), Massachusetts ($5,000), Michigan ($8,000), Minnesota ($25,000), New Jersey ($10,000), New York ($25,000), North Carolina ($10,000), Oklahoma ($10,000), Oregon ($5,000), Rhode Island ($3,000), South Carolina ($2,000), Utah ($5,000), Virginia ($5,000), Washington ($5,000), and Wisconsin ($4,000)

Membership Organizations (20)

Arkansas, District of Columbia, Georgia, Illinois, Kansas, Maine, Maryland, Michigan, Minnesota, New Jersey, New York, Ohio, Oklahoma, Oregon, Rhode Island, South Carolina, Utah, Virginia, West Virginia, and Wisconsin

Named Individuals (17)

Georgia, Illinois, Kansas, Maine, Maryland, Michigan, Minnesota, New Jersey, New York, Ohio, Oklahoma, Rhode Island, South Carolina, Utah, Virginia, West Virginia, and Wisconsin

Religious Organizations (16)

Arkansas, Connecticut, District of Columbia, Georgia, Kansas, Maryland, Massachusetts, Michigan, Minnesota, Missouri, North Carolina, Oklahoma, Oregon, South Carolina, Utah, and Wisconsin

Hospitals (10)

Connecticut, Kansas, Maine, Michigan, Missouri, North Carolina, Oregon, Rhode Island, Virginia, and West Virginia

Contract Requirements (28)

Arkansas, Connecticut, Georgia, Hawaii, Illinois, Indiana, Kansas, Maine, Maryland, Massachusetts, Michigan, New Hampshire, New Jersey, New York, North Carolina, North Dakota, Ohio, Oklahoma, Oregon, Pennsylvania, Rhode Island, South Carolina, Tennessee, Utah, Virginia, Washington, West Virginia, and Wisconsin

Prohibited Acts (33)

Alabama, Arkansas, Colorado, Connecticut, District of Columbia, Florida, Georgia, Hawaii, Illinois, Indiana, Kansas, Louisiana, Maine, Maryland, Massachusetts, Michigan, Minnesota, Nebraska, New Hampshire, New Jersey, New York, North Carolina, North Dakota, Oklahoma, Oregon, Pennsylvania, Rhode Island, South Carolina, Tennessee, Virginia, Washington, West Virginia, and Wisconsin

Reciprocal Agreement Provisions (13)

Arkansas, Hawaii, Illinois, Kansas, Maryland, Massachusetts, Minnesota, North Carolina, Oklahoma, Pennsylvania, South Carolina, Tennessee, and West Virginia

Advisory Councils (5)

District of Columbia, New York, Pennsylvania, South Carolina, and West Virginia

Principal Regulatory Office

Secretary of State (15)

Arkansas, Colorado, Georgia, Iowa, Kansas, Maryland, Nebraska, Nevada, New York, North Dakota, Pennsylvania, South Carolina, Tennessee, Washington, and West Virginia

Attorney General (13)

California, Illinois, Kentucky, Massachusetts, Michigan, Minnesota, Missouri, New Hampshire, New Jersey, New Mexico, Ohio, Oregon, and Texas

Other (12)

Connecticut, District of Columbia, Florida, Hawaii, Louisiana, Maine, North Carolina, Oklahoma, Rhode Island, Utah, Virginia, and Wisconsin

Appendix B

Exempt Organizations Charitable Solicitations Compliance Improvement
Program Study Checksheet – Phase II

I. Entity Data	National Office Hotline Phone for:

National Office Hotline Phone for:
- **Project and Checksheet**
  Questions - **566—6181**
- **Technical (fundraising)**
  Questions - **566—4332**

1. Name of Organization:

2. Street Address:

3. City, State, ZIP Code:

4. EIN: | | | − | | | | | | | |

5. Type of Return: ☐ Form 990 ☐ Form 990–PF

6. Tax Period: | | | | |

7. Foundation Code: | | |

8. Classification Code: | | | | |

9. Activity Codes   Per EO/BMF: _____ _____ _____
   Per Exam: _____ _____ _____

10. Income/Asset   Per EO/BMF: ___/___
    Codes   Per Exam: ___/___

II. Fundraising Activities Present?

11. Did you find the organization was involved in fundraising activities?   ☐ Yes   ☐ No
[Based upon the response to this item, please refer to "Note 2" in Attachment 5 of the Manual Supplement for further instruction for the completion of this checksheet.]

12. What was the nature of the fundraising activities? [Check the applicable activities listed below and give a brief description of the activities in the space below or complete the descriptive "items" mentioned which appear later on this checksheet.]:

Auction . . . . ☐
Musical Concert . . . . ☐
Spectator Sporting Event . . . . ☐
Luncheon, Dinner, or Banquet . . . . ☐
Carnival, Bazaar, or Fair . . . . ☐
Raffle, Lottery, or Sweepstakes . . . . ☐
Las Vegas or Monte Carlo Nights . . . . ☐
Bingo [and any other Games of Chance (items 39–45)] . . . . ☐
Charity Ball . . . . ☐
[Describe activity here.]:

Fashion Show . . . . ☐
Theatrical Show . . . . ☐
Thrift Store [or similar activity (items 56 – 60)] . . . . ☐
Membership Drive . . . . ☐
Awards Ceremony . . . . ☐
Cultural Exhibition . . . . ☐
Annual Solicitation Campaign . . . . ☐
Other (specify):[   ] . . . . . ☐

	Yes	No	N/A
13. Did the organization conduct any fundraising activities designed to solicit payments which were intended to be, in part, a gift and, in part, a payment for admission to the fundraising event, participation in the fundraising event, or for other benefits conferred on the donor? [If "Yes", please refer to items 62–67].	☐	☐	☐
14. Did the charity receive any "noncash" contributions with a fair market value greater than $500 from any donor(s)? [If "Yes", please refer to items 70 – 76].	☐	☐	☐
15. Did the charity sell, exchange, consume or otherwise dispose of any "noncash" contribution(s) within two years of receipt of the "noncash" property? [If "Yes", please refer to items 78–80].	☐	☐	☐

III. General Information on Fundraising Activities

	Yes	No	N/A
16. If the charity engaged in fundraising activities, complete items 17–25. Otherwise, enter an "X" in "N/A". . . . . ☐ N/A			
17. Did the charity acknowledge receipt of the cash donation in writing?	☐	☐	☐
18. Did the charity acknowledge receipt of the noncash donation in writing?	☐	☐	☐
19. Was an outside/professional fundraiser hired to conduct the fundraising program? [If "Yes", please refer to items 27–37].	☐	☐	☐

Charitable Solicitations Compliance Improvement Program Study Checksheet – Phase II

III. General Information on Fundraising Activities (Continued)

	Yes	No	N/A
20. Did the charity maintain any record(s) of the names and addresses of the donors?	☐	☐	☐
21. Did the charity maintain sample copies of the solicitation materials, advertisements of the fundraising event(s), tickets, receipts, or other evidence of payment received in connection with the fundraising activity(ies)?	☐	☐	☐
22. Did the charity maintain copies of script, transcripts, or other evidence of on-air solicitations for TV and/or radio fundraising solicitations?	☐	☐	☐
23. Did the charity indicate in membership literature or other written evidence that the "cost" of membership dues was tax deductible?	☐	☐	☐
24. If "Yes" to Item 23, were there any benefits associated with joining the charity as a member?	☐	☐	☐

25. Describe in the space below the benefits that a new member would receive in return for his/her membership contribution:

IV. Outside/Professional Fundraiser

26. If the charity hired an outside/professional fundraiser, complete Items 27-37. Otherwise, enter an "X" in "N/A", and go to Item 38. . . . . ☐ N/A

27. Who was the professional fundraiser? [Check the box at the right that best applies and provide the name and address]:

For-Profit Entity . . . ☐
Individual . . . . ☐
Tax Exempt Entity . . ☐
Other . . . . ☐
N/A . . . . ☐

28. Please provide the following information, as it relates to the fundraising activities of the "outside" fundraiser:

28(a). Total number of mailings . . . . _____

28(b). Total aggregate cost of the mailings . . . . $_____

28(c). Total number of donor responses to the mailings . . . . _____

28(d). Total dollar amount of contributions generated from the mailings . . . . $_____

	Yes	No
29. Was there a written agreement between the charity and the professional fundraiser? If "Yes", attach a copy of the agreement.	☐	☐
30. If "Yes" to Item 29, was the compensation arrangement based upon a flat fee or as a percentage of the income generated by the professional fundraiser? Please describe the arrangement in the space provided:	☐	☐
31. Was the charity created by an owner, officer, director, trustee, or employee of the professional fundraiser? If "Yes", please specify in the space provided:	☐	☐
32. Is any officer, director, trustee, or employee of the charity employed by or connected with the professional fundraiser in any ownership of business, investment venture, or family relationship? If "Yes", please explain in the space below:	☐	☐

Charitable Solicitations Compliance Improvement Program Study Checksheet – Phase II

IV. Outside/Professional Fundraiser (Continued)

	Yes	No
33. Did the charity have "approval" rights, as client of the professional fundraiser, over any of the fundraising program implemented by the professional fundraiser?	☐	☐
34. Did the professional fundraiser have check "writing" authority?	☐	☐
35. Did the professional fundraiser have check "cashing" authority?	☐	☐
36. Did the charity retain copies of fundraising materials prepared by the professional fundraiser? If "Yes", please attach copies of the fundraising materials.	☐	☐
37. Did the charity meet the "commensurate test" as set forth in Rev. Rul. 64–182?	☐	☐

V. Bingo and Other Games of Chance

	Yes	No	N/A
38. If the charity conducted bingo or other games of chance, complete items 39–48. Otherwise, enter an "X" in "N/A", then go to Item 49.			☐ N/A
39. Did the bingo activity meet the tests of IRC 513(f)(2), specifically including the requirements that the activity meet the definition of a "Bingo game"; the conduct of which is not an activity ordinarily carried out on a commercial basis; and the conduct of which does not violate any state or local law?	☐	☐	☐
40. If the tests under IRC 513(f)(2) were not met, did the charity timely file Form 990–T?	☐	☐	☐
41. If "No" to Item 40, did you secure the delinquent Form 990–T?	☐	☐	☐
42. Did the games of chance, other than bingo, take place in North Dakota? If "Yes", go to Item 43. If "No", go to Item 44.	☐	☐	☐
43. If the games of chance, other than bingo, were conducted in North Dakota, and the gross income was not reported on a filed Form 990–T, did the organization meet all the tests set forth in Section 311 of the Deficit Reduction Act of 1984? If "No", go to Item 44. [These tests specifically include the requirements that the games must be conducted by non-profit entities; that there must have been a state law (originally enacted on 4–22–77) in effect on 10–5–83, which permitted the conduct of such games of chance; and the games must not violate state or local law.]	☐	☐	☐
44. Did the charity timely file Form 990–T?	☐	☐	☐
45. If "No" to Item 44, did you secure the delinquent Form 990–T?	☐	☐	☐
46. Was the income from either bingo or any other games of chance subject to any of the UBI exceptions, e.g. volunteer labor, as described in IRC 513(a)? If "Yes", please specify the exception in the space provided.	☐	☐	☐
47. Did the charity timely file the proper information returns (Form 1099–MISC) and withholding returns (Form W2–G) for the winners of bingo and other games of chance?	☐	☐	☐
48. Did the charity hire outside contractors to specifically operate bingo and other games of chance?	☐	☐	☐

Charitable Solicitations Compliance Improvement Program Study Checksheet – Phase II

VI. Travel Tours

49. If the charity conducted travel tours, complete Items 50–54. Otherwise, enter an "X" in "N/A", then go to Item 55. . . . . [ ] N/A

	Yes	No	N/A
50. Did the promotional travel literature and/or other written documentation indicate that the tours were educational? [Please attach copies of the tour literature or documentation.]	[ ]	[ ]	[ ]
51. Did the promotional travel literature and/or other written documentation contain discussions of any social/recreational aspects of the tour?	[ ]	[ ]	[ ]
52. Did the charity have a contract or do business with a for–profit travel agency?	[ ]	[ ]	[ ]
53. If "Yes" to Item 52, did the charity receive any fee from the travel agency? If "Yes", please explain in the space below:	[ ]	[ ]	[ ]

54. Please indicate if the charity was related to the for–profit travel agency by means of:

54(a). Sharing the same address or building . . . . [ ]

54(b). Sharing the same office space, equipment, or personnel . . . . [ ]

54(c). Creator of charity and owner of for–profit entity . . . . [ ]

54(d). Officer, director, trustee, or employee of the charity and the travel agency . . . . [ ]

54(e). Presence of family ties between the charity and travel agency . . . . [ ]

54(f). No Relationship exists between charity and travel agency . . . . [ ]

54(g). Other, specify:[   ] . . . . [ ]

VII. Thrift Store or Similar Type Activity

55. If the charity operated a thrift or "second–hand" store, complete Items 56–60. Otherwise, enter an "X" in "N/A", then go to Item 61. . . . . [ ] N/A

	Yes	No	N/A
56. Did the charity solicit used clothing, furniture, etc. from donors for resale by a for–profit entrepreneur?	[ ]	[ ]	[ ]
57. Did the charity receive compensation from the for–profit entrepreneur? If "Yes", please describe the terms of the compensation agreement in the space below, i.e. flat fee, percent of revenues, etc.:	[ ]	[ ]	[ ]
58. Was there a co–venture, partnership, or similar type arrangement between the charity and the thrift store or similar type operation? If "Yes", please describe the arrangement in the space below and provide the name and address of the other entity:	[ ]	[ ]	[ ]
59. Did the charity receive any new goods from corporate inventories designated as surplus or not saleable by the corporation?	[ ]	[ ]	[ ]
60. If "Yes" to Item 59, please describe the goods received, including the fair market value and use made of the goods:	[ ]	[ ]	[ ]

Charitable Solicitations Compliance Improvement Program Study Checksheet – Phase II

VIII. Goods or Services Received in Exchange for a Charitable Contribution

61. If the charity gives goods or services for charitable donations, complete items 62–67. Otherwise, enter an "X" in "N/A", then go to Item 68. . . . . . ☐ N/A

62. What was the nature of the benefits, goods, or services given to the donor? Please indicate those goods or services that apply and give a brief description in the space below:

62(a). Retail merchandise .... ☐
62(b). New and donated merchandise received at an auction .... ☐
62(c). Tickets for a raffle, lottery, bingo, or other game of chance .... ☐
62(d). Tuition at a school or other educational institution .... ☐
62(e). Travel or other transportation .... ☐
62(f). Tickets to an athletic, cultural, entertainment, or other event .... ☐
62(g). Discounts on goods or services .... ☐
62(h). Free subscriptions to publications .... ☐
62(i). Preferential seating at a college or university athletic event .... ☐
62(j). Other, specify:[   ] ....
Description:

		Yes	No	N/A
63. Did the charity disclose the deductible amount or make reference to deductibility in its solicitations and/or promotional literature? [Please attach representative copies of the literature.]		☐	☐	☐
64. Did the charity disclose the deductible amount or refer to deductibility in any thank you letter, receipt, ticket, or other written receipt? [Please attach representative copies of receipts.]		☐	☐	☐

65. Did the charity disclose the deductible amount or make reference to deductibility in any other manner, e.g. via oral communication? If "Yes", please select the item that best describes the manner of oral communication: [Yes ☐ No ☐ N/A ☐]

65(a). Radio .... ☐
65(b). Television .... ☐
65(c). Door-to-door solicitation .... ☐
65(d). Other, specify:[   ] .... ☐

	Yes	No	N/A
66. Was the charity aware of Rev. Rul. 67–246 prior to the examination?	☐	☐	☐
67. Did the charity receive Publication 1391 in the mail in 1988? If "No", please provide a copy of the publication to the charity.	☐	☐	☐

IX. Noncash Contributions

68. If the charity received or disposed of any noncash charitable contributions, complete Items 69–80. Otherwise, enter an "X" in "N/A", then go to Item 81. ☐ N/A

69. If the charity received any noncash contributions in the year examined, complete items 70–76. Otherwise, enter an "X" in "N/A". . . . . ☐ N/A

70. Please attach a listing (if more than one item) of all noncash charitable contributions, whose fair market value (FMV) exceeded $500, given to the charity during the year examined. The listing should include the following:
70(a). Name and Address of donor:
70(b). Item Name:
70(c). Description of Item:
70(d). Date Item Received:
70(e). FMV: $

71. Who determined the FMV of the contributed noncash property? Select one below:

71(a). Donor .... ☐
71(b). Charity .... ☐
71(c). Independent Appraiser .... ☐
71(d). Other, specify:[   ] .... ☐

Charitable Solicitations Compliance Improvement Program Study Checksheet – Phase II

IX. Noncash Contributions (Continued)

	Yes	No	N/A
72. For contributed noncash property with a FMV of $5,000 or less, did the charity provide the donor with a receipt containing the following information? 72(a). Donee name, 72(b). Date and location of the contributed property, and 72(c). A description of the property in detail, including its value.	☐	☐	☐
73. Was there any kind of an agreement between the charity and donor concerning the use, sale, or other disposition of the property? If "Yes", please explain below:	☐	☐	☐
74. Did the charity complete Section B, Part I of Form 8283? (If "No", please explain below. If "Yes", complete Items 75 and 76.)	☐	☐	☐
75. Was Form 8283 signed by a properly authorized official of the charity?	☐	☐	☐
76. Did the charity retain a copy of Form 8283?	☐	☐	☐

77. If the charity disposed of any noncash property within two years of its receipt, complete Items 78–80. Otherwise, enter an "X" in "N/A". . . . . ☐ N/A

78. Please attach a listing (if more than one item) of all noncash donated property, valued at $500 or more, that was sold, exchanged, consumed, or otherwise disposed of during the year under examination, which the charity received within two years of the disposal date. The listing should include:
78(a). Description of the donated noncash property disposed of:
78(b). Date the charity received the property:
78(c). Date the property was disposed of:

	Yes	No	N/A
79. Did the charity timely file Form 8282, Noncash Charitable Contributions Donee Information?	☐	☐	☐
80. Did the charity furnish a copy of Form 8282 to the donor of the noncash property?	☐	☐	☐

X. Penalty Assessments

81. If any penalty was assessed against the charity, complete Item 82. Otherwise, enter an "X" in "N/A", then go to Item 83. . . . . ☐ N/A

82. Select the penalty(ies) which you assessed against the charity and give a brief explanation below:

82(a). § 6651(a)(1) – Failure to file tax return . . . . ☐
82(b). § 6652(a)(2) – Failure to pay tax . . . . ☐
82(c). § 6652(c)(1)(A)(ii) – Failure to file complete or accurate EO information return . . . . ☐
82(d). § 6661 – Substantial understatement of liability . . . . ☐
82(e). § 6700 – Promoting abusive tax shelters . . . . ☐
82(f). § 6701 – Aiding and abetting understatements of tax liability . . . . ☐
82(g). § 6721 – Failure to file certain information returns . . . . ☐
82(h). § 6722 – Failure to file certain payee statements . . . . ☐
82(i). § 6723 – Failure to include correct information on an information return or payee statement . . . . ☐
82(j). Other, specify [§   ] . . . . ☐

Please explain the reason for the assessment and state the amount of the penalty:

Appendix C

Form **1023**
(Rev. December 1989)
Department of the Treasury
Internal Revenue Service

Application for Recognition of Exemption
Under Section 501(c)(3) of the Internal Revenue Code

OMB No. 1545-0056

If exempt status is approved, this application will be open for public inspection.

Read the instructions for each Part carefully.
A User Fee must be attached to this application.

If the required information and appropriate documents are not submitted along with Form 8718 (with payment of the appropriate user fee), the application may be returned to you.

Part I — Identification of Applicant

1a Full name of organization (as shown in organizing document)	**2** Employer identification number **(If none, see instructions.)**
1b c/o Name (if applicable)	**3** Name and telephone number of person to be contacted if additional information is needed
1c Address (number and street)	( )
1d City or town, state, and ZIP code	**4** Month the annual accounting period ends

5 Date incorporated or formed	**6** Activity codes (See instructions.)	**7** Check here if applying under section: **a** ☐ 501(e) **b** ☐ 501(f) **c** ☐ 501(k)

8 Did the organization previously apply for recognition of exemption under this Code section or under any other section of the Code? . . . . ☐ **Yes** ☐ **No**
If "Yes," attach an explanation.

9 Has the organization filed Federal income tax returns or exempt organization information returns? . . . . . ☐ **Yes** ☐ **No**
If "Yes," state the form number(s), years filed, and Internal Revenue office where filed.

10 Check the box for your type of organization. BE SURE TO ATTACH A COMPLETE COPY OF THE CORRESPONDING DOCUMENTS TO THE APPLICATION BEFORE MAILING.

a ☐ Corporation— Attach a copy of your Articles of Incorporation, (including amendments and restatements) showing approval by the appropriate state official; also include a copy of your bylaws.

b ☐ Trust— Attach a copy of your Trust Indenture or Agreement, including all appropriate signatures and dates.

c ☐ Association— Attach a copy of your Articles of Association, Constitution, or other creating document, with a declaration (see instructions) or other evidence the organization was formed by adoption of the document by more than one person; also include a copy of your bylaws.

If you are a corporation or an unincorporated association that has not yet adopted bylaws, check here . . . . ▶ ☐

I declare under the penalties of perjury that I am authorized to sign this application on behalf of the above organization and that I have examined this application, including the accompanying schedules and attachments, and to the best of my knowledge it is true, correct, and complete.

Please Sign Here ▶

---------------------------------- ---------------------------------- ----------------------------------
(Signature) (Title or authority of signer) (Date)

For Paperwork Reduction Act Notice, see page 1 of the instructions.

Complete the Procedural Checklist (page 7 of the instructions) prior to filing.

Part II   **Activities and Operational Information**

1   Provide a detailed narrative description of all the activities of the organization—past, present, and planned. **Do not merely refer to or repeat the language in your organizational document.** Describe each activity separately in the order of importance. Each description should include, as a minimum, the following: (a) a detailed description of the activity including its purpose; (b) when the activity was or will be initiated; and (c) where and by whom the activity will be conducted.

2   What are or will be the organization's sources of financial support? List in order of size.

3   Describe the organization's fundraising program, both actual and planned, and explain to what extent it has been put into effect. (Include details of fundraising activities such as selective mailings, formation of fundraising committees, use of volunteers or professional fundraisers, etc.) Attach representative copies of solicitations for financial support.

Form 1023 (Rev. 12-89)   Page **3**

Part II   **Activities and Operational Information** *(Continued)*

4   Give the following information about the organization's governing body:

a Names, addresses, and titles of officers, directors, trustees, etc.   **b** Annual Compensation

c Do any of the above persons serve as members of the governing body by reason of being public officials or being
appointed by public officials?. . . . . ☐ **Yes**   ☐ **No**
If "Yes," name those persons and explain the basis of their selection or appointment.

d Are any members of the organization's governing body "disqualified persons" with respect to the organization
(other than by reason of being a member of the governing body) or do any of the members have either a
business or family relationship with "disqualified persons"? (See the Specific Instructions for line 4d.) . . . . . ☐ **Yes**   ☐ **No**
If "Yes," explain.

5   Does the organization control or is it controlled by any other organization? . . . . ☐ **Yes**   ☐ **No**
Is the organization the outgrowth of (or successor to) another organization, or does it have a special relationship
to another organization by reason of interlocking directorates or other factors? . . . . ☐ **Yes**   ☐ **No**
If either of these questions is answered "Yes," explain.

6   Does or will the organization directly or indirectly engage in any of the following transactions with any political
organization or other exempt organization (other than 501(c)(3) organizations): (a) grants; (b) purchases or
sales of assets; (c) rental of facilities or equipment; (d) loans or loan guarantees; (e) reimbursement arrangements; (f) performance of services, membership, or fundraising solicitations; or (g) sharing of facilities,
equipment, mailing lists or other assets, or paid employees?. ☐ **Yes**   ☐ **No**
If "Yes," explain fully and identify the other organization(s) involved.

7   Is the organization financially accountable to any other organization? . . . . ☐ **Yes**   ☐ **No**
If "Yes," explain and identify the other organization. Include details concerning accountability or attach copies of
reports if any have been submitted.

Part II   **Activities and Operational Information** *(Continued)*

8 What assets does the organization have that are used in the performance of its exempt function? (Do not include property producing investment income.) If any assets are not fully operational, explain their status, what additional steps remain to be completed, and when such final steps will be taken. If "None," indicate "N/A."

9a Will any of the organization's facilities or operations be managed by another organization or individual under a contractual agreement? . . . . ☐ **Yes**   ☐ **No**

b Is the organization a party to any leases? . . . . ☐ **Yes**   ☐ **No**

   If either of these questions is answered "Yes," attach a copy of each such contract and explain the relationship between the applicant and each of the other parties.

10 Is the organization a membership organization? . . . . ☐ **Yes**   ☐ **No**

   If "Yes," complete the following:

a Describe the organization's membership requirements and attach a schedule of membership fees and dues.

b Describe your present and proposed efforts to attract members and attach a copy of any descriptive literature or promotional material used for this purpose.

c What benefits do (or will) your members receive in exchange for their payment of dues?

11a If the organization provides benefits, services or products, are the recipients required, or will they be required, to pay for them? . . . . ☐ **N/A**   ☐ **Yes**   ☐ **No**

   If "Yes," explain; show how the charges are determined; and attach a copy of your current fee schedule.

b Does or will the organization limit its benefits, services or products to specific individuals or classes of individuals? . . . . ☐ **N/A**   ☐ **Yes**   ☐ **No**

   If "Yes," explain how the recipients or beneficiaries are or will be selected.

12 Does or will the organization attempt to influence legislation? . . . . ☐ **Yes**   ☐ **No**

   If "Yes," explain. Also, give an estimate of the percentage of the organization's time and funds which it devotes or plans to devote to this activity.

13 Does or will the organization intervene in any way in political campaigns, including the publication or distribution of statements? . . . . ☐ **Yes**   ☐ **No**

   If "Yes," explain fully.

Part III   Technical Requirements

1   Are you filing Form 1023 within 15 months from the end of the month in which you were created or formed?   . ☐ **Yes**   ☐ **No**
If you answer "Yes," do not answer questions 2 through 6.

2   If one of the exceptions to the 15-month filing requirement shown below applies, check the appropriate box and proceed to
question 7.
Exceptions—You are not required to file an exemption application within 15 months if the organization:

☐   **(a)** Is a church, interchurch organization, local unit of a church, a convention or association of churches, or an integrated
auxiliary of a church;

☐   **(b)** Is not a private foundation and normally has gross receipts of not more than $5,000 in each tax year; or,

☐   **(c)** Is a subordinate organization covered by a group exemption letter, but only if the parent or supervisory organization timely
submitted a notice covering the subordinate.

3   If you do not meet any of the exceptions in question 2, do you wish to request relief from the 15-month filing
requirement?   .   .   .   .   ☐ **Yes**   ☐ **No**

4   If you answer "Yes" to question 3, please give your reasons for not filing this application within 15 months from the end of the month
in which your organization was created or formed.

5   If you answer "No" to both questions 1 and 3 and do not meet any of the exceptions in question 2, your
qualification as a section 501(c)(3) organization can be recognized only from the date this application is filed
with your key District Director. Therefore, do you want us to consider your application as a request for
recognition of exemption as a section 501(c)(3) organization from the date the application is received and
not retroactively to the date you were formed?   .   .   .   .   ☐ **Yes**   ☐ **No**

6   If you answer "Yes" to question 5 above and wish to request recognition of section 501(c)(4) status for the period beginning with the
date you were formed and ending with the date your Form 1023 application was received (the effective date of your section
501(c)(3) status), check here ▶ ☐ and attach a completed page 1 of Form 1024 to this application.

Part III **Technical Requirements** *(Continued)*

---

7 Is the organization a private foundation?

☐ **Yes**   (Answer question 8.)

☐ **No**   (Answer question 9 and proceed as instructed.)

---

8 If you answer "Yes" to question 7, do you claim to be a private operating foundation?

☐ **Yes**   (Complete Schedule E)

☐ **No**

After answering this question, go to Part IV.

---

9 If you answer "No" to question 7, indicate the public charity classification you are requesting by checking the box below that most appropriately applies:

THE ORGANIZATION IS NOT A PRIVATE FOUNDATION BECAUSE IT QUALIFIES:

(a) ☐	As a church or a convention or association of churches (MUST COMPLETE SCHEDULE A.)	Sections 509(a)(1) and 170(b)(1)(A)(i)
(b) ☐	As a school (MUST COMPLETE SCHEDULE B).	Sections 509(a)(1) and 170(b)(1)(A)(ii)
(c) ☐	As a hospital or a cooperative hospital service organization, or a medical research organization operated in conjunction with a hospital (MUST COMPLETE SCHEDULE C).	Sections 509(a)(1) and 170(b)(1)(A)(iii)
(d) ☐	As a governmental unit described in section 170(c)(1).	Sections 509(a)(1) and 170(b)(1)(A)(v)
(e) ☐	As being operated solely for the benefit of, or in connection with, one or more of the organizations described in (a) through (d), (g), (h), or (i) (MUST COMPLETE SCHEDULE D).	Section 509(a)(3)
(f) ☐	As being organized and operated exclusively for testing for public safety.	Section 509(a)(4)
(g) ☐	As being operated for the benefit of a college or university that is owned or operated by a governmental unit.	Sections 509(a)(1) and 170(b)(1)(A)(iv)
(h) ☐	As receiving a substantial part of its support in the form of contributions from publicly supported organizations, from a governmental unit, or from the general public.	Sections 509(a)(1) and 170(b)(1)(A)(vi)
(i) ☐	As normally receiving not more than one-third of its support from gross investment income and more than one-third of its support from contributions, membership fees, and gross receipts from activities related to its exempt functions (subject to certain exceptions).	Section 509(a)(2)
(j) ☐	We are a publicly supported organization but are not sure whether we meet the public support test of block (h) or block (i). We would like the Internal Revenue Service to decide the proper classification.	Sections 509(a)(1) and 170(b)(1)(A)(vi) or Section 509(a)(2)

If you checked one of the boxes (a) through (f) in question 9, go to question 14.
If you checked box (g) in question 9, go to questions 11 and 12.
If you checked box (h), (i), or (j), go to question 10.

Part III **Technical Requirements** *(Continued)*

10 If you checked box (h), (i), or (j) in question 9, have you completed a tax year of at least 8 months?

☐ No—You must request an advance ruling by completing and signing 2 Forms 872-C and attaching them to your application.

☐ Yes—Indicate whether you are requesting:

☐ A definitive ruling (Answer question 11 through and including question 14.)

☐ An advance ruling (Answer questions 11 and 14 and attach 2 Forms 872-C completed and signed.)

11 If the organization received any unusual grants during any of the tax years shown in Part IV-A, attach a list for each year showing the name of the contributor; the date and the amount of the grant; and a brief description of the nature of each such grant.

12 If you are requesting a definitive ruling under section 170(b)(1)(A)(iv) or (vi), check here ▶ ☐ and:

a Enter 2% of line 8, column (e) of Part IV-A _____

b Attach a list showing the name and amount contributed by each person (other than a governmental unit or "publicly supported" organization) whose total gifts, grants, contributions, etc., were more than the amount you entered on line **12a** above.

13 If you are requesting a definitive ruling under section 509(a)(2), check here ▶ ☐ and:

a For each of the years included on lines 1, 2, and 9 of Part IV-A, attach a list showing the name of and amount received from each person who is a "disqualified person."

b For each of the years included on line 9 of Part IV-A, attach a list showing the name of and amount received from each payer (other than a "disqualified person") whose payments to the organization were more than $5,000. For this purpose, "payer" includes, but is not limited to, any organization described in sections 170(b)(1)(A)(i) through (vi) and any governmental agency or bureau.

14 Indicate if your organization is one of the following, and if so, complete the required schedule. (Submit only those schedules, if any, that apply to your organization. **Do not submit blank schedules.**)

	Yes	No	If "Yes," complete schedule:
Is the organization a church?			A
Is the organization, or any part of it, a school?			B
Is the organization, or any part of it, a hospital or medical research organization?			C
Is the organization a section 509(a)(3) supporting organization?			D
Is the organization an operating foundation?			E
Is the organization, or any part of it, a home for the aged or handicapped?			F
Is the organization, or any part of it, a child care organization?			G
Does the organization provide or administer any scholarship benefits, student aid, etc.?			H
Has the organization taken over, or will it take over, the facilities of a "for profit" institution?			I

Form 1023 (Rev. 12-89)

Part IV   **Financial Data**

Complete the financial statements for the current year and for each of the 3 years immediately before it. If in existence less than 4 years, complete the statements for each year in existence. **If in existence less than 1 year, also provide proposed budgets for the 2 years following the current year.**

A.—Statement of Revenue and Expenses

		Current tax year	3 prior tax years or proposed budget for 2 years			
		(a) From .... to	**(b)** 19	**(c)** 19	**(d)** 19	**(e) TOTAL**
Revenue	1 Gifts, grants, and contributions received (not including unusual grants—see instructions) . .					
	2 Membership fees received . .					
	3 Gross investment income (see instructions for definition) . .					
	4 Net income from organization's unrelated business activities not included on line 3					
	5 Tax revenues levied for and either paid to or spent on behalf of the organization					
	6 Value of services or facilities furnished by a governmental unit to the organization without charge (not including the value of services or facilities generally furnished the public without charge)					
	7 Other income (not including gain or loss from sale of capital assets) (attach schedule) . .					
	8 **Total** of lines 1 through 7 . . .					
	9 Gross receipts from admissions, sales of merchandise or services, or furnishing of facilities in any activity that is not an unrelated business within the meaning of section 513					
	10 **Total** of lines 8 and 9					
	11 Gain or loss from sale of capital assets (attach schedule) . . .					
	12 Unusual grants					
	13 **Total** revenue (add lines 10 through 12)					
Expenses	14 Fundraising expenses					
	15 Contributions, gifts, grants, and similar amounts paid (attach schedule) . .					
	16 Disbursements to or for benefit of members (attach schedule) .					
	17 Compensation of officers, directors, and trustees (attach schedule)					
	18 Other salaries and wages . . .					
	19 Interest					
	20 Occupancy (rent, utilities, etc.) .					
	21 Depreciation and depletion . .					
	22 Other (attach schedule) . . .					
	23 **Total** expenses					
	24 Excess of revenue over expenses (line 13 minus line 23)					

Form 1023 (Rev. 12-89)   Page **9**

Part IV   **Financial Data** *(Continued)*

	B.—Balance Sheet (at the end of the period shown)	Current tax year Date ....
	Assets	
1	Cash	
2	Accounts receivable, net	
3	Inventories	
4	Bonds and notes receivable (attach schedule)	
5	Corporate stocks (attach schedule)	
6	Mortgage loans (attach schedule)	
7	Other investments (attach schedule)	
8	Depreciable and depletable assets (attach schedule)	
9	Land	
10	Other assets (attach schedule)	
11	**Total assets**	
	Liabilities	
12	Accounts payable	
13	Contributions, gifts, grants, etc., payable	
14	Mortgages and notes payable (attach schedule)	
15	Other liabilities (attach schedule)	
16	**Total liabilities**	
	Fund Balances or Net Assets	
17	Total fund balances or net assets	
18	**Total liabilities and fund balances or net assets** (add line 16 and line 17)	

If there has been any substantial change in any aspect of your financial activities since the end of the period shown above, check the box and attach a detailed explanation .... ▶ ☐

Appendix D

Return of Organization Exempt From Income Tax

Under section 501(c) (except black lung benefit trust or private foundation)
of the Internal Revenue Code or section 4947(a)(1) trust

(See separate instructions.)

Department of the Treasury
Internal Revenue Service

Note: You may be required to use a copy of this return to satisfy state reporting requirements. See instruction E.

OMB No. 1545-0047

19 89

For the calendar year 1989, or fiscal year beginning	, 1989, and ending	, 19

Use IRS label. Other- wise, please print or type.	Name of organization	**A Employer identification number** (see instruction S)
	Address (number and street) or P.O. box number	**B State registration number** (see instruction E)
	City or town, state, and ZIP code	**C** If application for exemption is pending, check here ▶ . . . . ☐

D Check type of organization—Exempt under section ▶ ☐ 501(c)( ) (insert number),
OR ▶ ☐ section 4947(a)(1) trust (see instruction C7 and question 92.)

E Accounting method: ☐ Cash ☐ Accrual
☐ Other (specify) ▶

F Is this a group return (see instruction Q) filed for affiliates?. . . . . . . ☐ Yes ☐ No
If "Yes," enter the number of affiliates for which this return is filed _____
Is this a separate return filed by a group affiliate? . . . . ☐ Yes ☐ No

G If either answer in F is "Yes," enter four-digit group exemption number (GEN) ▶

H Check here ☐ if your gross receipts are normally not more than $25,000 (see instruction B11). You do not have to file a completed return with IRS; but if you received a Form 990 Package in the mail, you should file a return without financial data (see instruction A). **Some states require a completed return.**

Note: Form 990EZ is available for organizations with gross receipts less than $100,000 **and** total assets less than $250,000 at end of year.

501(c)(3) organizations and 4947(a)(1) trusts must also complete and attach Schedule A (Form 990). (See instructions.)

Part I Statement of Revenue, Expenses and Changes in Net Assets or Fund Balances

1	Contributions, gifts, grants, and similar amounts received:				
a	Direct public support	1a			
b	Indirect public support	1b			
c	Government grants	1c			
d	**Total** (add lines 1a through 1c) (attach schedule—see instructions)			1d	
2	Program service revenue (from Part VII, line 93)			2	
3	Membership dues and assessments			3	
4	Interest on savings and temporary cash investments			4	
5	Dividends and interest from securities.			5	
6a	Gross rents	6a			
b	Less: rental expenses	6b			
c	Net rental income (loss)			6c	
7	Other investment income (describe ▶)			7	
8a	Gross amount from sale of assets other than inventory	(A) Securities 8a	(B) Other 8a		
b	Less: cost or other basis and sales expenses	8b	8b		
c	Gain (loss) (attach schedule)	8c	8c	8d	
9	Special fundraising events and activities (attach schedule—see instructions):				
a	Gross revenue (not including $_____ of contributions reported on line 1a)	9a			
b	Less: direct expenses	9b			
c	Net income (line 9a less line 9b)			9c	
10a	Gross sales less returns and allowances	10a			
b	Less: cost of goods sold	10b			
c	Gross profit (loss) (attach schedule)			10c	
11	Other revenue (from Part VII, line 103)			11	
12	**Total revenue** (add lines 1d, 2, 3, 4, 5, 6c, 7, 8d, 9c, 10c, and 11)			12	
13	Program services (from line 44, column (B)) (see instructions) .			13	
14	Management and general (from line 44, column (C)) (see instructions)			14	
15	Fundraising (from line 44, column (D)) (see instructions)			15	
16	Payments to affiliates (attach schedule—see instructions)			16	
17	**Total expenses** (add lines 16 and 44, column (A)).			17	
18	Excess (deficit) for the year (subtract line 17 from line 12)			18	
19	Net assets or fund balances at beginning of year (from line 74, column (A))			19	
20	Other changes in net assets or fund balances (attach explanation)			20	
21	Net assets or fund balances at end of year (add lines 18, 19, and 20).			21	

Revenue (side label for lines 1–12)
Expenses (side label for lines 13–17)
Net Assets (side label for lines 18–21)

For Paperwork Reduction Act Notice, see page 1 of the instructions.

Form **990** (1989)

Part II | **Statement of Functional Expenses**

All organizations must complete column (A). Columns (B), (C), and (D) are required for section 501(c)(3) and (c)(4) organizations and 4947(a)(1) trusts but optional for others. (See instructions.)

Do not include amounts reported on line 6b, 8b, 9b, 10b, or 16 of Part I.	(A) Total	(B) Program services	(C) Management and general	(D) Fundraising
22 Grants and allocations (attach schedule)			/////	/////
23 Specific assistance to individuals			/////	/////
24 Benefits paid to or for members			/////	/////
25 Compensation of officers, directors, etc.				
26 Other salaries and wages				
27 Pension plan contributions				
28 Other employee benefits				
29 Payroll taxes				
30 Professional fundraising fees		/////	/////	
31 Accounting fees				
32 Legal fees			.	
33 Supplies				
34 Telephone				
35 Postage and shipping				
36 Occupancy				
37 Equipment rental and maintenance				
38 Printing and publications				
39 Travel				
40 Conferences, conventions, and meetings				
41 Interest				
42 Depreciation, depletion, etc. (attach schedule)				
43 Other expenses (itemize): a				
b				
c				
d				
e				
f				
44 Total functional expenses (add lines 22 through 43) Organizations completing columns B-D, carry these totals to lines 13-15				

(left margin label: Expenses)

Part III   Statement of Program Service Accomplishments (See instructions.)

Describe what was achieved in carrying out your exempt purposes. Fully describe the services provided; the number of persons benefited; or other relevant information for each program title. Section 501(c)(3) and (4) organizations must also enter the amount of grants to others.

Expenses
Required for section 501(c)(3) and (4) organizations, optional for others

a ....
....
....
.... (Grants and allocations $)

b ....
....
....
.... (Grants and allocations $)

c ....
....
....
.... (Grants and allocations $)

d ....
....
....
.... (Grants and allocations $)

e Other program services (attach schedule) . . . . (Grants and allocations $)
f Total (add lines a through e) (should equal line 44, column (B)). . . . . ▶

Part IV   **Balance Sheets**

Note: *Where required, attached schedules and amounts in the description column should be for end-of-year amounts only.*

		(A) Beginning of year		**(B)** End of year
Assets				
45	Cash—noninterest-bearing		45	
46	Savings and temporary cash investments		46	
47a	Accounts receivable 47a			
b	Less: allowance for doubtful accounts 47b		47c	
48a	Pledges receivable 48a			
b	Less: allowance for doubtful accounts 48b		48c	
49	Grants receivable		49	
50	Receivables due from officers, directors, trustees, and key employees (attach schedule)		50	
51a	Other notes and loans receivable (attach schedule) . 51a			
b	Less: allowance for doubtful accounts 51b		51c	
52	Inventories for sale or use		52	
53	Prepaid expenses and deferred charges		53	
54	Investments—securities (attach schedule)		54	
55a	Investments—land, buildings, and equipment: basis 55a			
b	Less: accumulated depreciation (attach schedule) 55b		55c	
56	Investments—other (attach schedule)		56	
57a	Land, buildings, and equipment: basis 57a			
b	Less: accumulated depreciation (attach schedule) . 57b		57c	
58	Other assets (describe ▶ _____)		58	
59	**Total assets** (add lines 45 through 58)		59	
Liabilities				
60	Accounts payable and accrued expenses		60	
61	Grants payable		61	
62	Support and revenue designated for future periods (attach schedule) . . .		62	
63	Loans from officers, directors, trustees, and key employees (attach schedule) .		63	
64	Mortgages and other notes payable (attach schedule)		64	
65	Other liabilities (describe ▶ _____)		65	
66	**Total liabilities** (add lines 60 through 65)		66	
Fund Balances or Net Assets				
Organizations that use fund accounting, check here ▶ ☐ and complete lines 67 through 70 and lines 74 and 75.				
67a	Current unrestricted fund		67a	
b	Current restricted fund		67b	
68	Land, buildings, and equipment fund		68	
69	Endowment fund		69	
70	Other funds (describe ▶ _____)		70	
Organizations that do not use fund accounting, check here ▶ ☐ and complete lines 71 through 75.				
71	Capital stock or trust principal		71	
72	Paid-in or capital surplus		72	
73	Retained earnings or accumulated income		73	
74	Total fund balances or net assets (see instructions)		74	
75	**Total liabilities and fund balances/net assets** (see instructions)		75	

Form 990 (1989)   Page **4**

Part V	List of Officers, Directors, and Trustees (List each one even if not compensated. See instructions.)				
(A) Name and address		**(B)** Title and average hours per week devoted to position	**(C)** Compensation (if not paid, enter zero)	**(D)** Contributions to employee benefit plans	**(E)** Expense account and other allowances
-------------------------------------					

Part VI	Other Information		Yes	No
76	Did you engage in any activity not previously reported to the Internal Revenue Service?	**76**		
	If "Yes," attach a detailed description of each activity.			
77	Were any changes made in the organizing or governing documents, but not reported to IRS?	**77**		
	If "Yes," attach a conformed copy of the changes.			
78a	Did your organization have unrelated business gross income of $1,000 or more during the year covered by this return?	**78a**		
b	If "Yes," have you filed a tax return on **Form 990-T**, Exempt Organization Business Income Tax Return, for this year?	**78b**		
c	At any time during the year, did you own a 50% or greater interest in a taxable corporation or partnership?	**78c**		
	If "Yes," complete Part IX.			
79	Was there a liquidation, dissolution, termination, or substantial contraction during the year? (See instructions.) .	**79**		
	If "Yes," attach a statement as described in the instructions.			
80a	Are you related (other than by association with a statewide or nationwide organization) through common membership, governing bodies, trustees, officers, etc., to any other exempt or nonexempt organization? (See instructions.)	**80a**		
b	If "Yes," enter the name of the organization ▶ -- -- and check whether it is ☐ exempt **OR** ☐ nonexempt.			
81a	Enter amount of political expenditures, direct or indirect, as described in the instructions.	**81a**		
b	Did you file **Form 1120-POL**, U.S. Income Tax Return for Certain Political Organizations, for this year? . . .	**81b**		
82a	Did you receive donated services or the use of materials, equipment, or facilities at no charge or at substantially less than fair rental value?	**82a**		
b	If "Yes," you may indicate the value of these items here. Do not include this amount as revenue in Part I or as an expense in Part II. See instructions for reporting in Part III . . .	**82b**		
83a	Did anyone request to see either your annual return or exemption application (or both)?	**83a**		
b	If "Yes," did you comply as described in the instructions? (See General Instruction L.)	**83b**		
84a	Did you solicit any contributions or gifts that were not tax deductible?	**84a**		
b	If "Yes," did you include with every solicitation an express statement that such contributions or gifts were not tax deductible? (See General Instruction N.)	**84b**		
85a	Section 501(c)(5) or (6) organizations.—Did you spend any amounts in attempts to influence public opinion about legislative matters or referendums? (See instructions and Regulations section 1.162-20(c).)	**85a**		
b	If "Yes," enter the total amount spent for this purpose	**85b**		
86	Section 501(c)(7) organizations.—Enter:			
a	Initiation fees and capital contributions included on line 12.	**86a**		
b	Gross receipts, included on line 12, for public use of club facilities (See instructions.) . . .	**86b**		
c	Does the club's governing instrument or any written policy statement provide for discrimination against any person because of race, color, or religion? (See instructions.)	**86c**		
87	Section 501(c)(12) organizations.—Enter amount of:			
a	Gross income received from members or shareholders	**87a**		
b	Gross income received from other sources (Do not net amounts due or paid to other sources against amounts due or received from them.)	**87b**		
88	Public interest law firms.—Attach information described in the instructions.			
89	List the states with which a copy of this return is filed ▶ ---			
90	During this tax year did you maintain any part of your accounting/tax records on a computerized system? . . .	**90**		
91	The books are in care of ▶ --------------------------- Telephone no. ▶ -------------------			
	Located at ▶ --			
92	Section 4947(a)(1) trusts filing Form 990 in lieu of **Form 1041**, U.S. Fiduciary Income Tax Return.— . . . . . Check here ▶ ☐ and enter the amount of tax-exempt interest received or accrued during the tax year. . . ▶ **92**			

Form 990 (1989)   Page 5

Part VII   Analysis of Income-Producing Activities

Enter gross amounts unless otherwise indicated.

93 Program service revenue:	Unrelated business income		Excluded by section 512, 513, or 514		(e) Related or exempt function income
	(a) Business code	(b) Amount	(c) Exclusion code	(d) Amount	
(a) _____					
(b) _____					
(c) _____					
(d) _____					
(e) _____					
(f) _____					
(g) Fees from government agencies					
94 Membership dues and assessments					
95 Interest on savings and temporary cash investments					
96 Dividends and interest on securities					
97 Net rental income (loss) from real estate:					
(a) debt-financed property					
(b) not debt-financed property					
98 Net rental income (loss) from personal property					
99 Other investment income					
100 Gain (loss) from sales of assets other than inventory					
101 Net income from special fundraising events					
102 Gross profit (loss) from sales of inventory					
103 Other revenue: (a) _____					
(b) _____					
(c) _____					
(d) _____					
(e) _____					
104 Subtotal (add columns (b), (d), and (e))					

105 **TOTAL** (add line 104, columns (b), (d), and (e)) . . . . ▶ _____

(Line 105 plus line 1d, Part I, should equal the amount on line 12, Part I.)

Part VIII   Relationship of Activities to the Accomplishment of Exempt Purposes

Line No. ▼	Explain below how each activity for which income is reported in column (e) of Part VII contributed importantly to the accomplishment of your exempt purposes (other than by providing funds for such purposes).

Part IX   Information Regarding Taxable Subsidiaries (Complete this Part if you answered "Yes" to question 78c)

Name, address, and employer identification number of corporation or partnership	Percentage of ownership interest	Nature of business activities	Total income	End-of-year assets

Please Sign Here

Under penalties of perjury, I declare that I have examined this return, including accompanying schedules and statements, and to the best of my knowledge and belief, it is true, correct, and complete. Declaration of preparer (other than officer) is based on all information of which preparer has any knowledge.

▶ _____ | _____   ▶   _____
Signature of officer   Date   Title

Paid Preparer's Use Only

Preparer's signature ▶		Date	Check if self-employed ▶ ☐
Firm's name (or yours if self-employed) and address ▶		ZIP code	

*U.S. Government Printing Office: 1990-262-151/00066

Table of Cases

Table of IRS Pronouncements

Revenue Ruling	Pages
54-243	447
55-676	393
56-152	392
56-511	387
59-330	401
64-182	369, 441
66-221	380
67-246	366, 372
67-325	439
69-268	393
69-545	24
69-574	387
69-633	395
71-477	438
71-581	393, 399
72-431	400, 404
73-504	435
75-201	401
75-472	390
76-204	24
78-84	24
78-85	24
78-144	393
80-108	416, 420
80-200	24
80-286	24
84-132	446
85-184	447

Revenue Procedures	Pages
72-54	439
75-50	439
82-23	375
83-23	424, 425
90-4	417

Private Letter Rulings	Page
7946001	403
8127019	401
8203134	406
8216009	401
8232011	406
8725056	414
8747066	415
8823109	415
8832003	374

General Counsel Memoranda	Page
39727	415

Index